Feminist Legal Theory

New Perspectives on Law, Culture, and Society
Robert W. Gordon and Margaret Jane Radin,
Series Editors

Mind, Machine, and Metaphor: An Essay on Artificial Intelligence and Legal Reasoning, Alexander E. Silverman

Rebellious Lawyering: One Chicano's Vision of Progressive Law Practice, Gerald P. López

Wittgenstein and Legal Theory,
edited by Dennis M. Patterson

Pragmatism in Law and Society,
edited by Michael Brint and William Weaver

Feminist Legal Theory: Readings in Law and Gender,
edited by Katharine T. Bartlett and Rosanne Kennedy

FORTHCOMING

Words That Wound: Critical Race Theory, Assaultive Speech, and the First Amendment, Mari J. Matsuda, Charles R. Lawrence III, Richard Delgado, and Kimberlè Williams Crenshaw

Intellect and Craft: Writings of Justice Hans Linde,
edited by Robert F. Nagel

Property and Persuasion: Normativity and Change in the Jurisprudence of Property, Carol M. Rose

Failed Revolutions: Why Good Intentions, Great Promise, and Boundless Energy Fail to Transform the World, Richard Delgado and Jean Stefancic

The Philosophy of International Law: A Human Rights Approach, Fernando R. Tesón

In Whose Name? Feminist Legal Theory and the Experience of Women, Christine A. Littleton

Feminist Legal Theory

Readings in Law and Gender

EDITED BY

Katharine T. Bartlett

Duke University School of Law

AND

Rosanne Kennedy

Australian National University

Westview Press

BOULDER • SAN FRANCISCO • OXFORD

New Perspectives on Law, Culture, and Society

Copyright © 1991 by Westview Press, Inc.

Published in 1991 in the United States of America by Westview Press, Inc., 5500 Central Avenue, Boulder, Colorado 80301-2847, and in the United Kingdom by Westview Press, 36 Lonsdale Road, Summertown, Oxford OX2 7EW

Library of Congress Cataloging-in-Publication Data
Feminist legal theory : readings in law and gender / edited by
  Katharine T. Bartlett and Rosanne Kennedy.
    p. cm.
  Includes bibliographical references and index.
  ISBN 0-8133-1247-7. ISBN 0-8133-1248-5 (pbk.).
  1. Women—Legal status, laws, etc. 2. Sex discrimination against
women. 3. Sex and law. 4. Feminist theory. 5. Feminism.
I. Bartlett, Katharine T. II. Kennedy, Rosanne.
K644.Z9F46 1991
346.01'34—dc20
[342.6134]   91-21830
                                                                                  CIP

Printed and bound in the United States of America

The paper used in this publication meets the requirements
of the American National Standard for Permanence of Paper
for Printed Library Materials Z39.48-1984.

10   9   8   7

To Annis, Sam, and Helen
K.T.B.

To Josephine and Robert Kennedy
R.K.

Contents

PART TWO
QUESTIONING THE LEGAL SUBJECT

PART THREE
FEMINISM AND CRITICAL THEORY

PART FOUR
TURNING FEMINIST METHOD INWARD

Contents

Credits

by The University of Chicago. All rights reserved. Reprinted by permission.

Chapter 10   Reprinted, with deletions of text and notes, from 55 U. Chi. L. Rev. 1 (1988). Copyright © 1988 by The University of Chicago. All rights reserved. Reprinted by permission.

Chapter 11   Reprinted, with deletions of text and notes, from 42 Stan. L. Rev. 581 (1990). Copyright © 1990 by the Board of Trustees of the Leland Stanford Junior University. Reprinted by permission.

Chapter 12   Reprinted, with deletions of text and notes, from 4 Berkeley Women's L.J. 191 (1989–1990). Copyright © 1990 by Berkeley Women's Law Journal. Reprinted by permission of the University of California Press Journals Department and Patricia A. Cain.

Chapter 13   Reprinted, with deletions of text and notes, by permission of The Yale Law Journal Company and Fred B. Rothman & Company from The Yale Law Journal, vol. 94, pp. 997–1114, and by permission of Clare Dalton.

Chapter 14   Reprinted, with deletions of text and notes, from Frances Olsen, *Statutory Rape: A Feminist Critique of Rights Analysis in Feminist Legal Theory: Readings in Gender and Law.* Published originally in 63 Texas Law Review 387–432 (1984). Copyright © 1984 by the Texas Law Review Association. Reprinted by permission.

Chapter 15   Reprinted, with deletions of text and notes, from Elizabeth M. Schneider, "The Dialectic of Rights and Politics: Perspectives from the Women's Movement," 61 N.Y.U. L. Rev. 589, 593–652 (1986). Reprinted by permission of the New York University Law Review.

Chapter 16   Reprinted, with deletions of text and notes, from 42 Stan. L. Rev. 617 (1990). Copyright © 1990 by the Board of Trustees of the Leland Stanford Junior University. Reprinted by permission.

Chapter 17   Reprinted, with deletions of notes, from 38 J. of Legal Educ. 47 (1988). Reprinted by permission.

Chapter 18   Reprinted, with deletions of text and notes, from 103 Harv. L. Rev. 829 (1990). Copyright © 1990 by the Harvard Law Review Association. Reprinted by permission.

Chapter 19   Reprinted, with deletions of text and notes, from 38 Buffalo L. Rev. 1 (1990). Reprinted by permission.

1

Introduction

*Katharine T. Bartlett
and Rosanne Kennedy*

Over the past decade, a type of scholarship known as "feminist legal theory" or "feminist jurisprudence" has begun to appear in law journals, at legal conferences, and in law school classrooms. Feminist legal theory draws from the experiences of women and from critical perspectives developed within other disciplines to offer powerful analyses of the relationship between law and gender and new understandings of the limits of, and opportunities for, legal reform. This theory, as a body, represents one of today's most significant challenges to contemporary law and legal institutions.

The first "women's rights" movement emerged from efforts by nineteenth-century women to secure the right to vote, to own property as married women, and to gain legal access to birth control. It was not until well into the 1960s, however, that the entry of large numbers of women into law schools and the legal profession and a series of important legal victories on behalf of women provided the momentum that could sustain a deeper and more comprehensive critique of law. In the 1970s, feminists advocated reforms in areas of law that were recognized as having a special impact on women, such as family law, employment, and rape. Both in courts and in legislatures, feminists challenged the empirical assumptions underlying many laws, such as those of female dependency and the unsuitability and unavailability of women for certain jobs, and succeeded in eliminating or changing laws and employment practices that discriminated against women.

Despite these successes, by the end of the 1980s the forward progress of feminist legal reform seemed stalled. The defeat of the Equal Rights Amendment, retrenchment in abortion rights, and a dramatic increase in reported violence against women demonstrated both the precariousness of feminist achievements and the difficulty of eliminating sexual subordination through conventional law reform. Some of these disappointments are part of a general conservative backlash against all progressive political reforms. Many feminists, however, see a more basic failure in the ability of the strategies and theoretical frameworks developed in the 1970s to bring about deeper, far-reaching change. In reassessing past strategies, feminists in law have focused a more critical eye upon the theoretical assumptions embedded in modern legal theory and in traditional legal doctrines and precedents. Feminist work in other traditions, including philosophy, psychoanalysis, political theory, and literary criticism, has stimulated this interest and suggested directions for further feminist legal theory.

This book gathers some of the most prominent and thought-provoking examples of the feminist legal scholarship of the last decade. Our aim was to include pieces that demonstrate both the breadth and depth of feminist scholarship, and in order to do so, some of the longer pieces had to be severely edited. Even so, we have had to omit many important works from this rich and diverse field. Many of these excellent articles are noted in suggestions for further reading following each of the parts.

Organizing these articles was also a challenge, especially since traditional categories of legal analysis continue to be exploded and new directions explored. No single organizational scheme succeeds in capturing the full range of contributions in this field without also freezing some of the very categories of analysis feminists are struggling to shed. We settled, nonetheless, on four categories: Sexual Difference and Equality Theory (Part One), Questioning the Legal Subject (Part Two), Feminism and Critical Theory (Part Three), and Turning Feminist Method Inward (Part Four). Before introducing these categories and the articles grouped within them, we first provide—primarily for the benefit of nonlawyers—an overview of the relationship between law and feminism, outlining some of the ways in which law limits as well as enables political and social reform.

The Constraints of Law

As an institution, law has both helped to implement and constrained feminist agendas. The law's guarantee of equality enabled feminists to articulate differences in the law's treatment of men and women and provided a structure through which feminists could pursue legal change. In examining the theoretical foundations of law, however, feminists have discovered that the mechanisms of legal reform are self-limiting, allowing change only to a point and even strengthening the roots of gender hierarchy that feminists seek to challenge. Understanding these constraints can help to explain why legal reform has achieved less for women than feminists had expected and can inform future feminist strategies.

One such constraint is the law's respect for precedent. Law may be changed, but because law purports to preserve institutional stability and continuity, reform must build from existing legal precedents and doctrines. For feminists, this requirement presents two problems. First, existing precedents are often decidedly androcentric, taking for granted and reinforcing a status quo that is more favorable to male interests than to female ones. Second, arguments that deviate significantly from precedent or accepted doctrine are often considered extreme and thus are less likely to be successful than moderate proposals.

As a consequence, debates among feminists over issues such as mandatory job security for pregnant women, maternal child custody preferences, and male-only combat rules often turn on questions of short-term versus long-term goals. In the short run, women seem to require changes in law if they are to compete with men in the workplace or in the courtroom. When these changes are viewed as unfair advantages or affirmative action, however, they end up perpetuating stereotypes about women, which in the long run limit women's opportunities. In the same way, a legal doctrine that appears promising and effective as a tool for immediate reform may limit the future capacity of law to meet women's needs. Abortion rights, for example, were won for women in 1973 under the legal doctrine that seemed at the time the most promising: the constitutional right of privacy. Grounding this right in privacy rather than antidiscrimination doctrine, however, permitted the Supreme Court to limit access to abortion by poor women and, further, reinforced the ideology that dominance and abuse within the "private" family are beyond the law's authority. This example and similar cases have taught feminists that a strategy of piecemeal reform often reinforces rather than weakens the institutional foundations of gender hierarchy, and that winning now frequently means accepting a loss somewhere down the line.

In addition to law's respect for precedent, the institutional context within which a feminist must practice law creates a tension between the immediate interests of clients and the broader interests of women generally. For example, evidence of the "battered woman's syndrome" to prove self-defense in a homicide case may be good politics because it educates the public about domestic violence and the extent to which homicide may be a justifiable response to sustained terror. In many jurisdictions, however, such a defense will have little chance of success and may contradict the safer "diminished-capacity" defense that the client may otherwise be able to establish. Moreover, the multiple interests of a disempowered client may be contradictory. For instance, even when a battered woman wins because of evidence of either the battered woman's syndrome or diminished capacity, she may lose if she experiences this defense as a humiliation, thereby increasing her sense of powerlessness and reinforcing her submission to a system weighted against her.

Law is constraining also in the extent to which it insists upon arguments it deems rational and coherent rather than ambiguous or contradictory. As feminists in diverse disciplines have shown, standards of what is rational reflect the interests of those who currently hold power, whose authority is affirmed by how neutral and inevitable these standards appear to be. Moreover, diverse demands on women often lead them to articulate claims and explanations in court that appear contradictory. For example, women in predominantly female occupations seeking to establish claims for comparable worth must reconcile the argument that they are underpaid with the admission that they have freely chosen these jobs. Likewise, courts prefer reductive, dichotomous legal categories to overlapping or ambiguous ones; consequently, a black woman claiming discrimination because of the combination of her race and sex may be unable to fit her claim to the law's narrow requirements of either race or sex discrimination.[1]

On the one hand, then, the conservative force of the law is powerful, forcing feminists to work within and even strengthen the very structures they must dismantle. On the other hand, as a tool of reform, law is often weak; changes in law generally fail to transform the social structures, ideologies, and divisions of labor upon which any meaningful change ultimately depends. Gender-neutral child custody laws, for example, have not equalized the burdens of raising children between men and women or even the proportion of mothers and fathers obtaining custody of their children at divorce. As Sylvia Law writes, "Achieving sex-based equality requires social movement for transformation of the family, childrearing arrangements, the economy, the wage labor market, and human consciousness. No constitutional principle mandates or allows courts to effectuate the range of changes needed to allow actual equality between men and women."[2] Stated simply, the depth and scope of transformation needed to end women's oppression cannot be achieved through law alone.

Despite the difficulties and costs of seeking change through law, law represents opportunities for feminism. Law is power. Whether women may choose to have abortions, whether they are safe on the streets or in their homes, and whether they may secure employment depend in large part on the options law makes available. Legal reform may create as well as resolve problems for feminism, and it may not instantaneously improve women's lives, but it is a necessary precondition for meaningful social change. As Kathryn Powers points out, "[The] intrusive, intersubjective, and symbolic qualities of modern law continually interact with social practices and relationships, making legal change an integral, necessary component of social change, even though changes in law are not solely determinative of the nature and direction of social change."[3]

How important is legal theory to meaningful social change? Some feminists are skeptical of theory, believing that improving women's lives will be achieved only by using law pragmatically as a concrete tool for reform. From this perspective, legal theory seems utopian, impractical, and unimportant to those outside the academy. The resulting tension between theorists and practitioners poses a challenge to feminist theory. Is theory a series of idle meanderings and self-indulgent speculations? Or is it a crucial component of feminist practice?

In answering these questions, feminist legal theorists point out that every practice has its theoretical assumptions, whether or not they are explicitly acknowledged. Only those who agree with the implicit assumptions, values, and beliefs of a given political or legal agenda can afford to disregard theory, since failing to identify and challenge these assumptions makes them appear all the more natural and inevitable. The failure of legal reform to secure lasting, fundamental change in hierarchical gender relationships demonstrates the inseparability of legal theory and practice. Although no single cause can explain this failure, the absence of theoretical understandings about the structure of law and its relationship to social change seems to be one important aspect of the problem. If feminists, for example, use employment discrimination doctrine to increase workplace opportunities for women without questioning its conventional categories of analysis or its androcentric approach to sexual difference, they will gain access to employment only on terms that continue to represent and reproduce men's social profiles more than women's.

Debates on legal issues command a potentially wide audience. The terms of these debates—over abortion rights, surrogate motherhood, and pregnancy leave, for example—transform social meanings, change minds, and, ultimately, shape culture. Feminist theorists can help to steer these debates by framing the issues in ways that make the most intellectual, political, and practical sense. In sum, feminist legal theory offers feminism access to a discursive domain that has significant influence over women's lives. In the remainder of this introduction, we summarize some of the primary themes and tensions in this body of theory.

Sexual Difference and Equality Theory

In Western liberal democracies, "equal rights" has long been a rallying cry for feminists, and U.S. feminists experienced many successes in the 1970s on the basis of equal rights doctrine. Despite these successes, many feminists have found equality doctrine a problematic foundation for legal reform. Equality doctrine requires comparisons, and the standard for comparison tends strongly to reflect existing societal norms. Thus, equality for women has come to mean equality with men—usually white, middle-class men. For feminism, this raises several questions: Do women want simply to be treated like men? Does equality require different treatment? Should equality be the primary goal of feminism, or are there more important values? At the heart of these questions is the issue of how feminists should define and respond to sexual difference. Should feminists ignore sexual differences in pursuing legal reform? Or should these differences be emphasized and used to compel affirmative treatment so that those who are "different" may achieve some functional equality with others? What are the alternatives?

Feminists pursuing equality have also had to face the contradictions of a society whose commitment to equality seems, at best, ambivalent. What does it mean to pursue equality in a society stratified by income, education, race, physical and mental ability, and age—as well as gender? Are feminist goals consistent with capitalism? Or does feminism require a more collective or socialist economic system?

In recent feminist legal theory, the search for equality has sparked considerable analysis and debate. In an incisive and now classic article, "The Equality Crisis: Some Reflections on Culture, Courts, and Feminism," Wendy Williams explores stereotypes of masculinity and femininity embedded in rules and statutes intended to protect women. Focusing on the examples of the male-only draft, statutory rape laws, and pregnancy, she argues that feminists have two choices: they can either claim equality for women on the basis of similarities between the sexes, or they can argue for special treatment for women on the basis of fundamental sexual differences. Insisting that "we cannot have it both ways," Williams favors stressing similarities between the sexes, since difference always means woman's difference, which provides the basis for treating women worse as well as better than men. She contends that by fighting only for the privileges associated with masculinity and not the risks, feminists reinforce cultural assumptions about femininity that ultimately sustain gender inequalities.

Many feminists have criticized Williams on the grounds that an equal treatment approach benefits women who meet male norms but not women who engage in traditional female activities like childbearing and childrearing. Several feminists have offered alternatives to the equal treatment approach to respond to the disadvantages women experience when they engage in such uniquely female activities.[4] Christine Littleton in "Reconstructing Sexual Equality" emphasizes not only those disadvantages faced by women as a result of their unique biological characteristics but also those resulting from women's social traits and characteristics. Littleton suggests as a feminist goal that all sexual differences be made "costless." To implement this goal, she proposes that for every gendered activity or trait, male and female complements be identified and equalized, so that the costs of having female characteristics or engaging in female activities will be no higher than the costs of comparable male characteristics and activities. Thus, for example, she suggests that a mother should receive honor, compensation, and reentry job preferences comparable to those accorded a military veteran.

A number of feminists have opposed the underlying assumptions of both antidiscrimination law and mainstream feminist theory. Kimberle Crenshaw in "Demarginalizing the Intersection of Race and Sex: A Black Feminist Critique of Antidiscrimination Doctrine, Feminist Theory, and Antiracist Politics" argues that antidiscrimination law constitutes a "top-down" structure whereby victims of discrimination must establish their claims according to categories that fail to recognize the relationships between race and sex. Thus, when black women are treated in ways different from either black men or white women, their discrimination claims will not be recognized on the basis of either race or sex. Crenshaw charges also that feminist theorists have ignored the intersection of race and sex, by blindly premising their analyses on the experiences of white women.

Some feminists have resisted the terms of the equality versus difference debate altogether. For Catharine MacKinnon, for example, equality doctrine not only fails in its present formulations but is structurally flawed in a rather permanent way, in that it permits differences between women and men to legitimate unequal and abusive conditions for women. In her essay "Difference and Dominance: On Sex Discrimination," MacKinnon argues that feminists should concentrate on identifying dominance—that is, the ways in which male domination and female subordination have been created and perpetuated— rather than differences between men and women.

Joan Williams in "Deconstructing Gender" also rejects terms of the equality debate, both criticizing the failure of "assimilationists" to take account of women's vulnerability to gender-related disabilities and disputing the description of women's differences offered by "relational feminists" because it falsely presents and reinforces women's traditional domesticity. Unlike MacKinnon, however, Williams retains the ideal of gender neutrality, arguing that gender must be neither ignored nor misrepresented but rather "deinstitutionalized."

The final article exploring issues of sexual difference and equality is Vicki Schultz's "Telling Stories About Women and Work." In this article, Schultz critically examines both conventional explanations for sex segregation in the workplace—the "conservative story" that women choose traditionally female jobs and the "liberal story" that employers discriminate against women in hiring. Schultz demonstrates how these alternative stories oversimplify and misrepresent the complex ways in which women's job preferences are structured by workplace factors, and she develops an alternative account that helps to redefine the proper scope of judicial authority for compelling workplace reforms.

Questioning the Legal Subject

The Anglo-U.S. legal system presupposes what is essentially a mythical being: a legal subject who is coherent, rational, and freely choosing, and who can, in ordinary circumstances, be held fully accountable for "his" actions. Thus, legal doctrines generally assume that an individual acts with clear intentions that are transparently available to himself and to others, on the basis of suppositions about what a "rational person" would do in similar circumstances. The law also assumes that the individual is essentially separate from others and exists in an antagonistic relation to society as a whole.

The liberal view of the subject so thoroughly permeates our culture that it seems both right and natural and, consequently, not a theory but a description of reality. Recently, however, feminists have attacked the law's assumptions about subjectivity in a variety of ways. In "On Being the Object of Property," Patricia Williams presents an epiphanic account of her search for her own identity that throws into question totalistic views of the subject. For Williams, the subject encompasses aspects that are splintered and fragmenting; for the black female subject, reclaiming one's personality necessitates the paradoxical task of reclaiming the roots of her disinheritance. Williams's essay demonstrates powerfully how the process of recovering these fragments can illuminate, among other things, the role the law plays in disguising "the full range of human potential" in favor of particular, constructed, "partializing" identities.

Some feminist attacks on the subject have helped to crystallize a debate within feminism over whether allegedly female attributes and values are essential, inherent characteristics, or whether they are primarily the result of processes of social construction. The view that traditionally female values and attributes are socially constructed and can thus be changed is implicit in most of the articles in this book. Catharine MacKinnon in "Feminism, Marxism, Method, and the State: Toward Feminist Jurisprudence" presents a "total" theory of male dominance that is explicitly based upon a strong concept of social construction.[5] She argues that female sexuality—to her, the crucial component of gender identity—is constructed by men, for their pleasure and benefit, through the process of objectification, whereby the male perspective is taken as neutral, nonsituated, universal, or "objective." According to MacKinnon, "[f]eminism affirms women's point of view by revealing, criticizing, and explains its impossibility." Through an analysis of how the law of rape reflects the male rather than the female subject, and how it defines "normal" sex in ways that protect male interests, MacKinnon purports to represent the "woman's standpoint." The feminism she advocates "seeks to define and pursue women's interest as the fate of all women bound together. It seeks to extract the truth of women's commonalities out of the lie that all women are the same."

In "Jurisprudence and Gender," Robin West, like MacKinnon, stresses the commonalities of women's situations. She pursues a line of analysis, however, radically different from MacKinnon's. According to West, modern legal theory—and modern law—is male because it assumes that individuals are essentially separate from one another. West maintains, in contrast, that women are essentially connected to other human beings, especially through the biologically based activities of pregnancy, breastfeeding, and heterosexual intercourse. "Cultural feminists," West explains, value this connectedness, whereas for "radical feminists," "women's connection to others is the source of women's misery." Finding validity in both of these responses, West urges a feminist jurisprudence that criticizes the failure of male jurisprudence to reflect the fundamental connectedness of women, and that reconstructs new legal concepts to take account of the complicated realities of women's experiences.

Because West contends that woman's "true nature" is grounded in female biology, she emphasizes the similarities rather than the differences among women. However, several feminists have objected to treating women as a homogeneous category. For example, in "Race and Essentialism in Feminist Legal Theory," Angela Harris argues that West and MacKinnon are "gender essentialists," in that their theories imply that woman has an essential core identity. They then describe this identity, Harris contends, in terms characteristic of white, middle-class women, thereby ignoring differences of race and class and reinforcing exclusions based upon these characteristics. Harris suggests three contributions that women of color can make to a postessentialist feminist theory: the insistence on a self that is multiplicitous rather than unitary; the realization that differences are relational rather than essential; and "the recognition that wholeness and commonality are acts of will and creativity, rather than passive discovery." In a parallel effort, Patricia Cain in "Feminist Jurisprudence: Grounding the Theories" traces the development of feminist thought and shows how, at each important stage, feminist scholarship has excluded and thereby marginalized the experiences of lesbians. Cain also argues that feminists must be more conscious of the process by which the reality of dominant groups within a movement comes to stand for the reality of a larger number of groups in that movement.

Feminism and Critical Theory

In debating the nature of the legal subject, feminists have been influenced by developments outside of law. For instance, West draws on Carol Gilligan's work in moral theory, Angela Harris on black feminist theory, and Catharine MacKinnon on Marxist political theory. Feminist legal theory has also been influenced by contemporary developments within law. In particular, one strain of feminist legal theory has emerged from a rapport with and in response to the critical legal studies movement (CLS). This movement, a postrealist coalition of legal theorists that emerged in the 1970s, has introduced recent Continental perspectives on language, meaning, power, and knowledge into law. Although CLS scholars pursue diverse projects, they share certain fundamental premises.

They accept the postmodern critique of rationalism in modern Western culture, reject the law's claim to neutrality, attack the hierarchical structures of democratic society, and lament the poverty of individualism. One of the methods favored by critical scholars is *deconstruction*—a process of examining allegedly neutral, universal concepts and principles to expose their constructed, contingent nature and the power relations lurking behind them.

Feminists affiliated with CLS have shown how the hierarchical opposition of masculine and feminine within such binary pairs as public/private, objective/ subjective, and form/substance creates and reinforces norms that favor male characteristics and values over female ones. Clare Dalton's deconstruction of the law applied to cohabitation contracts in "Deconstructing Contract Law," for example, demonstrates how the legal concepts of consent, objective intent, and consideration rest upon certain unstated notions about gender roles, sexuality, and private intentions—notions that create and reinforce male prerogative and female powerlessness in the family law setting.

CLS feminists have also focused on the critique of legal rights. As with the concept of equality, feminists have again discovered an uncomfortable paradox. On the one hand, many feminists agree with the CLS position that rights discourse is indeterminate, alienating, and supportive of the status quo. Adapting this view to feminist goals, Frances Olsen in "Statutory Rape: A Feminist Critique of Rights Analysis" argues that feminists have wrongly limited themselves to critiques that can be expressed in terms of existing rights, without considering the underlying commitments rights discourse entails. Rather than confining their visions to what can be articulated through traditional, question-begging legal doctrine, feminists, Olsen insists, should work toward reconstructing sexuality by calling for "what we really want."

On the other hand, most feminists agree that women and minorities have achieved some political and social gains through the use of rights claims.[6] Elizabeth Schneider in "The Dialectic of Rights and Politics: Perspectives from the Women's Movement," combines an appreciation for the insights of the CLS movement with an affirmation of the positive, regenerative force rights discourse plays within feminist theory and practice. Whereas CLS scholars argue that rights are opposed to politics, Schneider emphasizes the interrelationship between rights and political struggle and the positive interaction between theory and practice in the women's movement. Rights are not static, Schneider argues, but emerge in response to concrete political issues. Rights discourse, despite its limitations, has enabled women to form coalitions and to assert a collective identity based on common experiences. Because the language of rights shapes public discourse, feminists have been able to use it to express the politics and vision of their movement.

Despite certain similarities between the goals of feminist legal theory and CLS, some feminists are skeptical of CLS's use of critical theory, particularly deconstruction, which adopts a strategy of undecidability and seems to lead to interminable critique. As Deborah Rhode explains in "Feminist Critical Theories," feminists argue that although deconstruction is useful in exposing the ways in which Western philosophy has marginalized the feminine, a feminist politics cannot stop at critique, but must be prepared to take affirmative positions on a range of issues. The skepticism parallels the feminist wariness of poststructuralist critiques of the rational subject, which seem to vacate the category of the subject and with it feminism's unique claim to a politics grounded in women's experiences. Many feminists believe that politically, the women's movement needs to assert a collective identity and to project women as self-conscious political agents. Likewise, there is widespread agreement that although it is instructive for feminist theory to expose the implicit hierarchies and exclusions through which meanings are constituted, feminists also need to take the positive step of transforming institutional and social practices.

Turning Feminist Method Inward

One characteristic of some feminist legal theory has been its determination to engage in self-criticism and, in particular, to use its critical methods on feminism itself. In a piece that supported work such as that of Angela Harris and Patricia Cain, Martha Minow in "Feminist Reason: Getting It and Losing It" argues that feminists themselves perpetuate exclusions and hierarchies by failing to apply the insights gained from their own subordination to forms of subordination based upon factors other than gender. Minow examines the factors, including the psychological and cognitive needs to simplify, order, and control, that may lead feminists to repress their unstated reference points and privileged positions and to universalize the particularities of their experiences. She suggests that feminists might be able to overcome these tendencies by making "a pointed effort to see points of view" and to challenge any designation of "difference" that "seems to allocate benefits or burdens as though the results were natural rather than chosen."

In "Feminist Legal Methods," Katharine T. Bartlett explores similar themes in an effort to identify the methods that make the study and practice of law characteristically "feminist." She focuses on three methods—asking the woman question, feminist practical reasoning, and consciousness-raising—and then examines, pragmatically, the nature of the truth claims these methods entail. Bartlett moves through the possibilities of empiricism, standpoint epistemology, and postmodernism to argue in favor of "positionality," a posture that both recognizes the possibility of truth based upon experience, upon which politics is based, and the improvability of truth based upon the ongoing, self-critical practice of turning feminism's methods inward, on itself.

A more concrete form of self-criticism is apparent in the excerpt from Lucie White's "Subordination, Rhetorical Skills, and Sunday Shoes: Notes on the Hearing of Mrs. G." In this piece, White analyzes her role as lawyer in her representation of a black welfare recipient, Mrs. G., at a welfare fraud hearing. In the course of showing that formal procedural equality did not go far enough in removing the historical, social, and bureaucratic barriers Mrs. G. faced in her confrontation with the welfare bureaucracy, White examines how Mrs. G.'s resistance strategies were turned not only against that system but against her own lawyer as well. In so doing, White goes far in showing her own complicity and, by extension, the complicity of each of us in the complex and overlapping set of hierarchies that define contemporary society.

Conclusion

The essays in this book show that over the last decade, feminists have made significant progress in revealing the androcentricism of law, in bringing feminist perspectives to bear in the legal academy and in the courts, and in challenging some of the most cherished legal principles and doctrines. However, far from heralding an era of "postfeminism," these essays indicate how much work lies ahead. Although the increased presence of women in legal institutions seems to indicate that feminism has been successful, much of this progress has been deceptive. On a deeper level, justice for women remains elusive. Women still constitute the majority of the country's poor; new legal and medical ways are being found to control women's reproductive capacities; and patterns of violence against women have multiplied rather than diminished.

Feminists have opened many doors. It remains to be seen in the 1990s and beyond exactly what will be found behind them. It is to be hoped that the commitment of engaged feminists, such as those whose work is contained in this volume, will provide strength and insight for the battles ahead.

Notes

1. See Kimberle Crenshaw, "Demarginalizing the Intersection of Race and Sex: A Black Feminist Critique of Antidiscrimination Doctrine, Feminist Theory, and Antiracist Politics," 1989 U. Chi. Legal F. 139.

2. Sylvia Law, "Rethinking Sex and the Constitution," 132 U. Pa. L. Rev. 955, 956 (1984).

3. Kathryn L. Powers, "Sex Segregation and the Ambivalent Directions of Sex Discrimination Law," 1979 Wis. L. Rev. 55, 63.

4. See, e.g., Herma Hill Kay, "Models of Equality," 1985 U. Ill. L. Rev. 39 (1985) (arguing for equal treatment except during periods in which women are engaged in uniquely female activities such as pregnancy, breastfeeding, menstruation, and rape); Sylvia Law, "Rethinking Sex and the Constitution," 132 U. Pa. L. Rev. 955, 1007–13 (1984) (arguing for equal treatment except in areas relating to reproduction, where rules that have a significant impact in perpetuating sex-role constraints or the oppression of women could be upheld only if required to serve a compelling state purpose); Linda Krieger and Patricia Cooney, "The Miller-Wohl Controversy: Equal Treatment, Positive Action, and the Meaning of Women's Equality," 13 Golden Gate U. L. Rev. 513, 517 (1983) (rejecting the metaphysical, "idealist" view of equal treatment, in favor of a "dialectical and materialist approach").

5. The outlines for this theory were presented in another one of Catharine MacKinnon's groundbreaking essays, "Feminism, Marxism, Method, and the State: An Agenda for Theory," 7 Signs: J. of Women in Culture & Soc. 515 (1982).

6. Patricia Williams, for example, mounts an attack on the CLS critique of rights from the point of view of minorities, arguing that the language of needs, which CLS favors over rights discourse, has done nothing for blacks, whereas rights discourse has been politically effective. See "Alchemical Notes: Reconstructing Ideals from Deconstructed Rights," 22 Harv. C.R.-C.L. L. Rev. 410 (1987).

PART ONE

Sexual Difference
and Equality Theory

2

The Equality Crisis: Some Reflections on Culture, Courts, and Feminism [1982]

Wendy W. Williams

Introduction

To say that courts are not and never have been the source of radical social change is an understatement. They reflect, by and large, mainstream views, mostly after those views are well established, although very occasionally (as in *Brown v. Board of Education*, the great school desegregation case) the Court moves temporarily out ahead of public opinion. What women can get from the courts—what we have gotten in the past decade—is a qualified guarantee of equal treatment. We can now expect, for the most part, that courts will rule that the privileges the law explicitly bestows on men must also be made available to women.

Because courts, as institutions of circumscribed authority, can only review in limited and specific ways the laws enacted by elected representatives, their role in promoting gender equality is pretty much confined to telling legislators what they cannot do, or extending the benefit of what they have done, to women. In an important sense, then, courts will do no more than measure women's claim to equality against legal benefits and burdens that are an expression of white male middle-class interests and values.[2] This means, to rephrase the point, that women's equality as delivered by the courts can only be an integration into a pre-existing, predominantly male world. To the extent that women share those predominant values or aspire to share that world on its own terms, resort to the courts has, since the early 1970s, been the most efficient, accessible, and reliable mode of redress. But to the extent that the law of the public world must be reconstructed to reflect the needs and values of both sexes, change must be sought from legislatures rather than the courts. And women, whose separate experience has not been adequately registered in the political process, are the ones who must seek the change.

Nonetheless, I am going to talk about courts because what they do—what the Supreme Court does—is extremely important, for a number of reasons. (1) The way courts define equality, within the limits of their sphere, does indeed matter in the real world. (2) Legal cases have been and continue to be a focal point of debate about the meaning of equality; our participation in that debate and reflection upon it has enabled us to begin to form coherent overall theories of gender equality that inform our judgments about what we should seek from legislatures as well as courts. (3) The cases themselves, the participation they attract and the debate they engender, tell us important things about societal norms, cultural tensions, indeed, cultural limits concerning gender and sexual roles.

My thesis is that we (feminists) are at a crisis point in our evaluation of equality and women and that perhaps one of the reasons for the crisis is that, having dealt with the easy cases, we (feminists and courts) are now trying to cope with issues that touch the hidden nerves of our most profoundly embedded cultural values. . . .

I. A Brief History of Gender Equality and the Supreme Court

Just before the American Revolution, Blackstone, in the course of his comprehensive commentary on the common law, set forth the fiction that informed and guided the treatment of married women in the English law courts. When a woman married, her legal identity merged into that of her husband; she was civilly dead.[3] She couldn't sue, be sued,[4] enter into contracts,[5] make wills,[6] keep her own earnings,[7] control her own property.[8] She could not even protect her own physical integrity—her husband had the right to chastise her (although only with a switch no bigger than his thumb),[9] restrain her freedom,[10] and impose sexual intercourse upon her against her will.[11]

Beginning in the middle of the nineteenth century, the most severe civil disabilities were removed in this country by state married women's property acts.[12] Blackstone's unities fiction was for the most part replaced by a theory that recognized women's legal personhood but which assigned her a place before the law different and distinct from that of her husband. This was the theory of the separate spheres of men and women, under which the husband was the couple's representative in the public world and its breadwinner; the wife was the center of the private world of the family.[13] Because it endowed women with a place, role, and importance of their own, the doctrine of the separate spheres was an advance over the spousal unities doctrine. At the same time, however, it preserved and promoted the dominance of male over female.[14] The public world of men was governed by law while the private world of women was outside the law, and man was free to exercise his prerogatives as he chose.

Perhaps the best-known expression of the separate spheres ideology is Justice Bradley's concurring opinion in an 1873 Supreme Court case, *Bradwell v. Illinois*, which begins with the observation that "Civil law, as well as nature herself, has always recognized a wide difference in the respective spheres and destinies of man and woman"[15] and concludes, in ringing tones, that the "paramount destiny and mission of woman are to fulfill the noble and benign offices of wife and mother."[16] The separate spheres ideology was used in *Bradwell* to uphold the exclusion of women from legal practice. Thirty-five years later, in *Muller v. Oregon*,[17] it became the basis for upholding legislation governing the hours women were permitted to work in the paid labor force. Women's special maternal role, said the Court, justified special protections in the workplace.[18] As late as 1961, in a challenge by a criminal defendant, the Court upheld a statute creating an automatic exemption from jury duty for all women who failed to volunteer their names for the jury pool, saying, "[W]oman is still regarded as the center of home and family life. We cannot say that it is constitutionally impermissible for a State . . . to conclude that a woman should be relieved from the civil duty of jury service unless she herself determines that such service is consistent with her own special responsibilities."[19]

The separate spheres ideology was repudiated by the Supreme Court only in the last twelve years. The engine of destruction was, as a technical matter, the more rigorous standard of review that the Court began applying to sex discrimination cases beginning in 1971.[20] By 1976 the Court was requiring that sex-based classifications bear a "substantial" relationship to an "important" governmental purpose.[21] This standard, announced in *Craig v. Boren*, was not as strong as that used in race cases,[22] but it was certainly a far cry from the rational basis standard that had traditionally been applied to sex-based classifications.

As a practical matter, what the Court did was strike down sex-based classifications that were premised on the old breadwinner-homemaker, master-dependent dichotomy inherent in the separate spheres ideology. Thus, the Supreme Court insisted that women wage earners receive the same benefits for their families under military,[23] social security,[24] welfare,[25] and workers compensation[26] programs as did male wage earners; that men receive the same child care allowance when their spouses died as women did;[27] that the female children of divorce be entitled to support for the same length of time as male children, so that they too could get the education necessary for life in the public world;[28] that the duty of support through alimony not be visited exclusively on husbands;[29] that wives as well as husbands participate in the management of the community property;[30] and that wives as well as husbands be eligible to administer their deceased relatives' estates.[31]

All this happened in the little more than a decade that has elapsed since 1971. The achievement is not an insubstantial one. Yet it also seems to me that in part what the Supreme Court did was simply to recognize that the real world outside the courtroom had already changed. [Women] were in fact no longer chiefly housewife-dependents. The family wage no longer existed; for a vast number of two-parent families, two wage earners were an economic necessity. In addition, many families were headed by a single parent. It behooved the Court to account for this new reality and it did so by recognizing that the breadwinner-homemaker dichotomy was an outmoded stereotype.

II. Men's Culture:
Aggressor in War and Sex

Of course, not all of the Supreme Court cases involved the breadwinner-homemaker stereotype. The other cases can be grouped in several ways; for my purposes I will place them in two groups. One group is composed of the remedial or compensatory discrimination cases—the cases in which a statute treats women differently and better than men for the purpose of redressing past unequal treatment.[35] The other group, the focus of this paper, consists of the cases that don't really seem to fit into any neat category but share a common quality. Unlike the cases discussed above, they do not deal with laws that rest on an economic model of the family that no longer predominates; rather, they concern themselves with other, perhaps more basic, sex-role arrangements. They are what I would call, simply, the "hard" cases, and for the most part, they are cases in which a sex-based classification was upheld by the Court.[36] There are a number of ways one could characterize and analyze them. I want to view them from one of those possible perspectives, namely, what they tell us about the state of our culture with respect to the equality of men and women. What do they say about the cultural limits of the equality principle?

In the 1980–81 Term the Supreme Court decided three sex-discrimination cases. One was *Kirshberg v. Feenstra*,[37] a case which struck down the Louisiana statute that gave husbands total control over the couple's property. That, to my mind, was an easy case. It falls within the line of cases I have already described which dismantle the old separate spheres ideology. The other two cases were *Rostker v. Goldberg*,[38] the case which upheld the male-only draft registration law, and *Michael M. v. Superior Court*,[39] the case upholding the California statutory rape law. They are prime candidates for my hard-cases category.

Justice Rehnquist wrote the opinion of the Court in both *Rostker* and *Michael M.* In *Rostker*, the draft registration case, his reasoning was a simple syllogism. The purpose of the registration, he said, is to identify the draft pool.[40] The purpose of the draft is to provide combat troops.[41] Women are excluded from combat.[42] Thus, men and women are not similarly situated with respect to the draft,[43] and it is therefore constitutional to register males only.[44] Of course, the problem with his syllogism was that one of the premises—that the purpose of the draft is exclusively to raise combat troops—was and is demonstrably false,[45] but the manipulation of the facts of that case is not what I mean to focus on here.

In *Michael M.*, a 17 1/2-year-old man and a 16 1/2-year-old woman had sexual intercourse. The 17 1/2-year-old man was prosecuted under California's statutory rape law, which made such intercourse criminal for the man but not the woman.[46] Rehnquist, for a plurality of the Court, accepted the utterly dubious proposition put forward by the State of California that the purpose of the statutory rape statute was to prevent teenage pregnancies. The difference in treatment under the statute is justified, he said, because men and women are not similarly situated with respect to this purpose.[48] Because the young woman is exposed to the risk of pregnancy, she is deterred from sexual intercourse by that risk. The young man, lacking such a natural deterrent, needs a legal deterrent, which the criminal statute provides.[49]

I think that perhaps the outcomes of these two cases—in which the sex-based statutes were upheld—were foregone conclusions and that the only question, before they were decided, was *how* the court would rationalize the outcome. This is perhaps more obvious in the draft case than the statutory rape case, but applies, I think, to both. Let me explain.

Suppose you could step outside our culture, rise above its minutiae, and look at its great contours. Having done so, speculate for a moment about where society might draw the line and refuse to proceed further with gender equality. What does our culture identify as quintessentially masculine? Where is the locus of traditional masculine pride and self-identity? What can we identify in men's cultural experience that most divides it from women's cultural experience? Surely, one rather indisputable answer to that question is "war": physical combat and its modern equivalents. (One could also answer that preoccupation with contact sports is such a difference, but that is, perhaps, just a subset of physical combat.)

Not surprisingly, the Court in *Rostker* didn't come right out and say "We've reached our cultural limits." Yet I [find] it significant that even the Justices who dissented on the constitutionality of the draft registration law seemed to concede the constitutionality of excluding women from combat.[52] When Congress considered whether women should be drafted, it was much more forthright about its reasons and those reasons support my thesis. The Senate Armed Services Committee Report states:

> [T]he starting point for any discussion of the appropriateness of registering women for the draft is the question of the proper role of women in combat. The principle that women should not intentionally and routinely engage in combat *is fundamental, and enjoys wide support among our people.*[53]

In addition, the committee expressed three specific reasons for excluding women from combat. First, registering women for assignment to combat "would leave the actual performance of sexually mixed units as an experiment to be conducted in war with unknown risk—a risk that the committee finds militarily unwarranted and dangerous."[54] Second, any attempt to assign women to combat could "affect the national resolve at the time of mobilization."[55] Third, drafting women would "place unprecedented strains on family life."[56] The committee envisioned a young mother being drafted leaving a young father home to care for the family and concluded, "The committee is strongly of the view that such a result . . . is unwise and unacceptable to a large majority of our people."[57] To translate, Congress was worried that (1) sexually mixed units would not be able to function—perhaps because of sex in the foxhole? (2) if women were assigned to combat, the nation might be reluctant to go to war, presumably because the specter of women fighting would deter a protective and chivalrous populace; and (3) the idea that mom could go into battle and dad keep the home fires burning is simply beyond the cultural pale. In short, current notions of acceptable limits on sex-role behavior would be surpassed by putting women into combat.

But what about statutory rape? Not such a clear case, you say. I disagree. Buried perhaps a bit deeper in our collective psyches but no less powerful and perhaps even more fundamental than our definition of man as aggressor in war is man as aggressor in sex. The original statutory rape laws were quite explicitly based on this view. Then, as is true even today, men were considered the natural and proper initiators of sex. In the face of male sexual initiative, women could do one of two things, yield or veto, "consent" or decline. What normal women did not, *should* not, do was to initiate sexual contact, to be the sexual aggressor. The premise underlying statutory rape laws was that young women's chastity was precious and their naivete enormous. Their inability knowingly to consent to sexual intercourse meant that they required protection by laws which made their consent irrelevant but punished and deterred the "aggressive" male.

The Court's opinion, I believe, is implicitly based on stereotypes concerning male sexual aggression and female sexual passivity, despite Justice Rehnquist's express denial of that possibility.[63] His recitation of the facts of the case sets the stage for the sexual gender-role pigeon-holing that follows: "After being struck in the face for rebuffing petitioner's advances, Sharon," we are told, "*submitted* to sexual intercourse with petitioner."[64] Although, in theory, coercion and consent are relevant only to the crime of rape, not to statutory rape, we are thus provided with the details of this particular statutory rape case, details which cast Michael and Sharon as prototypes of the sexually aggressive male and the passive female.

But it is Rehnquist's description of the lower court opinion that most clearly reveals sex role assumptions that lead first the California high court and then the United States Supreme Court to uphold the legislation. He says, "Because *males alone* can 'physiologically cause the result which the law properly seeks to avoid [pregnancy], the California Supreme Court further held that the gender classification was readily justified as a means of identifying *offender* and *victim*."[65] The statement is remarkable for two (related) reasons. The first and most dramatic is the strangeness of the biological concept upon which it is based. Do the justices still believe that each sperm carries a homunculus—a tiny person—who need only be planted in the woman in order to grow? Are they ignorant of ova? Or has sex-role ideology simply outweighed scientific fact? Since no one has believed in homunculi for at least a century, it must be the latter. Driven by the stereotype of male as aggressor/offender and woman as passive victim, even the facts of conception are transformed to fit the image.

The second is the characterization of man and woman as "offender" and "victim." Statutory rape is, in criminal law terms, a clear instance of a victimless crime, since all parties are, by definition, voluntary participants. In what sense, then, can Rehnquist assert that the woman is victim and the man offender? One begins to get an inkling when, later, the Justice explains that the statutory rape law is "protective" legislation: "The statute here protects women from sexual intercourse at an age when those consequences are particularly severe."[68] His preconceptions become manifest when, finally, Rehnquist on one occasion calls the statute a "rape" statute[69]—by omitting the word "statutory" inadvertently exposing his hidden assumptions and underlining the belief structure which the very title of the crime, "statutory rape," lays bare.

What is even more interesting to me than the Court's resolution of these cases is the problem they cause for feminist analysis. The notion that men are frequently the sexual aggressors and that the law ought to be able to take that reality into account in very concrete ways is hardly one that feminists could reject out of hand (I'm thinking here of sexual harassment and forcible rape, among other things); it is therefore an area, like the others I'm about to discuss, in which we need to pay special attention to our impulses lest we inadvertently support and give credence to the very social constructs and behaviors we so earnestly mean to oppose. Should we, for example, defend traditional rape laws on the ground that rape, defined by law as penetration by the penis of the vagina, is a sexual offense the psychological and social consequences of which are so unique, severe, and rooted in age-old power relationships between the sexes that a gender-neutral law would fail in important ways to deal with the world as it really is? Or should we insist that equality theory requires that we reorganize our understanding of sexual crime, that unwanted sexual intrusion of types other than male-female sexual intercourse can similarly violate and humiliate the victim, and that legislation which defines sexual offenses in gender-neutral terms, because it resists our segregationist urges, and affirms our common humanity, is therefore what feminists should support? These are not easy questions, but they must be answered if feminist lawyers are to press a coherent theory of equality upon the courts in these hard cases.

As for *Rostker v. Goldberg*, the conflicts among feminists were overtly expressed. Some of us felt it essential that we support the notion that a single-sex draft was unconstitutional; others felt that feminists should not take such a position. These latter groups explicitly contrasted the female ethic of nurturance and life-giving with a male ethic of aggression and militarism and asserted that if we argued to the Court that single-sex registration is unconstitutional we would be betraying ourselves and supporting what we find least acceptable about the male world.

To me, this latter argument quite overtly taps qualities that the culture has ascribed to woman-as-childrearer and converts them to a normative value statement, one with which it is easy for us to sympathize. This is one of the circumstances in which the feeling that "I want what he's got but I don't want to be what he's had to be in order to get it" comes quickly to the surface. But I also believe that the reflexive response based on these deeper cultural senses leads us to untenable positions.

The single-sex laws upheld in *Michael M.* and *Rostker* ultimately do damage to women. For one thing, they absolve women of personal responsibility in the name of protection. There is a sense in which women have been victims of physical aggression in part because they have not been permitted to act as anything but victims.[78] For another, do we not acquire a greater right to claim our share from society if we too share its ultimate jeopardies? To me, *Rostker* never posed the question of whether women should be forced as men now are to fight wars, but whether we, like them, must take the responsibility for deciding whether or not to fight, whether or not to bear the cost of risking our lives, on the one hand, or resisting in the name of peace, on the other. And do we not, by insisting upon our differences at these crucial junctures, promote and reinforce the us-them dichotomy that permits the Rehnquists and the Stewarts to resolve matters of great importance and complexity by the simplistic, reflexive assertion that men and women "are simply not similarly situated?"

III. Women's Culture: Mother of Humanity

We have looked briefly at the male side of the cultural equation. What are the cultural limits on women's side? Step outside the culture again and speculate. If we find limits and conflicts surrounding the male role as aggressor in war and sex, what will be the trouble spots at the opposite pole? What does the culture identify as quintessentially female? Where does our pride and self-identity lie? Most probably, I think, somewhere in the realm of behaviors and concerns surrounding maternity.

I would expect the following areas to be the places where the move toward equality of the sexes might come into collision with cultural limits, both in judicial opinions and in ourselves: treatment of maternity in the workplace, the tender years presumption, and joint custody of children upon divorce. The issues surrounding pregnancy and maternity are the most difficult from a theoretical point of view and for that reason may be the best illustration of the conflict I am trying to explore.

Let me start again with a Supreme Court case. As discussed earlier, before 1971, the ideology of the separate spheres informed Supreme Court opinions; it allowed the courts to view men and women as basically on different life tracks and therefore never really similarly situated. That fundamentally dichotomous view which characterized man as breadwinner, woman as homemaker-childrearer, foreclosed the possibility that the courts could successfully apply an equality model to the sexes.

Once the Supreme Court took on the task of dismantling the statutory structure build upon the separate spheres ideology, it had to face the question of how to treat pregnancy itself. Pregnancy was, after all, the centerpiece, the linchpin, the essential feature of women's separate sphere.[83] The stereotypes, the generalizations, the role expectations were at their zenith when a woman became pregnant. Gender equality would not be possible, one would think, unless the Court was willing to examine, at least as closely as other gender-related rulemaking, those prescriptions concerning pregnancy itself. On the other hand, the capacity to bear a child is a crucial, indeed definitional, difference between women and men. While it is obvious that the sexes can be treated equally with respect to characteristics that they share, how would it be possible to apply the equality principle to a characteristic unique to women?

So what did the Court do? It drew the line at pregnancy. *Of course* it would take a more critical look at sex discrimination than it had in the past—but, it said, discrimination on the basis of pregnancy is not sex discrimination.[84] Now here was a simple but decisive strategy for avoiding the doctrinal discomfort that inclusion of pregnancy within the magic circle of stricter review would bring with it. By placing pregnancy altogether outside that class of phenomena labeled sex discrimination, the Court need not apply to classifications related to pregnancy the level of scrutiny it had already reserved, in cases such as *Reed v. Reed* and *Frontiero v. Richardson*, for gender classifications.[85] Pregnancy classifications would henceforth be subject only to the most casual review.

The position was revealed for the first time in 1974 in *Geduldig v. Aiello*,[86] a case challenging under the equal protection clause exclusion of pregnancy-related disabilities from coverage by an otherwise comprehensive state disability insurance program. The Court explained, in a footnote, that pregnancy classifications were not sex-based but were, instead, classifications based upon a physical condition and should be treated accordingly:

> The California insurance program does not exclude anyone from benefit eligibility because of gender *but merely removes one physical condition—pregnancy—from the list of compensable disabilities.* While it is true that only women can become pregnant, it does not follow that every legislative classification concerning pregnancy is a sex-based classification . . . Normal pregnancy is an objectively identifiable physical condition with unique characteristics . . . [L]awmakers are constitutionally free to include or exclude pregnancy from the coverage of legislation such as this on any reasonable basis, *just as with respect to any other physical condition.*[87]

The second time the Supreme Court said pregnancy discrimination is not sex discrimination was in *General Electric Company v. Gilbert*,[88] decided in 1976. *Gilbert* presented the same basic facts—exclusion of pregnancy-related disabilities from a comprehensive disability program—but this case was brought under Title VII rather than the equal protection clause. The Court nonetheless relied on *Geduldig*, saying that when Congress prohibited "sex discrimination," it didn't mean to include within the definition of that term pregnancy discrimination.[89]

There was, however, an additional theory available in *Gilbert* because it was a Title VII case that was not available in the equal protection case. That theory was that if an employer's rule has a disparate effect on women, even though there is no intent to discriminate, it might also violate Title VII. And did the Court find that the exclusion of pregnancy-related disabilities had a disparate effect on women? It did not.[90] Men and women, said Justice Rehnquist, received coverage for the disabilities they had in common. Pregnancy was an *extra* disability, since only women suffered it. To compensate women for it would give them more than men got. So here there was no disparate effect—the exclusion of pregnancy merely insured the basic equality of the program.[91]

The remarkable thing about this statement, like Rehnquist's later assertion in *Michael M.* that only men can "cause" pregnancy, is its peculiarly blinkered male vision. After all, men received coverage under General Electric's disability program for disabilities they did not have in common with women, including disabilities linked to exclusively male aspects of the human anatomy.[92] Thus, the only sense in which one can understand pregnancy to be "extra" is in some reverse-Freudian psychological fashion. Under Freud's interpretation, women were viewed by both sexes as inadequate men (men *minus*) because they lacked penises.[93] In Rehnquist's view, woman is now man *plus*, because she shares all his physical characteristics except that she also gets pregnant.

Under either of these extravagantly skewed views of the sexes, however, man is the measure against which the anatomical features of woman are counted and assigned value, and when the addition or subtraction is complete, woman comes out behind.

The corollary to *Gilbert* appeared in *Nashville Gas Co. v. Satty*,[94] decided in 1977. There the Court finally found a pregnancy rule that violated Title VII. The rule's chief characteristic was its gratuitously punitive effect. It provided that a woman returning from maternity leave lost all of the seniority she acquired *prior* to her leave.[95] Here, said Rehnquist, we have a case where women are not seeking extra benefits for pregnancy. Here's a case where a woman, now back at work and no longer pregnant, has actually had something taken away from her—her pre-pregnancy seniority—and she therefore suffers a burden that men don't have to bear.[96] This rule therefore has a disproportionate impact on women.

Roughly translated, *Gilbert* and *Satty* read together seemed to stand for the proposition that insofar as a rule deprives a woman of benefits for actual pregnancy, that rule is lawful under Title VII. If, on the other hand, it denies her benefits she had earned while not pregnant (and hence like a man) and now seeks to use upon return to her non-pregnant (male-like) status, it has a disproportionate effect on women and is not lawful.

In summary, then, the Court seems to be of the view that discrimination on the basis of pregnancy isn't sex discrimination. The Court achieves this by, on the one hand, disregarding the "ineluctible link" between gender and pregnancy, treating pregnancy as just another physical condition that the employer or state can manipulate on any arguably rational basis, and on the other hand, using woman's special place in "the scheme of human existence"[98] as a basis for treating her claim to benefits available to other disabled workers as a claim not to equal benefits but to special treatment. The equality principle, according to the Court, cannot be bent to such ends.

In reaction to *Gilbert* and, to a lesser extent, to *Satty*, Congress amended the definitions section of Title VII to provide that discrimination on the basis of pregnancy, childbirth, and related medical conditions was, for purposes of the Act, sex discrimination. The amendment, called the Pregnancy Discrimination Act (PDA),[99] required a rather radical change in approach to the pregnancy issue from that adopted by the Court. In effect, Title VII creates a general presumption that men and women are alike in all relevant respects and casts the burden on the employer to show otherwise in any particular case.[100] The PDA, likewise, rejects the presumption that pregnancy is so unique that special rules concerning it are to be treated as prima facie reasonable. It substitutes the contrary presumption that pregnancy, at least in the workplace context, is like other physical conditions which may affect workers. As with gender classifications in general, it places the burden of establishing pregnancy's uniqueness in any given instance on the employer. The amendment itself specifies how this is to be done:

> [W]omen affected by pregnancy, childbirth, or related medical conditions shall be treated the same for all employment-related purposes, including receipt of benefits

under fringe benefit programs, as other persons not so affected but similar in their ability or inability to work. . . .[101]

Under the PDA, employers cannot treat pregnancy less favorably than other potentially disabling conditions, but neither can they treat it more favorably. And therein lies the crisis.

At the time the PDA was passed, all feminist groups supported it. Special treatment of pregnancy in the workplace had always been synonymous with unfavorable treatment; the rules generally had the effect of forcing women out of the work force and back into the home when they became pregnant. By treating pregnancy discrimination as sex discrimination, the PDA required that pregnant women be treated as well as other wage earners who became disabled. The degree to which this assisted women depended on the generosity of their particular employers' sick leave or disability policy, but anything at all was better than what most pregnant women had had before.

The conflict within the feminist community arose because some states had passed legislation which, instead of placing pregnant women at a disadvantage, gave them certain positive protections. Montana, for example, passed a law forbidding employers to fire women who became pregnant and requiring them to give such women reasonable maternity leave.[104] The Miller-Wohl Company, an employer in that state, had a particularly ungenerous sick leave policy. Employees were entitled to no sick leave in their first year of employment and five days per year thereafter.[105] On August 1, 1979, the company hired a pregnant woman who missed four or five days over the course of the following three weeks because of morning sickness. The company fired her. She asserted her rights under the Montana statute. The company sought declaratory relief in federal court, claiming that Montana's special treatment statute was contrary to the equality principle mandated by the PDA and was therefore invalid under the supremacy clause of the constitution.[106]

Feminists split over the validity of the Montana statute. Some of us felt that the statute was, indeed, incompatible with the philosophy of the PDA.[107] Others of us argued that the PDA was passed to *help* pregnant women, which was also the objective of the Montana statute.[108] Underneath are very different views of what women's equality means; the dispute is therefore one of great significance for feminists.

The Montana statute *was* meant to help pregnant women. It was passed with the best of intentions. The philosophy underlying it is that pregnancy is central to a woman's family role and that the law should take special account of pregnancy to protect that role for the working wife. And those who supported the statute can assert with great plausibility that pregnancy is a problem that men don't have, an extra source of workplace disability, and that women workers cannot adequately be protected if pregnancy is not taken into account in special ways. They might also add that procreation plays a special role in human life, is viewed as a fundamental right by our society, and therefore is appropriately singled out on social policy grounds. The instinct to treat pregnancy as a special case is deeply imbedded in our culture, indeed in every culture. It seems natural, and *right*, to treat it that way.

Yet, at a deeper level, the Supreme Court in cases like *Gilbert*, and the feminists who seek special recognition for pregnancy, are starting from the same basic assumption, namely, that women have a special place in the scheme of human existence when it comes to maternity. Of course, one's view of how that basic assumption cuts is shaped by one's perspective. What businessmen, Supreme Court Justices, and feminists make of it is predictably quite different. But the same doctrinal approach that permits pregnancy to be treated *worse* than other disabilities is the same one that will allow the state constitutional freedom to create special *benefits* for pregnant women. The equality approach to pregnancy (such as that embodied in the PDA) necessarily creates not only the desired floor under the pregnant woman's rights but also the ceiling which the *Miller-Wohl* case threw into relief. It we can't have it both ways, we need to think carefully about which way we want to have it.

My own feeling is that, for all its problems, the equality approach is the better one. The special treatment model has great costs. First, as discussed above, is the reality that conceptualizing pregnancy as a special case permits unfavorable as well as favorable treatment of pregnancy. Our history provides too many illustrations of the former to allow us to be sanguine about the wisdom of urging special treatment.

Second, treating pregnancy as a special case divides us in ways that I believe are destructive in a particular political sense as well as a more general sense. On what basis can we fairly assert, for example, that the pregnant woman fired by Miller-Wohl deserved to keep her job when any other worker who got sick for any other reason did not? Creating special privileges of the Montana type has, as one consequence, the effect of shifting attention away from the employer's inadequate sick leave policy or the state's failure to provide important protections to all workers and focusing it upon the unfairness of protecting one class of worker and not others.

Third, as our experience with single-sex protective legislation earlier in this century demonstrated, what appear to be special "protections" for women often turn out to be, at best, a double-edged sword. It seems likely, for example, that the employer who wants to avoid the inconveniences and costs of special protective measures will find reasons not to hire women of childbearing age in the first place.[115]

Fourth, to the extent the state (or employers as proxies for the state) can lay claim to an interest in women's special procreational capacity for "the future well-being of the race," as *Muller v. Oregon* put it in 1908,[116] our freedom of choice about the direction of our lives is more limited than that of men in significant ways. This danger is hardly a theoretical one today. The Supreme Court has [shown a willingness] to permit restrictions on abortion in deference to the state's interest in the "potential life" of the fetus,[117] and private employers are adopting policies of exclusion of women of childbearing capacity in order to protect fetuses from exposure to possibly hazardous substances in the workplace.[118]

More fundamentally, though, this issue, like the others I discussed earlier, has everything to do with how, in the long run, we want to define women's and men's places and roles in society.

Implicit in the PDA approach to maternity issues is a stance toward parenthood and work that is decidedly different from that embodied in the special-treatment approach to pregnancy. For many years, the prototype of the enlightened employer maternity policy was one which provided for a mandatory unpaid leave of absence for the woman employee commencing four or five months before and extending for as long as six months after childbirth.[119] Such maternity leaves were firmly premised on that aspect of the separate spheres ideology which assigned motherhood as woman's special duty and prerogative; employers believed that women should be treated as severed from the labor force from the time their pregnancies became apparent until their children emerged from infancy.[120] Maternity leave was always based upon cultural constructs and ideologies rather than upon biological necessity, upon role expectations rather than irreducible differences between the sexes.

The PDA also has significant ideological content. It makes the prototypical maternity leave policy just described illegal. In its stead, as discussed above, is a requirement that the employer extend to women disabled by pregnancy the same disability or sick leave available to other workers. If the employer chooses to extend the leave time beyond the disability period, it must make such leaves available to male as well as to female parents. Title VII requires sex neutrality with respect to employment practices directed at parents.[123] It does not permit the employer to base policies on the separate spheres ideology. Accordingly, the employer must devise its policies in such a way that women and men can, if they choose, structure the allocation of family responsibilities in a more egalitarian fashion. It forecloses the assumption that women are necessarily and inevitably destined to carry the dual burden of homemaker and wage earner.

Statutes such as the Montana statute challenged in the *Miller-Wohl* case are rooted in the philosophy that women have a special and different role and deserve special and different treatment. Feminists can plausibly and forcibly claim that such laws are desirable and appropriate because they reflect the material reality of women's lives. We can lay claim to such accommodations based on the different pattern of our lives, our commitment to children, our cultural destiny. We can even resort to arguments based on biological imperatives and expect that at least some members of the Supreme Court might lend a sympathetic ear. Justice Stevens suggested one such approach in a footnote to his dissent in *Caban v. Mohammed*,[124] a case invalidating a law that granted to unwed mothers but denied to unwed fathers the right to withhold consent to adoption of their children. He observed:

> [T]here is some sociological and anthropological research indicating that by virtue of the symbiotic relationship between mother and child during pregnancy and the initial contact between mother and child directly after birth a physical and psychological bond immediately develops between the two that is not then present between the infant and the father or any other person. [Citations omitted.][125] [Brackets in original.]

Justice Stevens' seductive bit of science is useful for making my point, although other illustrations might do as well. Many women who have gone through childbirth have experienced the extraordinary sense of connection to their newborn that the literature calls "bonding."[126] It may be, as some have contended, that the monolithic role women have so long played has been triggered and sustained by this phenomenon, that the effect of this bonding has made it emotionally possible for women to submit to the stringent limitations imposed by law and culture upon the scope and nature of their aspirations and endeavors.[127] On the other hand, it seems entirely possible that the concept of exclusive mother-infant bonding—the latest variation on "maternal instinct"— is a social construct designed to serve ideological ends.[128]

Less than a century ago, doctors and scientists were generally of the view that a woman's intellect, her capacity for education, for reasoning, for public undertakings, was biologically limited.[129] While men were governed by their intellect, women were controlled by their uteruses.[130] No reputable scientist or doctor would make such claims today. But if women are now understood to share with men a capacity for intellectual development, is it not also possible that mother-infant bonding is, likewise, only half the story? What Justice Stevens overlooks is the evidence of the capacity of fathers (the exploration of whose nurturing potential is as new as their opportunity actively to participate in the birth of their children) to "bond" as well.

Again, the question is, are we clinging, without really reflecting upon it, to culturally dictated notions that underestimate the flexibility and potential of human beings of both sexes and which limit us as a class and as individuals?

IV: Conclusion: Confronting Yin and Yang

The human creature seems to be constructed in such a way as to be largely culture bound. We should not, therefore, be surprised that the creaky old justices on the Supreme Court and we somewhat less creaky feminists some-times—perhaps often—respond to the same basic characterizations of male and female—although, unquestionably, the justices tend sometimes to do different things with those basic characterizations than feminists would do. At this point, we need to think as deeply as we can about what we want the future of women and men to be. Do we want equality of the sexes—or do we want justice for two kinds of human beings who are fundamentally different? If we gain equality, will we lose the special sense of kinship that grows out of experiences central to our lives and not shared by the other sex? Are feminists defending a separate women's culture while trying to break down the barriers created by men's separate culture? Could we, even if we wanted to, maintain the one while claiming our place within the other? *Michael M.*, which yokes assumptions about male sexual aggression with the conclusion that the sexes are not similarly situated because of women's pregnancy, and the Senate report on the all-male draft, which suggests that what sends men to war and leaves women at home is a fundamental trade-off by which men are assigned to battle and women to child rearing, should give us pause. I for one suspect a deep but sometimes nearly invisible set of complementarities, a yin-yang of sex-role assumptions and assignments so complex and interrelated that we cannot successfully dismantle any of it without seriously exploring the possibility of dismantling it all. The "hard cases"—cases like *Michael M.*, *Rostker*, *Gilbert*, *Geduldig*, *Caban*—give us an opportunity to rethink our basic assumptions about women and men, assumptions sometimes buried beneath our consciousness. They allow us to ask afresh who we are, what we want, and if we are willing to begin to create a new order of things.

Notes

2. This point is probably an obvious one. Until very recently, women were not represented among the lawmakers. S. TOLCHIN & M. TOLCHIN, CLOUT: WOMANPOWER AND POLITICS 17 (1973) (in 1973, women constituted 52% of the population and 53% of the voting population, but only 3% of the country's elected officials). A deliberative body made up exclusively of men—or whites, the rich, or Catholics—no matter how strong their desire to represent "all of the people," will, at least sometimes, inadequately discern, much less build into their laws, provisions that reflect the needs and interests of women—or nonwhites, the poor, or Protestants. This is not to say that there is a monolithic "women's viewpoint" any more than there is a monolithic "men's viewpoint." Plainly there is not. Rather, it is to suggest that women's life experiences still differ sufficiently from men's that a diverse group of women would bring a somewhat different set of perceptions and insights to certain issues than would a similarly diverse group of men. . . .

3. 2 BLACKSTONE'S COMMENTARIES [444] (St. George Tucker ed. 1803). . . .

4. *Id.* at 442-43. The common law disability was not honored in the equity courts, where married women could sue and be sued in their own right. *See, e.g.*, 2 J. STORY, COMMENTARIES ON EQUITY JURISPRUDENCE 597-98 (1836) [hereinafter cited as STORY, EQUITY].

5. At common law, marriage destroyed the general contractual capacity of a woman. Because marriage deprived her of ownership of her personal property and control over her real property, she possessed nothing which could be bound by her contracts. R. MORRIS, STUDIES IN THE HISTORY OF AMERICAN LAW 173 (1959) [hereinafter cited as MORRIS, STUDIES]. . . . As was the case with other disabilities, the contractual incapacity of married women was somewhat mitigated under equitable principles. . . . 2 BISHOP, COMMENTARIES ON THE LAW at 418-20 §§ 528-32 (1875); . . . STORY, EQUITY, *supra* note 4, at 626-28. . . .

6. At common law, the wife could not make a will with respect to her real property, 2 BISHOP, COMMENTARIES ON THE LAW OF MARRIED WOMEN § 535, at 422 (1875), although equity would compel the heir of the wife to make a conveyance to the party to whom she sought by will to leaver her real property. STORY, EQUITY, *supra* note 4, at 615-16. . . .

7. . . . MORRIS, STUDIES, *supra* note 5, at 166-67; STORY, EQUITY, *supra* note 4, at 630. The wife's earnings, as personalty, became the husband's. Since the wife had a common law duty to provide services to her husband, *see* 1 J. BISHOP, MARRIAGE, DIVORCE AND SEPARATION §§ 1183-84, at 510 (1891), the fruits of her labors, including earned income, were his. *Id.* at § 1202, at 579.

8. 1 BISHOP, MARRIAGE, DIVORCE AND SEPARATION § 1202, at 579. Her husband acquired an estate in her real property by virtue of marriage, which entitled him to control the property as well as receive the profits from it. C. MOYNAHAN, INTRODUCTION TO THE LAW OF REAL PROPERTY 52-54 (1962). Again, equity modified the harshness of

the common law by permitting the creation of an equitable estate under certain circumstances. STORY, EQUITY, *supra* note 4, at 608–14.

9. *See, e.g.,* 2 BLACKSTONE, COMMENTARIES 444–45 (St. George Tucker ed. 1803). . . .

10. 1 BLACKSTONE, COMMENTARIES, 444 (St. George Tucker ed. 1803). . . .

11. The history of the common law rule that marriage was a defense to a charge of rape is traced in State v. Smith, 148 N.J. Super. 219, 372 A.2d 386 (Essex County Ct. 1977). Several states have abrogated this doctrine by statute. *See generally* Barry, *Spousal Rape: The Uncommon Law,* 66 A.B.A.J. 1088 (1980).

12. . . . These early separate estate acts were limited measures; they did not grant women a right to their own earnings nor a general contractual capacity. Those developments emerged in the final third of the century. New York, for example, created such rights in an 1860 amendment to the 1848 act. [Johnston, *Sex and Property: The Common Law Tradition, The Law School Curriculum, and Developments Toward Equality,* 47 N.Y.U. L. REV. 1033, 1066 (1972)].

13. *See, e.g.,* N. COTT, THE BONDS OF WOMANHOOD: "WOMAN'S SPHERE" IN NEW ENGLAND, 1780–1835, at 197–200 (1977).

14. Separate spheres ideology was used, for example, to justify denial of the vote to women, E. FLEXNER, CENTURY OF STRUGGLE: THE WOMEN'S RIGHTS MOVEMENT IN THE UNITED STATES 306 (rev. ed. 1975); to exclude them from the practice of law, Bradwell v. Illinois, 83 U.S. 130 (1873); and to excuse them from participation in jury service, Hoyt v. Florida, 368 U.S. 57 (1961).

The Court in Muller v. Oregon, 208 U.S. 412, 421–22, a case upholding limitations on the hours women were permitted to work, was quite explicit on the subject: "Still again, history disclosed the fact that woman has always been dependent upon man. He established his control at the outset by superior physical strength, and this control in various forms, with diminishing intensity, has continued to the present. . . . Though limitations upon personal and contractual rights may be removed by legislation, there is that in her disposition and habits of life which will operate against full assertion of those rights. She will still be where some legislation to protect her seems necessary to secure real equality of right."

15. 83 U.S. 130, 141 (1873).

16. *Id.*

17. 208 U.S. 412 (1908).

18. "[H]er physical structure and the proper discharge of her maternal functions— having in view not merely her own health, but the well-being of the race—justify legislation to protect her from the greed as well as the passion of man. . . . " *Id.* at 422.

19. Hoyt v. Florida, 368 U.S. 57, 62 (1961).

20. Reed v. Reed, 404 U.S. 71, 75 (1971). . . .

21. Craig v. Boren, 429 U.S. 190, 197 (1976). "[C]lassifications by gender must serve important governmental objectives and must be substantially related to the achievement of those objectives."

22. *Reed* had required that the gender-based classification bear a "fair and substantial relationship to the object of the legislation." 404 U.S. at 76. The typical articulation of the standard applicable to racial classifications was that the classification must be "necessary" to a "compelling state purpose." The effect of *Craig,* then, was to maintain the "substantial relationship" requirement of *Reed* and to add to it a heavier burden upon the state with respect to the state's purpose. The result was a standard consciously parallel in its elements to, but less stringent than, the racial classification standard.

23. Frontiero v. Richardson, 411 U.S. 677 (1973).

24. Califano v. Goldfarb, 430 U.S. 199 (1977).

25. Califano v. Westcott, 443 U.S. 76 (1979).

26. Wengler v. Druggists Mutual Insurance Co., 446 U.S. 142 (1980).

27. Weinberger v. Wiesenfeld, 420 U.S. 636 (1975).

28. Stanton v. Stanton, 421 U.S. 7 (1975).

29. Orr v. Orr, 440 U.S. 268 (1979).

30. Kirschberg v. Feenstra, 450 U.S. 455 (1981).

31. Reed v. Reed, 404 U.S. 71 (1971).

35. *See, e.g.*, Kahn v. Shevin, 416 U.S. 351 (1974) (Florida statute granting widows but not widowers property tax exemption constitutional because intended to assist sex financially most affected by spousal loss) and Califano v. Webster, 430 U.S. 313 (1977) (Social Security Act section creating benefit calculation formula more favorable to women than men held constitutional because intended to compensate women for wage discrimination). . . .

36. *See, e.g.*, Schlesinger v. Ballard, 419 U.S. 498 (1975) (Court upheld (5-4) law that results in discharge of male officers if twice passed over for promotion, but guarantees female officers 13-year tenure before discharge for lack of promotion); Rostker v. Goldberg, 453 U.S. 57 (1981); Michael M. v. Superior Court, 450 U.S. 464 (1981); Dothard v. Rawlinson, 443 U.S. 321 (1977); Geduldig v. Aiello, 417 U.S. 484 (1974): General Electric Corp. v. Gilbert, 429 U.S. 125 (1976); Nashville Gas Co. v. Satty, 434 U.S. 136 (1977). All of these cases were authored either by Justice Stewart or by Justice Rehnquist.
. . .

37. 450 U.S. 455 (1981).

38. 453 U.S. 57 (1981).

39. 450 U.S. 464 (1981).

40. 453 U.S. at 75.

41. *Id.* at 76.

42. *Id.* The Court pointed out that the Navy and Air Force combat exclusions are statutory; the Army and Marine Corps "precludes the use of women in combat as a matter of established policy." *Id.*

43. *Id.* at 78-79.

44. *Id.*

45. See dissent of Justice White, joined by Justice Brennan, *id.* at 85.

46. 450 U.S. at 466, California's statute, which renamed the crime "illegal intercourse" in 1970, proscribed the act of sexual intercourse "accomplished with female not the wife of the perpetrator, where the female is under the age of 18 years." CAL. PENAL CODE § 261.5 (West Supp. 1982).

48. 450 U.S. at 471.

49. *Id.* at 473. . . .

52. 453 U.S. at 83 (White J., dissenting, joined by Brennan, J.: "I assume what has not been challenged in this case—that excluding women from combat positions does not offend the Constitution"). *Id.* at 93 (Marshall, J., dissenting, joined by Brennan, J.: "Had appellees raised a constitutional challenge to the prohibition against assignment of women to combat, this discussion in the Senate Report might well provide persuasive reasons for upholding the restrictions. But the validity of the combat restrictions is not an issue we need decide in this case").

53. Department of Defense Authorization Act of 1981. S. Rep. No. 826, 96th Cong., 2d Sess., *reprinted in* U.S. CODE CONG. & AD. NEWS 2646, 2647 (emphasis added).

54. *Id.*

55. *Id.*

56. *Id.* at 2649.

57. *Id.*

63. "Contrary to [defendant's] assertions, the statute does not rest on the assumption that males are generally the aggressors." 450 U.S. at 475.

64. *Id.* at 467. Justice Blackmun, concurring, for some unknown reason graced posterity with extensive quotations from the transcript of the preliminary hearing (the actual details of the sexual liaison were not relevant to the constitutional issue presented to the court). The facts are a marvelous illustration of the cultural phenomenon of male initiator, female responder. But Justice Blackmun chose to delete (and Justice Rehnquist failed to mention) the young woman's specific response to the defendant's rather forceful request for sexual intercourse. Justice Mosk, of the California Supreme Court, supplies the detail: "In due course Michael told Sharon to remove her pants, and when at first she demurred he allegedly struck her twice. *Sharon testified she then said to herself, 'Forget it,' and decided to let him do as he wished.* The couple then had intercourse." *Id.* at 484-85; 25 Cal. 3d at 616, 159 Cal. Rptr, at 345, 601 P.2d at 577 (emphasis added). Sharon was not entirely in a passive-responsive mode, however. After Sharon and the defendant, Michael, had spent some time hugging and kissing in the bushes, Sharon's sister and two other young men approached them. Sharon declined to go home with her sister, who then left with one of the two. Sharon thereupon approached and began kissing Bruce, the other young man. When Bruce left, Sharon then rejoined Michael, whereupon the events giving rise to his prosecution transpired. 450 U.S. at 486-87; 25 Cal. 3d at 616, 159 Cal. Rptr. at 345, 601 P.2d at 577.

65. 450 U.S. at 467 (emphasis added).

68. 450 U.S. at 471-72. . . .

69. *Id.* at 475.

78. Susan Brownmiller observes that "Women are trained to be rape victims. . . . Rape seeps into our childhood consciousness by imperceptible degrees. Even before we learn to read we have become indoctrinated into a victim mentality." S. Brownmiller, Against Our Will: Men, Women and Rape 309 (1975).

83. *See, e.g.,* General Electric Co. v. Gilbert, 429 U.S. 125, 161-62 (1976) (Stevens, J., dissenting).

84. Geduldig v. Aiello, 417 U.S. 484, 496 n.20 (1974).

85. In Reed v. Reed, 404 U.S. 17 (1971), the Court said that sex classifications were "subject to scrutiny," *id.* at 75, and that such classifications must bear a "fair and substantial relation to the object of the legislation." *Id.* at 76 (quoting Royster Guano Co. v. Virginia, 253 U.S. 412, 415 (1920)). In Frontiero v. Richardson, 411 U.S. 677 (1973), the Court came within one vote of deciding that sex classifications were "suspect" and that the state must prove that such classifications were necessary to a compelling state interest, the standard it applied in race cases. In *Geduldig,* the Court said, "The dissenting opinion to the contrary, this case is thus a far cry from cases like Reed . . . and Frontiero . . . involving discrimination based upon gender as such." 417 U.S. at 496 n.20.

86. 417 U.S. 484.

87. *Id.* at 496-97 n.20 (emphasis added).

88. 429 U.S. 125.

89. *Id.* 135.

90. *Id.* at 136-40.

91. *Id.*

92. *Id.* at 152 (Brennan. J., dissenting).

93. *See, e.g.,* Whitbeck, *Theories of Sexual Difference,* in Women and Philosophy 68 (Gould & Wartofsky eds. 1976). . . .

94. 434 U.S. 136 (1977).

95. *Id.* at 137.
96. *Id.* at 142.
98. *Gilbert,* 429 U.S. at 139 n. 17. *See also Satty,* 434 U.S. at 142. . . .
99. 42 U.S.C. § 2000e(k) (Supp. IV 1980).
100. Thus, Title VII makes it an unlawful employment practice for an employer to classify on the basis of sex, 42 U.S.C. § 2000e-2(a), unless the employer can establish that sex is a "bona fide occupational qualification reasonably necessary to the normal operation of [the] particular business or enterprise," 42 U.S.C. § 2000e-2(e). The exception has been narrowly interpreted. *See* Dothard v. Rawlinson, 433 U.S. 321, 334 (1977) ("We are persuaded . . . that the bfoq exception was in fact meant to be an extremely narrow exception to the general prohibition of discrimination on the basis of sex.") Once the plaintiff establishes the existence of a sex-based classification, the burden of persuasion shifts to the employer to establish that sex is a bfoq. *See, e.g.,* Weeks v. Southern Bell Tel. and Tel. Co., 408 F.2d 228, 235 (5th Cir. 1969).
101. 42 U.S.C. § 2000e(k) (Supp. IV 1980).
104. MONT. CODE ANN. §§ 39-7-201 to 209 (1981). The law also provided that an employee disabled as a result of pregnancy was entitled to her accrued disability or leave benefits. *Id.* at 39-7-203(3). . . .
105. Miller-Wohl Co. v. Comm'r of Labor & Industry, State of Montana, 414 F. Supp. 1264, 1265 (D. Mont. 1981), *rev'd on procedural grounds.* 685 F.2d 1088 (9th Cir. 1982).
106. *Id.* The trial court held that the statute did not conflict with the PDA because employers could comply with the state act *and* avoid discrimination by extending to persons disabled for other reasons the protections the act guarantees to pregnant women.
107. I did, for example.
108. *See* brief *amicus curiae* submitted on behalf of Equal Rights Advocates, Inc., Employment Law Center, and California Fair Employment Practice Commission in *Miller-Wohl.*
115. Title VII does not permit such practices. As a practical matter, however, proof of such motivations is difficult. Actions based on a class sufficiently large to illuminate the hidden motivation are prohibitively expensive and complex.
116. 208 U.S. 412, 422. . . .
117. *See, e.g.,* Harris v. McRae, 448 U.S. 297, 325 (1980) . . . ; Maher v. Roe, 432 U.S. 464, 478–79 (1977). . . . *See also* Poelker v. Doe, 432 U.S. 519, 520–21 (1977).
118. *See generally* Williams, *Firing the Woman to Protect the Fetus: The Reconciliation of Fetal Protection with Employment Opportunity Goals Under Title VIII.* 69 GEO. L.J. 641, 647–50 (1981).
119. . . . NATIONAL INDUSTRIAL CONFERENCE BOARD, *Maternity Leaves of Absence,* 21 MANAGEMENT RECORD 232–34, 250–63 (1959). . . .
120. *See, e.g.,* MEYER, WOMEN AND EMPLOYEE BENEFITS 2, 4 (1978) (The reason many employers resist paying disability benefits for pregnancy-related disabilities is that "a specific group—mothers-to-be— . . . is widely regarded as being made up of terminal employees whose loyalty will be to their homes and children rather than to the corporation.")
123. *See* Phillips v. Martin Marietta Corp., 400 U.S. 542 (1971) (company policy prohibiting the hiring of mothers but not fathers of preschool-aged children violates section 703(a) of Title VII). . . .
124. 441 U.S. 380 (1979).
125. *Id.* at 405 n.10 (Stevens, J., dissenting).
126. I certainly number myself among those who have experienced this magical feeling and know, from many conversations with other mothers, that my experience is hardly

unique. It seems apparent, however, that my reaction is not universal. *See* J. BERNARD. THE FUTURE OF MOTHERHOOD 35 (1974). More importantly, falling in love with a child is apparently not limited to mothers or even to biological parents. . . .

127. *See, e.g.,* Rossi, *A Biosocial Perspective on Parenting,* DAEDALUS, Spring 1977, at 3–5.

128. *See, e.g.,* Arnay, *Maternal-Infant Bonding: The Politics of Falling in Love With Your Child,* 6 FEMINIST STUDIES 546 (1980). Arnay reviews the bonding literature and concludes that its claims have not been adequately established. *Id.* at 548–56. He warns that "Bonding theory lends legitimacy to the notion that women are the only appropriate attendants for children." *Id.* at 564. . . .

129. Both blacks and caucasian women were believed to have smaller and less convoluted brains and therefore restricted intellects. *See, e.g.,* J. HALLER & R. HALLER, THE PHYSICIAN AND SEXUALITY IN VICTORIAN AMERICA 53–61 (1978); S. GOULD, THE MISMEASURE OF MAN 103–107 (1981). Women who did exert their intellects were thought to endanger their reproductive organs and even, if they pursued careers, to desex themselves and become "mannish" women. *See* Smith-Rosenberg and Rosenberg, *The Female Animal: Medical and Biological Views of Woman and Her Role in Nineteenth-Century America,* 60 J. AM. HIST. 332 (1973): HALLER & HALLER, *supra, at* 60–61; B. EHRENREICH & D. ENGLISH, FOR HER OWN GOOD: 150 YEARS OF THE EXPERTS' ADVICE TO WOMEN 125–31 (1979).

Ehrenreich and English point out that men, too, were faced with a competition between their brains and their reproductive organs for their bodies' limited energy supply, but in the case of men, doctors recommended that they enhance their intellects by preserving their male fluids: "Since the mission of the male (the middle-class male, anyway) was to be a businessman, professor, lawyer, or gynecologist—he had to be careful to conserve all his energy for the 'higher functions.' Doctors warned men not to 'spend their seed' (the material essence of their energy) recklessly in marital relations, and of course not to let it dribble away in secret vice or prurient dreams." *Id.* at 126.

130. B. EHRENREICH & D. ENGLISH, *supra* note 129, at 120–25. . . .

3

Reconstructing Sexual Equality [1987]

Christine A. Littleton

. . .

Development of Feminist Legal Theory

. . .

Feminist Responses

Feminist legal theory has been primarily reactive, responding to the development of legal racial equality theory. The form of response, however, has varied. One response has been to attempt to equate legal treatment of sex with that of race and deny that there are in fact any significant natural differences between women and men; in other words, to consider the two sexes symmetrically located with regard to *any* issue, norm, or rule.[75] This response, which I term the "symmetrical" approach, classifies asymmetries as illusions, "overboard generalizations," or temporary glitches that will disappear with a little behavior modification. A competing response rejects this analogy, accepting that women and men are or may be "different," and that women and men are often asymmetrically located in society. This response, which I term the "assymmetrical" approach, rejects the notion that all gender differences are likely to disappear, or even that they should.

1. Symmetrical Models of Sexual Equality

Feminists theorists frequently take the symmetrical approach to sexual equality, not as an ideal, but as the only way to avoid returning to separate spheres ideology. For example, in her highly compelling defense of symmetry in the law, Wendy Williams warns that "we can't have it both ways, we need to think carefully about which way we want to have it."[78]

There are two models of the symmetrical vision—referred to here as "assimilation" and "androgyny." Assimilation, the model most often accepted by the courts, is based on the notion that women, given the chance, really are or could be just like men. Therefore, the argument runs, the law should require

35

social institutions to treat women as they already treat men—requiring, for example, that the professions admit women to the extent they are "qualified," but also insisting that women who enter time-demanding professions such as the practice of law sacrifice relationships (especially with their children) to the same extent that male lawyers have been forced to do.

Androgyny, the second symmetrical model, also posits that women and men are, or at least could be, very much like each other, but argues that equality requires institutions to pick some golden mean between the two and treat both sexes as androgynous persons would be treated. However, given that all of our institutions, work habits, and pay scales were formulated without the benefit of substantial numbers of androgynous persons, androgynous symmetry is difficult to conceptualize, and might require very substantial restructuring of many public and private institutions. In order to be truly androgynous within a symmetrical framework, social institutions must find a single norm that works equally well for all gendered characteristics. Part of my discomfort with androgynous models is that they depend on "meeting in the middle," while I distrust the ability of any person, and especially any court, to value women enough to find the "middle." Moreover, the problems involved in determining such a norm for even one institution are staggering. At what height should a conveyor belt be set in order to satisfy a symmetrical androgynous ideal?

Symmetry appears to have great appeal for the legal system, and this is not surprising. The hornbook definition of equal protection is "that those who are similarly situated be similarly treated,"[88] and many courts, following the Supreme Court's lead, have held that absent a showing of similarity, strict scrutiny is simply inapplicable.[89] Symmetrical analysis also has great appeal for liberal men,[90] to whom it appears to offer a share in the feminist enterprise. If perceived difference between the sexes is only the result of overly rigid sex roles, the men's liberty is at stake too. Ending this form of sexual inequality could free men to express their "feminine" side, just as it frees women to express their "masculine" side.

2. Asymmetrical Models of Sexual Equality

Asymmetrical approaches to sexual equality take the position that difference should not be ignored or eradicated. Rather, they argue that any sexually equal society must somehow deal with difference, problematic as that may be. Asymmetrical approaches include "special rights," "accommodation," "acceptance," and "empowerment."

The special rights model affirms that women and men *are* different, and asserts that cultural differences, such as childrearing roles, are rooted in biological ones, such as reproduction. Therefore, it states, society must take account of these differences and ensure that women are not punished for them. This approach, sometimes referred to as a "bivalent" model,[93] is closest to the "special treatment" pole of the asymmetrical/symmetrical equality debate. Elizabeth Wolgast, a major proponent of special rights, argues that women cannot be men's "equals" because equality by definition requires sameness.[94] Instead of equality, she suggests seeking justice, claiming special rights for women based on their special needs.[95]

The second asymmetrical model, accommodation, agrees that differential treatment of biological differences (such as pregnancy, and perhaps breastfeeding) is necessary, but argues that cultural or hard-to-classify differences (such as career interests and skills) should be treated under an equal treatment or androgynous model. Examples of accommodation models include Sylvia Law's approach to issues of reproductive biology[96] and Herma Hill Kay's "episodic" approach to the condition of pregnancy.[97] These approaches could also be characterized as "symmetry, with concessions to asymmetry where necessary." The accommodationists limit the asymmetry in their models to biological differences because, like Williams, they fear a return to separate spheres ideology should asymmetrical theory go too far.[98]

My own attempt to grapple with difference, which I call an "acceptance" model,[99] is essentially asymmetrical. While not endorsing the notion that cultural differences between the sexes are biologically determined, it does recognize and attempt to deal with both biological and social differences. Acceptance does not view sex differences as problematic per se, but rather focuses on the ways in which differences are permitted to justify inequality. It asserts that eliminating the unequal consequences of sex differences is more important than debating whether such differences are "real," or even trying to eliminate them altogether.

Unlike the accommodationists, who would limit asymmetrical analysis to purely biological differences, my proposal also requires equal acceptance of cultural differences. The reasons for this are twofold. First, the distinction between biological and cultural, while useful analytically, is itself culturally based. Second, the inequality experienced by women is often presented as a necessary consequence of cultural rather than of biological difference. If, for instance, women do in fact "choose" to become nurses rather than real estate appraisers,[100] it is not because of any biological imperative. Yet, regardless of the reasons for the choice, they certainly do not choose to be paid less. It is the consequences of gendered difference, and not its sources, that equal acceptance addresses.

If, as it appears from Gilligan's studies,[101] women and men tend to develop somewhat differently in terms of their values and inclinations, each of these modes of development must be equally valid and valuable. In our desire for equality, we should not be forced to jettison either; rather, we should find some way to value both. That such different modes do not perfectly correspond to biological sex does not prevent them from being typed socially as "male" and "female," and neither should it prevent us from demanding that they be equally valued. Thus, if women currently tend to assume primary responsibility for childrearing, we should not ignore that fact in an attempt to prefigure the rosy day when parenting is fully shared. We should instead figure out how to assure that equal resources, status, and access to social decisionmaking flow to those women (and few men) who engage in this socially female behavior.

The focus of equality as acceptance, therefore, is not on the question of whether women are different, but rather on the question of how the social fact of gender asymmetry can be dealt with so as to create some symmetry in the lived-out experience of all members of the community. I do not think it matters so much whether differences are "natural" or not; they are built into our structures and selves in either event. As social facts, differences are created by the interaction of person with person or person with institution; they inhere in the relationship, not in the person. On this view, the function of equality is to make gender differences, perceived or actual, costless relative to each other, so that anyone may follow a male, female, or androgynous lifestyle according to their natural inclination or choice without being punished for following a female lifestyle or rewarded for following a male one.

As an illustration of this approach, consider what many conceive to be the paradigm difference between men and women—pregnancy. No one disputes that only women become pregnant, but symmetrical theorists analogize pregnancy to other events, in order to preserve the unitary approach of symmetrical theory. Such attempts to minimize difference have the ironic result of obscuring more fundamental similarities.

In *California Federal Savings & Loan Association v. Guerra (Cal. Fed.)*,[105] Lillian Garland, a receptionist at California Federal tried to return to her job after the birth of her child. The bank refused to reinstate her, and she sued under the California Fair Employment and Housing Act (FEHA).[106] That law requires that employees temporarily disabled by pregnancy be given an unpaid leave of up to four months, with guaranteed reinstatement in their original job or its equivalent.[107] The bank in turn sued in federal court, claiming that the FEHA was preempted by Title VII of the Civil Rights Act of 1964,[108] as amended by the Pregnancy Discrimination Act (PDA). The PDA requires only that employers treat pregnancy the same as any other disability.[109] California Federal argued that the PDA prevented California from enforcing its pregnancy disability leave requirements against firms that did not provide these benefits for disabilities unrelated to pregnancy.[110]

In addition to narrow questions of statutory interpretation, *Cal. Fed.* raised more fundamental questions about the meaning of equal employment opportunity for women. Citing the dangers of separate spheres ideology raised by "protectionist" legislation, the national ACLU filed an amicus brief arguing that the California law should be struck down, and that the remedy should provide for job-protected leave for all temporarily disabled employees, whatever the source of their disability.[111] California feminist groups, such as Equal Rights Advocates, filed on the other side of the debate, arguing that the California law guaranteed equality of opportunity, and was thus consistent with federal law and policy.[112]

Missing in these arguments, however, was any recognition that working men and women shared a more fundamental right than the right to basic disability leave benefits or job protection. The Coalition for Reproductive Equality in the Workplace (CREW) advanced the position that working women and men share a right to procreative choice in addition to an interest in disability leave.[113] In order to ensure equal exercise of procreative rights, it argued, an employer must provide leave adequate to the effects of pregnancy.

The California statute eliminates barriers to equality in both procreation and employment faced by women who cannot afford to lose their jobs when they decide to become parents. Male employees who become fathers and female employees who become mothers are thus enabled to combine procreation and employment to the same extent.[114]

This form of acceptance, unlike those that analogize pregnancy to disability, emphasizes the basic commonality of procreation as a human endeavor involving both women and men. By recognizing pregnancy as "different" from other causes of disability, it supports efforts to equalize the position of working women and men with respect to this fundamental right.[115]

The foregoing asymmetrical models, including my own, share the notion that, regardless of their differences, women and men must be treated as full members of society. Each model acknowledges that women may need treatment different than that accorded to men in order to effectuate their membership in important spheres of social life; all would allow at least some such claims, although on very different bases, and probably in very different circumstances.

A final asymmetrical approach, "empowerment," rejects difference altogether as a relevant subject of inquiry.[117] In its strongest form, empowerment claims that the subordination of women to men has itself constructed the sexes, and their differences. For example, Catharine MacKinnon argues:

> [I]t makes a lot of sense that women might have a somewhat distinctive perspective on social life. We may or may not speak in a different voice—I think that the voice that we have been said to speak in is in fact in large part the 'feminine' voice, the voice of the victim speaking without consciousness. But when we understand that women are *forced* into this situation of inequality, it makes a lot of sense that we should want to negotiate, since we lose conflicts. It makes a lot of sense that we should want to urge values of care, because it is what we have been valued for. We have had little choice but to be valued this way.[118]

A somewhat weaker version of the claim is that we simply do not and cannot know whether there are any important differences between the sexes that have not been created by the dynamic of domination and subordination. In either event, the argument runs, we should forget about the question of differences and focus directly on subordination and domination. If a law, practice, or policy contributes to the subordination of women or their domination by men, it violates equality. If it empowers women or contributes to the breakdown of male domination, it enhances equality.

The reconceptualization of equality as antidomination, like the model of equality as acceptance, attempts to respond directly to the concrete and lived-out experience of women. Like other asymmetrical models, it allows different treatment of women and men when necessary to effectuate its overall goal of ending women's subordination. However, it differs substantially from the acceptance model in its rejection of the membership, belonging, and participatory aspects of equality.

3. *The Difference That Difference Makes*

Each of the several models of equality discussed above, if adopted, would have a quite different impact on the structure of society. If this society wholeheartedly embraced the symmetrical approach of assimilation—the point of view that "women are just like men"—little would need to be changed in our economic or political institutions except to get rid of lingering traces of irrational prejudice, such as an occasional employer's preference for male employees. In contrast, if society adopted the androgyny model, which views both women and men as bent out of shape by current sex roles and requires both to conform to an androgynous model, it would have to alter radically its methods of resource distribution. In the employment context, this might mean wholesale revamping of methods for determining the "best person for the job." Thus, while assimilation would merely require law firms to hire women who have managed to get the same credentials as the men they have traditionally hired, androgyny might insist that the firm hire only those persons with credentials that would be possessed by someone neither "socially male" nor "socially female."[124]

If society adopted an asymmetrical approach such as the accommodation model, no radical restructuring would be necessary. Government would need only insist that women be given what they need to resemble men, such as time off to have babies and the freedom to return to work on the same rung of the ladder as their male counterparts. If, however, society adopted the model of equality as acceptance, which seeks to make difference costless, it might additionally insist that women and men who opt for socially female occupations, such as child-rearing, be compensated at a rate similar to those women and men who opt for socially male occupations, such as legal practice. Alternatively, such occupations might be restructured to make them equally accessible to those whose behavior is culturally coded "male" or "female."

The different models also have different potential to challenge the phallocentrism of social institutions. No part of the spectrum of currently available feminist legal theory is completely immune to the feminist critique of society as phallocentric. We cannot outrun our history, and that history demonstrates that the terms of social discourse have been set by men who, actively or passively, have ignored women's voices—until even the possibility of women having a voice has become questionable. Nevertheless, the models do differ with respect to the level at which the phallocentrism of the culture reappears.

Under the assimilationist approach, for example, women merit equal treatment only so far as they can demonstrate that they are similar to men. The assimilation model is thus fatally phallocentric. To the extent that women cannot or will not conform to socially male forms of behavior, they are left out in the cold. To the extent they do or can conform, they do not achieve equality as women, but as social males.

Similarly, empowerment and androgyny (an asymmetrical and a symmetrical approach, respectively) both rely on central concepts whose current meaning is phallocentrically biased. If "power" and "neutrality" (along with "equality") were not themselves gendered concepts, the empowerment and androgyny approaches would be less problematic. But our culture conceives of power as power used by men, and creates androgynous models "tilted" toward the male. As Carrie Menkel-Meadow put it, the trouble with marble cake is that it never has enough chocolate; the problem with androgyny is that it never has enough womanness.[131] Similarly, empowering women without dealing with difference, like assimilation, too easily becomes simply sharing male power more broadly.

Equality as acceptance is not immune from phallocentrism in several of its component concepts. However, these concepts are not necessarily entailed by theory and may be replaced with less biased concepts as they reveal themselves through the process of equalization. For example, in discussing employment-related applications of the model, I use the measures already existing in that sphere—money, status, and access to decisionmaking. These measures of value are obviously suspect. Nevertheless, my use of them is contingent. Acceptance requires only that culturally coded "male" and "female" complements be equally valued; it does not dictate the coin in which such value should be measured. By including access to decisionmaking as part of the measure, however, the theory holds out the possibility that future measures of value will be created by women and men *together*. Thus, acceptance strives to create the preconditions necessary for sexually integrated debate about a more appropriate value system.

The various models of equality arise out of common feminist goals and enterprises: trying to imagine what a sexually equal society would look like, given that none of us has ever seen one; and trying to figure out ways of getting there, given that the obstacles to sexual equality are so many and so strong.

The perception among feminist legal thinkers that the stakes in the symmetrical vs. asymmetrical debate are high is correct. Difference indeed makes a difference. Yet, the frantic nature of the debate about difference between the sexes makes the divergent views within feminist legal thought appear as a deadly danger rather than an exciting opportunity. The label "divisive" gets slapped on before the discussion even gets underway.

We need to recognize difference among women as diversity rather than division, and difference between women and men as opportunity rather than danger. Audre Lorde calls for the recognition of difference among women in terms that should apply to all human difference:

> As a tool of social control, women have been encouraged to recognize only one area of human difference as legitimate, those differences which exist between women and men. And we have learned to deal across those differences with the urgency of all oppressed subordinates. . . . We have recognized and negotiated these differences, even when this recognition only continued the old dominant/ subordinate mode of human relationship, where the oppressed must recognize the masters' difference in order to survive.
>
> *But our future survival is predicated upon our ability to relate within equality.*[135]

There must be choices beyond those of ignoring difference or accepting inequality. So long as difference itself is so expensive in the coin of equality, we approach the variety of human experience with blinders on. Perhaps if difference were not so costly, we, as feminists, could think about it more clearly. Perhaps if equality did not require uniformity, we, as women, could demand it less ambivalently.

Equality and Difference

.   .   .

Feminist Critique of Equality

The phallocentricity of equality is most apparent in the extraordinary difficulty the legal system has had dealing with the fact that women (and *not* men) conceive and bear children. Indeed, it would not be necessary to go further than to establish that the legal system *has* had difficulty with this fact in order to ground the claim that equality analysis is phallocentric. It is, however, necessary to go beyond a simple recounting of the law in this area in order to lay out the particular ways in which the phallocentricity is manifested.

. . . [T]he Supreme Court's decision in *Reed v. Reed*[139] marked its acceptance of the "assimilationist" model of sexual equality. That decision was profoundly assimilationist in that the Court rejected as "irrational" the view that women might be different from men with respect to their ability to handle the traditionally "male" responsibilities of estate administration.

The first cases to reach the Supreme Court after its about-face in *Reed* did not present questions that challenged this assimilationist model. In *Craig v. Boren*,[142] for example, the Court saw the differences in driving patterns of male and female teenage drinkers not as a significant difference, but rather as one that could readily be ignored, thus failing to provide a substantial "fit" between the difference and the differential classification. Similarly, those classifications that were upheld by the Court were justified as temporary measures to reduce differences that were not intractable. Thus, in *Kahn v. Shevin*,[143] Florida's tax subsidy to widows (and not widowers) was upheld as a reasonable attempt to compensate the spouse who would most severely feel the economic loss of the other partner to the marriage, a difference that would disappear once sex discrimination is gone from our society. Temporary alleviation of socially created (and socially remediable) differences between the sexes is simple affirmative action. Its goal is symmetry of the sexes, achieved through temporary asymmetrical treatment. Under this view, had men been irrationally discriminated against in employment, it might just as easily have been the widowers rather than the widows who needed the tax break.

When challenges arose to pregnancy-based classifications, however, the Court was faced with a difference that it could not ignore or treat as created by irrational discrimination. In *Geduldig v. Aiello*[145] and *General Electric Co. v. Gilbert*,[146] the Supreme Court announced, apparently with a straight face, that singling out pregnancy for disadvantageous treatment was not discrimination on the basis of *sex*. Underlying both opinions was the unarticulated assumption that pregnancy was a real difference, and that equality was therefore simply inapplicable. As Justice Stewart stated in *Geduldig*, "There is no risk from which men are protected and women are not. Likewise, there is no risk from which women are protected and men are not."[148]

The Court's equality analysis could thus deal with overboard generalizations, questions of closeness of fit, and even temporary affirmative action, but a generalization of difference between the sexes that was accurate, and permanently so, was beyond the pale. The first strand of the feminist critique of equality addresses this failing, asserting that *equality analysis defines as beyond its scope precisely those issues that women find crucial to their concrete experience as women.*

Legal equality analysis "runs out" when it encounters "real" difference, and only becomes available if and when the difference is analogized to some experience men can have too. Legislative overruling of *Gilbert* by the Pregnancy Discrimination Act was thus accomplished by making pregnancy look similar to something men experienced as well—disability. Given the way employment is structured, pregnancy renders a woman unable to work for a few days to a few months, just like illness and injury do for men. However, what makes pregnancy a *disability* rather than, say, an additional ability, is the structure of work, not reproduction. Normal pregnancy may make a woman unable to "work" for days, weeks or months, but it also makes her able to reproduce. From whose viewpoint is the work that she cannot do "work," and the work that she is doing *not* work? Certainly not from hers.

Thus, the second strand of the feminist critique of equality states: *Difference, which is created by the relationship of women to particular and contingent social structures, is taken as natural (that is, unchangeable and inherent), and it is located solely in the woman herself.* It is not impossible to imagine a definition of "work" that includes the "labor" of childbirth; nor is it impossible to imagine a workplace setting in which pregnancy would not be disabling.

Analogizing pregnancy to disability has created new difficulties for a legal system trying to apply an assimilationist model of equality. In *California Federal Savings & Loan Association v. Guerra*,[154] an employer challenged a mandatory pregnancy leave statute, arguing that the law could be regarded as equal treatment, rather than a special bonus for women, only where men already have a right to disability leave for other reasons. Underlying the employer's argument was the assumption that the workplace is itself a gender-neutral institution that must treat all workers evenhandedly. Evenhanded treatment requires treating each worker the same as her coworkers, which means extending leave to all workers regardless of cause or denying leave to all. This reasoning falls prey to the second strand of the critique by assuming that if women have other needs for disability leave, it is because *they* are different.

It also gives rise to a third objection: that an institution structured so that women are inevitably disadvantaged by its facially neutral policies is itself phallocentric. Thus, *the third strand of the critique challenges the assumed gender-neutrality of social institutions, as well as the notion that practices must distinguish themselves from "business as usual" in order to be seen as unequal.*

The inability of traditional equality analysis to cope with difference is not limited to biological differences in the workplace. Purporting to follow state constitutional equal rights amendments, many state courts have visited severe hardship on women in marital dissolution proceedings. In case after case, women who have spent most of the marriage as full-time homemakers and mothers are treated as "equal" to their male partners who have spent those years developing a career.[156] In setting alimony awards, courts have refused even to consider the possibility that the woman might find herself at a competitive disadvantage in the job market—a disadvantage directly related to the work she performed during the marriage. Instead, the parties are treated "equally," and any prior disadvantaging of the women vis-a-vis the workplace is completely ignored.[157]

To summarize, from a feminist viewpoint, current equality analysis is phallocentrically biased in three respects: (1) it is inapplicable once it encounters "real" differences; (2) it locates difference in women, rather than in relationships; and (3) it fails to question the assumptions that social institutions are gender-neutral, and that women and men are therefore similarly related to those institutions. What the three strands of this critique share is their focus on "difference." A reconstructed equality analysis—one that seeks to eliminate, or at least reduce, the phallocentrism of the current model—must at some point deal with each strand of the critique. Thus, from a theoretical standpoint, symmetrical equality models, with their insistence that difference be ignored, eradicated or dissolved, are not responsive to the feminist critique of equality.

. . .

Equality as Acceptance

The model of equality as acceptance responds to the first strand of the feminist critique of equality by insisting that equality can in fact be applied *across* difference. It is not, however, a "leveling" proposal. Rather, equality as acceptance calls for equalization across only those differences that the culture has encoded as gendered complements. The theory of comparable worth provides one example of this, and the field of athletics yields another.

Most proponents of comparable worth have defined the claim along the following lines: jobs that call for equally valuable skills, effort, and responsibility should be paid equally, even though they occur in different combinations of predominantly female and predominantly male occupations.[172] Thus, when an employer has defined two job classifications as gendered complements, the employer should pay the same to each. Equality as acceptance makes the broader claim that *all* behavioral forms that the culture (not just the employer) has encoded as "male" and "female" counterparts should be equally rewarded. Acceptance would thus support challenges to the overvaluation of "male" skills (and corresponding undervaluation of "female" ones) by employers, rather than limiting challenges to unequal application of an existing valuation or to the failure to make such a valuation.

In the sphere of athletics, equality as acceptance would support an argument that equal resources be allocated to male and female sports programs regardless of whether the sports themselves are "similar." In this way, women's equality in athletics would not depend on the ability of individual women to assimilate themselves to the particular sports activities traditionally engaged in by men.

Under the model of equality as acceptance, equality analysis does not end at the discovery of a "real" difference. Rather, it attempts to assess the "cultural meaning" of that difference, and to determine how to achieve equality despite it. This formulation responds to the second strand of the feminist critique by locating difference in the relationship between women and men rather than in women alone, as accommodation arguably does. Acceptance would thus provide little support for the claim that traditionally male sports (such as football) should be modified so as to accommodate women (or vice versa). Equality as acceptance does not prescribe the superiority of socially female categories, nor even the superiority of androgynous categories. It does, however, affirm the equal validity of men's and women's lives.

Finally, equality as acceptance responds to the third strand of the feminist critique by acknowledging that women and men frequently stand in assymetrical positions to a particular social institution. It recognizes that women are frequently disadvantaged by facially neutral practices and insists that such asymmetries be reflected in resource allocation. To carry forward the athletics example, equality as acceptance would support an equal division of resources between male and female programs rather than dividing up the available sports budget per capita. Since women and men do not stand symmetrically to the social institution of athletics, per capita distribution would simply serve to perpetuate the asymmetry, diverting more resources to male programs, where the participation rate has traditionally been high, and away from female programs, where the participation rate has been depressed both by women's exclusion from certain sports and by the subordination of those activities women have developed for themselves.

It may be apparent from the preceding paragraphs that equal acceptance as a legal norm does not automatically produce one and only one "right answer" to difficult questions of equality. Instead, it provides support for new remedial strategies as well as a method of uncovering deeper layers of inequality.

Acceptance, Not Accommodation

Asymmetrical equality theorists have usually been taken to mean that male institutions should take account of women's differences by accommodating those differences. "Reasonable accommodation" can be asked of a court (although the people usually being asked to be "reasonable" are those asking for accommodation), and if the choice truly is between accommodation and nothing, "half a loaf" *is* better than none.

The problem with accommodation, however, is that it implicitly accepts the prevailing norm as generally legitimate, even as it urges that "special circumstances" make the norm inappropriate for the particular individual or class seeking accommodation. In addition, it falls prey to the feminist critique of equality by labeling women as deviant from the norm, thus locating the difference in women. Assimilated women are particularly vulnerable to this misperception, and are all too often persuaded to drop valid demands for inclusion on their own terms by the response that they are asking for "an exception."

The distinction between accommodation and acceptance may be illustrated by a rather commonplace example. I remember a feminist lawyer walking up to a podium to deliver a speech. The podium was high enough that she could not reach the microphone. While arrangements were being modified, she pointedly noted, "Built for a man!" Accommodation is a step platform brought for her to stand on. Acceptance is a podium whose height is adjustable.

.   .   .

Making Difference Costless

.   .   .

Differently Gendered Complements

The problem of identifying gendered complements lies along two axes of difference. One axis measures the "source" of differences, ranging from the clearly biological to the clearly social (with a great deal of controversy in between). The other measures the degree of overlap between the sexes, and runs from more-to-less differences on one end to yes-or-no differences on the other.

For gender differences that are more-or-less, there is a significant degree of overlap between the sexes. Height is one of these. Not all women would have been disaffirmed by the too-high podium that was "build for a man," and not all men would have been affirmed by it. But more women than men in this society would have had the feminist lawyer's experience. Additionally, differences of the more-or-less variety are easier to deny, since there is always some woman over six feet or some man under five, and a great number of both in between. These differences are also easier to "match," because shorter and taller are both measures of the same concededly shared human characteristic of height.

For yes-or-no gender differences, there is no overlap at all. The primary example of this is, of course, pregnancy. No man can become pregnant, and most women can. However, women who have never had the capacity for pregnancy are not thereby made either biologically or socially male, even when the dominant culture has tended to view them as "not women." Thus, although it is useful for purposes of analysis to separate yes-or-no differences from more-or-less ones, they represent two poles of the same spectrum.

Disparate treatment analysis under Title VII allows individuals who are exceptions to the "rule" of their biological sex to be socially classed with the other sex. Thus, tall women must be treated the same as tall men, and short men the same as short women. As the podium example demonstrates, phallocentrism in such cases usually involves setting the norm by reference to the center of the male bell curve. When the norm is set by reference to the female bell curve, the same analysis applies; men who can type must be allowed into socially female secretarial positions.

To establish a prima facie case of discrimination under disparate treatment analysis, a plaintiff must show:

> (i) that [the plaintiff] belongs to a racial minority [or is a woman]; (ii) that he [or she] applied and was qualified for a job for which the employer was seeking applicants; (iii) that, despite [plaintiff's] qualifications, he [or she] was rejected;

and (iv) that, after [plaintiff's] rejection, the position remained open and the employer continued to seek applicants from persons of complainant's qualifications.[236]

Requiring a female complainant to establish "qualifications" for a traditionally male job is to require her to establish that she is socially male, at least in this context.

Disparate impact analysis, on the other hand, allows socially female women to bring equality claims if the job qualification containing the gendered norm is irrelevant to the applicant's ability to perform the job. No showing of direct intent to discriminate is required.[237] Under disparate impact doctrine, then, a woman can establish discrimination by demonstrating that women as a class are more severely affected than men by a facially neutral employment practice, such as a height requirement. The employer can, however, justify the discriminatory impact by demonstrating that the practice is "job related" or necessary to the employer's business.[239] Moreover, the relevance of the practice is tested solely by reference to the way the job is already structured.[240] Thus, even disparate impact analysis—as currently practiced—does not allow for challenges to male bias in the structure of businesses, occupations, or jobs.[241]

Equality as acceptance would support challenges to government and employer policies and practices that use male norms even when such norms are considered job-related, necessary to the business, or "substantially related to an important governmental interest." Unlike the more radical version of the model of androgyny referred to above, however, acceptance would not necessarily require the *elimination* of such norms. Acceptance could instead be achieved by inventing complementary structures containing female norms. For example, assume an employer successfully defends its 5'9" minimum height requirement as necessary to the job of sorting widgets as they pass on a conveyor belt. Equality as acceptance could be achieved by restructuring the job itself—in this case, by changing the height of the conveyor belt or by adding a second belt. Alternatively, the employer could defend the requirement by demonstrating that equal job opportunities exist in the plant for applicants shorter than 5'9". Acceptance would thus permit de facto sex segregation in the workplace, but *only* if the predominantly male and predominantly female jobs have equal pay, status, and opportunity for promotion into decisionmaking positions.

Yes-or-no differences do not yield so readily to matching. This has helped focus the "equal treatment/special treatment" debate on pregnancy—specifically, on the question of whether requiring employers to grant pregnancy leaves for women violates the equal rights of men, who can never take advantage of such leaves. If pregnancy were a more-or-less difference, such as disabling heart trouble or childcare responsibility, it would be easy for the current legal system to answer this question. Since it is a yes-or-no difference, however, the legal system runs in circles: the Supreme Court in *Geduldig v. Aiello*[246] said pregnancy is different, so women can be punished for it; the federal district court in *Cal. Fed.*[247] said pregnancy is not different, so women should not benefit from it; the Supreme Court, affirming the Ninth Circuit in *Cal. Fed.*,[248] said pregnancy is different, so men are not hurt by taking account of it.

I think that the appropriate unit of analysis in yes-or-no cases is *interaction* of the sexes rather than comparison. Even with rapidly developing reproductive technology, it is still necessary for some part of a woman to interact with some part of a man to produce a pregnancy. In that interaction, the gendered complements are pregnancy for the woman and fewer sperm cells for the man. Since pregnancy almost always results in some period of disability for the woman, making the sex difference costless with respect to the workplace requires that money, status, and opportunity for advancement flow equally to the womb-donating woman and the sperm-donating man (himself an equal contributor to the procreative act).[249]

Both average height and pregnancy lie near the biological pole of the source axis; these differences are clearly biological. Their existence and degree of overlap are less problematic as an empirical matter than differences lying closer to the cultural pole. The clearly cultural differences, on the other hand, are more problematic, primarily because they are even more likely than biological differences to give rise to stereotypes that harm women. Arguments for ignoring difference are also more plausible with reference to the cultural axis. Because these differences are acquired, they can presumably be done away with, if not for us then for our children or grandchildren.[252] This combination of danger and plausibility has led several sex equality theorists to place themselves toward the middle of the symmetrical vs. asymmetrical debate.[253] I am, however, either brave or foolhardy enough to believe that even cultural differences can be made accessible to equality analysis.

Cultural differences of the more-or-less variety can be dealt with along the same general lines as biological differences that overlap. Under acceptance, marital dissolution decrees, for example, could value the contributions of the non-earner spouse (usually, but not always, the woman), take into account services in the home performed after divorce, and treat realistically the expenses necessarily incurred by the custodial parent. These measures would go further toward reducing the potentially devastating economic impact of divorce for women than current experiments, such as presumptions in favor of joint custody.

Cultural differences of the yes-or-no variety are easier to identify than those of the more-or-less, but harder to deal with. Fortunately, there are relatively few of them (far fewer than there were a few decades ago). The most visible is employment in the armed services. Women are excluded from draft registration, and female volunteers are excluded from combat positions.

Just as gendered complements in the "biological" realm come from our current perceptions of biology, so must gendered complements in the "cultural" realm come from our current perceptions of culture. The traditional gender divide sets up "warrior" in its cultural sense directly opposite "mother" in its cultural sense.[257] The "cult of motherhood" resembles the "glory of battle" in a number of ways. Both occupations involve a lot of unpleasant work, along with a real sense of commitment to a cause beyond oneself that is culturally gussied up and glamorized culturally to cover up the unpleasantness involved. Both involve danger and possible death. And, of course, the rationale most frequently given for women's exclusion from combat is their capacity for motherhood.[260]

Making this gender difference less costly could mean requiring the government to pay mothers the same low wages and generous benefits as most soldiers.[261] It could also mean encouraging the use of motherhood as an unofficial prerequisite for governmental office. As a paying occupation with continuing status perks, many more men might be induced to stay home and raise their children. Alternatively, but less likely, making difference costless could mean ceasing to pay combat troops.

For example, in *Personnel Administrator v. Feeney*,[264] the Supreme Court upheld Massachusetts' lifetime veteran's preference against an equal protection challenge, reasoning that Massachusetts had not intended that preference to lock women into lower-level and dead-end civil service positions, regardless of this obvious effect. Under an equality as acceptance model, a state's failure to provide equal preference for the gendered female complement to military service would be evidence of intentional discrimination. Thus, even without additional constitutional or statutory enactment, a change in the Court's underlying model of equality could alter the result in actual cases.

Matching gendered complements in order to equalize across cultural differences may sound like marching directly into the valley of the stereotypes. Those who consider Carol Gilligan's discovery of "a different voice" sexist are not likely to find this appealing. Nevertheless, allow me to make two disclaimers. First, almost all cultural differences are, or could easily be, "more or less." Lots of biological men exhibit socially female characteristics (for which they are all too often punished); at least as many biological women exhibit socially male ones (for which they are often rewarded, although they are simultaneously punished for not having the biological form to match); and many more women and men fall in the middle, exhibiting no readily identifiable "male" or "female" behavior patterns. Second, what is objectionable about stereotypes is not that they are *never* true, but rather that they are not *always* true. Demonstrating that not every woman with children is primarily responsible for their care may help those women who do not have such responsibility to compete for certain jobs, but it does little to help those women struggling to hold down two jobs, only one of which is paid.

Disclaimers aside, what is relevant for this exercise is not the accuracy or inaccuracy of any set of gendered complements, but rather how the complements reward or punish those who are perceived to fall on one side or the other. Studies of sex-segregated work places tend to show that there is a high correlation between employer perceptions of gender differences and the segregation patterns themselves.[267] These perceived gender differences, such as lifting strength and small-muscle dexterity, are of the more-or-less type, and tend to fall toward the middle of the "source" axis.[268] Requiring individual testing alleviates segregation to some extent, but it only helps those women who do not fit the female stereotype (at the expense, of course, of those men who do not fit the male stereotype). However, the main problem with sex segregation is that promotion patterns and pay scales are determined by entry-level job classifications. Thus, those women who do fit the female stereotype (of, say, low lifting strength and high small-muscle dexterity) are stuck. They are not harmed by the "female" job classification as such; they are harmed by the disparity in pay and opportunity for promotion that goes along with it. And the disparity in promotion opportunities continues the cycle of overvaluation of "male" characteristics and undervaluation of "female" ones, because employers will continue to select those biological men and women who are socially male.

If, alternatively, both "male" and "female" entry-level positions paid the same and offered the same promotion opportunities, individual testing would not matter so much. Indeed, assuming proportionate numbers of openings, applicants might well self-select into the classification that better utilizes their particular strengths and minimizes their particular weaknesses. If so, the segregation pattern would gradually break down unless employers actively and, legally speaking, "intentionally" sought to maintain it. Moreover, even if self-selection by individual skills did not occur, a better sex mix at the management level would eventually have a significant impact throughout the firm.

As Frances Olsen sets forth in *The Sex of Law*, we tend to think in dichotomies, and those dichotomies are both sexualized (with one side masculine and the other feminine) and hierarchicized (with one side in each pair superior).[269] She argues that the sexualization and hierarchicization should be attacked simultaneously, to the end of deconstructing the dichotomies themselves. While I do not disagree with this goal, I do think Olsen's strategy is impractical. Dichotomies that purport to describe gender differences are, I think, only likely to fall apart once they no longer accurately describe differences in pay scales, hiring patterns, or promotion ladders. Additionally, since we presently think in these dichotomies, we may as well use them to help us in our struggle to discard them.

The rigidity of sexualized dichotomies does appear to be gradually breaking down in many areas. Whether the strategy I am suggesting would impede that breakdown is discussed below. With regard to the practical problem of implementation, however, the true breakdown of any particular male-female dichotomy is not a problem, but a benefit. It puts us one step closer toward eliminating them entirely.

Reifying Gender

The theoretical problem of the above discussion is, of course, the danger that using gendered complements overtly (I remain convinced that we use them covertly all the time) will strengthen the gender divide. This danger seems real, although perhaps overstated if the rest of my analysis holds. As I have urged throughout this Article, it is not gender difference, but the difference gender makes, that creates a divide. Instead of division, there might easily be a continuum stretching beyond the current poles—the "polymorphous perversity" that Jeff Goldstein posits in the erotic arena[270] or the "reds and greens and blues" that Frances Olsen imagines within a liberated androgyny.[271] If the status of "victim" were not so debilitating in socially real terms, we would be able to laugh at the argument that the Minneapolis antipornography ordinance paints women as victims of male violence. Similarly, if the location of a person, action, or characteristic on the "female" side of the divide did not entail her/

his/its immediate devaluation, then the mere identification of a law's beneficiaries as "women" would not divert us from a deeper and more practical analysis of its relative advantages and disadvantages.

There is yet another layer, however, to the critique of reifying gender. Not only is the socially female a constructed category, but that social construction was historically created in the absence of women, or at least without their participation. Therefore, runs the criticism, the socially female cannot be claimed as truly belonging to women, because it has been men who have done the defining. How, then, can I claim it as valuable on behalf of *women?*

I am not claiming that women's authentic voice would value everything that has been assigned to us by social definition. I literally do not know what I would say about my selfhood had I not been raised in a phallocentric culture—and neither does anyone else. However, as long as identification with socially female attributes is more "expensive" than identification with socially male ones—when taking parental leave shunts you off the partnership track, crying in a meeting shuts off the discussion, breastfeeding makes you unacceptable at the restaurant table—we are not ever going to be in a position to find out what women would value for themselves.

The social construction of "woman" has not just been a matter of men taking the best for themselves and assigning the rest to women. It has also been a matter of perceiving the "worst" as being whatever women were perceived to be.[276] This interaction can be disrupted either by revaluing what women have been perceived to be, or by reassigning the attributes that comprise the social sexes, or both. . . . So long as equality analysis takes place in [a phallocentric society], reassignment of social sex attributes must itself operate unequally. My claim is also based on the quasi-empirical observation that women are willing to pay an increasingly heavy price to maintain at least some socially female modes of being, and that men are unwilling, or unasked, to pay a similar price to take them on. To take one example, reassigning childcare has not thus far meant assigning it to men or even sharing it with them; it has meant assigning it to poorer women. Despite a rapid increase in the number of married women in the full-time labor force, men's contributions to household tasks have remained astonishingly low.[279] For the sexual dialectic to yield anything transformative, we have got to take our social finger off one end of the scale.

As indicated above, making gender difference costless, even in the skewed terms by which we now measure "cost," seems just as likely to decrease the overlap between biological and social sex as ignoring what we perceive as gender difference in the hope that it will disappear or be "transformed." If it costs most men and women the same to stay home with the baby, parenting is more likely to be shared. (Currently, women have less to lose than men by foregoing paid employment for unpaid childcare, since both women's salaries *and* expectations are generally lower.) And if the social rewards of childrearing are closer to those of what we now think of as employment, making the two compatible can proceed from two directions instead of one.

It is, of course, possible that "social transvestitism" will not occur to any great extent, even if it becomes relatively costless. Perhaps biological or cultural imperatives do play a larger role than power and economics. I doubt it. But if it does turn out that, given a flat cost curve, most biological women opt for social womanhood and most biological men opt for social manhood and very few explore new modes of social existence, I'm not sure I'd care very much. The modernists may enjoy mixing things up for its own sake; me, I'm only in it for the equality. . . .

Notes

75. In the 1970's, the first wave of feminist litigators chose this approach, and this led to the rather counterintuitive use of male plaintiffs in most of the major constitutional sex discrimination cases of the 1970's. *See e.g.,* Califano v. Goldfarb, 430 U.S. 199 (1977); Weinberger w. Wiesenfeld, 420 U.S. 636 (1975); Kahn v. Shevin, 416 U.S. 351 (1974). For a sympathetic interpretation of this phenomenon, see Cole, *Strategies of Difference: Litigating for Women's Rights in a Man's World,* 2 J.L. & INEQUALITY 33, 53–92 (1984).

78. Williams, *The Equality Crisis* [: *Some Reflections on Culture, Courts, and Feminism,* 7 WOMEN'S RTS. L. REP. 175, 196 (1982) (hereinafter Williams, *The Equality Crisis*)]. . . .

88. Tussman & tenBroek, *The Equal Protection of the Laws,* 37 CALIF. L. REV. 341, 344 (1949). . . .

89. *See e.g.,* Rostker v. Goldberg, 453 U.S. 57 (1981); Michael M. v. Superior Court, 450 U.S. 464 (1981) (both holding strict scrutiny inapplicable to classifications based on actual or legal differences between the sexes).

90. The least critical symmetrical approaches are found in the work of male legal theorists. Richard Wasserstrom, for example, envisions the sexually equal society as one in which biological sex is "no more significant then eye color," and in which asking whether a new baby is a boy or a girl is no more common than asking whether it has large or small feet. Wasserstrom, [*Racism, Sexism, and Preferential Treatment: An Approach to the Topics,* 24 UCLA L. REV. 581, 606 (1977)]. . . .

93. *See* Scales, [*Towards a Feminist Jurisprudence,* 56 IND. L.J. 375, 430–34 (1981)]; *see also* E. WOLGAST, EQUALITY AND THE RIGHTS OF WOMEN 61–63 (1980).

94. E. WOLGAST, *supra* note 93, at 122. . . .

95. . . . *Id.* at 157. . . .

96. Law, *Rethinking Sex and the Constitution,* 132 U. PA. L. REV. 955, 1007–13 (1984) (calling for equal treatment in all areas *except* reproduction, where an analysis based on an empowerment approach . . . should be adopted).

97. Kay, *Equality and Difference: the Case of Pregnancy.* 1 BERKELEY WOMEN'S L.J. 1, 27–37 (1985) (sex differences should be ignored, *except* during the time a female is actually pregnant).

98. *See, e.g., id.* at 22 (distinguishing the author's approach from one that might support separate spheres).

99. At one time, I called this model of equality one of "affirmation." *See* C. Littleton, Alternative Models of Sexual Equality. Address delivered at the Clara Brett Martin Workshop. University of Toronto (1984) (on file with the author). I have changed the terminology, however, because I am not advocating a "celebration" of women's difference, or even pushing the subversive potential of "jouissance." *See* [INTRODUCTION TO NEW FRENCH FEMINISMS: AN ANTHOLOGY 3 (E. Marks & I. de Courtivron eds. 1980)]; D. Cornell, Equality and Gender Difference: Towards a Critical Theory of Equality 17 (1983) (unpublished manuscript on file with the author). Such celebrations look too much like embracing our oppression when women do it, and too much like condescension

when men do. Nor am I calling for an inversion of the hierarchical ordering of male and female modes of being (although I might not object to one). It does, however, seem affirming to be simply (simply?) accepted for what one is, not pushed into one side or the other of the great gender divide by economic and social pressures. At the risk of making it sound like too little to ask, then, I have chosen to call the model one of "acceptance".

100. See Lemons v. City & County of Denver, 17 Fair Empl. Prac. Cas. (BNA) 906 (D. Colo. Apr. 17, 1978) (rejecting a comparable worth claim that paying nurses less tha[n] real estate appraisers violates Title VII).

101. See C. GILLIGAN, [IN A DIFFERENT VOICE (1982)].

105. 107 S. Ct. 683 (1987).

106. CAL. GOV'T CODE §§ 12900–12996 (West 1980 & Supp. 1987).

107. § 12945(b)(2).

108. 42 U.S.C. §§ 2000e-10 to -17 (1982).

109. Pub. L. No. 95-555, 92 Stat, 2076 (1978) (codified at 42 U.S.C. § 2000e(k)).

. . .

110. *Cal. Fed.*, 107 S. Ct. at 688, 692.

111. Brief for the ACLU as amicus curiae, *Ca. Fed.*, 107 S. Ct. 683 (1987) (No. 85-494). In this case, the Union did not represent the views of its largest affiliate, the ACLU of Southern California, which has consistently supported the pregnancy disability legislation. See id. at A-2. The National Organization for Women made a similar argument, suggesting that state and federal law could be reconciled by requiring the employer to provide leave for disability arising from any source. Brief for the National Organization for Women as amicus curiae. *Cal. Fed.*, 107 S. Ct. 683 (1987) (No. 85-494).

112. Brief for Equal Rights Advocates as amicus curiae, *Cal. Fed.*, 107 S. Ct. 683 (1987) (No. 85-494).

113. Brief for the Coalition for Reproductive Equality in the Workplace (CREW) as amicus curiae, *Cal. Fed.*, 107 S. Ct. 683 (1987) (No. 85-494). I was the attorney of record for CREW, and the principal author of the CREW amicus brief.

114. *Id.* at 36–37.

115. The *Cal. Fed.* opinion, authored by Justice Marshall, does much to bring together the asymmetrical and symmetrical equality arguments. As alternative holdings, the opinion first defends the California law as consistent with equal employment opportunity. "By 'taking pregnancy into account.' California's pregnancy disability leave statute allows women, as well as men, to have families without losing their jobs." 107 S. Ct. as 694. The Court then states that the employer can satisfy both California law and demands for symmetry by providing leave for all forms of disability. *Id.* at 694–95.

117. This model has been articulated most fully by Catharine MacKinnon, and draws heavily on the work of radical feminist theorists such as Andrea Dworkin. See C. MACKINNON [SEXUAL HARASSMENT OF WORKING WOMEN (1979)] (examining sexual harassment in context of male power structure); MacKinnon, *Feminism, Marxism, Method and the State: Toward Feminist Jurisprudence,* 8 SIGNS 635 (1983) (examining how traditional theories of "the state" perpetuate male power to exclude women's perspective) . . . ; A. DWORKIN, OUR BLOOD 96–111 (1976); A. DWORKIN, PORNOGRAPHY: MEN POSSESSING WOMEN 13–24 (1979). . . .

118. DuBois, Dunlap, Gilligan, MacKinnon, & Menkel-Meadow, *Feminist Discourse, Moral Values, and the Law—A Conversation,* 34 BUFFALO L. REV. 11, 27 (1985)] (emphasis added).

124. See Rossi, [*Sexual Equality: The Beginning of Ideology,* in BEYOND SEX ROLE STEREOTYPES 80, 87 (A. Kaplan & J. Bean eds. 1976)].

131. A. Allen, C. Littleton & C. Menkel-Meadow, Law in a Different Voice, 15th National Conference on Women and the Law, Address by C. Menkel-Meadow (Mar. 31, 1984) (tape on file with the author.)

135. A. LORDE, *Age, Race, Class and Sex: Women Redefining Difference*, in SISTER OUTSIDER, 114, 122 [1984] (emphasis added).

139. 404 U.S. 71 (1971).

142. 429 U.S. 190 (1976). . . .

143. 416 U.S. 351 (1974).

145. 417 U.S. 484 (1974).

146. 429 U.S. 125 (1976).

148. 417 U.S. at 496–97.

154. 107 S. Ct. 683 (1987). . . .

156. Such "equality with a vengeance" has been exhaustively documented by Lenore Weitzman, a sociologist who spent several years studying the concrete effects of California's adoption of "no fault" divorce. L. WEITZMAN, THE DIVORCE REVOLUTION (1985).

157. Weitzman's findings indicate that one year after divorce, the standard of living of male ex-spouses rises 43%, while the standard of living of female ex-spouses fails 73%. Weitzman, *The Economics of Divorce: Social and Economic Consequences of Property, Alimony, and Child Support*, 28 UCLA L. REV. 1181, 1251 (1980). She blames this economic disaster not on the concept of "no fault" divorce itself, but on the state legislature's failure to take into account the male and female partners to marriage usually stand in asymmetrical positions with respect to the job market. *See* Stix, *Disasters of the No-Fault Divorce*, L.A. Times, Nov. 7, 1985, § V, at 3, col. 1.

172. Note, *Comparable Worth—A Necessary Vehicle for Pay Equity*, 68 MARQ. L. REV. 93, 98 n.33 (1984). . . .

236. McDonnell-Douglas Corp. v. Green, 411 U.S. 792, 802 (1973). . . .

237. Griggs v. Duke Power Co., 401 U.S. 424 (1971).

239. *Griggs*, 401 U.S. at 429, 431.

240. A court might question an employer's *post hoc* characterization of a job, *see* Diaz v. Pan Am. World Airways, Inc., 442 F.2d 385 (5th Cir.) (finding the purpose of the airline business to be safe transportation, not comforting passengers), *cert. denied*, 404 U.S. 950 (1971), but it will still evaluate the business as it is, not as it might be if it were not male-biased.

241. This does not mean that Title VII could not be interpreted to allow such challenges, only that its current interpretation does not, Wendy Williams' optimistic reading to the contrary. *See* Williams, *Equality's Riddle: Pregnancy and the Equal Treatment/Special Treatment Debate*, 13 N.Y.U. REV. L. & SOC. CHANGE 325, 331 (1985) . . . (disparate impact analysis is a doctrinal tool useful for "squeez[ing] the male tilt out a purportedly neutral legal structure").

246. 417 U.S. 484 (1974).

247. California Fed. Sav. & Loan Ass'n v. Guerra. 33 Empl. Prac. Dec. (CCH) ¶ 34,227 (1984), *rev'd* 758 F.2d 390 (9th Cir. 1985), *aff'd*, 107 S. Ct. 683 (1987). . . .

248. 107 S. Ct. 683 (1987).

249. Equality as acceptance does not itself dictate whether this acceptance should be accomplished by (1) female and male workers sharing the disadvantage that the workplace now visits on women alone—perhaps through requiring male employees to take on without extra pay some portion of the work of the absent female employees; (2) eliminating the disadvantage to women through some form of pregnancy leave rights; or (3) reshaping the structure itself so that no disadvantage arises at all—through more radical time-shifting, time-sharing work schedules or through elimination of the workplace-home

dichotomy. While equality as acceptance would support arguments for all three, option (2) is probably the most viable currently.

252. Why bother with making these differences costless relative to each other if we can get rid of them altogether? My response is similar to that given to androgyny as an equality model: getting rid of difference in a system of male dominance means getting rid of *women's* differences. For example, "equality" in private law firm practice seems to mean that both women and men who take parenting leave fail to make partner; "equality" in academia seems to mean that both women and men whose research field is women's studies are not considered "serious" scholars. *Cf.* Lynn v. Regents of the Univ. of Calif., 656 F.2d 1337 (9th Cir. 1981) (university's disdain for women's studies is evidence of sex discrimination), *cert. denied.* 459 U.S. 823 (1982). Similarly, my female students are consistently counseled to wear gray or navy blue "power suits" to job interviews (often with little string or silk "ties").

Until such time as "getting rid of sex differences" has some chance of operating equally, it is an empty (perhaps deadening) promise for women. Moreover, it does not seem particularly unfair for women to demand a little equality now, for ourselves, without waiting for our grandchildren to "grow up free." Nor does it seem unjustified for women to be accepted as equal members of this society in spite of our cultural skewing—after all, men are skewed too, albeit differently. Of course, there is the obligatory fallback position that the opportunity for "social transvestitism" I envision as a result of this strategy will actually hasten the day that sex differences cease to operate for most people. However, societies are not build by or for people who may never exist, nor even for the purpose of creating such people.

253. *See e.g.,* Kay, *supra* note 97; Law, *supra* note 96 (both advocating a symmetrical model as the norm, with some area of asymmetry).

257. Williams, *The Equality Crisis, supra* note [78], at 190.

260. *See e.g.,* S. REP. No. 826, 96th Cong., 2d Sess. 159, 161, *reprinted in* 1980 U.S. CODE CONG. & ADMIN. NEWS 2612, 2649-51. *But see* C. ENLOE, [DOES KHAKI BECOME YOU? 15 (1983)] (women in combat would confuse men's certainty about their male identity).

261. Aid to Families with Dependent Children (AFDC) programs might be the culture's partial recognition of the importance of the occupation of childcare. However, that AFDC payments are seen as a response to need, rather than an earned income, makes them vulnerable to political windshifting. . . . In addition, social labeling of AFDC payments as "charity" rather than earnings has a necessary impact on recipients' self-image and sense of worth. Altering the basis and measurement of AFDC payments by making them the equivalent of military pay could go a long way toward alleviating both the feminization of poverty and the negative impact of social welfare programs on the purported beneficiaries. Additionally, the educational programs available in the military and by virtue of financial assistance following military service are far superior to the paltry "job training" programs currently available to welfare recipients.

264. 442 U.S. 256 (1979).

267. *See* W. Biebly & J. Baron, Men and Women at Work: Sex Segregation and Statistical Discrimination 27-28 (1985) (unpublished manuscript on file with the author).

. . .

268. *Id.* at 22-33.

269. Olsen, [The Sex of Law 1-4 (1984)].

270. Goldstein, *Pornography and Its Discontents,* Village Voice, Oct. 16, 1984, at 19, 44.

271. Olsen, [*The Family and the Market: A Study of Ideology and Legal Reform,* 96 HARV. L. REV. 1497, 1598 (1983)]. Olsen describes androgyny as arising from the synergism

of male and female, rather than their union, and thus yielding characteristics not otherwise displayed by either. How this process is to take place is not explained.

276. Does the Dictionary of Occupation Titles rate childcare as unskilled work because it "really" is, or only because those speaking in the public discourse never saw or formalized the instruction that took place every day that we watched our mothers or cared for younger children ourselves? *See* Briggs, *Guess Who Has the Most Complex Job?, reprinted in* B. BABCOCK. A. FREEDMAN, E. NORTON & S. ROSS, [SEX DISCRIMINATION AND THE LAW 203 (1973)]. If the reply is that childcare is "instinctual," then so is tool-use, but neither point is relevant. Modern human childrearing is as different from instinctual parental behavior as modern human tool use is different from its instinctual counterpart.

279. P. ROOS, GENDER & WORK 13-19 (1985).

4

Demarginalizing the Intersection of Race and Sex: A Black Feminist Critique of Antidiscrimination Doctrine, Feminist Theory, and Antiracist Politics [1989]

Kimberle Crenshaw

One of the very few Black women's studies books is entitled *All the Women Are White, All the Blacks Are Men, But Some of Us Are Brave.*[1] I have chosen this title as a point of departure in my efforts to develop a Black feminist criticism because it sets forth a problematic consequence of the tendency to treat race and gender as mutually exclusive categories of experience and analysis.[3] . . . I want to examine how this tendency is perpetuated by a single-axis framework that is dominant in antidiscrimination law and that is also reflected in feminist theory and antiracist politics.

I will center Black women in this analysis in order to contrast the multidimensionality of Black women's experience with the single-axis analysis that distorts these experiences. Not only will this juxtaposition reveal how Black women are theoretically erased, it will also illustrate how this framework imports its own theoretical limitations that undermine efforts to broaden feminist and antiracist analyses. With Black women as the starting point, it becomes more apparent how dominant conceptions of discrimination condition us to think about subordination as disadvantage occurring along a single categorical axis. I want to suggest further that this single-axis framework erases Black women in the conceptualization, identification and remediation of race and sex discrimination by limiting inquiry to the experiences of otherwise-privileged members of the group. In other words, in race discrimination cases, discrimination tends to be viewed in terms of sex- or class-privileged Blacks; in sex discrimination cases, the focus is on race- and class-privileged women.

This focus on the most privileged group members marginalizes those who are multiply-burdened and obscures claims that cannot be understood as resulting from discrete sources of discrimination. I suggest further that this focus on otherwise-privileged group members creates a distorted analysis of racism and sexism because the operative conceptions of race and sex become grounded in experiences that actually represent only a subset of a much more complex phenomenon.

After examining the doctrinal manifestations of this single-axis framework, I will discuss how it contributes to the marginalization of Black women in feminist theory and in antiracist politics. I argue that Black women are sometimes excluded from feminist theory and antiracist policy discourse because both are predicated on a discrete set of experiences that often does not accurately reflect the interaction of race and gender. These problems of exclusion cannot be solved simply by including Black women within an already established analytical structure. Because the intersectional experience is greater than the sum of racism and sexism, any analysis that does not take intersectionality into account cannot sufficiently address the particular manner in which Black women are subordinated. Thus, for feminist theory and antiracist policy discourse to embrace the experiences and concerns of Black women, the entire framework that has been used as a basis for translating "women's experience" or "the Black experience" into concrete policy demands must be rethought and recast.

As examples of theoretical and political developments that miss the mark with respect to Black women because of their failure to consider intersectionality, I will briefly discuss the feminist critique of rape and separate spheres ideology, and the public policy debates concerning female-headed households within the Black community.

I. The Antidiscrimination Framework

A. *The Experience of Intersectionality and the Doctrinal Response*

One way to approach the problem of intersectionality is to examine how courts frame and interpret the stories of Black women plaintiffs. While I cannot claim to know the circumstances underlying the cases that I will discuss, I nevertheless believe that the way courts interpret claims made by Black women is itself part of Black women's experience and, consequently, a cursory review of cases involving Black female plaintiffs is quite revealing. To illustrate the difficulties inherent in judicial treatment of intersectionality, I will consider three Title VII[4] cases: *DeGraffenreid v General Motors*,[5] *Moore v Hughes Helicopters*[6] and *Payne v Travenol*.[7]

1. DeGraffenreid v General Motors

In *DeGraffenreid*, five Black women brought suit against General Motors, alleging that the employer's seniority system perpetuated the effects of past discrimination against Black women. Evidence adduced at trial revealed that General Motors simply did not hire Black women prior to 1964 and that all of the Black women hired after 1970 lost their jobs in a seniority-based layoff during a subsequent recession. The district court granted summary judgment for the defendant, rejecting the plaintiffs' attempt to bring a suit not on behalf of Blacks or women, but specifically on behalf of Black women. The court stated:

> [P]laintiffs have failed to cite any decisions which have stated that Black women are a special class to be protected from discrimination. The Court's own research has failed to disclose such a decision. The plaintiffs are clearly entitled to a remedy if they have been discriminated against. However, they should not be allowed to combine statutory remedies to create a new 'super-remedy' which would give them relief beyond what the drafters of the relevant statutes intended. Thus, this lawsuit must be examined to see if it states a cause of action for race discrimination, sex discrimination, or alternatively either, but not a combination of both.[8]

Although General Motors did not hire Black women prior to 1964, the court noted that "General Motors has hired . . . female employees for a number of years prior to the enactment of the Civil Rights Act of 1964."[9] Because General Motors did hire women—albeit *white women*—during the period that no Black women were hired, there was, in the court's view, no sex discrimination that the seniority system could conceivably have perpetuated.

After refusing to consider the plaintiffs' sex discrimination claim, the court dismissed the race discrimination complaint and recommended its consolidation with another case alleging race discrimination against the same employer.[10] The plaintiffs responded that such consolidation would defeat the purpose of their suit since theirs was not purely a race claim, but an action brought specifically on behalf of Black women alleging race *and* sex discrimination. The court, however, reasoned:

> The legislative history surrounding Title VII does not indicate that the goal of the statute was to create a new classification of 'black women' who would have greater standing than, for example, a black male. The prospect of the creation of new classes of protected minorities, governed only by the mathematical principles of permutation and combination, clearly raises the prospect of opening the hackneyed Pandora's box.[11]

Thus, the court apparently concluded that Congress either did not contemplate that Black women could be discriminated against as "Black women" or did not intend to protect them when such discrimination occurred.[12] The court's refusal in *DeGraffenreid* to acknowledge that Black women encounter combined race and sex discrimination implies that the boundaries of sex and race discrimination doctrine are defined respectively by white women's and Black men's experiences. Under this view, Black women are protected only to the extent that their experiences coincide with those of either of the two groups.[13] Where their experiences are distinct, Black women can expect little protection as long as approaches, such as that in *DeGraffenreid*, which completely obscure problems of intersectionality prevail.

2. Moore v Hughes Helicopters, Inc.

Moore v Hughes Helicopters, Inc.[14] presents a different way in which courts fail to understand or recognize Black women's claims. *Moore* is typical of a number of cases in which courts refused to certify Black females as class representatives in race *and* sex discrimination actions.[15] In *Moore*, the plaintiff alleged that the employer, Hughes Helicopter, practiced race and sex discrimination in promotions to upper-level craft positions and to supervisory jobs. Moore introduced statistical evidence establishing a significant disparity between men and women, and somewhat less of a disparity between Black and white men in supervisory jobs.[16]

Affirming the district court's refusal to certify Moore as the class representative in the sex discrimination complaint on behalf of all women at Hughes, the Ninth Circuit noted approvingly:

> . . . Moore had never claimed before the EEOC that she was discriminated against as a female, *but only* as a Black female. . . . [T]his raised serious doubts as to Moore's ability to adequately represent white female employees.[17]

The curious logic in *Moore* reveals not only the narrow scope of antidiscrimination doctrine and its failure to embrace intersectionality, but also the centrality of white female experiences in the conceptualization of gender discrimination. One inference that could be drawn from the court's statement that Moore's complaint did not entail a claim of discrimination "against females" is that discrimination against Black females is something less than discrimination against females. More than likely, however, the court meant to imply that Moore did not claim that *all* females were discriminated against *but only* Black females. But even thus recast, the court's rationale is problematic for Black women. The court rejected Moore's bid to represent all females apparently because her attempt to specify her race was seen as being at odds with the standard allegation that the employer simply discriminated "against females."

The court failed to see that the absence of a racial referent does not necessarily mean that the claim being made is a more inclusive one. A white woman claiming discrimination against females may be in no better position to represent all women than a Black woman who claims discrimination as a Black female and wants to represent all females. The court's preferred articulation of "against females" is not necessarily more inclusive—it just appears to be so because the racial contours of the claim are not specified.

The court's preference for "against females" rather than "against Black females" reveals the implicit grounding of white female experiences in the doctrinal conceptualization of sex discrimination. For white women, claiming sex discrimination is simply a statement that but for gender, they would not have been disadvantaged. For them there is no need to specify discrimination as *white* females because their race does not contribute to the disadvantage for which they seek redress. The view of discrimination that is derived from this grounding takes race privilege as a given.

Discrimination against a white female is thus the standard sex discrimination claim; claims that diverge from this standard appear to present some sort of hybrid claim. More significantly, because Black females' claims are seen as hybrid, they sometimes cannot represent those who may have "pure" claims of sex discrimination. The effect of this approach is that even though a challenged policy or practice may clearly discriminate against all females, the fact that it has particularly harsh consequences for Black females places Black female plaintiffs at odds with white females.

Moore illustrates one of the limitations of antidiscrimination law's remedial scope and normative vision. The refusal to allow a multiply-disadvantaged class to represent others who may be singularly-disadvantaged defeats efforts to restructure the distribution of opportunity and limits remedial relief to minor adjustments within an established hierarchy. Consequently, "bottom-up" approaches, those which combine all discriminatees in order to challenge an entire employment system, are foreclosed by the limited view of the wrong and the narrow scope of the available remedy. If such "bottom-up" intersectional representation were routinely permitted, employees might accept the possibility that there is more to gain by collectively challenging the hierarchy rather than by each discriminatee individually seeking to protect her source of privilege within the hierarchy. But as long as antidiscrimination doctrine proceeds from the premise that employment systems need only minor adjustments, opportunities for advancement by disadvantaged employees will be limited. Relatively privileged employees probably are better off guarding their advantage while jockeying against others to gain more. As a result, Black women—the class of employees which, because of its intersectionality, is best able to challenge all forms of discrimination—are essentially isolated and often required to fend for themselves.

In *Moore*, the court's denial of the plaintiff's bid to represent all Blacks and females left Moore with the task of supporting her race and sex discrimination claims with statistical evidence of discrimination against Black females alone.[18] Because she was unable to represent white women or Black men, she could not use overall statistics on sex disparity at Hughes, nor could she use statistics on race. Proving her claim using statistics on Black women alone was no small task, due to the fact that she was bringing the suit under a disparate impact theory of discrimination.[19]

The court further limited the relevant statistical pool to include only Black women who it determined were qualified to fill the openings in upper-level labor jobs and in supervisory positions.[20] According to the court, Moore had not demonstrated that there were any qualified Black women within her bargaining unit or the general labor pool for either category of jobs.[21] Finally, the court stated that even if it accepted Moore's contention that the percentage of Black females in supervisory positions should equal the percentage of Black females in the employee pool, it still would not find discriminatory impact.[22] Because the promotion of only two Black women into supervisory positions would have achieved the expected mean distribution of Black women within that job category, the court was "unwilling to agree that a prima facie case of disparate impact ha[d] been proven."[23]

The court's rulings on Moore's sex and race claim left her with such a small statistical sample that even if she had proved that there were qualified Black women, she could not have shown discrimination under a disparate impact theory. *Moore* illustrates yet another way that antidiscrimination doctrine essentially erases Black women's distinct experiences and, as a result, deems their discrimination complaints groundless.

3. Payne v Travenol

Black female plaintiffs have also encountered difficulty in their efforts to win certification as class representatives in some race discrimination actions. This problem typically arises in cases where statistics suggest significant disparities between Black and white workers and further disparities between Black men and Black women. Courts in some cases[24] have denied certification based on logic that mirrors the rationale in *Moore*: The sex disparities between Black men and Black women created such conflicting interests that Black women could not possibly represent Black men adequately. In one such case, *Payne v Travenol*,[25] two Black female plaintiffs alleging race discrimination brought a class action suit on behalf of all Black employees at a pharmaceutical plant.[26] The court refused, however, to allow the plaintiffs to represent Black males and granted the defendant's request to narrow the class to Black women only. Ultimately, the district court found that there had been extensive racial discrimination at the plant and awarded back pay and constructive seniority to the class of Black female employees. But, despite its finding of general race discrimination, the court refused to extend the remedy to Black men for fear that their conflicting interests would not be adequately addressed;[27] the Fifth Circuit affirmed.[28]

Notably, the plaintiffs in *Travenol* fared better than the similarly-situated plaintiff in *Moore*: They were not denied use of meaningful statistics showing an overall pattern of race discrimination simply because there were no men in their class. The plaintiffs' bid to represent all Black employees, however, like Moore's attempt to represent all women employees, failed as a consequence of the court's narrow view of class interest.

Even though *Travenol* was a partial victory for Black women, the case specifically illustrates how antidiscrimination doctrine generally creates a dilemma for Black women. It forces them to choose between specifically articulating the intersectional aspects of their subordination, thereby risking their ability to represent Black men, or ignoring intersectionality in order to state a claim that would not lead to the exclusion of Black men. When one considers the political consequences of this dilemma, there is little wonder that many people within the Black community view the specific articulation of Black women's interests as dangerously divisive.

In sum, several courts have proved unable to deal with intersectionality, although for contrasting reasons. In *DeGraffenreid*, the court refused to recognize the possibility of compound discrimination against Black women and analyzed their claim using the employment of white women as the historical base. As a consequence, the employment experiences of white women obscured the distinct discrimination that Black women experienced.

Conversely, in *Moore*, the court held that a Black woman could not use statistics reflecting the overall sex disparity in supervisory and upper-level labor jobs because she had not claimed discrimination as a woman, but "only" as a Black woman. The court would not entertain the notion that discrimination experienced by Black women is indeed sex discrimination—provable through disparate impact statistics on women.

Finally, courts, such as the one in *Travenol*, have held that Black women cannot represent an entire class of Blacks due to presumed class conflicts in cases where sex additionally disadvantaged Black women. As a result, in the few cases where Black women are allowed to use overall statistics indicating racially disparate treatment Black men may not be able to share in the remedy.

Perhaps it appears to some that I have offered inconsistent criticisms of how Black women are treated in antidiscrimination law: I seem to be saying that in one case, Black women's claims were rejected and their experiences obscured because the court refused to acknowledge that the employment experience of Black women can be distinct from that of white women, while in other cases, the interests of Black women are harmed because Black women's claims were viewed as so distinct from the claims of either white women or Black men that the court denied to Black females representation of the larger class. It seems that I have to say that Black women are the same and harmed by being treated differently, or that they are different and harmed by being treated the same. But I cannot say both.

This apparent contradiction is but another manifestation of the conceptual limitations of the single-issue analyses that intersectionality challenges. The point is that Black women can experience discrimination in any number of ways and that the contradiction arises from our assumptions that their claims of exclusion must be unidirectional. Consider an analogy to traffic in an intersection, coming and going in all four directions. Discrimination, like traffic through an intersection, may flow in one direction, and it may flow in another. If an accident happens in an intersection, it can be caused by cars traveling from any number of directions and, sometimes, from all of them. Similarly, if a Black woman is harmed because she is in the intersection, her injury could result from sex discrimination or race discrimination.

Judicial decisions which premise intersectional relief on a showing that Black women are specifically recognized as a class are analogous to a doctor's decision at the scene of an accident to treat an accident victim only if the injury is recognized by medical insurance. Similarly, providing legal relief only when Black women show that their claims are based on race or on sex is analogous to calling an ambulance for the victim only after the driver responsible for the injuries is identified. But it is not always easy to reconstruct an accident: Sometimes the skid marks and the injuries simply indicate that they occurred simultaneously, frustrating efforts to determine which driver caused the harm. In these cases the tendency seems to be that no driver is held responsible, no treatment is administered, and the involved parties simply get back in their cars and zoom away.

To bring this back to a non-metaphorical level, I am suggesting that Black women can experience discrimination in ways that are both similar to and different from those experienced by white women and Black men. Black women sometimes experience discrimination in ways similar to white women's experiences; sometimes they share very similar experiences with Black men. Yet often they experience double-discrimination—the combined effects of practices which discriminate on the basis of race, and on the basis of sex. And sometimes, they experience discrimination as Black women—not the sum of race and sex discrimination, but as Black women.

Black women's experiences are much broader than the general categories that discrimination discourse provides. Yet the continued insistence that Black women's demands and needs be filtered through categorical analyses that completely obscure their experiences guarantees that their needs will seldom be addressed.

B. The Significance of Doctrinal Treatment of Intersectionality

DeGraffenreid, Moore and *Travenol* are doctrinal manifestations of a common political and theoretical approach to discrimination which operates to marginalize Black women. Unable to grasp the importance of Black women's intersectional experiences, not only courts, but feminist and civil rights thinkers as well have treated Black women in ways that deny both the unique compoundedness of their situation and the centrality of their experiences to the larger classes of women and Blacks. Black women are regarded either as too much like women or Blacks and the compounded nature of their experience is absorbed into the collective experiences of either group or as too different, in which case Black women's Blackness or femaleness sometimes has placed their needs and perspectives at the margin of the feminist and Black liberationist agendas.

While it could be argued that this failure represents an absence of political will to include Black women, I believe that it reflects an uncritical and disturbing acceptance of dominant ways of thinking about discrimination. Consider first the definition of discrimination that seems to be operative in antidiscrimination law: Discrimination which is wrongful proceeds from the identification of a specific class or category; either a discriminator intentionally identifies this category, or a process is adopted which somehow disadvantages all members of this category.[29] According to the dominant view, a discriminator treats all people within a race or sex category similarly. Any significant experiential or statistical variation within this group suggests either that the group is not being discriminated against or that conflicting interests exist which defeat any attempts to bring a common claim.[30] Consequently, one generally cannot combine these categories. Race and sex, moreover, become significant only when they operate to explicitly *disadvantage* the victims; because the *privileging* of whiteness or maleness is implicit, it is generally not perceived at all.

Underlying this conception of discrimination is a view that the wrong which antidiscrimination law addresses is the use of race or gender factors to interfere with decisions that would otherwise be fair or neutral. This process-based definition is not grounded in a bottom-up commitment to improve the substantive conditions for those who are victimized by the interplay of numerous factors. Instead, the dominant message of antidiscrimination law is that it will regulate only the limited extent to which race or sex interferes with the process of determining outcomes. This narrow objective is facilitated by the top-down strategy of using a singular "but for" analysis to ascertain the effects of race or sex. Because the scope of antidiscrimination law is so limited, sex and race discrimination have come to be defined in terms of the experiences of those who are privileged *but for* their racial or sexual characteristics. Put differently, the paradigm of sex discrimination tends to be based on the experiences of white women; the model of race discrimination tends to be based on the experiences of the most privileged Blacks. Notions of what constitutes race and sex discrimination are, as a result, narrowly tailored to embrace only a small set of circumstances, none of which include discrimination against Black women.

To the extent that this general description is accurate, the following analogy can be useful in describing how Black women are marginalized in the interface between antidiscrimination law and race and gender hierarchies: Imagine a basement which contains all people who are disadvantaged on the basis of race, sex, class, sexual preference, age and/or physical ability. These people are stacked—feet standing on shoulders—with those on the bottom being disadvantaged by the full array of factors, up to the very top, where the heads of all those disadvantaged by a singular factor brush up against the ceiling. Their ceiling is actually the floor above which only those who are *not* disadvantaged in any way reside. In efforts to correct some aspects of domination, those above the ceiling admit from the basement only those who can say that "but for" the ceiling, they too would be in the upper room. A hatch is developed through which those placed immediately below can crawl. Yet this hatch is generally available only to those who—due to the singularity of their burden and their otherwise privileged position relative to those below—are in the position to crawl through. Those who are multiply-burdened are generally left below unless they can somehow pull themselves into the groups that are permitted to squeeze through the hatch.

As this analogy translates for Black women, the problem is that they can receive protection only to the extent that their experiences are recognizably similar to those whose experiences tend to be reflected in antidiscrimination doctrine. If Black women cannot conclusively say that "but for" their race or "but for" their gender they would be treated differently, they are not invited to climb through the hatch but told to wait in the unprotected margin until they can be absorbed into the broader, protected categories of race and sex.

Despite the narrow scope of this dominant conception of discrimination and its tendency to marginalize those whose experiences cannot be described within its tightly-drawn parameters, this approach has been regarded as the appropriate framework for addressing a range of problems. In much of feminist theory and, to some extent, in antiracist politics, this framework is reflected in the belief that sexism or racism can be meaningfully discussed without paying attention to the lives of those other than the race-, gender- or class-privileged. As a result, both feminist theory and antiracist politics have been organized, in part, around the equation of racism with what happens to the Black middle-class or to Black men, and the equation of sexism with what happens to white women.

Looking at historical and contemporary issues in both the feminist and the civil rights communities, one can find ample evidence of how both communities' acceptance of the dominant framework of discrimination has hindered the development of an adequate theory and praxis to address problems of inter-sectionality. This adoption of a single-issue framework for discrimination not only marginalizes Black women within the very movements that claim them as part of their constituency but it also makes the illusive goal of ending racism and patriarchy even more difficult to attain.

II. Feminism and Black Women: "Ain't We Women?"

Oddly, despite the relative inability of feminist politics and theory to address Black women substantively, feminist theory and tradition borrow considerably from Black women's history. For example, "Ain't I a Woman" has come to represent a standard refrain in feminist discourse.[31] Yet the lesson of this powerful oratory is not fully appreciated because the context of the delivery is seldom examined. I would like to tell part of the story because it establishes some themes that have characterized feminist treatment of race and illustrates the importance of including Black women's experiences as a rich source for the critique of patriarchy.

In 1851, Sojourner Truth declared "Ain't I a Woman?" and challenged the sexist imagery used by male critics to justify the disenfranchisement of women.[32] The scene was a Women's Rights Conference in Akron, Ohio; white male hecklers, invoking stereotypical images of "womanhood," argued that women were too frail and delicate to take on the responsibilities of political activity. When Sojourner Truth rose to speak, many white women urged that she be silenced, fearing that she would divert attention from women's suffrage to emancipation. Truth, once permitted to speak, recounted the horrors of slavery, and its particular impact on Black women:

> Look at my arms! I have ploughed and planted and gathered into barns, and no man could head me—and ain't I a woman? I would work as much and eat as much as a man—when I could get it—and bear the lash as well! And ain't I a woman? I have born thirteen children, and seen most of 'em sold into slavery, and when I cried out with my mother's grief, none but Jesus heard me—and ain't I a woman?[33]

By using her own life to reveal the contradiction between the ideological myths of womanhood and the reality of Black women's experience, Truth's oratory provided a powerful rebuttal to the claim that women were categorically weaker than men. Yet Truth's personal challenge to the coherence of the cult of true womanhood was useful only to the extent that white women were willing to reject the racist attempts to rationalize the contradiction—that because Black women were something less than real women, their experiences had no bearing on true womanhood. Thus, this 19th-century Black feminist challenged not only patriarchy, but she also challenged white feminists wishing to embrace Black women's history to relinquish their vestedness in whiteness.

Contemporary white feminists inherit not the legacy of Truth's challenge to patriarchy but, instead, Truth's challenge to their forbearers. Even today, the difficulty that white women have traditionally experienced in sacrificing racial privilege to strengthen feminism renders them susceptible to Truth's critical question. When feminist theory and politics that claim to reflect *women's* experience and *women's* aspirations do not include or speak to Black women, Black women must ask: "Ain't *We* Women?" If this is so, how can the claims that "women are," "women believe" and "women need" be made when such claims are inapplicable or unresponsive to the needs, interests and experiences of Black women?

The value of feminist theory to Black women is diminished because it evolves from a white racial context that is seldom acknowledged. Not only are women of color in fact overlooked, but their exclusion is reinforced when *white* women speak for and as *women*. The authoritative universal voice—usually white male subjectivity masquerading as non-racial, non-gendered objectivity[34]—is merely transferred to those who, but for gender, share many of the same cultural, economic and social characteristics. When feminist theory attempts to describe women's experiences through analyzing patriarchy, sexuality, or separate spheres ideology, it often overlooks the role of race. Feminists thus ignore how their own race functions to mitigate some aspects of sexism and, moreover, how it often privileges them over and contributes to the domination of other women.[35] Consequently, feminist theory remains *white*, and its potential to broaden and deepen its analysis by addressing non-privileged women remains unrealized.

An example of how some feminist theories are narrowly constructed around white women's experiences is found in the separate spheres literature. The critique of how separate spheres ideology shapes and limits women's roles in the home and in public life is a central theme in feminist legal thought.[36] Feminists have attempted to expose and dismantle separate spheres ideology by identifying and criticizing the stereotypes that traditionally have justified the disparate societal roles assigned to men and women. Yet this attempt to debunk ideological justifications for *women's* subordination offers little insight into the domination of *Black* women. Because the experiential base upon which many feminist insights are grounded is white, theoretical statements drawn from them are overgeneralized at best, and often wrong.[38] Statements such as "men and women are taught to see men as independent, capable, powerful; men and women are taught to see women as dependent, limited in abilities, and passive,"[39] are common within this literature. But this "observation" overlooks the anomalies created by crosscurrents of racism and sexism. Black men and women live in a society that creates sex-based norms and expectations which racism operates simultaneously to deny; Black men are not viewed as powerful, nor are Black women seen as passive. An effort to develop an ideological explanation of gender domination in the Black community should proceed from an understanding of how crosscutting forces establish gender norms and how the conditions of Black subordination wholly frustrate access to these norms. Given this understanding, perhaps we can begin to see why Black women have been dogged by the stereotype of the pathological matriarch[40] or why there have been those in the Black liberation movement who aspire to create institutions and to build traditions that are intentionally patriarchal.[41]

Because ideological and descriptive definitions of patriarchy are usually premised upon white female experiences, feminists and others informed by feminist literature may make the mistake of assuming that since the role of Black women in the family and in other Black institutions does not always resemble the familiar manifestations of patriarchy in the white community, Black women are somehow exempt from patriarchal norms. For example, Black women have traditionally worked outside the home in numbers far exceeding the labor participation rate of white women.[42] An analysis of patriarchy that highlights the history of white women's exclusion from the workplace might permit the inference that Black women have not been burdened by this particular gender-based expectation. Yet the very fact that Black women must work conflicts with norms that women should not, often creating personal, emotional and relationship problems in Black women's lives. Thus, Black women are burdened not only because they often have to take on responsibilities that are not traditionally feminine but, moreover, their assumption of these roles is sometimes interpreted within the Black community as either Black women's failure to live up to such norms or as another manifestation of racism's scourge upon the Black community.[43] This is one of the many aspects of intersectionality that cannot be understood through an analysis of patriarchy rooted in white experience.

Another example of how theory emanating from a white context obscures the multidimensionality of Black women's lives is found in feminist discourse on rape. A central political issue on the feminist agenda has been the pervasive problem of rape. Part of the intellectual and political effort to mobilize around this issue has involved the development of a historical critique of the role that law has played in establishing the bounds of normative sexuality and in regulating female sexual behavior.[44] Early carnal knowledge statutes and rape laws are understood within this discourse to illustrate that the objective of rape statutes traditionally has not been to protect women from coercive intimacy but to protect and maintain a property-like interest in female chastity.[45] Although feminists quite rightly criticize these objectives, to characterize rape law as reflecting male control over female sexuality is for Black women an oversimplified account and an ultimately inadequate account.

Rape statutes generally do not reflect *male* control over *female* sexuality, but *white* male regulation of *white* female sexuality.[46] Historically, there has been absolutely no institutional effort to regulate Black female chastity.[47] Courts in some states had gone so far as to instruct juries that, unlike white women, Black women were not presumed to be chaste.[48] Also, while it was true that the attempt to regulate the sexuality of white women placed unchaste women outside the law's protection, racism restored a fallen white woman's chastity where the alleged assailant was a Black man.[49] No such restoration was available to Black women.

The singular focus on rape as a manifestation of male power over female sexuality tends to eclipse the use of rape as a weapon of racial terror.[50] When Black women were raped by white males, they were being raped not as women generally, but as Black women specifically: Their femaleness made them sexually vulnerable to racist domination, while their Blackness effectively denied them any protection.[51] This white male power was reinforced by a judicial system in which the successful conviction of a white man for raping a Black woman was virtually unthinkable.[52]

In sum, sexist expectations of chastity and racist assumptions of sexual promiscuity combined to create a distinct set of issues confronting Black women.[53] These issues have seldom been explored in feminist literature nor are they prominent in antiracist politics. The lynching of Black males, the institutional practice that was legitimized by the regulation of white women's sexuality, has historically and contemporaneously occupied the Black agenda on sexuality and violence. Consequently, Black women are caught between a Black community that, perhaps understandably, views with suspicion attempts to litigate questions of sexual violence, and a feminist community that reinforces those suspicions by focusing on white female sexuality.[54] The suspicion is compounded by the historical fact that the protection of white female sexuality was often the pretext for terrorizing the Black community. Even today some fear that antirape agendas may undermine antiracist objectives. This is the paradigmatic political and theoretical dilemma created by the intersection of race and gender: Black women are caught between ideological and political currents that combine first to create and then to bury Black women's experiences.

III. When and Where I Enter: Integrating an Analysis of Sexism into Black Liberation Politics

Anna Julia Cooper, a 19th-century Black feminist, coined a phrase that has been useful in evaluating the need to incorporate an explicit analysis of patriarchy in any effort to address racial domination.[55] Cooper often criticized Black leaders and spokespersons for claiming to speak for the race, but failing to speak for Black women. Referring to one of Martin Delaney's public claims that where he was allowed to enter, the race entered with him, Cooper countered: "Only the Black Woman can say, when and where I enter . . . then and there the whole Negro race enters with me."[56]

Cooper's words bring to mind a personal experience involving two Black men with whom I had formed a study group during our first year of law school. One of our group members, a graduate from Harvard College, often told us stories about a prestigious and exclusive men's club that boasted memberships of several past United States presidents and other influential white males. He was one of its very few Black members. To celebrate completing our first-year exams, our friend invited us to join him at the club for drinks. Anxious to see this fabled place, we approached the large door and grasped the brass door ring to announce our arrival. But our grand entrance was cut short when our friend sheepishly slipped from behind the door and whispered that he had forgotten a very important detail. My companion and I bristled, our training as Black people having taught us to expect yet another barrier to our inclusion; even an informal one-Black-person quota at the establishment was not unimaginable. The tension broke, however, when we learned that *we* would not be excluded because of our race, but that I would have to go around to the back door because I was a female. I entertained the idea of making a scene to dramatize the fact that my humiliation as a female was no less painful and my exclusion no more excusable than had we all been sent to the back door because we were Black. But, sensing no general assent to this proposition, and also being of the mind that due to our race a scene would in some way jeopardize all of us, I failed to stand my ground. After all, the Club was about to entertain its first Black guests—even though one would have to enter through the back door.[57]

Perhaps this story is not the best example of the Black community's failure to address problems related to Black women's intersectionality seriously. The story would be more apt if Black women, and only Black women, had to go around to the back door of the club and if the restriction came from within, and not from the outside of the Black community. Still this story does reflect a markedly decreased political and emotional vigilance toward barriers to Black women's enjoyment of privileges that have been won on the basis of race but continue to be denied on the basis of sex.[58]

The story also illustrates the ambivalence among Black women about the degree of political and social capital that ought to be expended toward challenging gender barriers, particularly when the challenges might conflict with the antiracism agenda. While there are a number of reasons—including antifeminist ones—why gender has not figured directly in analyses of the subordination of Black Americans, a central reason is that race is still seen by many as the primary oppositional force in Black lives. If one accepts that the social experience of race creates both a primary group identity as well as a shared sense of being under collective assault, some of the reasons that Black feminist theory and politics have not figured prominently in the Black political agenda may be better understood.[60]

The point is not that African Americans are simply involved in a more important struggle. Although some efforts to oppose Black feminism are based on this assumption, a fuller appreciation of the problems of the Black community will reveal that gender subordination does contribute significantly to the destitute conditions of so many African Americans and that it must therefore be addressed. Moreover, the foregoing critique of the single-issue framework renders problematic the claim that the struggle against racism is distinguishable from, much less prioritized over, the struggle against sexism. Yet it is also true that the politics of racial otherness that Black women experience along with Black men prevent Black feminist consciousness from patterning the development of white feminism. For white women, the creation of a consciousness that was distinct from and in opposition to that of white men figured prominently in the development of white feminist politics. Black women, like Black men, live in a community that has been defined and subordinated by color and culture.[61] Although patriarchy clearly operates within the Black community, presenting yet another source of domination to which Black women are vulnerable, the racial context in which Black women find themselves makes the creation of a political consciousness that is oppositional to Black men difficult.

Yet while it is true that the distinct experience of racial otherness militates against the development of an oppositional feminist consciousness, the assertion of racial community sometimes supports defensive priorities that marginalize Black women. Black women's particular interests are thus relegated to the periphery in public policy discussions about the presumed needs of the Black community. The controversy over the movie *The Color Purple* is illustrative. The animating fear behind much of the publicized protest was that by portraying domestic abuse in a Black family, the movie confirmed the negative stereotypes of Black men.[62] The debate over the propriety of presenting such an image on the screen overshadowed the issue of sexism and patriarchy in the Black community. Even though it was sometimes acknowledged that the Black community was not immune from domestic violence and other manifestations of gender subordination, some nevertheless felt that in the absence of positive Black male images in the media, portraying such images merely reinforced racial stereotypes.[63] The struggle against racism seemed to compel the subordination of certain aspects of the Black female experience in order to ensure the security of the larger Black community.

The nature of this debate should sound familiar to anyone who recalls Daniel Moynihan's diagnosis of the ills of Black America.[64] Moynihan's report depicted a deteriorating Black family, foretold the destruction of the Black male householder and lamented the creation of the Black matriarch. His conclusions prompted a massive critique from liberal sociologists[65] and from civil rights leaders.[66] Surprisingly, while many critics characterized the report as racist for its blind use of white cultural norms as the standard for evaluating Black families, few pointed out the sexism apparent in Moynihan's labeling Black women as pathological for their "failure" to live up to a white female standard of motherhood.[67]

The latest versions of a Moynihanesque analysis can be found in the Moyers televised special, *The Vanishing Black Family*,[68] and, to a lesser extent, in William Julius Wilson's *The Truly Disadvantaged*.[69] In *The Vanishing Black Family*, Moyers presented the problem of female-headed households as a problem of irresponsible sexuality, induced in part by government policies that encouraged family breakdown.[70] The theme of the report was that the welfare state reinforced the deterioration of the Black family by rendering the Black male's role obsolete. As the argument goes, because Black men know that someone will take care of their families, they are free to make babies and leave them. A corollary to the Moyers view is that welfare is also dysfunctional because it allows poor women to leave men upon whom they would otherwise be dependent.

Most commentators criticizing the program failed to pose challenges that might have revealed the patriarchal assumptions underlying much of the Moyers report. They instead focused on the dimension of the problem that was clearly recognizable as racist.[71] White feminists were equally culpable. There was little, if any, published response to the Moyers report from the white feminist community. Perhaps feminists were under the mistaken assumption that since the report focused on the Black community, the problems highlighted were racial, not gender based. Whatever the reason, the result was that the ensuing debates over the future direction of welfare and family policy proceeded without significant feminist input. The absence of a strong feminist critique of the Moynihan/Moyers model not only impeded the interests of Black women, but it also compromised the interests of growing numbers of white women heads of household who find it difficult to make ends meet.[72]

William Julius Wilson's *The Truly Disadvantaged* modified much of the moralistic tone of this debate by reframing the issue in terms of a lack of marriageable Black men.[73] According to Wilson, the decline in Black marriages is not attributable to poor motivation, bad work habits or irresponsibility but instead is caused by structural economics which have forced Black unskilled labor out of the work force. Wilson's approach represents a significant move away from that of Moynihan/Moyers in that he rejects their attempt to center the analysis on the morals of the Black community. Yet, he too considers the proliferation of female-headed households as dysfunctional *per se* and fails to explain fully why such households are so much in peril. Because he incorporates no analysis of the way the structure of the economy and the workforce subordinates the interests of women, especially childbearing Black women, Wilson's suggested reform begins with finding ways to put Black men back in the family.[74] In Wilson's view, we must change the economic structure with an eye toward providing more Black jobs for Black men. Because he offers no critique of sexism, Wilson fails to consider economic or social reorganization that directly empowers and supports these single Black mothers.[75]

My criticism is not that providing Black men with jobs is undesirable; indeed, this is necessary not only for the Black men themselves, but for an entire community, depressed and subject to a host of sociological and economic ills that accompany massive rates of unemployment. But as long as we assume that the massive social reorganization Wilson calls for is possible, why not think about it in ways that maximize the choices of Black women?[76] A more complete theoretical and political agenda for the Black underclass must take into account the specific and particular concerns of Black women; their families occupy the bottom rung of the economic ladder, and it is only through placing them at the center of the analysis that their needs and the needs of their families will be directly addressed.[77]

IV. Expanding Feminist Theory and Antiracist Politics by Embracing the Intersection

If any real efforts are to be made to free Black people of the constraints and conditions that characterize racial subordination, then theories and strategies purporting to reflect the Black community's needs must include an analysis of sexism and patriarchy. Similarly, feminism must include an analysis of race if it hopes to express the aspirations of non-white women. Neither Black liberationist politics nor feminist theory can ignore the intersectional experiences of those whom the movements claim as their respective constituents. In order to include Black women, both movements must distance themselves from earlier approaches in which experiences are relevant only when they are related to certain clearly identifiable causes (for example, the oppression of Blacks is significant when based on race, of women when based on gender). The praxis of both should be centered on the life chances and life situations of people who should be cared about without regard to the source of their difficulties.

I have stated earlier that the failure to embrace the complexities of compoundedness is not simply a matter of political will, but is also due to the influence of a way of thinking about discrimination which structures politics so that struggles are categorized as singular issues. Moreover, this structure imports a descriptive and normative view of society that reinforces the status quo.

It is somewhat ironic that those concerned with alleviating the ills of racism and sexism should adopt such a top-down approach to discrimination. If their efforts instead began with addressing the needs and problems of those who are most disadvantaged and with restructuring and remaking the world where necessary, then others who are singularly disadvantaged would also benefit. In addition, it seems that placing those who currently are marginalized in the center is the most effective way to resist efforts to compartmentalize experiences and undermine potential collective action.

It is not necessary to believe that a political consensus to focus on the lives of the most disadvantaged will happen tomorrow in order to recenter discrimination discourse at the intersection. It is enough, for now, that such an effort would encourage us to look beneath the prevailing conceptions of discrimination and to challenge the complacency that accompanies belief in the effectiveness of this framework. By so doing, we may develop language which is critical of the dominant view and which provides some basis for unifying activity. The goal of this activity should be to facilitate the inclusion of marginalized groups for whom it can be said: "When they enter, we all enter."

Notes

1. Gloria T. Hull, et al, eds (The Feminist Press, 1982).

3. The most common linguistic manifestation of this analytical dilemma is represented in the conventional usage of the term "Blacks and women." Although it may be true that some people mean to include Black women in either "Blacks" or "women," the context in which the term is used actually suggests that often Black women are not considered. See, for example, Elizabeth Spelman, *The Inessential Woman* 114–15 (Beacon Press, 1988) (discussing an article on Blacks and women in the military where "the racial identity of those identified as 'women' does not become explicit until reference is made to Black women, at which point it also becomes clear that the category of women excludes Black women"). It seems that if Black women were explicitly included, the preferred term would be either "Blacks and white women" or "Black men and all women."

4. Civil Rights Act of 1964, 42 USC § 2000e, et seq as amended (1982).

5. 413 F Supp 142 (E D Mo 1976).

6. 708 F2d 475 (9th Cir 1983).

7. 673 F2d 798 (5th Cir 1982).

8. *DeGraffenreid*, 413 F Supp at 143.

9. Id at 144.

10. Id at 145. In *Mosley v General Motors*, 497 F Supp 583 (E D Mo 1980), plaintiffs, alleging broad-based racial discrimination at General Motors' St. Louis facility, prevailed in a portion of their Title VII claim. The seniority system challenged in *DeGraffenreid*, however, was not considered in *Mosley*.

11. Id at 145.

12. Interestingly, no case has been discovered in which a court denied a white male's attempt to bring a reverse discrimination claim on similar grounds—that is, that sex and race claims cannot be combined because Congress did not intend to protect compound classes. White males in a typical reverse discrimination case are in no better position than the frustrated plaintiffs in *DeGraffenreid*: If they are required to make their claims separately, white males cannot prove race discrimination because white women are not discriminated against, and they cannot prove sex discrimination because Black males are not discriminated against. Yet it seems that courts do not acknowledge the compound nature of most reverse discrimination cases. That Black women's claims automatically raise the question of compound discrimination and white males' "reverse discrimination" cases do not suggest that the notion of compoundedness is somehow contingent upon an implicit norm that is not neutral but is white male. Thus, Black women are perceived as a compound class because they are two steps removed from a white male norm, while white males are apparently not perceived to be a compound class because they somehow represent the norm.

13. I do not mean to imply that all courts that have grappled with this problem have adopted the *DeGraffenreid* approach. Indeed, other courts have concluded that Black women are protected by Title VII. See, for example, *Jefferies v Harris Community Action Ass'n.*, 615 F2d 1025 (5th Cir 1980). I do mean to suggest that the very fact that the Black women's claims are seen as aberrant suggests that sex discrimination doctrine is centered in the experiences of white women. Even those courts that have held that Black women are protected seem to accept that Black women's claims raise issues that the "standard" sex discrimination claims do not. See Elaine W. Shoben, *Compound Discrimination: The Interaction of Race and Sex in Employment Discrimination*, 55 NYU I. Rev 793, 803–04 (1980) (criticizing the *Jefferies* use of a sex-plus analysis to create a subclass of Black women).

14. 708 F2d 475.

15. See also *Moore v National Association of Securities Dealers*, 27 EPD (CCH) ¶ 32,238 (D DC 1981); but see *Edmondson v Simon*, 86 FRD 375 (N D Ill 1980) (where the court was unwilling to hold as a matter of law that no Black female could represent without conflict the interests of both Blacks and females).

16. 708 F2d at 479. Between January 1976 and June 1979, the three years in which Moore claimed that she was passed over the promotion, the percentage of white males occupying first-level supervisory positions ranged from 70.3 to 76.8%; Black males from 8.9 to 10.9%; white women from 1.8 to 3.3%; and Black females from 0 to 2.2%. The overall male/female ratio in the top five labor grades ranged from 100/0% in 1976 to 98/1.8% in 1979. The white/Black ratio was 85/3.3% in 1976 and 79.6/8% in 1979. The overall ratio of men to women in supervisory positions was 98.2 to 1.8% in 1976 to 93.4 to 6.6% in 1979; the Black to white ratio during the same time period was 78.6 to 8.9% and 73.6 to 13.1%

For promotions to the top five labor grades, the percentages were worse. Between 1976 and 1979, the percentage of white males in these positions ranged from 85.3 to 77.9%; Black males 3.3 to 8%; white females from 0 to 1.4%, and Black females from 0 to 0%. Overall, in 1979, 98.2% of the highest level employees were male; 1.8% were female.

17. 708 F2d at 480 (emphasis added).

18. Id at 484–86.

19. Under the disparate impact theory that prevailed at the time, the plaintiff had to introduce statistics suggesting that a policy or procedure disparately affects the members of a protected group. The employer could rebut that evidence by showing that there was a business necessity supporting the rule. The plaintiff then countered the rebuttal by showing that there was a less discriminatory alternative. See, for example, *Griggs v Duke Power*, 401 US 424 (1971); *Connecticut v Teal*, 457 US 440 (1982).

A central issue in a disparate impact case is whether the impact proved is statistically significant. A related issue is how the protected group is defined. In many cases a Black female plaintiff would prefer to use statistics which include white women and/or Black men to indicate that the policy in question does in fact disparately affect the protected class. If, as in *Moore*, the plaintiff may use only statistics involving Black women, there may not be enough Black women employees to create a statistically significant sample.

20. Id at 484.

21. The court buttressed its finding with respect to the upper-level labor jobs with statistics for the Los Angeles Metropolitan Area which indicated that there were only 0.2% Black women within comparable job categories. Id at 485 n 9.

22. Id at 486.

23. Id.

24. See *Strong v Arkansas Blue Cross & Blue Shield, Inc.*, 87 FRD 496 (E D Ark 1980); *Hammons v Folger Coffee Co.*, 87 FRD 600 (W D Mo 1980); *Edmondson v Simon*, 86 FRD 375 (N D Ill 1980); *Vuyanich v Republic National Bank of Dallas*, 82 FRD (N D Tex 1979); *Colston v Maryland Cup Corp.*, 26 Fed Rules Serv 940 (D Md 1978).

25. 416 F Supp 248 (N D Miss 1976).

26. The suit commenced on March 2, 1972, with the filing of a complaint by three employees seeking to represent a class of persons allegedly subjected to racial discrimination at the hands of the defendants. Subsequently, the plaintiffs amended the complaint to add an allegation of sex discrimination. Of the original named plaintiffs, one was a Black male and two were Black females. In the course of the three-year period between the filing of the complaint and the trial, the only named male plaintiff received permission of the court to withdraw for religious reasons. Id at 250.

27. As the dissent in *Travenol* pointed out, there was no reason to exclude Black males from the scope of the remedy *after* counsel had presented sufficient evidence to support a finding of discrimination against Black men. If the rationale for excluding Black males was the potential conflict between Black males and Black females, then "[i]n this case, to paraphrase an old adage, the proof of plaintiffs' ability to represent the interests of Black males was in the representation thereof." 673 F2d at 837–38.

28. 673 F2d 798 (5th Cir 1982).

29. In much of antidiscrimination doctrine, the presence of intent to discriminate distinguishes unlawful from lawful discrimination. See *Washington v Davis*, 426 US 229, 239–45 (1976) (proof of discriminatory purposes required to substantiate Equal Protection violation). Under Title VII, however, the Court has held that statistical data showing a disproportionate impact can suffice to support a finding of discrimination. See *Griggs*, 401 US at 432. Whether the distinction between the two analyses will survive is an open question. See *Wards Cove Packing Co., Inc. v Atonio*, 109 S Ct 2115, 2122–23 (1989) (plaintiffs must show more than mere disparity to support a prima facie case of disparate impact). For a discussion of the competing normative visions that underlie the intent and effects analyses, see Alan David Freeman, *Legitimizing Racial Discrimination Through Antidiscrimination Law: A Critical Review of Supreme Court Doctrine*, 62 Minn L Rev 1049 (1978).

30. See, for example, *Moore*, 708 F2d at 479.

31. See Phyliss Palmer, *The Racial Feminization of Poverty: Women of Color as Portents of the Future for All Women,* Women's Studies Quarterly 11:3-4 (Fall 1983) (posing the question of why "white women in the women's movement had not created more effective and continuous alliances with Black women" when "simultaneously . . . Black women [have] become heroines for the women's movement, a position symbolized by the consistent use of Sojourner Truth and her famous words, "Ain't I a Woman?"").

32. See Paula Giddings, *When and Where I Enter: The Impact of Black Women on Race and Sex in America* 54 (William Morrow and Co, Inc, 1st ed 1984).

33. Eleanor Flexner, *Century of Struggle: The Women's Rights Movement in the United States* 91 (Belknap Press of Harvard University Press, 1975). See also Bell Hooks, *Ain't I a Woman* 159-60 (South End Press, 1981).

34. "'Objectivity' is itself an example of the reification of white male thought." Hull et al, eds, *But Some of Us Are Brave* at XXV (cited in note 1).

35. For example, many white females were able to gain entry into previously all white male enclaves not through bringing about a fundamental reordering of male versus female work, but in large part by shifting their "female" responsibilities to poor and minority women.

36. Feminists often discuss how gender-based stereotypes and norms reinforce the subordination of women by justifying their exclusion from public life and glorifying their roles within the private sphere. Law has historically played a role in maintaining this subordination by enforcing the exclusion of women from public life and by limiting its reach into the private sphere. See, for example, Deborah L. Rhode, *Association and Assimilation,* 81 Nw U L Rev 106 (1986); Frances Olsen, *From False Paternalism to False Equality: Judicial Assaults on Feminist Community, Illinois 1869-95,* 84 Mich L Rev 1518 (1986); Martha Minow, *Foreword: Justice Engendered,* 101 Harv L Rev 10 (1987); Nadine Taub and Elizabeth M. Schneider, *Perspectives on Women's Subordination and the Role of Law,* in David Kairys, ed, *The Politics of Law* 117-39 (Pantheon Books, 1982).

38. This criticism is a discrete illustration of a more general claim that feminism has been premised on white middle-class women's experience. For example, early feminist texts such as Betty Friedan's *The Feminine Mystique* (W. W. Norton, 1963), placed white middle-class problems at the center of feminism and thus contributed to its rejection within the Black community. See Hooks, *Ain't I a Woman* at 185-96 (cited in note 33) (noting that feminism was eschewed by Black women because its white middle-class agenda ignored Black women's concerns).

39. Richard A. Wasserstrom, *Racism, Sexism and Preferential Treatment: An Approach to the Topics,* 24 UCLA L Rev 581, 588 (1977). I chose this phrase not because it is typical of most feminist statements of separate spheres; indeed, most discussions are not as simplistic as the bold statement presented here. See, for example, Taub and Schneider, *Perspectives on Women's Subordination and the Role of Law* at 117-39 (cited in note 36).

40. For example, Black families have sometimes been cast as pathological largely because Black women's divergence from the white middle-class female norm. The most infamous rendition of this view is found in the Moynihan report which blamed many of the Black community's ills on a supposed pathological family structure. [See note 64.]

41. See Hooks, *Ain't I a Woman* at 94-99 (cited in note 33) (discussing the elevation of sexist imagery in the Black liberation movement during the 1960s).

42. See generally Jacqueline Jones, *Labor of Love, Labor of Sorrow: Black Women, Work, and the Family from Slavery to the Present* (Basic Books, 1985); Angela Davis, *Women, Race and Class* (Random House, 1981).

43. As Elizabeth Higginbotham noted, "women, who often fail to conform to 'appropriate' sex roles, have been pictured as, and made to feel, inadequate—even though

as women, they possess traits recognized as positive when held by men in the wider society. Such women are stigmatized because their lack of adherence to expected gender roles is seen as a threat to the value system." Elizabeth Higginbotham, *Two Representative Issues in Contemporary Sociological Work on Black Women*, in Hull, et al, eds, *But Some of Us Are Brave* at 95 (cited in note 1).

44. See generally Susan Brownmiller, *Against Our Will* (Simon and Schuster, 1975); Susan Estrich, *Real Rape* (Harvard University Press, 1987).

45. See Brownmiller, *Against Our Will* at 17; see generally Estrich, *Real Rape*.

46. One of the central theoretical dilemmas of feminism that is largely obscured by universalizing the white female experience is that experiences that are described as a manifestation of male control over females can be instead a manifestation of dominant group control over all subordinates. The significance is that other nondominant men may not share in, participate in or connect with the behavior, beliefs or actions at issue, and may be victimized themselves by "male" power. In other contexts, however, "male authority" might include nonwhite men, particularly in private sphere contexts. Efforts to think more clearly about when Black women are dominated as *women* and when they are dominated as *Black women* are directly related to the question of when power is *male* and when it is *white male*.

47. See Note, *Rape, Racism and the Law*, 6 Harv Women's L J 103, 117–23 (1983) (discussing the historical and contemporary evidence suggesting that Black women are generally not thought to be chaste). See also Hooks, *Ain't I a Woman* at 54 (cited in note 33) (stating that stereotypical images of Black womanhood during slavery were based on the myth that "all black women were immoral and sexually loose"); Beverly Smith, *Black Women's Health: Notes for a Course*, in Hull et al, eds, *But Some of Us Are Brave* at 110 (cited in note 1) (noting that ". . . white men for centuries have justified their sexual abuse of Black women by claiming that we are licentious, always 'ready' for any sexual encounter").

48. The following statement is probably unusual only in its candor: "What has been said by some of our courts about an unchaste female being a comparatively rare exception is no doubt true where the population is composed largely of the Caucasian race, but we would blind ourselves to actual conditions if we adopted this rule where another race that is largely immoral constitutes an appreciable part of the population." *Dallas v State*, 76 Fla 358, 79 So 690 (1918), quoted in Note, 6 Harv Women's L J at 121 (cited in note 47).

Espousing precisely this view, one commentator stated in 1902: "I sometimes hear of a virtuous Negro woman but the idea is so absolutely inconceivable to me . . . I cannot imagine such a creature as a virtuous Negro woman." Id at 82. Such images persist in popular culture. See Paul Grein, *Taking Stock of the Latest Pop Record Surprises*, LA Times § 6 at 1 (July 7, 1988) (recalling the controversy in the late 70s over a Rolling Stones recording which included the line "Black girls just wanna get fucked all night").

. . .

49. Because of the way the legal system viewed chastity, Black women could not be victims of forcible rape. One commentator has noted that "[a]ccording to governing [stereotypes], chastity could not be possessed by Black women. Thus, Black women's rape charges were automatically discounted, and the issue of chastity was contested only in cases where the rape complainant was a white woman." Note, 6 Harv Women's L J at 126 (cited in note 47). Black women's claims of rape were not taken seriously regardless of the offender's race. A judge in 1912 said: "This court will never take the word of a nigger against the word of a white man [concerning rape]." Id at 120. On the other hand, lynching was considered an effective remedy for a Black man's rape of a white woman. Since rape of a white woman by a Black man was "a crime more horrible than

death," the only way to assuage society's rage and to make the woman whole again was to brutally murder the Black man. Id at 125.

50. See *The Rape of Black Women as a Weapon of Terror*, in Gerda Lerner, ed, *Black Women in White America* 172–93 (Pantheon Books, 1972). See also Brownmiller, *Against Our Will* (cited in note 44). Even where Brownmiller acknowledges the use of rape as racial terrorism, she resists making a "special case" for Black women by offering evidence that white women were raped by the Klan as well. Id at 139. Whether or not one considers the racist rape of Black women a "special case," such experiences are probably different. In any case, Brownmiller's treatment of the issue raises serious questions about the ability to sustain an analysis of patriarchy without understanding its multiple intersections with racism.

51. Lerner, *Black Women in White America* at 173.

52. See generally, Note, 6 Harv Women's L J at 103 (cited in note 47).

53. Paula Giddings notes the combined effect of sexual and racial stereotypes: "Black women were seen having all of the inferior qualities of white women without any of their virtues." Giddings, *When and Where I Enter* at 82 (cited in note 32).

54. Susan Brownmiller's treatment of the Emmett Till case illustrates why antirape politicization makes some African Americans uncomfortable. Despite Brownmiller's quite laudable efforts to discuss elsewhere the rape of Black women and the racism involved in much of the hysteria over the Black male threat, her analysis of the Till case places the sexuality of white women, rather than racial terrorism, at center stage. Brownmiller states: "Rarely has one single case exposed so clearly as Till's the underlying group-male antagonisms over access to women, for what began in Bryant's store should not be misconstrued as an innocent flirtation. . . . In concrete terms, the accessibility of all white women was on review." Brownmiller, *Against Our Will* at 272 (cited in note 44).

Later, Brownmiller argues: "And what of the wolf whistle, Till's 'gesture of adolescent bravado'? We are rightly aghast that a whistle could be cause for murder but we must also accept that Emmett Till and J. W. Millam shared something in common. They both understood that the whistle was no small tweet of hubba-hubba or melodious approval for a well-turned ankle. Given the deteriorated situation . . . it was a deliberate insult just short of physical assault, a last reminder to Carolyn Bryant that this black boy, Till, had a mind to possess her." Id at 273.

While Brownmiller seems to categorize the case as one that evidences a conflict over possession, it is regarded in African American history as a tragic dramatization of the South's pathological hatred and fear of African Americans. Till's body, mutilated beyond recognition, was viewed by thousands so that, in the words of Till's mother, "the world could see what they did to my boy." Juan Williams, *Standing for Justice*, in *Eyes on the Prize* 44 (Viking, 1987). The Till tragedy is also regarded as one of the historical events that bore directly on the emergence of the Civil Rights movement. "[W]ithout question it moved black America in a way the Supreme Court ruling on school desegregation could not match." Id. As Williams later observed, "the murder of Emmitt Till had a powerful impact on a generation of blacks. It was this generation, those who were adolescents when Till was killed, that would soon demand justice and freedom in a way unknown in America before." Id at 57. Thus, while Brownmiller looks at the Till case and sees the vicious struggle over the possession of a white woman, African Americans see the case as a symbol of the insane degree to which whites were willing to suppress the Black race. While patriarchal attitudes toward women's sexuality played a supporting role, to place white women center stage in this tragedy is to manifest such confusion over racism as to make it difficult to imagine that the white antirape movement could be sensitive to more subtle racial tensions regarding Black women's participation in it.

55. See Anna Julia Cooper, *A Voice from the South* (Negro Universities Press, 1969 reprint of the Aldine Printing House, Ohio, 1892).

56. Id at 31.

57. In all fairness, I must acknowledge that my companion accompanied me to the back door. I remain uncertain, however, as to whether the gesture was an expression of solidarity or an effort to quiet my anger.

58. To this one could easily add class.

60. For a comparative discussion of Third World feminism paralleling this observation, see Kumari Jayawardena, *Feminism and Nationalism in the Third World* 1–24 (Zed Books Ltd, 1986). Jayawardena states that feminism in the Third World has been "accepted" only within the central struggle against international domination. Women's social and political status has improved most when advancement is necessary to the broader struggle against imperialism.

61. For a discussion of how racial ideology creates a polarizing dynamic which subordinates Blacks and privileges whites, see Kimberle Crenshaw, *Race, Reform and Retrenchment: Transformation and Legitimation in Antidiscrimination Law*, 101 Harv L Rev 1331, 1371–76 (1988).

62. Jack Matthews, *Three Color Purple Actresses Talk About Its Impact*, LA Times § 6 at 1 (Jan 31, 1986); Jack Matthews, *Some Blacks Critical of Spielberg's Purple*, LA Times § 6 at 1 (Dec 20, 1985). But see Gene Siskel, *Does Purple Hate Men?*, Chicago Tribune § 13 at 16 (Jan 5, 1986); Clarence Page, *Toward a New Black Cinema*, Chicago Tribune § 5 at 3 (Jan 12, 1986).

63. A consistent problem with any negative portrayal of African Americans is that they are seldom balanced by positive images. On the other hand, most critics overlooked the positive transformation of the primary male character in *The Color Purple*.

64. Daniel P. Moynihan, *The Negro Family: The Case for National Action* (Office of Policy Planning and Research, United States Department of Labor, 1965).

65. See Lee Rainwater and William L. Yancey, *The Moynihan Report and the Politics of Controversy* 427–29 (MIT Press, 1967) (containing criticism of the Moynihan Report by, among others, Charles E. Silberman, Christopher Jencks, William Ryan, Laura Carper, Frank Riessman and Herbert Gans).

66. Id at 395–97 (critics included Martin Luther King, Jr., Benjamin Payton, James Farmer, Whitney Young, Jr. and Bayard Rustin).

67. One of the notable exceptions is Jacquelyne Johnson Jackson, *Black Women in a Racist Society*, in *Racism and Mental Health* 185–86 (University of Pittsburgh Press, 1973).

68. *The Vanishing Black Family* (PBS Television Broadcast, January 1986).

69. William Julius Wilson, *The Truly Disadvantaged: The Inner City, The Underclass and Public Policy* (The University of Chicago Press, 1987).

70. Columnist Mary McGrory, applauding the show, reported that Moyers found that sex was as common in the Black ghetto as a cup of coffee. McGrory, *Moynihan was Right 21 Years Ago*, The Washington Post B1 and B4 (Jan 26, 1986). George Will argued that oversexed Black men were more of a menace than Bull Conner, the Birmingham Police Chief who in 1968 achieved international notoriety by turning fire hoses on protesting school children. George Will, *Voting Rights Won't Fix It*, The Washington Post A23 (Jan 23, 1986).

My guess is that the program has influenced the debate about the so-called underclass by providing graphic support to pre-existing tendencies to attribute poverty to individual immorality. During a recent and memorable discussion on the public policy implications of poverty in the Black community, one student remarked that nothing can be done about Black poverty until Black men stop acting like "roving penises," Black women stop having babies "at the drop of a hat," and they all learn middle-class morality. The student cited the Moyers report as her source.

71. Although the nearly exclusive focus on the racist aspects of the program poses both theoretical and political problems, it was entirely understandable given the racial nature of the subsequent comments that were sympathetic to the Moyers view. As is typical in discussions involving race, the dialogue regarding the Moyers program covered more than just the issue of Black families; some commentators took the opportunity to indict not only the Black underclass, but the Black civil rights leadership, the war on poverty, affirmative action and other race-based remedies. See, for example, Will, *Voting Rights Won't Fix It* at A23 (cited in note 70).

72. Their difficulties can also be linked to the prevalence of an economic system and family policy that treat the nuclear family as the norm and other family units as aberrant and unworthy of societal accommodation.

73. Wilson, *The Truly Disadvantaged* at 96 (cited in note 69).

74. Id at 154 (suggestions include macroeconomic policies which promote balanced economic growth, a nationally-oriented labor market strategy, a child support assurance program, a child care strategy, and a family allowances program which would be both means tested and race specific).

75. Nor does Wilson include an analysis of the impact of gender on changes in family patterns. Consequently, little attention is paid to the conflict that may result when gender-based expectations are frustrated by economic and demographic factors. This focus on demographic and structural explanations represent an effort to regain the high ground from the Moyers/Moynihan approach which is more psycho-social. Perhaps because psycho-social explanations have come dangerously close to victim-blaming, their prevalence is thought to threaten efforts to win policy directives that might effectively address deteriorating conditions within the working class and poor Black communities. See Kimberle Crenshaw, *A Comment on Gender, Difference, and Victim Ideology in the Study of the Black Family,* in *The Decline of Marriage Among African Americans: Causes, Consequences and Policy Implications* (forthcoming 1989).

76. For instance, Wilson only mentions in passing the need for day care and job training for single mothers. Wilson at 153 (cited in note 69). No mention at all is made of other practices and policies that are racist and sexist, and that contribute to the poor conditions under which nearly half of all Black women must live.

77. Pauli Murray observes that the operation of sexism is at least the partial cause of social problems affecting Black women. See Murray, *The Liberation of Black Women,* in Jo Freeman, ed, *Women: A Feminist Perspective* 351–62 (Mayfield Publishing Co, 1975).

5

Difference and Dominance:
On Sex Discrimination [1984]

Catharine A. MacKinnon

What is a gender question a question of? What is an equality question a question of? These two questions underlie applications of the equality principle to issues of gender, but they are seldom explicitly asked. I think it speaks to the way gender has structured thought and perception that mainstream legal and moral theory tacitly gives the same answer to them both: these are questions of sameness and difference. The mainstream doctrine of the law of sex discrimination that results is, in my view, largely responsible for the fact that sex equality law has been so utterly ineffective at getting women what we need and are socially prevented from having on the basis of a condition of birth: a chance at productive lives of reasonable physical security, self-expression, individuation, and minimal respect and dignity. Here I expose the sameness/ difference theory of sex equality, briefly show how it dominates sex discrimination law and policy and underlies its discontents, and propose an alternative that might do something.

According to the approach to sex equality that has dominated politics, law, and social perception, equality is an equivalence, not a distinction, and sex is a distinction. The legal mandate of equal treatment—which is both a systemic norm and a specific legal doctrine—becomes a matter of treating likes alike and unlikes unlike; and the sexes are defined as such by their mutual unlikeness. Put another way, gender is socially constructed as difference epistemologically; sex discrimination law bounds gender equality by difference doctrinally. A built-in tension exists between this concept of equality, which presupposes sameness, and this concept of sex, which presupposes difference. Sex equality thus becomes a contradiction in terms, something of an oxymoron, which may suggest why we are having such a difficult time getting it.

Upon further scrutiny, two alternate paths to equality for women emerge within this dominant approach, paths that roughly follow the lines of this tension. The leading one is: be the same as men. This path is termed gender neutrality doctrinally and the single standard philosophically. It is testimony to how substance gets itself up as form in law that this rule is considered formal equality. Because this approach mirrors the ideology of the social world, it is considered abstract, meaning transparent of substance; also for this reason it is considered not only to be *the* standard, but *a* standard at all. It is so far the leading rule that the words "equal to" are code for, equivalent to, the words "the same as"—referent for both unspecified.

To women who want equality yet find that you are different, the doctrine provides an alternate route: be different from men. This equal recognition of difference is termed the special benefit rule or special protection rule legally, the double standard philosophically. It is in rather bad odor. Like pregnancy, which always calls it up, it is something of a doctrinal embarrassment. Considered an exception to true equality and not really a rule of law at all, this is the one place where the law of sex discrimination admits it is recognizing something substantive. Together with the Bona Fide Occupational Qualification (BFOQ), the unique physical characteristic exception under ERA policy, compensatory legislation, and sex-conscious relief in particular litigation, affirmative action is thought to live here.[1]

The philosophy underlying the difference approach is that sex *is* a difference, a division, a distinction, beneath which lies a stratum of human commonality, sameness. The moral thrust of the sameness branch of the doctrine is to make normative rules conform to this empirical reality by granting women access to what men have access to: to the extent that women are no different from men, we deserve what they have. The differences branch, which is generally seen as patronizing but necessary to avoid absurdity, exists to value or compensate women for what we are or have become distinctively as women (by which is meant, unlike men) under existing conditions.

My concern is not with which of these paths to sex equality is preferable in the long run or more appropriate to any particular issue, although most discourse on sex discrimination revolves about these questions as if that were all there is. My point is logically prior: to treat issues of sex equality as issues of sameness and difference *is to take a particular approach.* I call this the difference approach because it is obsessed with the sex difference. The main theme in the fugue is "we're the same, we're the same, we're the same." The counterpoint theme (in a higher register) is "but we're different, but we're different, but we're different." Its underlying story is: on the first day, difference was; on the second day, a division was created upon it; on the third day, irrational instances of dominance arose. Division may be rational or irrational. Dominance either seems or is justified. Difference *is.*

There is a politics to this. Concealed is the substantive way in which man has become the measure of all things. Under the sameness standard, women are measured according to our correspondence with man, our equality judged by our proximity to his measure. Under the difference standard, we are measured according to our lack of correspondence with him, our womanhood judged by our distance from his measure. Gender neutrality is thus simply the male standard, and the special protection rule is simply the female standard, but do not be deceived: masculinity, or maleness, is the referent for both. Think about it like those anatomy models in medical school. A male body is the human body; all those extra things women have are studied in ob/gyn. It truly is a situation in which more is less. Approaching sex discrimination in this way—as if sex questions are difference questions and equality questions are sameness questions—provided two ways for the law to hold women to a male standard and call that sex equality.

Having been very hard on the difference answer to sex equality questions, I should say that it takes up a very important problem: how to get women access to everything we have been excluded from, while also valuing everything that women are or have been allowed to become or have developed as a consequence of our struggle either not to be excluded from most of life's pursuits or to be taken seriously under the terms that have been permitted to be our terms. It negotiates what we have managed in relation to men. Legally articulated as the need to conform normative standards to existing reality, the strongest doctrinal expression of its sameness idea would prohibit taking gender into account in any way.

Its guiding impulse is: we're as good as you. Anything you can do, we can do. Just get out of the way. I have to confess a sincere affection for this approach. It has gotten women some access to employment and education, the public pursuits, including academic, professional, and blue-collar work; the military; and more than nominal access to athletics. It has moved to change the dead ends that were all we were seen as good for and has altered what passed for women's lack of physical training, which was really serious training in passivity and enforced weakness. It makes you want to cry sometimes to know that it has had to be a mission for many women just to be permitted to do the work of this society, to have the dignity of doing jobs a lot of other people don't even want to do.

The issue of including women in the military draft has presented the sameness answer to the sex equality question in all its simple dignity and complex equivocality. As a citizen, I should have to risk being killed just like you. The consequences of my resistance to this risk should count like yours. The undercurrent is: what's the matter, don't you want me to learn to kill . . . just like you? Sometimes I see this as a dialogue between women in the afterlife. The feminist says to the soldier, "we fought for your equality." The soldier says to the feminist, "oh, no, *we* fought for *your* equality."

Feminists have this nasty habit of counting bodies and refusing not to notice their gender. As applied, the sameness standard has mostly gotten men the benefit of those few things women have historically had—for all the good they did us. Almost every sex discrimination case that has been won at the Supreme Court level has been brought by a man.[10] Under the rule of gender neutrality, the law of custody and divorce has been transformed, giving men an equal chance at custody of children and at alimony.[11] Men often look like better "parents" under gender-neutral rules like level of income and presence of nuclear family, because men make more money and (as they say) initiate the building of family units.[12] In effect, they get preferred because society advantages them before they get into court, and law is prohibited from taking that preference into account because that would mean taking gender into account. The group realities that make women more in need of alimony are not permitted to matter, because only individual factors, gender-neutrally considered, may matter. So the fact that women will live their lives, as individuals, as members of the group women, with women's chances in a sex-discriminatory society, may not count, or else it is sex discrimination. The equality principle in this guise mobilizes the idea that the way to get things for women is to get them for men. Men have gotten them. Have women? We still have not got equal pay,[13] or equal work,[14] far less equal pay for equal work,[15] and we are close to losing separate enclaves like women's schools through this approach.[16]

Here is why. In reality, which this approach is not long on because it is liberal idealism talking to itself, virtually every quality that distinguishes men from women is already affirmatively compensated in this society. Men's physiology defines most sports,[17] their needs define auto and health insurance coverage, their socially designed biographies define workplace expectations and successful career patterns, their perspectives and concerns define quality in scholarship, their experiences and obsessions define merit, their objectification of life defines art, their military service defines citizenship, their presence defines family, their inability to get along with each other—their wars and rulerships—defines history, their image defines god, and their genitals define sex. For each of their differences from women, what amounts to an affirmative action plan is in effect, otherwise known as the structure and values of American society. But whenever women are, by this standard, "different" from men and insist on not having it held against us, whenever a difference is used to keep us second class and we refuse to smile about it, equality law has a paradigm trauma and it's crisis time for the doctrine.

What this doctrine has apparently meant by sex inequality is not what happens to us. The law of sex discrimination that has resulted seems to be looking only for those ways women are kept down that have *not* wrapped themselves up as a difference—whether original, imposed, or imagined. Start with original: what to do about the fact that women actually have an ability men still lack, gestating children in utero. Pregnancy therefore is a difference. Difference doctrine says it is sex discrimination to give women what we need, because only women need it. It is not sex discrimination not to give women what we need because then only women will not get what we need. Move into imposed: what to do about the fact that most women are segregated into low-paying jobs where there are not men. Suspecting that the structure of the marketplace will be entirely subverted if comparable worth is put into effect, difference doctrine says that because there is no man to set a standard from which women's treatment is a deviation, there is no sex discrimination here, only sex difference. Never mind that there is no man to compare with because no man would do that job if he had a choice, and of course he has because he is a man, so he won't.[19]

Now move into the so-called subtle reaches of the imposed category, the de facto area. Most jobs in fact require that the person, gender neutral, who is qualified for them will be someone who is not the primary caretaker of a preschool child. Pointing out that this raises a concern of sex in a society in which women are expected to care for the children is taken as day one of taking gender into account in the structuring of jobs. To do that would violate the rule against not noticing situated differences based on gender, so it never emerges that day one of taking gender into account was the day the job was structured with the expectation that its occupant would have no child care responsibilities. Imaginary sex differences—such as between male and female applicants to administer estates or between males aging and dying and females aging and dying[21]—I will concede, the doctrine can handle.

I will also concede that there are many differences between women and men. I mean, can you imagine elevating one half of a population and denigrating the other half and producing a population in which everyone is the same? What the sameness standard fails to notice is that men's differences from women are equal to women's differences from men. There is an *equality* there. Yet the sexes are not socially equal. The difference approach misses the fact that hierarchy of power produces real as well as fantasied differences, differences that are also inequalities. What is missing in the difference approach is what Aristotle missed in his empiricist notion that equality means treating likes alike and unlikes unlike, and nobody has questioned it since. Why should you have to be the same as a man to get what a man gets simply because he is one? Why does maleness provide an original entitlement, not questioned on the basis of *its* gender, so that it is women—women who want to make a case of unequal treatment in a world men have made in their image (this is really the part Aristotle missed)—who have to show in effect that they are men in every relevant respect, unfortunately mistaken for women on the basis of an accident of birth?

The women that gender neutrality benefits, and there are some, show the suppositions of this approach in highest relief. They are mostly women who have been able to construct a biography that somewhat approximates the male norm, at least on paper. They are the qualified, the least of sex discrimination's victims. When they are denied a man's chance, it looks the most like sex bias. The more unequal society gets, the fewer such women are permitted to exist. Therefore, the more unequal society gets, the *less* likely the difference doctrine is to be able to do anything about it, because unequal power creates both the appearance and the reality of sex differences along the same lines as it creates its sex inequalities.

The special benefits side of the difference approach has not compensated for the differential of being second class. The special benefits rule is the only place in mainstream equality doctrine where you get to identify as a woman and not have that mean giving up all claim to equal treatment—but it comes close. Under its double standard, women who stand to inherit something when their husbands die have gotten the exclusion of a small percentage of the inheritance tax, to the tune of Justice Douglas waxing eloquent about the difficulties of all women's economic situation.[22] If we're going to be stigmatized as different, it would be nice if the compensation would fit the disparity. Women have also gotten three more years than men get before we have to be advanced or kicked out of the military hierarchy, as compensation for being precluded from combat, the usual way to advance.[23] Women have also gotten excluded from contact jobs in male-only prisons because we might get raped, the Court taking the viewpoint of the reasonable rapist on women's employment opportunities.[24] We also get protected out of jobs because of our fertility. The reason is that the job has health hazards, and somebody who might be a real person some day and therefore could sue—that is, a fetus—might be hurt if women, who apparently are not real persons and therefore can't sue either for the hazard to our health or for the lost employment opportunity, are given jobs that subject our bodies to possible harm.[25] Excluding women is always an option if equality feels in tension with the pursuit itself. They never seem to think of excluding men. Take combat.[26] Somehow it takes the glory out of the foxhole, the buddiness out of the trenches, to imagine us out there. You get the feeling they might rather end the draft, they might even rather not fight wars at all than have to do it with us.

The double standard of these rules doesn't give women the dignity of the single standard; it also does not (as the differences standard does) suppress the gender of its referent, which is, of course, the female gender. I must also confess some affection for this standard. The work of Carol Gilligan on gender differences in moral reasoning[27] gives it a lot of dignity, more than it has ever had, more, frankly, than I thought it ever could have. But she achieves for moral reasoning what the special protection rule achieves in law: the affirmative rather than the negative valuation of that which has accurately distinguished women from men, by making it seem as though those attributes, with their consequences, really are somehow ours, rather than what male supremacy has attributed to us for its own use. For women to affirm difference, when difference means dominance, as it does with gender, means to affirm the qualities and characteristics of powerlessness.

Women have done good things, and it is a good thing to affirm them. I think quilts are art. I think women have a history. I think we create culture. I also know that we have not only been excluded from making what has been considered art; our artifacts have been excluded from setting the standards by which art is art. Women have a history all right, but it is a history both of what was and of what was not allowed to be. So I am critical of affirming what we have been, which necessarily is what we have been permitted, as if it is women's, ours, possessive. As if equality, in spite of everything, already ineluctably exists.

I am getting hard on this and am about to get harder on it. I do not think that the way women reason morally is morality "in a different voice."[28] I think it is morality in a higher register, in the feminine voice. Women value care because men have valued us according to the care we give them, and we could probably use some. Women think in relational terms because our existence is defined in relation to men. Further, when you are powerless, you don't just speak differently. A lot, you don't speak. Your speech is not just differently articulated, it is silenced. Eliminated, gone. You aren't just deprived of a language with which to articulate your distinctiveness, although you are; you are deprived of a life out of which articulation might come. Not being heard is not just a function of lack of recognition, not just that no one knows how to listen to you, although it is that; it is also silence of the deep kind, the silence of being prevented from having anything to say. Sometimes it is permanent. All I am saying is that the damage of sexism is real, and reifying that into differences is an insult to our possibilities.

So long as these issues are framed this way, demands for equality will always appear to be asking to have it both ways: the same when we are the same, different when we are different. But this is the way men have it: equal and different too. They have it the same as women when they are the same and want it, and different from women when they are different and want to be, which usually they do. Equal and different too would only be parity. But under male supremacy, while being told we get it both ways, both the specialness of the pedestal and an even chance at the race, the ability to be a woman and a person, too, few women get much benefit of either.

There is an alternative approach, one that threads its way through existing law and expresses, I think, the reason equality law exists in the first place. It provides a second answer, a dissident answer in law and philosophy, to both the equality question and the gender question. In this approach, an equality question is a question of the distribution of power. Gender is also a question of power, specifically of male supremacy and female subordination. The question of equality, from the standpoint of what it is going to take to get it, is at root a question of hierarchy, which—as power succeeds in constructing social perception and social reality—derivatively becomes a categorical distinction, a difference. Here, on the first day that matters, dominance was achieved, probably by force. By the second day, division along the same lines had to be relatively firmly in place. On the third day, if not sooner, differences were demarcated, together with social systems to exaggerate them in perception and in fact, *because* the systematically differential delivery of benefits and deprivations required making no mistake about who was who. Comparatively speaking, man has been resting ever since. Gender might not even code as difference, might not mean distinction epistemologically, were it not for its consequences for social power.

I call this the dominance approach, and it is the ground I have been standing on in criticizing mainstream law. The goal of this dissident approach is not to make legal categories trace and trap the way things are. It is not to make rules that fit reality. It is critical of reality. Its task is not to formulate abstract standards that will produce determinate outcomes in particular cases. Its project is more substantive, more jurisprudential than formulaic, which is why it is difficult for the mainstream discourse to dignify it as an approach to doctrine or to imagine it as a rule of law at all. It proposes to expose that which women have had little choice but to be confined to, in order to change it.

The dominance approach centers on the most sex-differential abuses of women as a gender, abuses that sex equality law in its difference garb could not confront. It is based on a reality about which little of a systematic nature was known before 1970, a reality that calls for a new conception of the problem of sex inequality. This new information includes not only the extent and intractability of sex segregation into poverty, which has been known before, but the range of issues termed violence against women, which has not been. It combines women's material desperation, through being relegated to categories of jobs that pay nil, with the massive amount of rape and attempted rape— 44 percent of all women—about which virtually nothing is done;[30] the sexual assault of children—38 percent of girls and 10 percent of boys—which is apparently endemic to the patriarchal family;[31] the battery of women that is systematic in one quarter to one third of our homes;[32] prostitution, women's fundamental economic condition, what we do when all else fails, and for many women in this country, all else fails often;[33] and pornography, an industry that traffics in female flesh, making sex inequality into sex to the tune of eight billion dollars a year in profits largely to organized crime.[34]

These experiences have been silenced out of the difference definition of sex equality largely because they happen almost exclusively to women. Understand: for this reason, they are considered *not* to raise sex equality issues. Because this treatment is done almost uniquely to women, it is implicitly treated as a difference, the sex difference, when in fact it is the socially situated subjection of women. The whole point of women's social relegation to inferiority as a gender is that for the most part these things aren't done to men. Men are not paid half of what women are paid for doing the same work on the basis of their equal difference. Everything they touch does not turn valueless because they touched it. When they are hit, a person has been assaulted. When they are sexually violated, it is not simply tolerated or found entertaining or defended as the necessary structure of the family, the price of civilization, or a constitutional right.

Does this differential describe the sex difference? Maybe so. It does describe the systematic relegation of an entire group of people to a condition of inferiority and attribute it to their nature. If this differential were biological, maybe biological intervention would have to be considered. If it were evolutionary, perhaps men would have to evolve differently. Because I think it is political, I think its politics construct the deep structure of society. Men who do not rape women have nothing wrong with their hormones. Men who are made sick by pornography and do not eroticize their revulsion are not underevolved. This social status in which we can be used and abused and trivialized and humiliated and bought and sold and passed around and patted on the head and put in place and told to smile so that we look as though we're enjoying it all is not what some of us have in mind as sex equality.

This second approach—which is not abstract, which is at odds with socially imposed reality and therefore does not look like a standard according to the standard for standards—became the implicit model for racial justice applied by the courts during the sixties. It has since eroded with the erosion of judicial commitment to racial equality. It was based on the realization that the condition of Blacks in particular was not fundamentally a matter of rational or irrational differentiation on the basis of race but was fundamentally a matter of white supremacy, under which racial differences became invidious as a consequence.[35] To consider gender in this way, observe again that men are as different from women as women are from men, but socially the sexes are not equally powerful. To be on the top of a hierarchy is certainly different from being on the bottom, but that is an obfuscatingly neutralized way of putting it, as a hierarchy is a great deal more than that. If gender were merely a question of difference, sex inequality would be a problem of mere sexism, of mistaken differentiation, of inaccurate categorization of individuals. This is what the difference approach thinks it is and is therefore sensitive to. But if gender is an inequality first, constructed as a socially relevant differentiation in order to keep that inequality in place, then sex inequality questions are questions of systematic dominance, of male supremacy, which is not at all abstract and is anything but a mistake.

If differentiation into classifications, in itself, is discrimination, as it is in difference doctrine, the use of law to change group-based social inequalities becomes problematic, even contradictory. This is because the group whose situation is to be changed must necessarily be legally identified and delineated, yet to do so is considered in fundamental tension with the guarantee against legally sanctioned inequality. If differentiation is discrimination, affirmative action, and any legal change in social inequality, is discrimination—but the existing social differentiations which constitute the inequality are not? This is only to say that, in the view that equates differentiation with discrimination, changing an unequal status quo is discrimination, but allowing it to exist is not.

Looking at the difference approach and the dominance approach from each other's point of view clarifies some otherwise confusing tensions in sex equality debates. From the point of view of the dominance approach, it becomes clear that the difference approach adopts the point of view of male supremacy on the status of the sexes. Simply by treating the status quo as "the standard," it invisibly and uncritically accepts the arrangements under male supremacy. In this sense, the difference approach is masculinist, although it can be expressed in a female voice. The dominance approach, in that it sees the inequalities of the social world from the standpoint of the subordination of women to men, is feminist.

If you look through the lens of the difference approach at the world as the dominance approach imagines it—that is, if you try to see real inequality through a lens that has difficulty seeing an inequality as an inequality if it also appears as a difference—you see demands for change in the distribution of power as demands for special protection. This is because the only tools that the difference paradigm offers to comprehend disparity equate the recognition of a gender line with an admission of lack of entitlement to equality under law. Since equality questions are primarily confronted in this approach as matters of empirical fit[36]—that is, as matters of accurately shaping legal rules (implicitly modeled on the standard men set) to the way the world is (also implicitly modeled on the standard men set)—any existing differences must be negated to merit equal treatment. For ethnicity as well as for gender, it is basic to mainstream discrimination doctrine to preclude any true diversity among equals or true equality within diversity.

To the difference approach, it further follows that any attempt to change the way the world actually is looks like a moral question requiring a separate judgment of how things ought to be. This approach imagines asking the following disinterested question that can be answered neutrally as to groups: against the weight of empirical difference, should we treat some as the equals of others, even when they may not be entitled to it because they are not up to standard? Because this construction of the problem is part of what the dominance approach unmasks, it does not arise with the dominance approach, which therefore does not see its own foundations as moral. If sex inequalities are approached as matters of imposed status, which are in need of change if a legal mandate of equality means anything at all, the question whether women should be treated unequally means simply whether women should be treated as less. When it is exposed as a naked power question, there is no separable question of what ought to be. The only real question is what is and is not a gender question. Once no amount of difference justifies treating women as subhuman, eliminating that is what equality law is for. In this shift of paradigms, equality propositions become no longer propositions of good and evil, but of power and powerlessness, no more disinterested in their origins or neutral in their arrival at conclusions than are the problems they address.

There came a time in Black people's movement for equality in this country when slavery stopped being a question of how it could be justified and became a question of how it could be ended. Racial disparities surely existed, or racism would have been harmless, but at that point—a point not yet reached for issues of sex—no amount of group difference mattered anymore. This is the same point at which a group's characteristics, including empirical attributes, become constitutive of the fully human, rather than being defined as exceptions to or as distinct from the fully human. To one-sidedly measure one group's differences against a standard set by the other incarnates partial standards. The moment when one's particular qualities become part of the standard by which humanity is measured is a millennial moment.

To summarize the argument: seeing sex equality questions as matters of reasonable or unreasonable classification is part of the way male dominance is expressed in law. If you follow my shift in perspective from gender as difference to gender as dominance, gender changes from a distinction that is presumptively valid to a detriment that is presumptively suspect. The difference approach tries to map reality; the dominance approach tries to challenge and change it. In the dominance approach, sex discrimination stops being a question of morality and starts being a question of politics.

You can tell if sameness is your standard for equality if my critique of hierarchy looks like a request for special protection in disguise. It's not. It envisions a change that would make possible a simple equal chance for the first time. To define the reality of sex as difference and the warrant of equality as sameness is wrong on both counts. Sex, in nature, is not a bipolarity; it is a continuum. In society it is made into a bipolarity. Once this is done, to require that one be the same as those who set the standard—those which one is already socially defined as different from—simply means that sex equality is conceptually designed never to be achieved. Those who most need equal treatment will be the least similar, socially, to those whose situation sets the standard as against which one's entitlement to be equally treated is measured. Doctrinally speaking, the deepest problems of sex inequality will not find women "similarly situated"[37] to men. Far less will practices of sex inequality require that acts be intentionally discriminatory.[38] All that is required is that the status quo be maintained. As a strategy for maintaining social power first structure reality unequally, then require that entitlement to alter it be grounded on a lack of distinction in situation; first structure perception so that different equals inferior, then require that discrimination be activated by evil minds who *know* they are treating equals as less.

I say, give women equal power in social life. Let what we say matter, then we will discourse on questions of morality. Take your foot off our necks, then we will hear in what tongue women speak. So long as sex equality is limited by sex difference, whether you like it or don't like it, whether you value it or seek to negate it, whether you stake it out as a grounds for feminism or occupy it as the terrain of misogyny, women will be born, degraded, and die. We would settle for that equal protection of the laws under which one would be born, live, and die, in a country where protection is not a dirty word and equality is not a special privilege.

Notes

1. The Bona Fide Occupational Qualification (BFOQ) exception to Title VII of the Civil Rights Act of 1964, 42 U.S.C. § 2000 e-(2)(e), permits sex to be a job qualification when it is a valid one. The leading interpretation of the proposed federal Equal Rights Amendment would, pursuing a similar analytic structure, permit a "unique physical characteristic" exception to its otherwise absolute embargo on taking sex into account. Barbara Brown, Thomas I. Emerson, Gail Falk, and Ann E. Freedman, "The Equal Rights Amendment: A Constitutional Basis for Equal Rights for Women," 80 *Yale Law Journal* 893 (1971).

10. David Cole, "Strategies of Difference: Litigating for Women's Rights in a Man's World," 2 *Law & Inequality: A Journal of Theory and Practice* 34 n.4 (1984) (collecting cases).

11. Devine v. Devine, 398 So. 2d 686 (Ala. Sup. Ct. 1981); Danielson v. Board of Higher Education, 358 F. Supp. 22 (S.D.N.Y. 1972); Weinberger v. Wiesenfeld, 420 U.S. 636 (1975); Stanley v. Illinois, 405 U.S. 645 (1971); Caban v. Mohammed, 441 U.S. 380 (1979); Orr v. Orr, 440 U.S. 268 (1979).

12. Lenore Weitzman, "The Economics of Divorce: Social and Economic Consequences of Property, Alimony and Child Support Awards," 28 U.C.L.A. *Law Review* 1118, 1251 (1982), documents a decline in women's standard of living of 73 percent and an increase in men's of 42 percent within a year after divorce.

13. Equal Pay Act, 29 U.S.C. § 206(d)(1) (1976) guarantees pay equality, as does case law, [but consider the data on pay gaps: Comparing the median income of the sexes from twenty-five to fifty-four years of age, 1975 to 1983, the U.S. Department of Labor Women's Bureau reports than in 1975, women made $8,155.00 to men's $14,105.00; in 1983, women made $15,349.66 to men's $24,458.33. U.S. Department of Labor, Women's Bureau, *Time of Change: 1983 Handbook of Women Workers*, Bulletin 298, 456 (1983). The same publication notes that "among professionals in 1981, men earned 54% more

than did women." Id. at 92. In 1981, men's overall earnings exceeded women's by 68.8 percent. Id at 93. The Equal Pay Act was passed in 1963].

14. Examples include Christenson v. State of Iowa, 563 F.2d 353 (8th Cir. 1977); Gerlach v. Michigan Bell Tel. Co., 501 F. Supp. 1300 (E.D. Mich. 1980); Odomes v. Nucare, Inc., 653 F.2d 246 (6th Cir. 1981) (female nurse's aide denied Title VII remedy because her job duties were not substantially similar to those of better-paid male orderly); Power v. Barry County, Michigan, 539 F. Supp. 721 (W.D. Mich. 1982); Spaulding v. University of Washington, 740 F. 2d 686 (9th Cir. 1984).

15. County of Washington v. Gunther, 452 U.S. 161 (1981) permits a comparable worth–type challenge where pay inequality can be proven to be a correlate of intentional job segregation. *See also* Lemons v. City and County of Denver, 17 FEP Cases 910 (D. Colo. 1978), *aff'd*, 620 F.2d 228 (10th Cir. 1977), *cert. denied*, 449 U.S. 888 (1980); AFSCME v. State of Washington, 770 F.2d 1401 (9th Cir. 1985). *See generally* Carol Jean Pint, "Value, Work and Women," 1 *Law & Inequality: A Journal of Theory and Practice* 159 (1983).

16. Combine the result in Bob Jones University v. United States, 461 U.S. 547 (1983) with Mississippi University for Women v. Hogan, 458 U.S. 718 (1982), and the tax-exempt status of women-only schools is clearly threatened.

17. A particularly pungent example comes from a case in which the plaintiff sought to complete in boxing matches with men, since there were no matches sponsored by the defendant among women. A major reason that preventing the woman from competing was found not to violate her equality rights was that the "safety rules and precautions [were] developed, designed, and tested in the context of all-male competition." Lafler v. Athletic Board of Control, 536 F. Supp. 104, 107 (W.D. Mich. 1982). As the court put it: "In this case, the real differences between the male and female anatomy are relevant in considering whether men and women may be treated differently with regard to their participating in boxing. The plaintiff *admits* that she wears a protective covering for her breasts while boxing. Such a protective covering . . . would violate Rule Six, Article 9 of the Amateur Boxing Federation rules currently in effect. The same rule *requires* contestants to wear a protective cup, a rule obviously designed for the unique anatomical characteristics of men." Id. at 106 (emphasis added). The rule is based on the male anatomy, therefore not a justification for the discrimination but an example of it. This is not considered in the opinion, nor does the judge discuss whether women might benefit from genital protection, and men from chest guards, as in some other sports.

19. Most women work at jobs mostly women do, and most of those jobs are paid less than jobs that mostly men do. *See, e.g.*, Pint, note 15 above, at 162–63 nn.19, 20 (collecting studies). To the point that men may not meet the male standard themselves, one court found that a union did not fairly represent its women in the following terms: "As to the yard and driver jobs, defendants suggest not only enormous intellectual requirements, but that the physical demands of those jobs are so great as to be beyond the capacity of any female. Again, it is noted that plaintiffs' capacity to perform those jobs was never tested, despite innumerable requests therefore. It is also noted that defendants have never suggested *which* of the innumerable qualifications they list for these jobs (for the first time) the plaintiffs might fail to meet. The court, however, will accept without listing here the extraordinary catalogue of feats which defendants argue must be performed in the yard, and as a driver. That well may be. However, one learns from this record that one cannot be too weak, too sick, too old and infirm, or too ignorant to perform these jobs, *so long as one is a man.* The plaintiffs appear to the layperson's eye to be far more physically fit than many of the drivers who moved into the yard, over the years, according to the testimony of defense witnesses . . . In short, they were all at least as fit as the men with serious physical deficits and disabilities who

held yard jobs." Jones v. Cassens Transport, 617 F. Supp. 869, 892 (1985) (emphasis in original).

21. Reed v. Reed, 404 U.S. 71 (1971) held that a statute barring women from administering estates is sex discrimination. If few women were taught to read and write, as used to be the case, the gender difference would not be imaginary in this case, yet the social situation would be even more sex discriminatory than it is now. Compare City of Los Angeles v. Manhart, 434 U.S. 815 (1978), which held that requiring women to make larger contributions to their retirement plan was sex discrimination, in spite of the allegedly proven sex difference that women on the average outlive men.

22. Kahn v. Shevin, 416 U.S. 351, 353 (1974).

23. Schlesinger v. Ballard, 419 U.S. 498 (1975).

24. Dothard v. Rawlinson, 433 U.S. 321 (1977); *see also* Michael M. v. Sonoma County Superior Court, 450 U.S. 464 (1981).

25. Doerr v. B.F. Goodrich, 484 F. Supp. 320 (N.D. Ohio 1979). Wendy Webster Williams, "Firing the Woman to Protect the Fetus: The Reconciliation of Fetal Protection with Employment Opportunity Goals Under Title VII," 69 *Georgetown Law Journal* 641 (1981). *See also* Hayes v. Shelby Memorial Hospital, 546 F. Supp. 259 (N.D. Ala. 1982); Wright v. Olin Corp., 697 F.2d 1172 (4th Cir. 1982).

26. Congress requires the Air Force (10 U.S.C. § 8549 [1983]) and the Navy (10 U.S.C. § 6015 [1983]) to exclude women from combat, with some exceptions. Owens v. Brown, 455 F. Supp. 291 (D.D.C. 1978), had previously invalidated the prior Navy combat exclusion because it prohibited women from filling jobs they could perform and inhibited Navy's discretion to assign women on combat ships. The Army excludes women from combat based upon its own policies under congressional authorization to determine assignment (10 U.S.C. § 3012 [e] [1983]).

27. Carol Gilligan, *In a Different Voice* (1982).

28. Id.

30. Diana Russell and Nancy Howell, "The Prevalence of Rape in the United States Revisited," 8 *Signs: Journal of Women in Culture and Society* 689 (1983) (44 percent of women in 930 households were victims of rape or attempted rape at some time in their lives).

31. Diana Russell, "The Incidence and Prevalence of Intrafamilial and Extrafamilial Sexual Abuse of Female Children," 7 *Child Abuse & Neglect: The International Journal* 133 (1983).

32. R. Emerson Dobash and Russell Dobash, *Violence against Wives: A Case against the Patriarchy* (1979); Bruno v. Codd, 90 Misc. 2d 1047, 396 N.Y.S. 2d 974 (Sup. Ct. 1977), *rev'd*, 64 A.D. 2d 582, 407 N.Y.S. 2d 165 (1st Dep't 1978), *aff'd* 47 N.Y. 2d 582, 393 N.E. 2d 976, 419 N.Y.S. 2d 901 (1979).

33. Kathleen Barry, *Female Sexual Slavery* (1979); Moira K. Griffin, "Wives, Hookers and the Law: The Case for Decriminalizing Prostitution," 10 *Student Lawyer* 18 (1982); Report of Jean Fernand-Laurent, Special Rapporteur on the Suppression of the Traffic in Persons and the Exploitation of the Prostitution of Others (a United Nations report), in *International Feminism: Networking against Female Sexual Slavery* 130 (Kathleen Barry, Charlotte Bunch, and Shirley Castley eds.) (Report of the Global Feminist Workshop to Organize against Traffic in Women, Rotterdam, Netherlands, Apr. 6–15, 1983 [1984]).

34. Galloway and Thornton, "Crackdown on Pornography—A No-Win Battle," *U.S. News and World Report*, June 4, 1984, at 84. *See also* "The Place of Pornography," *Harper's*, November 1984, at 31 (citing $7 billion per year).

35. Loving v. Virginia, 388 U.S. 1 (1967), first used the term "white supremacy" in invalidating an antimiscegenation law as a violation of equal protection. The law equally forbade whites and Blacks to intermarry. Although going nowhere near as far, courts

in the athletics area have sometimes seen that "same" does not necessarily mean "equal" nor does "equal" require "same." In a context of sex inequality like that which has prevailed in athletic opportunity, allowing boys to compete on girls' teams may diminish overall sex equality. "Each position occupied by a male reduces the female participation and increases the overall disparity of athletic opportunity which generally exists." Petrie v. Illinois High School Association, 394 N.E. 2d 855, 865 (Ill. 1979). "We conclude that to furnish exactly the same athletic opportunities to boys as to girls would be most difficult and would be detrimental to the compelling governmental interest of equalizing general athletic opportunities between the sexes." Id.

36. The scholars Tussman and tenBroek first used the term "fit" to characterize the necessary relation between a valid equality rule and the world to which it refers. J. Tussman and J. tenBroek, "The Equal Protection of the Laws," 37 *California Law Review* 341 (1949).

37. Royster Guano Co. v. Virginia, 253 U.S. 412, 415 (1920): "[A classification] must be reasonable, not arbitrary, and must rest upon some ground of difference having a fair and substantial relation to the object of the legislation, so that all persons similarly circumstanced shall be treated alike." Reed v. Reed, 404 U.S. 71, 76 (1971): "Regardless of their sex, persons within any one of the enumerated classes . . . are similarly situated . . . By providing dissimilar treatment for men and women who are thus similarly situated, the challenged section violates the Equal Protection Clause."

38. Washington v. Davis, 426 U.S. 229 (1976) and Personnel Administrator of Massachusetts v. Feeney, 442 U.S. 256 (1979) require that intentional discrimination be shown for discrimination to be shown.

6

Deconstructing Gender [1989]

Joan C. Williams

Introduction

Mid-century feminism, now often referred to somewhat derisively as assimilationism, focused on providing opportunities to women in realms traditionally preserved for men. In the 1980s two phenomena have shifted feminists' attention from assimilationists' focus on how individual women are *like* men to a focus on gender *differences*, on how women as a group differ from men as a group. The first is the feminization of poverty, which dramatizes the chronic and increasing economic vulnerability of women. Feminists now realize that the assimilationists' traditional focus on gender-neutrality may have rendered women more vulnerable to certain gender-related disabilities that have important economic consequences. The second phenomenon that plays a central role in the current feminist imagination is that of career women "choosing" to abandon or subordinate their careers so they can spend time with their small children. These phenomena highlight the fact that deep-seated social differences continue to encourage men and women to make quite different choices with respect to work and family. Thus, "sameness" scholars are increasingly confronted by the existence of gender differences.

Do these challenges to assimilationism prove that we should stop trying to kid ourselves and admit the "real" differences between men and women, as the popular press drums into us day after day, and as the "feminism of difference" appears to confirm? Do such phenomena mean that feminists' traditional focus on gender-neutrality is a bankrupt ideal? I will argue no on both counts, taking an approach quite different from that ordinarily taken by feminists on the sameness side of the spectrum. "Sameness" feminists usually have responded to the feminists of difference by reiterating their basic insight that individual men and women can be very similar. While true, this is not an adequate response to the basic insight of "difference" feminists: that gender exists, that men and women differ as groups. . . .

[On the other hand, I disagree with] the widely influential description of gender advocated by Carol Gilligan. . . . In particular I reject Gilligan's core

95

claim that women are focused on relationships while men are not. To the extent this claim pinpoints actual gender differences, . . . it merely reflects the oppressive realities of the current gender system. Beyond that, Gilligan's claim is inaccurate and serves to perpetuate our traditional blindness to the ways in which men are nurturing and women are competitive and power-seeking.

I. The Feminism of Difference

A. Introduction

The most influential source for the feminism of difference is Carol Gilligan's book, in which Gilligan argues that women speak "in a different voice."[12] Women are portrayed as nurturers, defined by their relationships and focused on contextual thinking; men are depicted as abstract thinkers, defined by individual achievement. We should listen to women's "voice," argue Gilligan and her followers, because women's culture offers the basis for a transformation of our society, a transformation based on the womanly values of responsibility, connection, selflessness, and caring, rather than on separation, autonomy, and hierarchy.[13]

One reason why the feminism of difference has proved so persuasive is that it has claimed for women two of the central critiques of twentieth-century thought. In a strain of argument particularly popular in law reviews, feminists characterize traditional Western epistemology as "male" and identify the twentieth-century critique of that epistemology as an integral part of "women's voice."[14] Gilligan and her followers also identify with women a critique of possessive individualism whose implications have been spelled out in *Equal Employment Opportunity Commission (EEOC) v. Sears, Roebuck & Co.*[15]

B. The New Epistemology as Women's Voice

Gilligan's description is often presented as a rediscovery of obvious differences between men and women we knew about all along. In fact, even feminists of difference disagree about what are the "obvious" differences between men and women. Gilligan's description of women has been so widely adopted that it is easy to overlook the fact that other feminists of difference have offered a sharply different version of women's true nature. Some radical feminists, more influential ten years ago than today, have espoused a view of women dramatically different from Gilligan's. Often using witch imagery, they stress women's intuition, their sexual power, and their alliance with deep forces of irrationality.[18]

This portrait of woman as id derives largely from the pre-modern stereotype of woman as the "weaker vessel."[19] Before the mid-eighteenth century, women were viewed not only as physically weaker than men; their intellectual and moral frailty meant they needed men's guidance to protect them from the human propensity for evil. Women's intense sexuality and their fundamental irrationality meant they were in need of outside control, because women in their weakness could be easily tempted. The darkest expression of the traditional view that women unsupervised quickly slipped into collusion with evil was the persecution (during some periods, massive in scale) of women as witches.[20]

This traditional stereotype of women crystallized after the early modern period into some traditional truths about women. As the *philosophies* of the Enlightenment celebrated logic and reason, women's intellectual inferiority came to be expressed as an inability to engage in rigorous, abstract thinking. The Enlightenment also celebrated reason over emotion, and women's pre-modern alliance with the devil was transmuted into the view that women's limited ability for rational thought meant they were fundamentally emotional creatures.

These stereotypes have provided the link for many feminists of difference between women and the critique of traditional Western epistemology.[21] This critique, which I have elsewhere called the new epistemology,[22] consists of a broad and diverse intellectual movement that rejects a range of long-standing Western verities, some dating to the Enlightenment, and others all the way back to Plato. Perhaps the core element of the new epistemology is its rejection of an absolute truth accessible through rigorous, logical manipulation of abstractions.[23] Feminists of difference have characterized the new epistemology with women's voice, noting that women traditionally have been thought to eschew abstraction for sensitivity to context, and to eschew logic for a faith in emotion and intuition as tools of thought.

On closer inspection, however, the traditional stereotype of women as overly emotional and incapable of rational, abstract thought is quite different from the critique proffered by the new epistemology: feminists are being highly selective in the aspects of the traditional stereotype they choose to stress. It is true there are some similarities between the traditional stereotype of women and the new epistemology. Both share a sense of the limitations of pure logic and a faith in contextual thinking. But feminists of difference submerge the fact that the thinkers who have developed the new epistemology have, by and large, been cerebral and detached in the extreme. Neither they nor the new epistemology fits the traditional stereotype of women as too emotional for sustained rational thought. What the new epistemologists are talking about is a new kind of rationality, one not so closely tied to abstract, transcendental truths, one that does not exclude so much of human experience as Western rationality traditionally has done. The ideal they propose represents a broadening of traditional intellectual life, whereas the traditional caricature of women as emotional and irrational represents a formal marginalization of those characteristics of human personality that the Western tradition has devalued.[26]

Thus, this attempt to rehabilitate traditional stereotypes as "women's voice," and to associate women's voice with the new epistemology, fails to come to terms with the extent to which the gender stereotypes were designed to marginalize women. These stereotypes no doubt articulated some values shunted aside by Western culture. But the circumstances of their birth mean they presented a challenge to predominant Western values that was designed to fail, and to marginalize women in the process.

At a simpler level, the attempt to claim the new epistemology for women is unconvincing simply because the new epistemology has been developed largely by men. These include philosophers from Frederick Nietzsche and the American pragmatists to Martin Heidegger and Ludwig Wittgenstein, all of whom helped develop the movement's critique of absolutes.[27] Important figures in developing the new epistemology's view of truths as necessarily partial and contextual include the fathers of post-Newtonian physics (Albert Einstein and Max Planck), the linguists Benjamin Whorf and Ferdinand de Saussure, and Wittgenstein, who rejected the "picture theory" that Truth is an objective picture of reality in favor of the view that a multiplicity of truths exists as an integral part of culture and context.[28]

. . . In what sense, then, is this vast epistemological shift "feminist" or even "feminine"? The simple answer is that the new epistemology is not in any meaningful way "women's voice."

C. Women's Voice and the Critique of Possessive Individualism

1. The Feminism of Difference as a Resurgence of Domesticity

The traditional stereotype of women, designed to justify women's subservience in a society that saw hierarchies as natural and desirable, came during the course of the eighteenth century to seem inconsistent with the emerging political philosophy of liberalism, which held all men as equal.[30] Gradually a new gender ideology, the ideology of domesticity, developed in which women continued to be viewed as weaker than men physically and intellectually, but were newly extolled as more moral than men.[31]

Gilligan echoes domesticity's "discovery" of women's higher morality. Unlike the Victorians, Gilligan does not argue explicitly that women's morality is of a higher order: she articulates her ideal as a "dialectic mixture" of the male and female "voices." Yet commentators have noted the striking resemblance between Gilligan's ideal morality and her description of female emotional maturity.[32] An emotionally mature woman, it seems, will reach Gilligan's ideal moral state automatically, while men will attain it only through a fundamental restructuring of their gender identity.

A close analysis of the traits Gilligan attributes to women suggests that she and other scholars who share her view of women offer domesticity with a difference. These "relational feminists,"[33] as they have been aptly called, reclaim the compliments of Victorian gender ideology while rejecting its insults. Thus, relational feminists agree with the Victorians that women are more nurturing than men ("focused on relationships"), less tied to the questionable virtues of capitalism, and ultimately more moral than men. But they disagree with the Victorians' view that women are also more passive than men, less competent, more timid and naturally demure.

Relational feminism has had a pervasive impact on women's history, and it is a historian of women who has best illustrated its relation to the ideology of domesticity. One of the major achievements of relational feminism in women's history is Suzanne Lebsock's subtle and persuasive study of a small Virginia town before the Civil War. In *The Free Women of Petersburg,* Lebsock summarizes her conclusions about women's values in the pre–Civil War period as follows:[34]

> [H]ere, in one list, are the documentable components of a women's value system. Women, more than men, noticed and responded to the needs and merits of particular persons. This showed in their tendency to reward favorite slaves and to distribute their property unevenly among their heirs. It also showed in their ability to make independent judgments about their own fitness to administer estates. Women were particularly sensitive to the interests of other women and to their precarious economic position; this was demonstrated in favoritism toward female heirs and in the establishment of separate estates. As their real estate and credit transactions suggest, women wanted financial security for themselves as well as for others. Beyond that they were not as ego-invested as were men in the control of wealth. Our list grows a bit longer if we add the more ambiguous evidence derived from women's vanguard action in providing relief to the poor and in promoting religion. Women as a group were more invested than were men in Christian communities and the life of the spirit. And in their efforts to give assistance to the poor, both personalism and regard for other women surfaced again; the poor were mainly women and children, most of whom cannot have "deserved" their poverty.
>
> The people who wrote the antebellum period's popular literature have been trying to tell us all along that women were different from men, better than men in some respects. Perhaps it is time we took their message more seriously.[35]

Lebsock's book, published shortly after Gilligan's, comes to some strikingly similar conclusions. Both authors conclude that women are more focused on relationships than are men, and both suggest that women's is a higher morality. But Lebsock differs from Gilligan, and from most other relational feminists, in her awareness that she is reclaiming stereotypes from domesticity. Unlike scholars who have glossed over the Victorians' negative characterizations of women, Lebsock confronts them directly, and her conclusions are instructive. She asserts that women were not uniformly inept; many were active and competent as executors of their husbands' estates. Nor were they passive as investors; only risk-averse. When it comes to the positive attributes of Victorian gender stereotypes, Lebsock's conclusions differ. She concludes that women were characterized by a "personalism" that made them more sensitive to slaves, the poor, and vulnerability in other women, less involved in capitalist values and (consequently?) more moral than men.

Lebsock thus rejects the insults of Victorian gender ideology but embraces those elements complimentary to women. So do most feminists of difference, though few make their selectivity so clear. Moreover, relational feminists often seem unaware of their own selectivity. "Perhaps it is time we took [the antebellum] message more seriously," Lebsock argues, forgetting the half of the antebellum message she rejects. In this she is joined by the majority of relational feminists.[37]

Given the decision to rehabilitate domesticity's gender stereotypes, it is not surprising that relational feminists choose domesticity's compliments over its insults. But this veils the deeper question: Why return to domesticity at all?

In answer let us start with a telling exchange between Carol Gilligan and Catharine MacKinnon in the 1984 "conversation" held at the Buffalo School of Law.[38] In a discussion of Jake, Gilligan's typical male, and Amy, her typical female, Gilligan argued that her goal was to assimilate Amy's voice into the mainstream of society. MacKinnon responded that her goal was more to have Amy develop a new voice, one that "would articulate what she cannot now, because his foot is on her throat." Gilligan's Amy, said MacKinnon, "is articulating the feminine. And you are calling it hers. That's what I find infuriating." "No," replied Gilligan, "I am saying she is articulating a set of values which are very positive."[39]

Note Gilligan's assumption that because what she has found is "very positive," she cannot have found "the feminine"—i.e. conventional gender stereotypes derived from domesticity. MacKinnon is right that what Gilligan has found is femininity; Gilligan is right that there is something positive there.

2. Domesticity as a Critique of Possessive Individualism[40]

The conventional wisdom among the "sameness" contingent is that relational feminists in their celebration of women's voice are simply basking in self-congratulation. I think this misses the mark. Relational feminists' interest in "the feminine" stems from its transformative potential.[42] Relational feminists find enshrined in domesticity "female" values that, they believe, will enable women to achieve equality not by buying into the male world on male terms, but by transforming the world in women's image. Thus Kathy Ferguson in The Feminist Case Against Bureaucracy[43] asserts that feminist theory "can provide for a reconceptualization of some of the most basic terms of political life."[44] Carrie Menkel-Meadow, a leading disciple of Gilligan within the legal community, hopes to restructure the legal system to express the values of "Portia's" voice.[45] Robin West recommends a new focus on connectedness and intimacy.[46] Other relational feminists go further and argue that women's voice is the best hope for the future of the planet. But Suzanne Lebsock, as usual, says it best: "If we find that all along women have managed to create and sustain countercultures, then the chances increase that as women come to power, a more humane social order will indeed come with them."[47]

For all these feminists, this "more humane social order" entails a new ethic of care[48] based on a focus on relationships, not competition; on negotiation, not combat; on community, not individual self-interest.[49] "What is needed," concludes the early and influential feminist of difference Elizabeth Wolgast, "is another model. . . . We need a model that acknowledges . . . other kinds of interest than self-interest."[50] A more recent legal feminist echoes this thought, noting his aspiration "to transform our polity and its underlying assumptions from the alienated world of atomistic competition to an interconnected world of mutual cooperation."[51] The model being rejected is possessive individualism.

If we examine the transformation proposed by relational feminists, we uncover a critique of this model that dates back to the original version of domesticity. Historians have long known that domestic ideology presented a challenge to the capitalist mainstream of American society. Said Daniel Scott Smith in 1973:

Instead of postulating woman as an atom in competitive society, [the Victorians] viewed women as a person in the context of relationships with others. By defining the family as a community, this ideology allowed women to engage in something of a critique of male, materialistic, market society and simultaneously proceed to seize power within the family.[52]

In 1977, historian Nancy Cott worked out in detail the way domesticity functioned as an internal critique of capitalism. She linked the invention of domestic ideology with changes in work patterns that accompanied the industrial revolution. Cott argued that domesticity developed in conjunction with the shift from traditional "task-oriented" work, which mixed labor and leisure, to modern "time-disciplined" wage labor, which isolates work both temporarily and geographically from family life. She argued that domestic ideology set up the home as a haven from the heartless world of nineteenth-century capitalism.

In accentuating the split between "work" and "home" and proposing the latter as a place of salvation, the canon of domesticity tacitly acknowledged the capacity of modern work to desecrate the human spirit. Authors of domestic literature, especially the female authors, denigrated business and politics as arenas of selfishness, exertion, embarrassment, and degradation of soul. These rhetoricians suggested what Marx's analysis of alienated labor in the 1840s would assert, that "the worker . . . feels at ease only outside work, and during work he is outside himself. He is at home when he is not working and when he is working he is not at home." The canon of domesticity embodied a protest against that advance of exploitation and pecuniary values.[53]

Cott's description of domesticity as a *"cri de coeur* against modern work relations" suggests that domesticity has from the beginning functioned as an internal critique of Western capitalism.[54] Gilligan and her followers carry on this tradition in their visions of the future that extol connection, cooperation, and community (the "values of the web") and aspire to overcome competition and self-interest.[55]

Gilligan picks up not only domesticity's claim that women offer an alternative to capitalism, but also its stereotype of men as capitalists *par excellence*. "For men," Gilligan asserts, "the moral imperative appears . . . as an injunction to respect the rights of others and thus to protect from interference the rights to life and self-fulfillment.[56] By labelling as "male" the "morality of rights and noninterference," Gilligan links men with the liberal ideology that underlies American capitalism.[57] Gilligan also attributes to men the liberal premise that the world is one of "people standing alone,"[58] arguing, in effect, that men accept liberalism's vision of society as a set of preconstituted individuals who choose to associate for limited purposes. Hence Jake, Gilligan's typical male, is "concerned with limiting interference" and places a high value on separation and autonomy.[59] Gilligan associates the male voice with the pursuit of self-interest, and, therefore, with capitalism's central tenet that this pursuit will benefit society as a whole.[60]

Relational feminism is better understood as a critique of possessive individualism than as a description of what men and women are actually like. Gilligan
herself acknowledges this when she refuses to associate her "voices" with males
and females. Yet Gilligan appears not to heed her own warnings on this point,
for in the remainder of her book she invariably associates men with one voice
and women with the other, and often makes sweeping statements about the
way men and women "are."[62] Gilligan's inconsistent signals about whether she
is talking about women or "the feminine" have left relational feminism with
the potential to be used as a weapon against women. As evidence of this, I
next turn to the *Sears* case, a clear example of the perils of modern domesticity.

3. EEOC v. Sears: *The Perils of Modern Domesticity*

In *EEOC v. Sears, Roebuck & Co.*,[63] Sears argued successfully that women
were underrepresented in its relatively high-paying commission sales positions
not because Sears had discriminated against them, but because women lacked
"interest" in commission sales. Sears used the language of relational feminism
to support its core argument that women's focus on relationships at home and
at work makes them choose to sacrifice worldly advancement in favor of a
supportive work environment and limited hours that accommodate their devotion
to family.[64] An unmistakable undertone is Sears' subtle intimation that women's
sacrifice is limited, since their "different voice" makes the fast track unappealing.
Women's "ethic of care" enables them to rise above the fray, so they are not
truly hurt when they are excluded from high-powered, competitive jobs in
commission sales.[65]

The brilliance of Sears' lawyers lies in their success in enshrining gender
stereotypes at the core of Title VII.[66] *Sears* provides a dramatic illustration of
the power or relational feminism to provide a respectable academic language
in which to dignify traditional stereotypes. The case holds the potential to
transform Title VII law in a way that pits gender discrimination plaintiffs
against stereotypes in a battle the stereotypes are designed to win, for in effect
Sears establishes a legal assumption that all women fit gender stereotypes and
imposes on plaintiffs a burden to disprove that assumption as part of their
prima facie case. Understanding the potential impact of *Sears* requires some
background in Title VII law.

The usual focus of a Title VII class action lawsuit is on statistics comparing
the proportion of women in a given job category with the proportion of women
in the relevant labor market. Statistics are direct proof that a facially neutral
hiring policy has a disparate impact on a group protected under Title VII.[67]
Statistics also are evidence of intent, as is illustrated by the "billiard ball"
example. Say one begins with a barrel containing 50 black and 50 white billiard
balls. If balls were removed in a random fashion, one would expect half black
and half white balls to be chosen. The further the results are from a 50/50
split, the greater the likelihood some other factor is at work. Because defendants
who discriminate are rarely open about it, the law helps plaintiffs through a
presumption that the "other factor" involved is discrimination. Thus, courts
have required only evidence of a statistically significant disparity by a plaintiff

to establish a prima facie case of discrimination.[68] Thereafter, the burden shifts to the defendant to articulate some nondiscriminatory reason for the disparity documented.[69]

In contrast to courts prior to *Sears*, both the trial and appellate *Sears* courts required the EEOC to prove not only statistical disparities but also men's and women's "equal interest."[70] Under *Sears*, therefore, a class of gender discrimination plaintiffs cannot prove their prima facie case simply by proving a disparity between the proportion of women in the relevant labor market and the proportion of women in the jobs at issue. Instead they have the additional burden of establishing what percentage of women in the otherwise relevant labor market was truly "interested" in the jobs at issue.

Sears based its argument, first, upon testimony of managers, one of whom made the now famous claim that women did not want commission sales jobs because such salesmen were required to work outside the store and women do not like to go out when "it's snowing or raining or whatever."[71] The managers' testimony was bolstered by a sociologist who testified about a survey of Sears employees,[72] by a writer on women's issues,[73] and by historian Rosalind Rosenberg, who cited Gilligan and other relational feminists to support her assertion that the EEOC's "assumption that women and men have identical interests and aspirations regarding work is incorrect. Historically, men and women have had different interests, goals and aspirations regarding work."[74]

To support this statement, Rosenberg offered portraits of men and women that closely echoed Gilligan's. Women she depicted as "humane and nurturing," focused on relationships, and averse to capitalist virtues such as competition.[75] Again echoing Gilligan, she painted men as competitive and motivated by self-interest: possessive individualists *par excellence.*[76]

Sears proceeded to use against women the gender stereotypes rehabilitated by relational feminism. The implication of Sears' successful use of domesticity's insults is that relational feminists delude themselves if they think they can rehabilitate domesticity's compliments without its insults. To relational feminists, the key point of domesticity may be women's higher morality; to Sears managers it was that women are weak and dependent, delicate and passive.

A closer look at the trial transcript dramatizes the power of these stereotypes once unleashed, for it shows how Sears systematically used stereotypes to override information about the desires and the aspirations of actual women. The most obvious example of this occurs in the testimony of Joan Haworth, Sears' major statistical witness, who argued that even female applicants who appeared to be interested in commission sales, in fact, were not interested. When the EEOC challenged this statement, Haworth chose three applications that indicated background and experience in commission sales and explained how she knew none was truly interested.[78] The EEOC located two of the three women Haworth discussed, both of whom testified they had in fact been seeking jobs in commission sales.[79] The trial judge glossed over this rebuttal in his opinion.[80]

Sears also systematically discounted interests expressed by female applicants in "male" jobs such as auto sales. Haworth, who argued that those applicants were puffing up their interest, guarded against this by "normalizing" the scores of female applicants. Her methodology functioned to ensure that sales applicants who indicated interest in working both in "male" areas such as auto sales and in "female" areas such as the baby department had their "male" interests systematically discounted.[81]

Sears' attorneys had help from the trial judge in policing gender stereotypes.[82] Judge John A. Nordberg, a Reagan appointee, played an active role in shaping the evidence to support his eventual holdings that women lack interest in "male" jobs. Whenever EEOC witnesses made statements about women's commitment to the home and their lack of commitment to wage labor that contradicted gender stereotypes, Nordberg insisted they specify the precise percentage of women whose interests diverged from those of women in general (i.e., from gender stereotypes). Here's one example from the testimony of historian Alice Kessler-Harris, who countered Rosenberg's testimony by arguing that women generally have taken higher paying jobs when they became available despite the mandates of domesticity.

> Could I just interrupt for one second, Dr. Harris, or Kessler-Harris. This is what I have said to others, and if you had sat through all the testimony, you would understand the reason for my saying this. One of the difficulties in analyzing and dealing with the evidence in the case is a tendency of witnesses to use the phrase "men and women" as though it is 100 percent of men or 100 percent of women. I think that the testimony makes it clear that there are a range of personalities, interests, experiences, achievements, and everything in both sexes. . . . And what this case in a sense is getting down to, because of the statistical nature of the case, is percentages. It would be very helpful to me during the course of your testimony to try to quantify the percentage or the proportion or possible number that you are dealing with in any particular thing that you say. I [know] it is hard, because you are, in a sense, seeking to generalize. But it makes it very difficult when it is asserted that either women so and so or men so and so, when we all know that it isn't 100 percent correct.[83]

Judge Nordberg repeated the same point as a constant refrain to the testimony of EEOC witnesses. Women behave like this, they testified. What percentage, Nordberg asked again and again.[84] When Sears witnesses made generalized statements about women that *confirmed* stereotypes derived from domesticity, Nordberg's concern for quantification evaporated. I found no instance in which Nordberg felt the need for this type of quantification from Sears witnesses.[85] Nordberg's opinion shows why: he adopted the argument advanced by Sears (through Rosalind Rosenberg) that women who did not fit conventional stereotypes were a marginal group of (uppity?) college women. No statistical evidence supported this assertion.[86]

Nordberg's insistence on quantification in effect required plaintiffs to specify the precise percentage of women interested in nontraditional jobs such as commission sales. By not requiring Sears to provide equivalent proof of the specific percentage of women who *fit* gender stereotypes, the *Sears* district court opinion in effect establishes a legal presumption that all women fit traditional gender stereotypes. The Seventh Circuit opinion wholeheartedly adopted this approach.[87]

Sears' doctrinal innovation clashes at a fundamental level with the thrust of Title VII. *Sears* allows information about *gender,* about women *as a group,* to be used to establish a legal presumption about individual plaintiffs consolidated into a class. This is inappropriate because Title VII is designed to protect women who do not fit gender stereotypes, who want to work as physicists, or in auto sales. Title VII's underlying goal is to protect women who want nontraditional work. Establishing a legal presumption that every class of female plaintiffs conforms to gender stereotypes frustrates this goal.

Sears is thus a dramatic reversal of existing Title VII law and should be overruled. From a theoretical standpoint, *Sears* shows the power of gender stereotypes to overshadow evidence about actual women. *Sears* also shows how relational feminism's critique of possessive individualism serves to marginalize both women and the critique itself.

Unlike the critique of capitalism from traditional radical discourse, domesticity's critique does not compel its followers to confront capitalist practice and to change it. Instead, an abiding tenet of domesticity is that women's aversion to capitalist virtues makes them "choose" home and family. This is an argument that encourages women to "choose" economic marginalization and celebrate that choice as a badge of virtue. This analysis of domesticity as an ideology designed to enlist women in their own oppression will be more fully developed later. For now the important thing is how Sears mobilized domesticity's critique of possessive individualism against women.

One can see how domesticity's compliments add up to its critique: women reject crass competition; they favor a friendly, cooperative, working environment over mere material advancement; they value their commitments to family over career success.[91] Sears' argument demonstrates how domesticity's critique of possessive individualism rests on a claim that women are psychologically unsuited to the economic mainstream. All Sears did was pick this up and use it to argue that women are psychologically unsuited to work in commission sales.

Sears . . . shows that domesticity's power derives from its ability to make arguments about women's "choice" vaguely complimentary instead of clearly insulting. When defendants prior to *Sears* tried to mobilize the interest argument, they met with little success because their "interest" arguments so clearly mobilized racist or sexist insults. For example, the assertion in a 1976 race discrimination case that blacks lacked interest in law enforcement evidently smacked too much of a claim that blacks are lazy and shiftless, or inherently not law-abiding.[92] In another case, the defendant's argument that women did not need the vocational training available to men since women choose unskilled jobs anyway also struck a jarring note.[93] In both cases, the interest argument evidently struck the courts as a blatant attempt to use against minorities the insulting stereotypes to which they traditionally have been subjected. Sears' lawyers succeeded because they used against women not the insults but the compliments of domesticity. Once the interest argument was linked with women's *virtues,* the trial judge and the conservative Seventh Circuit found it easier to frame complimentary holdings asserting that women choose their relative poverty, while framing their argument as a paean to female virtue.[94]

If *Sears* contains some disturbing messages for relational feminists, it also contains a comforting one: that by giving up domesticity's critique of possessive individualism, they are abandoning a singularly ineffective critique. A key source of the attraction of "women's voice" for feminists and other progressive thinkers is that, in a society where radicals have had trouble being taken seriously, relational feminism offers a critique of capitalism that avoids the perceived stridency of traditional radical discourse. It is Marxism you can take home to mother.[95] But, as *Sears* shows, this strength is also a weakness, for what domesticity offers is a singularly "domesticated" critique that accepts the notion that anyone who rejects the values of contemporary capitalism freely chooses to eschew the spoils of capitalist endeavor. As traditional radical discourse makes clear, the whole point of critiquing capitalism is to challenge the way in which wealth is created and distributed. Domesticity's critique is designed to evade the central issue of whether society should be transformed.

.   .   .

II. Challenging the Gendered
Structure of Wage Labor

The challenge to "male norms" offered by the feminism of difference is comprised of two quite different elements. The first is the critique of "male" behavior and values, which in essence is the critique of possessive individualism. A second element is the critique of men's traditional life patterns. Like the first, this second critique has traditionally been linked with domesticity, but it need not be. In this section, I present an analysis that challenges the desirability of men's traditional life patterns without linking the critique to domestic ideology.

A rejection of men's traditional life patterns entails a fundamental challenge to the structure of wage labor. . . . Western wage labor is premised on an ideal worker with no child care responsibilities.[101] In this system men and women workers are allocated very different roles. Men are raised to believe they have the right and the responsibility to perform as ideal workers. Husbands as a group therefore do far less child care, and earn far more, than their wives. Women are raised with complementary assumptions. They generally feel that they are entitled to the pleasure of spending time with their children while they are small. Moreover, even upon their return to work, the near-universal tendency is to assume that women's work commitment must be defined to accommodate continuing child-care responsibilities.

This gender system results in the impoverishment of women, since it leads mothers systematically to "choose" against performing as ideal workers in order to ensure that their children receive high-quality care. . . .

. . . Women's choices show the system's success in persuading women to buy into their own economic marginalization. Openly discriminatory treatment based on the notion that "women should stay at home" shows how gender ideology serves to police the gender system by eliminating options that would loosen the grip of gender roles. In sum, women's choices show how women perpetuate the gender system themselves; discrimination shows how others join them in policing the gender system.

The impoverishment of women that results from the current gender system has been well documented.[119] Lenore Weitzman has shown that women experience a 73 percent decline in their standard of living in the year after divorce; men experience a concomitant 42 percent rise in living standards.[120] Statistics on the feminization of poverty also are well known. Three out of every five people with incomes below the poverty line are women.[121] Three-fourths of all black families below the poverty line are headed by women.[122] Two out of every three poor elderly people are women.[123] Almost one in three female-headed households is poor; only about one in eighteen male-headed households is.[124] The average income of female-headed families is less than half that of male-headed families. Moreover, families composed of women and children are ten times more likely to stay poor than are families where a male is present.[125]

The feminization of poverty reflects the way the gendered labor system invented at the time of the Industrial Revolution has adapted to modern conditions. In a world where many more women than ever before are raising children without significant financial assistance from men, the gender system has taken on a more repressive dynamic than at any time since its invention.

Why is this so difficult to see? In large part because of the ideology that women's disadvantaged position results from choices made by women themselves. Alexis de Tocqueville offered an early version of this argument over a century ago.

> In America, a woman loses her independence forever in the bonds of matrimony. While there is less constraint on girls there than anywhere else, a wife submits to stricter obligations. For the former, her father's house is a home of freedom and pleasure; for the latter, her husband's is almost a cloister.
>
> . . . .
>
> . . . [Yet, the American woman] herself has freely accepted the yoke. She suffers her new state bravely, for she has chosen it.[126]

The modern form of this argument is the contemporary celebration of women who either subordinate their careers or abandon them altogether because they "know their own priorities." "[A] woman shouldn't have to apologize for her priorities," said Betty Friedan in a recent interview on "sequencing," *i.e.*, women dropping out of professional life for the period when their children are young.[127] News articles on "sequencing" seem invariably to point to women such as Jeane J. Kirkpatrick, Sandra Day O'Connor, and D.C. Circuit Chief Judge Patricia Wald, each of whom took from five to fifteen years off to stay home with young children.[128] Only occasionally do these articles note that such women are the exception.[129] I suspect most women would take years off their careers if they could be guaranteed that upon their return they could become an ambassador to the United Nations, a Supreme Court Justice, or a D.C. Circuit Court judge. . . .

. . . Decoded, the current talk about women's priorities is a translation into new language of domesticity's old argument that women's values lead them to make different choices. The persistence of this classic argument makes it imperative for feminists to analyze why the argument has abiding persuasiveness. The approach most useful to an analysis of women's "choice" is Antonio Gramsci's concept of cultural hegemony.[134] Gramsci painted a complex picture of how the dominant culture rules with the consent of the governed by shaping a "hegemony" of values, norms, perceptions, and beliefs that "helps mark the boundaries of permissible discourse, discourages the clarification of social alternatives, and makes it difficult for the dispossessed to locate the source of their unease, let alone remedy it."[135]

Gramsci's thought suggests that feminists can approach women's culture as a system of cultural hegemony. Marxist feminists have long argued that domesticity is a capitalist tool to privatize the costs of workers at the expense of women for the benefit of the employers.[136] Gramsci's analysis offers needed subtlety by focusing on the complexities surrounding women's consent. For Gramsci consent is a complex state fraught with ambiguities, a " 'contradictory consciousness' mixing approbation and apathy, resistance and resignation."[137]

Gramsci's analysis of consent suggests that feminists must come to terms with the ways in which women's culture has served to enlist women's support in perpetuating existing power relations. As historian T.J. Jackson Lears has expressed it:

> The idea that less powerful folk may be unwitting accomplices in the maintenance of existing inequalities runs counter to much of the social and cultural historiography of the last fifteen years, which has stressed the autonomy and vitality of subordinate cultures. Discovering nearly inexhaustible resources for resistance to domination, many social historians have been reluctant to acknowledge the possibility that their subjects may have been muddled by assimilation to the dominant culture— perhaps even to the point of believing and behaving against their own best interests.[138]

Women's historians and other feminists have illustrated this reluctance. In their effort to do justice to the dignity of women, they resoundingly rejected the image of women as victims, and instead have celebrated women's "nearly inexhaustible resources for resistance."[139] Now that this refusal to see women as victims has been transposed into a blame-the-victim argument through the rhetoric of choice, there is an acute need for a more balanced view of women's culture. . . .

Feminists need to arm women to resist the argument that women's economic marginalization is the product of their own choice. Challenging this argument should be easy, since, in fact, in our deeply gendered system men and women face very different choices indeed. Whereas women, in order to be ideal workers, have to choose not to fulfill their "family responsibilities," men do not. The question women ask themselves is this: Should I make professional sacrifices for the good of my children? In order for the wife's "choice" to be equivalent to her husband's, she would first have to be in a position to ask herself whether or not she would choose to be an ideal worker if her husband would choose to stay home with the children. Second, she would have to pose the question in a context where powerful social norms told her he was peculiarly suited to raising children. When we speak of women's "choices" to subordinate their careers, we are so blinded by gender prescriptions that we can forget that the husband's decision to be an ideal worker rests upon the assumption that his wife will choose not to be in order to allow him that privilege. This is true whether the wife eschews a career altogether or whether (in the modern pattern) she merely subordinates her career to child-care responsibilities. The point is that the husband is doing neither. Women know that if *they* do not sacrifice *no one* will, whereas men assume that if *they* do not, *women* will.

Thus women do not enjoy the same choices as men. But the underlying point is a deeper one: that society is structured so that everyone, regardless of sex, is limited to two unacceptable choices—men's traditional life patterns or economic marginality. Under the current structure of wage labor, people are limited to being ideal workers, which leaves them with inadequate time to devote to parenting, and being primary parents condemned to relative poverty (if they are single parents) or economic vulnerability (if they are currently married to an ideal worker). Wage labor does not have to be structured in this way. . . .

Women can work without insisting on a redefinition of the ideal worker, but most can do so only at the cost of failing to fulfill the ideal. This is not happening. Consequently, what we are seeing today is the adjustment of the gender system to these new conditions in a way that ensures women's continued relegation to the margins of economic life. We are living through a reinvention of the gender system, when we as feminists should be proposing a paradigm shift that entails a redesign of wage labor to take parenting activities into account. There are three basic options for changing the status quo. One is for each individual woman to rebel against the traditional demand that she sacrifice in order for her husband to be an ideal worker. But what will that mean: that *she* will become the ideal worker and he will play the supportive role? This is an alternative most men would find unthinkable because they are socially conditioned to believe that the option to be an ideal worker is their birthright. Most women, moreover, would find this option unattractive because society has nourished in them the belief that it is their birthright to be able to take time off the grind and enjoy their children while they are small.

A second alternative is for both men and women to give a little, so that they share the family responsibilities that preclude ideal worker status. But then neither husband nor wife functions as an ideal worker—a risky strategy in an age of economic uncertainty.

The only remaining alternative is to challenge the structure of wage labor. Since the current structure, and the gender system of which it is a part, increasingly condemns women to poverty, this should be at the core of a feminist program.

Such a program would build upon many reforms that currently exist. These include programs such as day care, flex-time, and four-day work weeks, organized labor contracts that provide for unconditional personal days that can be used for care of sick children, as well as paid maternity leave (for the physical disability associated with childbirth) and parental leave. More sweeping proposals are those offered by noted child care specialists Benjamin Spock and Penelope Leach,[168] and by noted economist Heidi Hartmann, who advocates a six-hour work day for all workers.[169]

Feminists' goal must be to redesign wage labor to take account of reproduction. Such a goal today seems utopian—but then the eight-hour work day seemed utopian in the mid-nineteenth century.[170] The notion that the wage-labor system should take account of the human life cycle has always faced the argument that such "private costs" as aging or raising children are of no concern to employers. Even in the United States, this view has been successfully challenged: old age is now acknowledged as a reality, and wage-labor expectations have been modified accordingly. That, too, once seemed a utopian goal.[171] But expectations change: hegemony is never complete. Feminists should begin to work both towards cultural change and towards the kind of small, incremental steps that will gradually modify the wage-labor system to acknowledge the reality of society's reproductive needs.

III. Refocusing the Debate

A. *From Gender-Neutrality to Deinstitutionalizing Gender*

"Sameness" feminists' focus on the similarities between individual men and individual women led them to advocate "gender-neutral" categories that do not rely on gender stereotypes to differentiate between men and women. Recent feminists have challenged the traditional goal of gender neutrality on the grounds that it mandates a blindness to gender that has left women in a worse position than they were before the mid-twentieth-century challenge to gender roles.

This argument has been made in two different ways. Scholars such as Martha Fineman have argued that liberal feminists' insistence on gender-neutrality in the formulation of "no-fault" divorce laws has led to courts' willful blindness to the ways in which marriage systematically helps men's, and hurts women's, careers.[172] Catharine MacKinnon has generalized this argument. She argues that because women are systematically disadvantaged by their sex, properly designed remedial measures can legitimately be framed by reference to sex.[173]

MacKinnon's "inequality approach" would allow for separate standards for men and women so long as "the policy or practice in question [does not] integrally contribute[ ] to the maintenance of an underclass or a deprived position because of gender status."[174] The strongest form her argument takes is that adherence to gender roles disadvantages women: Why let liberal feminists' taboo against differential treatment of women eliminate the most effective solution to inequality?

This debate is graced by a core truth and massive confusion. The core truth is that an insistence on gender neutrality by definition precludes protection for women victimized by gender.

The confusion stems from the use of the term gender neutrality. One *could* argue that problems created by the gendered structure of wage labor, or other aspects of the gender system, should not be remedied through the use of categories that identify the protected group by reference to the gender roles that have disadvantaged them. For example, one could argue that workers whose careers were disadvantaged by choices in favor of child care should not be given the additional support they need to "catch up" with their former spouses, on the grounds that the group protected inevitably would be mostly female, and this could reinforce the stereotype that women need special protections. Yet I know of no feminist of any stripe who makes this argument, which would be the position of someone committed to gender neutrality.

Traditionally, feminists have insisted not upon a blindness to gender, but on opposition to the traditional correlation between sex and gender. MacKinnon's crucial divergence is that she accepts the use of sex as a proxy for gender. Thus MacKinnon sees nothing inherently objectionable about protecting workers who have given up ideal worker status due to child-care responsibilities by offering protections to *women*.[175] Her inequality approach allows disadvantages produced by *gender* to be remedied by reference to *sex*. This is in effect an acceptance and a reinforcement of the societal presumption that the social role of primary caretaker is necessarily correlated with possession of a vagina.

MacKinnon's approach without a doubt would serve to reinforce and to legitimize gender stereotypes that are an integral part of the increasingly oppressive gender system. Let's focus on a specific example. Scholars have found that the abolition of the maternal presumption in child-custody decisions has had two deleterious impacts on women.[176] First, in the 90 percent of the cases where mothers received custody,[177] mothers often find themselves bargaining away financial claims in exchange for custody of the children. Even if the father does not want custody, his lawyer often will advise him to claim it in order to have a bargaining chip with which to bargain down his wife's financial claims. Second, the abolition of the maternal preference has created situations where a father who wants custody often wins even if he was not the primary caretaker prior to the divorce—on the grounds that he can offer the children a better life because he is richer than his former wife. In these circumstances, the ironic result of a mother's sacrifice of ideal worker status for the sake of her children is that she ultimately loses the children.

While these results are no doubt infuriating, do they merit a return to a maternal presumption, as MacKinnon's approach seems to imply? No: the deconstruction of gender, by highlighting the chronic and increasing oppressiveness of the gender system, demonstrates the undesirability of the inequality approach, which would reinforce the gender system in both a symbolic way and a practical one. On a symbolic level, the inequality approach would reinforce and legitimize the traditional assumption that childrearing is "naturally" the province of women. MacKinnon's rule also would reinforce gender mandates in a very concrete way. Say a father chose to give up ideal worker status in order to undertake primary child care responsibility. MacKinnon's rule fails to help him, because the rule is framed in terms of biology, not gender. The result: a strong message to fathers that they should not deviate from established gender roles. MacKinnon's rule operates to reinforce the gender system.

What we need, then, is a rule that avoids the traditional correlation between gender and sex, a rule that is *sex-* but not *gender*-neutral. The traditional goal, properly understood, is really one of *sex*-neutrality, or, more descriptively, one of deinstitutionalizing gender.[178] It entails a systematic refusal to institutionalize gender in any form. This approach mandates not an enforced blindness to gender, but rather a refusal to reinforce the traditional assumption that adherence to gender roles flows "naturally" from biological sex. Reinforcing that assumption reinforces the grip of the gender system as a whole.

For an example that highlights the distinction between gender neutrality and deinstitutionalization, let us return to our "divorce revolution" example. It is grossly unfair for courts suddenly to pretend that gender roles within marriage do not exist once a couple enters the courtroom, and the deinstitutionalization of gender does not require it. What is needed is not a gender-neutral rule but one that avoids the traditional shorthand of addressing gender by reference to sex.

This analysis shows that the traditional commitment, which is really one to deinstitutionalizing gender rather than to gender neutrality, need not preclude rules that protect people victimized by gender. People disadvantaged by gender can be protected by properly naming the group: in this case, not mothers, but anyone who has eschewed ideal worker status to fulfill child-care responsibilities.[179] One court, motivated to clear thinking by a legislature opposed to rules that addressed gender disabilities by reference to sex, has actually framed child-custody rules in this way.[180]

The traditional goal is misstated by the term "gender neutrality." The core feminist goal is not one of pretending gender does not exist. Instead, it is to deinstitutionalize the gendered structure of our society. There is no reason why people disadvantaged by gender need to be suddenly disowned. The deconstruction of gender allows us to protect them by reference to their social roles instead of their genitals.

B. *Deconstructing Difference*

How can this be done? Certainly the hardest task in the process of deconstructing gender is to begin the long and arduous process of seeing through the descriptions of men and women offered by domesticity. Feminists need to explain exactly how the traditional descriptions of men and women are false. This is a job for social scientists, for a new Carol Gilligan in reverse, who can focus the massive literature on sex stereotyping in a way that dramatizes that Gilligan is talking about metaphors, not actual people.[181] Nonetheless, I offer some thoughts on Gilligan's central imagery: that women are focused on relationships while men are not. As I see it, to the extent this is true, it is merely a restatement of male and female gender roles under the current gender system. Beyond that, it is unconvincing.

This is perhaps easiest to see from Gilligan's description of men as empty vessels of capitalist virtues—competitive and individualistic and espousing liberal ideology to justify this approach to life. Gilligan's description has an element of truth as a description of *gender*: it captures men's sense of entitlement to ideal worker status and their gendered choice in favor of their careers when presented with the choice society sets up between child-care responsibilities and being a "responsible" worker.

Similarly, Gilligan's central claim that women are more focused on relationships reflects gender verities. It is true in the sense that women's lives are shaped by the needs of their children and their husbands—but this is just a restatement of the gender system that has traditionally defined women's social existence in terms of their husbands' need to eliminate child-care and other responsibilities that detract from their ability to function as ideal workers. And when we speak of women's focus on relationships with *men*, we also reflect the underlying reality that the only alternative to marriage for most women—certainly for most mothers—has traditionally been poverty, a state of affairs that continues in force to this day.[182]

The kernel of truth in Gilligan's "voices," then, is that Gilligan provides a description of gender differences related to men's and women's different roles with respect to wage labor and child care under the current gender regime. Yet we see these true gender differences through glasses framed by an ideology that distorts our vision. To break free of traditional gender ideology, we need at the simplest level to see how men nurture people and relationships and how women are competitive and powerful. This is a task in which we as feminists will meet considerable resistance, both from inside and outside the feminist movement.

Our difficulty in seeing men's nurturing side stems in part from the word "nurture." Although its broadest definition is "the act of promoting development or growth,"[183] the word derives from nursing a baby, and still has overtones of "something only a mother can do." Yet men are involved in all kinds of relationships in which they promote another's development in a caring way: as fathers, as mentors, as camp counselors, as boy scout leaders. These relationships may have a somewhat different emotional style and tone than do those of women and often occur in somewhat different contexts: that is the gender difference. But a blanket assertion that women are nurturing while men are not reflects more ideology than reality.

So does the related claim that women's voice involves a focus on relationships that is lacking in men. Men focus on relationships, too. How they can be said not to in a culture that deifies romantic love as much as ours does has always mystified me. Perhaps part of what resonates in the claim that men do not focus on relationships is that men *as a group* tend to have a different style than do women: whereas women tend to associate intimacy with self-disclosure, men tend not to.[185] This may be why women forget about the role that relationships play in men's lives, from work relationships, to solidarity based on spectator sports, to time spent "out with the boys."[186] These relationships may not look intimate to women, but they are often important to men.

Ideology not only veils men's needy side, it also veils the competitive nature of many women who want power as avidly as men. "Feminists have long been fiercely critical of male power games, yet we have often ignored or concealed our own conflicts over money, control, position, and recognition. . . . It is time to end the silence."[187] The first step, as those authors note, is to acknowledge the existence of competition in women's lives. Women's desire for control may be exercised in running "a tight ship" on a small income, in tying children to apron strings, or in nagging husbands—the classic powerplay of the powerless.[188] Note how these examples tend to deprecate women's desire for power. These are the stereotypes that come to mind because they confirm the ideology that "real" women don't need power. These are ways women's yearning for power has been used as evidence against them, as evidence they are not worthy as wives, as mothers, or as women. Feminists' taboo against competition has only reinforced the traditional view that real women don't need power. Yet women's traditional roles have always required them to be able to wield power with self-confidence and subtlety. Other cultures recognize that dealing with a two-year-old is one of the great recurring power struggles in the cycle of human life. But not ours. We are too wrapped up in viewing childrearing as nurturing, as something opposed by its nature to authoritative wielding of power, to see that nurturing involves a sophisticated use of power in a hierarchical relationship. The differences between being a boss and a mother in this regard are differences in degree as well as in kind.

Moving ever closer to the bone, we need to reassess the role of power in relationships based on romantic love. The notion that a marriage involves complex ongoing negotiations over power may seem shocking. But if we truly are committed to a deconstruction of traditional gender verities, we need to stop blinding ourselves to nurturing outside the home and to power negotiations within it.

Conclusion

The first message of this article is that feminists uncomfortable with relational feminism cannot be satisfied with their conventional response: "When we get a voice, we don't all say the same thing."[191] The traditional focus on how individuals diverge from gender stereotypes fails to come to terms with gender similarities of women as a group. I have tried to present an alternative response. By taking gender seriously, I have reached conclusions very different from those of the relational feminists. I have not argued that gender differences do not exist; only that relational feminists have misdescribed them.

Relational feminism, I have argued, can best be understood as encompassing two critiques: the critique of possessive individualism and the critique of absolutes. Both are better stated in nongendered terms, though for different reasons. Feminists are simply incorrect when they claim the critique of absolutes as women's voice, since that critique has been developed by men, and its ideal is different from the traditional stereotype of women as emotional and illogical.

Relational feminism's linkage of women to the critique of possessive individualism is trickier. If all relational feminists claim is that elite white men are disproportionately likely to buy more completely into the ideology that controls access to wealth, in one sense this is true. I would take it on faith that a higher proportion of elite white males buy into possessive individualism than do black males, working class and poor males, or women of all groups. Indeed, in the last twenty years writers have documented that these marginalized groups have developed their own cultures that incorporate critiques of mainstream culture.[192] "One very important difference between white people and black people is that white people think you are your work," a black informant told an anthropologist in the 1970s. "Now a black person has more sense than that. . . ."[193] Marginalized groups necessarily have maintained a more critical perspective on possessive individualism in general, and the value of wage labor in particular, than did white males who had most to gain by taking the culture's dominant ideology seriously.[194] Moreover, the attitude of white women towards wage labor reflects their unique relationship with it. Traditionally, married white women, even many working-class women, had a relationship to wage labor that only a very few leisured men have ever had: these women viewed wage labor as something that had to prove its worth in their lives, because the option not to work remained open to them psychologically (if, at times, not economically).

Fewer blacks and women have made the virtues of possessive individualism a central part of their self-definition, and this is a powerful force for social change. But blacks as a group and women as a group have these insights not because they are an abiding part of "the" black family or of women's "voice." These are insights black culture and women's culture bring from their history of exclusion. We want to preserve the insights but abandon the marginalization that produced them: to become part of a mainstream that learns from our experience. The *Sears* case shows how these insights' transformative potential can easily backfire if the critiques can be marginalized as constitutive of a semi-permanent part of the black or female personality.

Relational feminists help diffuse the transformative potential of the critique of possessive individualism by championing a gendered version of that critique. The simple answer is that they should not say they are talking about women if they admit they aren't. Once they admit they are talking about *gender*, they have to come to terms with domesticity's hegemonic role in enlisting women in their own oppression.

The approach of deconstructing gender requires women to give up their claims to special virtue. But it offers ample compensation. It highlights the fact that women will be vulnerable until we redesign the social ecology, starting with a challenge to the current structure of wage labor. The current structure may not have been irrational in the eighteenth century, but it is irrational today. Challenging it today should be at the core of a feminist program.

The message that women's position will remain fundamentally unchanged until labor is restructured is both a hopeful and a depressing one. It is depressing because it shows that women will remain economically vulnerable in the absence of fundamental societal change. Yet it is hopeful because, if we heed it, we may be able to unite as feminists to seize the opportunity offered by mothers' entry into the work force, instead of frittering it away rediscovering traditional (and inaccurate) descriptions of gender differences.

Notes

12. C. GILLIGAN, IN A DIFFERENT VOICE 24–63 (1982). Gilligan is only the most famous of the scholars who have defined gender in psychological terms. Her findings parallel, and presumably were influenced by, the work of Jean Baker Miller, *see* J.B. MILLER, TOWARD A NEW PSYCHOLOGY OF WOMEN (2d ed. 1986); *see also* N. CHODOROW, THE REPRODUCTION OF MOTHERING: PSYCHOANALYSIS AND THE SOCIOLOGY OF GENDER (1978). All three authors focus in different ways on "connectedness" as a crucial (if not the crucial) gender difference. *See* C. GILLIGAN, *supra*, at 8–9; J.B. MILLER, *supra*, at 83, 148 n.1; N. CHODOROW, *supra*, at 90–91, 167–70, 178–79. But only Chodorow seems clearly to recognize that what she is talking about is the psychological construction of gender and its costs for women. *Id.* at 213–19.

It is important to place Gilligan's work into historical context. Though I take issue with her conclusions about women's voice, I endorse her fundamental motivation, namely to reverse the previous practice of ignoring women altogether, or treating any differences between men and women as reflecting women's inadequacy. Gilligan's primary contribution was to articulate a modern challenge to "male norms."

13. *See* C. GILLIGAN, *supra* note 12, at 19–21, 64–66, 70–71, 82–83.

14. *See, e.g.*, Scales, *The Emergence of Feminist Jurisprudence: An Essay*, 95 YALE L.J. 1373 (1986); Matsuda, *Liberal Jurisprudence and Abstracted Visions of Human Nature: A Feminist Critique of Rawls' Theory of Justice*, 16 N. MEX. L. REV. 613 (1986); Kornhauser, *The Rhetoric of the Anti-Progressive Income Tax Movement: A Typical Male Reaction*, 86 MICH. L. REV. 465 (1987); Areen, *A Need for Caring* (Book Review), 86 MICH. L. REV. 1067, 1073 (1988).

15. 628 F. Supp. 1264 (N.D. Ill. 1986), *affd.*, 839 F.2d 302 (7th Cir. 1988).

18. *See, e.g.*, M. DALY, PURE LUST xii, 4–7 (1984); M. DALY, GYN/ECOLOGY 202–22 (1978). The French feminists combine elements of domesticity with elements of this earlier image of women. *See, e.g.*, L. IRIGARAY, THIS SEX WHICH IS NOT ONE 29, 208–11 (1985).

19. For an introduction, see A. FRASER, THE WEAKER VESSEL 1–6 (1984); N. COTT, THE BONDS OF WOMANHOOD: "WOMAN'S SPHERE" IN NEW ENGLAND, 1780–1835, at 201–04 (1977).

20. C. KARLSEN, THE DEVIL IN THE SHAPE OF A WOMAN 154–81 (1987); J. DEMOS, ENTERTAINING SATAN 60–64, 197–209, 394–95 (1982); J. KLAITS, SERVANTS OF SATAN 51–59 (1985); G.R. QUAIFE, WANTON WENCHES AND WAYWARD WIVES 14–15, 182–83 (1979); L. ULRICH, GOOD WIVES 96–99, 106–12 (1980); Bloch, *Untangling the Roots of Modern Sex Roles: A Survey of Four Centuries of Change*, 4 SIGNS: J. WOMEN CULTURE & SOCY. 237, 240–41 (1978); Demos, *Husbands and Wives, reprinted in* J. FRIEDMAN & W. SHADE, OUR AMERICAN SISTERS: WOMEN IN AMERICAN LIFE AND THOUGHT 41–42 (1982). . . .

21. *See generally* A. JAGGAR, FEMINIST POLITICS AND HUMAN NATURE 364–84 (1983); A FEMINIST PERSPECTIVE IN THE ACADEMY (E. Langland & W. Gove eds. 1981); S. HARDING, THE SCIENCE QUESTION IN FEMINISM (1986); C. MCMILLAN, WOMEN, REASON, AND NATURE (1982); Vickers, *Memoirs of an Ontological Exile: The Methodological Rebellions of Feminist Research, in* FEMINISM IN CANADA: FROM PRESSURE TO POLITICS (G. Ginn & A. Miles eds. 1982).

22. *See* Williams, *Critical Legal Studies: The Death of Transcendence and the Rise of the New Langdells,* 62 N.Y.U. L. REV. 429 (1987).

23. *Id.* at 432–34.

26. The most sophisticated of the feminist scholars who link traditional rationalism with males is the historian of science (a scientist herself) Evelyn Fox Keller. *See* E.F. KELLER, REFLECTIONS ON GENDER AND SCIENCE 61–65 (1985). Keller convincingly argues that the ideology of science developed as part and parcel of a new gender system in the early modern era. But this does not establish, as she and others seem to assume, that the new epistemology (which is a critique of that system of science in the sense that science built upon the tenets of traditional epistemology) is "female" in any meaningful sense.

27. *See* Williams, *supra* note 22, at 435–39.

28. *See id.* at 439–53.

30. *See* Bloch, *supra* note 20, at 241 (hierarchy as natural); L. KERBER, WOMEN OF THE REPUBLIC: INTELLECT AND IDEOLOGY IN REVOLUTIONARY AMERICA 13–15 (1980). Kerber describes the initial accommodation between liberalism and gender in the concept of republican motherhood. *See* L. KERBER, *supra*, at 265–88.

31. *See* Baker, *The Domestication of Politics: Women and American Political Society, 1780–1920,* 89 AM. HIST. REV. 620 (1984); N. COTT, *supra* note 19; Bloch, *supra* note 20, at 249–50. This description is an oversimplification. Domesticity changed the image of white, middle-class women, but the older stereotype lived on. It continued to be applied to lower-class women, to black women, and to white middle-class women who violated the code of female behavior mandated by domesticity. These themes are astutely explored in Hall, *"The Mind That Burns in Each Body": Women, Rape and Racial Violence,* and Peiss, *"Charity Girls" and City Pleasures: Historical Notes on Working-Class Sexuality, 1880–1920,* in POWERS OF DESIRE (A. Snitow, C. Stansell & S. Thompson eds. 1983).

32. *See* Auerbach, Blum Smith & Williams, *Commentary on Gilligan's In A Different Voice,* 11 FEM. STUD. 149, 156–59 (1985); *see also* Ehrenreich, *Accidental Suicide* (Book Review), ATLANTIC, Oct. 1986, at 98, 100 (Gilligan's work being used "to re-open the old case for women's absolute moral superiority"); Kerber, *Some Cautionary Words for Historians,* 11 SIGNS: J. WOMEN CULTURE & SOCY. 304, 309 (1986).

33. Often, *Defining Feminism: A Comparative Approach,* 14 SIGNS: J. WOMEN CULTURE & SOCY. 119, 135 (1988).

34. S. LEBSOCK, THE FREE WOMEN OF PETERSBURG: STATUS AND CULTURE IN A SOUTHERN TOWN, 1784–1860 (1984). . . .

35. *Id.* at 142–43.

37. The one Victorian compliment relational feminists have rejected is the view of women as passionless. The classic study of the different cultural meaning of asexuality is Cott, *Passionlessness: An Interpretation of Victorian Sexual Ideology, 1790–1850,* in N. COTT & E. PLECK, A HERITAGE OF HER OWN (1979).

38. Conversation between Carol Gilligan and Catharine MacKinnon, Mitchell Lecture Series, State University of New York at Buffalo School of Law (Nov. 20, 1984), *reprinted in [James McCormick Mitchell Lecture: Feminist Discourse, Moral Values, and the Law— A Conversation,* 34 BUFFALO L. REV. 11 (1985) (hereinafter *A Conversation)].*

39. *Id.* at 74–75.

40. The term "possessive individualism" comes from C.B. MACPHERSON, THE PO-LITICAL THEORY OF POSSESSIVE INDIVIDUALISM 3, 263–64 (1962). The term refers to the liberal premises that society consists of market relations, and that freedom means freedom from any relations with others except those relations the individual enters voluntarily with a view to his own self-interest.

42. Although Gilligan herself sends mixed messages, . . . her recent comments show that she diverges from many of her followers in a significant way on the issue of the transformative potential of "women's voice." She has from the beginning acknowledged that both men and women face challenges, though they are different ones, in achieving emotional maturity. Men need to appreciate relationships while women need to realize that a caring and nurturing outlook should include their own, as well as others', needs. See A Conversation, supra note [38], at 35, 45–46.

43. K. FERGUSON, [THE FEMINIST CASE AGAINST BUREAUCRACY (1984)].

44. Id. at 166. . . .

45. Menkel-Meadow, [Portia in a Different Voice: Speculations on a Woman's Lawyering Process, 1 BERK. WOMEN'S L.J. 39, 43 (1985)]. . . .

46. See West, [Jurisprudence and Gender, 55 U. CHI. L. REV. 1, 65 (1988)].

47. S. LEBSOCK, supra note 34, at 144. Lebsock's claims are modest: "This is a hopeful vision," she continues, "but not necessarily a utopian one; we may be talking about the realm of small improvement." Other feminists are more openly utopian. An example is Representative Patricia Schroeder's statement that "doing something about women's poverty won't make the gender gap disappear. Women will still worry that unless we change the old caveman rules, we will all be blown up." O'Reilly, Getting a Gender Message, Time, July 25, 1983, at 12. Other feminists are more aggressive in their claims for the transformative potential of women's voice. See, e.g., West, supra note [46], at 65.

48. See N. NODDINGS, [CARING (1984)]; Areen, supra note 14.

49. See, e.g., Karst, [Woman's Constitution, 1984 DUKE L.J. 447], 486–95; Menkel-Meadow, supra note [45], at 50–55; C. GILLIGAN, supra note 12, at 29; West, supra note [46], at 37. West makes it explicit that she sees feminism as the way out of liberalism (within which category she includes critical legal studies, as the "unofficial story"). How feminists differ from critical legal scholars in their yearning for a vision of community and connection she makes less clear.

50. E. WOLGAST, [EQUALITY AND THE RIGHTS OF WOMEN 156 (1980)].

51. Comments of Paul J. Spiegelman, A Conversation, supra note [38] at 36.

52. Smith, Family Limitation, Sexual Control, and Domestic Feminism in Victorian America, in A HERITAGE OF HER OWN, supra note 37, at 222, 238–39. Cf. N. CHODOROW, supra note 12, at 213.

53. N. COTT, supra note 19, at 67–68; see also C. LASCH, HAVEN IN A HEARTLESS WORLD: THE FAMILY BESIEGED (1977).

54. N. COTT, supra note 19, at 70; see also Baker, supra note 31, at 620.

55. C. GILLIGAN, supra note 12, at 17, 62–63.

56. Id. at 100.

57. Id. at 22.

58. Id. at 29.

59. Id. at 38.

60. Id. at 35, 79.

62. Nel Noddings is more successful than most relational feminists at following through her statement that the "caring" ethics she advocates is available, and in fact practiced, by both men and women. See N. NODDINGS, supra note [48], at 2.

63. 628 F. Supp. 1264 (N.D. Ill. 1986), affd., 839 F.2d 302 (7th Cir. 1988).

64. This argument was made most clearly through the testimony of Rosalind Rosenberg. See Offer of Proof Concerning the Testimony of Dr. Rosalind Rosenberg at paras. 11, 16–22. EEOC v. Sears (No. 79-C-4373). Sears' testimony at times made it seem that all women prefer part-time work.

65. See id. at paras. 16–22. Another Title VII defendant successfully used a similar interest argument in EEOC v. General Tel. Co. of Northwest, Inc., 40 Fair Empl. Prac

Cas. (BNA) 1533 (W.D. Wash. 1985), *affd.*, 45 Fair Empl. Prac. Cas. (BNA) 1888 (9th Cir. 1988) (unpublished opinion).

66. 42 U.S.C. §§ 2000e-2000e-17 (1982).

67. I'm simplifying for clarity. In individual cases, of course, what the relevant labor market is can be a subject of hot contention. *See* D. BALDUS & J. COLE, STATISTICAL PROOF OF DISCRIMINATION 44–49, 102–41 (1980).

68. For a good general discussion, see Boardman & Vining, *The Role of Probative Statistics in Employment Discrimination Cases*, 46 LAW & CONTEMP. PROBS., Autumn 1983, at 189; for an advanced discussion, see D. BALDUS & J. COLE, *supra* note 67, at 26–31, 290–93.

69. *See* D. BALDUS & J. COLE, *supra* note 67, at 27.

70. *See* 628 F. Supp. at 1305–15; 839 F.2d at 320–21.

71. Trial Transcript at 8439, Testimony of Ray Graham, EEOC v. Sears, Roebuck & Co., 628 F. Supp. 1264 (N.D. Ill. 1986) (No. 79-C-4373), *affd.*, 839 F.2d 302 (7th Cir. 1988). Graham, Sears' corporate director of equal opportunity, repeatedly expressed the opinion that some jobs (hardware, for example) have "natural appeal" for men, *id.* at 8435, while others (draperies) are "a natural" for women, *id.* at 8432. His assessments were based on assertions that women are averse to competition, *id.* at 8433, and pressure, *id.* at 8434–35.

72. *See* EEOC v. Sears, 628 F. Supp. at 1308–13.

73. 628 F. Supp. at 1307.

74. Offer of Proof Concerning the Testimony of Dr. Rosalind Rosenberg, at para. 1, EEOC *v. Sears* (No. 79-C-4373).

75. *Id.* at paras. 16–22.

76. *Id.*

78. Trial Transcript at 14625–29, Testimony of Joan Haworth, EEOC *v. Sears* (No. 79-C-4373). . . .

79. One stated, "[C]ommission sales is exactly what I was looking for and was the reason I came to Sears and put in an application." Written Testimony of Lura L. Nader at 1, EEOC *v. Sears* (No. 79-C-4373). *See also* Written Testimony of Alice Howland at 4.

80. Judge Nordberg's opinion discounted these witnesses' testimony on the ground that the EEOC had not proven that they were discriminated against. EEOC v. Sears, 628 F. Supp. 1264, 1318 (N.D. Ill. 1986), *affd.*, 839 F.2d 302 (7th Cir. 1988). This of course was not the purpose for which these witnesses' testimony was submitted.

81. This arose in Sears' lawyers' analysis of Sears' Applicant Interview Guides (AIG's), in which applicants were asked to rate their interest in selling various categories of items from one to five in terms of interest, experience, and skill. In Judge Nordberg's words, "The scores were normalized to take into account that some applicants might inflate their scores to increase their chances of being hired." 628 F. Supp. at 1322. Normalization is a commonly used statistical technique, but two of EEOC's experts testified they had never seen it used as Dr. Haworth used it.

The normalization procedure only registered the applicant in a category if the applicant gave herself a rating for each of the three dimensions (interest, skill and experience) that was 125% of her average rating for that dimension on all other AIG activities. For example, if an individual rated herself four for each of interest, experience, and skill in home improvement, this rating would be counted only if her average rating for all other activities covered by the AIGs was not greater than 3.2 for each of interest, experience, and skill. This procedure penalized people with varied interests and experience. It was therefore likely to penalize women with interest or experience in nontraditional work unless those women both disclaimed interest in and had never done traditional women's work. Thus women's interest in nontraditional work was systematically discounted. Consequently, a woman who had held a low-paying sales position of the type in which women retail workers are disproportionately concentrated would be likely to have any interest she expressed, or experience she had, in commission sales discounted. Since men are less likely to have experience or interest in (lower-paying) women's work, their interest in higher-paying jobs traditionally held by men was much less likely to be discounted. *Compare* Judge Nordberg's analysis, 628 F. Supp. at 1322 n.79, *with* Brief of the Equal Employment Opportunity Commission as Appellant at 41–42, EEOC v. Sears, 839 F.2d 302 (7th Cir. 1988).

82. Sears also had help from the EEOC. The Agency's decision not to provide testimony from victims of discrimination made it much easier for Sears to make general arguments on the basis of stereotypes. The EEOC's position is that if it had provided witnesses, the trial judge would have discounted their testimony on the grounds that the witnesses were too few in number or were otherwise unrepresentative of the nationwide class. Brief of the Equal Employment Opportunity Commission as Appellant at 151–53, EEOC v. Sears, 839 F.2d 302 (7th Cir. 1988). However, the testimony of live women interested in nontraditional jobs might have made it more awkward for the courts of accept Sears' assertions about women's interests. Maybe not, of course; *see supra* notes 78–79. But the existence of victim testimony so labelled would at the least have required the Seventh Circuit to write its opinion differently. It relied heavily on the lack of testimony from "real" victims. *See* 839 F.2d at 310–12.

83. Trial Transcript at 16501–02, EEOC v. Sears (No. 79-C-4373).

84. For example, Nordberg repeated this point to Alice Kessler-Harris six times. Trial Transcript, *passim*, EEOC v. Sears (No. 79-C-4373).

85. I have not read the entire 19,000-page transcript. However, I note that Nordberg never pressed Sears's complementary witness Rosalind Rosenberg to attach a percentage to her claims about women, although those claims often were as unqualified as Kessler-Harris', or more so. To Rosenberg, Nordberg stressed the need to qualify her statements by designating the time period to which they applied. Trial Transcript at 10374–76, EEOC v. Sears (No. 79-C-4373). That objection was much easier to meet: it is easier for a historian to limit generalized statements to a given century than to specify what precise percentage of women during a given period wanted nontraditional jobs (or otherwise diverged from women's traditional roles).

86. *See* 628 F. Supp. at 1314–15; Offer of Proof Concerning the Testimony of Dr. Rosalind Rosenberg, para. 23, EEOC v. Sears (No. 79-C-4373).

87. *See* 839 F.2d at 320–21.

91. *Compare* Offer of Proof Concerning the Testimony of Dr. Rosalind Rosenberg, EEOC v. Sears (No. 79-C-4373), at paras. 19(c), 20(a) (women reject competitiveness) *and* para. 19(a) ("Women tend to be more interested than men in the cooperative, social aspects of the work situation.") *with* para. 10 ("Even as they have entered the labor force in increasing numbers, women have retained their historic commitment to the home.").

92. Castro v. Beecher, 334 F. Supp. 930, 936 (D. Mass. 1971).

93. Glover v. Johnston, 478 F. Supp. 1075, 1086–88 (E.D. Mich. 1979), *affd. sub nom.* Cornish v. Johnson, 774 F.2d 1161 (6th Cir. 1985), *cert. denied*, 478 U.S. 1020 (1986).

94. *See* EEOC v. Sears, 628 F. Supp. 1264, 1307–08 (N.D. Ill. 1986); 839 F.2d 302, 320–21 (7th Cir. 1988).

95. This phrase was first applied to Antonio Gramsci. *See* Romano, *But Was He a Marxist?* (Book Review), VILLAGE VOICE, Mar. 29, 1983, at 41, *quoted in* Lears, *The Concept of Cultural Hegemony: Problems and Possibilities*, 90 AM. HIST. REV. 567 (1985).

101. I would like to thank Ann Freeman for insights and encouragement in developing this argument, of which she has a somewhat different version. Mary Joe Frug has

articulated the core insight that Western wage labor assumes a worker with no child care responsibilities in her seminal study. Frug, *Securing Job Equality for Women: Labor Market Hostility to Working Mothers*, 59, B.U.L. REV. 55 (1979). . . .

119. *See* L. WEITZMAN, [THE DIVORCE REVOLUTION 337-56 (1985)]; *see also* R. EISLER, DISSOLUTION: NO-FAULT DIVORCE, MARRIAGE, AND THE FUTURE OF WOMEN 20-54 (1977); Levin, *Virtue Does Not Have Its Reward for Women in California*, 61 WOMEN LAW. J. 55, 57 (1975); Prager, *Shifting Perspectives on Marital Property Law*, in RETHINKING THE FAMILY: SOME FEMINIST QUESTIONS 111, 123 (B. Thorne & M. Yablom eds., 1982). . . .

120. L. WEITZMAN, *supra* note [119], at 337-56. *See also* Burtless, *Comments on Income for the Single Parent: Child Support, Work, and Welfare*, in GENDER IN THE WORKPLACE 263 (C. Brown & J. Pechman eds. 1987); Blair, [*Women Who Divorce: Are They Getting a Fair Deal?* WOMAN'S DAY, May 27, 1986, at 36].

121. Eisenstein, *The Sexual Politics of the New Right: Understanding the "Crisis of Liberalism" for the 1980s, reprinted in* FEMINIST THEORY: A CRITIQUE OF IDEOLOGY 77 [(N. Keohane, M. Rosaldo & B. Gelpi eds. 1981)].

122. Pearce, [*Welfare Is Not for Women: Toward a Model of Advocacy To Meet the Needs of Women in Poverty*, 19 CLEARINGHOUSE REV. 412, 413 (1985)].

123. Eisenstein, *supra* note 121, at 91.

124. Figures for households not headed by females are from the National Advisory Council in Economic Opportunity study, which reported that 39% of all female-headed households live under the poverty line. *See* Blair, *supra* note [120] at 40.

125. Pearce, *supra* note [122] at 413.

126. A. DE TOCQUEVILLE, DEMOCRACY IN AMERICA 568 (J. Mayer & M. Lerner eds. 1966).

127. *See* Rimer, [*Sequencing: Putting Careers on Hold*, N.Y. Times, Sept. 23, 1988, at A21, col. 1].

128. *See, e.g.*, Fierst, [*Careers and Kids*, Ms. MAGAZINE, May 1988], at 62-63; Rimer, *supra* note [127].

129. *See, e.g.*, Rimer, *supra* note [127]. *See also* Torry, *Female Lawyers Face Persistent Bias*, ABA Told, Wash. Post, Aug. 9, 1988, at A1, A4 ("women are not increasing their representation among partnerships, judgeships and tenured law faculty positions in nearly the percentages their numbers and class rank would indicate" in part due to the fact "they are forced to sacrifice career advancement . . . to have children").

134. Good introductions to Gramsci are A. GRAMSCI, SELECTIONS FROM THE PRISON NOTEBOOKS (Q. Hoare & G. Smith eds. & trans. 1971); W. ADAMSON, HEGEMONY AND REVOLUTION: A STUDY OF ANTONIO GRAMSCI'S POLITICAL AND CULTURAL THEORY (1980); J. CAMMETT, ANTONIO GRAMSCI AND THE ORIGINS OF ITALIAN COMMUNISM (1967); A. DAVIDSON, ANTONIO GRAMSCI: TOWARDS AN INTELLECTUAL BIOGRAPHY (1977); J. FEMIA, GRAMSCI'S POLITICAL THOUGHT (1981); T. NEMETH, GRAMSCI'S PHILOSOPHY: A CRITICAL STUDY (1980).

135. Lears, *supra* note 95, at 569-70.

136. This has long been noted by Marxists. *See, e.g.*, Hartmann, [*The Unhappy Marriage of Marxism and Feminism: Towards a More Progressive Union*, in WOMEN AND REVOLUTION 28 (L. Sargent ed. 1981)]; *see also* Harding, *What Is the Real Material Base of Patriarchy and Capital?*, in WOMEN AND REVOLUTION 130 (L. Sargent ed. 1981).

137. Lears, *supra* note 95, at 570.

138. *Id.* at 573 (footnote omitted).

139. *Id.*

168. "Go after our industries!" advises Doctor Spock. He recommends more flexibility in hours, six-hour work days and subsidized day care. Both Penelope Leach, a psychology

Ph.D., and Dr. T. Barry Brazelton believe that current trends have potentially adverse psychological consequences for today's families. Brazelton has stressed the need for improved pay for day care workers; Leach advocates extensive paid maternity leave (6 months) and part-time work by both parents (next 18 months). See Work and Families, WASHINGTON PARENT 1, 3, 5 (Nov. 1988) (report of a panel discussion in Boston, Apr. 1988). See also Brazelton, Stress for Families Today, INFANT MENTAL HEALTH J., Spring 1988, at 65.

169. See Hartmann, Achieving Economic Equity for Women, in WINNING AMERICA: IDEAS AND LEADERSHIP FOR THE 1990s, 99 (M. Raskin & C. Hartman, eds. 1988).

170. "In 1840, the average work week in the United States was 78 hours." Frug, supra note 101, at 97 n.248 (citing Northrup, The Reduction in Hours, in HOURS OF WORK (C. Dankert, F. Mann & H. Northrup eds. 1965)).

171. See A. EPSTEIN, THE CHALLENGE OF THE AGED vii (1976); see also C. MEYER, SOCIAL SECURITY: A CRITIQUE OF RADICAL REFORM PROSPECTS 9 (1987).

172. Fineman, Implementing Equality: Ideology, Contradiction and Social Change, 1983 WIS. L. REV. 789, 791; Levin, supra note 119, at 55. See also Finley, [Transcending Equality Theory: A Way Out of the Maternity and the Workplace Debate, 86 COLUM L. REV. 1118, 1148–63 (1986)].

173. [C. MACKINNON], SEXUAL HARASSMENT [OF WORKING WOMEN: A CASE OF SEX DISCRIMINATION 100–41 (1979)] (discussing Phillips v. Martin Marietta Corp., 400 U.S. 542 (1971)); [C. MACKINNON, FEMINISM UNMODIFIED 35–36 (1987)].

174. SEXUAL HARASSMENT, supra note [173], at 117. See Taub, Book Review, 80 COLUM. L. REV. 1686 (1980).

175. SEXUAL HARASSMENT, supra note [173], at 122–24.

176. See Polikoff, Why Mothers Are Losing: A Brief Analysis of Criteria Used in Child Custody Determinations, 7 WOMEN'S RTS. L. REP. 235 (1982); L. WEITZMAN, supra note [119], 217, 310–18.

177. See Polikoff, supra note 176, at 236. Fathers now win an estimated one-half to two-thirds of all custody battles. See Salholtz, [Feminism's Identity Crisis, NEWSWEEK, Mar. 31, 1988], at 59.

178. Experts agree. See Polikoff, supra note 176, at 237. See also Kay, [Equality and Difference: A Perspective on No-Fault Divorce and Its Aftermath, 56 U. CIN. L. REV. 1, 24, 79 (1987)].

The term "deinstitutionalizing gender" is Alison Jaggar's. Jaggar, On Sexual Equality, 84 ETHICS 275, 276 (1975). Jaggar's position appears to have changed. See A. JAGGAR, supra note 21, at 148.

179. Of course, most of those protected will be women, and that in itself will reinforce the notion that women "are really different but we're not allowed to say so."

Though this is a drawback of sex-neutral standards, it does not obviate the need for them. Such standards are useful because they address pressing social issues without bowing to a central tenet of gender ideology, namely that gender roles are necessarily correlated with biology, and without penalizing men who choose to play gender roles ordinarily assigned to females.

Nonetheless sex-neutral standards designed to address gender-produced disabilities have very real limitations: they no doubt will tend to reinforce the connection between biology and gender in people's minds. This limitation simply highlights the need to link short-term solutions, such as sex-neutral protections for those disadvantaged by gender, with a long-term strategy challenging basic tenets of the gender system as a whole.

180. See Garska v. McCoy, 278 S.E.2d 357, 360–63 (W. Va. 1981), cited in Williams, The Equality Crisis: Some Reflections on Culture, Courts and Feminism, 7 WOMEN'S RTS. L. REP. 175, 190 n.80 (1982).

181. For a recent survey of studies on sex differences, see I. FRIEZE, J. PARSONS, P. JOHNSON, D. RUBLE, & G. ZELLMAN, WOMEN AND SEX ROLES: A SOCIAL PSYCHOLOGICAL PERSPECTIVE 45-68 (1978). For a readily accessible survey of the literature, see Taub, *Keeping Women in Their Place: Stereotyping Per Se as a Form of Employment Discrimination,* 21 B.C. L. REV. 345, 349-61 (1980).

Although this is not the place to do it, it is also time to bring up out of the footnotes law reviews' treatment of the numerous and cogent critiques of Gilligan's methodology and conclusions. *See, e.g.,* Auerbach, Blum, Smith & Williams, [*Commentary on Gilligan's* In a Different Voice, 11 FEM. STUD. 149 (1985)]; Broughton, *Women's Rationality And Men's Virtues: A Critique of Gender Dualism in Gilligan's Theory of Moral Development,* 50 SOC. RES. 597 (1983); Flanagan & Adler, *Impartiality and Particularity,* 50 SOC. RES. 576 (1983); Kerber, Greeno, Maccoby, Luria, Stack & Gilligan, On In a Different Voice: *An Interdisciplinary Forum,* 11 SIGNS: J. WOMEN CULTURE & SOCY. 304 (1986); Nails, *Social-Scientific Sexism: Gilligan's Mismeasure of Man,* 50 SOC. RES. 643 (1983). The interesting thing from a cultural standpoint is how little impact these critiques have made on the widespread acceptance of Gilligan's theories.

182. *See* C. MACKINNON, [FEMINISM UNMODIFIED, *supra* note 173], at 39. MacKinnon has begun the task of diffusing the "naturalness" of gender stereotypes about women.

183. THE AMERICAN HERITAGE DICTIONARY (William Morris ed. 1970).

185. *See* Rubin & Shenker, *Friendship, Proximity, and Self-disclosure,* 46 J. PERSONALITY 1-22 (1978).

186. The irony is that, as recently as twenty years ago, male bonding was celebrated. Perhaps the celebration of women's culture can be viewed as a response by women who as youngsters were informed (as I was) that women were too petty and competitive to enjoy the kind of deep and lasting friendships males experienced. See E. L. RANELAGH, MEN ON WOMEN (1985).

187. COMPETITION: A FEMINIST TABOO? 1 (V. Miner & H. Longino eds. 1987).

188. Literature provides a rich source of examples of men as nurturers and women as power-hungry, for those of us who are not sociologists. *See, e.g.,* P. ROSE, PARALLEL LIVES: FIVE VICTORIAN MARRIAGES 8-9 (1983).

191. Comments of Ellen Du Bois, in A Conversation, *supra* note [38], at 73.

192. *See, e.g.,* Janeway, *Women and the Uses of Power,* in THE FUTURE OF DIFFERENCE (H. Eisenstein & A. Jardine eds. 1985).

193. J.L. GWALTNEY, DRYLONGSOUL: A SELF-PORTRAIT OF BLACK AMERICA 173-74 (1981), *quoted in* S. Harley, "When Your Work Is Not Who You Are": The Development of a Working-Class Consciousness Among Afro-American Women, Paper given at the Conference On Women in the Progressive Era, sponsored by the American Historical Association in conjunction with the National Museum of American History (Mar. 10-12, 1988).

194. *See generally* THE NEW HISTORY: THE 1980S AND BEYOND (T. Rabb & R. Rotberg eds. 1982).

7

Telling Stories About Women and Work: Judicial Interpretations of Sex Segregation in the Workplace in Title VII Cases Raising the Lack of Interest Argument [1990]

Vicki Schultz

Introduction

How do we make sense of that most basic feature of the world of work, sex segregation on the job? That it exists is part of our common understanding. Social science research has documented, and casual observation confirmed, that men work mostly with men, doing "men's work," and women work mostly with women, doing "women's work."[1] We know also the serious negative consequences segregation has for women workers. Work traditionally done by women has lower wages, less status, and fewer opportunities for advancement than work done by men. Despite this shared knowledge, however, we remain deeply divided in our attitudes toward sex segregation on the job. What divides us is how we interpret this reality, the stories we tell about its origins and meaning. Why does sex segregation on the job exist? Who is responsible for it? Is it an injustice, or an inevitability?

In *EEOC v. Sears, Roebuck & Co.*,[3] the district court interpreted sex segregation as the expression of women's own choice. The Equal Employment Opportunity Commission (EEOC) sued Sears under title VII of the Civil Rights Act of 1964.[4] The EEOC claimed that Sears had engaged in sex discrimination in hiring and promotion into commission sales jobs, reserving these jobs mostly for men while relegating women to much-lower-paying noncommission sales jobs.[5] Like most employment discrimination plaintiffs, the EEOC relied heavily on statistical evidence to prove its claims. The EEOC's statistical studies showed that Sears had severely underhired women sales applicants for the most lucrative commission sales positions,[6] even after controlling for potential sex differences in qualifications.

Although the statistical evidence exposed a long-standing pattern of sex segregation in Sears' salesforce, the court refused to attribute this pattern to sex discrimination. The judge concluded that the EEOC's statistical analyses were "virtually meaningless," because they were based on the faulty assumption that female sales applicants were as "interested" as male applicants in commission sales jobs. Indeed, the EEOC had "turned a blind eye to reality," for Sears had proved that women sales applicants preferred lower-paying noncommission sales jobs.[10] The judge credited various explanations for women's "lack of interest" in commission sales, all of which rested on conventional images of women as "feminine" and nurturing, unsuited for the vicious competition in the male-dominated world of commission selling.[11] In the court's eyes, Sears had done nothing to segregate its salesforce; it had merely honored the preexisting employment preferences of working women themselves. . . .

Neither the issues nor the outcome in *Sears* are new. For almost two decades, employers have argued successfully that they had no role in creating sex segregation in their workforces. "It's not our fault," they say. "We don't exclude women from men's jobs. In fact, we've been trying to move women into those jobs. The trouble is, women won't apply for them—they just aren't interested. They grow up wanting to do women's work, and we can't force them to do work they don't want to do."[14] Almost half the courts to consider the issue have accepted this explanation and attributed women's disadvantaged place in the workplace to their own lack of interest in more highly valued nontraditional jobs. . . .

. . . The women who predominate in these cases are working-class women. Many are women of color, seeking jobs traditionally held by men rather than jobs held by white women.[18] Working-class women have shared the experience of being marginalized at work, but being unable to opt out.[19] They have made a high priority of ending job segregation, for they want work that will enable them to support themselves their families with security, while providing challenge, a sense of accomplishment, and control over their own lives. Our society, however, has long viewed these women as inauthentic workers, uncommitted to wage work as an important life interest and source of identity. This view has justified relegating them to dead-end, female-dominated jobs at the lowest rung of the economic ladder.

Title VII promised working women change. But, consciously or unconsciously, courts have interpreted the statute with some of the same assumptions that have historically legitimated women's economic disadvantage. Most centrally, courts have assumed that women's aspirations and identities as workers are shaped exclusively in private realms that are independent of and prior to the workworld. By assuming that women form stable job aspirations before they begin working, courts have missed the ways in which employers contribute to creating women workers in their images of who "women" are supposed to be. Judges have placed beyond the law's reach the structural features of the workplace that gender jobs and people, and disempower women from aspiring to higher-paying nontraditional employment. . . .

[This approach was not inevitable. Before the first sex discrimination case raising the lack of interest argument was decided, the courts had already decided a landmark series of race discrimination cases addressing the same argument. In these early race discrimination cases, the courts applied evidentiary standards that presumed that continuing patterns of racial segregation were attributable to historical labor market discrimination, rather than to minorities' independent preferences for lower-paying, less-challenging jobs. This approach recognized that human choices are never formed in a vacuum, and that people's work aspirations are inevitably shaped by the job opportunities that have historically been available to them as well as by their experiences in the work structures and relations of which they have been a part. By acknowledging that work aspirations and identities are shaped in the context of what larger institutional and legal environments define as possible, early courts refused to allow employers to escape responsibility for the collective history of labor market discrimination by pinning the blame on its victims.[103] If judges had been unwilling to take such an approach, employers would have simply rationalized the status quo as the expression of minorities' own work choices.

To a large extent, this rationalization of the status quo has occurred in sex discrimination cases. Courts have been unwilling to take an approach that situates women's work aspirations in the context of historical labor market discrimination. Instead, they have attributed women's aspirations exclusively to their early socialization. This view has led them to insist that plaintiffs produce anecdotal evidence that the employer discriminated against individual women. Anecdotal evidence has become central, not because it allows judges to estimate with any accuracy whether women's work interests differ systematically from men's, but because it signifies that society has progressed sufficiently to produce women who grow up aspiring to "men's work." The individual victim has come to symbolize the "modern" woman, that genderless creature entitled to the law's protection.

But the judicial focus on the victim has left the majority of working women in the wake of the law. Within the interpretive framework embraced by conservative and liberal courts alike, employers' practices are defined as discriminatory only insofar as they prevent individual women from realizing preexisting preferences for nontraditional work—and not because those practices are part of a larger workplace environment in which most women have never been able to dream of the possibility of doing such work.

Stories about Women and Work:
A Rhetorical Study of the Two Competing
Judicial Interpretations of Sex Segregation

.   .   .

A. The Conservative Story of Choice

The conservative story of choice is the familiar one told by the *Sears* court: women are "feminine," nontraditional work is "masculine," and therefore women do not want to do it. The story rests on an appeal to masculinity and femininity as oppositional categories. Women are "feminine" because that is the definition of what makes them women. Work itself is endowed with the imagined human characteristics of masculinity or femininity based on the sex of the workers who do it. "Femininity" refers to a complex of womanly traits and aspirations that by definition precludes any interest in the work of men. Even though the story always follows this same logic, the story changes along class lines in the way it is told. Cases involving blue-collar work emphasize the "masculinity" of the work, drawing on images of physical strength and dirtiness. Cases involving white-collar work focus on the "femininity" of women, appealing to traits and values associated with domesticity.

In the blue-collar context, the story begins by describing the work in heavily gendered terms. Courts invoke oppositional images of work as heavy versus light, dirty versus clean, and explicitly align the left side of the equation with masculinity (while implicitly aligning the right side with femininity). Thus, nontraditional jobs in bakeries are described as "hot, heavy, and hard work."[187] Males, of course, do this "heavy work", while females do the "lighter," "less demanding" work.[188] Work in a cardboard box factory is "dirty and somewhat heavy"; the factory is located in a "very poor section of the city," where women fear to tread.[189] Road maintenance work is "outside laboring work" that is "physically demanding and generally unappealing" to women.[190] Working as a food inspector for a railroads association is characterized as "nocturnal prowling in railroad yards inspecting rotten food" that is not "attractive" to "young women."[191]

In such cases, conservative courts did not bother to question whether the work fit the gendered characteristics ascribed to it. Indeed, employers did not assert that being male was a bona fide occupational qualification for these jobs.[192] Although some of these jobs may have required considerable physical strength, the courts made no inquiry into whether this was true and if so, whether only men had sufficient strength to perform them. Similarly, although some of the settings may have been dirty, a tolerance for dirt is surely not a "job qualification" possessed only by men. Within the story of coercion, nontraditional work is simply reified, endowed with characteristics typically thought of as masculine, as though there were a natural connection between dirty, heavy work and manhood itself. Ironically, courts associated such work with masculinity even in some cases where the employer's traditionally female jobs involved equally dirty and physically demanding work.[193]

Once the court described the work in reified, masculine terms, women's lack of interest followed merely as a matter of "common sense." "The defendant manufactures upholstered metal chairs,"[194] said one court. "Common sense tells us that few women have the skill or the desire to be a welder or a metal fabricator, and that most men cannot operate a sewing machine and have no desire to learn."[195] Or, as another court put it, "Common practical knowledge tells us that certain work in a bakery operation is not attractive to females. . . . The work is simply not compatible with their personal interests and capabilities."[196] In these blue-collar cases, the courts almost never state their specific assumptions about women workers' traits or attitudes. Just what is it about women's "personal interests" that causes them not to want to be welders or bakers? Interestingly, employers and courts almost never invoke women's family roles as the reason for their lack of interest in male-dominated blue-collar jobs.[197] They appeal instead to a much broader conception of femininity that draws on physical images of weakness and cleanliness and applies even to women without family responsibilities.

While in blue-collar cases, the story begins by describing the work as "masculine," in white-collar cases, it begins instead by describing women as "feminine." In the white-collar context, courts invoke social and psychological characteristics rather than physical images. In particular, employers invoke women's domestic roles to explain their lack of interest in traditionally male white-collar work,[198] and conservative courts accept these explanations. In *Gillespie v. Board of Education of North Little Rock*,[199] the court explained why women teachers did not want to be promoted to administrative positions as follows:

> [M]ales who are pursuing careers in education are often the principal family breadwinners. Women . . . , on the other hand, have frequently taken teaching jobs to supplement family income and leave when this is no longer necessary or they are faced with the exigencies of raising a family. We regard this as a logical explanation and find as a matter of fact that there has been no discrimination in the North Little Rock School District.[200]

In some cases, the appeal to women's domestic roles is less direct, but even broader in its implications. In *Sears*,[201] for example, the court invoked women's experience in the family as the underlying cause of a whole host of "feminine" traits and values that lead them to prefer lower-paying noncommission sales jobs. According to the court,

> Women tend to be more interested than men in the social and cooperative aspects of the workplace. Women tend to see themselves as less competitive. They often view non-commission sales as more attractive than commission sales, because they can enter and leave the job more easily, and because there is more social contact and friendship, and less stress in noncommission selling.[202]

To support these generalizations, the court cited the testimony of the historian Sears hired as an expert witness,[203] who attributed the "nurturing" aspects of women's personalities directly to their historic domestic roles.[204] This reasoning transforms the observation that women have been family caretakers into the far more general proposition that they do not aspire to nontraditional work.

Even though the white-collar story begins by portraying women as "feminine," the story nonetheless depends on a contrasting image of nontraditional white-collar work as "masculine." In the *Sears* case, women were romanticized as friendly and noncompetitive, but this mattered only because such traits were the opposite of the ones allegedly needed for successful commission selling. Sears's retail testing manual described a commission salesperson as a "special breed of cat" who has a "sharper intellect" and "more powerful personality" than noncommission salesworkers,[205] someone who is "active" and "has a lot of drive," has "considerable physical vigor," and "likes work which requires physical energy."[206] Sears also administered to sales applicants a test that included such questions as, "Do you have a low-pitched voice?," "Do you swear often?," "Have you ever done any hunting?," and "Have you played on a football team?"[207] Yet, it did not occur to the court to ask whether Sears had used the sales manual and test to construct the job in masculine terms.[208] Like the courts in blue-collar cases, the judge simply took for granted that the gendered characteristics Sears ascribed to the commission sales position were an inherent, necessary part of the job. Once the court endowed the job with these stereotypically masculine characteristics, it became a foregone conclusion that women would find it unappealing.

In the end, the logic of the story of choice converges in blue-collar and white-collar cases. It makes no difference that in blue-collar cases gender is described in physical imagery, while in white collar cases gender is described in social and psychological terms. In both contexts, the story portrays gender as so complete and natural as to render invisible the processes through which gender is socially constructed by employers. The story is powerful because it appeals to the widely held perception that the sexes are different. It extends this perception into an account of gendered job aspirations: if women have different physical characteristics or have had different life experiences from men, then they must have different work interests, too. There is no room for the possibility that women are different from men in certain respects, yet still aspire to the same types of work. If gender is all-encompassing, it is also so natural as to be unalterable. Women's preferences for "feminine" work are so central to the definition of womanhood itself that they remain unchanged (and unchangeable), regardless of what women experience at work. Because there is no room for change, employers do not and cannot and contribute to shaping women's job preferences.

The flip side of the coin is that work itself is somehow inherently "masculine" or "feminine," apart from anything employers do to make it that way. With the world neatly compartmentalized into gendered people and jobs, sex segregation becomes easy to explain. Women bring to the workplace their preexisting preferences for traditionally female work, and employers merely honor those preferences. In the story of choice, workplace segregation implies no oppression or even disadvantage for women. Courts telling this story often describe women's jobs as "more desirable" than men's jobs, even where the women's jobs pay lower wages, afford less prestige, and offer fewer opportunities for advancement than the men's.[209] The implicit point of reference for evaluating the desirability of the work is, of course, the courts' own construction of women's point of view: no court would describe women's work as more desirable to men. The moral of the conservative story is that working women choose their own economic disempowerment.

B. *The Liberal Story of Coercion*

Like their conservative counterparts, liberal courts assume that women form their job preferences before they begin working. This shared assumption, however, drives liberal courts to a rhetoric that is the opposite of conservative rhetoric. Whereas the conservative story has a strong account of gender that implies a preference for "feminine" work, the liberal story has no coherent account of gender. To the contrary, liberal courts suppress gender difference, because the assumption of stable preexisting preferences means that they can hold employers responsible for sex segregation only by portraying women as ungendered subjects who emerge from early life realms with the same experiences and values, and therefore the same work aspirations, as men.

The liberal story centers around the prohibition against stereotyping. Courts reject the lack of interest argument by reasoning that "Title VII was intended to override stereotypical views" of women.[210] "[T]o justify failure to advance women because they did not want to be advanced is the type of stereotyped characterization which will not stand."[211] This anti-stereotyping reasoning is the classic rhetoric of gender neutrality: it invokes the familiar principle that likes are to be treated alike.[212] The problem lies in determining the extent to which women are "like" men. On its face, the anti-stereotyping reasoning seems to deny the existence of group-based gender differences and assert that, contrary to the employer's contention, the women in the proposed labor pool are no less interested than the men in nontraditional work. Below the surface, however, this reasoning reflects a basic ambiguity (and ambivalence) about the extent of gender differences. For the anti-stereotyping rule may be interpreted to admit that the women are *as a group* less interested than men in nontraditional work, and to assert only that some *individual* women may nonetheless be exceptions who do not share the preferences of most women. Under this individualized approach, the employer is forbidden merely from presuming that *all* women are so "different" from men that they do not aspire to nontraditional work.[213]

This individualized approach finds support in a number of cases, which emphasize the exceptional woman who does not "share the 'characteristics generally attributed to [her] group.' "[214] Some courts condemn employers who raise the lack of interest argument for "stereotyping" all women as being uninterested in nontraditional work.[215] Other courts reject the interest argument by observing that although some women do not desire nontraditional jobs, others do.[216] These courts reason that "Title VII rights are not peculiar to the individual, and are not lost or forfeited because some members of protected classes are unable or unwilling to undertake certain jobs."[217] Logically, however, this reasoning does not suffice to refute the lack of interest argument. The employer is not asserting that no individual woman in interested in nontraditional work, but rather that, within the pool of eligible workers, the women are as a group sufficiently less interested than men to explain their underrepresentation.

The focus on individual women thus serves a largely symbolic function. The liberal story invokes the image of the victim, the modern woman who comes to the labor market with a preexisting interest in nontraditional work, to signify the presence of a new social order in which the sexes are equal and ungendered. In this brave new world free of gender, women emerge from pre-work realms with the same life experiences and values, and therefore the same work aspirations, as men. The liberal story suppresses gender difference *outside* the workplace to attribute sex segregation *within* the workplace to employer coercion. Insofar as women approach the labor market with the same experiences and values as men, they must have the same job preferences as men, and to the extent that women end up severely underrepresented in nontraditional jobs, the employer must have discriminated.

The symbolic use of the victim, however, does not resolve the underlying issue of how representative of other women the victim is. This poses no practical difficulty when the only women who testify are the plaintiff's witnesses, who say that the employer prevented them from realizing their preferences for nontraditional jobs. But when employers present testimony from other women, who say that they are happier doing traditionally female jobs and that they would not take more highly rewarded nontraditional jobs even if offered, the liberal story confronts a dilemma. Often, liberal courts have simply characterized these women as unrepresentative of the larger group of women in the labor pool.[219] But they have no way of explaining why these women should be considered less representative of most women than the victims, or how they came to have more gendered job aspirations than other women. Because liberal courts have no coherent explanation for gender difference, more conservative courts can easily portray the victims, rather than those satisfied with traditionally female work, as the anomalous, unrepresentative group.[220]

Indeed, at a conceptual level, the liberal suppression of gender difference actually reinforces the conservative story. Because the liberal story assumes that women form their job preferences through pre-work socialization, it accepts the notion that only women who are socialized the same as men desire such work. To secure legal victory under the liberal approach, women must present themselves as ungendered subjects without a distinctive history, experience, culture or identity. But this approach only validates the conservative notion that women who are "different" ("feminine") in nonwork aspects automatically have "different" ("feminine") work preferences, as well.

The EEOC's position in *Sears* illustrates this dynamic. The EEOC emphasized that, contrary to the district court's findings, it had *not* assumed that female sales applicants were as interested as males in commission sales jobs. Instead, the EEOC had recognized that the women were less interested than the men, and it had controlled for sex differences in interest by isolating the subgroup of female applicants who were similar to the males on a number of different background characteristics and who therefore could be presumed to be equally interested in commission sales.[221] The EEOC argued that "men and women who are alike with respect to [these] . . . characteristics . . . would be similar with respect to their interest in commission sales."[222] Judge Cudahy, in a dissent from the Seven Circuit's opinion, agreed.[223] Although he condemned the majority and the district court for "stereotyping" women,[224] his acceptance of the EEOC's argument suggests that the only women whose job interests were being inaccurately stereotyped were those whose earlier life experiences resembled men's.[225] Judge Cudahy's and the EEOC's position assumed that the women had formed specific preferences for commission or noncommission sales work before they applied at Sears. Indeed, Judge Cudahy expressed this assumption explicitly, emphasizing that the EEOC's case would have been much stronger if it had produced "even a handful of witnesses to testify that Sears had frustrated their *childhood dreams* of becoming commission sellers."[226] Once this assumption was accepted, it was impossible to analyze seriously the extent to which Sears had shaped the women's preferences. The only alternative was to identify the illusive group of women whose personal histories were so similar to men's that one might safely presume that they had been socialized to prefer the same jobs.

This liberal approach faces two strategic difficulties that leave working women vulnerable to the conservative explanation for segregation. The first may be termed a credibility problem. Insofar as the liberal story relies on an image of women as "ungendered," it is less believable than the conservative story. Like most people, judges tend to find implausible the suggestion that women have the same characteristics, experiences, and values as men. Employers are able to turn this perception to their advantage, by pointing out that even feminists have acknowledged that our sexist society socializes girls and women into "feminine" roles. In *Sears*, for example, the historian retained by Sears was able to cite the feminist consciousness-raising movement to the company's advantage, asserting that the very need for consciousness-raising was premised on the "recognition that men and women have internalized different personality traits and different attitudes."[228] In the end, it made no difference that the EEOC had controlled for sex differences in background, for the judge believed that even women whose life experiences resembled men's remained sufficiently "different" that they lacked interest in commission sales jobs.[229] The conservative story thus capitalizes on the widely-held perception of gender difference to imply that because girls are pressured to conform to "feminine" sex roles, adult women will aspire automatically to "feminine" work.

This same dynamic emerges more subtly in connection with the "different family roles" explanation for women's underrepresentation in nontraditional jobs. The liberal approach refuses to credit this explanation, but it fails to make clear whether this refusal is based on a denial that women have heavier family responsibilities than men or rather a rejection of the notion that women's concededly heavier family responsibilities lead them to choose female-dominated jobs.[230] This ambiguity weakens the liberal story, for women do assume a greater burden than men for sustaining family life.[231] Again, the result is greater credibility for the conservative story, which clearly acknowledges that domestic labor is gendered. The flaw in the conservative story is not that it unfairly "stereotypes" women as family caretakers, but rather that it portrays women's domestic roles as the fulfillment of a broader set of unalterable "feminine" values that dictates a preference for lower-paying, traditionally female jobs.

This leads to the second, related problem with the liberal story. Because it denies gender difference, the liberal approach misses the ways in which employers draw upon societal gender relations to produce sex segregation at work. The liberal prohibition against stereotyping assumes that the problem is that the employer has inaccurately identified the job interests of (at least some exceptional) women who have already formed preferences for nontraditional work. By stopping at this level of analysis, however, liberal courts fail to inquire into or discover the deeper processes through which employers actively shape women's work aspirations along gendered lines. The liberal approach to discriminatory recruiting exemplifies this overly narrow focus. Through their recruiting strategies, employers do more than simply publicize job vacancies to those who are already interested: they actually stimulate interest among those they hope to attract to the jobs. The harm of sexually discriminatory recruiting is not only, or even primarily, that it fails to provide information about nontraditional job openings to women who have already formed an interest in those jobs. The deeper harm of discriminatory recruiting is that it is part of a larger process of investing nontraditional jobs with such a masculinized image and culture that many women will never picture themselves as the sort of person the employer has in mind and will therefore never actualize their potential interest in such jobs.[232] Evidence shows that sex-segregated advertising depicting the "Man for the Job" in explicitly masculine terms has precisely this effect.[233] Nonetheless, even though courts have uniformly held that title VII prohibits sex-segregated advertising,[234] only two courts have come close to identifying its deeper harm.[235] Most have simply noted that it violates title VII's mandate of gender-neutral treatment, and have not really analyzed the nature of the injury.[236]

Just as sex-segregated advertising constructs an artificial masculine culture around nontraditional work, so, too, does word-of-mouth recruiting. Drawing on doctrine developed in the race discrimination context, a few liberal courts have invoked the discriminatory impact of word-of-mouth recruiting as a rationale for rejecting the lack of interest argument. These courts might have acknowledged that the harm of word-of-mouth recruiting is not merely that it fails to disseminate job information to women who are already interested in the work, but that it also actively (if informally) shapes the potential interest of women in applying. Word-of-mouth recruiting signals to women that they would be unwelcome in an occupational culture so masculine that the employer relies on male employees to recruit new workers through mostly male networks. However, the few courts that have condemned word-of-mouth recruiting have not extended their reasoning this far. They have portrayed word-of-mouth recruiting not as an active means of creating a gendered occupational culture, but rather as a passive failure to provide women formally equal access to information about job opportunities. They have reasoned that when the employer fails to publicize vacancies for nontraditional jobs, women who are already interested in those jobs will be less likely than men to be told about openings by existing male employees.[237]

Though these liberal courts deserve credit for recognizing that lack of awareness of opportunity poses a barrier for women seeking nontraditional jobs,[238] their failure to identify the deeper gender dynamics has restricted application of the word-of-mouth recruiting doctrine and left it on shaky ground. Ironically, other courts have used the liberal rhetoric of gender neutrality against itself to transform the word-of-mouth recruiting doctrine into a defense of sex segregation. In *Wilkins v. University of Houston*,[239] the plaintiffs alleged that "new faculty members often were selected through operation of an 'old boy network' by which exclusively male or male-dominated recruitment committees" overlooked women.[240] The evidence showed that as many as fifteen percent of all faculty openings had been filled with "preselected" candidates the same day the vacancy was announced, and almost half of all faculty positions had been filled by men without any women being considered.[241] The plaintiffs invoked a long line of Fifth Circuit race discrimination doctrine condemning these practices as discriminatory. But the court dismissed this doctrine as irrelevant, reasoning that "the obstacle of widespread segregation faced by potential black employees . . . is not present for women seeking university faculty positions . . . [because] . . . women . . . have been educated at the same institutions and by the same professors as their male counterparts."[242] In the world portrayed by the Fifth Circuit, old-boy networks are not part of college life; female students are just as likely as males to be favored by their (mostly male) professors.[243] By failing to recognize that gender dynamics permeate social life, the court blinded itself to the processes through which employers extend and strengthen those same dynamics into the workplace itself. In an effort to ground title VII in a vision of a gender-neutral world, the liberal story thus renders invisible the mechanisms of reproducing sex segregation at work.[244]

C. *The Need for a New Story*

. . . There is a need for a new story to make sense of sex segregation in the workplace. Gender conditioning in pre-work realms is too slender a reed to sustain the weight of sex segregation. To explain sex segregation, the law needs an account of how employers actively construct gendered job aspirations— and jobs—in the workplace itself.

An Alternative Account of Gender and Work

[A rich body of sociological research supports an alternative account of sex segregation in the workplace.] Unlike the liberal story, this account recognizes the reality of gender in social life. It acknowledges that women and men are subjected to different expectations and experiences, and that, as a result, they tend to express preferences for different types of work early in their lives. But unlike the conservative story, the new account does not find sex-role conditioning so monolithic or so powerful that it dictates irrevocably gendered job aspirations. Girls may be taught to be "feminine," but this does not imply that adult women will aspire only to traditionally female work throughout their adult lives. Rather, women's work preferences are formed, and created, and recreated in response to changing work conditions.

This new account traces gendered work attitudes and behaviors to organizational structures and cultures in the workplace. Like all workers, women adapt their work aspirations and orientations rationally and purposefully, but always within and in response to the constraints of organizational arrangements not of their own making. Providing women the formal opportunity to enter nontraditional jobs is a necessary but insufficient condition to empower them to claim those jobs, because deeper aspects of work systems pose powerful disincentives for women to enter and remain in nontraditional employment. The new account of work and gender thus reverses the causation implicit in the current judicial framework. Sex segregation persists not because most women bring to the workworld fixed preferences for traditionally female jobs, but rather because employers structure opportunities and incentives and maintain work cultures and relations so as to disempower most women from aspiring to and succeeding in traditionally male jobs.

The new account suggests a more transformative role for the law in dismantling sex segregation at work. Once we realize that women's work aspirations are shaped not solely by amorphous "social" forces operating in pre-work realms, but primarily by the structures of incentives and social relations within work organizations, it becomes clear that title VII can play a major role producing the needed changes. Title VII cases challenging segregation seek to alter (at least indirectly) the very structural conditions that prevent women from developing and realizing aspirations for higher-paid, more challenging nontraditional jobs. By attributing women's aspirations to forces external and prior to the workworld, courts deny their own ability to (re)construct workplace arrangements and the work aspirations that arise out of those arrangements. In a very real sense, the legal system has perpetuated the status quo of sex segregation by refusing to acknowledge its own power to dismantle it. . . .

. . .

1. The Structures of Mobility and Reward for Traditionally Female Jobs. It is an old insight that people who are placed in jobs that offer little opportunity for growth or upward mobility will adapt to their situations by lowering their work aspirations and commitment and turning their energies elsewhere. . . . Female-dominated jobs tend to be on distinct promotional ladders that offer far less opportunity for advancement than do male-dominated jobs.[298] In light of these unequal mobility structures, "[w]omen in low-mobility . . . situations develop attitudes and orientations that are sometimes said to be characteristic of those people as individuals or 'women as a group,' but that can more profitably be viewed as universal *human* responses to blocked opportunities."[299]

Kanter's study of secretaries in a major industrial corporation vividly portrays this point. The corporation recruited its secretaries from parochial high schools, attended mostly by young women accustomed to taking orders and who had had little opportunity to develop habits of independence and initiative. Once hired, secretaries had no opportunity to move upward in the organization. They could not switch to the managerial track. Their own ladder was short, with their formal rank derivative of their bosses': climbing to "the top" meant only snaring a boss who was higher up in the managerial hierarchy. Bosses rewarded secretaries for their attitudes instead of their skills, for their loyalty instead of their talent. An analysis of their performance evaluations showed that bosses valued them most highly for "enthusiasm" and "personal service orientation." In exchange, secretaries were offered non-utilitarian, symbolic rewards—such as "praise" and "love"—rather than money or career advance-ment.[300]

Looking at the corporation's secretaries, one would observe a group of women who tended to display work attitudes and behaviors that are commonly perceived to be attributes of "femininity." Many were narrowly devoted to their individual bosses, timid and self-effacing, dependent on praise, and given to emotionality and gossip. But it was their position within the organization and the structure of incentives attached to their jobs that led them to develop these orientations.[301] To be good secretaries, they were required to display the "feminine" behaviors that are commonly viewed as an extension of women's intrinsic personalities.[302]

. . . Kanter's secretaries adjusted to their realistically nonexistent possibility of advancement by rating the desirability of promotion relatively low.[303] Similarly, they began to value social relations at work over the intrinsic aspects of the job itself, developing close relationships with their peers in a counterculture that valued mutual aid and loyalty over individual mobility and "success."[304] The corporation's "folk wisdom" maintained that only women would be worried about taking a promotion because it would mean leaving their friends. But the men in low-opportunity positions exhibited the same concern.[305] Thus, women's work aspirations and orientations are, like men's, shaped by their opportunities for mobility and the social organization of their jobs.[306]

The stories of blue-collar tradeswomen illustrate the converse effect on women's aspirations, created by the opportunity to enter nontraditional jobs offering higher wages, challenge, and the chance for advancement. These women's interest and commitment to nontraditional work seemed almost fortuitous, the by-product of being lucky enough to encounter some opportunity to move into a job offering greater personal growth and rewards. However, the fact that they encountered such an opportunity was not mere happenstance, but a direct consequence of the fact that their employers felt legal pressures to hire women.[307] Many of these women cited the significance of affirmative action in influencing them to pursue nontraditional work. For them, sex-neutral recruiting efforts would have been insufficient. It was important for them to hear that the employer was actively seeking *women* workers—not just looking for workers in general (which they would have understood to mean men). When they heard that some nontraditional job was opening up specifically for women,[308] or saw other women performing nontraditional work,[309] or made contact with com-munity-based programs designed specifically to attract and support women in nontraditional work,[310] it occurred to many of them for the first time that they could aspire to nontraditional jobs.

Once they began doing nontraditional jobs, these women became highly motivated workers who defined work as a central life interest and who valued the intrinsic aspects of their work. Although many of the women had originally moved into nontraditional work because they needed the money, the job quickly became more than a paycheck. The women in Walshok's study valued four things most highly about their work: (1) productivity, or "a feeling of having done something constructive, of having accomplished something with one's time";[311] (2) challenge, or "a new or unusual experience, that requires a woman to stretch herself, to reach, to grow";[312] (3) autonomy, or the opportunity to work independently and to exercise discretion about how to control the timing and sequencing of one's work;[313] and (4) relatedness, or "feeling as if one's in 'the swim of things,' in the 'mainstream' of life."[314] Indeed, women may appreciate these features of nontraditional work even more than men do, because they contrast so favorably with the characteristics of female-dominated jobs available to working-class women.[315]

If there is tragedy in this account of how work aspirations and behaviors come to be gendered, there is also potential for hope. If women's work orientations are attributable not to their individual "feminine" characteristics, but rather to the structures of mobility and rewards attached to jobs, then the obvious solution is to change those structures.[316] Classwide title VII suits challenging sex discrimination in promotion hold the promise to do just that. In alleging that women on the female job ladder are systematically being denied promotion into better jobs on the male job ladder, plaintiffs are seeking to restructure internal career ladders so as to create new paths up and out of entry-level female jobs for all women (and not just an exceptional few).[317] Courts can order remedies that will prompt employers to restructure those ladders in ways that will infuse women workers with new hopes and aspirations.[318] In doing so, they may also stimulate employers to redefine the content of entry-level jobs traditionally done by women in less stereotypically feminine terms.[319]

Unfortunately, the courts all too often fail to respond, and in the process, they reproduce the very rationalizations for the two-tier system that keeps so many women in their place. When courts accept employers' arguments that women in female jobs lack interest in being promoted, they reinforce the sexist notion that there is something about womanhood itself that endows women with a penchant for low-paying, dead-end jobs. By refusing to intervene, they permit employers to continue to structure career ladders in ways that will encourage women to develop the depressed aspirations that can later be identified as "proof" that they preferred to be stuck at the bottom all along. Through their statements and their actions, these courts undercut women's ability to form and exercise the very choice they purport to defend.

2. The Work Cultures of Traditionally Male Jobs. While separate-but-unequal job structures encourage women to lower their work aspirations, they also imply that segregation is natural in a way that encourage male workers to adopt proprietary attitudes toward "their" jobs. These attitudes encapsulate male-dominated jobs in a web of social relations that are hostile and alienating to women who dare to upset the "natural" order of segregation. I refer to the entire bundle of practices and processes through which these relations are created and sustained as harassment.[320] Overtly sexual behavior is only the tip of a tremendous iceberg that confronts women in nontraditional jobs.[321] They face a wide-ranging set of behaviors and attitudes by their male supervisors and co-workers that make the culture of nontraditional work hostile and alienating.[322] The following statement by a woman welder captures a sense of what is involved:

It's a form of harassment every time I pick up a sledgehammer and that prick laughs at me, you know. It's a form of harassment when the journeyman is supposed to be training me and it's real clear to me that he does not want to give me any information whatsoever. . . . It's a form of harassment to me when the working foreman puts me in a dangerous situation and tells me to do something in an improper way and then tells me, Oh, you can't do that! It's a form of harassment when someone takes a tool out of my hand and said, Oh, I'm going to show you . . . and he grabs the sledgehammer from my hand and proceeded to . . . show me how to do this thing . . . you know, straighten up a post . . . it's nothing to it, you just bang it and it gets straight. . . . It's a form of harassment to me when they call me honey and I have to tell them every day, don't call me that, you know, I have a name printed right on my thing. . . . Ah, you know, it's all a form of harassment to me. It's not right. They don't treat each other that way. They shouldn't treat me that way.[323]

Harassment is a structural feature of the workplace that sex segregation engenders.[324] It creates a serious disincentive for women to enter and remain in nontraditional jobs. Even overtly sexual harassment is widespread.[325] Furthermore, women in male-dominated occupations are more likely to be subjected to harassment than are women in other occupations.[326] Women in female jobs understand that they will be likely to experience harassment if they attempt to cross the gender divide;[327] they may conclude that the price of deviance is too high. Harassment is also driving the small number of women in nontraditional jobs away.[328] Blue-collar tradeswomen report that women are leaving the trades because they cannot tolerate the hostile work cultures,[329] and there are signs that this is occurring in male-dominated professions as well.[330]

One of the most debilitating forms of harassment is conduct that interferes with a woman's ability to do her job. In nontraditional blue-collar occupations, virtually all the training is acquired informally on the job. Thus, a woman's ability to succeed depends on the willingness of her supervisors and co-workers to teach her the relevant skills. Yet women's stories of being denied proper training are legion.[331] Indeed, it is sometimes difficult to distinguish inadequate training from deliberate sabotage of women's work performance, both of which can endanger a woman's physical safety.[332] To the extent that foremen and co-workers succeed in undermining womens's job performance, they convert the notion that women are not cut out for nontraditional work into a self-fulfilling prophecy.

In nontraditional white-collar occupations, male workers—including elite professionals—also guard their territory against female incursion. Their conduct, too, runs the gamut from overtly sexual behavior,[333] to discriminatory work assignments and performance evaluations, to day-to-day personal interactions that send women the message that they are "different" and "out of place."[334] The white-collar equivalent of work sabotage may lie in evaluating women's work by differential and sexist standards, a practice which occurs even within the upper echelons of professional life.[335] Whatever men's motivations or sources of insecurity,[336] harassment is a central process through which the image of nontraditional work as "masculine" is sustained. If there are no women in the job, then the work's content can be described exclusively in terms of the "manly" personal characteristics of the men who do it. On the other hand, if women can do the work, it becomes far more difficult to define the job with reference to stereotypically masculine images.[337] As one female pipefitter observed:

> For a long time I wasn't allowed to do certain types of jobs . . . Some of the men would take the tools out of my hands. You see it is just very hard for them to work with me because they're really into proving their masculinity and being tough. And when a woman comes on a job that can work, get something done as fast and efficiently, as well, as they can, it really affects them. Somehow if a woman can do it, it ain't that masculine, not that tough.[338]

By driving women out of nontraditional jobs, harassment reinforces the idea that women are inferior workers who cannot meet the demands of a "man's job." More subtly, for women who stay in nontraditional jobs, harassment exaggerates gender differences to remind them that they are women who are out of place in a man's workworld. By labelling the women as "freaks" or "deviants,"[339] and simultaneously pressuring them to conform to the dominant male culture,[340] men mediate the contradiction posed by the presence of women doing "masculine" work. Thus, harassing behavior that marks nontraditionally employed women workers as exceptions for their gender—yet still *women* and therefore never quite as competent or as committed as the men—enables men to continue to define "their" work (and themselves) in masculine terms.

Cynthia Cockburn's study of engineers illustrates this process.[341] By defining women as inherently incapable of possessing technological competence, the men appropriated engineering as a masculine preserve. They viewed the relationship between manhood and technology in essentialist terms, as a natural affinity between "man" and "machine."[342] "In contrast to the way the men [perceived] themselves—as striving, achieving, engaging in the public sphere of work— they [viewed] women as static, domestic, private people, as nonworkers."[343] They defined women as "aspect[s] of the decor" who "create a pleasant atmosphere,"[344] as interested in and good at "boring and repetitive tasks,"[345] and as soft, weak creatures who " 'couldn't do' the *man*handling" required to master technology.[346] They exceptionalized the few women engineers as "performing seals," who must have been "train[ed] . . . up a bit" by some man behind the scene.[347] They also created an occupational culture built around "sexual stories, references and innuendo that are directly objectifying and exploitative of women."[348] By creating such a hostile work culture, the men ensured that few women would try to invade "their" jobs. They could then point to the absence of women as evidence that these jobs demand "masculine" skills and abilities not possessed by women.[349]

This analysis of the relationship between harassment and the "masculinity" of nontraditional work makes clear why many women are reluctant to apply for such work. Women understand that behind the symbolism of masculinized job descriptions lies a very real force: the power of men to harass, belittle, ostracize, dismiss, marginalize, discard, and just plain hurt them as workers. The legal system does not adequately protect women from this harassment and abuse.[350] Courts have erected roadblocks to recovery, abandoning women to

cope with hostile work environments on their own. The general attitude of
the legal system seems to mirror that held by many male workers and managers:[351]
if women want to venture into a man's workworld, they must take it as they
find it.[352]

The legal system thus places women workers in a Catch-22 situation. Women
are disempowered from pursuing or staying in higher-paid nontraditional jobs
because of the hostile work cultures. The only real hope for making those
work cultures more hospitable to women lies in dramatically increasing the
proportion of women in those jobs. Eliminating those imbalances is, of course,
what title VII lawsuits challenging segregation promise. But when women
workers bring these suits, too often the courts tell them that they are
underrepresented in nontraditional jobs not because the work culture is threatening or alienating, but rather because their own internalized sense of "femininity" has led them to avoid those jobs.

And so the cycle continues. A few women continue to move in and out
the "revolving door," with little being done to stop them from being shoved
back out almost as soon as they enter. The majority of working women stand
by as silent witnesses, their failure to enter used to confirm that they "chose"
all along to remain on the outside. There is no need for a sign on the door.
Women understand that they enter at their own risk.

Conclusion: The Implications
of the New Account for the Law

. . . The new account [of gender and work] has three implications for legal
analysis that, taken together, transform the current judicial framework for
interpreting sex segregation.

First, the new account frees courts to reject the conservative "choice"
explanation without resorting to the liberal suppression of gender difference.
Once judges acknowledge that women's early work preferences remain tentative
and temporary, they need not deny the force of gender in social life to hold
employers responsible for sex segregation in their workforces. Courts may
acknowledge that our society pressures girls to conform to appropriately
"feminine" roles, that it is women who assume the lion's share of the load of
caring for families, and even that it is important to most women to think of
themselves as "feminine," for none of these observations imply that women
will aspire only to the lower-paying, dead-end jobs considered appropriate for
their sex. To put it more positively, courts may acknowledge that women have
a distinctive history, culture and identity, without concluding as a corollary
that they are marginal workers content to do only unremunerative, unchallenging
jobs. The new account thus frees courts to portray "women" and "workers"
as involving no contradiction in terms.

Second, the new account demands deeper judicial scrutiny of the way
employers have structured their workplaces. Once the assumption that women
approach the labor market with fixed job preferences is abandoned, it will no
longer do to conceptualize discrimination in terms of whether the employer

has erected specific "barriers" that prevent individual women from exercising their preexisting preferences. Employers do not simply erect "barriers" to already-formed preferences: they create the workplace structures and relations out of which those preferences arise in the first place. Thus, in resolving the lack of interest argument, courts must look beyond whether the employer has provided women the formal opportunity to enter nontraditional jobs. Judges should be skeptical about employers' claims to have made efforts to attract women to nontraditional work. Such efforts are likely to be ineffective unless they enlist the participation of community organizations that serve working women and employ creative strategies to describe the work in terms that will appeal to women. Moreover, even extensive recruiting efforts will fail if the firm manages only to convey an all-too-accurate picture or organizational life that serves more as a warning than a welcome to women. Through its hiring criteria, training programs, performance evaluation standards, mobility and reward structures, response to harassment, and its managers' and male workers' day-to-day attitudes and actions, the firm may have created an occupational culture that debilitates most women from aspiring to nontraditional jobs. These sorts of work cultures can be changed, but only if courts recognize that the employers' practices create a disempowering culture for women. . . .

[This leads to the third and most fundamental implication of the new account:] that the legal system is itself inevitably implicated in creating women's work preferences. Once we understand that women form their job preferences in response to employers' practices, it becomes clear that courts participate in shaping women's job preferences all the time. Preference shaping is an avoidable part of the job judges do whenever they decide title VII cases challenging workplace segregation. Every time a plaintiff brings such a case, the legal system is confronted with a decision whether to affirm or alter the status quo. When courts accept the lack of interest argument, they permit employers to organize their workplaces in ways that disable women from forming an interest in nontraditional work. When courts impose liability instead, they prompt employers to restructure their workplaces in ways that empower women to aspire to nontraditional jobs. Judicial decisions that reject the lack of interest argument also create a climate in which it is more likely that employers not involved in litigation will undertake genuine affirmative action through creative efforts to dismantle old patterns of sexual hierarchy. That such efforts can free women's aspirations is clear from the reports of nontraditional women workers. Thus, judges' decisions are embedded in the fabric of organizational life through which women's hopes and dreams as workers are woven.

The new account of gender and work thus reminds judges that they, too, are the authors of women's work aspirations. This should bring a new sensitivity to the way judges exercise their responsibility to resolve the lack of interest issue. If this is a daunting responsibility, it is one that courts have been assuming since the very earliest days of title VII enforcement. Courts can acknowledge their own constitutive power and use it to help create a workworld in which the majority of working women are empowered to choose the more-highly-rewarded work that title VII has long been promising them. To create that world, they must refuse to proclaim that women already have that choice.

Notes

1. Although the degree of sex segregation declined modestly during the 1970's, work remains highly segregated by sex. Throughout the 1980's, for example, roughly 60% of all men and women workers would have been required to switch to occupations atypical for their sex to achieve sex-integrated occupations. *See, e.g.,* J. JACOBS, REVOLVING DOORS: SEX SEGREGATION AND WOMEN'S CAREERS 20, 28–29 (1989); Beller, *Trends in Occupational Segregation by Sex and Race, 1960–1981,* in SEX SEGREGATION IN THE WORKPLACE: TRENDS, EXPLANATIONS, REMEDIES II (B. Reskin ed. 1984) [hereinafter SEX SEGREGATION IN THE WORKPLACE]. As recently as 1985, over two-thirds of working women were employed in occupations in which at least 70% of the workers were female. *See* Jacobs, *Long-Term Trends in Occupational Segregation by Sex,* 95 AM. J. SOC. 160, 160 (1989). These estimates of occupational segregation understate the degree of sex segregation, because even workers employed in apparently sex-neutral occupations often work in industries, firms, departments, and jobs that are highly segregated by sex. *See, e.g.,* Bielby & Barron, *A Woman's Place Is with Other Women: Sex Segregation Within Organizations,* in SEX SEGREGATION IN THE WORKPLACE, *supra,* at 27, 35 (1982) (finding that in a random sample of 393 California firms, 90% of the workers were in job titles to which only one sex was assigned); Gutek & Morasch, *Sex Ratios, Sex-Role Spillover, and Sexual Harassment of Women at Work,* J. SOC. ISSUES, Winter 1982, at 55, 61–62 (finding that in a representative sample of 1232 Los Angeles workers, 42% of the women in male dominated occupations were nonetheless in female-dominated jobs). For general discussions of sex segregation at work, see B. BERGMANN, THE ECONOMIC EMERGENCE OF WOMEN (1986); P. ENGLAND & G. FARKAS, HOUSEHOLDS, EMPLOYMENT, AND GENDER: A SOCIAL, ECONOMIC AND DEMOGRAPHIC VIEW 121–196 (1986); J. JACOBS, *supra;* WOMEN'S WORK, MEN'S WORK: SEX SEGREGATION ON THE JOB (B. Reskin & H. Hartmann eds. 1986) [hereinafter WOMEN'S WORK, MEN'S WORK].

3. 628 F. Supp. 1264 (N.D. Ill. 1986), *aff'd,* 839 F.2d 302 (7th Cir. 1988).

4. Title VII is the major federal statute prohibiting discrimination in employment. It prohibits employers with 15 or more employees from discriminating on the basis of race, color, religion, sex, or national origin. *See* 42 U.S.C. secs. 2000e to 2000e-17 (1982).

5. Between 1973 and 1980, the median hourly wages for first-year commission salesworkers were about twice as high as those for all noncommission salesworkers. *See* Plaintiff's Pretrial Brief—Commission Sales Issues at 27, EEOC v. Sears, Roebuck & Co., 628 F. Supp. 1264 (N.D. Ill. 1986) (No. 79-C-4373).

6. Between 1973 and 1980, for example, women constituted 61% of all full-time sales applicants at Sears, but only 27% of the newly-hired full-time commission salesworkers. In contrast, women made up approximately 75% of Sears' noncommission salesforce. Brief for the Equal Employment Opportunity Comm'n as Appellant at 7, EEOC v. Sears, Roebuck & Co., 839 F.2d 302 (7th Cir. 1988) (Nos. 86-1519 and 86-1621) [hereinafter EEOC Brief].

10. *See* EEOC v. Sears, Roebuck & Co., 628 F. Supp. at 1324–25. The judge reached this conclusion despite evidence that women who worked at Sears needed to maximize their incomes. For example, a 1981 survey of married women employed in noncommission sales jobs showed that 28% had unemployed husbands, 35% had husbands who earned below the $20,260 national median income for men, and an additional 19% had husbands who earned below $25,000 per year. *See* Written Testimony of Eileen Appelbaum at 18–19 & n.27, EEOC v. Sears, Roebuck & Co., 628 F. Supp. 1264 (N.D. Ill. 1986) (No. 79-C-4373).

11. According to the judge, women shunned the "big ticket," "hard" lines of merchandise, such as home improvements, hardware, and men's clothing, which were

more likely to be sold on commission at Sears; they felt more comfortable with the "small ticket," soft lines, such as jewelery, cosmetics, and women's clothing, which were sold on a commission basis. *See Sears,* 628 F. Supp. at 1306. In addition, women "disliked the perceived 'dog-eat-dog competition' " and "financial risk" of commission sales, preferring the "security" and more "enjoyable and friendly" nature of noncommission sales. *See id.* at 1307.

14. Employers also resort to this argument to justify sex segregation outside the litigation context. As one researcher summarized managers' views, "The conclusion is: 'It's not our fault'. . . . [E]veryone places the blame far away from the workplace. A unanimous chorus repeats: it's the parents' fault, it's the teachers' fault, it's the fault of the careers advisers. And of course, fundamentally, it's women's fault: 'they are their own worst enemies.'" C. COCKBURN, MACHINERY OF DOMINANCE: WOMEN, MEN AND TECHNICAL KNOW-HOW 165 (1985). For similar descriptions of how managers have rationalized segregation, see V. BEECHEY & T. PERKINS, A MATTER OF HOURS: WOMEN, PART-TIME WORK AND THE LABOUR MARKET 102–19 (1987); and L. HOWE, PINK COLLAR WORKERS: INSIDE THE WORLD OF WOMEN'S WORK 90–91 (1977).

18. . . . Since the enactment of title VII, women of color have made far more progress entering occupations traditionally held by white women than they (or white women) have made in entering occupations traditionally held by men. Researchers typically estimate the extent of occupational segregation with a construct called the index of dissimilarity, which measures the proportion of workers who would have to switch to occupations atypical for their sex or race in order for occupations to be integrated. While the index of race segregation between minority women and white women workers declined substantially from 46.8 in 1960 to 17.2 in 1981, the index of sex segregation between minority women and minority men declined much more modestly during the same period from 54.0 to 47.9. *See* Albelda, *Occupational Segregation by Race and Gender, 1958–81,* 39 INDUS. & LAB. REL. REV. 404, 405–06 (1986). Similarly, while the index of race segregation between minority men and white men declined from 38.4 in 1960 to 23.8 in 1981, the index of sex segregation between white women and white men declined more modestly from 59.6 to 53.0. *See id.* The greatest difference in occupational distribution between any two groups was, of course, between minority women and white men: the index of segregation began at 67.2 in 1960 and declined to only 58.1 in 1981. *See id.* . . .

19. Historically, African-American women, immigrant women, and low-income native-born white women have engaged in wage work in large numbers, despite being relegated to undesirable jobs. *See, e.g.,* J. JONES, [LABOR OF LOVE, LABOR OF SORROW: BLACK WOMEN, WORK, AND THE FAMILY FROM SLAVERY TO THE PRESENT (1985)]; S. KENNEDY, IF ALL WE DID WAS TO WEEP AT HOME: A HISTORY OF WHITE WORKING CLASS WOMEN IN AMERICA (1979); A. KESSLER-HARRIS, OUT TO WORK: A HISTORY OF WAGE EARNING WOMEN IN THE UNITED STATES (1982); Milkman, *A Statistical Portrait,* in 2 N. HEWITT, WOMEN, FAMILIES, AND COMMUNITIES: READINGS IN AMERICAN HISTORY 249 (1989). Estimates of women's historical labor force participation are known to be too low because of the U.S. Census Bureau's practices of undercounting work done by women. *See, e.g.,* Bose, *Devaluing Women's Work: The Undercount of Women's Employment in 1900 and 1980,* in HIDDEN ASPECTS OF WOMEN'S WORK [95 (C. Bose, R. Feldberg & N. Sokoloff eds. 1987)].

103. This early race discrimination law may, however, have taken sex segregation as a given. Most of the cases involved jobs held by white men, and the courts probably did not envision women of color as among those who had been discriminatorily denied these jobs. In one case, the Second Circuit vacated a 30% hiring goal because it was based on the entire population of minorities in the local area, and thus included minority

women. Noting casually that "women have never sought to become steamfitters," the court held: "Absent racial discrimination, . . . the non-white members of the Union would have been drawn from the *male* workforce over 18 years of age in the Union's jurisdiction." Rios v. Enterprise Ass'n Steamfitters Local 638, 501 F.2d 622, 632 (2d Cir. 1974) (emphasis added). In other cases, minority women are mentioned only in connection with clerical jobs. *See, e.g.* United States v. Central Motor Lines, 338 F. Supp. 532, 548–52 (W.D.N.C. 1971). . . .

187. EEOC v. Mead Foods, Inc., 466 F. Supp. 1, 3 (W.D. Okla. 1977).

188. *See id.* at 4.

189. EEOC v. Service Container Corp., 19 Fair Empl. Prac. Cas. (BNA) 1614, 1616 (W.D. Okla. 1976). . . .

190. Mazus v. Department of Transp., 489 F. Supp. 376, 388 (M.D. Pa. 1979), *aff'd,* 629 F.2d 870 (3d Cir. 1980), *cert. denied,* 449 U.S. 1126 (1981).

191. St. Marie v. Eastern R.R. Ass'n, 650 F.2d 395, 403 (2d Cir. 1981).

192. [With the bona fide occupational qualification defense, the employer seeks to justify an overt policy of excluding all women by proving that "all or substantially all women would be unable to perform safely and efficiently the duties of the job involved." Weeks v. Southern Bell Tel. & Tel. Co., 408 F.2d 228, 235 (5th Cir. 1969), or that "the essence of the business operation would be undermined by not hiring members of one sex exclusively." Diaz v. Pan Am. World Airways, 442 F.2d 385, 388 (5th Cir. 1971), *cert. denied,* 404 U.S. 950 (1971); *accord* Dothard v. Rawlinson, 433 U.S. 321, 333 91977) (citing *Weeks* and *Diaz* formulations approvingly).]

193. In EEOC v. H.S. Camp & Sons, Inc., 542 F. Supp. 411 (M.D. Fla. 1982), for example, a meat processing plant explicitly barred women from a number of departments, on the ground that the jobs there were too physically demanding for women. The court accepted this reasoning, even though the company produced no evidence other than the owner's subjective opinion that women were incapable of doing these jobs. *See id.* at 429. Ironically, the company did hire women for other lower-paying departments in which the jobs appeared to require equal physical strength. Women predominated in the meat packing department, for instance, where they were required to carry boxes of meat weighing from 80 to 90 pounds. In the all-male receiving department, by contrast, the men did not rely on brute strength but used hydraulic jacks to unload heavy boxes from delivery trucks. In addition, the company had hired no women for at least three other departments which, according to the court's own description, required no particular physical prowess. *See id.* at 422.

194. Logan v. General Fireproofing Co., 6 Fair Empl. Prac. Cas. (BNA) 140, 144 (W.D.N.C. 1972).

195. *Id.*

196. EEOC v. Mead Foods, Inc., 466 F. Supp. 1, 3 (W.D. Okla. 1977).

197. I found only one blue-collar case in which an employer appealed to women's family roles to explain their alleged preferences for traditionally female work. *See* Parker v. Siemens-Allis, 601 F. Supp. 1377, 1385 (E.D. Ark. 1985) (noting the company's assertion in its affirmative action plan that women prefer electrical wiring to higher-paid machine-shop work because the former is "clean . . . [and] routine work, which once learned, gives the female the opportunity to plan the family budget, menu and other responsibilities directly related to family ties").

198. *See, e.g.,* Kraszewski v. State Farm. Ins. Co., 38 Fair Empl. Prac. Cas. (BNA) 197, 222 (N.D. Cal. 1985); EEOC v. Akron National Bank & Trust Co., 497 F. Supp. 733, 748 (N.D. Ohio 1980). It is not clear why employers use different explanations for sex segregation in the blue-collar and white-collar contexts. Perhaps employers have realized that it would be implausible to try to attribute sex segregation to women's

domestic roles in blue-collar settings, in which women with family responsibilities have long labored in jobs that demand as much of their time as the higher-paid jobs done by men. *See generally* L. WEINER, FROM WORKING GIRL TO WORKING MOTHER 86–87 (1985) (describing the relegation of married women to lower-paid blue-collar work before 1940). In numerous cases in this study, women were assigned to lower-paying female jobs in factories, even though those jobs were apparently on the same shifts as the higher-paying, male-dominated jobs. *See, e.g., Parker,* 601 F. Supp. at 1385; Chrapliwy v. Uniroyal, Inc., 458 F. Supp. 252, 266 (N.D. Ind. 1977); Ostapowicz v. Johnson Bronze Co., 369 F. Supp. 522, 527 (W.D. Pa. 1973), *aff'd in part and vacated in part on the other grounds,* 541 F.2d 394 (3d Cir. 1976); *cert. denied,* 429 U.S. 1041 (1977); *see also* Mitchell v. Mid-Continent Spring Co., 583 F.2d 275, 279 (4th Cir. 1978), *cert. denied,* 441 U.S. 922 (1979) (noting that plant permitted male-only machine set-up employees to transfer between the day and night shifts, but refused to permit female-only machine operators to do so, because "'there was a shortage of men. However, females were easier to hire'"). Conversely, employers may have realized that they could not plausibly defend women's absence from white-collar work with images of physical difference, because white-collar work is light, clean work of the type associated with femininity in the blue-collar context. Thus, in white-collar cases, employers have had to resort to imputed social and psychological characteristics to ground their conceptions of femininity and masculinity.

199. 528 F. Supp. 433 (E.D. Ark. 1981), *aff'd on other grounds,* 692 F.2d 529 (8th Cir. 1982).

200 *Id.* at 437.

201. EEOC v. Sears, Roebuck & Co., 628 F. Supp. 1264 (N.D. Ill. 1986), *aff'd,* 839 F.2d 302 (7th Cir. 1988).

202. *Id.* at 1308.

203. *See id.* at 1308 & n.42.

204. Rosalind Rosenberg was the historian who testified for Sears. The gist of her testimony is captured in the following excerpts: "Women's role in American society and in the American family unit has fostered the development of 'feminine' values that have been internalized by women themselves. . . . Throughout American history women have been trained from earliest childhood to develop the humane and nurturing values expected of the American mother. Women's participation in the labor force is affected by the values they have internalized. For example: Women tend to be more relationship-centered and men tend to be more work-centered. Women tend to be more interested than men in the cooperative, social aspects of the work situation. These differences in female and male self-perception present difficulties for women in traditionally masculine occupations." Offer of Proof Concerning the Testimony of Dr. Rosalind Rosenberg, EEOC v. Sears, Roebuck & Co., 628 F. Supp. 1264 (N.D. Ill. 1986) (No. C-4373) [hereinafter Testimony of Rosalind Rosenberg].

205. *Sears,* 628 F. Supp. at 1290.

206. *Id.* at 1300.

207. *Id.* at 1300 n.29.

208. The fact that Sears' characterization of the commission sales job varied dramatically from the way the job was defined in an earlier era shows that there is nothing necessary or inevitable about the way Sears characterized it. Susan Porter Benson has shown that from 1890 to 1940, when department stores were eager to attract women to retail sales jobs (including commission sales) in the expanding service sector, managers defined the essence of "good selling" in terms of stereotypically feminine traits rather than the masculine traits emphasized by Sears. *See* S. PORTER BENSON, COUNTER CULTURES: SALESWOMEN, MANAGERS, AND CUSTOMERS IN AMERICAN DEPARTMENT STORES 1890–1940, at 130–31 (1986).

209. *See, e.g.,* EEOC v. H.S. Camp & Sons, Inc., 542 F. Supp. 411, 446 (M.D. Fla. 1982); EEOC v. Mead Foods, Inc., 466 F. Supp. 1, 4 (W.D. Okla. 1977).

210. EEOC v. Cook Paint & Varnish Co., 24 Fair Empl. Prac. Cas. (BNA) 51, 56 (W.D. Mo. 1980).

211. Ostapowicz v. Johnson Bronze Co., 369 F. Supp. 522, 537 (W.D. Pa. 1973), *aff'd in part and vacated in part on other grounds,* 541 F.2d 394 (3d Cir. 1976), *cert. denied,* 429 U.S. 1041 (1977).

212. *See* C. MacKinnon, Sexual Harassment of Working Women 122–23 (1978).

213. The Supreme Court has adopted this form of anti-stereotyping reasoning in both the title VII and fourteenth amendment contexts. *See, e.g.,* City of Los Angeles Dep't of Water & Power v. Manhart, 435 U.S. 702, 707–08 (1978) (holding that under title VII "[e]ven a true generalization about the class in an insufficient reason for disqualifying an individual to whom the generalization does not apply"); Frontiero v. Richardson, 411 U.S. 677 (1973) (adopting a similar rationale in the fourteenth amendment context).

214. *Ostapowicz,* 369 F. Supp. at 537.

215. *See, e.g.,* Mitchell v. Mid-Continent Spring Co., 583 F.2d 275, 281–83 (6th Cir. 1978), *modified,* 587 F.2d 841 (6th Cir. 1978), *cert. denied,* 441 U.S. 922 (1979); EEOC v. Cook Paint & Varnish Co., 24 Fair Empl. Prac. Cas. (BNA) 28, 51, 56 (W.D. Mo. 1980); EEOC v. Rath Packing Co., 40 Fair Empl. Prac. Cas, (BNA) 559, 565 (S.D. Iowa 1979), *aff'd in part and rev'd in part on other grounds,* 787 F.2d 318 (8th Cir. 1986); Chrapliwy v. Uniroyal, Inc., 458 F. Supp. 252, 262–63 (N.D. Ind. 1977).

216. *See, e.g.,* Kohne v. Imco Container Co., 480 F. Supp. 1015, 1027–28 (W.D. Va. 1979); *Ostapowicz,* 369 F. Supp. at 537–38.

217. *Rath,* 40 Fair Empl. Prac. Cas. (BNA) at 566; *accord Mitchell,* 583 F.2d at 281; *Chrapliwy,* 458 F. Supp. at 278.

219. *See, e.g.,* Palmer v. Shultz, 815 F.2d 84, 110 (D.D.C. 1987); *Kohne,* 480 F. Supp. at 1027–28 & n.6 (W.D. Va. 1979); *Rath,* 40 Fair Empl. Prac. Cas. (BNA) at 565–66; *Ostapowicz,* 369 F. Supp. at 537–38. Employers tend to present testimony from women who were hired for traditionally female jobs, rather than from women who were rejected from employment altogether, as examples of women who "prefer" traditionally female work. But as Judge Thornberry has observed, the fact that women already working in traditionally female jobs have grown accustomed to them says little about whether women who were denied employment altogether "might well have taken [nontraditional jobs], if not precluded from doing so by a discriminatory hiring policy." Durant v. Owens-Illinois Glass Co., 656 F.2d 89, 91 (5th Cir. 1981) (Thornberry, J., dissenting).

220. As one court who accepted the lack of interest argument stated: "To be sure there are some females who would be interested in this type of physical [road maintenance] work, but a reliable percentage has not yet been developed." Mazus v. Department of Transp. 489 F. Supp. 376, 388 (M.D. Pa. 1979), *aff'd,* 629 F.2d 870 (3d Cir. 1980), *cert. denied,* 449 U.S. 1126 (1981). *See also* EEOC v. Sears, Roebuck & Co., 628 F. Supp. 1264, 1314 (N.D. Ill. 1966) (dismissing the EEOC's historical examples of women who have responded to nontraditional job opportunities as isolated instances involving only "small groups of unusual women" rather than "the majority of women"), *aff'd,* 839 F.2d 302 (7th Cir. 1988).

221. *See* EEOC Brief, *supra* note 6, at 127, 141. Among the characteristics the EEOC controlled for in its statistical analyses were age, education, job applied for, job type experience, product line experience, and expanded commission sales experience.

222. *See* EEOC Brief, *supra* note 6, at 38.

223. *See* EEOC v. Sears Roebuck & Co., 839 F.2d 302, 360–66 (7th Cir. 1988) (Cudahy, J., concurring in part and dissenting in part).

224. *See id.* at 361–62.

225. *See id.* at 362.

226. *Id.* (emphasis added).

228. Testimony of Dr. Rosalind Rosenberg, *supra* note 204, at 766; *see also* Davis v. City of Dallas, 483 F. Supp. 54, 61 (N.D. Tex. 1979) (attributing women's failure to apply for police work to "job preferences . . . born of attitudes conditioned by societal sexist values").

229. *See* EEOC v. Sears, Roebuck & Co., 628 F. Supp. 1264, 1302–08 (N.D. Ill. 1986), *aff'd,* 839 F.2d 302 (7th Cir. 1988).

230. *See, e.g.,* Palmer v. Shultz, 815 F.2d 84, 111 (D.C. Cir. 1987); EEOC v. Akron Nat'l Bank & Trust Co., 497 F. Supp. 733, 748 (N.D. Ohio 1980). *But see* Kraszewski v. State Farm Ins. Co., 38 Fair Empl. Prac. Cas (BNA) 197, 221 (N.D. Cal 1985) (acknowledging that women were interested in careers as insurance sales agents "despite difficult family situations").

231. Studies have universally found that women do far more childcare and other domestic work than men and that married men increase their share of housework very little in response to increases in their wives' paid employment. *See, e.g.,* B. BERGMANN, *supra* note 1, at 261–69; S. BERK, THE GENDER FACTORY: THE APPORTIONMENT OF WORK IN AMERICAN HOUSEHOLDS (1985); M. GEERKEN & W. GOVE, AT HOME AND AT WORK: THE FAMILY'S ALLOCATION OF LABOR (1983). *See generally* P. ENGLAND & G. FARKAS, *supra* note 1, at 94–99 (1986) (summarizing these studies and the prevailing explanations for men's low participation in housework).

232. This process works in the opposite direction, too, when employers create low-paying jobs and then recruit in a way that is designed to attract women. After title VII took effect a number of employers in the cases in this study transferred some of the responsibilities of an exclusively-male job to a new, much-lower-paid job, and then proceeded to construct the new job as a "female" job by recruiting and hiring all or mostly women. *See, e.g.,* Peltier v. City of Fargo, 396 F. Supp. 710, 713 (D.N.D. 1975), *aff'd in part and rev'd in part on other grounds,* 533 F.2d 374 (8th Cir. 1976) (involving a female car marker position carved out of a police officer job); Wetzel v. Liberty Mutual Ins. Co., 372 F. Supp. 1146, 1150–51 (W.D. Pa. 1974) (involving a female claims representative position carved out of a claims adjuster job), *aff'd,* 511 F.2d 199 (3d Cir. 1975), *vacated and remanded on other grounds,* 424 U.S. 737 (1976). There is evidence that managers construct new jobs as "female" by designing their recruiting strategies and even their location decisions specifically with women in mind, so that they may take advantage of the fact that women are a cheap source of labor. *See* Kelley, *Commentary: The Need to Study the Transformation of Job Structures,* in SEX SEGREGATION IN THE WORKPLACE, *supra* note 1, at 261, 264. Some multinational corporations justify hiring women for the least skilled jobs in ideological terms, citing women's "natural patience" and "manual dexterity"; they justify paying women low wages by claiming the women do not need to work and will quit when they get married anyway. *See* A. FUENTES & B. EHRENREICH, WOMEN IN THE GLOBAL FACTORY 11–15 (1983).

233. A classic study by Bem and Bem illustrates this point. Whereas only 5% of the women surveyed expressed interest in nontraditional telephone "lineman" and "frameman" jobs when the ad described those jobs in sex-biased language, 25% expressed interest when the language was sex-neutral, and fully 45% expressed interest when the ad was written to appeal to women. Bem & Bem, *Does Sex-biased Job Advertising 'Aid and Abet' Sex Discrimination,* 3 J. APPLIED SOC. PSYCHOLOGY 6 (1973). Even apparently sex-neutral language can communicate to women that they are not who the employer had in mind for the job. Cockburn describes the following ad for an electronics engineer: "Enthusiasm, along with creativity, drive and a clear understanding of your personal

contribution are needed in a business where technological limits are constantly being tested and new frontiers broken and explored." C. COCKBURN, *supra* note 14, at 181. As Cockburn states. "On the face of it, this is not discriminatory wording. But women know how women are usually defined—not with words like 'drive,' 'limits,' 'test'. [A] woman . . . is likely to read [this] as addressed not to women but to men. To many women it will be more of a warning than an invitation." *Id.*

234. It was not until 1969, however, that the EEOC guidelines on sex discrimination prohibited employers from placing neutrally-worded advertisements under "Male" or "Female" newspaper headings. Compare 29 C.F.R. 1604.4(b) (1966) (permitting advertising placements under "Male" and "Female" headings to convey "that some occupations are considered more attractive to persons of one sex than the other") *with* 29 C.F.R. 1604.5 (1989) (prohibiting such placements unless sex is a bona fide occupational qualification for the job).

235. See Wetzel 372 F. Supp. at 1150-1151, 1154 (recognizing that the company's use of separate, heavily gendered recruiting brochures was designed to communicate to women that the only position appropriate for them was the lower-paying claims representative job, but not the higher-paying claims adjuster job); *see also* Kraszewski v. State Farm Ins. Co., 38 Fair Empl. Prac. Cas. (BNA) 197, 230-31 (N.D. Cal. 1985) (using a similar analysis).

236. *See, e.g.,* Chrapliwy v. Uniroyal, Inc., 458 F. Supp. 252, 266-67, 284 (N.D. Ind. 1977); Hill v. Western Elec. Co., 12 Fair Empl. Prac. Cas. (BNA) 1175, 1179 (E.D. Va. 1976), *aff'd in part and rev'd in part on other grounds,* 596 F.2d 99 (4th Cir.), *cert. denied,* 444 U.S. 929 (1979); Peltier v. City of Fargo, 396 F. Supp. 710, 727 (D.N.D. 1975), *aff'd in part and rev'd in part on other grounds,* 533 F.2d 374 (8th Cir. 1976). . . .

237. As one court stated, "[n]o notices of vacancies were ever posted, nor had the Union ever recommended any of its women members for these positions [as meat-cutters]. Consequently plaintiffs were never informed of the vacancies for which they could apply." Babrocky v. Jewel Food Co., 773 F.2d 857, 867 (7th Cir. 1985). . . .

238. An extensive literature documents that male workers are more likely to share job information with other men than with women. For this reason, men are more likely to secure their jobs through personal contacts, while women are more likely to use formal job-search methods. For a summary of this literature, see Roos & Reskin, *Institutional Factors Contributing to Sex Segregation in the Workplace,* in SEX SEGREGATION IN THE WORKPLACE, cited above in note 1, at 235, 241-42, 245-46.

239. 654 F.2d 388 (5th Cir. 1981), *vacated on other grounds,* 459 U.S. 809 (1982).

240. See id. at 399.

241. See id. at 396 n.8, 399.

242. Id. at 400.

243. This, of course, is not true. The New York Times reported the findings of a recent study which is only "the latest in a steady stream of research over the last two decades showing that while they may be sitting side by side, male and female [college students] have substantially different educational experiences." Fiske, Lessons, N.Y. Times, Apr. 11, 1990, at B8, col. 1. . . .

244. Other courts also have refused to characterize word-of-mouth recruiting as sexually discriminatory. In EEOC v. Service Container Corp., 19 Fair Empl. Prac. Cas. (BNA) 1614 (W.D. Okla. 1976), for example, the plaintiff contended that the plant's reliance on its almost-exclusively male workforce to recruit new shop workers discriminated against women. The court disposed of this contention in a sentence, noting that the plaintiff herself "came to work as a referral." See id. at 1616. But the plaintiff had applied because she had learned specifically that the plant was replacing another female worker, not because she had heard that the plant was hiring workers generally. See id.

298. *See* Hartmann, *Internal Labor Markets and Gender: A Case Study of Promotion*, in GENDER IN THE WORKPLACE 59, 59–66 (C. Brown & J. Pechman eds. 1987) (reviewing studies documenting the existence of separate internal career ladders for men and women); Roos & Reskin, *supra* note 238, at 248–51 (same).

299. R. KANTER, MEN AND WOMEN OF THE CORPORATION 159 (1977) (emphasis in original). *See also* Laws, *Psychological Dimensions of Labor Force Participation of Women*, in EQUAL EMPLOYMENT OPPORTUNITY AND THE AT&T CASE [125, 141 (P. Wallace ed. 1976)] ("When women lower their occupational aspirations, this may reflect a realistic assessment of their chances for success").

300. *See* R. KANTER, *supra* note 299, at 69–91.

301. *See id.* at 91–99.

302. There are several ways in which employers have structured traditionally female jobs so as to require or encourage women to display behaviors that are commonly viewed as preexisting attributes of womanhood. *See, e.g.,* V. BEECHEY & T. PERKINS, *supra* note 14, at 45–76, 77–101 (showing how employers have built gender into the way they structure hours, achieving flexibility in male jobs by adding overtime to full-time jobs, but doing so in female jobs by constructing them as part-time); S. COHN, THE PROCESS OF OCCUPATIONAL SEX-TYPING 91–115 (1985) (showing how employers have forced women to quit work when they marry as a way of lowering labor costs in certain female jobs and have legitimated such "marriage bars" by describing women as uncommitted to wage work); B. GUTEK, SEX AND THE WORKPLACE 134–36, 142–46 (1985) (showing how employers have built sexual attractiveness into the very definition of what is required to do traditionally female job).

303. Kanter found that the mean score on a measure of motivation to be promoted was lower for non-managerial women workers (mostly secretaries) than for non-managerial men. However, the men's objective prospects for promotion were also better. Indeed, the women consistently rated their promotional prospects as more desirable than likely. They believed they had no chance of escaping low-level, female-dominated jobs. *See* R. KANTER, *supra* note 299, at 140–42.

304. *See id.* at 149–52.

305. *See id.* at 151.

306. *See id.* at 159.

307. Many women understood that they had obtained their jobs only as a result of legal pressures. *See, e.g.,* M. MARTIN, HARD-HATTED WOMEN: STORIES OF STRUGGLE AND SUCCESS IN THE TRADES 150 (1988) ("The company was pushing affirmative action, because it had a class-action suit brought against it by a group of women in the mines in 1973. I was hired four years after the suit was filed, but even then, there were only a few women working for the company."); *id.* at 71 ("The process of entering the San Francisco Police Department . . . started for me in 1973. That's when community groups got together and filed a suit to open up the job to women and minorities . . . ")

308. As one former secretary explained: "I didn't think about non-traditional work until I heard the carpenters were looking for women. . . . But as soon as the possibility was mentioned, my imagination went with it." J. SCHROEDEL, ALONE IN A CROWD: WOMEN IN THE TRADES TELL THEIR STORIES 35 (1985).

309. One woman described the transformative power of seeing women doing non-traditional work as follows: "When I came out here I fell in with some women who worked in the trades and they had some potlucks for women in the building trades and I went there and I saw all these women and I was real excited—I thought, 'Oh, yeah, that's who I am, I'm like those women over there.'" M. WALSHOK, BLUE-COLLAR WOMEN: PIONEERS ON THE MALE FRONTIER 137–38 (1981); *see also id.* at 163–64 (describing a similar transformation).

310. One woman who became a sailor explained: "[I]t wasn't until I moved to Seattle when I was surrounded by organizations and groups that seemed encouraging of this—just seeing flyers about workshops on women in nontraditional trades, having Mechanica available where you could learn the details about steps in joining a union. That's when it became a real possibility." J. SCHROEDEL, *supra* note 308, at 77; *see also* M. WALSHOK, *supra* note 309, at 167–68 (discussing the importance of community-based programs in inspiring and helping women enter nontraditional trades); Law, *"Girls Can't Be Plumbers"— Affirmative Action for Women in Construction: Beyond Goals and Quotas,* 24 HARV. C.R.-C.L.L. REV. 45, 45–46, 53–55, 72–76 (1989) (same).

311. M. WALSHOK, *supra* note 309, at 140.

312. *Id.* at 142.

313. *Id.* at 147–48.

314. *Id.* at 145. Other studies have reported that women in blue-collar trades value the challenge, freedom, and intrinsic rewards of the job, just as their male co-workers do. *See, e.g.,* K. DEAUX & J. ULLMAN, WOMEN OF STEEL: FEMALE BLUE-COLLAR WORKERS IN THE BASIC STEEL INDUSTRY 131–33 (1983). The women speak movingly of the exhilaration that comes with freedom and challenge on the job. M. MARTIN, *supra* note 307, at 167–68. One female firefighter stated: "For nine days, I was part of the biggest [fire] incident I ever expect to see. . . . I've never worked as hard as I did on some of those hot afternoons, pulling hose lines around in the mud and rocks. . . . Events that demand everything you can give leave you with an unconquerable feeling of exuberance that lasts well beyond the fatigue. Given the choice, there was no place in the world I would rather have been." *Id.; see also* J. SCHROEDEL, *supra* note 308, at 14 ("That is the greatest feeling in the world—the music, the sun, and wheeling along the freeway [in my truck]. . . . I like being on the road where you haven't got somebody looking over your shoulder, bitching all the time.").

315. *See* M. WALSHOK, *supra* note 309, at xix–xx.

316. For suggestions for how to change work structures in ways that will both reduce sex segregation and improve the quality of worklife for all workers, *see* C. COCKBURN, cited above in note 14, at 242–44; and R. KANTER, cited above in note 299, at 267–84.

317. In several cases, plaintiffs have alleged that women in entry-level female jobs were systematically denied promotion of transfer into higher-paid male jobs in separate career ladders. *See, e.g.,* Kyriazi v. Western Electric Co., 461 F. Supp. 894 (D.N.J. 1978), *aff'd on other grounds,* 647 F.2d 388 (3d Cir. 1981); Wetzel v. Liberty Mutual Ins. Co., 372 F. Supp. 1146 (W.D. Pa. 1974), *aff'd,* 511 F.2d 199 (3d Cir.), *vacated and remanded on other grounds,* 424 U.S. 1146 (1976); *see also* B. BERGMANN, *supra* note 1, at 106–10 (discussing these two cases). In other cases, women employed in what we think of as nontraditional positions (such as management) have alleged that they were disproportionately denied promotion into the upper echelons or were given discriminatory work assignments that decreased their chances for promotion later. *See, e.g.,* Palmer v. Shultz, 815 F.2d 84 (D.C. Cir. 1987); Leisner v. New York Tel. Co., 358 F. Supp. 359 (S.D.N.Y. 1973).

[318]. [There are many documented cases of dramatic increases in female participation in nontraditional jobs in response to court orders and court-supervised consent decrees. *See, e.g.,* COUNCIL ON ECONOMIC PRIORITIES, WOMEN AND MINORITIES IN BANKING: SHORTCHANGE/UPDATE 68 (1976) (recording a 166% increase in female participation in managerial, professional, technical and salesworker jobs, and an even greater increase in female participation in blue-collar jobs, at a major bank between 1971 and 1975); K. DEAUX & J. ULLMAN, [*supra* note 314, at 85] (recording a 170% increase in female participation in production, maintenance, and craft positions in two steel mills between 1976 and 1979); Appendix D. in EQUAL EMPLOYMENT OPPORTUNITY AND THE AT&T

CASE, *supra* note 299, at 343 (recording a 119% increase in female participation in craft jobs and a 46% increase in female participation in managerial jobs between 1973 and the end of 1974).]

319. *See* G. NIELSEN, FROM SKY GIRL TO FLIGHT ATTENDANT: WOMEN AND THE MAKING OF A UNION 81–103 (1982) (describing how early title VII decisions helped redefine the flight attendant job in less patronizing, more professional terms).

320. In contrast to my definition of harassment, the legal system focuses on conduct that is explicitly "sexual" in nature. EEOC guidelines, for example, define harassment in these terms: "[U]nwelcome *sexual* advances, requests for *sexual* favors, and other verbal or physical conduct of a *sexual* nature . . . when (1) submission to such conduct is made explicitly or implicitly a term or condition of an individual's employment, (2) submission to or rejection of such conduct by an individual is used as the basis for employment decisions affecting such individual, or (3) such conduct has the purpose or effect of unreasonably interfering with an individual's work performance or creating an intimidating, hostile, or offensive work environment." EEOC Guidelines on Discrimination Because of Sex, 29 C.F.R. sec. 1604.11(a) (1989) (emphasis added). Drawing on the guidelines, legal doctrine recognizes two different types of sexual harassment: (1) "quid pro quo" harassment, in which women workers are asked to grant sexual favors at the risk of forfeiting some employment benefit; and (2) "hostile environment harassment," in which conduct by supervisors or co-workers is "sufficiently severe or pervasive to alter the conditions of [the victim's] employment and create an abusive work environment." Meritor Savings Bank v. Vinson, 477 U.S. 57, 67 (1986) (quoting Hanson v. Dundee, 686 F.2d 849, 904 (11th Cir. 1982)); *see also* C. MACKINNON, *supra* note 212, at 32–47 (describing these forms of harassment).

321. For women in male-dominated jobs, harassment is less likely to take the form of supervisors' demands for sexual favors and more likely to take the form of sexual taunts and other actions by co-workers that are part of a larger pattern of hostility intended to drive the women away. Foremen and supervisors usually tolerate or cooperate in the harassment. *See* Crull, *Searching for the Causes of Sexual Harassment: an Examination of Two Prototypes,* in HIDDEN ASPECTS, *supra* note 19, at 225, 228–30; Pollack, *Sexual Harassment: Women's Experience vs. Legal Definitions,* 13 HARV. WOMEN'S L.J. 35, 37, 50 n. 51 (1990).

322. *See* M. MARTIN, *supra* note 307, at 10. This broader form of harassment is so much a part of the "normal" environment of traditionally male-dominated trades that some researchers do not even attempt to measure it. Mary Walshok observed, for example, that it is "normal" for men in blue-collar trades "to question the sincerity of the woman's interest and commitment to a man's job, to wonder about whether or not the woman was going to get married and take off or get pregnant, to question whether the woman had technical or mechanical competence or the physical strength and agility to do the job, and to resent women because they perceived them as taking away a job from one of their own." M. WALSHOK, *supra* note 309, at 211. This led Walshok to define the "negative work environments" as those that go beyond this "normal" treatment to involve "actual acts of hostility or sabotage, withholding of opportunities for information and training, persistent sexual innuendos, and open harassment." *Id.* at 211–12. Even using this narrow definition, Walshok found that approximately half of the women had negative relationships with their supervisors and co-workers during their first year on the job. *See id.* at 188, 221.

323. *Id.* at 221–22.

324. The literature documenting the effects of skewed sex ratios on work groups makes this clear. *See, e.g.,* B. GUTEK, *supra* note 302, at 129–52; R. KANTER, *supra* note 299, at 206–42.

325. This literature is now far too extensive to cite. Some of the earliest surveys documenting the existence of sexual harassment are described in C. MACKINNON, *supra* note 212, at 26–30. More recent studies include B. GUTEK, cited above in note 302; U.S. MERIT SYSTEM PROTECTION BD., SEXUAL HARASSMENT IN THE FEDERAL WORKPLACE: IS IT A PROBLEM? (1981); and U.S. MERIT SYSTEM PROTECTION BD., SEXUAL HARASSMENT IN THE FEDERAL WORKPLACE: AN UPDATE (1988).

326. *See, e.g.,* Gutek & Morasch, *supra* note 1, at 67–68 (finding that women in male-dominated occupations and jobs were more likely to report harassment and to have experienced negative consequences from it than women in other work settings); Martin, *Sexual Harassment: The Link Joining Gender Stratification, Sexuality, and Women's Economic Status,* in WOMEN: A FEMINIST PERSPECTIVE 57, 61 (J. Freeman 4th ed. 1989) (citing studies showing that the greater the proportion of men in a work group, the more likely women were to be harassed).

327. *See, e.g.,* O'Farrell & Harlan, *Craftworkers and Clerks: The Effect of Male Co-Worker Hostility on Women's Satisfaction with Nontraditional Jobs,* 29 SOC. PROBS. 252, 259 (1982) (finding that half the women in white-collar, female-dominated occupations who considered moving into blue-collar, male-dominated occupations expected that they would be subjected to harassment if they did so).

328. *See, e.g.,* B. GUTEK, *supra* note 302, at 119 ("By making insulting comments and touching women sexually, some men may try to 'make life miserable' for women in the [nontraditional] jobs, encouraging them to leave. The relatively high turnover rate among women in [these jobs] suggests that this is a successful strategy to force women out."); GUTEK & MORASCH, *supra* note 1, at 68 (finding that 20% of women in nontraditional work quit a job at some point because of sexual harassment, while only 9% of the larger sample did so). . . .

329. *See, e.g.,* M. MARTIN, *supra* note 307, at 11; Eisenberg, *Women Hard Hats Speak Out,* NATION, Sept. 18, 1989, at 272–73; Pollack, *supra* note 321, at 37–38.

330. A recent newspaper article noted, for example, that a growing number of women engineers have become so discouraged by their discriminatory treatment that they are leaving engineering to pursue alternative careers. *See* Arundel, *Stagflation for Female Engineers,* N.Y. Times, Oct. 1, 1989, at F32. Other studies have documented the disproportionate attrition of women from law firms, *see, e.g.,* Menkel-Meadow, *Exploring a Research Agenda on the Feminization of the Legal Profession: Theories of Gender and Social Change,* 14 LAW & SOC. INQUIRY 289, 307 (1989); Weisenhaus, *Still a Long Way to Go for Women, Minorities,* Nat'l L. J., Feb. 8, 1988, at 48, and there is evidence that women leave in part because of discrimination. *See, e.g.,* Liefland, *Career Patterns of Male and Female Lawyers,* 35 BUFFALO L. REV. 601, 609–611 (1986); Quade, *Myth v. Ms.: Why Women Leave the Law,* 13 BARRISTER 28 (1986).

331. In Walshok's study, when the women were asked about the negative aspects of their job during the first year, the most frequently voiced criticism (expressed by 68% of the women) was that they felt they were being trained poorly. *See* M. WALSHOK, *supra* note 309, at 188.

332. Stories like carpenter Sue Eisenberg's are still far too common: "For some men, getting rid of the invaders was a personal mission. Ron, one of my first foremen, constantly warned me of the ways I might get killed in this dangerous trade: be electrocuted, have my head severed from my body, be boiled alive by steam. Without giving any instruction on how to do it safely, he told me one day to open up a 200-foot-long-snake. . . . A snake is a thin piece of steel, used by electricians to pull wires through pipes. It comes tightly coiled, bound with wire ties, and if not opened carefully, will spring apart with great force. 'I had a Chinese kid open one up,' Ron told the crew, laughing. 'He got it caught up his nose and wound up in the hospital. Quit right

after that.' I haven't opened up a snake since without remembering how I sweated through it that first time, while my co-workers hid." Eisenberg, *supra* note 329, at 272. For other stories of how women have been subjected to acts by foremen or co-workers that threatened them with, or caused them, physical harm, see, for example, M. MARTIN, *supra* note 307, at 33–34 ("[The men] didn't want the women to replace them, so they pulled stunts. Someone cut the chain holding up a big motor mount I was welding. It fell down on me and burned my arm to the bone."); *id.* at 257 ("I had to start checking all the parts on my machine because Dick would loosen stuff on it, which could kill you."); J. SCHROEDEL, cited above in note 308, at 256–57 ("I went in the women's room, and I cried, because a man pushed me under a machine. . . . The men admit they think it's a man's job and a woman has no right out there.").

333. For example, one of Atlanta's most prestigious corporate law firms, King & Spaulding, planned to hold a "wet-T-shirt" contest featuring its female summer associates, even while the firm faced a sex discrimination lawsuit in the Supreme Court. *See* Burleigh & Goldberg, *Breaking the Silence: Sexual Harassment in Law Firms*, A.B.A. J., Aug. 1989, at 46. (The lawsuit was Hishon v. King & Spaulding, 467 U.S. 69 (1984)). After complaints, the firm decided to hold a swimsuit competition instead. One of the firm's partner's later told the Wall Street Journal that the "winner" of the competition had been offered a job upon graduation, remarking: "She has the body we'd like to see more of." Burleigh & Goldberg, *supra*, at 46.

334. In one recent case, the lone female resident in a general surgery program was forced to endure sexual advances and touching; sexually explicit drawings of her body and other pornography in public meeting rooms; her supervisors' refusal to talk to her, permit her to operate, or assign her work tasks; discriminatory standards for evaluating her performance; sabotage of her work, including falsification of medical records to make it appear as though she and another female resident had made an error, *see* Lipsett v. University of Puerto Rico, 864 F.2d 881, 886–94 (1st Cir. 1988), and "a constant verbal attack, one which challenged their capacity as women to be surgeons, and questioned the legitimacy of their being in the Program at all," *id.* at 905.

335. *See, e.g.*, Price-Waterhouse v. Hopkins, 109 S.Ct. 1775 (1989). Ann Hopkins sued Price-Waterhouse, perhaps the nation's most prestigious public accounting firm, claiming that she was discriminatorily denied partnership. Among other outstanding achievements, she had helped secure a multi-million dollar contract with the Department of State, an accomplishment that none of the other candidates for partnership that year had matched. *See id.* at 1782. But, when it came time to consider her for partnership, her male colleagues evaluated her by criteria by which no man would be judged: "One partner described her as 'macho' . . . ; another suggested that she 'overcompensated for being a woman' . . . ; a third advised her to take 'a course at charm school'. . . . Several partners criticized her use of profanity . . . [Another advised her] to 'walk more femininely, talk more femininely, dress more femininely, wear make-up, have her hair styled, and wear jewelry.' " *Id.* (citations omitted).

336. Some researchers emphasize that men are motivated by economic incentives, because they feel that their job security and high wages are threatened by the presence of women. *See, e.g.*, R. MILKMAN, GENDER AT WORK: THE DYNAMICS OF JOB SEGREGATION BY SEX DURING WORLD WAR II 7–8, 158 (1987). Other writers have stressed more patriarchal motives, arguing that traditional sex roles "spill over" into the workplace. *See, e.g.*, B. GUTEK, *supra* note 302, at 149–51.

337. *See* V. BEECHEY & T. PERKINS, *supra* note 14, at 102–119; C. WILLIAMS, GENDER DIFFERENCES AT WORK: WOMEN AND MEN IN NONTRADITIONAL OCCUPATIONS 88–103 (1989). These studies show how the cultural constructions of the same job vary depending upon whether men or women do it. For example, one machine tools company that

employed only men as crane operators explained that women did not want to drive cranes because "that was hot, heavy, dirty work and women didn't do that sort of work." V. BEECHEY & T. PERKINS, *supra* note 14, at 105. But another such company that employed women defined the job in feminine terms, and suggested that women were actually better crane operators because they had a "sensitive touch" learned through knitting. *See id.* at 106.

338. J. SCHROEDEL, *supra* note 308, at 20–21; *see also* C. WILLIAMS, *supra* note 337, at 61 (noting that the Marine Corps segregates basic training because "[r]egardless of whether training standards are compromised in fact, the sight of women mastering the feats of basic training makes it appear that the training is not rigorous enough").

339. One of the tactics men use to make nontraditional women workers feel deviant is "lesbian-baiting." M. MARTIN, *supra* note 307, at 14. Lesbian-baiting is only one extreme example, however, of behavior intended to divide and alienate women. *See* Pollack, *supra* note 321, at 78 & n.178.

340. Kanter discusses how male workers subject token women to "loyalty tests," in which they are required to affirm their loyalty to the dominant culture by turning against other women. Pressuring women to tolerate sexist jokes and comments are examples. R. KANTER, *supra* note 299, at 227–29. Racist jokes and comments are often used in the same manner. The invitation to participate in racist "humor" is one of the ways white women are often "welcomed into the club." M. MARTIN, *supra* note 307, at 13. The pervasive racism of many nontraditional blue-collar environments of course makes them particularly difficult for women of color, who often encounter a virulent combination of sexual and racial stereotyping. For some of their stories, see *id.*, at 71–80, 118–21, 150–55, 187–92; J. SCHROEDEL, *supra* note 308, at 99–139. One of the most shocking stories is police officer Rose Melendez's. One night her partner drove her to a secluded area and stopped the patrol car. When Melendez asked why they were stopping, he said he wanted to shoot rats. He then opened his shirt, pulled out a handgun, and pointed it directly at her, saying "I just want to see how fast you women cops can run." M. MARTIN, *supra* note 307, at 74.

341. *See* C. COCKBURN, *supra* note 14.

342. *Id.* at 172.

343. *Id.* at 185.

344. *Id.*

345. *Id.* at 186.

346. *Id.* at 101 (emphasis in original).

347. *Id.* at 188.

348. *Id.* at 176.

349. The contradictions within the men's ideological justifications are exposed as the men's careers unfold. Early in their careers, when they do hands-on machine work, male engineers defend the masculinity of their jobs in terms of a hard/soft dichotomy that defines "hard," physical work as masculine and "soft," intellectual work as feminine. In middle age, however, many of these same engineers must move on to managerial desk jobs that they once denigrated as unmanly. *Id.* at 195. They then adopt an intellectual/ non-intellectual dichotomy that, ironically, associates masculinity with the intellectual and femininity with the physical. *See id.* at 196–97.

350. It remains unclear, for example, whether hostile but not sexually explicit behavior of the type so often encountered by nontraditional women workers even falls within title VII's definition of sexual harassment. *Compare* McKinney v. Dole, 765 F.2d 1129 (D.C. Cir. 1985) (holding that actions that are hostile but not explicitly sexual may constitute sexual harassment prohibited by title VII) *with* Rabidue v. Osceola Refining Co., 805 F.2d 611, 619 (6th Cir. 1986) (implicitly refusing to recognize as harassment

hostile conduct that is not explicitly sexual in nature). For a discussion of this issue, see Austin, *Employer Abuse, Worker Resistance, and the Tort*, 41 STAN. L. REV. 1, 12–13 (1988); Pollack, cited above in note 321, at 75 & n.164.

351. *See, e.g.,* Collins & Blodgett, *Sexual Harassment: Some See It . . . Some Won't*, 59 HARV. BUS. REV. 76, 90 (1981) (noting that majority of managers responding to a survey said that women employees should be able to handle on their own whatever sexual harassment they face).

352. The clearest expression of this attitude appears in the Sixth Circuit's opinion in Rabidue v. Osceola Refining Co., 805 F.2d 611 (6th Cir. 1986), *cert. denied*, 481 U.S. 1041 (1987). The plaintiff was the only woman with managerial responsibilities over male employees in a refining company. Despite the fact that the work environment was extremely hostile and degrading to women, the court held that it was not so offensive as to have interfered with the work performance, or to have affected seriously the "psychological well-being of, a reasonable employee." *Id.* at 620. To support this holding, the majority quoted favorably the following passage from the district court's opinion: ". . . [I]t cannot seriously be disputed that in some environments, humor and language are rough hewn and vulgar. Sexual jokes, sexual conversation and girlie magazines may abound. Title VII was not meant to—or can—change this. . . . Title VII is the federal court mainstay in the struggle for equal employment opportunity for the female workers of America. But . . . Title VII was [not] designed to bring about a magical transformation in the social mores of American workers." *Id.* at 620–21 (quoting Osceola v. Rabidue, 584 F. Supp. 419, 430 (E.D. Mich. 1984)).

Further Reading for Part One

Equality and Liberal Theory

Feminist equality theory in the 1970s modeled itself explicitly after the antidiscrimination doctrine developed in earlier decades to handle race discrimination. This scholarship is exemplified in Judge Ruth Ginsburg's defense of an Equal Rights Amendment to the U.S. Constitution, especially in "Gender and the Constitution," 44 *U. Cin. L. Rev.* 1 (1975), and "Sex Equality and the Constitution," 52 *Tulane L. Rev.* 451 (1978); see also Barbara Brown, Thomas Emerson, Gail Falk, and Ann Freedman, "The Equal Rights Amendment: A Constitutional Basis for Equal Rights for Women," 80 *Yale L.J.* 871 (1971), and Richard Wasserstrom, "Racism, Sexism, and Preferential Treatment: An Approach to the Topics," 24 *U.C.L.A. L. Rev.* 581 (1977).

A fuller explanation by Wendy Williams of how the equal rights approach is applied to pregnancy is found in "Equality's Riddle: Pregnancy and the Equal Treatment/Special Treatment Debate," 13 *N.Y.U. Rev. Law & Soc. Change* 325 (1985). See also Wendy Williams and Nadine Taub, "Will Equality Require More than Assimilation, Accommodation, or Separation from the Existing Social Structure?" 37 *Rutgers L. Rev.* 825 (1985), which argues that Title VII affirmative action analysis, aimed at removing the effects of past discrimination, is preferable to the permanent institution of "special" or "favored" treatment for women, and Wendy Williams, "Firing the Woman to Protect the Fetus: The Reconciliation of Fetal Protection with Employment Opportunity Goals Under Title VII," 69 *Geo. L.J.* 641 (1981), which applies the antidiscrimination principles of Title VII to fetal protection rules.

Cynthia Fuchs Epstein explains how feminist approaches that stress similarities between men and women are required, rather than proved inadequate, by the significant disparities in the material circumstances of men's and women's lives; see *Deceptive Distinctions: Sex, Gender, and the Social Order* (1988). In a more controversial defense of the equal rights model, Wendy Kaminer argues that the feminist abandonment of equal rights is an expression of various modern anxieties, especially women's anxiety over reproduction; see *A Fearful Freedom: Women's Flight from Equality* (Reading, Mass.: Addison-Wesley, 1990). For a more conventional defense of liberal feminism, see David Kirp, Mark Yudof, and Marlene Franks, *Gender Justice* (Chicago: Univ. of Chicago Press, 1986).

The most comprehensive overview of the successes and failures of the equal rights approach in American law is Deborah L. Rhode's *Justice and Gender: Sex Discrimination and the Law* (Cambridge: Harvard Univ. Press, 1989). Works from other disciplines that explore liberal feminism and its alternatives include Alison Jaggar's classic work *Feminist Politics and Human Nature* (Totowa, N.J.: Rowman & Allenheld, 1983); Rosemarie Tong's *Feminist Thought: A Comprehensive Introduction* (Boulder, Colo.: Westview, 1989); Josephine

Donovan's *Feminist Theory: The Intellectual Traditions of American Feminism* (New York: Ungar, 1985); and a collection edited by Anne Phillips, *Feminism and Equality* (New York: New York Univ. Press, 1987). Zillah Eisenstein's books are also helpful in exploring the many faces of liberal feminism, including both its contradictions and its radical potential: *Feminism and Sexual Equality: Crisis in Liberal America* (New York: Monthly Review Press, 1984); *The Radical Future of Liberal Feminism* (Boston: Northeastern Univ. Press, 1986); *The Female Body and the Law* (Berkeley: Univ. of California Press, 1988). See also Jennifer Nedelsky, "Reconceiving Autonomy: Sources, Thoughts, and Possibilities," 1 *Yale J. L. & Feminism* 7 (1989), which attempts to revise the view of autonomy upon which liberal theory is premised, and Elizabeth Fox-Genovese, *Feminism Without Illusions: A Critique of Individualism* (Chapel Hill: University of North Carolina Press, 1991), which pursues a parallel attack on the premise of liberal individualism.

Equality and Woman's Difference

One of the earliest statements of the "special treatment" or "special rights" approach to equality was Elizabeth H. Wolgast's *Equality and the Rights of Women* (Ithaca, N.Y.: Cornell Univ. Press, 1980). Other examples include Ann Scales, "Toward a Feminist Jurisprudence," 56 *Indiana L.J.* 375 (1980–1981); Kathryn Powers, "Sex Segregation and the Ambivalent Directions of Sex Discrimination," 1979 *Wis. L. Rev.* 55; Linda Krieger and Patricia Cooney, "The *Miller-Wohl* controversy: Equal Treatment, Positive Action, and the Meaning of Women's Equality," 13 *Golden Gate U.L. Rev.* 513 (1983); and Herma Hill Kay, "Equality and Difference: The Case of Pregnancy," 1 *Berkeley Women's L.J.* (1985). See also Kay, "Models of Equality," 1985 *Ill. L. Rev.* 39.

Not all of the feminist writing based upon an emphasis of women's differences or "special" needs has related to pregnancy. Deborah Rhode in "Association and Assimilation," 81 *Nw. U.L. Rev.* 10 (1986), suggests a defense of all-women's schools, based in part on women's particular needs. Nancy Erickson in "The Feminist Dilemma over Unwed Parents' Custody Rights: The Mother's Rights Must Take Priority," 2 *L. & Inequality* 477 (1984), defends the position that mothers' rights should take priority in custody disputes with unwed fathers. Martha Fineman has written extensively about the institutional biases against women in custody decisionmaking and the need for woman-centered approaches to custody law. See especially her "Dominant Discourse, Professional Language, and Legal Change in Child Custody Decisionmaking," 101 *Harv. L. Rev.* 727 (1988); "Implementing Equality: Ideology, Contradiction, and Social Change: A Study of Rhetoric and Results in the Regulation of the Consequences of Divorce," 1983 *Wis. L. Rev.* 789; "The Politics of Custody and the Transformation of American Custody Decisionmaking," 22 *U.C. Davis L. Rev.* 829 (1989); and, with Anne Opie, "The Uses of Social Science Data in Legal Policymaking: Custody Determinations at Divorce," 1987 *Wis. L. Rev.* 107. A book that explores the failure of the neutrality principle for women in the family more generally is Susan Moller Okin, *Justice, Gender, and Family* (New York: Basic Books, 1989).

Feminist thinking about how women are different from men has expanded beyond the often-cited work by Carol Gilligan, *In a Different Voice: Psychological Theory and Women's Development* (Cambridge: Harvard Univ. Press, 1982), and Nancy Chodorow, *The Reproduction of Mothering: Psychoanalysis and the Sociology of Gender* (Berkeley: Univ. of California Press, 1978). *Mapping the Moral Domain: A Contribution of Women's Thinking to Psychological Theory and Education* (Cambridge: Harv. Univ. Pres, 1988) is a collection of essays edited by Carol Gilligan, Janie Victoria Ward, and Jill McLean Taylor that extend and revise the implications of Gilligan's earlier research. In *Making Connections: The Relational Worlds of Adolescent Girls at Emma Willard School* (Cambridge:

Harv. Univ. Press, 1990), Gilligan and coauthors Nona P. Lyons and Trudy J. Hanmer explore the findings of a long-term, intense study of the social processes of identity formation among a group of privileged, female adolescents. Another related work on women's differences is Mary Field Belenky, Blythe McVicker Clinchy, Nancy Rule Goldberger, and Jill Mattuck Tarule, *Women's Ways of Knowing: The Development of Self, Voice, and Mind* (New York: Basic Books, 1986). For a collection of essays by Nancy Chodorow that show the development of her psychoanalytic theories about the construction of gender roles, see *Feminism and Psychoanalytic Theory* (New Haven: Yale Univ. Press, 1989).

Some feminist legal scholars have used Gilligan's research to suggest that the greater participation of women in law—as law students, law professors, practicing attorneys, and judges—will help transform law by reflecting a greater emphasis on care and responsibility. Carrie Menkel-Meadow has written extensively on changes women have brought to legal education and the lawyering profession. See "Portia in a Different Voice: Speculations on a Woman's Lawyering Process," 1 *Berkeley Women's L.J.* 39 (1985), and "Feminist Legal Theory, Critical Legal Studies, and Legal Education or 'The Fem-Crits Go to Law School,'" 38 *J. Legal Educ.* 61 (1985). One of the first empirical studies meant to test speculations in this area is Dana and Rand Jack's *Moral Vision and Professional Decisions: The Changing Values of Women and Men Lawyers* (New York: Cambridge Univ. Press, 1989). Jane Maslow Cohen in "Feminism and Adaptive Heroinism: The Paradigm of Portia as a Means of Introduction," 25 *Tulsa L.J.* 657 (1990), stresses the normative relevance of this project by exploring questions of a feminist professional ethos in the practice of law.

Judith Resnik in "On the Bias: A Comment on Feminist Theory and Judging," 61 *So. Cal. L. Rev.* 1877 (1988), offers a provocative study of the implications of feminist theory for judging, using the work of Gilligan, West, Rosemary Reuther, and Sara Ruddick. In "Housekeeping: The Nature and Allocation of Work in Federal Trial Courts," 24 *Ga. L. Rev.* 909 (1990), Resnik analyzes the gender implications of the divisions in federal trial court work between the "important" cases and routine "housekeeping" duties. Pat Cain in "Good and Bad Bias: A Comment on Feminist Theory and Judging," 61 *So. Cal. L. Rev.* 1845 (1988), considers the subject of judging with particular attention to the question of whether there is a legitimate distinction between "good" and "bad" bias. Also linking Gilligan's research to judging, Suzannah Sherry argues in "Civic Virtue and the Feminine Voice in Constitutional Adjudication," 72 *Va. L. Rev.* 543 (1986), that there is a distinctively "feminine" jurisprudence, apparent even among conservative female judges such as Justice Sandra Day O'Connor, which is characterized by a focus on responsibility and human interdependency rather than abstract and universal principles.

Examples of legal scholarship promoting values of care and responsibility as a basis for substantive legal reforms include Lucinda Finley, "Transcending Equality Theory: A Way Out of the Maternity and the Workplace Debate," 86 *Colum. L. Rev.* 1118 (1986), which argues in favor of greater collective responsibility for pregnant women and families; Leslie Bender, "Feminist (Re)Torts: Thoughts on the Liability Crisis, Mass Torts, Power, and Responsibilities," 1990 *Duke L.J.* 848, which reconceptualizes mass tort law following similar principles; and Katharine T. Bartlett, "Re-Expressing Parenthood," 98 *Yale L.J.* 293 (1988), which urges a shift in ideology and rhetoric from rights to responsibilities in the area of child custody law.

A famous, fascinating, and sometimes tense exchange among feminist scholars about the implications of Gilligan's research for the law was published as the 1984 James McCormick Mitchell Lecture at the law school of the State University of New York in Buffalo. See Ellen C. DuBois, Marcy C. Dunlap, Carol J. Gilligan, Catharine A. MacKinnon, and Carrie J. Menkel-Meadow, "Feminist Discourse, Moral Values, and the Law—A

Conversation," 34 *Buffalo L. Rev.* 11 (1985). Kathleen Daly in "Criminal Justice Ideologies and Practices in Different Voices: Some Feminist Questions About Justice," 17 *International J. Soc. L.* 1 (1989), challenges Gilligan's model of gender-specific moral reasoning in the context of criminal law and practice. For a collection of essays edited by Eva Kittay and Diana Meyers that evaluates the most recent research in men's and women's moral reasoning and the philosophical implications of this research, see *Women and Moral Theory* (Totowa, N.J.: Rowman & Littlefield, 1987); for another exploration of the philosophical implications, see Jean Grimshaw, *Philosophy and Feminist Thinking* (Minneapolis: Univ. of Minnesota Press, 1986).

Equality and Dominance

Catharine MacKinnon's dominance approach to equality analysis was first set forth in her path-breaking work defining sexual harassment as discrimination based on sex, *Sexual Harassment of Working Women: A Case of Sex Discrimination* (New Haven: Yale Univ. Press, 1979). Some feminist scholars have developed approaches related to MacKinnon's dominance approach. These include Stephanie Wildman's "participatory perspective," found in "The Legitimation of Sex Discrimination: A Critical Response to Supreme Court Jurisprudence," 63 *Ore. L. Rev.* 265 (1984); Ruth Colker's "anti-subordination" principle, found in "Anti-Subordination Above All: Sex, Race, and Equal Protection," 61 *N.Y.U. L. Rev.* 1003 (1986); and Sylvia Law's "perpetuation of oppression" test, found in "Rethinking Sex and the Constitution," 132 *U. Pa. L. Rev.* 955, 1008–1009 (1984). Ann Scales has relied more directly on MacKinnon's dominance perspective in "The Emergence of Feminist Jurisprudence: An Essay," 95 *Yale L.J.* 1373 (1986), and "Militarism, Male Dominance and Law: Feminist Jurisprudence as Oxymoron?" 12 *Harv. Women's L.J.* 25 (1989). Nancy Ehrenreich in "Pluralist Myths and Powerless Men: The Ideology of Reasonableness in Sexual Harassment Law," 99 *Yale L.J.* 1177 (1990), questions why the "reasonable person" test in sexual harassment law "is still seen as the prototypical expression of the law's fairness and objectivity rather than . . . as a mechanism for facilitating the coercive exercise of social power," and Jane Aiken in "Differentiating Sex from Sex: The Male Irresistible Impulse," 12 *N.Y.U Rev. Law & Soc. Change* 357 (1983–1984), applies MacKinnon's dominance approach by showing how the concept of the uncontrollable male sexual impulse facilitates the continued disregard of women's rights in the law. See also Iris Marion Young, *Justice and the Politics of Difference* (Princeton, N.J.: Princeton Univ. Press, 1990), which presents a political philosophy based upon the concepts of domination and oppression. Further references to MacKinnon's dominance approach in the context of pornography, and response thereto, are found in the Further Reading section following Part Two.

Equality and Racial Difference

The subject of how the law should approach the discrimination claims of individuals who are both women and black or members of other minority groups is receiving increasing attention in feminist legal scholarship. Judy Scales-Trent in "Black Women and the Constitution: Finding Our Place, Asserting Our Rights," 24 *Harv. C.R.-C.L. L. Rev.* 9 (1989), and "Comparable Worth: Is This a Theory for Black Workers?" 8 *Women's Rts. L. Rep.* 51 (1984–1985), and Cathy Scarborough in "Conceptualizing Black Women's Employment Experiences," 98 *Yale L.J.* 1457 (1989), offer particularly forceful critiques of the interaction between race and sex in the employment law context. Numerous other articles challenge the law's current ability to deal with issues that confront black women in ways not experienced either by black men or by white women. Katrina Grider in "Hair Salons and Racial Stereotypes: The Impermissible Use of Racially Discriminatory Pricing Schemes," 12 Harv. Women's L.J. 75 (1989), for example, examines in the context of discriminatory pricing schemes at hair salons how laws purporting to protect blacks in fact submerge ethnic and cultural diversities, offering protection to blacks only insofar as they are the same as whites. Jennifer Wriggins in "Rape, Racism, and the Law," 6 Harv. Women's L.J. 103 (1983), analyzes the extent to which rape law presupposes the black rapist and the white female victim, thus targeting black men for punishment and leaving black women particularly vulnerable and without redress. See also Kristin Bumiller, "Rape as a Legal Symbol: An Essay on Sexual Violence and Racism," 42 U. Miami L. Rev. 75 (1987), which argues that the cultural meaning of rape is "rooted in a symbiosis of racism and sexism that has tolerated the acting out of male aggression against women and, in particular, black women," and Barbara Omolade, "Black Women, Black Men, and Tawana Brawley—The Shared Condition," 12 Harv. Women's L.J. 11 (1989), which criticizes white feminists for ignoring the special problems of black female rape victims.

Equality, Home, and Work

The EEOC v. Sears case has been the subject of considerable feminist scholarship concerned with sexual difference and equality. One of the most widely known articles is Joan Scott's "Deconstructing Equality-Versus-Difference: Or, The Uses of Post-Structuralist Theory for Feminism," 14 Fem. Stud. 33, 44 (Spring 1988), which explores the destructive impact of the debate between equality and difference in the context of sex segregation in the workplace. Instead of engaging in this debate, Scott argues, feminists should be engaged in "the unmasking of the power relationship constructed by posing equality as the antithesis of difference." Lucinda Finley in "Transcending Equality Theory: A Way Out of the Maternity and the Workplace Debate," 86 Colum. L. Rev. 1118 (1986), advocates a move away from the identification of sameness and difference in workplace debates, toward a focus on social responsibility. Sheila McCloud, who also focuses on workplace issues, finds all models of sexual equality to be "idealist," in the sense that their success depends upon conditions that simply do not exist; in "Feminism's Idealist Error," 14 N.Y.U. Rev. Law & Soc. Change 277 (1986), McCloud urges feminist strategies to identify what women really need for their material and economic advancement in the workplace.

Among other important works in law exploring gendered workplace injustices, Mary Joe Frug's "Securing Job Equality for Women: Labor Market Hostility to Working Mothers," 59 Boston U. L. Rev. 55 (1979), is a scathing, still-relevant critique of workplace hostility to women. Regina Austin stresses abuse in her analysis of workplace discrimination, "Employer Abuse, Worker Resistance, and the Tort of International Infliction of Emotional Distress," 41 Stan. L. Rev. 1 (1988). Articles that demonstrate powerfully the extent to which the "neutral" workplace is, in fact, deeply male-centered, and the inadequacy of existing antidiscrimination law to deal with the gender bias that permeates the workplace, include Kathyrn Abrams, "Gender Discrimination and the Transformation of Workplace Norms," 42 Vanderbilt L. Rev. 1183 (1989); Nancy Dowd, "Work and Family: The Gender Paradox and the Limitations of Discrimination Analysis: Restructuring the Workplace," 24 Harv. C.R.-C.L. L. Rev. 79 (1989); and Maxine Eichner, "Getting Women Work That Isn't Women's Work: Challenging Gender Biases in the Workplace Under Title VII," 97 Yale L.J. 1397 (1988).

Two collections provide rich discussions of many work and family issues. One is a symposium about legislative approaches to work and the family found at 26 Harv. J.

Legis. 295 (1989). The other is a collection of essays edited by Naomi Gerstel and Harriet Gross, *Families and Work* (Philadelphia: Temple Univ. Press, 1987), which provides an interdisciplinary set of perspectives on the relationship between work, family, and the economy. From the social sciences, the most recent studies of sex segregation and pay inequities in the workplace include Sara M. Evans and Barbara J. Nelson, *Wage Justice: Comparable Worth and the Paradox of Technocratic Reform* (Chicago: Univ. of Chicago Press, 1989); Jerry A. Jacobs, *Revolving Doors: Sex Segregation and Women's Careers* (Stanford, Calif.: Stanford Univ. Press, 1989); Alice Kessler-Harris, *A Woman's Wage: Historical Meanings and Social Consequences* (Lexington: Univ. Press of Kentucky, 1990); *Pay Equity: Empirical Inquiries,* ed. Robert T. Michael, Heidi I. Hartmann, and Brigid O'Farrell (Washington, D.C.: National Academy Press, 1989); and Christine L. Williams, *Gender Differences at Work: Women and Men in Nontraditional Occupations* Berkeley: Univ. of California Press, 1989).

Sylvia Law in "Women, Work, Welfare, and the Preservation of Patriarchy," 131 *U. Pa. L. Rev.* 1249 (1983), offers a powerful analysis of how federal labor and welfare policy coalesce to "resolve" the work-family conflict in favor of impeding women's access to the wage labor market. A more recent collection of essays on this subject is *Women, the State, and Welfare,* ed. Linda Gordon (Madison: Univ. of Wisconsin Press, 1990).

PART TWO

Questioning the Legal Subject

8

On Being the Object of Property [1988]

Patricia J. Williams

On Being Invisible

Reflections

For some time I have been writing about my great-great-grandmother. I have considered the significance of her history and that of slavery from a variety of viewpoints on a variety of occasions: in every speech, in every conversation, even in my commercial transactions class. I have talked so much about her that I finally had to ask myself what it was I was looking for in this dogged pursuit of family history. Was I being merely indulgent, looking for roots in the pursuit of some genetic heraldry, seeking the inheritance of being special, different, unique in all that primogeniture hath wrought?

I decided that my search was based in the utility of such a quest, not mere indulgence, but a recapturing of that which had escaped historical scrutiny, which had been overlooked and underseen. I, like so many blacks, have been trying to pin myself down in history, place myself in the stream of time as significant, evolved, present in the past, continuing into the future. To be without documentation is too unsustaining, too spontaneously ahistorical, too dangerously malleable in the hands of those who would rewrite not merely the past but my future as well. So I have been picking through the ruins for my roots.

What I know of my mother's side of the family begins with my great-great-grandmother. Her name was Sophie and she lived in Tennessee. In 1850, she was about twelve years old. I know that she was purchased when she was eleven by a white lawyer named Austin Miller and was immediately impregnated by him. She gave birth to my great-grandmother Mary, who was taken away from her to be raised as a house servant.[1] I know nothing more of Sophie (she was, after all, a black single mother—in today's terms—suffering the anonymity of yet another statistical teenage pregnancy). While I don't remember what I was told about Austin Miller before I decided to go to law school, I do remember that just before my first day of class, my mother said, in a voice full of secretive reassurance, "The Millers were lawyers, so you have it in your blood."[2]

When my mother told me that I had nothing to fear in law school, that law was "in my blood," she meant it in a very complex sense. First and foremost, she meant it defiantly; she meant that no one should make me feel inferior because someone else's father was a judge. She wanted me to reclaim that part of my heritage from which I had been disinherited, and she wanted me to use it as a source of strength and self-confidence. At the same time, she was asking me to claim a part of myself that was the dispossessor of another part of myself; she was asking me to deny that disenfranchised little black girl of myself that felt powerless, vulnerable and, moreover, rightly felt so.

In somewhat the same vein, Mother was asking me not to look to her as a role model. She was devaluing that part of herself that was not Harvard and refocusing my vision to that part of herself that was hard-edged, proficient, and Western. She hid the lonely, black, defiled-female part of herself and pushed me forward as the projection of a competent self, a cool rather than despairing self, a masculine rather than a feminine self.

I took this secret of my blood into the Harvard milieu with both the pride and the shame with which my mother had passed it along to me. I found myself in the situation described by Marguerite Duras, in her novel *The Lover*: "We're united in a fundamental shame at having to live. It's here we are at the heart of our common fate, the fact that [we] are our mother's children, the children of a candid creature murdered by society. We're on the side of society which has reduced her to despair. Because of what's been done to our mother, so amiable, so trusting, we hate life, we hate ourselves."[3]

Reclaiming that from which one has been disinherited is a good thing. Self-possession in the full sense of that expression is the companion to self-knowledge. Yet claiming for myself a heritage the weft of whose genesis is my own disinheritance is a profoundly troubling paradox.

Images

A friend of mine practices law in rural Florida. His office is in Belle Glade, an extremely depressed area where the sugar industry reigns supreme, where blacks live pretty much as they did in slavery times, in dormitories called slave ships. They are penniless and illiterate and have both a high birth rate and a high death rate.

My friend told me about a client of his, a fifteen-year-old young woman pregnant with her third child, who came seeking advice because her mother had advised a hysterectomy—not even a tubal ligation—as a means of birth control. The young woman's mother, in turn, had been advised of the propriety of such a course in her own case by a white doctor some years before. Listening to this, I was reminded of a case I worked on when I was working for the Western Center on Law and Poverty about eight years ago. Ten black Hispanic women had been sterilized by the University of Southern California–Los Angeles County General Medical Center, allegedly without proper consent, and in most instances without even their knowledge.[4] Most of them found out what had been done to them upon inquiry, after a much-publicized news story in which an intern charged that the chief of obstetrics at the hospital pursued a policy of recommending Caesarian delivery and simultaneous sterilization for any pregnant woman with three or more children and who was on welfare. In the course of researching the appeal in that case, I remember learning that one-quarter of all Navajo women of childbearing age—literally all those of childbearing age ever admitted to a hospital—have been sterilized.[5]

As I reflected on all this, I realized that one of the things passed on from slavery, which continues in the oppression of people of color, is a belief structure rooted in a concept of black (or brown, or red) anti-will, the antithetical embodiment of pure will. We live in a society in which the closest equivalent of nobility is the display of unremittingly controlled willfulness. To be perceived as unremittingly will-less is to be imbued with an almost lethal trait.

Many scholars have explained this phenomenon in terms of total and infantilizing interdependency of dominant and oppressed.[6] Consider, for example, Mark Tushnet's distinction between slave law's totalistic view of personality and the bourgeois "pure will" theory of personality: "Social relations in slave society rest upon the interaction of owner with slave; the owner, having total dominion over the slave. In contrast, bourgeois social relations rest upon the paradigmatic instance of market relations, the purchase by a capitalist of a worker's personality. Slave relations are total, engaging the master and slave in exchanges in which each must take account of the entire range of belief, feeling, and interest embodied by the other; bourgeois social relations are partial, requiring only that participants in a market evaluate their general productive characteristics without regard to aspects of personality unrelated to production."[7]

Although such an analysis is not objectionable in some general sense, the description of master-slave relations as "total" is, to me, quite troubling. Such a choice of words reflects and accepts—at a very subtle level, perhaps—a historical rationalization that whites had to, could do, and did do everything for these simple, above-animal subhumans. It is a choice of vocabulary that fails to acknowledge blacks as having needs beyond those that even the most "humane" or "sentimental" white slavemaster could provide.[8] In trying to describe the provisional aspect of slave law, I would choose words that revealed its structure as rooted in a concept of, again, black anti-will, the polar opposite of pure will. I would characterize the treatment of blacks by whites in whites' law as defining blacks as those who had no will. I would characterize that treatment not as total interdependency, but as a relation in which partializing judgments, employing partializing standards of humanity, impose generalized inadequacy on a race: if pure will or total control equals the perfect white person, then impure will and total lack of control equals the perfect black man or woman. Therefore, to define slave law as comprehending a "total" view of personality implicitly accepts that the provision of food, shelter, and clothing (again assuming the very best of circumstances) is the whole requirement of humanity. It assumes also either that psychic care was provided by slave owners (as though a slave or an owned psyche could ever be reconciled with mental health) or that psyche is not a significant part of a whole human.

Market theory indeed focuses attention away from the full range of human potential in its pursuit of a divinely willed, invisibly handed economic actor. Master-slave relations, however, focused attention away from the full range of black human potential in a somewhat different way: it pursued a vision of blacks as simple-minded, strong-bodied economic actants.[9] Thus, while blacks had an indisputable generative force in the marketplace, their presence could not be called activity; they had no active role in the market. To say, therefore, that "market relations disregard the peculiarities of individuals, whereas slave relations rest on the mutual recognition of the humanity of master and slave"[10] (no matter how dialectical or abstracted a definition of humanity one adopts) is to posit an inaccurate equation: if "disregard for the peculiarities of individuals" and "mutual recognition of humanity" are polarized by a "whereas," then somehow regard for peculiarities of individuals must equal recognition of humanity. In the context of slavery this equation mistakes whites' overzealous and oppressive obsession with projected specific peculiarities of blacks for actual holistic regard for the individual. It overlooks the fact that most definitions of humanity require something beyond mere biological sustenance, some healthy measure of autonomy beyond that of which slavery could institutionally or otherwise conceive. Furthermore, it overlooks the fact that both slave and bourgeois systems regarded certain attributes as important and disregarded certain others, and that such regard and disregard can occur in the same glance, like the wearing of horseblinders to focus attention simultaneously toward and away from. The experiential blinders of market actor and slave are focused in different directions, yet the partializing ideologies of each makes the act of not seeing an unconscious, alienating component of seeing. Restoring a unified social vision will, I think, require broader and more scattered resolutions than the simply symmetry of ideological bipolarity.

Thus, it is important to undo whatever words obscure the fact that slave law was at least as fragmenting and fragmented as the bourgeois worldview— in a way that has persisted to this day, cutting across all ideological boundaries. As "pure will" signifies the whole bourgeois personality in the bourgeois worldview, so wisdom, control, and aesthetic beauty signify the whole white personality in slave law. The former and the latter, the slavemaster and the Burgermeister, are not so very different when expressed in those terms. The reconciling difference is that in slave law the emphasis is really on the inverse rationale: that irrationality, lack of control, and ugliness signify the whole slave personality. "Total" interdependence is at best a polite way of rationalizing such personality splintering; it creates a bizarre sort of yin-yang from the dross of an oppressive schizophrenia of biblical dimension. I would just call it schizophrenic, with all the baggage that connotes. That is what sounds right to me. Truly total relationships (as opposed to totalitarianism) call up images of whole people dependent on whole people; an interdependence that is both providing and laissez-faire at the same time. Neither the historical inheritance of slave law nor so-called bourgeois law meets that definition.

None of this, perhaps, is particularly new. Nevertheless, as precedent to anything I do as a lawyer, the greatest challenge is to allow the full truth of partializing social constructions to be felt for their overwhelming reality—reality that otherwise I might rationally try to avoid facing. In my search for roots, I must assume, not just as history but as an ongoing psychological force, that, in the eyes of white culture, irrationality, lack of control, and ugliness signify not just the whole slave personality, not just the whole black personality, but me.

Vision

Reflecting on my roots makes me think again and again of the young woman in Belle Glade, Florida. She told the story of her impending sterilization, according to my friend, while keeping her eyes on the ground at all times. My friend, who is white, asked why she wouldn't look up, speak with him eye to eye. The young woman answered that she didn't like white people seeing inside her.

My friend's story made me think of my own childhood and adolescence: my parents were always telling me to look up at the world; to look straight at people, particularly white people; not to let them stare me down; to hold my ground; to insist on the right to my presence no matter what. They told me that in this culture you have to look people in the eye because that's how you tell them you're their equal. My friend's story also reminded me how very difficult I had found that looking-back to be. What was hardest was not just that white people saw me, as my friend's client put it, but that they looked through me, that they treated me as though I were transparent.

By itself, seeing into me would be to see my substance, my anger, my vulnerability, and my wild raging despair—and that alone is hard enough to show, to share. But to uncover it and to have it devalued by ignore-ance, to hold it up bravely in the organ of my eyes and to have it greeted by an impassive stare that passes right through all that which is me, an impassive stare that moves on and attaches itself to my left earlobe or to the dust caught in the rusty vertical geysers of my wiry hair or to the breadth of my freckled brown nose—this is deeply humiliating. It re-wounds, relives the early childhood anguish of uncensored seeing, the fullness of vision that is the permanent turning-away point for most blacks.

The cold game of equality-staring makes me feel like a thin sheet of glass: white people see all the worlds beyond me but not me. They come trotting at me with force and speed; they do not see me. I could force my presence, the real me contained in those eyes, upon them, but I would be smashed in the process. If I deflect, if I move out of the way, they will never know I existed.

Marguerite Duras, again in *The Lover*, places the heroine in relation to the family. "Every day we try to kill one another, to kill. Not only do we not talk to one another, we don't even look at one another. When you're being looked at you can't look. To look is to feel curious, to be interested, to lower yourself."[11]

To look is also to make myself vulnerable; yet not to look is to neutralize the part of myself which is vulnerable. I look in order to see, and so I must look. Without that directness of vision, I am afraid I will will my own blindness, disinherit my own creativity, and sterilize my own perspective of its embattled, passionate insight.

On Ardor

The Child

One Saturday afternoon not long ago, I sat among a litter of family photographs telling a South African friend about Marjorie, my godmother and my mother's cousin. She was given away by her light-skinned mother when she was only six. She was given to my grandmother and my great-aunts to be raised among her darker-skinned cousins, for Marjorie was very dark indeed. Her mother left the family to "pass," to marry a white man—Uncle Frederick, we called him with trepidatious presumption yet without his ever knowing of our existence—an heir to a meat-packing fortune. When Uncle Frederick died thirty years later and the fortune was lost, Marjorie's mother rejoined the race, as the royalty of resentful fascination—Lady Bountiful, my sister called her—to regale us with tales of gracious upper-class living.

My friend said that my story reminded him of a case in which a swarthy, crisp-haired child was born, in Durban, to white parents. The Afrikaner government quickly intervened, removed the child from its birth home, and placed it to be raised with a "more-suitable," browner family.

When my friend and I had shared these stories, we grew embarrassed somehow, and our conversation trickled away into a discussion of laissez-faire economics and governmental interventionism. Our words became a clear line, a railroad upon which all other ideas and events were tied down and sacrificed.

The Market

As a teacher of commercial transactions, one of the things that has always impressed me most about the law of contract is a certain deadening power it exercises by reducing the parties to the passive. It constrains the lively involvement of its signatories by positioning enforcement in such a way that parties find themselves in a passive relationship to a document: it is the contract that governs, that "does" everything, that absorbs all responsibility and deflects all other recourse.

Contract law reduces life to fairy tale. The four corners of the agreement become parent. Performance is the equivalent of obedience to the parent. Obedience is dutifully passive. Passivity is valued as good contract-socialized behavior; activity is caged in retrospective hypotheses about states of mind at the magic moment of contracting. Individuals are judged by the contract unfolding rather than by the actors acting autonomously. Nonperformance is disobedience; disobedience is active; activity becomes evil in contrast to the childlike passivity of contract conformity.

One of the most powerful examples of all this is the case of Mary Beth Whitehead, mother of Sara—of so-called Baby M. Ms. Whitehead became a vividly original actor *after* the creation of her contract with William Stern;

unfortunately for her, there can be no greater civil sin. It was in this upside-down context, in the picaresque unboundedness of breachor, that her energetic grief became hysteria and her passionate creativity was funneled, whorled, and reconstructed as highly impermissible. Mary Beth Whitehead thus emerged as the evil stepsister who deserved nothing.

Some time ago, Charles Reich visited a class of mine.[12] He discussed with my students a proposal for a new form of bargain by which emotional "items"— such as praise, flattery, acting happy or sad—might be contracted for explicitly. One student, not alone in her sentiment, said, "Oh, but then you'll just feel obligated." Only the week before, however (when we were discussing the contract which posited that Ms. Whitehead "will not form or attempt to form a parent-child relationship with any child or children"), this same student had insisted that Ms. Whitehead must give up her child, because she had *said* she would: "She was obligated!" I was confounded by the degree to which what the student took to be self-evident, inalienable gut reactions could be governed by illusions of passive conventionality and form.

It was that incident, moreover, that gave me insight into how Judge Harvey Sorkow, of New Jersey Superior Court, could conclude that the contract that purported to terminate Ms. Whitehead's parental rights was "not illusory."[13]

(As background, I should say that I think that, within the framework of contract law itself, the agreement between Ms. Whitehead and Mr. Stern was clearly illusory.[14] On the one hand, Judge Sorkow's opinion said that Ms. Whitehead was seeking to avoid her *obligations*. In other words, giving up her child became an actual obligation. On the other hand, according to the logic of the judge, this was a service contract, not really a sale of a child; therefore delivering the child to the Sterns was an "obligation" for which there was no consideration, for which Mr. Stern was not paying her.)

Judge Sorkow's finding the contract "not illusory" is suggestive not just of the doctrine by that name, but of illusion in general, and delusion, and the righteousness with which social constructions are conceived, acted on, and delivered up into the realm of the real as "right," while all else is devoured from memory as "wrong." From this perspective, the rhetorical tricks by which Sara Whitehead became Melissa Stern seem very like the heavy-worded legalities by which my great-great-grandmother was pacified and parted from her child. In both situations, the real mother had no say, no power; her powerlessness was imposed by state law that made her and her child helpless in relation to the father. My great-great-grandmother's powerlessness came about as the result of a contract to which she was not a party; Mary Beth Whitehead's powerlessness came about as a result of a contract that she signed at a discrete point of time—yet which, over time, enslaved her. The contract-reality in both instances was no less than magic: it was illusion transformed into not-illusion. Furthermore, it masterfully disguised the brutality of enforced arrangements in which these women's autonomy, their flesh and their blood, were locked away in word vaults, without room to reconsider—*ever*.

In the months since Judge Sorkow's opinion, I have reflected on the similarities of fortune between my own social positioning and that of Sara Melissa Stern

Whitehead. I have come to realize that an important part of the complex magic that Judge Sorkow wrote into his opinion was a supposition that it is "natural" for people to want children "like" themselves. What this reasoning raised for me was an issue of what, exactly, constituted this "likeness"? (What would have happened, for example, if Ms. Whitehead had turned out to have been the "passed" descendant of my "failed" godmother Marjorie's mother? What if the child she bore had turned out to be recessively and visibly black? Would the sperm of Mr. Stern have been so powerful as to make this child "his" with the exclusivity that Judge Sorkow originally assigned?) What constitutes, moreover, the collective understanding of "un-likeness"?

These questions turn, perhaps, on not-so-subtle images of which mothers should be bearing which children. Is there not something unseemly, in our society, about the spectacle of a white woman mothering a black child? A white woman giving totally to a black child; a black child totally and demandingly dependent for everything, for sustenance itself, from a white woman. The image of a white woman suckling a black child; the image of a black child sucking for its life from the bosom of a white woman. The utter interdependence of such an image; the selflessness, the merging it implies; the giving up of boundary; the encompassing of other within self; the unbounded generosity, the interconnectedness of such an image. Such a picture says that there is no difference; it places the hope of continuous generation, of immortality of the white self in a little black face.

When Judge Sorkow declared that it was only to be expected that parents would want to breed children "like" themselves, he simultaneously created a legal right to the same. With the creation of such a "right," he encased the children conforming to "likeliness" in protective custody, far from whole ranges of taboo. Taboo about touch and smell and intimacy and boundary. Taboo about ardor, possession, license, equivocation, equanimity, indifference, tolerance, rancor, dispossession, innocence, exile, and candor. Taboo about death. Taboos that amount to death. Death and sacredness, the valuing of body, of self, of other, of remains. The handling lovingly in life, as in life; the question of the intimacy versus the dispassion of death.

In effect, these taboos describe boundaries of valuation. Whether something is inside or outside the marketplace of rights has always been a way of valuing it. When a valued object is located outside the market, it is generally understood to be too "priceless" to be accommodated by ordinary exchange relationships; when, in contrast, the prize is located within the marketplace, all objects outside become "valueless." Traditionally, the Mona Lisa and human life have been the sorts of subjects removed from the fungibility of commodification, as "priceless." Thus when black people were bought and sold as slaves, they were placed beyond the bounds of humanity. And thus, in the twistedness of our brave new world, when blacks have been thrust out of the market and it is white children who are bought and sold, black babies have become "worthless" currency to adoption agents—"surplus" in the salvage heaps of Harlem hospitals.

The Imagination

"Familiar though his name may be to us, the storyteller in his living immediacy is by no means a present force. He has already become something remote from us and something that is getting even more distant. . . . Less and less frequently do we encounter people with the ability to tell a tale properly. . . . It is as if something that seemed inalienable to us, the securest among our possessions, were taken from us: the ability to exchange experiences."[15]

My mother's cousin Marjorie was a storyteller. From time to time I would press her to tell me the details of her youth, and she would tell me instead about a child who wandered into a world of polar bears, who was prayed over by polar bears, and in the end eaten. The child's life was not in vain because the polar bears had been made holy by its suffering. The child had been a test, a message from god for polar bears. In the polar bear universe, she would tell me, the primary object of creation was polar bears, and the rest of the living world was fashioned to serve polar bears. The clouds took their shape from polar bears, trees were designed to give shelter and shade to polar bears, and humans were ideally designed to provide polar bears with meat.[16]

The truth, the truth, I would laughingly insist as we sat in her apartment eating canned fruit and heavy roasts, mashed potatoes, pickles and vanilla pudding, cocoa, Sprite, or tea. What about roots and all that, I coaxed. But the voracity of her amnesia would disclaim and disclaim and disclaim; and she would go on telling me about the polar bears until our plates were full of emptiness and I became large in the space which described her emptiness and I gave in to the emptiness of words.

On Life and Death

Sighing into Space

There are moments in my life when I feel as though a part of me is missing. There are days when I feel so invisible that I can't remember what day of the week it is, when I feel so manipulated that I can't remember my own name, when I feel so lost and angry that I can't speak a civil word to the people who love me best. Those are the times when I catch sight of my reflection in store windows and am surprised to see a whole person looking back. Those are the times when my skin becomes gummy as clay and my nose slides around on my face and my eyes drip down to my chin. I have to close my eyes at such times and remember myself, draw an internal picture that is smooth and whole; when all else fails, I reach for a mirror and stare myself down until the features reassemble themselves like lost sheep.

Two years ago, my godmother Marjorie suffered a massive stroke. As she lay dying, I would come to the hospital to giver her her meals. My feeding her who had so often fed me became a complex ritual of mirroring and self-assembly. The physical act of holding the spoon to her lips was not only a rite of nurture and of sacrifice, it was the return of a gift. It was a quiet bowing to the passage of time and the doubling back of all things. The quiet woman who listened to my woes about work and school required now that I bend my head down close to her and listen for mouthed word fragments, sentence crumbs. I bent down to give meaning to her silence, her wandering search for words.

She would eat what I brought to the hospital with relish; she would reject what I brought with a turn of her head. I brought fruit and yogurt, ice cream and vegetable juice. Slowly, over time, she stopped swallowing. The mashed potatoes would sit in her mouth like cotton, the pudding would slip to her chin in slow sad streams. When she lost not only her speech but the power to ingest, they put a tube into her nose and down to her stomach, and I lost even that medium by which to communicate. No longer was there the odd but reassuring communion over taste. No longer was there some echo of comfort in being able to nurture one who nurtured me.

The increment of decay was like a little newborn death. With the tube, she stared up at me with imploring eyes, and I tried to guess what it was that she would like. I read to her aimlessly and in desperation. We entertained each other with the strange embarrassed flickering of our eyes. I told her stories to fill the emptiness, the loneliness, of the white-walled hospital room.

I told her stories about who I had become, about how I had grown up to know all about exchange systems, and theories of contract, and monetary fictions. I spun tales about blue-sky laws and promissory estoppel, the wispy-feathered complexity of undue influence and dark-hearted theories of unconscionability. I told her about market norms and life economy and the thin razor's edge of the bartering ethic. Once upon a time, I rambled, some neighbors of mine included me in their circle of barter. They were in the habit of exchanging eggs and driving lessons, hand-knit sweaters and computer programming, plumbing and calligraphy. I accepted the generosity of their inclusion with gratitude. At first, I felt that, as a lawyer, I was worthless, that I had no barterable skills and nothing to contribute. What I came to realize with time, however, was that my value to the group was not calculated by the physical items I brought to it. These people included me because they wanted me to be part of their circle, they valued my participation apart from the material things I could offer. So I gave of myself to them, and they gave me fruit cakes and dandelion wine and smoked salmon, and in their giving, their goods became provisions. Cradled in this community whose currency was a relational ethic, my stock in myself soared. My value depended on the glorious intangibility, the eloquent invisibility of my just being *part* of the collective; and in direct response I grew spacious and happy and gentle.

My gentle godmother. The fragility of life; the cold mortuary shelf.

Dispassionate Deaths

The hospital in which my godmother died is now filled to capacity with AIDS patients. One in sixty-one babies born there, as in New York City generally, is infected with AIDS antibodies.[17] Almost all are black or Hispanic. In the Bronx, the rate is one in forty-three.[18] In Central Africa, experts estimate that, of children receiving transfusions for malaria-related anemia, "about 1000 may have been infected with the AIDS virus in each of the last five years."[19] In Congo, 5 percent of the entire population is infected.[20] The *New York Times* reports that "the profile of Congo's population seems to guarantee the continued spread of AIDS."[21]

In the Congolese city of Pointe Noir, "the annual budget of the sole public health hospital is estimated at about $200,000—roughly the amount of money spent in the United States to care for four AIDS patients."[22]

The week in which my godmother died is littered with bad memories. In my journal, I made note of the following:

> *Good Friday*: Phil Donahue has a special program on AIDS. The segues are:
>
> a. from Martha, who weeps at the prospect of not watching her children grow up
>
> b. to Jim, who is not conscious enough to speak just now, who coughs convulsively, who recognizes no one in his family any more
>
> c. to Hugh who, at 85 pounds, thinks he has five years but whose doctor says he has weeks
>
> d. to an advertisement for denture polish ("If you love your Polident Green/then gimmeeya SMILE!")
>
> e. and then one for a plastic surgery salon on Park Avenue ("The only thing that's expensive is our address")
>
> f. and then one for what's coming up on the five o'clock news (Linda Lovelace, of *Deep Throat* fame, "still recovering from a double mastectomy and complications from silicone injections" is being admitted to a New York hospital for a liver transplant)
>
> g. and finally one for the miracle properties of all-purpose house cleaner ("Mr. Cleeean/is the man/behind the shine/is it wet or is it dry?" I note that Mr. Clean, with his gleaming bald head, puffy musculature and fever-bright eyes, looks like he is undergoing radiation therapy). Now back to our show.
>
> h. "We are back now with Martha," (who is crying harder than before, sobbing uncontrollably, each jerking inhalation a deep unearthly groan). Phil says, "Oh honey, I hope we didn't make it worse for you."
>
> *Easter Saturday*: Over lunch, I watch another funeral. My office windows overlook a graveyard as crowded and still as a rush-hour freeway. As I savor pizza and milk, I notice that one of the mourners is wearing an outfit featured in the window of Bloomingdale's (59th Street store) only since last weekend. This thread of recognition jolts me, and I am drawn to her in sorrow; the details of my own shopping history flash before my eyes as I reflect upon the sober spree that brought her to the rim of this earthly chasm, her slim suede heels sinking into the soft silt of the graveside.
>
> *Resurrection Sunday*: John D., the bookkeeper where I used to work, died, hit on the head by a stray but forcefully propelled hockey puck. I cried copiously at his memorial service, only to discover, later that afternoon when I saw a black rimmed photograph, that I had been mourning the wrong person. I had cried because the man I *thought* had died is John D. the office messenger, a bitter unfriendly man who treats me with disdain; once I bought an old electric typewriter from him which never worked. Though he promised nothing, I have harbored deep dislike since then; death by hockey puck is only one of the fates I had

imagined for him. I washed clean my guilt with buckets of tears at the news of what I thought was his demise.

The man who did die was small, shy, anonymously sweet-featured and innocent. In some odd way I was relieved; no seriously obligatory mourning to be done here. A quiet impassivity settled over me and I forgot my grief.

Holy Communion

A few months after my godmother died, my Great Aunt Jag passed away in Cambridge, at ninety-six the youngest and the last of her siblings, all of whom died at ninety-seven. She collapsed on her way home from the polling place, having gotten in her vote for "yet another Kennedy." Her wake was much like the last family gathering at which I had seen her, two Thanksgivings ago. She was a little hard of hearing then and she stayed on the outer edge of the conversation, brightly, loudly, and randomly asserting enjoyment of her meal. At the wake, cousins, nephews, daughters-in-law, first wives, second husbands, great-grand-nieces gathered round her casket and got acquainted all over again. It was pouring rain outside. The funeral home was dry and warm, faintly spicily clean-smelling; the walls were solid, dark, respectable wood; the floors were cool stone tile. On the door of a room marked "No Admittance" was a sign that reminded workers therein of the reverence with which each body was held by its family and prayed employees handle the remains with similar love and care. Aunt Jag wore yellow chiffon; everyone agreed that laying her out with her glasses on was a nice touch.

Afterward, we all went to Legal Seafoods, her favorite restaurant, and ate many of her favorite foods.

On Candor

Me

I have never been able to determine my horoscope with any degree of accuracy. Born at Boston's now-defunct Lying-In Hospital, I am a Virgo, despite a quite poetic soul. Knowledge of the *hour* of my birth, however, would determine not just my sun sign but my moons and all the more intimate specificities of my destiny. Once upon a time, I sent for my birth certificate, which was retrieved from the oblivion of Massachusetts microfiche. Said document revealed that an infant named Patricia Joyce, born of parents named Williams, was delivered into the world "colored." Since no one thought to put down the hour of my birth, I suppose that I will never know my true fate.

In the meantime, I read what text there is of me.

My name, Patricia, means patrician. Patricias are noble, lofty, elite, exclusively educated, and well mannered despite themselves. I was on the cusp of being Pamela, but my parents knew that such a me would require lawns, estates, and hunting dogs too.

I am also a Williams. Of William, whoever he was: an anonymous white man who owned my father's people and from whom some escaped. That rupture is marked by the dark-mooned mystery of utter silence.

Williams is the second most common surname in the United States; Patricia is *the* most common prename among women born in 1951, the year of my birth.

Them

In the law, rights are islands of empowerment. To be un-righted is to be disempowered, and the line between rights and no rights is most often the line between dominators and oppressors. Rights contain images of power, and manipulating those images, either visually or linguistically, is central in the making and maintenance of rights. In principle, therefore, the more dizzyingly diverse the images that are propagated, the more empowered we will be as a society.

In reality, it was a lovely polar bear afternoon. The gentle force of the earth. A wide wilderness of islands. A conspiracy of polar bears lost in timeless forgetting. A gentleness of polar bears, a fruitfulness of polar bears, a silent black-eyed interest of polar bears, a bristled expectancy of polar bears. With the wisdom of innocence, a child threw stones at the polar bears. Hungry, they rose from their nests, inquisitive, dark-souled, patient with foreboding, fearful in tremendous awakening. The instinctual ferocity of the hunter reflected upon the hunted. Then, proud teeth and warrior claws took innocence for wilderness and raging insubstantiality for tender rabbit breath.

In the newspapers the next day, it was reported that two polar bears in the Brooklyn Zoo mauled to death an eleven-year-old boy who had entered their cage to swim in the moat. The police were called and the bears were killed.[23]

In the public debate that ensued, many levels of meaning emerged. The rhetoric firmly established that the bears were innocent, naturally territorial, unfairly imprisoned, and guilty. The dead child (born into the urban jungle of a black, welfare mother and a Hispanic alcoholic father who had died literally in the gutter only six weeks before) was held to a similarly stern standard. The police were captured, in a widely disseminated photograph,[24] shooting helplessly, desperately, into the cage, through three levels of bars, at a pieta of bears; since this image, conveying much pathos, came nevertheless not in time to save the child, it was generally felt that the bears had died in vain.[25]

In the egalitarianism of exile, pluralists rose up as of one body, with a call to buy more bears, control juvenile delinquency, eliminate all zoos, and confine future police.[26]

In the plenary session of the national meeting of the Law and Society Association, the keynote speaker unpacked the whole incident as a veritable laboratory of emergent rights discourse. Just seeing that these complex levels of meaning exist, she exulted, should advance rights discourse significantly.[27]

At the funeral of the child, the presiding priest pronounced the death of Juan Perez not in vain, since he was saved from growing into "a lifetime of crime." Juan's Hispanic-welfare-black-widow-of-an-alcoholic mother decided then and there to sue.

The Universe Between

How I ended up at Dartmouth College for the summer is too long a story to tell. Anyway, there I was, sharing the town of Hanover, New Hampshire, with about two hundred prepubescent males enrolled in Dartmouth's summer basketball camp, an all-white, very expensive, affirmative action program for the street-deprived.

One fragrant evening, I was walking down East Wheelock Street when I encountered about a hundred of these adolescents, fresh from the courts, wet, lanky, big-footed, with fuzzy yellow crew cuts, loping toward Thayer Hall and food. In platoons of twenty-five or so, they descended upon me, jostling me, smacking me, and pushing me from the sidewalk into the gutter. In a thoughtless instant, I snatched off my brown silk headrag, my flag of African femininity and propriety, my sign of meek and supplicatory place and presentation. I released the armored rage of my short nappy hair (the scalp gleaming bare between the angry wire spikes) and hissed: "Don't I exist for you?! See Me! And deflect, godammit!" (The quaint professionalism of my formal English never allowed the rage in my head to rise so high as to overflow the edges of my text.)

They gave me wide berth. They clearly had no idea, however, that I was talking to them or about them. They skirted me sheepishly, suddenly polite, because they did know, when a crazed black person comes crashing into one's field of vision, that it is impolite to laugh. I stood tall and spoke loudly into their ranks: "I have my rights!" The Dartmouth Summer Basketball Camp raised its collective eyebrows and exhaled, with a certain tested nobility of exhaustion and solidarity.

I pursued my way, manumitted back into silence. I put distance between them and me, gave myself over to polar bear musings. I allowed myself to be watched over by bear spirits. Clean white wind and strong bear smells. The shadowed amnesia; the absence of being; the presence of polar bears. White wilderness of icy meateaters heavy with remembrance; leaden with undoing; shaggy with the effort of hunting for silence; frozen in a web of intention and intuition. A lunacy of polar bears. A history of polar bears. A pride of polar bears. A consistency of polar bears. In those meandering pastel polar bear moments, I found cool fragments of white-fur invisibility. Solid, black-gummed, intent, observant. Hungry and patient, impassive and exquisitely timed. The brilliant bursts of exclusive territoriality. A complexity of messages implied in our being.

Notes

1. For a more detailed account of the family history to this point, see Patricia Williams, "Grandmother Sophie," *Harvard Blackletter* 3 (1986): 79.

2. Patricia Williams, "Alchemical Notes: Reconstructing Ideals from Deconstructed Rights," *Harvard Civil Rights–Civil Liberties Law Review* 22 (1987): 418.

3. Marguerite Duras, *The Lover* (New York: Harper & Row, 1985), 55.

4. *Madrigal v. Quilligan*, U.S. Court of Appeals, 9th Circuit, Docket no. 78-3187, October 1979.

5. This was the testimony of one of the witnesses. It is hard to find official confirmation for this or any other sterilization statistic involving Native American women. Official statistics kept by the U.S. Public Health Service, through the Centers for Disease Control in Atlanta, come from data gathered by the National Hospital Discharge Survey, which covers neither federal hospitals nor penitentiaries. Services to Native American women living on reservations are provided almost exclusively by federal hospitals. In addition, the U.S. Public Health Service breaks down its information into only three categories: "White," "Black," and "Other." Nevertheless, in 1988, the Women of All Red Nations Collective of Minneapolis, Minnesota, distributed a fact sheet entitled "Sterilization Studies of Native American Women," which claimed that as many as 50 percent of all Native American women of childbearing age have been sterilized. According to "Surgical Sterilization Surveillance: Tubal Sterilization and Hysterectomy in Women aged 15–44, 1979–1980," issued by the Centers for Disease Control in 1983, "In 1980, the tubal sterilization rate for black women . . . was 45 percent greater than that for white women" (7). Furthermore, a study released in 1984 by the Division of Reproductive Health of the Center for Health Promotion and Education (one of the Centers for Disease Control) found that, as of 1982, 48.8 percent of Puerto Rican women between the ages of 15 and 44 had been sterilized.

6. See, generally, Stanley Elkins, *Slavery* (New York: Grosset & Dunlap, 1963); Kenneth Stampp, *The Peculiar Institution* (New York: Vintage, 1956): Winthrop Jordan, *White over Black* (Baltimore: Penguin Books, 1968).

7. Mark Tushnet, *The American Law of Slavery* (Princeton, N.J.: Princeton University Press, 1981), 6. There is danger, in the analysis that follows, of appearing to "pick" on Tushnet. That is not my intention, nor is it to impugn the body of his research, most of which I greatly admire. The choice of this passage for analysis has more to do with the randomness of my reading habits; the fact that he is one of the few legal writers to attempt, in the context of slavery, a juxtaposition of political theory with psychoanalytic theories of personality; and the fact that he is perceived to be of the political left, which simplifies my analysis in terms of its presumption of sympathy, i.e., that the constructions of thought revealed are socially derived and unconscious rather than idiosyncratic and intentional.

8. In another passage, Tushnet observes: "The court thus demonstrated its appreciation of the ties of sentiment that slavery could generate between master and slave and simultaneously denied that those ties were relevant in the law" (67). What is noteworthy about the reference to "sentiment" is that it assumes that the fact that emotions could grow up between slave and master is itself worth remarking: slightly surprisingly, slightly commendable for the court to note (i.e., in its "appreciation")—although "simultaneously" with, and presumably in contradistinction to, the court's inability to take official cognizance of the fact. Yet, if one really looks at the ties that bound master and slave, one has to flesh out the description of master-slave with the ties of father-son, father-daughter, half-sister, half-brother, uncle, aunt, cousin, and a variety of de facto foster relationships. And if one starts to see those ties as more often than not intimate family ties, then the terminology "appreciation of . . . sentiment . . . between master and slave" becomes a horrifying mockery of any true sense of family sentiment, which is utterly, utterly lacking. The court's "appreciation," from this enhanced perspective, sounds blindly cruel, sarcastic at best. And to observe that courts suffused in such "appreciation" could simultaneously deny its legal relevance seems not only a truism; it misses the point entirely.

9. "Actants have a kind of phonemic, rather than a phonetic role: they operate on the level of function, rather than content. That is, an actant may embody itself in a particular character (termed an acteur) or it may reside in the function of more than

one character in respect of their common role in the story's underlying 'oppositional' structure. In short, the deep structure of the narrative generates and defines its actants at a level beyond that of the story's surface content" (Terence Hawkes, *Structuralism and Semiotics* [Berkeley: University of California Press, 1977], 89).

10. Tushnet, 69.

11. Duras, 54.

12. Charles Reich is author of *The Greening of America* (New York: Random House, 1970) and professor of law at the University of San Francisco Law School.

13. See, generally, In the Matter of Baby "M," A Pseudonym for an Actual Person, Superior Court of New Jersey, Chancery Division, Docket no. FM-25314-86E, March 31, 1987. This decision was appealed, and on February 3, 1988, the New Jersey Supreme Court ruled that surrogate contracts were illegal and against public policy. In addition to the contract issue, however, the appellate court decided the custody issue in favor of the Sterns but granted visitation rights to Mary Beth Whitehead.

14. An illusory promise is an expression cloaked in promissory terms, but which, upon closer examination, reveals that the promisor has committed himself not at all" (J. Calamari and J. Perillo, *Contracts*, 3d ed. [St. Paul: West Publishing, 1987], 228).

15. Walter Benjamin, "The Storyteller," in *Illuminations*, ed. Hannah Arendt (New York: Schocken, 1969), 83.

16. For an analysis of similar stories, see Richard Levins and Richard Lewontin, *The Dialectical Biologist* (Cambridge, Mass.: Harvard University Press, 1985), 66.

17. B. Lambert, "Study Finds Antibodies for AIDS in 1 in 61 Babies in New York City," *New York Times* (January 13, 1988), sec. A.

18. Ibid.

19. "Study Traces AIDS in African Children," *New York Times* (January 22, 1988), sec. A.

20. J. Brooke, "New Surge of AIDS in Congo May Be an Omen for Africa," *New York Times* (January 22, 1988), sec. A.

21. Ibid.

22. Ibid.

23. J. Barron, "Polar Bears Kill a Child at Prospect Park Zoo," *New York Times* (May 20, 1987), sec. A.

24. *New York Post* (May 22, 1987), p. 1.

25. J. Barron, "Officials Weigh Tighter Security at Zoos in Parks," *New York Times* (May 22, 1987), sec. B.

26. Ibid.

27. Patricia Williams, "The Meaning of Rights" (address to the annual meeting of the Law and Society Association, Washington, D.C., June 6, 1987).

9

Feminism, Marxism, Method, and the State: Toward Feminist Jurisprudence [1983]

Catharine A. MacKinnon

I

Feminism has no theory of the state. It has a theory of power: sexuality is gendered as gender is sexualized. Male and female are created through the erotization of dominance and submission. The man/woman difference and the dominance/submission dynamic define each other. This is the social meaning of sex and the distinctively feminist account of gender inequality.[1] Sexual objectification, the central process within this dynamic, is at once epistemological and political. The feminist theory of knowledge is inextricable from the feminist critique of power because the male point of view forces itself upon the world as its way of apprehending it.

The perspective from the male standpoint[3] enforces woman's definition, encircles her body, circumlocutes her speech, and describes her life. The male perspective is systemic and hegemonic. The content of the signification "woman" is the content of women's lives. Each sex has its role, but their stakes and power are not equal. If the sexes are unequal, and perspective participates in situation, there is no ungendered reality or ungendered perspective. And they are connected. In this context, objectivity—the nonsituated, universal standpoint, whether claimed or aspired to—is a denial of the existence or potency of sex inequality that tacitly participates in constructing reality from the dominant point of view. Objectivity, as the epistemological stance of which objectification is the social process, creates the reality it apprehends by defining as knowledge the reality it creates through its way of apprehending it. Sexual metaphors for knowing are no coincidence.[4] The solipsism of this approach does not undercut its sincerity, but it is interest that precedes method.

Feminism criticizes this male totality without an account of our capacity to do so or to imagine or realize a more whole truth. Feminism affirms women's point of view by revealing, criticizing, and explaining its impossibility. This is not a dialectical paradox. It is a methodological expression of women's situation, in which the struggle for consciousness is a struggle for world: for a sexuality, a history, a culture, a community, a form of power, an experience of the sacred.

If women had consciousness or world, sex inequality would be harmless, or all women would be feminist. Yet we have something of both, or there would be no such thing as feminism. Why can women know that this—life as we have known it—is not all, not enough, not ours, not just? Now, why don't all women?[5]

The practice of a politics of all women in the face of its theoretical impossibility is creating a new process of theorizing and a new form of theory. Although feminism emerges from women's particular experience, it is not subjective or partial, for no interior ground and few if any aspects of life are free of male power. Nor is feminism objective, abstract, or universal.[6] It claims no external ground or unsexed sphere of generalization or abstraction beyond male power, nor transcendence of the specificity of each of its manifestations. How is it possible to have an engaged truth that does not simply reiterate its determinations? Disengaged truth only reiterates *its* determinations. Choice of method is choice of determinants—a choice which, for women as such, has been unavailable because of the subordination of women. Feminism does not begin with the premise that it is unpremised. It does not aspire to persuade an unpremised audience because there is no such audience. Its project is to uncover and claim as valid the experience of women, the major content of which is the devalidation of women's experience.

This defines our task not only because male dominance is perhaps the most pervasive and tenacious system of power in history, but because it is metaphysically nearly perfect.[7] Its point of view is the standard for point-of-viewlessness, its particularity the meaning of universality. Its force is exercised as consent, its authority as participation, its supremacy as the paradigm of order, its control as the definition of legitimacy. Feminism claims the voice of women's silence, the sexuality of our eroticized desexualization, the fullness of "lack," the centrality of our marginality and exclusion, the public nature of privacy, the presence of our absence. This approach is more complex than transgression, more transformative than transvaluation, deeper than mirror-imaged resistance, more affirmative than the negation of our negativity. It is neither materialist nor idealist; it is feminist. Neither the transcendence of liberalism nor the determination of materialism works for us. Idealism is too unreal; women's inequality is enforced, so it cannot simply be thought out of existence, certainly not by us. Materialism is too real; women's inequality has never not existed, so women's equality never has. That is, the equality of women to men will not be scientifically provable until it is no longer necessary to do so. Women's situation offers no outside to stand on or gaze at, no inside to escape to, too much urgency to wait, no place else to go, and nothing to use but the twisted tools that have been shoved down our throats. If feminism is revolutionary, this is why.

Feminism has been widely thought to contain tendencies of liberal feminism, radical feminism, and socialist feminism. But just as socialist feminism has often amounted to marxism applied to women, liberal feminism has often amounted to liberalism applied to women. Radical feminism is feminism. Radical feminism—after this, feminism unmodified—is methodologically post-marxist.[8] It moves to resolve the marxist-feminist problematic on the level of method. Because its method emerges from the concrete conditions of all women as a sex, it dissolves the individualist, naturalist, idealist, moralist structure of liberalism, the politics of which science is the epistemology. Where liberal feminism sees sexism primarily as an illusion or myth to be dispelled, an inaccuracy to be corrected, true feminism sees the male point of view as fundamental to the male power to create the world in its own image, the image of its desires, not just as its delusory end product. Feminism distinctively as such comprehends that what counts as truth is produced in the interest of those with power to shape reality, and that this process is as pervasive as it is necessary as it is changeable. Unlike the scientific strain in marxism or the Kantian imperative in liberalism, which in this context share most salient features, feminism neither claims universality nor, failing that, reduces to relativity. It does not seek a generality that subsumes its particulars or an abstract theory or a science of sexism. It rejects the approach of control over nature (including us) analogized to control over society (also including us) which has grounded the "science of society" project as the paradigm for political knowledge since (at least) Descartes. Both liberalism and marxism have been subversive on women's behalf. Neither is enough. To grasp the inadequacies for women of liberalism on one side and marxism on the other is to begin to comprehend the role of the liberal state and liberal legalism[9] within a post-marxist feminism of social transformation.

As feminism has a theory of power but lacks a theory of the state, so marxism has a theory of value which (through the organization of work in production) becomes class analysis, but a problematic theory of the state. Marx did not address the state much more explicitly than he did women. Women were substratum, the state epiphenomenon.[10] Engels, who frontally analyzed both, and together, presumed the subordination of women in every attempt to reveal its roots, just as he presupposed something like the state, or state-like social conditions, in every attempt to expose its origins.[11] Marx tended to use the term "political" narrowly to refer to the state or its laws, criticizing as exclusively political interpretations of the state's organization or behavior which took them as sui generis. Accordingly, until recently, most marxism has tended to consider political that which occurs between classes, that is, to interpret as "the political" instances of the marxist concept of inequality. In this broad sense, the marxist theory of social inequality has been its theory of politics. This has not so much collapsed the state into society (although it goes far in that direction) as conceived the state as determined by the totality of social relations of which the state is one determined and determining part— without specifying which, or how much, is which.

In this context, recent marxist work has tried to grasp the specificity of the institutional state: how it wields class power, or transforms class society, or responds to approach by a left aspiring to rulership or other changes. While liberal theory has seen the state as emanating power, and traditional marxism has seen the state as expressing power constituted elsewhere, recent marxism, much of it structuralist, has tried to analyze state power as specific to the state as a form, yet integral to a determinate social whole understood in class terms. This state is found "relatively autonomous." This means that the state, expressed through its functionaries, has a definite class character, is definitely capitalist or socialist, but also has its own interests which are to some degree independent of those of the ruling class and even of the class structure. The state as such, in this view, has a specific power and interest, termed "the political," such that class power, class interest expressed by and in the state, and state behavior, although inconceivable in isolation from one another, are nevertheless not linearly or causally linked or strictly coextensive. Such work locates "the specificity of the political" in a mediate "region" between the state as its own ground of power (which alone, as in the liberal conception, would set the state above or apart from class) and the state as possessing no special supremacy or priority in terms of power, as in the more orthodox marxist view.

The idea that the state is relatively autonomous, a kind of first among equals of social institutions, has the genius of appearing to take a stand on the issue of reciprocal constitution of state and society while straddling it. Is the state essentially autonomous of class but partly determined by it, or is it essentially determined by class but not exclusively so? Is it relatively constrained within a context of freedom or relatively free within a context of constraint? As to who or what fundamentally moves and shapes the realities and instrumentalities of domination, and where to go to do something about it, what qualifies what is as ambiguous as it is crucial. Whatever it has not accomplished, however, this literature has at least relieved the compulsion to find all law—directly or convolutedly, nakedly or clothed in unconscious or devious rationalia—to be simply bourgeois, without undercutting the notion that it is determinately driven by interest.

A methodologically post-marxist feminism must confront, on our own terms, the issue of the relation between the state and society, within a theory of social determination adequate to the specificity of sex. Lacking even a tacit theory of the state of its own, feminist practice has instead oscillated between a liberal theory of the state on the one hand and a left theory of the state on the other. Both treat law as the mind of society: disembodied reason in liberal theory, reflection of material interest in left theory. In liberal moments the state is accepted on its own terms as a neutral arbiter among conflicting interests. The law is actually or potentially principled, meaning predisposed to no substantive outcome, thus available as a tool that is not fatally twisted. Women implicitly become an interest group within pluralism, with specific problems of mobilization and representation, exit and voice, sustaining incremental gains and losses. In left moments, the state becomes a tool of dominance and repression, the law legitimizing ideology, use of the legal system a form of utopian idealism or gradualist reform, each apparent gain deceptive or cooptive, and each loss inevitable.

Applied to women, liberalism has supported state intervention on behalf of women as abstract persons with abstract rights, without scrutinizing the content of these notions in gendered terms. Marxism applied to women is always on the edge of counseling abdication of the state as an arena altogether—and with it those women whom the state does not ignore or who are, as yet, in no position to ignore it. Feminism has so far accepted these constraints upon its alternatives: either the state, as primary tool of women's betterment and status transformation, without analysis (hence strategy) for it as male; or civil society, which for women has more closely resembled a state of nature. The state, with it the law, has been either omnipotent or impotent: everything or nothing.

The feminist posture toward the state has therefore been schizoid on issues central to women's survival: rape, battery, pornography, prostitution, sexual harassment, sex discrimination, abortion, the Equal Rights Amendment, to name a few. Attempts to reform and enforce rape laws, for example, have tended to build on the model of the deviant perpetrator and the violent act, as if the fact that rape is a crime means that the society is against it, so law enforcement would reduce or delegitimize it. Initiatives are accordingly directed toward making the police more sensitive, prosecutors more responsive, judges more receptive, and the law, in words, less sexist. This may be progressive in the liberal or the left senses, but how is it empowering in the feminist sense? Even if it were effective in jailing men who do little different from what nondeviant men do regularly, how would such an approach alter women's rapability? Unconfronted are *why* women are raped and the role of the state in that. Similarly, applying laws against battery to husbands, although it can mean life itself, has largely failed to address, as part of the strategy for state intervention, the conditions that produce men who systematically express themselves violently toward women, women whose resistance is disabled, and the role of the state in this dynamic. Criminal enforcement in these areas, which suggesting that rape and battery are deviant, punishes men for expressing the images of masculinity that mean their identity, for which they are otherwise trained, elevated, venerated, and paid. These men must be stopped. But how does that change them or reduce the chances that there will be more like them? Liberal strategies entrust women to the state. Left theory abandons us to the rapists and batterers. The question for feminism is not only whether there is a meaningful difference between the two, but whether either is adequate to the feminist critique of rape and battery as systemic and to the role of the state and the law within that system.

Feminism has descriptions of the state's treatment of the gender difference, but no analysis of the state as gender hierarchy. We need to know. What, in gender terms, are the state's norms of accountability, sources of power, real constituency? Is the state to some degree autonomous of the interests of men or an integral expression of them? Does the state embody and serve male interests in its form, dynamics, relation to society, and specific policies? Is the state constructed upon the subordination of women? If so, how does male power become state power? Can such a state be made to serve the interests of those upon whose powerlessness its power is erected? Would a different relation between state and society, such as may pertain under socialism, make a difference? If not, is masculinity inherent in the state form as such, or is some other form of state, or some other way of governing, distinguishable or imaginable? In the absence of answer to such questions, feminism has been caught between giving more power to the state in each attempt to claim it for women and leaving unchecked power in the society to men. Undisturbed, meanwhile, like the assumption that women generally consent to sex, is the assumption that we consent to this government. The question for feminism, for the first time on its own terms, is: what is this state, from women's point of view?

As a beginning, I propose that the state is male in the feminist sense. The law sees and treats women the way men see and treat women. The liberal state coercively and authoritatively constitutes the social order in the interest of men as a gender, through its legitimizing norms, relation to society, and substantive policies. It achieves this through embodying and ensuring male control over women's sexuality at every level, occasionally cushioning, qualifying, or de jure prohibiting its excesses when necessary to its normalization. Substantively, the way the male point of view frames an experience is the way it is framed by state policy. To the extent possession is the point of sex, rape is sex with a woman who is not yours, unless the act is so as to make her yours. If part of the kick of pornography involves eroticizing the putatively prohibited, obscenity law will putatively prohibit pornography enough to maintain its desirability without ever making it unavailable or truly illegitimate. The same with prostitution. As male is the implicit reference for human, maleness will be the measure of equality in sex discrimination law. To the extent that the point of abortion is to control the reproductive sequelae of intercourse, so as to facilitate male sexual access to women, access to abortion will be controlled by "a man or The Man." Gender, elaborated and sustained by behavioral patterns of application and administration, is maintained as a division of power.

Formally, the state is male in that objectivity is its norm. Objectivity is liberal legalism's conception of itself. It legitimizes itself by reflecting its view of existing society, a society it made and makes by so seeing it, and calling that view, and that relation, practical rationality. If rationality is measured by point-of-viewlessness, what counts as reason will be that which corresponds to the way things are. Practical will mean that which can be done without changing anything. In this framework, the task of legal interpretation becomes "to perfect the state as mirror of the society."[17] Objectivist epistemology is the law of law. It ensures that the law will most reinforce existing distributions of power when it most closely adheres to its own highest ideal of fairness. Like the science it emulates, this epistemological stance can not see the social specificity of reflection as method or its choice to embrace that which it reflects. Such law not only reflects a society in which men rule women; it rules in a male way: "The phallus means everything that sets itself up as a mirror."[18] The rule form, which unites scientific knowledge with state control in its conception of what law is, institutionalizes the objective stance as jurisprudence. A closer look at the substantive law of rape in light of such an argument suggests that the relation between objectification (understood as the primary process of the subordination of women) and the power of the state is the relation between the personal and the political at the level of government. This is not because the state is presumptively the sphere of politics. It is because the state, in part through law, institutionalizes male power. If male power is systemic, it *is* the regime.

II

Feminists have reconceived rape as central to women's condition in two ways. Some see rape as an act of violence, not sexuality, the threat of which intimidates all women.[20] Others see rape, including its violence, as an expression of male sexuality, the social imperatives of which define all women.[21] The first, formally in the liberal tradition, comprehends rape as a displacement of power based on physical force onto sexuality, a preexisting natural sphere to which domination is alien. Thus, Susan Brownmiller examines rape in riots, wars, pogroms, and revolutions; rape by police, parents, prison guards; and rape motivated by racism—seldom rape in normal circumstances, in everyday life, in ordinary relationships, by men as men.[22] Women are raped by guns, age, white supremacy, the state—only derivatively by the penis. The more feminist view to me, one which derives from victims' experiences, sees sexuality as a social sphere of male power of which forced sex is paradigmatic. Rape is not less sexual for being violent; to the extent that coercion has become integral to male sexuality, rape may be sexual to the degree that, and because, it is violent.

The point of defining rape as "violence not sex" or "violence against women" has been to separate sexuality from gender in order to affirm sex (heterosexuality) while rejecting violence (rape). The problem remains what it has always been: telling the difference. The convergence of sexuality with violence, long used at law to deny the reality of women's violation, is recognized by rape survivors, with a difference: where the legal system has seen the intercourse in rape, victims see the rape in intercourse. The uncoerced context for sexual expression become as elusive as the physical acts come to feel indistinguishable. Instead of asking, what is the violation of rape, what if we ask, what is the nonviolation of intercourse? To tell what is wrong with rape, explain what is right about sex. If this, in turn, is difficult, the difficulty is as instructive as the difficulty men have in telling the difference when women see one. Perhaps the wrong of rape has proven so difficult to articulate because the unquestionable starting point has been that rape is definable as distinct from intercourse, when for women it is difficult to distinguish them under conditions of male dominance.[25]

Like heterosexuality, the crime of rape centers on penetration.[26] The law to protect women's sexuality from forcible violation/expropriation defines the protected in male genital terms. Women do resent forced penetration. But penile invasion of the vagina may be less pivotal to women's sexuality, pleasure or violation, than it is to male sexuality. This definitive element of rape centers upon a male-defined loss, not coincidentally also upon the way men define loss of exclusive access. In this light, rape, as legally defined, appears more a crime against female monogamy than against female sexuality. Property concepts fail fully to comprehend this,[27] however, not because women's sexuality is not, finally, a thing, but because it is never ours. The moment we "have" it—"have sex" in the dual sexuality/gender sense—it is lost as ours. This may explain the male incomprehension that, once a woman has had sex, she loses anything when raped. To them we *have nothing* to lose. Dignitary harms, because nonmaterial, are remote to the legal mind. But women's loss through rape is

avoide
ony notion
of issued
selection

not only less tangible, it is less existent. It is difficult to avoid the conclusion that penetration itself is known to be a violation and that women's sexuality, our gender definition, is itself stigmatic. [If this is so, the pressing question for explanation is not why some of us accept rape but why any of us resent it.]

The law of rape divides the world of women into spheres of consent according to how much say we are legally presumed to have over sexual access to us by various categories of men. Little girls may not consent; wives must. If rape laws existed to enforce women's control over our own sexuality, as the consent defense implies, marital rape would not be a widespread exception, nor would statutory rape proscribe all sexual intercourse with underage girls regardless of their wishes. The rest of us fall into parallel provinces: good girls, like children, are unconsenting, virginal, rapable; bad girls, like wives, are consenting, whores, unrapable. The age line under which girls are presumed disabled from withholding consent to sex rationalizes a condition of sexual coercion women never outgrow. As with protective labor laws for women only, dividing and protecting the most vulnerable becomes a device for not protecting everyone. Risking loss of even so little cannot be afforded. Yet the protection is denigrating and limiting (girls may not choose to be sexual) as well as perverse (girls are eroticized as untouchable; now reconsider the data on incest).

If the accused knows us, consent is inferred. The exemption for rape in marriage is consistent with the assumption underlying most adjudications of forcible rape: to the extent the parties relate, it was not really rape, it was personal. As the marital exemptions erode, preclusions for cohabitants and voluntary social companions may expand. In this light, the partial erosion of the marital rape exemption looks less like a change in the equation between women's experience of sexual violation and men's experience of intimacy, and more like a legal adjustment to the social fact that acceptable heterosexual sex is increasingly not limited to the legal family. So although the rape law may not now always assume that the woman consented simply because the parties are legally one, indices of closeness, of relationship ranging from nodding acquaintance to living together, still contraindicate rape. Perhaps this reflects men's experience that women they know meaningfully consent to sex with them. That cannot be rape; rape must be by someone else, someone unknown. But *women* experience rape most often by men we know.[30] Men believe that it is less awful to be raped by someone one is close to: "The emotional trauma suffered by a person victimized by an individual with whom sexual intimacy is shared as a normal part of an ongoing martial relationship is not nearly as severe as that suffered by a person who is victimized by one with whom that intimacy is not shared."[31] But women feel as much, if not more, traumatized by being raped by someone we have known or trusted, someone we have shared at least an illusion of mutuality with, than by some stranger. In whose interest is it to believe that it is not so bad to be raped by someone who has fucked you before as by someone who has not? Disallowing charges of rape in marriage may also "remove a substantial obstacle to the resumption of normal marital relations."[32] Depending upon your view of normal. Note that the obstacle to normalcy here is not the rape but the law against it. Apparently someone besides feminists finds sexual victimization and sexual intimacy not all that contradictory. Sometimes I think women and men live in different cultures.

Having defined rape in male sexual terms, the law's problem, which becomes the victim's problem, is distinguishing rape from sex in specific cases. The law does this by adjudicating the level of acceptable force starting just above the level set by what is seen as normal male sexual behavior, rather than at the victim's, or women's, point of violation. Rape cases finding insufficient force reveal that acceptable sex, in the legal perspective, can entail a lot of force. This is not only because of the way specific facts are perceived and interpreted, but because of the way the injury itself is defined as illegal. Rape is a sex crime that is not a crime when it looks like sex. To seek to define rape as violent, not sexual, is understandable in this context, and often seems strategic. But assault that is consented to is still assault; rape consented to is intercourse. The substantive reference point implicit in existing legal standards is the sexually normative level of force. Until this norm is confronted as such, no distinction between violence and sexuality will prohibit more instances of women's ex-perienced violation than does the existing definition. The question is what is *seen as* force, hence as violence, in the sexual arena. Most rapes, as women live them, will not be seen to violate women until sex and violence are confronted as mutually definitive. It is not only men convicted of rape who believe that the only thing they did different from what men do all the time is get caught.

The line between rape and intercourse commonly centers on some measure of the woman's "will." But from what should the law know woman's will? Like much existing law, Brownmiller tends to treat will as a question of consent and consent as a factual issue of the presence of force.[33] Proof problems aside, force and desire are not mutually exclusive. So long as dominance is eroticized, they never will be. Women are socialized to passive receptivity; may have or perceive no alternative to acquiescence; may prefer it to the escalated risk of injury and the humiliation of a lost fight; submit to survive. Some eroticize dominance and submission; it beats feeling forced. Sexual intercourse may be deeply unwanted—the woman would never have initiated it—yet no force may be present. Too, force may be used, yet the woman may want the sex—to avoid more force or because she, too, eroticizes dominance. Women and men know this. Calling rape violence, not sex, thus evades, at the moment it most seems to confront, the issue of who controls women's sexuality and the dominance/submission dynamic that has defined it. When sex is violent, women may have lost control over what is done to us, but absence of force does not ensure the presence of that control. Nor, under conditions of male dominance, does the presence of force make an interaction nonsexual. If sex is normally something men do to women, the issue is less whether there was force and more whether consent is a meaningful concept.[34]

To explain women's gender status as a function of rape, Brownmiller argues that the threat of rape benefits all men.[35] She does not specify in what way. Perhaps it benefits them sexually, hence as a gender: male initiatives toward women carry the fear of rape as support for persuading compliance, the resulting appearance of which has been called consent. Here the victims' perspective grasps what liberalism applied to women denies: that forced sex as sexuality is not exceptional in relations between the sexes but constitutes the social meaning of gender: "Rape is a man's act, whether it is male or a female man and whether it is a man relatively permanently or relatively temporarily; and being raped is a woman's experience, whether it is a female or a male woman and whether it is a woman relatively permanently or relatively temporarily."[36] To be rap*able*, a position which is social, not biological, defines what a woman *is*.

Most women get the message that the law against rape is virtually unenforceable as applied to them. Our own experience is more often delegitimized by this than the law is. Women radically distinguish between rape and experiences of sexual violation, concluding that we have not "really" been raped if we have ever seen or dated or slept with or been married to the man, if we were fashionably dressed or are not provably virgin, if we are prostitutes, if we put up with it or tried to get it over with, if we were force-fucked over a period of years. If we probably couldn't prove it in court, it wasn't rape. The distance between most sexual violations of women and the legally perfect rape measures the imposition of someone else's definition upon women's experiences. Rape, from women's point of view, is not prohibited; it is regulated. Even women who know we have been raped do not believe that the legal system will see it the way we do. We are often not wrong. Rather than deterring or avenging rape, the state, in many victims' experiences, perpetuates it. Women who charge rape say they were raped twice, the second time in court. If the state is male, this is more than a figure of speech.

The law distinguishes rape from intercourse by the woman's lack of consent coupled with a man's (usually) knowing disregard of it. A feminist distinction between rape and intercourse, to hazard a beginning approach, lies instead in the *meaning* of the act from women's point of view. What is wrong with rape is that it is an act of the subordination of women to men. Seen this way, the issue is not so much what rape "is" as the way its social conception is shaped to interpret particular encounters. Under conditions of sex inequality, with perspective bound up with situation, whether a contested interaction is rape comes down to whose meaning wins. If sexuality is relational, specifically if it is a power relation of gender, consent is a communication under conditions of inequality. It transpires somewhere between what the woman actually wanted and what the man comprehended she wanted. Instead of capturing this dynamic, the law gives us linear statics face to face. Nonconsent in law becomes a question of the man's force or the woman's resistance or both.[37] Rape, like many crimes and torts, requires that the accused possess a criminal mind (mens rea) for his acts to be criminal. The man's mental state refers to what he actually understood at the time or to what a reasonable man should have understood under the circumstances. The problem is this: the injury of rape lies in the meaning of the act to its victims, but the standard for its criminality lies in the meaning of the same act to the assailants. Rape is only an injury from women's point of view. It is only a crime from the male point of view, explicitly including that of the accused.

Thus is the crime of rape defined and adjudicated from the male standpoint, that is, presuming that (what feminists see as) forced sex is sex. Under male supremacy, of course, it is. What this means doctrinally is that the man's perceptions of the woman's desires often determine whether she is deemed violated. This might be like other crimes of subjective intent if rape were like other crimes. But with rape, because sexuality defines gender, the only difference between assault and (what is socially considered) noninjury is the meaning of the encounter to the woman. Interpreted this way, the legal problem has been to determine whose view of that meaning constitutes what really happened, as if what happened objectively exists to be objectively determined, thus as if this task of determination is separable from the gender of the participants and the gendered nature of their exchange. Thus, even though the rape law oscillates between subjective tests and more objective standards invoking social reasonableness, it uniformly presumes a single underlying reality, not a reality split by divergent meanings, such as those inequality produces. Many women are raped by men who know the meaning of their acts to women and proceed anyway.[38] But women are also violated every day by men who have no idea of the meaning of their acts to women. To them, it is sex. Therefore, to the law, it is sex. That is the single reality of what happened. When a rape prosecution is lost on a consent defense, the woman has not only failed to prove lack of consent, she is not considered to have been injured at all. Hermeneutically unpacked, read: because he did not perceive she did not want him, she was not violated. She had sex. Sex itself cannot be an injury. Women consent to sex every day. Sex makes a woman a woman. Sex is what women are *for*.

To a feminist analysis, men set sexual mores ideologically and behaviorally, define rape as they imagine the sexual violation of women through distinguishing it from their image of what they normally do, and sit in judgment in most accusations of sex crimes. So rape comes to mean a strange (read Black) man knowing a woman does not want sex and going ahead anyway. But men are systematically conditioned not even to notice what women want. They may have not a glimmer of women's indifference or revulsion. Rapists typically believe the woman loved it.[39] Women, as a survival strategy, must ignore or devalue or mute our desires (particularly lack of them) to convey the impression that the man will get what he wants regardless of what we want. In this context, consider measuring the genuineness of consent from the individual assailant's (or even the socially reasonable, i.e., objective man's) point of view.

Men's pervasive belief that women fabricate rape charges after consenting to sex makes sense in this light. To them, the accusations *are* false because, to them, the facts describe sex. To interpret such events as rapes distorts their experience. Since they seldom consider that their experience of the real is anything other than reality, they can only explain the woman's version as maliciously invented. Similarly, the male anxiety that rape is easy to charge and difficult to disprove (also widely believed in the face of overwhelming evidence to the contrary) arises because rape accusations express one thing men cannot seem to control: the meaning to women of sexual encounters.

Thus do legal doctrines, incoherent or puzzling as syllogistic logic, become coherent as ideology. For example, when an accused wrongly but sincerely believes that a woman he sexually forced consented, he may have a defense of mistaken belief or fail to satisfy the mental requirement of knowingly proceeding against her will.[40] One commentator notes, discussing the conceptually similar issue of revocation of prior consent (i.e., on the issue of the conditions under which women are allowed to control access to their sexuality from one time to the next): "Even where a woman revokes prior consent, such is the male ego that, seized of an exaggerated assessment of his sexual prowess, a man might genuinely believe her still to be consenting; resistance may be misinterpreted as enthusiastic cooperation; protestations of pain or disinclination, a spur to more sophisticated or more ardent love-making; a clear statement to stop, taken as referring to a particular intimacy rather than the entire performance."[41] This equally vividly captures common male readings of women's indications of disinclination under all kinds of circumstances.[42] Now reconsider to what extent the man's perceptions should determine whether a rape occurred. From whose standpoint, and in whose interest, is a law that allows one person's conditioned unconsciousness to contraindicate another's experienced violation? This aspect of the rape law reflects the sex inequality of the society not only in conceiving a cognizable injury from the viewpoint of the reasonable rapist, but in affirmatively rewarding men with acquittals for not comprehending women's point of view on sexual encounters.

Whether the law calls this coerced consent or mistake of fact, the more the sexual violation of women is routine, the more beliefs equating sexuality with violation become reasonable, and the more honestly women can be defined in terms of our fuckability. It would be comparatively simple if the legal problem were limited to avoiding retroactive falsification of the accused's state of mind. Surely there are incentives to lie. But the deeper problem is the rape law's assumption that a single, objective state of affairs existed, one which merely needs to be determined by evidence, when many (maybe even most) rapes involve honest men and violated women. When the reality is split—a woman is raped but not by a rapist?—the law tends to conclude that a rape *did not happen.* To attempt to solve this by adopting the standard of reasonable belief without asking, on a substantive social basis, to whom the belief is reasonable and why—meaning, what conditions make it reasonable—is one-sided: male-sided. What is it reasonable for a man to believe concerning a woman's desire for sex when heterosexuality is compulsory? Whose subjectivity becomes the objectivity of "what happened" is a matter of social meaning, that is, it has been a matter of sexual politics. One-sidedly erasing women's violation or dissolving the presumptions into the subjectivity of either side are alternatives dictated by the terms of the object/subject split, respectively. These are alternatives that will only retrace that split until its terms are confronted as gendered to the ground.

Desirability to men is commonly supposed to be a woman's form of power. This echoes the view that consent is women's form of control over intercourse, different but equal to the custom of male initiative. Look at it: man initiates, woman chooses. Even the ideal is not mutual. Apart from the disparate consequences of refusal, or openness of original options, this model does not envision a situation the woman controls being placed in, or choices she frames, yet the consequences are attributed to her as if the sexes began at arm's length, on equal terrain, as in the contract fiction. Ambiguous cases of consent are often archetypically referred to as "half won arguments in parked cars."[43] Why not half lost? Why isn't half enough? Why is it an argument? Why do men still want "it," feel entitled to "it," when women don't want them? That sexual expression is even framed as a matter of woman's consent, without exposing these presuppositions, is integral to gender inequality. Woman's so-called power presupposes her more fundamental powerlessness.[44]

III

The state's formal norms recapitulate the male point of view on the level of design. In Anglo-American jurisprudence, morals (value judgments) are deemed separable and separated from politics (power contests), and both from adjudication (interpretation). Neutrality, including judicial decision making that is dispassionate, impersonal, disinterested, and precedential, is considered desirable and descriptive. Courts, forums without predisposition among parties and with no interest of their own, reflect society back to itself resolved. Government of laws not men limits partiality with written constraints and tempers force with reasonable rule following. This law aspires to science: to the immanent generalization subsuming the emergent particularity, to prediction and control of social regularities and regulations, preferably codified. The formulaic "tests" of "doctrine" aspire to mechanism, classification to taxonomy. Courts intervene only in properly "factualized" disputes, cognizing social conflicts as if collecting empirical data. But the demarcations between morals and politics, the personality of the judge and the judicial role, bare coercion and the rule of law, tend to merge in women's experience. Relatively seamlessly they promote the dominance of men as a social group through privileging the form of power—the perspective on social life—feminist consciousness reveals as socially male. The separation of form from substance, process from policy, role from theory and practice, echoes and reechoes at each level of the regime its basic norm: objectivity.

Consider a central example. The separation of public from private is as crucial to the liberal state's claim to objectivity as its inseparability is to women's claim to subordination. Legally, it has both formal and substantive dimensions. The state considers formal, not substantive, the allocation of public matters to itself to be treated objectively, of private matters to civil society to be treated subjectively. Substantively, the private is defined as a right to "an inviolable personality,"[47] which is guaranteed by ensuring "autonomy or control over the intimacies of personal identity."[48] It is hermetic. It means that which is inaccessible to, unaccountable to, and unconstructed by anything beyond itself. Intimacy occurs in private; this is supposed to guarantee original symmetry of power. Injuries arise in violating the private sphere, not within and by and because of it. Private means consent can be presumed unless disproven. To contain a systematic inequality contradicts the notion itself. But feminist consciousness has exploded the private. For women, the measure of the intimacy has been the measure of the oppression. To see the personal as political means to see the private as public. On this level, women have no privacy to lose or to guarantee. We are not inviolable. Our sexuality, meaning gender identity, is not only violable, it *is* (hence we are) our violation. Privacy is everything women as women have never been allowed to be or to have; at the same time the private is everything women have been equated with and defined in terms of *men's* ability to have. To confront the fact that we have no privacy is to confront our private degradation as the public order. To fail to recognize this place of the private in women's subordination by seeking protection behind a right to that privacy is thus to be cut off from collective verification and state support in the same act.[49] The very place (home, body), relations (sexual), activities (intercourse and reproduction), and feelings (intimacy, selfhood) that feminism finds central to women's subjection form the core of privacy doctrine. But when women are segregated in private, one at a time, a law of privacy will tend to protect the right of men "to be let alone,"[50] to oppress us one at a time. A law of the private, in a state that mirrors such a society, will translate the traditional values of the private sphere into individual women's right to privacy, subordinating women's collective needs to the imperatives of male supremacy.[51] It will keep some men out of the bedrooms of other men.

Liberalism converges with the left at this edge of the feminist critique of male power. Herbert Marcuse speaks of "philosophies which are 'political' in the widest sense—affecting society as a whole, demonstrably transcending the sphere of privacy."[52] This does and does not describe the feminist political: "Women both have and have not had a common world."[53] Isolation in the home and intimate degradation, women share. The private sphere, which confines and separates us, is therefore a political sphere, a common ground of our inequality. In feminist translation, the private is a sphere of battery, marital rape, and women's exploited labor; of the central social institutions whereby women are deprived of (as men are granted) identity, autonomy, control, and self-determination; and of the primary activity through which male supremacy is expressed and enforced. Rather than transcending the private as a predicate to politics, feminism politicizes it. For women, the private necessarily transcends the private. If the most private also most "affects society as a whole," the separation between public and private collapses as anything other than potent ideology. The failure of marxism adequately to address intimacy on the one hand, government on the other, is the same failure as the indistinguishability between marxism and liberalism on questions of sexual politics.

Interpreting further areas of law, a feminist theory of the state will reveal that the idealism of liberalism and the materialism of the left have come to much the same for women. Liberal jurisprudence that the law should reflect society and left jurisprudence that all law does or can do is reflect existing social relations will emerge as two guises of objectivist epistemology. If objectivity is the epistemological stance of which women's sexual objectification is the social process, its imposition the paradigm of power in the male form, then the state will appear most relentless in imposing the male point of view when it comes closest to achieving its highest formal criterion of distanced aperspectivity. When it is most ruthlessly neutral, it will be most male; when it is most sex blind, it will be most blind to the sex of the standard being applied. When it most closely conforms to precedent, to "facts," to legislative intent, it will most closely enforce socially male norms and most thoroughly preclude questioning their content as having a point of view at all. Abstract rights will authorize the male experience of the world. The liberal view that law is society's text, its rational mind, expresses this in a normative mode; the traditional left view that the state, and with it the law, is superstructural or epiphenomenal expresses it in an empirical mode. Both rationalize male power by presuming that it does not exist, that equality between the sexes (room for marginal corrections conceded) is society's basic norm and fundamental description. Only feminism grasps the extent to which the opposite is true: that antifeminism is as normative as it is empirical. Once masculinity appears as a specific position, not just as the way things are, its judgments will be revealed in process and procedure, as well as adjudication and legislation. Perhaps the objectivity of the liberal state has made it appear "autonomous of class." Including, but beyond, the bourgeois in liberal legalism, lies what is male about it. However autonomous of class the liberal state may appear, it is not autonomous of sex. Justice will require change, not reflection—a new jurisprudence, a new relation between life and law.

Notes

1. Much has been made of the distinction between sex and gender. Sex is thought the more biological, gender the more social. The relation of each to sexuality varies. Since I believe sexuality is fundamental to gender and fundamentally social, and that biology is its social meaning in the system of sex inequality, which is a social and political system that does not rest independently on biological differences in any respect, the sex/gender distinction looks like a nature/culture distinction. I use sex and gender relatively interchangeably.

3. Male is a social and political concept, not a biological attribute. As I use it, it has *nothing whatever* to do with inherency, preexistence, nature, inevitability, or body as such. It is more epistemological than ontological, undercutting the distinction itself, given male power to conform being with perspective. . . . The perspective from the male standpoint is not always each man's opinion, although most men adhere to it, nonconsciously and without considering it a point of view, as much because it makes sense of their experience (the male experience) as because it is in their interest. It is rational for them. A few men reject it; they pay. Because it is the dominant point of view and defines rationality, women are pushed to see reality in its terms, although this denies their vantage point as women in that it contradicts (at least some of) their lived experience. Women who adopt the male standpoint are passing, epistemologically speaking. This is not uncommon and is rewarded. The intractability of maleness as a form of dominance suggests that social constructs, although they flow from human agency, can be less plastic than nature has proven to be. If experience trying to do so is any guide, it may be easier to change biology than society.

4. In the Bible, to know a woman is to have sex with her. You acquire carnal knowledge. Many scholarly metaphors elaborate the theme of violating boundaries to appropriate from inside to carry off in usable form: "a penetrating observation," "an incisive analysis," "piercing the veil." Mary Ellman writes, "The male mind . . . is assumed to function primarily like a penis. Its fundamental character is seen to be

aggression, and this quality is held essential to the highest or best working of the intellect" *(Thinking about Women* [New York: Harcourt, Brace, Jovanovich, 1968], p. 23). Feminists are beginning to understand that to know has meant to fuck. See Evelyn Fox Keller, "Gender and Science," *Psychoanalysis and Contemporary Thought* 1, no. 3 (1978): 409–33, esp. 413; and Helen Roberts, ed., *Doing Feminist Research* (London: Routledge & Kegan Paul, 1981). The term "to fuck" uniquely captures my meaning because it refers to sexual activity without distinguishing rape from intercourse. At least since Plato's cave, visual metaphors for knowing have been central to Western theories of knowledge, the visual sense prioritized as a mode of verification. The relationship between visual appropriation and objectification is now only beginning to be explored. "The knowledge gained through still photographs will always be . . . a semblance of knowledge, a semblance of wisdom, as the act of taking pictures is a semblance of wisdom, a semblance of rape. The very muteness of what is, hypothetically, comprehensible in photographs is what constitutes their attraction and provocativeness" (Susan Sontag, *On Photography* [New York: Farrar, Straus & Giroux, 1980] p. 24. . . .

5. Feminism aspires to represent the experience of all women as women see it, yet criticizes antifeminism and misogyny, including when it appears in female form. This tension is compressed in the epistemic term of art "the standpoint of all women." We are barely beginning to unpack it. Not all women agree with the feminist account of women's situation, nor do all feminists agree with any single rendition of feminism. Authority of interpretation—the claim to speak as a woman—thus becomes methodologically complex and politically crucial for the same reasons. Consider the accounts of their own experience given by right-wing women and lesbian sadomasochists. How can patriarchy be diminishing to women when women embrace and defend their place in it? How can dominance and submission be violating to women when women eroticize it? Now what is the point of view of the experience of all women? Most responses in the name of feminism, stated in terms of method, either (1) simply regard some women's views as "false consciousness," or (2) embrace any version of women's experience that a biological female claims as her own. The first approach treats some women's views as unconscious conditioned reflections of their oppression, complicitous in it. Just as science devalues experience in the process of uncovering its roots, this approach criticizes the substance of a view because it can be accounted for by its determinants. But if both feminism and antifeminism are responses to the condition of women, how is feminism exempt from devalidation by the same account? That feminism is critical, and antifeminism is not, is not enough, because the question is the basis on which we know something is one or the other when women, all of whom share the condition of women, disagree. The false consciousness approach begs this question by taking women's self-reflections as evidence of their stake in their own oppression, when the women whose self-reflections are at issue question whether their condition is oppressed at all. The second response proceeds as if women are free. Or, at least, as if we have considerable latitude to make, or to choose, the meanings if not the determinants of our situation. Or, that the least feminism can do, since it claims to see the world through women's eyes, is to validate the interpretations women choose. Both responses arise because of the unwillingness, central to feminism, to dismiss some women as simply deluded while granting other women the ability to see the truth. These two resolutions echo the object/subject split: objectivity (my consciousness is true, yours false, never mind why) or subjectivity (I know I am right because it feels right to me, never mind why). This is determinism answered with transcendence, traditional marxism with traditional liberalism, dogmatism with tolerance. The first approach claims authority on the basis of its lack of involvement, asserting its view independent of whether the described concurs—sometimes because it does not. It also has no account, other than its alleged lack of involvement, of its own

ability to provide such an account. How can some women see the truth and other women not? The second approach claims authority on the basis of its involvement. It has no account for different interpretations of the same experience or any way of choosing among conflicting ones, including those between women and men. It tends to assume that women, as we are, have power and are free in exactly the ways feminism, substantively, has found we are not. Thus, the first approach is one-sidedly outside when there is no outside, the second one-sidedly inside when someone (probably a woman) is inside everything, including every facet of sexism, racism, and so on. So our problem is this: the false consciousness approach cannot explain experience as it is experienced by those who experience it. The alternative can only reiterate the terms of that experience. This is only one way in which the object/subject split is fatal to the feminist enterprise.

6. To stress: the feminist criticism is not that the objective stance fails to be truly objective because it has social content, all the better to exorcise that content in the pursuit of the more truly point-of-viewless viewpoint. The criticism is that objectivity is largely accurate to its/the/a world, which world is criticized; and that it becomes more accurate as the power it represents and extends becomes more total. Analogous criticisms have arisen in the natural sciences, without being seen as threatening to the "science of society" project, or calling into question that project's tacit equation between natural and social objects of knowledge. What if we extend Heisenberg's uncertainty principle to social theory? (Werner Heisenberg, *The Physical Principles of the Quantum Theory* [Chicago: University of Chicago Press, 1930], pp. 4, 20, 62–65). What of the axiomatic method after Gödel's proof? (See Ernest Nagel and James R. Newman, *Gödel's Proof* [New York: New York University Press, 1958].)

7. Andrea Dworkin helped me express this.

8. I mean to imply that contemporary feminism that is not methodologically post-marxist is not radical, hence not feminist on this level. For example, to the extent Mary Daly's *Gyn/Ecology: The Metaethics of Radical Feminism* (Boston: Beacon Press, 1978) is idealist in method—meaning that the subordination of women is an idea such that to think it differently is to change it—it is formally liberal no matter how extreme or insightful. To the extent Shulamith Firestone's analysis (*The Dialectic of Sex: The Case for Feminist Revolution* [New York: William Morrow & Co., 1972]) rests on a naturalist definition of gender, holding that women are oppressed by our bodies rather than their social meaning, her radicalism, hence her feminism, is qualified. Susan Griffin's *Pornography and Silence: Culture's Revolt against Nature* (San Francisco: Harper & Row Publishers, 1982) is classically liberal in all formal respects including, for instance, the treatment of pornography and eros as a distinction that is fundamentally psychological rather than interested, more deeply a matter of good and bad (morality) than of power and powerlessness (politics). Andrea Dworkin's work, esp. *Pornography: Men Possessing Women* (New York: Perigee Books, 1981), and Adrienne Rich's poetry and essays, exemplify feminism as a methodological departure. This feminism seeks to define and pursue women's interest as the fate of all women bound together. It seeks to extract the truth of women's commonalities out of the lie that all women are the same. If whatever a given society defines as sexual defines gender, and if gender means the subordination of women to men, "woman" means—is not qualified or undercut by—the uniqueness of each woman and the specificity of race, class, time, and place. In this sense, lesbian feminism, the feminism of women of color, and socialist feminism are converging in a feminist politics of sexuality, race, and class, with a left to right spectrum of its own. This politics is struggling for a practice of unity that does not depend upon sameness without dissolving into empty tolerance, including tolerance of all it exists to change whenever that appears embodied in one of us. A new community begins here. As critique, women's communality describes a fact of male supremacy, of sex "in itself": no woman escapes the meaning

of being a woman within a gendered social system, and sex inequality is not only pervasive but may be universal (in the sense of never having not been in some form) although "intelligible only in . . . locally specific forms" (M. Z. Rosaldo, "The Use and Abuse of Anthropology: Reflections on Feminism and Cross-cultural Understanding," *Signs: Journal of Women in Culture and Society* 5, no. 3 [Spring 1980]: 389–417, 417). For women to become a sex "for ourselves" moves community to the level of vision.

9. See Karl Klare, "Law-Making as Praxis," *Telos* 12, no. 2 (Summer 1979): 123–35; Judith Shklar, *Legalism* (Cambridge, Mass.: Harvard University Press, 1964). To examine law as state is not to decide that all relevant state behavior occurs in legal texts. I do think that legal decisions expose power on the level of legitimizing rationale, and that law, as words in power, is central in the social erection of the liberal state.

10. Karl Marx, *Capital, Selected Works*, 3 vols. (Moscow: Progress Publishers, 1969), 2:120, 139–40; *The German Ideology* (New York: International Publishers, 1972), pp. 48–52; *Introduction to Critique of Hegel's Philosophy of Right*, ed. Joseph O'Malley, trans. Annette Jolin (Cambridge: Cambridge University Press, 1970), p. 139; Marx to P. V. Annenkov, 1846, in *The Poverty of Philosophy* (New York: International Publishers, 1963), pp. 179–93, 181.

11. I am criticizing Engels's assumptions about sexuality and women's place, and his empiricist method, and suggesting that the two are linked. Friedrich Engels, *Origin of the Family, Private Property and the State* (New York: International Publishers, 1942).

17. Laurence Tribe, "Constitution as Point of View" (Harvard Law School, Cambridge, Mass., 1982, mimeographed), p. 13.

18. Madeleine Gagnon, "Body I," in *New French Feminisms*, ed. Elaine Marks and Isabelle de Courtivron (Amherst, Mass.: University of Massachusetts Press, 1980), p. 180.
. . .

20. Susan Brownmiller, *Against Our Will: Men, Women and Rape* (New York: Simon & Schuster, 1976), p. 15.

21. Diana E. H. Russell, *The Politics of Rape: The Victim's Perspective* (New York: Stein & Day, 1977); Andrea Medea and Kathleen Thompson, *Against Rape* (New York: Farrar, Straus & Giroux, 1974); Lorenne M. G. Clark and Debra Lewis, *Rape: The Price of Coercive Sexuality* (Toronto: The Women's Press, 1977); Susan Griffin, "Rape, The All-American Crime," *Ramparts* (September 1971), pp. 26–35; Ti-Grace Atkinson connects rape with "the institution of sexual intercourse" (*Amazon Odyssey: The First Collection of Writings by the Political Pioneer of the Women's Movement* [New York: Links Books, 1974], pp. 13–23). Kalamu ya Salaam, "Rape: A Radical Analysis from the African-American Perspective," in *Our Women Keep Our Skies from Falling* (New Orleans: Nkombo, 1980), pp. 25–40.

22. Racism, clearly, is everyday life. Racism in the United States, by singling out Black men for allegations of rape of white women, has helped obscure the fact that it is men who rape women, disproportionately women of color.

25. "Since we would not want to say that there is anything morally wrong with sexual intercourse per se, we conclude that the wrongness of rape rests with the matter of the woman's consent" (Carolyn M. Shafer and Marilyn Frye, "Rape and Respect," in [*Feminism and Philosophy*, ed. Mary Vetterling-Braggin, Frederick A. Elliston, and Jane English (Totowa, N.J.: Littlefield, Adams & Co., 1977)], p. 334. "Sexual contact is not inherently harmful, insulting or provoking. Indeed, ordinarily it is something of which we are quite fond. The difference between ordinary sexual intercourse and rape is that ordinary sexual intercourse is more or less consented to while rape is not" ([Michael] Davis, ["What's So Bad about Rape?" paper presented at Annual Meeting of the Academy of Criminal Justice Sciences, Louisville, Ky., March 1982], p. 12).

26. Sec. 213.0 of the *Model Penal Code* (Official Draft and Revised Comments 1980), like most states, defines rape as sexual intercourse with a female who is not the wife

of the perpetrator "with some penetration however slight." Impotency is sometimes a defense. Michigan's gender-neutral sexual assault statute includes penetration by objects (sec. 520a[h]; 520[b]). See *Model Penal Code*, annotation to sec. 213.1(d) (Official Draft and Revised Comments 1980).

27. Although it is true that men possess women and that women's bodies are, socially, men's things, I have not analyzed rape as men treating women like property. In the manner of many socialist-feminist adaptations of marxian categories to women's situation, that analysis short-circuits analysis of rape as male sexuality and presumes rather than develops links between sex and class. We need to rethink sexual dimensions of property as well as property dimensions of sexuality.

30. Pauline Bart found that women were more likely to be raped—that is, less able to stop a rape in progress—when they knew their assailant, particularly when they had a prior or current sexual relationship ("A Study of Women Who Both Were Raped and Avoided Rape," *Journal of Social Issues* 37, no. 4 [1981]: 123–37, 132). . . .

31. Answer Brief for Plaintiff-Appellee at 10, People v. Brown, 632 P.2d 1025 (Colo. 1981).

32. Brown, 632 P.2d at 1027 (citing Comment, "Rape and Battery between Husband and Wife," *Stanford Law Review* 6 [1954]: 719–28, 719, 725).

33. Brownmiller (n. 20 above), pp. 8, 196, 400–407, 427–36.

34. See Carol Pateman, "Women and Consent," *Political Theory* 8, no. 2 (May 1980): 149–68.

35. Brownmiller (n. 20 above), p. 5.

36. Shafer and Frye (n. 25 above), p. 334. Battery of wives has been legally separated from marital rape not because assault by a man's fist is so different from assault by a penis. Both seem clearly violent. I am suggesting that both are also sexual. Assaults are often precipitated by women's noncompliance with gender requirements. See R. Emerson Dobash and Russell Dobash, *Violence against Wives: A Case against the Patriarchy* (New York: Free Press, 1979), pp. 14–20. Nearly all incidents occur in the home, most in the kitchen or bedroom. Most murdered women are killed by their husbands, most in the bedroom. The battery cycle accords with the rhythm of heterosexual sex (see Leonore Walker, *The Battered Woman* [New York: Harper & Row Publishers, 1979], pp. 19–20). The rhythm of lesbian S/M appears similar (Samois, eds., *Coming to Power* [Palo Alto, Calif.: Up Press, 1981]). Perhaps most interchange between genders, but especially violent ones, make sense in sexual terms. However, the larger issue for the relation between sexuality and gender, hence sexuality and violence generally, including both war and violence against women, is: What *is* heterosexuality? If it is the erotization of dominance and submission, altering the participants' gender is comparatively incidental. If it is males over female, gender matters independently. Since I see heterosexuality as the fusion of the two, but with gender a social outcome (such that the acted upon is feminized, is the "girl" regardless of sex, the actor correspondingly masculinized), battery appears sexual on a deeper level. In baldest terms, sexuality is violent, so violence is sexual, violence against women doubly so. If this is so, wives are beaten, as well as raped, *as women*—as the acted upon, as gender, meaning sexual, objects. It further follows that all acts *by anyone* which treat a woman according to her object label "woman" are *sexual* acts. The extent to which sexual acts are acts of objectification remains a question of our account of our freedom to make our own meanings. It is clear, at least, that it is centering sexuality upon genitality that distinguishes battery from rape at exactly the juncture that both the law, and seeing rape as violence not sex, does.

37. Even when nonconsent is not a legal element of the offense (as in Michigan), juries tend to infer rape from evidence of force or resistance.

38. This is apparently true of undetected as well as convicted rapists. Samuel David Smithyman's sample, composed largely of the former, contained self-selected respondents

to his ad, which read: "Are you a rapist? Researchers Interviewing Anonymously by Phone to Protect your Identity. Call . . . ." Presumably those who chose to call defined their acts as rapes, at least at the time of responding ("The Undetected Rapist" [Ph.D. diss., Claremont Graduate School, 1978], pp. 54–60, 63–76, 80–90, 97–107).

39. "Probably the single most used cry of rapist to victim is 'You bitch . . . slut . . . you know you want it. You *all* want it' and afterward, 'there now, you really enjoyed it, didn't you?'" (Nancy Gager and Cathleen Schurr, *Sexual Assault: Confronting Rape in America* [New York: Grosset & Dunlap, 1976], p. 244).

40. See Director of Public Prosecutions v. Morgan, 2411 E.R.H.L. 347 (1975); Pappajohn v. The Queen, 11 D.L.R. 3d 1 (1980); People v. Mayberry, 15 Cal. 3d 143, 542 P.2d 1337 (1975).

41. Richard H. S. Tur, "Rape: Reasonableness and Time," *Oxford Journal of Legal Studies* 3 (Winter 1981): 432–41, 441. Tur, in the context of the Morgan and Pappajohn cases, says the "law ought not to be astute to equate wickedness and wishful, albeit mistaken, thinking" (p. 437). In feminist analysis, a rape is not an isolated or individual or moral transgression but a terrorist act within a systematic context of group subjection, like lynching.

42. See Silke Vogelmann-Sine et al., "Sex Differences in Feelings Attributed to a Woman in Situations Involving Coercion and Sexual Advances," *Journal of Personality* 47, no. 3 (September 1979): 420–31, esp. 429–30.

43. Note, "Forcible and Statutory Rape: An Exploration of the Operation and Objectives of the Consent Standard," *Yale Law Journal* 62 (1952): 55–56.

44. A similar analysis of sexual harassment suggests that women have such "power" only so long as we behave according to male definitions of female desirability, that is, only so long as we accede the definition of our sexuality (hence, ourselves, as gender female) to male terms. We have this power only so long as we remain powerless.

47. S. D. Warren and L. D. Brandeis, "The Right to Privacy," *Harvard Law Review* 4 (1890): 193–205.

48. Tom Gerety, "Redefining Privacy," *Harvard Civil Right–Civil Liberties Law Review* 12, no. 2 (Spring 1977): 236.

49. Harris v. McRae, 448 U.S. 287 (1980), which holds that withholding public funds for abortions does not violate the federal constitutional right to privacy, illustrates. See Zillah Eisenstein, *The Radical Future of Liberal Feminism* (New York: Longman, Inc., 1981), p. 240.

50. Robeson v. Rochester Folding Box Co., 171 NY 538 (1902); Cooley, *Torts*, sec. 135, 4th ed. (Chicago: Callaghan & Co., 1932).

51. This argument learned a lot from Tom Grey's article, "Eros, Civilization and the Burger Court," *Law and Contemporary Problems* 43, no. 3 (Summer 1980): 83–99.

52. Herbert Marcuse, "Repressive Tolerance," in *A Critique of Pure Tolerance*, ed. Robert Paul Wolff, Barrington Moore, Jr., and Herbert Marcuse (Boston: Beacon Press, 1965), pp. 81–117, esp. p. 91.

53. Adrienne Rich, "Conditions for Work: The Common World of Women," in *Working It Out: Twenty-three Women Writers, Artists, Scientists, and Scholars Talk about Their Lives and Work*, ed. Sara Ruddick and Pamela Daniels (New York: Pantheon Books, 1977), pp. xiv–xxiv, esp. p. xiv.

10

Jurisprudence and Gender [1988]

Robin West

Introduction

What is a human being? Legal theorists must, perforce, answer this question: jurisprudence, after all, is about human beings. The task has not proven to be divisive. In fact, virtually all modern American legal theorists, like most modern moral and political philosophers, either explicitly or implicitly embrace what I will call the "separation thesis" about what it means to be a human being: a "human being," whatever else he is, is physically separate from all other human beings. I am one human being and you are another, and that distinction between you and me is central to the meaning of the phrase "human being." Individuals are, in the words of one commentator, "distinct and not essentially connected with one another."[1] We are each physically "boundaried"— this is the trivially true meaning of the claim that we are all individuals. In Robert Nozick's telling phrase, the "root idea" of any acceptable moral or political philosophy is that "there are individuals with separate lives."[2] Although Nozick goes on to derive from this insight an argument for the minimal state, the separation thesis is hardly confined to the libertarian right. According to Roberto Unger, premiere spokesperson for the communitarian left, "[t]o be conscious is to have the experience of being *cut off* from that about which one reflects: it is to be a subject that stands over against its objects . . . . *The subjective awareness of separation . . . defines consciousness.*"[3] The political philosopher Michael Sandel has recently argued that most (not all) modern political theory is committed to the proposition that "[w]hat separates us is in some important sense prior to what connects us—epistemologically prior as well as morally prior. We are distinct individuals first, and then we form relationships and engage in co-operative arrangements with others; hence the priority of plurality over unity."[4] The same commitment underlies virtually all of our legal theory. Indeed, Sandel's formulation may be taken as a definitive restatement of the "separation thesis" that underlies modern jurisprudence.

The . . . purpose of this essay is to put forward the global and critical claim that by virtue of their shared embrace of the separation thesis, all of our modern legal theory—by which I mean "liberal legalism" and "critical legal theory" collectively—is essentially and irretrievably masculine. [My use of "I" above was inauthentic, just as the modern, increasing use of the female pronoun in liberal and critical legal theory, although well-intended, is empirically and experientially false] For the cluster of claims that jointly constitute the "separation thesis"—the claim that human beings are, definitionally, distinct from one another, the claim that the referent of "I" is singular and unambiguous, the claim that the word "individual" has an uncontested biological meaning, namely that we are each physically individuated from every other, the claim that we are individuals "first," and the claim that what separates us is epistemologically and morally prior to what connects us—while "trivially true" of men, [is] patently untrue of women. Women are not essentially, necessarily, inevitably, invariably, always, and forever separate from other human beings: women, distinctively, are quite clearly "connected" to another human life when pregnant. In fact, women are in some sense "connected" to life and to other human beings during at least four recurrent and critical material experiences: the experience of pregnancy itself; the invasive and "connecting" experience of heterosexual penetration, which may lead to pregnancy; the monthly experience of menstruation, which represents the potential from pregnancy; and the post-pregnancy experience of breast-feeding. Indeed, perhaps the central insight of feminist theory of the last decade has been that women are "essentially connected," not "essentially separate," from the rest of human life, both materially, through pregnancy, intercourse, and breast-feeding, and existentially, through the moral and practical life. [If by "human beings" legal theorists mean women as well as men, then the "separation thesis" is clearly false. If, alternatively, by "human beings" they mean those for whom the separation thesis is true, then women are not human beings. It's not hard to guess which is meant. . . .]

Rejects
separation
thesis as
applied to
women.

SYLLOGISM:
P: Human
beings are those
for whom sep.
thesis is true.
P: Women are
not "essentially separate" (because of the interconnectedness of our biology)
C: Women are not human beings.

Masculine Jurisprudence and Feminist Theory

The by now very well publicized split in masculine jurisprudence between legal liberalism and critical legal theory can be described in any number of ways. The now standard way to describe the split is in terms of politics: "liberal legal theorists" align themselves with a liberal political philosophy which entails, among other things, allegiance to the Rule of Law and to Rule of Law virtues, while "critical legal theorists," typically left wing and radical, are skeptical of the Rule of Law and the split between law and politics which the Rule of Law purportedly delineates. Critical legal theorists are potentially far more sensitive to the political underpinnings of purportedly neutral legalistic constructs than are liberal legalists. I think this traditional characterization is wrong for a number of reasons: liberal theorists are not necessarily politically naive, and critical theorists are not necessarily radical. However, my purpose is not to critique it. [Instead, I want to suggest another way to understand the divisions in modern legal theory.]

An alternative description of the difference (surely not the only one) is that liberal legal theory and critical legal theory provide two radically divergent phenomenological descriptions of the paradigmatically male experience of the inevitability of separation of the self from the rest of the species, and indeed from the rest of the natural world. Both schools . . . accept the separation thesis; they both view human beings as materially (or physically) separate from each other, and both view this fact as fundamental to the origin of law. But their accounts of the subjective experience of physical separation from the other—an individual other, the natural world, and society—are in nearly diametrical opposition. Liberal legalists, in short, describe an inner life enlivened by freedom and autonomy from the separate other, and threatened by the danger of annihilation by him. Critical legal theorists, by contrast, tell a story of inner lives dominated by feelings of alienation and isolation from the separate other, and enlivened by the possibility of association and community with him. These differing accounts of the subjective experience of being separate from others, I believe, are at the root of at least some of the divisions between critical and liberal legal theorists. . . .

I will start with the liberal description of separation, because it is the most familiar, and surely the most dominant. According to liberal legalism, the inevitability of the individual's material separation from the "other," entails, first and foremost, an existential state of highly desirable and much valued freedom: because the individual is *separate* from the other, he is *free* of the other. Because I am separate from you, *my* ends, *my* life, *my* path, *my* goals are necessarily my own. Because I am separate, I am "autonomous." Because I am separate, I am existentially free (whether or not I am politically free). And, of course, this is true not just of me, but of everyone: it is the universal human condition. We are each separate and we are all separate, so we are each free and we are all free. We are, that is, equally free.

This existential condition of freedom in turn entails the liberal's conception of value. Because we are all free and we are each equally free, we should be treated by our government as free, and as equally free. The individual must be treated by his government (and by others) in a way that respects his equality and his freedom. The government must honor at the level of politics the existential claim made above: that my ends are *my* ends; that I cannot be forced to embrace your ends as my own. Our separation entails our freedom which in turn entails our right to establish and pursue our own concept of value, independent of the concept of value pursued or favored by others. Ronald Dworkin puts the point in this way:

> What does it mean for the government to treat its citizens as equals? *That is . . . the same question as the question of what it means for the government to treat all its citizens as free, or as independent, or with equal dignity . . . .* [To accord with this demand, a government must] be neutral on what might be called the question of the good life. . . .[5]

Because of the dominance of liberalism in this culture, we might think of autonomy as the "official" liberal value entailed by the physical, material condition of inevitable separation from the other: separation from the other entails my freedom from him, and that in turn entails my political right to autonomy. I can form my own conception of the good life, and pursue it. Indeed, any conception of the good which I form, will necessarily be *my* conception of the good life. That freedom must be respected. Because I am free, I value and have a right to autonomy. . . .

Autonomy, freedom and equality collectively constitute what might be called the "up side" of the subjective experience of separation. Autonomy and freedom are both entailed by the separation thesis, and autonomy and freedom both feel very good. However, there's a "down side" to the subjective experience of separation as well. Physical separation from the other entails not just my freedom; it also entails my vulnerability. Every other discrete, separate individual—because he is the "other"—is a source of danger to me and a threat to my autonomy. I have reason to fear you solely by virtue of the fact that I am me and you are you. You are not me, so by definition my ends are not your ends. Our ends might conflict. You might try to frustrate my pursuit of my ends. In an extreme case, you might even try to kill me—you might cause my annihilation.

Annihilation by the other, we might say, is the official *harm* of liberal theory, just as autonomy is its official value. Hobbes, of course, gave the classic statement of the terrifying vulnerability that stems from our separateness from the other:

> Nature hath made men so equall, in the faculties of body, and mind; as that though there bee found one man sometimes manifestly stronger in body, or of quicker mind then [sic] another; yet when all is reckoned together, the difference between man, and man, is not so considerable, as that one man can thereupon claim to himselfe any benefit, to which another may not pretend, as well as he. . . .[7]

Bruce Ackerman gives a more modern rendition, but the message is essentially the same:

> So long as we live, there can be no escape from the struggle for power. *Each of us must control his body and the world around it.* However modest these personal claims, they are forever at risk in a world of scarce resources. Someone, somewhere, will—if given the chance—take the food that sustains or the heart that beats within. . . .[8]

Thus, according to liberal legalism, the subjective experience of physical separation from the other determines both what we value (autonomy) and what we fear (annihilation). . . .

Now, Critical Legal Theory diverges from liberal legalism on many points, but one striking contrast is this: critical theorists provide a starkly divergent phenomenological description of the subjective experience of separation. According to our critical legal theorists, the separate individual is indeed, in Sandel's phrase, "epistemologically prior to the collective." Like liberal legalists, critical legal theorists also view the individual as materially separate from the rest of human life. But according to the critical theorist, what the material state of separation existentially entails is not a perpetual celebration of autonomy,

PLT's
individuals
fear not
annihilation,
but alienation.

but rather, a perpetual longing for community, or attachment, or unification, or connection. The separate individual strives to connect with the "other" from whom he is separate. The separate individual lives in a state of perpetual dread not of annihilation by the other, but of the alienation, loneliness, and existential isolation that his material separation from the other imposes upon him. The individual strives through love, work, and government to achieve a unification with the other, the natural world, and the society from which he was originally and continues to be existentially separated. The separate individual seeks *community*—not autonomy—and dreads isolation and alienation from the other— not annihilation by him. If we think of liberalism's depiction of the subjectivity of separation as the official story, then, we might think of this alternative description of the subjectivity of separation as the unofficial story. It is the subterranean, unofficial story of the unrecognized and—at least by liberals— slightly detested subjective craving of lost individuals.

. . . Robert Unger describes the terror that separation inflicts upon the individual in this way:

> Consciousness, then, is the sign of the self's distance from the world. If one could imagine this separateness from nature in its pure form, before it was counterbalanced by the effects of human activity, its sign would be the experience of terror before the strangeness of the world. *Because this terror is the mark of that very separation between self and nature upon which consciousness itself is based,* it has never been driven completely out of conscious life. On the contrary, the strength of the social bond, the willingness to accept almost every form of degradation and enslavement at the hands of society, owes much to the need men have of belonging to a social world in which the foreignness of a pre-human nature does not prevail.[10]

Indeed, the individual longs to reestablish connection with the other in spite of the very real possibility (acknowledged by most if not all critical theorists) that that other might, at any moment, frustrate his ends, threaten his autonomy, or annihilate him. But this longing for community survives in the face of an even more powerful source of resistance. The longing for attachment to the other persists in spite of the dominant liberal culture's adamant denial of the desire's existence. Peter Gabel describes the longing for connection in this way:

> . . . [W]e are constituted as social beings by the desire to be recognized by others in an empowering, life-giving way. It is this fundamental experiential need that animates a baby's search for "eye-contact" with mother as well as the organizational efforts of adults who try to form into groups to vitalize their work-situations through the achievement of solidarity. While our actions are obviously also motivated by other factors . . . it is the desire to *connect* through this confirming or genuine reciprocity that gives to our actions their distinctive social energy, impelling us out toward the other even when . . . the likelihood of success seems very small.[11]

. . .

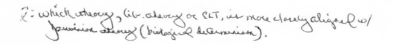

Q: which theory, lib. theory or PLT, is more closely aligned w/ feminism theory (biological determinism).

To summarize: according to liberal legalism, each of us is physically separate from every other, and because of that separation, we value our autonomy from the other and fear our annihilation by him. I have called these our "officially" recognized values and harms. Critical legal theory tells the unofficial story. According to critical legal theory, we are indeed physically separate from the other, but what that existentially entails is that we dread the alienation and isolation from the separate other, and long for connection with him. While liberal culture officially and publicly claims that we love our autonomy and fear the other, subjective life belies this claim. Subjectively, and in spite of the dominant culture's insistence to the contrary, we long to establish some sort of human connection with the other in order to overcome the pain of isolation and alienation which our separateness engenders. These two contrasting stories of the subjective experience of perpetual separation from the rest of human life might be schematized in this way.

	(The Official Story) LIBERAL LEGALISM	(The Unofficial Story) CRITICAL LEGALISM
VALUE (or Longing):	Autonomy	Connection; Community
HARM (or Dread):	Annihilation; Frustration	Alienation; Isolation

Let me now turn to feminist theory. Although the legal academy is for the most part unaware of it, modern feminist theory is as fundamentally divided as legal theory. One way to characterize the conflict—the increasingly standard way to characterize the conflict—is that while most modern feminists agree that women are different from men and agree on the importance of the difference, feminists differ over which differences between men and women are most vital. According to one group of feminists, sometimes called "cultural feminists," the important difference between men and women is that women raise children and men don't. According to a second group of feminists, now called "radical feminists," the important difference between men and women is that women get fucked and men fuck: "women," definitionally, are "those from whom sex is taken," just as workers, definitionally, are those from whom labor is taken. Another way to put the difference is in political terms. Cultural feminists appear somewhat more "moderate" when compared with the traditional culture: from a mainstream non-feminist perspective, cultural feminists appear to celebrate many of the same feminine traits that the traditional culture has stereotypically celebrated. Radical feminists, again from a mainstream perspective, appear more separatist, and, in contrast with standard political debate, more alarming. They also appear to be more "political" in a sense which perfectly parallels the critical theory-liberal theory split described above: radical feminists appear to be more attuned to power disparities between men and women than are cultural feminists.

I think this traditional characterization is wrong on two counts. First, cultural feminists no less than radical feminists are well aware of women's powerlessness vis-a-vis men, and second, radical feminism, as I will later argue, is as centrally concerned with pregnancy as it is with intercourse. But again, instead of arguing against this traditional characterization of the divide between radical and cultural feminism, I want to provide an alternative. My alternative characterization structurally (although not substantively) parallels the characterization of the difference between liberal and critical legalism. Underlying both radical and cultural feminism is a conception of women's existential state that is grounded in women's potential for physical, material connection to human life, just as underlying both liberal and critical legalism is a conception of men's existential state that is grounded in the inevitability of men's physical separation from the species. I will call the shared conception of women's existential lives the "connection thesis." The divisions between radical and cultural feminism stem from divergent accounts of the subjectivity of the potential for connection, just as what divides liberal from critical legal theory are divergent accounts of the subjectivity of the inevitability of separation.

The "connection thesis" is simply this: Women are actually or potentially materially connected to other human life. Men aren't. This material fact has existential consequences. While it may be true *for men* that the individual is "epistemologically and morally prior to the collectivity," it is not true for women. The potential for material connection with the other defines women's subjective, phenomenological and existential state, just as surely as the inevitability of material separation from the other defines men's existential state. Our potential for material connection engenders pleasures and pains, values and dangers, and attractions and fears, which are entirely different from those which follow, for men, from the necessity of separation. Indeed, it is the rediscovery of the multitude of implications from this material difference between men and women which has enlivened (and divided) both cultural and radical feminism in this decade (and it is those discoveries which have distinguished both radical and cultural feminism from liberal feminism). As Carol Gilligan notes, this development is somewhat paradoxical: during the same decade that liberal feminist political activists and lawyers pressed for equal (meaning same) treatment by the law, feminist theorists in non-legal disciplines rediscovered women's differences from men.[13] Thus, what unifies radical and cultural feminist theory (and what distinguishes both from liberal feminism) is the discovery, or rediscovery, of the importance of women's fundamental material difference from men. As we shall see, neither radical feminists nor cultural feminists are entirely explicit in their embrace of the connection thesis. But both groups, implicitly if not explicitly, adhere to some version of it.

If both cultural and radical feminists hold some version of the connection thesis, then one way of understanding the issues that divide radical and cultural feminists, different from the standard account given above, is that while radical and cultural feminists agree that women's lives are distinctive in their potential for material connection to others, they provide sharply contrasting accounts of the subjective experience of the material and existential state of connection. According to cultural feminist accounts of women's subjectivity, women value intimacy, develop a capacity for nurturance, and an ethic of care for the "other" with which we are connected, just as we learn to dread and fear separation from the other. Radical feminists tell a very different story. According to radical feminism, women's connection with the "other" is above all else invasive and intrusive: women's potential for material "connection" invites invasion into the physical integrity of our bodies, and intrusion into the existential integrity of our lives. Although women may "officially" value the intimacy of connection, we "unofficially" dread the intrusion it inevitably entails, and long for the individuation and independence that deliverance from that state of connection would permit. Paralleling the structure above, I will call these two descriptions feminism's official and unofficial stories of women's subjective experience of physical connection.

In large part due to the phenomenal success of Carol Gilligan's book *In a Different Voice*, cultural feminism may be the most familiar of these two feminist strands, and for that reason *alone*, I call it feminism's "official story." "Cultural feminism" (in this country and among academics) is in large part defined by Gilligan's book. Defined as such, cultural feminism begins not with a commitment to the "material" version of the connection thesis (as outlined above), but rather, with a commitment to its more observable existential and psychological consequences. Thus limited, we can put the cultural feminist point this way: women have a "sense" of existential "connection" to other human life which men do not. That sense of connection in turn entails a way of learning, a path of moral development, an aesthetic sense, and a view of the world and of one's place within it which sharply contrasts with men's. To reverse Sandel's formulation, for women, connection is "prior," both epistemologically and, therefore, morally, to the individual. . . .

Why are men and women different in this essential way? The cultural feminist explanation for women's heightened sense of connection is that women are more "connected" to life than are men because it is women who are the primary caretakers of young children. A female child develops her sense of identity as "continuous" with her caretaker's, while a young boy develops a sense of identity that is distinguished from his caretaker's. Because of the gender alignment of mothers and female children, young girls "fuse" their growing sense of identity with a sense of sameness with and attachment to the other, while because of the gender distinction between mothers and male children, young boys "fuse" their growing sense of identity with a sense of difference and separation from the other. This turns out to have truly extraordinary and far reaching consequences, for both cognitive and moral development. Nancy Chodorow explains:

> [This means that] [g]irls emerge from this period with a basis for "empathy" built into their primary definition of self in a way that boys do not . . . . [G]irls come to experience themselves as less differentiated than boys, as more continuous with and related to the external object-world and as differently oriented to their inner object-world as well.[15]

Women are therefore capable of a degree of physical as well as psychic *intimacy* with the other which greatly exceeds men's capacity. Carol Gilligan finds that:

The fusion of identity and intimacy . . . [is] clearly articulated . . . in [women's] . . . self-descriptions. In response to the request to describe themselves, . . . women describe a relationship, depicting their identity *in* the connection of future mother, present wife, adopted child, or past lover. Similarly, the standard of moral judgement that informs their assessment of self is a standard of relationship, an ethic of nurturance, responsibility, and care . . . [In] women's descriptions, identity is defined in a context of relationship and judged by a standard of responsibility and care. Similarly, morality is seen by these women as arising from the experience of connection and conceived as a problem of inclusion rather than one of balancing claims.[16]

[handwritten margin note: MORALITY: PROBLEM OF INCLUSION v. BALANCING CLAIMS]

. . .

Thus, according to Gilligan (and her subjects), women view themselves as fundamentally connected to, not separate from, the rest of life. This difference permeates virtually every aspect of our lives. According to the vast literature on difference now being developed by cultural feminists, women's cognitive development, literary sensibility, aesthetic taste, and psychological development, no less than our anatomy, are all fundamentally different from men's, and are different in the same way: unlike men, we view ourselves as connected to, not separate from, the other. As a consequence, women's ways of knowing are more "integrative" than men's; women's aesthetic and critical sense is "embroidered" rather than "laddered;" women's psychological development remains within the sphere of "attachment" rather than "individuation."

The most significant aspect of our difference, though, is surely the moral difference. According to cultural feminism, women are more nurturant, caring, loving and responsible to others than are men. This capacity for nurturance and care dictates the moral terms in which women, distinctively, construct social relations: women view the morality of actions against a standard of responsibility to others, rather than against a standard of rights and autonomy from others. As Gilligan puts it:

> The moral imperative . . . [for] women is an injunction to care, a responsibility to discern and alleviate the "real and recognizable trouble" of this world. For men, the moral imperative appears rather as an injunction to respect the rights of others and thus to protect from interference the rights to life and self-fulfillment.[18]

Cultural feminists, to their credit, have reidentified these differences as women's strengths, rather than women's weaknesses. Cultural feminism does not simply *identify* women's differences—patriarchy too insists on women's differences—it celebrates them. Women's art, women's craft, women's narrative capacity, women's critical eye, women's ways of knowing, and women's heart, are all, for the cultural feminist, redefined as things to celebrate. Quilting, cultural feminism insists, is not just something women do; it is art, and should be recognized as such. Integrative knowledge is not a confused and failed attempt to come to grips with the elementary rules of deductive logic; it is a way of knowledge and should be recognized as such. Women's distinctive aesthetic sense is as valid as men's. Most vital, however, for cultural feminism is the claim that intimacy is not just something women *do*, it is something human beings *ought* to do. Intimacy is a source of value, not a private hobby. It is morality, not habit.

To pursue my structural analogy to masculine legal theory, then, intimacy and the ethic of care constitute the entailed *values* of the existential state of connection with others, just as autonomy and freedom constitute the entailed values of the existential state of separation from others for men. Because women are fundamentally connected to other human life, women value and enjoy intimacy with others (just as because men are fundamentally separate from other human life men value and enjoy autonomy). Because women are connected with the rest of human life, intimacy with the "other" comes naturally. Caring, nurturance, and an ethic of love and responsibility for life is second nature. Autonomy, or freedom from the other constitutes a value for men because it reflects an existential state of being: separate. Intimacy is a value for women because it reflects an existentially connected state of being.

Intimacy, the capacity for nurturance and the ethic of care constitute what we might call the "up side" of the subjective experience of connection. It's all good. Intimacy feels good, nurturance is good, and caring for others morally is good. But there's a "down side" to the subjective experience of connection. There's danger, harm, and fear entailed by the state of connection as well as value. Whereas men fear annihilation from the separate other (and consequently have trouble achieving intimacy), women fear separation from the connected other (and consequently have trouble achieving independence). Gilligan makes the point succinctly: "Since masculinity is defined through separation while femininity is defined through attachment, male gender identity is threatened by intimacy while female gender identity is threatened by separation."[19] Separation, then, might be regarded as the official harm of cultural feminism. When a separate self must be asserted, women have trouble asserting it. . . .

. . . It seems quite plausible that women are more psychically connected to others in just the way Gilligan describes and for just the reason she expounds. Mothers raise children, and as a consequence girls, and not boys, think of themselves as continuous with, rather than separate from, that first all-important "other"—the mother. But this psychological and developmental explanation just raises—it does not answer—the background material question: why do women, rather than men, raise, nurture, and cook for children? What is the cause of this difference?

Although Gilligan doesn't address the issue, other cultural feminists have, and their explanations converge, I believe, implicitly if not explicitly, on a material, or mixed material-cultural, and not just a cultural answer: women *raise* children—and hence raise girls who are more connected and nurturant, and therefore more likely to be nurturant caretakers themselves—because it is women who bear children. Women are not inclined to abandon an infant they've carried for nine months and then delivered. If so, then women are ultimately more "connected"—psychically, emotionally, and morally—to other human beings because women, as children were raised by women and women raise children/because women, uniquely, are physically and materially "connected" to those human beings when the human beings are fetuses and then infants. Women are/more empathic to the lives of others because women are physically tied to the/lives of others in a way which men are not. Women's moral voice is one of/responsibility, duty and care for others because women's material circumstance is one of responsibility, duty and care for those who are first physically attached, then physically dependent, and then emotionally interdependent. [Women think in terms of the needs of others rather than the rights of others because women materially, and then physically, and then psychically, provide for the needs of others.] Lastly, women fear separation from the other rather than annihilation by him, and "count" it as a harm, because women experience the "separating" pain of childbirth and more deeply feel the pain of the maturation and departure of adult children.

Although this material explanation of women's difference now overtly dominates at least some forms of French cultural feminism, it still plays a largely implicit, rather than explicit role in United States cultural feminism, although that status is changing. There are several reasons for the reluctance of American cultural feminists to explicitly embrace a material version of the connection thesis. The first is totally external to feminism, and is, rather, internal to the academic community for which Gilligan's book was written and in which it was received. It is an academic allegiance to empirical rather than phenomenological explanations of social phenomena. [Material explanations require a willingness to engage in a form of speculative inquiry which is contrary to now dominant academic modes of proof.]

The second, and I believe major, reason for the resistance to material explanations of women's difference in American feminism is primarily strategic: American feminists of all stripes are wary of identifying the material fact of pregnancy as the root of moral, aesthetic, and cognitive difference, because, as liberal feminist and law professor Wendy Williams correctly notes, "most of the disadvantages imposed on women, in the workforce and elsewhere, derive from this central reality of the capacity of women to become pregnant *and the real and supposed implications of this reality.*"[22] The response to this "central reality" among American liberal feminists and American feminist lawyers has been to deny or minimize the importance of the pregnancy difference, thus making men and women more "alike," so as to force the legal system to treat men and women similarly.

Although a review of the history of liberal feminism is well beyond the scope of this essay, suffice it to say that there is a growing awareness amongst even liberal feminist legal theorists that this strategy has to some extent backfired. It has become increasingly clear that feminists must attack the burdens of pregnancy and its attendant differences, rather than denying the uniqueness of pregnancy. . . .[23]

Outside of the legal community . . . there is less reluctance among even U.S. cultural feminists to embrace /material explanations\ both of women's moral distinctiveness and political oppression. Let me mention just three examples, each from different disciplines. First, poet and scholar Adrienne Rich, who has surely done more than any other American feminist to lay bare the issues surrounding mandatory motherhood within conditions of patriarchy, . . . suggests the centrality of motherhood and the physicality of pregnancy to women's lives, to women's existential sense of connection, and ultimately of course to feminism:

> . . . . [M]otherhood is the great mesh in which all human relations are entangled, in which lurk our most elemental assumptions about love and power. . . .[24]

Marilyn French has also begun to bring an overtly material explanation both of women's "difference" and of women's oppression out of the background and into the forefront of American cultural feminism. Women have a different moral voice, French argues, because women are fundamentally committed to the preservation and survival of life, while men are committed to the goal of transcendence. Although French insists, correctly, that this existential difference is in no sense biologically *mandated* (men could become more nurturant and women could become more independent), it is nevertheless biologically *grounded*: it reflects natural and material facts, and reflects our natural and pre-legal history. Women are tied to nature and the life of the other, French argues, while men are fearful of nature and seek to transcend it rather than preserve it. . . .[25]

Similarly, and finally, in *Caring: A Feminine Approach to Ethics and Moral Education*,[28] Stanford philosopher and cultural feminist Nel Noddings endorses a biological and material explanation of women's different moral voice:

[C]learly, mothering and caring are deeply related. Several contemporary writers have raised a question that seems odd at first glance: Why is it that women in our society do the mothering? . . . . The biological view holds that women, having given birth and entered lactation, are naturally nurturant toward their infants. The socialization view denies arguments for nature, instinct, and natural nurturance and insists that mothering is a role—something learned. Finally, the psychological view suggested by Nancy Chodorow holds that the tendency for girls to want to mother, and to actually engage in mothering, is the result of deep psychological processes established in close and special relationships with their own mothers.

The socialization view, as an explanatory theory, seems nonsense. We are not nearly so successful at socializing people into roles as we are at reproducing mothering in women. Mothering is not a role but a relationship. The psychological view, however, seems very strong. . . . One difficulty [with it] is that those endorsing psychological views have felt the need to set aside or minimize biological arguments. It is true that a woman's natural inclination to mother a newborn does not explain why she continues to mother a child into adolescence or why she mothers other people's half-grown children. But it may well be that a completely adequate theory will have to embrace both biological and psychological factors.[29]

Whether we embrace a material or a purely developmental explanation of women's heightened connection with the other, however, the "story" of women's relationship with the other as told by cultural feminists [contrasts] in virtually every particular with the story of men's relationship to the other as told by liberals. . . .

. . . If, as I have suggested, cultural feminism is our dominant feminist dogma, then this account of the nature of women's lives constitutes the "official text" of feminism, just as liberal legalism constitutes the official text of legalism.

These two "official stories" sharply contrast. Whereas according to liberal legalism, men value autonomy from the other and fear annihilation by him, women, according to cultural feminism, value intimacy with the other and fear separation from her. Women's sense of connection with others determines our special competencies and special vulnerabilities, just as men's sense of separation from others determines theirs. Women value and have a special competency for intimacy, nurturance, and relational thinking, and a special vulnerability to and fear of isolation, separation from the other, and abandonment, just as men value and have a special competency for autonomy, and a special vulnerability to and fear of annihilation.

Against the cultural feminist backdrop, the story that radical feminists tell of women's invaded, violated lives is "subterranean" in the same sense that, against the backdrop of liberal legalism, the story critical legal theorists tell of men's alienation and isolation from others is subterranean. According to radical feminism, women's connection to others is the source of women's misery, not a source of value worth celebrating. For cultural feminists, women's connectedness to the other (whether material or cultural) is the source, the heart, the root, and the cause of women's different morality, different voice, different "ways of knowing," different genius, different capacity for care, and different ability to nurture. For radical feminists, that same potential for connection—experienced materially in intercourse and pregnancy, but experienced existentially in all spheres of life—is the source of women's debasement, powerlessness, subjugation, and misery. It is the cause of our pain, and the reason for our stunted lives. Invasion and intrusion, rather than intimacy, nurturance and care, is the "unofficial" story of women's subjective experience of connection.

Thus, modern radical feminism is unified among other things by its insistence on the invasive, oppressive, destructive implications of women's material and existential connection to the other. So defined, radical feminism (of modern times) begins not with the eighties critique of heterosexuality, but rather in the late sixties, with Shulamith Firestone's angry and eloquent denunciation of the oppressive consequences for women of the physical condition of pregnancy. Firestone's assessment of the importance and distinctiveness of women's reproductive role parallels Marilyn French's. Both view women's physical connection with nature and with the other as in some sense the "cause" of patriarchy. But their analyses of the chain of causation sharply contrast. For French, women's reproductive role—the paradigmatic experience of physical connection to nature, to life and to the other, and thus the core of women's moral difference—is also the cause of patriarchy, primarily because of men's fear of and contempt for nature. Firestone has a radically different view. Pregnancy is indeed the paradigmatic experience of physical connection, and it is indeed the core of women's difference, but according to Firestone, it is for that reason *alone* the cause of women's oppression. Male contempt has nothing (at first) to do with it. *Pregnancy itself,* independent of male contempt, is invasive, dangerous

[margin note: AD. FEM "invasion" radical other intimacy is why unofficial story of women's experience of connection.]

and oppressive; it is an assault on the physical integrity and privacy of the body. For Firestone, the strategic implication of this is both clear and clearly

Wow! → material. The technological separation of reproduction from the female body is the necessary condition for women's liberation.[31]

In a moment, I will turn to heterosexual intercourse, for it is intercourse, rather than pregnancy, which consumes the attention of the modern radical feminism of our decade. But before doing so it's worth recognizing that the original radical feminist case for reproductive freedom did not turn on rights of "privacy" (either of the doctor-patient relationship, or of the marriage, or of the family), or rights to "equal protection," or rights to be free of "discrimination." It did not turn on rights at all. Rather, the original feminist argument for reproductive freedom turned on the definitive radical feminist insight that pregnancy—the invasion of the body by the other to which women are distinctively vulnerable—is an injury and ought to be treated as such. Pregnancy connects us with life, as the cultural feminist insists, but that connection is not something to celebrate; it is that very connection that hurts us. This argument, as I will argue later, is radically incommensurate with liberal legal ideology. There's no legal category that fits it. But it is nevertheless the radical argument—that pregnancy is a dangerous, psychically consuming, existentially intrusive, and physically invasive assault upon the body which in turn leads to a dangerous, consuming, intrusive, invasive assault on the mother's self-identity—that best captures women's own sense of the injury and danger of pregnancy, whether or not it captures the law's sense of what an unwanted pregnancy involves, or why women should have the right to terminate it.

The radical feminist argument for reproductive freedom appears in legal argument only inadvertently or surreptitiously, but it does on occasion appear. It appeared most recently in the phenomenological descriptions of unwanted pregnancies collated in the *Thornburgh* amicus brief recently filed by the National Abortion Rights Action League ("NARAL").[32] The descriptions of pregnancy collated in that peculiarly non-legal legal document are filled with metaphors of invasion—metaphors, of course, because we lack the vocabulary to name these harms precisely. Those descriptions contrast sharply with the "joy" that cultural feminists celebrate in pregnancy, childbirth and child-raising. The invasion of the self by the other emerges as a source of oppression, not a source of moral value.

"During my pregnancy," one [woman] explains, "I was treated *like a baby machine—an incubator without feelings.*"[33] "Then I got pregnant again," another woman writes,

> This one would be only 13 months younger than the third child. I was faced with the unpleasant fact that I could not stop the babies from coming no matter what I did. . . . *You cannot possibly know what it is like to be the helpless pawn of nature.* I am a 71 year old widow.[34]

"Almost exactly a decade ago," writes another, "I learned I was pregnant. . . . I was sick in my heart and I thought I would kill myself. *It was as if I* had been told my body had been invaded with cancer. It seemed that very wrong."[35]

One woman speaks directly, without metaphor: "On the ride home from the clinic, the relief was enormous. I felt happy for the first time in weeks. I had a future again. *I had my body back.*"[36]

According to these women's self-descriptions, when the unwanted baby arrives, the injury is again one of invasion, intrusion and limitation. The *harm* of an unwanted pregnancy is that the baby will elicit a *surrender* (not an end) of the mother's life. The *fear* of unwanted pregnancy is that one will lose control of one's individuated being (not that one will die). Thus, one woman writes, "I was like any other woman who had an unintended pregnancy, I was terrified and felt as though my life was out of my control."[37]

This danger, and the fear of it, is gender-specific. It is a fear which grips women, distinctively, and it is a fear about which men, apparently, know practically nothing. Another woman writes:

> I was furiously angry, dismayed, dismal, by turns. I could not justify an abortion on economic grounds, on grounds of insufficient competence or on any other of a multitude of what might be perceived as "legitimate" reasons. But I kept being struck by the ultimate unfairness of it all. I could not conceive of any event which would so profoundly impact upon any man. Surely my husband would experience some additional financial burden, and additional "fatherly" chores, but his whole future plan was not hostage to this unchosen, undesired event. Basically his life would remain the same progression of ordered events as before.[38]

And another:

> Being a mother is hard at any age but being a teenager makes it harder. . . . Things I may have wanted to do before getting pregnant, like college and a career are different now. Before I think about my dreams, I have to think about taking care of a baby. . . . I could be making plans for my future, but instead I'm making plans for my baby's future.[39]

Conversely, women who had abortions felt able to form their own destiny. One woman wrote: "Personally legal abortion allowed me the choice as a teenager living on a very poor Indian Reservation to finish growing up and make something of my life."[40] And another:

> I was not glad that I was faced with an unwanted, unplanned pregnancy, however I am glad that I made the decision to have an abortion. The experience was a very positive one for me. It helped me learn that I am a person and I can make independent decisions. Had I not had the abortion I would have probably ended up a single mother struggling for survival and dealing with a child that I was not ready for.[41]

As noted above, radical feminism of the eighties has focused more on intercourse than on pregnancy. But this may represent less of a divergence than it first appears. From the point of view of the "connection thesis," what

[margin note: Unwanted pregnancies are a loss of one's body; a loss of control.]

• Radical feminism uses the act of intercourse as on material explanation / evidence of the dominance / invasiveness of the patriarchy.

the radical feminists of the eighties find objectionable, invasive, and oppressive about heterosexual intercourse, is precisely what the radical feminists of the sixties found objectionable, invasive, and oppressive about pregnancy and motherhood. According to the eighties radical critique, intercourse, like pregnancy, blurs the physical boundary between self and other, and that blurring of boundaries between self and other constitutes a profound invasion of the self's physical integrity. That invasion—the "dissolving of boundaries"—is something to condemn, not celebrate. Andrea Dworkin explains:

> Sexual intercourse is not intrinsically banal, though pop-culture magazines like *Esquire* and *Cosmopolitan* would suggest that it is. It is intense, often desperate. The internal landscape is violent upheaval, a wild and ultimately cruel disregard of human individuality, . . . no respecter of boundaries. . . .
> Sometimes, the skin comes off in sex. *The people merge, skinless. The body loses its boundaries.* . . . There is no physical distance, no self-consciousness, nothing withdrawn or private or alienated, no existence outside physical touch. The skin collapses as a boundary—it has no meaning. . . . Instead, there is necessity, nothing else—being driven, physical immersion in "each other" but with no experience of "each other" as separate entities coming together. . . .
> The skin is a line of demarcation, a periphery, the fence, the form, the shape, the first clue to identity in a society . . . , and, in purely physical terms, the formal precondition for being human. It is a thin veil of matter separating the outside from the inside. . . . The skin is separation, individuality, the basis for corporeal privacy, ...[42]

material explanation of invasiveness of intercourse.

Women, distinctively, lose this "formal precondition for being human" and they lose it in intercourse:

> A human being has a body that is inviolate; and when it is violated, it is abused. A woman has a body that is penetrated in intercourse: permeable, its corporeal solidness a lie. The discourse of male truth—literature, science, philosophy, pornography—calls that penetration *violation*. This it does with some consistency and some confidence. *Violation* is a synonym for intercourse. At the same time, the penetration is taken to be a use, not an abuse; a normal use; it is appropriate to enter her, to push into ("violate") the boundaries of her body. She is human, of course, but by a standard that does not include physical privacy. She is, in fact, human by a standard that precludes physical privacy, since to keep a man out altogether and for a lifetime is deviant in the extreme, a psychopathology, a repudiation of the way in which she is expected to manifest her humanity.[43]

A ⟶ Like pregnancy, then, intercourse is invasive, intrusive and violative, and like pregnancy it is therefore the cause of women's oppressed, invaded, intruded, violated, and debased lives. Dworkin concludes:

> This is nihilism; or this is truth. He has to push in past boundaries. There is the outline of a body, distinct, separate, its integrity an illusion, a tragic deception, because unseen there is a slit between the legs, and he has to push into it. There is never a real privacy of the body that can co-exist with intercourse: with being entered. The vagina itself is muscled and the muscles have to be pushed apart.

The thrusting is persistent invasion. She is opened up, split down the center. She is occupied—physically, internally, in her privacy . . . .

She, a human being, is supposed to have a privacy that is absolute; except that she, a woman, has a hole between her legs that men can, must, do enter. This hole, her hole, is synonymous with entry. A man has an anus that can be entered, but his anus is not synonymous with entry. A woman has an anus that can be entered, but her anus is not synonymous with entry. The slit between her legs, so simple, so hidden—frankly, so innocent—for instance, to the child who looks with a mirror to see if it could be true—is there an entrance to her body down there? . . .—that slit which means entry into her—intercourse—appears to be the key to women's lower human status. By definition, . . . she is intended to have a lesser privacy, a lesser integrity of the body, a lesser sense of self, . . . [and] this lesser privacy, this lesser integrity, this lesser self, establishes her lesser significance. . . . She is defined by how she is made, that hole, which is synonymous with entry; and intercourse, the act fundamental to existence, has consequences to her being that may be intrinsic, not socially imposed.[44]

[handwritten margin note: ← Recognition of a right to privacy vs. the hypocritical act of intercourse]

[handwritten margin note: ✗]

Although Dworkin herself does not draw the parallel, for both Dworkin and Firestone, women's potential for material connection with the other—whether through intercourse or pregnancy—constitutes an invasion upon our physical bodies, an intrusion upon our lives, and consequently an assault upon our existential freedom, whether or not it is also the root of our moral distinctiveness (the claim cultural feminism makes on behalf of pregnancy), or the hope of our liberation (the claim sexual liberationists make on behalf of sex). Both intercourse and pregnancy are literal, physical, material invasions and occupations of the body. The fetus, like the penis, literally occupies my body. In the extremes, of course, both unwanted heterosexual intercourse and unwanted pregnancy can be life threatening experiences of physical invasion. An unwanted fetus, no less than an unwanted penis, invades my body, violates my physical boundaries, occupies my body and can potentially destroy my sense of self. Although the culture does not recognize them as such, the physical and existential invasions occasioned by unwanted pregnancy and intercourse are real harms. They are events we should fear. They are events which any sane person should protect herself against. What unifies the radical feminism of the sixties and eighties is the argument that women's potential for material, physical connection with the other constitutes an invasion which is a very real harm causing very real damage, and which society ought to recognize as such.

The material, sporadic violation of a woman's body occasioned by pregnancy and intercourse implies an existential and pervasive violation of her privacy, integrity and life projects. According to radical feminists, women's longings for individuation, physical privacy, and independence go well beyond the desire to avoid the dangers of rape or unwanted pregnancy. Women also long for liberation from the oppression of intimacy (and its attendant values) which both cultural feminism and most women officially, and wrongly, overvalue. Intimacy, in short, is *intrusive*, even when it isn't life threatening (perhaps *especially* when it isn't life threatening). An unwanted pregnancy is disastrous, but even a *wanted* pregnancy and motherhood are intrusive. The child *intrudes*, just as the fetus invades.

Similarly, while unwanted heterosexual intercourse is disastrous, even wanted heterosexual intercourse is intrusive. The penis occupies the body and "divides the woman" internally, to use Andrea Dworkin's language, in consensual intercourse no less than in rape. It preempts, challenges, negates, and *renders impossible* the maintenance of physical integrity and the formation of a unified self. The deepest unofficial story of radical feminism may be that intimacy—the official value of cultural feminism—is itself oppressive. Women secretly, unofficially, and surreptitiously long for the very individuation that cultural feminism insists women fear: the freedom, the independence, the individuality, the sense of wholeness, the confidence, the self-esteem, and the security of identity which can only come from a life, a history, a path, a voice, a sexuality, a womb, and a body of one's own. Dworkin explains:

> In the experience of intercourse, she loses the capacity for integrity because her body—the basis of privacy and freedom in the material world for all human beings—is entered and occupied; the boundaries of her physical body are—neutrally speaking—violated. What is taken from her in that act is not recoverable, and she spends her life—wanting, after all to have something—pretending that pleasure is in being reduced through intercourse to insignificance . . . . She learns to eroticize powerlessness and self-annihilation. The very boundaries of her own body become meaningless to her, and even worse, useless to her. The transgression of those boundaries comes to signify a sexually charged degradation into which she throws herself, having been told, convinced, that identity, for a female, is there—somewhere beyond privacy and self-respect.[45]

Radical feminism, then, is unified by a particular description of the subjectivity of the material state of connection. According to that description, women dread intrusion and invasion, and long for an independent, individualized, *separate* identity. While women may indeed "officially" value intimacy, what women unofficially crave is physical privacy, physical integrity, and sexual celibacy—in a word, physical exclusivity. In the moral realm, women officially value contextual, relational, caring, moral thinking, but secretly wish that everyone would get the hell out of our lives so that we could pursue our own projects—we loathe the intrusion that intimacy entails. In the epistemological and moral realms, while women officially value community, the web, the spinning wheel, and the weave, we privately crave solitude, self-regard, self-esteem, linear thinking, legal rights, and principled thought.

The contrasting accounts of women's subjective lives that emerge from modern feminist theory's rediscovery of women's difference might be schematized in this way:

	CULTURAL FEMINISM	RADICAL FEMINISM
VALUE (or Longing):	Intimacy	Individuation; Integrity
HARM (or Dread):	Separation	Invasion; Intrusion

Finally, then, we can schematize the contrast between the description of the "human being" that emerges from modern legal theory, and the description of women that emerges from modern feminism:

	THE OFFICIAL STORY (Liberal legalism and cultural feminism)		THE UNOFFICIAL STORY (Critical legalism and radical feminism)	
	Value	Harm	Longing	Dread
LEGAL THEORY (human beings)	Autonomy	Annihilation; Frustration	Attachment; Connection	Alienation
FEMINIST THEORY (women)	Intimacy	Separation	Individuation	Invasion; Intrusion

[margin note: Lib. leg. v. cult. feminism]

As the diagram reveals, the descriptions of the subjectivity of human existence told by feminist theory and legal theory contrast at every point. There is no overlap. First, and most obviously, the "official" descriptions of human beings' subjectivity and women's subjectivity contrast rather than compare. According to liberal theory, human beings respond aggressively to their natural state of relative physical equality. In response to the great dangers posed by their natural aggression, they abide by a sharply anti-naturalist morality of autonomy, rights, and individual spheres of freedom, which is intended to and to some extent does curb their natural aggression. They respect a civil state that enforces those rights against the most egregious breaches. The description of women's subjectivity told by cultural feminism is much the opposite. According to cultural feminism, women inhabit a realm of natural *inequality*. They are physically stronger than the fetus and the infant. Women respond to their natural inequality over the fetus and infant not with aggression, but with nurturance and care. That natural and nurturant response evolves into a naturalist moral ethic of care which is consistent with women's natural response. The substantive moralities consequent to these two stories, then, unsurprisingly, are also diametrically opposed. The autonomy that human beings value and the rights they need as a restriction on their natural hostility to the equal and separate other are in sharp contrast to the intimacy that women value, and the ethic of care that represents not a limitation upon, but an extension of, women's natural nurturant response to the dependent, connected other.

[margin note: need for laws as defined by legal theory]

[margin note: Basically, the way the system is viewed, is opposite to how women viewed things]

The subterranean descriptions of subjectivity that emerge from the unofficial stories of radical feminism and critical legalism also contrast rather than compare. According to the critical legalists, human beings respond to their natural state of physical separateness not with aggression, fear and mutual suspicion, as liberalism holds, but with longing. Men suffer from a perpetual dread of isolation and alienation and a fear of rejection, and harbor a craving for community, connection, and association. Women, by contrast, according to radical feminism, respond to their natural state of material connection to the other with a craving for individuation and a loathing for invasion. Just as clearly, the subterranean dread men have of alienation (according to critical legalism) contrasts sharply with the subterranean dread that women have of invasion and intrusion (according to radical feminism).

The *responses* of human beings and women to these subterranean desires also contrast in substance, although, interestingly, the responses are structurally similar. According to both critical legalism and radical feminism, human beings and women, respectively, for the most part deny the subterranean desires that permeate their lives. Instead, they collaborate, to some degree, in the official culture's elaborate attempt to deny while partially accommodating the intensity of those felt needs. Both do so for the same reason: both human beings and women deny their subterranean desires because of a fear—legitimately grounded— that the subterranean need, if asserted, will be met by either violence or rejection by the dominant culture. The dominant male culture condemns as aberrant the man who needs others, just as the dominant female culture condemns the woman who wants to exist apart from others. Thus, men deny their need for attachment and women deny their need for individuation. The mechanisms by which the two groups effect the denial are fundamentally opposed in substance, albeit structurally parallel. According to critical theory, human beings deny their need for attachment primarily through the distancing and individuating assertion of individual rights. It is the purpose and content of those rights to largely deny the human need for attachment and communion with the other. According to radical feminism, women deny their need for individuation through the "intimating" mechanisms of romance, sentiment, familial ideology, the mystique of motherhood, and commitment to the false claims of affective attachment. It is the purpose and content of romance and familial ideology to largely deny women's need for individuation, separation, and individual identity.

Somewhat less obviously, the "unofficial" description of subjectivity provided by each side is not simply the equivalent of the "official" description of the other, although they are often mistaken as such. The mistaken belief that they are is responsible, I think, for the widespread and confused claim that critical legal studies already *is* feminist because the critical scholars' description of subjectivity converges with the cultural feminists' description of subjectivity, and the less widespread but equally confused claim that radical feminism is "just" liberalism, for the parallel reason.

First, the subjectivity depicted by critical legalism—the craving for connection and the dread of alienation—is not the subjectivity depicted by cultural feminism—the capacity for intimacy, the ethic of care, and the fear of separation. It is not hard to see the basis for the confused claim that cultural feminism's depiction of feminine subjectivity mirrors critical conceptions of the subjective experience of masculinity, though. There are two reasons for this confused identification. First, as Duncan Kennedy correctly notes, liberalism is indeed the rhetoric of the status quo. The description of subjectivity upon which critical legalists insist—"withdrawn selves" who cringe from autonomy and secretly crave community—contrasts sharply with the description of subjectivity endorsed by dominant, mainstream liberal ideology. The critics' description of subjective life is not well regarded by people in power, to put the point lightly.

Indeed, it is somewhat despised. Vis-a-vis liberal ideology, it is truly radical. It is underground. Similarly, women and women's values, to put the point lightly, are underground, despised, opposed, or at best undervalued by people in power. Vis-a-vis *feminism*, cultural feminism may be "dominant," but vis-a-vis *liberalism*, cultural feminism is at least as deeply underground and disapproved as critical legalism, if not more so. Cultural feminism and critical legalism share the outsider's status.

Further, the potential for connection which women naturally have and which cultural feminism celebrates, is in a sense the *goal* of critical legalism's alienated hero. For that reason, perhaps, the critical description of subjectivity may be confusedly identified as feminist. Nevertheless, the identification is over-stated. Unger explains the human being's natural goal of connection, or "natural harmony" in this way:

> In what sense and to what extent can . . . natural harmony be achieved by man? Take first the problem of reconciliation to the nonhuman world. The moral, artistic, and religious traditions of many cultures emphasize the persistence of men's desire to see themselves as members of a community of natural, and, above all, of living things.
>
> Because of its sexual aspect, love helps man overcome the distinction between self and nature within his own person. As a conscious and indeterminate being, he is distinguished by his relative freedom from the instincts or natural inclinations. These inclinations are the natural element within him. Insofar as he undergoes them, he is a natural being, and, insofar as he is free from them, he is more than a natural being. The natural inclinations, like the drives for food and sex, appear as a tyrannical fate; they impose limits and demands on what consciousness can accomplish.
>
> But in love, the union of persons, which represents an ideal of the relation between self and others, is consummated through the natural inclination of sex. It is not the case in love that the more a man is a natural being, the less is he distinctively human. On the contrary, the gap between mind and natural disposition is bridged. By satisfying the ideal of his relation with others and thereby becoming more human, he also becomes more completely natural.[46]

But Unger's explanation reveals the difference, not the sameness, between the intimacy women value the and "connection" that men seek. Women do not value love and intimacy *because* it "helps us overcome the distinction between self and nature." On the contrary, women value love and intimacy because they express the unity of self and nature within our own selves. More generally, women do not struggle toward connection with others, against what turn out to be insurmountable obstacles. Intimacy is not something which women fight to become capable of. We just do it. It is ridiculously easy. It is also, I suspect, qualitatively beyond the pale of male effort. The difference might be put pictorially: the intimacy women value is a sharing of intersubjective territory that preexists the effort made to identify it. The connection that I suspect men strive for does not preexist the effort, and it is not a sharing of space; at best it is an adjacency. Gilligan inadvertently sums the difference between the community critical legal studies insists that men surreptitiously seek, and the intimacy that cultural feminism insists that women value: "The discovery now being celebrated by men in mid-life of the importance of intimacy, relationships, and care is something that women have known from the beginning."[47]

Similarly, the dread of alienation that (according to critical legal studies) permeates men's lives is not the same as the fear of isolation and separation from the other that characterizes women's lives. The fear of separation, for women, is fundamental, physical, economic, empathic, and psychological, as well as psychic. Separation from one's infant will kill the infant to whom the mother has been physically and then psychically connected, and therefore a part of the mother will die as well; separation from one's community may have similarly life threatening consequences. The alienation men dread is not the fear that oneself or the one with whom one is in symbiosis will be threatened. The alienation that men dread is a sorrow over a fundamental, basic, "first" existential state of being. The longing to overcome alienation is a socially constructed reaction against the natural fact of individuation. More bluntly—love, for men, is an acquired skill; separation (and therefore autonomy) is what comes naturally. The separation that endangers women, by contrast, is what is socially constructed—attachment is natural. Separation, and the dread of it, is the response to the natural (and pleasant) state of connection.

Second, the description of women's subjective nature, aspirations, and fears drawn by radical feminism is not the same as the description of "human nature" employed by liberalism. It is not hard, however, to see the basis for this confusion. Both radical feminism and liberalism view the other as a danger to the self: liberalism identifies the other as a threat to autonomy and to life itself; radical feminism identifies the other as a threat to individuation and to physical integrity. It is hardly surprising, then, that radical feminists borrow heavily from liberalism's protective armor of rights and distance. From the radical feminist point of view, "liberal rights-talk," so disparaged by critical legalists, is just fine, and it would be even better if it protected women against the dangers that characterize their lives, as well as protecting men against the dangers that characterize their lives.

The structural similarity ends there, though. The *invasion* and *intrusion* that women dread from the penetrating and impregnating potential of the connected other is not the same as the annihilation and frustration by the separate other that men fear. Men's greatest fear is that of being wiped out—of being killed. The fear of sexual and fetal invasion and intrusion that permeates women's lives is not the fear of annihilation or frustration. The fear of sexual and fetal invasion is the fear of being occupied *from within*, not annihilated from without; of having one's self overcome, not ended; of having one's own physical and material life taken over by the pressing physical urgency of another, not ended by the conflicting interests of another; of being, in short, overtaken, occupied, displaced, and invaded, not killed. Furthermore, the intrusiveness of less damaging forms of intimacy—"wanted" intimacy—is not equivalent to the lesser form of annihilation liberalism recognizes: having one's ends frustrated by the conflicting ends of the other. I do not fear having my "ends" frustrated; I fear having my ends "displaced" before I even formulate them. I fear that I will be refused the right to be an "I" who fears. I fear than my ends will not be my own. I fear that the phrase "my ends" will prove to be (or already is) oxymoronic. I fear I will never feel the freedom, or have the space, to become an ends-making creature.

Similarly, the individuation prized by radical feminism is not the same as the autonomy liberalism heralds, although it may be a precondition of it. The "autonomy" praised by liberalism is one's right to pursue one's own ends. "Individuation," as understood by radical feminism, is the right *to be* the sort of creature who might have and then pursue one's "own" ends. Women's longing for individuation is a longing for a transcendent state of individuated being against that which is internally contrary, given, fundamental, and first. Autonomy is something which is natural to men's existential state and which the state might protect. Individuation, by contrast, is the material pre-condition of autonomy. Individuation is what you need to be before you can even begin to think about what you need to be free.

These, then, are the differences between the "human beings" assumed by legal theory and women, as their lives are now being articulated by feminist theory. The human being, according to legal theory, values autonomy and fears annihilation, while at the same time he subjectively dreads the alienation that his love of autonomy inevitably entails. Women, according to feminist theory, value intimacy and fear separation, while at the same time longing for the individuation which our fear of separation precludes, and dreading the invasion which our love of intimacy entails. The human being assumed or constituted by legal theory precludes the woman described by feminism.

Fundamental Contradictions

. . . Both [legal theory and feminist theory] appear to offer internally contradictory descriptions of men and women's subjectivity respectively. The "official story" of subjectivity proffered by liberal legalism conflicts with the account of the subjectivity of separation put forward by critical legal theory, just as the "official story" of cultural feminism conflicts with radical feminists' contrasting account of the subjectivity of connection. . . .

[One] explanation for the contradiction between official value and subjective life that recurs in both critical legal theory and in radical feminism centers on the psychoanalytic concept of "denial", and its political corollary, "collaboration." Thus, both Andrea Dworkin and Catharine MacKinnon (and numerous other radical feminists) have argued that the high regard in which women hold physical, heterosexual intimacy constitutes a form of denial, bad faith, and, ultimately, collaboration with patriarchy. Dworkin presents the argument in its greatest detail. Women claim to find intimacy in intercourse, Dworkin argues, because women must, after all, "have something." Women claim to enjoy intercourse (and mislabel it as "intimacy") because women have become "alienated from freedom" as a result of our fear of self-assertion. This fear is not groundless—it is based for the most part on all-too-accurate memories of either threatened or actual violent reactions to an attempted asserting of sexual independence. But it is nevertheless a form of cowardice. Women who claim to value heterosexual intimacy deny their desire for freedom because they fear a reenactment of a primary, and extremely painful experience of violent, sexual oppression. In a word, they collaborate. . . .[48]

Critical theorist Peter Gabel has given a perfectly parallel explanation of the attraction of autonomous, rights-focused, individuated liberal values in spite of the acutely painful longing for connection which in fact permeates men's lives. Gabel's argument structurally compares with Dworkin's, although it contrasts with it substantively. Thus, whereas Dworkin argues that women deny their desire for *freedom*, and distance themselves from it through a false commitment to *intimacy*, Gabel argues that human beings deny their craving for attachment with the other, and distance themselves from it through a false commitment to *rights.* As women deny their desire for freedom because of a fear that by asserting that desire they risk violent invasion, so human beings, according to Gabel, deny their desire for attachment because they fear that by exposing their deeper and truer need for connection, they will leave themselves vulnerable to the pain of rejection. This fear is rooted in an unconsciously embedded memory from infancy, just as women's fear of their own desire for freedom is rooted in a memory of male violence. At some point in early infancy, according to Gabel, the other (read: the mother) rejected him. That rejection was painful and humiliating. The individual denies his need for connection because he refuses to risk the reenactment of such a painful, humiliating, and embarrassing rejection, just as the woman denies her need for physical indi-viduation because she refuses to risk the reenactment of rape. So instead he creates a false self, defined by liberal "rights." In a word, he collaborates. . . .[49]

As Gabel by now must surely be aware, his account of the source of "our" alienation from the other is deeply gendered. The story he tells of attachment, separation, longing, rejection, repression, humiliation and then alienation is a story of male development, not female. But structurally, his argument is not at all gendered. Dworkin's and Gabel's arguments employ precisely the same logical structure. Dworkin, like Gabel, argues that women engage in massive denial, identification, and collaboration with the powers that cause their alien-ation. . . .

Both Gabel's and Dworkin's explanations, I believe, are ultimately unsatisfying, and although they are exploring subtantively opposed phenomena, they are unsatisfying for the same reason. Both claims fail to do justice to the complexity of the phenomenology that they are seeking to explain. Others have argued, and I think persuasively, that Gabel's explanation of the disempowered's "collaborative" embrace of rights fails to capture the phenomenological experience of rights as an empowering and even communitarian tool for disempowered peoples.[51] I will not pursue that argument here. I do want to argue, though, that Dworkin's parallel insistence that women's enjoyment of heterosexual intercourse constitutes a form of collaboration fails to capture the phenome-nological experience of intercourse as one of positive intimacy, rather than an

agree .

experience that is inevitably destructive of "all that is creative within us." Women often, and perhaps increasingly, experience heterosexual intercourse as freely chosen intimacy, not invasive bondage. A radicalism that flatly denies the reality of such a lived experience runs the risk of making itself unintelligible and irrelevant to all people, not to mention the audience that matters most: namely, those women for whom intercourse is not free, not chosen, and anything but intimate, and who have no idea that it either could be or should be both. . . .

Now, it is . . . true—emphatically true—that neither motherhood nor intercourse have been "released" from patriarchy. Until they are, there is no project more vital to our understanding of women's present oppression than the description of the subjective experience of motherhood, and of intercourse, within the patriarchical institutions that render those activities compulsory. . . . We need to be aware—to be made aware—of those institutions *as institutions* that constrain as they define the act. But . . . that is not all we need to understand. Feminists also need to understand what it means to mother and to enjoy intercourse within aspirational conditions of freedom, for it is those conditions which potentially and increasingly, for many of us, define the nature of those events. When we reach this understanding, or at least strive for it, we will have a better understanding of what non-institutional and non-patriarchal intercourse and motherhood might be and might ultimately become.

Of course, to . . . borrow from [Adrienne] Rich, to catch even a glimpse of mothering or intercourse within a non-patriarchal culture requires a "quantum leap" of imagination. It requires, most of all, the ability to imagine ourselves in a society in which women are in full possession of our bodies:

> [T]he "quantum leap" [of imagination] implies that even as we try to deal with backlash and emergency, we are imagining the new: a future in which women are powerful, full of our own power, not the old patriarchal power-over but the power-to-create, power-to-think, power-to-articulate and concretize our visions and transform our lives and those of our children. . . .[53]

Yet we make small versions of these "quantum leaps" every day. We continue to mother and to want to mother in spite of the compulsory nature of institutional motherhood. We also make small versions of the same "quantum leap" with respect to intercourse. Women do, increasingly, freely engage in heterosexual intercourse in spite of the compulsory nature of the institution of intercourse. Increasingly, we have a sense of what intercourse feels like when "released" from compulsory heterosexuality. Explanations that rest on denial of the possibility that equality and freedom can define intercourse and motherhood fail to incorporate real glimpses that we increasingly have of a world without the present oppressive institutions. They consequently endanger the seriousness and the truth of the radical feminist insight that many women, indeed most women, define their intimate relationships within the confines of necessity rather than possibility, and within the dictates of compulsion, rather than choice.

The second possible explanation of contradiction between the official story and true subjectivity centers on the Gramscian and Marxist concept of legitimation and apology. Thus, Catharine MacKinnon argues that "intimacy" simply legitimates invasion, and that cultural feminism's celebration of intimacy is, in essence, simply apology for patriarchy:

> For women to affirm difference, when difference means dominance, as it does with gender, means to affirm the qualities and characteristics of powerlessness. . . .[54]

This explanation has a parallel in critical legal theory. According to critical legalists, the dominant class legitimates the oppressive reality of alienation by relabelling alienation as freedom, just as cultural feminism, according to MacKinnon, relabels invasion as intimacy. Indeed, it is a recurrent claim in critical legal theory that the rhetoric of autonomy and freedom found in nineteenth century contract law, like the rhetoric of good faith and fulfilled expectations in twentieth century contract law, all operate to deny the true human need for connection and collectivity:

> The legitimating image of classical contract law in the nineteenth century was the ideal of free competition as the consequence of wholly voluntary interactions among many private persons, all of whom were in their nature free and equal to one another. . . . [T]his was denial and apology. It did not take account of the practical limitations on market freedom and equality arising from class position or unequal distribution of wealth. . . .[55]

Again, both MacKinnon's argument and the parallel critical legal claim are unsatisfying, and for the same reason. Both claims fail to do justice to the complexity of the opposing vision they attack. For while it is true that liberalism's commitment to individualism echoes capitalism's legitimating myth of market freedom, this doesn't come anywhere near the whole story. The commitment to individualism that pervades *part* of liberalism and of liberal culture exists *in spite of* capitalism's actual disdain for true individualism, not because of capitalism's false claim to freedom. Liberalism has always had a radical commitment to a true individualism which is not in any sense apologist; liberal individualism in at least some of its historical and modern forms undercuts, rather than relegitimates, capitalist super-structure. Similarly, women's ethic of care, and commitment to the value of nurturance and intimacy celebrated by cultural feminism, exists *in spite of* patriarchy's contempt for and under-valuation of those values, not because of their false claim to honor women's separate sphere. While it is of course true that cultural feminism's celebration of women's ethic of care echoes patriarchy's celebration of separate spheres, the former is hardly an apology for the latter. The differences between cultural feminism and patriarchy are the all-important ones: patriarchy devalues women, and cultural feminism does not. Patriarchy celebrates women's different sphere in order to reinforce women's powerlessness. Cultural feminism does not.

Critical legal theorists have developed a third account of the contradiction between liberal values and subjective desire: the contradiction is based on a real, lived contradiction grounded in material, unreconstructed reality. I believe this explanation is the strongest of the three, though, as far as I know, it has no parallel in feminist theory. Both Roberto Unger and Duncan Kennedy have argued, with considerable force, that the "contradiction" between liberalism's claim that human beings value autonomy and fear the other, and critical theory's opposing claim that they desire connection with the other and dread their alienation from him, reflects a real contradiction in our subjective, material, and natural lives. It is not then (solely) the product of either psychoanalytic denial or Gramscian legitimation. The contradiction is an *experiential* contradiction, not a logical contradiction. The difference is important.

According to Kennedy, we value *both* autonomy and connection, and fear *both* annihilation by the other and alienation from him, and all for good reason. The other is both necessary to our continued existence and a threat to that continued existence. While it is true that the dominant liberal story of autonomy and annihilation serves to perpetuate the status quo, it does not follow from that fact that the subjective desires for freedom and security which those liberal values reify are entirely *false*. Rather, Kennedy argues, collectivity is both essential to our identity and an obstacle to it. We have contradictory desires and values because our essential human condition—physical separation from the collectivity which is necessary to our identity—is itself contradictory. It is that essential human condition which carries the seeds of our twin fears of alienation and annihilation, as well as our twin desires for autonomy and attachment:

> Here is an initial statement of the fundamental contradiction: . . . Others (family, friends, bureaucrats, cultural figures, the state) are necessary if we are to become persons at all—they provide us the stuff of our selves and protect us in crucial ways against destruction. Even when we seem to ourselves to be most alone, others are with us, incorporated in us through processes of language, cognition and feeling that are, simply as a matter of biology, collective aspects of our individuality. Moreover, we are not always alone. We sometimes experience fusion with others, in groups of two or even two million, and it is good rather than a bad experience.
>
> But at the same time that it forms and protects us, the universe of others (family, friendship, bureaucracy, culture, the state) threatens us with annihilation and urges upon us forms of fusion that are quite plainly bad rather than good. . . . Numberless conformities, large and small abandonments of self to others, are the price of what freedom we experience in society. And the price is a high one.[57]

.   .   .

The strength of Duncan Kennedy's work is that he has not just asserted the existence of this fundamental contradiction, but has shown its permeation through a remarkably wide range of legal materials. The structurally parallel claim in feminist theory that I think radical feminists should explore, is that women "officially" value intimacy (and fear separation) in spite of subjective desires to the contrary not (solely) because of the legitimating power of patriarchal ideology, nor (solely) because of the power of denial, but rather, because women's existential and material circumstance is *itself* one of contradiction. The potentiality for physical connection with others that uniquely characterizes women's lives has within it the seeds of *both* intimacy and invasion, and therefore women rightly value the former while we dread and fear the latter, just as the necessity of physical separation, for men, carries within it the seeds of *both* intimacy and alienation, and men rightly value the former and dread the latter. If this is right, then *all four* accounts of human experience—liberal legalism, critical legalism, cultural feminism and radical feminism—are saying something true about human experience. Liberal legalism and critical legalism both describe something true about male experience, and cultural feminism and radical feminism both describe something true about female experience. If Kennedy is right, then men simply live with an experiential contradiction. In a parallel fashion, cultural feminism and radical feminism may both be *true* although contradictory. The contradiction between them may be experiential rather than logical. Women may both value intimacy and dread the intrusion and invasion which intimacy implies; and women may both fear separation and long for the individualization which separation would bring. . . .

Minimally, I want to suggest that feminists should think about the possibility that the notion of a "fundamental" experienced contradiction, grounded in the material and existential state of connection with the other, might help us explain women's subjective lives, as well as close the broadening gap between cultural and radical feminist theory. The presence of such a contradiction, for example, explains why some women see the possibility of intimacy in pornographic depictions of female sexual submission while others see the threat of invasion (and it would explain why many women see both). The presence of a contradiction underlying women's subjective lives also clarifies the existential basis of many of the apparent tensions in feminist legal reforms. It explains why women insist upon and embrace an ethic of care and the right to have children without economic hardship, while at the same time fighting for rights of individuation, physical privacy, and freedom. Finally, it explains the complex relationship between the emerging feminist legal theory and dominant legal theory: it explains, for example, why legal feminists are both attracted to liberal rights of individuation, physical privacy, and individual security, and at the same time are threatened by them. The contradiction explains why feminists understand, and even sympathize with, critical legal theory's rights critique, but will never endorse it. . . .

Of course, there is a major difference between the presence of contradiction in legal theory and the presence of contradiction in feminist theory. Even if it is true that women, like men, live within the parameters of a contradiction, women live within the parameters of this fundamental contradiction *within the oppressive conditions of patriarchy*. Men don't (although men do live within the parameters of the oppressive conditions of capitalism). Therefore, feminists need to develop not just an examination of the experience of the contradiction between invasion and intimacy to which our potential for connection gives rise, but also a description of how patriarchy effects, twists, perverts, and surely to some extent causes that contradiction. We also need, however, to imagine how the contradiction would be felt outside of patriarchy, and we need to reflect on our own experiences of non-patriarchal mothering, intercourse, and intimacy to generate such imaginings. For while women's bodies may continue to be "materially connected" to others as long as they are women's bodies, they need not forever by *possessed* by others. Our connection to the other is a function of our material condition; our possession by the other, however, is a function of patriarchy. We need to imagine both having power over our bodies and power over our contradictory material state. We need to imagine how this fundamental contradiction would feel outside of the context of the dangers and fears that patriarchy requires. Adrienne Rich asks, of non-constrained, non-compulsory, truly chosen motherhood in a world free of patriarchy:

> What would it mean to mother in a society where women were deeply valued and respected, in a culture which was woman-affirming? What would it mean to bear and raise children in the fullness of our power to care for them, provide for them, in dignity and pride? . . . What would it mean to mother in a society which was making full use of the spiritual, intellectual, emotional, physical gifts of women, in all our difference and diversity? What would it mean to mother in a society which laid no stigma upon lesbians, so that women grew up with real emotional and erotic options in the choice of life companions and lovers? What would it mean to live and die in a culture which affirmed both life and death, in which both the living world and the bodies of women were released at last from centuries of violation and control? This is the quantum leap of the radical feminist vision.[61]

We need to ask these questions of intercourse as well. What would intercourse feel like, or *be*, in a world in which it was freely chosen? What would it mean to have intercourse in a world in which women's pleasures were honored, and women's injuries were cared for, and women's labor was compensated? And finally we need to ask these questions of intimacy generally. How would the "contradiction" between invasion and intimacy feel in a world free of the fear of male sexual aggression? Would intimacy be entirely non-threatening where there was no reason to fear rape? Would individuation be as enticing where intercourse and motherhood were not mandatory? Would separation be as harmful where familial association was not the assumed form of women's lives? How would the contradiction between intimacy and intrusion feel, if we had no reason to fear the more life threatening forms of invasion? We need to ask these questions, but we also need to *answer* them. The answers, I suspect, must come at least in part from the non-patriarchal relationships in our own lives. We should not be surprised when, as we look at those lives, we see and feel contradictions, not just within the structures of patriarchy, but behind them, through them, and beyond them as well.

Feminist Jurisprudence

By the claim that modern jurisprudence is "masculine," I mean two things. First, I mean that the values, the dangers, and what I have called the "fundamental contradiction" that characterize women's lives are not reflected at any level whatsoever in contracts, torts, constitutional law, or any other field of legal doctrine. The values that flow from women's material potential for physical connection are not recognized as values by the Rule of Law, and the dangers attendant to that state are not recognized as dangers by the Rule of Law.

First, the Rule of Law does not value intimacy—its official value is autonomy. The material consequence of this theoretical undervaluation of women's values in the material world is that women are economically *impoverished*. The value women place on intimacy reflects our existential and material circumstance; women will act on that value whether it is compensated or not. But it is not. Nurturant, intimate labor is neither valued by liberal legalism nor compensated by the market economy. It is not compensated in the home and it is not compensated in the workplace—wherever intimacy is, there is no compensation. Similarly, separation of the individual from his or her family, community, or children is not understood to be a harm, and we are not protected against it. The Rule of Law generally and legal doctrine in its particularity are coherent reactions to the existential dilemma that follows from the liberal's description of the male experience of material separation from the other: the Rule of Law acknowledges the danger of annihilation and the Rule of Law protects the value of autonomy. Just as assuredly, the Rule of Law is *not a coherent reaction* to the existential dilemma that follows from the material state of being connected to others, and the values and dangers attendant to that condition. It neither recognizes nor values intimacy, and neither recognizes nor protects against separation.

Nor does the Rule of Law recognize, in any way whatsoever, muted or unmuted, occasionally or persistently, overtly or covertly, the contradiction which characterizes women's, but not men's, lives: while we value the intimacy we find so natural, we are endangered by the invasion and dread the intrusion in our lives which intimacy entails, and we long for individuation and independence. Neither sexual nor fetal invasion of the self by the other is recognized as a harm worth bothering with. Sexual invasion through rape is understood to be a harm, and is criminalized as such, only when it involves some other harm: today, when it is accompanied by violence that appears in a form men understand (meaning a plausible threat of annihilation); in earlier times, when it was understood as theft of another man's property. But marital rape, date rape, acquaintance rape, simple rape, unaggravated rape, or as Susan Estrich wants to say "real rape"[62] are either not criminalized, or if they are, they are not punished—to do so would force a recognition of the concrete, experiential harm to identity formation that sexual invasion accomplishes.

Similarly, fetal invasion is not understood to be harmful, and therefore the claim that I ought to be able to protect myself against it is heard as nonsensical. The argument that the right to abortion mirrors the right of self defense falls on deaf ears for a reason: the analogy is indeed flawed. The right of self defense is the right to protect the body's security against annihilation liberally understood, not invasion. But the danger an unwanted fetus poses is not to the body's security at all, but rather to the body's integrity. Similarly, the woman's fear is not that she will die, but that she will cease to be or never become a self. The danger of unwanted pregnancy is the danger of invasion by the other, not of annihilation by the other. In sum, the Rule of Law does not recognize the danger of invasion, nor does it recognize the individual's need for, much less entitlement to, individuation and independence from the intrusion which heterosexual penetration and fetal invasion entails. The material consequence of this lack of recognition in the real world is that women are *objectified*— regarded as creatures who can't be harmed.

The second thing I mean to imply by the phrase "masculine jurisprudence" is that both liberal and critical legal theory, which is about the relation between law and life, is about men and not women. The reason for this lack of parallelism, of course, is hardly benign neglect. Rather, the distinctive values women hold, the distinctive dangers from which we suffer, and the distinctive contradictions that characterize our inner lives are not reflected in legal theory because legal theory (whatever else it's about) is about actual, real life, enacted, legislated, adjudicated law, and women have, from law's inception, lacked the power to make law protect, value, or seriously regard our experience. Jurisprudence is "masculine" because jurisprudence is about the relationship between human beings and the laws we actually have, and the laws we actually have are "masculine" both in terms of their intended beneficiary and in authorship. Women are absent from jurisprudence because women *as human beings* are absent from the law's protection: jurisprudence does not recognize us because law does not protect us. The implication for this should be obvious. We will not have a genuinely ungendered jurisprudence (a jurisprudence "unmodified" so to speak) until we have legal doctrine that takes women's lives as seriously as it takes men's. . . .

It does not follow, however, that there is no such thing as feminist legal theory. Rather, I believe what is now inaccurately called "feminist jurisprudence" consists of two discrete projects. The first project is the unmasking and critiquing of the patriarchy behind purportedly ungendered law and theory, or, put differently, the uncovering of what we might call "patriarchal jurisprudence" from under the protective covering of "jurisprudence." The primary purpose of the critique of patriarchal jurisprudence is to show that jurisprudence and legal doctrine protect and define men, not women. Its second purpose is to show how women—that is, people who value intimacy, fear separation, dread invasion, and crave individuation—have fared under a legal system which fails to value intimacy, fails to protect against separation, refuses to define invasion as a harm, and refuses to acknowledge the aspirations of women for individuation and physical privacy.

The second project in which feminist legal theorists engage might be called "reconstructive jurisprudence." The last twenty years have seen a substantial amount of feminist law reform, primarily in the areas of rape, sexual harassment, reproductive freedom, and pregnancy rights in the workplace. For strategic reasons, these reforms have often been won by characterizing women's injuries as analogous to, if not identical with, injuries men suffer (sexual harassment as a form of "discrimination;" rape as a crime of "violence"), or by characterizing women's longing as analogous to, if not identical with, men's official values (reproductive freedom—which ought to be grounded in a right to individuation— conceived instead as a "right to privacy," which is derivative of the autonomy right). This misconceptualization may have once been a necessary price, but it is a high price, and, as these victories accumulate, an increasingly unnecessary one. Reconstructive feminist jurisprudence should set itself the task of rearticulating these new rights in such a way as to reveal, rather than conceal their origin in women's distinctive existential and material state of being. . . .

[handwritten margin note: Isn't this similar to the tonal pointing practice of changing personal pronouns.]

Conclusion: Toward a Jurisprudence Unmodified

The "separation thesis," I have argued, is drastically untrue of women. What's worth noting by way of conclusion is that it is not entirely true of men either. First, it is not true materially. Men are connected to another human life prior to the cutting of the umbilical cord. Furthermore, men are somewhat connected to women during intercourse, and men have openings that can be sexually penetrated. Nor is the separation thesis necessarily true of men existentially. As Suzanna Sherry has shown, the existence of the entire classical republican tradition belies the claim that masculine biology mandates liberal values.[75] More generally, as Dinnerstein, Chodorow, French, and Gilligan all insist, material biology does not *mandate* existential value: men *can* connect to other human life. Men can nurture life. Men can mother. Obviously, men can care, and love, and support, and affirm life. Just as obviously, however, most men don't. One reason that they don't, of course, is male privilege. Another reason, though, may be the blinders of our masculinist utopian visionary. Surely one of the most important insights of feminism has been that biology is indeed destiny when we are unaware of the extent to which biology is narrowing our fate, but that *biology is destiny only to the extent of our ignorance.* As we become increasingly aware, we become increasingly free. As we become increasingly free, we, rather than biology, become the authors of our fate. Surely this is true both of men and women.

On the flip side, the "connection thesis" is also not entirely true of women, either materially or existentially. Not all women become pregnant, and not all women are sexually penetrated. Women can go through life fundamentally unconnected to other human life. Women can also go through life fundamentally unconcerned with other human life. Obviously, as the liberal feminist movement firmly established, many women can and do individuate, speak the truth, develop integrity, pursue personal projects, embody freedom, and attain an atomistic liberal individuality. Just as obviously, most women don't. Most women are indeed forced into motherhood and heterosexuality. One reason for this is utopian blinders: women's lack of awareness of existential choice in the face of what are felt to be biological imperatives. But that is surely not the main reason. The primary reason for the stunted nature of women's lives is male power.

Perhaps the greatest obstacle to the creation of a feminist jurisprudence is that feminist jurisprudence must simultaneously confront both political and conceptual barriers to women's freedom. The political barrier is surely the most pressing. Feminists must first and foremost counter a profound power imbalance, and the way to do that is through law and politics. But jurisprudence—like law—is persistently utopian and conceptual as well as apologist and political: jurisprudence represents a constant and at least at times a sincere attempt to articulate a guiding utopian vision of human association. Feminist jurisprudence must respond to these utopian images, correct them, improve upon them, and participate in them as utopian images, not just as apologies for patriarchy. Feminism must envision a post-patriarchal world, for without such a vision we have little direction. We must use that vision to construct our present goals, and we should, I believe, interpret our present victories against the backdrop of that vision. That vision is not necessarily androgynous; surely in a utopian world the presence of differences between people will be cause only for celebration. In a utopian world, all forms of life will be recognized, respected and honored. A perfect legal system will protect against harms sustained by all forms of life, and will recognize life affirming values generated by all forms of being. Feminist jurisprudence must aim to bring this about and, to do so, it must aim to transform the images as well as the power. Masculine jurisprudence must become humanist jurisprudence, and humanist jurisprudence must become a jurisprudence unmodified.

Notes

1. Naomi Scheman, Individualism and the Objects of Psychology, in Sandra Harding and Merrill B. Hintikks, eds., Discovering Reality 225, 237 (1983).

2. Robert Nozick, Anarchy, State, and Utopia 33 (1974).

3. Roberto Mangabeira Unger, Knowledge and Politics 200 (1976) (citation omitted) (emphasis added).

4. Michael J. Sandel, Liberalism and the Limits of Justice 133 (1982).

5. Ronald Dworkin, A Matter of Principle 191 (1985) (capitalization omitted) (emphasis added).

7. Thomas Hobbes, Leviathan 183–84 (C.B. Macpherson, ed. 1968).

8. Bruce A. Ackerman, Social Justice in the Liberal State 3 (1980) (emphasis added).

10. Unger, Knowledge and Politics at 201 (emphasis added) (cited in note 3).

11. Peter Gabel, The Phenomenology of Rights-Consciousness and the Pact of the Withdrawn Selves, 62 Tex.L.Rev. 1563, 1566-7 (1984) (citation omitted).

13. Carol Gilligan, In a Different Voice 6–8 (1982).

15. Nancy Chodorow, The Reproduction of Mothering 167 (1978).

16. Gilligan, In a Different Voice at 159–60 (cited in note 13).

18. Id. at 100.

19. Id. at 8.

22. Discrimination on the Basis of Pregnancy, 1977, Hearings on S. 995 Before the Subcommittee on Labor of the Senate Committee on Human Resources, 95th Cong., 1st Sess. 123 (1977) (remarks of Professor Wendy Williams) (emphasis added).

23. [See] Lucinda M. Finley, Transcending Equality Theory: A Way Out of the Maternity and the Workplace Debate, 86 Colum.L.Rev. 1118, 1139–40 (1986). . . .

24. Adrienne Rich, On Lies, Secrets, and Silence 260–63 (1979) . . . (emphasis added).

25. Marilyn French, Beyond Power 482-83 (1985).

28. Nel Noddings, Caring (1984).

29. Id. at 128.

31. Shulamith Firestone, The Dialectic of Sex (1970).

32. Amicus Brief for the National Abortion Rights Action League, et al., Thornburgh v. American College of Obstetricians and Gynecologists, Nos. 84-495 and 84-1379 ("NARAL Amicus Brief") (on file at The University of Chicago Law Review). For the Supreme Court opinion, see 476 U.S. 747 (1986).

33. NARAL Amicus Brief at 13 (emphasis added).

34. Id. at 19 (emphasis added).

35. Id. at 28 (emphasis added).

36. Id. at 29 (emphasis added).

37. Id. at 29.

38. Id. at 29.

39. Id. at 24.

40. Id. at 29.

41. Id.

42. Andrea Dworkin, Intercourse 21-22 (1987) (emphasis added).

43. Id. at 122.

44. Id. at 122-23 (emphasis added on the words "and intercourse, the act," otherwise emphasis is original).

45. Id. at 137-38.

46. Unger, Knowledge and Politics at 205-06 (cited in note 3).

47. Gilligan, In a Different Voice at 17 (cited in note 13).

48. Dworkin, Intercourse at 141-42 (cited in note 42).

49. Gabel, 62 Tex.L.Rev. at 1567-69 (cited in note 11). . . .

51. See, e.g., Patricia Williams, Alchemical Notes: Reconstructed Ideals from Deconstructed Rights, 22 Harv.Civ.Rts.-Civ.Liberties Law Review 401 (1987) and Richard Delgado, The Ethereal Scholar: Does Critical Legal Studies Have What Minorities Want?, 22 Harv.Civ.Rts.-Civ.Liberties Law Review 301 (1987).

53. [Rich, On Lies, Secrets, and Silence] at 271-72 [cited in note 24].

54. Catharine A. MacKinnon, Feminism Unmodified 39 (1987).

55. Peter Gabel and Jay M. Feinman, Contract Law as Ideology, in David Kairys, ed., The Politics of Law 172, 176 (1982) (citation omitted).

57. Duncan Kennedy, The Structure of Blackstone's Commentaries, 28 Buffalo L.Rev. 209, 211-12 (1979).

61. Rich, On Lies, Secrets, and Silence at 272-73 (cited in note 24).

62. Susan Estrich, Real Rape (1987).

75. [Suzanna Sherry, Civic Virtue and the Feminine Voice in Constitutional Litigation, 72 Va.L.Rev. 543, 584 (1986)].

11

Race and Essentialism in Feminist Legal Theory [1990]

Angela P. Harris

bein alive & bein a woman & bein colored is a metaphysical dilemma[1]
—ntozake shange

Introduction

A. *Prologue: The Voices in Which We Speak*

1. Funes the Memorious

In *Funes the Memorious*,[2] Borges tells of Ireneo Funes, who was a rather ordinary young man (notable only for his precise sense of time) until the age of nineteen, when he was thrown by a half-tamed horse and left paralyzed but possessed of perfect perception and a perfect memory.

After his transformation, Funes

> knew by heart the forms of the southern clouds at dawn on the 30th of April, 1882, and could compare them in his memory with the mottled streaks on a book in Spanish binding he had only seen once and with the outlines of the foam raised by an oar in the Rio Negro the night before the Quebracho uprising. These memories were not simple ones; each visual image was linked to muscular sensations, thermal sensations, etc. He could reconstruct all his dreams, all his half-dreams. Two or three times he had reconstructed a whole day; he never hesitated, but each reconstruction had required a whole day.[3]

Funes tells the narrator that after his transformation he invented his own numbering system. "In place of seven thousand thirteen, he would say (for example) *Máximo Pérez*; in place of seven thousand fourteen, *The Railroad*; other numbers were Luis Melián Lafinur, Olimar, sulphur, the reins, the whale, the gas, the caldron, Napoleon, Agustín de Vedia."[4] The narrator tries to explain to Funes "that this rhapsody of incoherent terms was precisely the opposite of a system of numbers. I told him that saying 365 meant saying three hundreds, six tens, five ones, an analysis which is not found in the 'numbers' *The Negro Timoteo* or *meat blanket*. Funes did not understand me or refused to understand me."[5]

In his conversation with Funes, the narrator realizes that Funes' life of infinite unique experiences leaves Funes no ability to categorize: "With no effort, he had learned English, French, Portuguese and Latin. I suspect, however, that he was not very capable of thought. To think is to forget differences, generalize, make abstractions. In the teeming world of Funes, there were only details, almost immediate in their presence."[6] For Funes, language is only a unique and private system of classification, elegant and solipsistic. The notion that language, made abstract, can serve to create and reinforce a community is incomprehensible to him.

2. "We the People"

Describing the voice that speaks the first sentence of the Declaration of Independence, James Boyd White remarks:

> It is not a person's voice, not even that of a committee, but the "unanimous" voice of "thirteen united States" and of their "people." It addresses a universal audience—nothing less than "mankind" itself, located neither in space nor in time—and the voice is universal too, for it purports to know about the "Course of human events" (all human events?) and to be able to discern what "becomes necessary" as a result of changing circumstances.[7]

The Preamble of the United States Constitution, White argues, can also be heard to speak in this unified and universal voice. This voice claims to speak

> for an entire and united nation and to do so directly and personally, not in the third person or by merely delegated authority. . . . The instrument thus appears to issue from a single imaginary author, consisting of all the people of the United States, including the reader, merged into a single identity in this act of self-constitution. "The People" are at once the author and the audience of this instrument.[8]

Despite its claims, however, this voice does not speak for everyone, but for a political faction trying to constitute itself as a unit of many disparate voices; its power lasts only as long as the contradictory voices remain silenced.

In a sense, the "I" of Funes, who knows only particulars, and the "we" of "We the People," who know only generalities, are the same. Both voices are monologues; both depend on the silence of others. The difference is only that the first voice knows of no others, while the second has silenced them.

3. Law and Literature

The first voice, the voice of Funes, is the voice toward which literature sometimes seems driven. In an essay, Cynthia Ozick describes a comment she once overheard at a party: "For me, the Holocaust and a corncob are the same."[9] Ozick understands this comment to mean that for a writer, all experience is equal. Literature has no moral content, for it exists purely in the domain of the imagination, a place where only aesthetics matter. Thus, a poet may freely replace the Holocaust with a corncob, just as Funes replaces "7013" with *Máximo Pérez*. Poetic language is only a game of words; the poet need not and in fact should not worry about social responsibility. Literary language is purely self-referential.

Law, however, has not been much tempted by the sound of the first voice. Lawyers are all too aware that legal language is not a purely self-referential game, for "legal interpretive acts signal and occasion the imposition of violence upon others."[10] In their concern to avoid the social and moral irresponsibility of the first voice, legal thinkers have veered in the opposite direction, toward the safety of the second voice, which speaks from the position of "objectivity" rather than "subjectivity," "neutrality" rather than "bias." This voice, like the voice of "We the People," is ultimately authoritarian and coercive in its attempt to speak for everyone.[11]

In both law and literature there are theorists who struggle against their discipline's grain. Literary theorists such as Henry Louis Gates, Jr., Gayatri Spivak, and Abdul JanMohamed are attempting to "read specific verbal and visual texts against complex cultural codes of power, assertion, and domination which these texts both reflect and, indeed, reinforce."[12] Legal theorists such as Mari Matsuda, Pat Williams, and Derrick Bell juxtapose the voice that "allows theorists to discuss liberty, property, and rights in the aspirational mode of liberalism with no connection to what those concepts mean in real people's lives"[13] with the voices of people whose voices are rarely heard in law. In neither law nor literature, however, is the goal merely to replace one voice with its opposite. Rather, the aim is to understand both legal and literary discourse as the complex struggle and unending dialogue between these voices.

The metaphor of "voice" implies a speaker. I want to suggest, however, that both the voices I have described come from the same source, a source I term "multiple consciousness." It is a premise of this article that we are not born with a "self," but rather are composed of a welter of partial, sometimes contradictory, or even antithetical "selves." A unified identity, if such can ever exist, is a product of will, not a common destiny or natural birthright. Thus, consciousness is "never fixed, never attained once and for all";[14] it is not a final outcome or a biological given, but a process, a constant contradictory state of becoming, in which both social institutions and individual wills are deeply implicated. A multiple consciousness is home both to the first and second voices, and all the voices in between.

As I use the phrase, "multiple consciousness" as reflected in legal or literary discourse is not a golden mean or static equilibrium between two extremes, but rather a process in which propositions are constantly put forth, challenged, and subverted. Cynthia Ozick argues that "a redemptive literature, a literature that interprets and decodes the world, beaten out for the sake of humanity, must wrestle with its own body, with its own flesh and blood, with its own life."[15] Similarly, Mari Matsuda, while arguing that in the legal realm "[h]olding on to a multiple consciousness will allow us to operate both within the abstractions of standard jurisprudential discourse, *and* within the details of our own special knowledge,"[16] acknowledges that "this constant shifting of con- sciousness produces sometimes madness, sometimes genius, sometimes both."[17]

B. Race and Essentialism in Feminist Legal Theory

1. Methodology

In this article, I discuss some of the writings of feminist legal theorists Catharine MacKinnon and Robin West. I argue that their work, though powerful and brilliant in many ways, relies on what I call gender essentialism—the notion that a unitary, "essential" women's experience can be isolated and described independently of race, class, sexual orientation, and other realities of experience. The result of this tendency toward gender essentialism, I argue, is not only that some voices are silenced in order to privilege others (for this is an inevitable result of categorization, which is necessary both for human communication and political movement), but that the voices that are silenced turn out to be the same voices silenced by the mainstream legal voice of "We the People"—among them, the voices of black women.

This result troubles me for two reasons. First, the obvious one: As a black woman, in my opinion the experience of black women is too often ignored both in feminist theory and in legal theory, and gender essentialism in feminist legal theory does nothing to address this problem. A second and less obvious reason for my criticism of gender essentialism is that, in my view, contemporary legal theory needs less abstraction and not simply a different sort of abstraction. To be fully subversive, the methodology of feminist legal theory should challenge not only law's content but its tendency to privilege the abstract and unitary voice, and this gender essentialism also fails to do.

In accordance with my belief that legal theory, including feminist legal theory, is in need of less abstraction, in this article I destabilize and subvert the unity of MacKinnon's and West's "woman" by introducing the voices of black women, especially as represented in literature. Before I begin, however, I want to make three cautionary points to the reader. First, my argument should not be read to accuse either MacKinnon or West of "racism" in the sense of personal antipathy to black people. Both writers are steadfastly anti-racist, which in a sense is my point. Just as law itself, in trying to speak for all persons, ends up silencing those without power, feminist legal theory is in danger of silencing those who have traditionally been kept from speaking, or who have been ignored when they spoke, including black women. The first step toward avoiding this danger is to give up the dream of gender essentialism.

Second, in using a racial critique to attack gender essentialism in feminist legal theory, my aim is not to establish a new essentialism in its place based on the essential experience of black women. Nor should my focus on black women be taken to mean that other women are not silenced either by the mainstream culture or by feminist legal theory. Accordingly, I invite the critique and subversion of my own generalizations.

Third and finally, I do not mean in this article to suggest that either feminism or legal theory should adopt the voice of Funes the Memorious, for whom every experience is unique and no categories or generalizations exist at all. Even a jurisprudence based on multiple consciousness must categorize; without categorization each individual is as isolated as Funes, and there can be no moral responsibility or social change. My suggestion is only that we make our categories explicitly tentative, relational, and unstable, and that to do so is all the more important in a discipline like law, where abstraction and "frozen" categories are the norm. Avoiding gender essentialism need not mean that the Holocaust and a corncob are the same.

2. Feminist Legal Theory

> As a Black lesbian feminist comfortable with the many different ingredients of my identity, and a woman committed to racial and sexual freedom from oppression, I find I am constantly being encouraged to pluck out some one aspect of myself and present this as the meaningful whole, eclipsing or denying the other parts of self.[18]
> —Audre Lorde

The need for multiple consciousness in feminist movement—a social movement encompassing law, literature, and everything in between—has long been apparent. Since the beginning of the feminist movement in the United States, black women have been arguing that their experience calls into question the notion of a unitary "women's experience."[19] In the first wave of the feminist movement, black women's[20] realization that the white leaders of the suffrage movement intended to take neither issues of racial oppression nor black women themselves seriously was instrumental in destroying or preventing political alliances between black and white women within the movement.[21] In the second wave, black women are again speaking loudly and persistently,[22] and at many levels our voices have begun to be heard. Feminists have adopted the notion of multiple consciousness as appropriate to describe a world in which people are not oppressed only or primarily on the basis of gender, but on the bases of race, class, sexual orientation, and other categories in inextricable webs.[23] Moreover, multiple consciousness is implicit in the precepts of feminism itself. In Christine Littleton's words, "[f]eminist method starts with the very radical act of taking women seriously, believing that what we say about ourselves and our experience is important and valid, even when (or perhaps especially when) it has little or no relationship to what has been or is being said *about* us."[24] If a unitary "women's experience" or "feminism" must be distilled, feminists must ignore many women's voices.[25]

In feminist legal theory, however, the move away from univocal toward multivocal theories of women's experience and feminism has been slower than in other areas. In feminist legal theory, the pull of the second voice, the voice of abstract categorization, is still powerfully strong: "We the People" seems in danger of being replaced by "We the Women." And in feminist legal theory, as in the dominant culture, it is mostly white, straight, and socioeconomically privileged people who claim to speak for all of us. Not surprisingly, the story they tell about "women," despite its claim to universality, seems to black women to be peculiar to women who are white, straight, and socioeconomically privileged—a phenomenon Adrienne Rich terms "white solipsism."[27]

Elizabeth Spelman notes:

> [T]he real problem has been how feminist theory has confused the condition of
> one group of women with the condition of all.
>   . . . A measure of the depth of white middle-class privilege is that the apparently
> straightforward and logical points and axioms at the heart of much of feminist
> theory guarantee the direction of its attention to the concerns of white middle-
> class women.[28]

The notion that there is a monolithic "women's experience" that can be
described independent of other facets of experience like race, class, and sexual
orientation is one I refer to in this essay as "gender essentialism."[29] A corollary
to gender essentialism is "racial essentialism"—the belief that there is a monolithic
"Black Experience," or Chicano Experience." The source of gender and racial
essentialism (and all other essentialisms, for the list of categories could be
infinitely multiplied) is the second voice, the voice that claims to speak for all.
The result of essentialism is to reduce the lives of people who experience
multiple forms of oppression to addition problems: "racism + sexism = straight
black women's experience," or "racism + sexism + homophobia = black
lesbian experience."[30] Thus, in an essentialist world, black women's experience
will always be forcibly fragmented before being subjected to analysis, as those
who are "only interested in race" and those who are "only interested in gender"
take their separate slices of our lives.

Moreover, feminist essentialism paves the way for unconscious racism. Spelman
puts it this way:

> [T]hose who produce the "story of woman" want to make sure they appear in
> it. The best way to ensure that is to be the storyteller and hence to be in a
> position to decide which of all the many facts about women's lives ought to go
> into the story, which ought to be left out. Essentialism works well in behalf of
> these aims, aims that subvert the very process by which women might come to
> see where and how they wish to make common cause. For essentialism invites
> me to take what I understand to be true of me "as a woman" for some golden
> nugget of womanness all women have as women; and it makes the participation
> of other women inessential to the production of the story. How lovely: the many
> turn out to be one, and the one that they are is me.[31]

In a racist society like this one, the storytellers are usually white, and so
"woman" turns out to be "white woman."

Why, in the face of challenges from "different" women and from feminist
method itself, is feminist essentialism so persistent and pervasive? I think the
reasons are several. Essentialism is intellectually convenient, and to a certain
extent cognitively ingrained. Essentialism also carries with it important emotional
and political payoffs. Finally, essentialism often appears (especially to white
women) as the only alternative to chaos, mindless pluralism (the Funes trap), and
the end of the feminist movement. In my view, however, as long as feminists,
like theorists in the dominant culture, continue to search for gender and racial
essences, black women will never be anything more than a crossroads between

two kinds of domination, or at the bottom of a hierarchy of oppressions; we will always be required to choose pieces of ourselves to present as wholeness. . . .

Modified Women and Unmodified Feminism: Black Women in Dominance Theory

Catharine MacKinnon describes her "dominance theory," like the Marxism with which she likes to compare it, as "total": "[T]hey are both theories of the totality, of the whole thing, theories of a fundamental and critical under-pinning of the whole they envision."[35] Both her dominance theory (which she identifies as simply "feminism") and Marxism "focus on that which is most one's own, that which most makes one the being the theory addresses, as that which is most taken away by what the theory criticizes. In each theory you are made who you are by that which is taken away from you by the social relations the theory criticizes."[36] In Marxism, the "that" is work; in feminism, it is sexuality.

MacKinnon defines sexuality as "that social process which creates, organizes, expresses, and directs desire, creating the social beings we know as women and men, as their relations create society."[37] Moreover, "the organized expro-priation of the sexuality of some for the use of others defines the sex, woman. Heterosexuality is its structure, gender and family its congealed forms, sex roles its qualities generalized to social persona, reproduction a consequence, and control its issue."[38] Dominance theory, the analysis of this organized expro-priation, is a theory of power and its unequal distribution.

In MacKinnon's view, "[t]he idea of gender difference helps keep the reality of male dominance in place."[39] That is, the concept of gender difference is an ideology which masks the fact that genders are socially constructed, not natural, and coercively enforced, not freely consented-to. Moreover, "the social relation between the sexes is organized so that men may dominate and women must submit and this relation is sexual—in fact, is sex."[40]

For MacKinnon, male dominance is not only "perhaps the most pervasive and tenacious system of power in history, but . . . it is metaphysically nearly perfect."[41] The masculine point of view is point-of-viewlessness; the force of male dominance "is exercised as consent, its authority as participation, its supremacy as the paradigm of order, its control as the definition of legitimacy."[42] In such a world, the very existence of feminism is something of a paradox. "Feminism claims the voice of women's silence, the sexuality of our eroticized desexualization, the fullness of 'lack,' the centrality of our marginality and exclusion, the public nature of privacy, the presence of our absence."[43] The wonder is how feminism can exist in the face of its theoretical impossibility.

In MacKinnon's view, men have their foot on women's necks,[44] regardless of race or class, or of mode of production: "Feminists do not argue that it means the same to women to be on the bottom in a feudal regime, a capitalist regime, and a socialist regime; the commonality argued is that, despite real changes, bottom is bottom."[45] As a political matter, moreover, MacKinnon is quick to insist that there is only one "true," "unmodified" feminism: that which analyzes women *as women*, not as subsets of some other group and not as gender-neutral beings.[46]

Despite its power, MacKinnon's dominance theory is flawed by its essentialism. MacKinnon assumes, as does the dominant culture, that there is an essential "woman" beneath the realities of differences between women[47]—that in describing the experiences of "women" issues of race, class, and sexual orientation can therefore be safely ignored, or relegated to footnotes.[48] In her search for what is essential womanhood, however, MacKinnon rediscovers white womanhood and introduces it as universal truth. In dominance theory, black women are white women, only more so.

Essentialism in feminist theory has two characteristics that ensure that black women's voices will be ignored. First, in the pursuit of the essential feminine, Woman leached of all color and irrelevant social circumstance, issues of race are bracketed as belonging to a separate and distinct discourse—a process which leaves black women's selves fragmented beyond recognition. Second, feminist essentialists find that in removing issues of "race" they have actually only managed to remove black women—meaning that white women now stand as the epitome of Woman. Both processes can be seen at work in dominance theory.

MacKinnon begins *Signs I* promisingly enough: She says she will render "Black" in upper-case, because she does not regard

> Black as merely a color of skin pigmentation, but as a heritage, an experience, a cultural and personal identity, the meaning of which becomes specifically stigmatic and/or glorious and/or ordinary under specific social conditions. It is as much socially created as, and at least in the American context no less specifically meaningful or definitive than, any linguistic, tribal, or religious ethnicity, all of which are conventionally recognized by capitalization.[49]

By the time she has finished elaborating her theory, however, black women have completely vanished; remaining are only white women with an additional burden.

A. Dominance Theory and the Bracketing of Race

MacKinnon repeatedly seems to recognize the inadequacy of theories that deal with gender while ignoring race, but having recognized the problem, she repeatedly shies away from its implications. Thus, she at times justifies her essentialism by pointing to the essentialism of the dominant discourse: "My suggestion is that what we have in common is not that our conditions have no particularity in ways that matter. But we are all measured by a male standard for women, a standard that is not ours."[50] At other times she deals with the challenge of black women by placing it in footnotes. For example, she places in a footnote without further comment the suggestive, if cryptic, observation that a definition of feminism "of coalesced interest and resistance" has tended both to exclude and to make invisible "the diverse ways that many women—notably Blacks and working-class women—have *moved* against their determinants."[51] In another footnote generally addressed to the problem of relating Marxism to issues of gender and race, she notes that "[a]ny relationship *between* sex and race tends to be left entirely out of account, since they are considered parallel 'strata,' "[52] but this thought simply trails off into a string cite to black feminist and social feminist writings.

Finally, MacKinnon postpones the demand of black women until the arrival of a "general theory of social inequality";[53] recognizing that "gender in this country appears partly to comprise the meaning of, as well as bisect, race and class, even as race and class specificities make up, as well as cross-cut, gender,"[54] she nevertheless is prepared to maintain her "colorblind" approach to women's experience until that general theory arrives (presumably that is someone else's work).

The results of MacKinnon's refusal to move beyond essentialism are apparent in the most tentative essay in *Whose Culture? A Case Note on Martinez v. Santa Clara Pueblo.*[55] Julia Martinez sued her Native American tribe, the Santa Clara Pueblo, in federal court, arguing that a tribal ordinance was invalid under a provision of the Indian Civil Rights Act guaranteeing equal protection of the laws. The ordinance provided that if women married outside the Pueblo, the children of that union were not full tribal members. Martinez married a Navajo man, and her children were not allowed to vote or inherit her rights in communal land. The United States Supreme Court held that this question was a matter of Indian sovereignty to be resolved by the tribe.[56]

MacKinnon starts her discussion with an admission: "I find *Martinez* a difficult case on a lot of levels, and I don't usually find cases difficult."[57] She concludes that the Pueblo ordinance was wrong, because it "did nothing to address or counteract the reasons why Native women were vulnerable to white male land imperialism through marriage—it gave in to them, by punishing the *woman*, the Native person."[58] Yet she reaches her conclusion, as she admits, without knowledge other than "word of mouth" of the history of the ordinance and its place in Santa Clara Pueblo culture.

MacKinnon has Julia Martinez ask her tribe, "Why do you make me choose between my equality as woman and my cultural identity?"[59] But she, no less than the tribe, eventually requires Martinez to choose; and the correct choice is, of course, that Martinez's female identity is more important than her tribal identity. MacKinnon states,

> [T]he aspiration of women to be no less than men—not to be punished where a man is glorified, not to be considered damaged or disloyal where a man is rewarded or left in peace, not to lead a derivative life, but to do everything and be anybody at all—is an aspiration indigenous to women across place and across time.[60]

What MacKinnon does not recognize, however, is that though the aspiration may be everywhere the same, its expression must depend on the social historical circumstances. In this case, should Julia Martinez be content with struggling for change from within,[61] or should the white government have stepped in "on her behalf"? What was the meaning of the ordinance within Pueblo discourse, as opposed to a transhistorical and transcultural feminist discourse? How did it come about and under what circumstances? What was the status of women within the tribe, both historically and at the time of the ordinance and at the present time, and was Martinez's claim heard and understood by the tribal authorities or simply ignored or derided? What were the Pueblo traditions about children of mixed parentage,[62] and how were those traditions changing? In a jurisprudence based on multiple consciousness, rather than the unitary consciousness of MacKinnon's dominance theory, these questions would have to be answered before the ordinance could be considered on its merits and even before the Court's decision to stay out could be evaluated. MacKinnon does not answer these questions, but leaves the essay hanging with the idea that the male supremacist ideology of some Native American tribes may be adopted from white culture and therefore invalid.[64] MacKinnon's tentativeness may be due to not wanting to appear a white cultural imperialist, speaking for a Native American tribe, but to take up Julia Martinez's claim at all is to take that risk. Without a theory that can shift focus from gender to race and other facets of identity and back again, MacKinnon's essay is ultimately crippled. Martinez is made to choose her gender over her race, and her experience is distorted in the process.

B. Dominance Theory and White Women as All Women

The second consequence of feminist essentialism is that the racism that was acknowledged only in brackets quietly emerges in the feminist theory itself—both a cause and an effect of creating "Woman" from white woman. In MacKinnon's work, the result is that black women become white women only more so.

In a passage in *Signs I*, MacKinnon borrows a quote from Toni Cade Bambara describing a black woman with too many children and no means with which to care for them as "grown ugly and dangerous from being nobody for so long," and then explains:

> By using her phrase in altered context, I do not want to distort her meaning but to extend it. Throughout this essay, I have tried to see if women's condition is shared, even when contexts or magnitudes differ. (Thus, it is very different to be "nobody" as a Black woman than as a white lady, but neither is "somebody" by male standards.) This is the approach to race and ethnicity attempted throughout. I aspire to include all women in the term "women" in some way, without violating the particularity of any woman's experience. Whenever this fails, the statement is simply wrong and will have to be qualified or the aspiration (or the theory) abandoned.[66]

I call this the "nuance theory" approach to the problem of essentialism[67]: by being sensitive to the notion that different women have different experiences, generalizations can be offered about "all women" while qualifying statements, often in footnotes, supplement the general account with the subtle nuances of experience that "different" women add to the mix. Nuance theory thus assumes the commonality of all women—differences are a matter of "context" or "magnitude"; that is, nuance.

The problem with nuance theory is that by defining black women as "different," white women quietly become the norm, or pure, essential woman.[68] Just as MacKinnon would argue that being female is more than a "context" or a "magnitude" of human experience,[69] being black is more than a context or magnitude of all (white) women's experience. But not in dominance theory. For instance, MacKinnon describes how a system of male supremacy has constructed "woman":

> Contemporary industrial society's version of her is docile, soft, passive, nurturant, vulnerable, weak, narcissistic, childlike, incompetent, masochistic, and domestic, made for child care, home care, and husband care. . . . Women who resist or fail, including those who never did fit—for example, black and lower-class women who cannot survive if they are soft and weak and incompetent, assertively self-respecting women, women with ambitions of male dimensions—are considered less female, lesser women.[70]

In a peculiar symmetry with this ideology, in which black women are something less than women, in MacKinnon's work black women become something more than women. In MacKinnon's writing, the word "black," applied to women, is an intensifier: If things are bad for everybody (meaning white women), then they're even worse for black women. Silent and suffering, we are trotted onto the page (mostly in footnotes) as the ultimate example of how bad things are.[71]

Thus, in speaking of the beauty standards set for (white) women, MacKinnon remarks, "Black women are further from being able concretely to achieve the standard that no woman can ever achieve, or it would lose its point."[72] The frustration of black women at being unable to look like an "All-American" woman is in this way just a more dramatic example of all (white) women's frustration and oppression. When a black woman speaks on this subject, however, it becomes clear that a black woman's pain at not being considered fully feminine is different qualitatively, not merely quantitatively, from the pain MacKinnon describes. It is qualitatively different because the ideology of beauty concerns not only gender but race. Consider Toni Morrison's analysis of the influence of standards of white beauty on black people in *The Bluest Eye*.[73] Claudia MacTeer, a young black girl, muses, "Adults, older girls, shops, magazines, newspapers, window signs—all the world has agreed that a blue-eyed, yellow-haired, pink-skinned doll was what every girl child treasured."[74] Similarly, in the black community, "high yellow" folks represent the closest black people can come to beauty, and darker people are always "lesser. Nicer, brighter, but still lesser."[75] Beauty is whiteness itself; and middle-class black girls

> go to land-grant colleges, normal schools, and learn how to do the white man's work with refinement: home economics to prepare his food; teacher education to instruct black children in obedience; music to soothe the weary master and entertain his blunted soul. Here they learn the rest of the lesson begun in those

soft houses with porch swings and pots of bleeding heart: how to behave. The careful development of thrift, patience, high morals, and good manners. In short, how to get rid of the funkiness. The dreadful funkiness of passion, the funkiness of nature, the funkiness of the wide range of human emotions.

Wherever it erupts, this Funk, they wipe it away; where it crusts, they dissolve it; wherever it drips, flowers, or clings, they find it and fight it until it dies. They fight this battle all the way to the grave. The laugh that is a little too loud; the enunciation a little too round; the gesture a little too generous. They hold their behind in for fear of a sway too free; when they wear lipstick, they never cover the entire mouth for fear of lips too thick, and they worry, worry, worry about the edges of their hair.[76]

Thus, Pecola Breedlove, born black and ugly, spends her lonely and abused childhood praying for blue eyes.[77] Her story ends in despair and the fragmentation of her mind into two isolated speaking voices, not because she's even further away from ideal beauty than white women are, but because Beauty *itself* is white, and she is not and can never be, despite the pair of blue eyes she eventually believes she has. There is a difference between the hope that the next makeup kit or haircut or diet will bring you salvation and the knowledge that nothing can. The relation of black women to the ideal of white beauty is not a more intense form of white women's frustration: It is something other, a complex mingling of racial and gender hatred from without, self-hatred from within.

MacKinnon's essentialist, "color-blind" approach also distorts the analysis of rape that constitutes the heart of *Signs II*. By ignoring the voices of black female theoreticians of rape, she produces an ahistorical account that fails to capture the experience of black women.

MacKinnon sees sexuality as "a social sphere of male power of which forced sex is paradigmatic."[78] As with beauty standards, black women are victimized by rape just like white women, only more so: "Racism in the United States, by singling out Black men for allegations of rape of white women, has helped obscure the fact that it is men who rape women, disproportionately women of color."[79] In this peculiar fashion MacKinnon simultaneously recognizes and shelves racism, finally reaffirming that the divide between men and women is more fundamental and that women of color are simply "women plus." MacKinnon goes on to develop a powerful analysis of rape as the subordination of women to men, with only one more mention of color: "[R]ape comes to mean a strange (read Black) man knowing a woman does not want sex and going ahead anyway."[80]

This analysis, though rhetorically powerful, is an analysis of what rape means to white women masquerading as a general account; it has nothing to do with the experience of black women.[81] For black women, rape is a far more complex experience, and an experience as deeply rooted in color as in gender.

For example, the paradigm experience of rape for black women has historically involved the white employer in the kitchen or bedroom as much as the strange black man in the bushes. During slavery, the sexual abuse of black women by white men was commonplace.[82] Even after emancipation, the majority of working black women were domestic servants for white families, a job which made them uniquely vulnerable to sexual harassment and rape.[83]

Moreover, as a legal matter, the experience of rape did not even exist for black women. During slavery, the rape of a black woman by any man, white or black, was simply not a crime.[84] Even after the Civil War, rape laws were seldom used to protect black women against either white or black men, since black women were considered promiscuous by nature.[85] In contrast to the partial or at least formal protection white women had against sexual brutalization, black women frequently had no legal protection whatsoever. "Rape," in this sense, was something that only happened to white women; what happened to black women was simply life.

Finally, for black people, male and female, "rape" signified the terrorism of black men by white men, aided and abetted, passively (by silence) or actively (by "crying rape"), by white women. Black women have recognized this aspect of rape since the nineteenth century. For example, social activist Ida B. Wells analyzed rape as an example of the inseparability of race and gender oppression in *Southern Horrors: Lynch Law in All Its Phases*, published in 1892. Wells saw that both the law of rape and Southern miscegenation laws were part of a patriarchal system through which white men maintained their control over the bodies of all black people: "[W]hite men used their ownership of the body of the white female as a terrain on which to lynch the black male."[86] Moreover, Wells argued, though many white women encouraged interracial sexual relationships, white women, protected by the patriarchal idealization of white womanhood, were able to remain silent, unhappily or not, as black men were murdered by mobs.[87] Similarly, Anna Julia Cooper, another nineteenth-century theorist, "saw that the manipulative power of the South was embodied in the southern patriarch, but she describes its concern with 'blood,' inheritance, and heritage in entirely female terms and as a preoccupation that was transmitted from the South to the North and perpetuated by white women."[88]

Nor has this aspect of rape become purely a historical curiosity. Susan Estrich reports that between 1930 and 1967, 89 percent of the men executed for rape in the United States were black;[89] a 1968 study of rape sentencing in Maryland showed that in all 55 cases where the death penalty was imposed the victim had been white, and that between 1960 and 1967, 47 percent of all black men convicted of criminal assaults on black women were immediately released on probation.[90] The case of Joann Little is testimony to the continuing sensitivity of black women to this aspect of rape. As Angela Davis tells the story:

> Brought to trial on murder charges, the young Black woman was accused of killing a white guard in a North Carolina jail where she was the only woman inmate. When Joann Little took the stand, she told how the guard had raped her in her cell and how she had killed him in self-defense with the ice pick he had used to threaten her. Throughout the country, her cause was passionately supported by individuals and organizations in the Black community and within the young women's movement, and her acquittal was hailed as an important victory made possible by this mass campaign. In the immediate aftermath of her acquittal, Ms. Little issued several moving appeals on behalf of a Black man named Delbert Tibbs, who awaited execution in Florida because he had been falsely convicted of raping a white woman.

Many Black women answered Joann Little's appeal to support the cause of Delbert Tibbs. But few white women—and certainly few organized groups within the anti-rape movement—followed her suggestion that they agitate for the freedom of this Black man who had been blatantly victimized by Southern racism.[91]

The rift between white and black women over the issue of rape is highlighted by the contemporary feminist analyses of rape that have explicitly relied on racist ideology to minimize white women's complicity in racial terrorism.[92]

Thus, the experience of rape for black women includes not only a vulnerability to rape and a lack of legal protection radically different from that experienced by white women, but also a unique ambivalence. Black women have simultaneously acknowledged their own victimization and the victimization of black men by a system that has consistently ignored violence against women while perpetrating it against men.[93] The complexity and depth of this experience is not captured, or even acknowledged, by MacKinnon's account.

MacKinnon's essentialist approach recreates the paradigmatic woman in the image of the white woman, in the name of "unmodified feminism." As in the dominant discourse, black women are relegated to the margins, ignored or extolled as "just like us, only more so." But "Black women are not white women with color."[94] Moreover, feminist essentialism represents not just an insult to black women, but a broken promise—the promise to listen to women's stories, the promise of feminist method.

Robin West's "Essential Woman"

While MacKinnon's essentialism is pervasive but covert, Robin West expressly declares her essentialism. In the last section of *The Difference in Women's Hedonic Lives: A Phenomenological Critique of Feminist Legal Theory*,[95] West argues:

> Both the liberal and the radical legalist have accepted the Kantian assumption that *to be human* is to be in some sense autonomous—meaning, minimally, to be differentiated, or individuated, from the rest of social life.
>
> Underlying and underscoring the poor fit between the proxies for subjective well-being endorsed by liberals and radicals—choice and power—and women's subjective, hedonic lives is the simple fact that women's lives—*because of our biological, reproductive role*—are drastically at odds with this fundamental vision of human life. Women's lives are *not* autonomous, they are profoundly relational.[96]

In West's view, women are ontologically distinct from men, because "Women, and *only* women, and *most* women, transcend *physically* the differentiation or individuation of biological self from the rest of human life trumpeted as the norm by the entire Kantian tradition."[97] That is, because only women can bear children, and because women have the social responsibility for raising children, our selves are profoundly different from male selves. "To the considerable degree that our potentiality for motherhood defines ourselves, women's lives are relational, not autonomous. As mothers we nurture the weak and we depend upon the strong. More than do men, we live in an interdependent and hierarchical natural web with others of varying degrees of strength."[98]

This claim about women's essential connectedness to the world becomes the centerpiece of *Jurisprudence and Gender.*[99] West begins the article with the question, "What is a human being?" She then asserts that "perhaps the central insight of feminist theory of the last decade has been that wom[e]n are 'essentially connected,' not 'essentially separate,' from the rest of human life, both materially, through pregnancy, intercourse, and breast-feeding, and existentially, through the moral and practical life."[100] For West, this means that "all of our modern legal theory—by which I mean 'liberal legalism' and 'critical legal theory' collectively—is essentially and irretrievably masculine."[101] This is so because modern legal theory relies on the "separation thesis," the claim that human beings are distinct individuals first and form relationships later.[102]

Black women are entirely absent from West's work. . . . However, . . . the bracketing of issues of race leads to the installation of white women on the throne of essential womanhood.

West's claims are clearly questionable on their face insofar as the experience of some women—"mothers"—is asserted to stand for the experience of all women. As with MacKinnon's theory, West's theory necessitates the stilling of some voices—namely, the voices of women who have rejected their "biological, reproductive role"—in order to privilege others. One might also question the degree to which motherhood, or our potential for it, defines us. For purposes of this article, however, I am more interested in the conception of self that underlies West's account of "women's experience."

West argues that the biological and social implications of motherhood shape the selfhood of all, or at least most, women. This claim involves at least two assumptions.[104] First, West assumes (as does the liberal social theory she criticizes) that everyone has a deep, unitary "self" that is relatively stable and unchanging. Second, West assumes that this "self" differs significantly between men and women but is the same for all women and for all men despite differences of class, race, and sexual orientation: that is, that this self is deeply and primarily gendered. In a later part of the article, I will argue that black women can bring the experience of a multiple rather than a unitary self to feminist theory. Here I want to argue that the notion that the gender difference is primary to an individual's selfhood is one that privileges white women's experience over the experience of black women.

The essays and poems in *This Bridge Called My Back*[106] describe experiences of women of color that differ radically from one another. Some contributors are Lesbians; some are straight; some are class-privileged, and others are not. What links all the writings, however, is the sense that the self of a woman of color is not primarily a female self or a colored self, but a both-and self. In her essay "Brownness,"[107] Andrea Canaan describes both-and experience:

> The fact is I am brown and female, and my growth and development are tied to the entire community. I must nurture and develop brown self, woman, man, and child. I must address the issues of my own oppression and survival. When I

separate them, isolate them, and ignore them, I separate, isolate, and ignore myself.
I am a unit. A part of brownness.[108]

A personal story may also help to illustrate the point. At a 1988 meeting of
the West Coast "fem-crits," Pat Cain and Trina Grillo asked all the women
present to pick out two or three words to describe who they were. None of
the white women mentioned their race; all of the women of color did.

In this society, it is only white people who have the luxury of "having no
color"; only white people have been able to imagine that sexism and racism
are separate experiences. Far more for black women than for white women,
the experience of self is precisely that of being unable to disentangle the web
of race and gender—of being enmeshed always in multiple, often contradictory,
discourses of sexuality and color. The challenge to black women has been the
need to weave the fragments, our many selves, into an integral, though always
changing and shifting, whole: a self that is neither "female" nor "black," but
both-and. West's insistence that every self is deeply and primarily gendered,
then, with its corollary that gender is more important to personal identity than
race, is finally another example of white solipsism. By suggesting that gender
is more deeply embedded in self than race, her theory privileges the experience
of white people over all others,[111] and thus serves to reproduce relations of
domination in the larger culture. Like MacKinnon's essential woman, West's
essential woman turns out to be white.

.   .   .

Beyond Essentialism: Black Women
and Feminist Theory

*[O]ur future survival is predicated upon our ability to relate within equality. As women,
we must root out internalized patterns of oppression within ourselves if we are to move
beyond the most superficial aspects of social change. Now we must recognize differences
among women who are our equals, neither inferior nor superior, and devise ways to
use each others' difference to enrich our visions and our joint struggles.*[124]

—Audre Lorde

In this part of the article, I want to talk about what black women can bring
to feminist theory to help us move beyond essentialism and toward multiple
consciousness as feminist and jurisprudential method. In my view, there are at
least three major contributions that black women have to offer post-essentialist
feminist theory: the recognition of a self that is multiplicitous, not unitary; the
recognition that differences are always relational rather than inherent; and the
recognition that wholeness and commonality are acts of will and creativity,
rather than passive discovery.

A. The Abandonment of Innocence

Black women experience not a single inner self (much less one that is
essentially gendered), but many selves. This sense of a multiplicitous self is not
unique to black women, but black women have expressed this sense in ways

that are striking, poignant, and potentially useful to feminist theory. bell hooks describes her experience in a creative writing program at a predominantly white college, where she was encouraged to find "her voice," as frustrating to her sense of multiplicity.

> It seemed that many black students found our situations problematic precisely because our sense of self, and by definition our voice, was not unilateral, monologist, or static but rather multi-dimensional. We were as at home in dialect as we were in standard English. Individuals who speak languages other than English, who speak patois as well as standard English, find it a necessary aspect of self-affirmation not to feel compelled to choose one voice over another, not to claim one as more authentic, but rather to construct social realities that celebrate, acknowledge, and affirm differences, variety.[125]

This experience of multiplicity is also a sense of self-contradiction, of containing the oppressor within oneself. In her article *On Being the Object of Property*,[126] Patricia Williams writes about herself writing about her great-great-grandmother, "picking through the ruins for my roots."[127] What she finds is a paradox: She must claim for herself "a heritage the weft of whose genesis is [her] own disinheritance."[128] William's great-great-grandmother, Sophie, was a slave, and at the age of about eleven was impregnated by her owner, a white lawyer named Austin Miller. Their daughter Mary, William's great-grandmother, was taken away from Sophie and raised as a house servant.

When Williams went to law school, her mother told her, "The Millers were lawyers, so you have it in your blood."[129] Williams analyzes this statement as asking her to acknowledge contradictory selves:

> [S]he meant that no one should make me feel inferior because someone else's father was a judge. She wanted me to reclaim that part of my heritage from which I had been disinherited, and she wanted me to use it as a source of strength and self-confidence. At the same time, she was asking me to claim a part of myself that was the dispossessor of another part of myself; she was asking me to deny that disenfranchised little black girl of myself that felt powerless, vulnerable and, moreover, rightly felt so.[130]

The theory of black slavery, Williams notes, was based on the notion that black people are beings without will or personality, defined by "irrationality, lack of control, and ugliness."[131] In contrast, "wisdom, control, and aesthetic beauty signify the whole white personality in slave law."[132] In accepting her white self, her lawyer self, Williams must accept a legacy of not only a disinheritance but a negation of her black self: To the Millers, her forebears, the Williamses, her forebears, did not even have selves as such.

Williams's choice ultimately is not to deny either self, but to recognize them both, and in so doing to acknowledge guilt as well as innocence. She ends the piece by invoking "the presence of polar bears"[133]: bears that mauled a child to death at the Brooklyn Zoo and were subsequently killed themselves, bears judged in public debate as simultaneously "innocent, naturally territorial, unfairly imprisoned, and guilty."[134]

This complex resolution rejects the easy innocence of supposing oneself to be an essential black self with a legacy of oppression by the guilty white Other. With such multilayered analyses, black women can bring to feminist theory stories of how it is to have multiple and contradictory selves, selves that contain the oppressor as well as the oppressed.[135]

B. Strategic Identities and "Difference"

A post-essentialist feminism can benefit not only from the abandonment of the quest for a unitary self, but also from Martha Minow's realization that difference—and therefore identity—is always relational, not inherent.[136] Zora Neale Hurston's work is a good illustration of this notion.

In an essay written for a white audience, *How It Feels to Be Colored Me*,[137] Hurston argues that her color is not an inherent part of her being, but a response to her surroundings. She recalls the day she "became colored"—the day she left her home in an all-black community to go to school: "I left Eatonville, the town of the oleanders, as Zora. When I disembarked from the river-boat at Jacksonville, she was no more. It seemed that I had suffered a sea change. I was not Zora of Orange County any more, I was now a little colored girl."[138] But even as an adult, Hurston insists, her colored self is always situational: "I do not always feel colored. Even now I often achieve the unconscious Zora of Eatonville before the Hegira. I feel most colored when I am thrown against a sharp white background."[139]

As an example, Hurston describes the experience of listening to music in a jazz club with a white male friend:

> My pulse is throbbing like a war drum. I want to slaughter something—give pain, give death to what, I do not know. But the piece ends. The men of the orchestra wipe their lips and rest their fingers. I creep back slowly to the veneer we call civilization with the last tone and find the white friend sitting motionless in his seat, smoking calmly.
>
> "Good music they have here," he remarks, drumming the table with his fingertips.
>
> Music. The great blobs of purple and red emotion have not touched him. He has only heard what I felt. He is far away and I see him but dimly across the ocean and the continent that have fallen between us. He is so pale with his whiteness then and I am *so* colored.[140]

In reaction to the presence of whites—both her white companion and the white readers of her essay—Hurston invokes and uses the traditional stereotype of black people as tied to the jungle, "living in the jungle way."[141] Yet in a later essay for a black audience, *What White Publishers Won't Print*,[142] she criticizes the white "folklore of 'reversion to type' ":

> This curious doctrine has such wide acceptance that it is tragic. One has only to examine the huge literature on it to be convinced. No matter how high we may *seem* to climb, put us under strain and we revert to type, that is, to the

bush. Under a superficial layer of western culture, the jungle drums throb in out veins.[143]

The difference between the first essay, in which Hurston revels in the trope of black persons as primitive, and the second essay, in which she deplores it, lies in the distinction between an identity that is contingent, temporary, and relational, and an identity that is fixed, inherent, and essential. Zora as jungle woman is fine as an argument, a reaction to her white friend's experience: what is abhorrent is the notion that Zora can always and only be a jungle woman. One image is in flux, "inspired" by a relationship with another; the other is static, unchanging, and ultimately reductive and sterile rather than creative.

Thus, "how it feels to be colored Zora" depends on the answer to these questions: " 'Compared to what? As of when? Who is asking? In what context? For what purpose? With what interests and presuppositions?' What Hurston rigorously shows is that questions of difference and identity are always functions of a specific interlocutionary situation—and the answers, matters of strategy rather than truth."[146] Any "essential self" is always an invention; the evil is in denying its artificiality.

To be compatible with this conception of the self, feminist theorizing about "women" must similarly be strategic and contingent, focusing on relationships, not essences. One result will be that men will cease to be a faceless Other and reappear as potential allies in political struggle. Another will be that women will be able to acknowledge their differences without threatening feminism itself. In the process, as feminists begin to attack racism and classism and homophobia, feminism will change from being only about "women as women" (modified women need not apply), to being about all kinds of oppression based on seemingly inherent and unalterable characteristics. We need not wait for a unified theory of oppression; that theory can be feminism.

C. Integrity as Will and Idea

> Because each had discovered years before that they were neither white nor male, and that all freedom and triumph was forbidden to them, they had set about creating something else to be.[151]
>
> —Toni Morrison

Finally, black women can help feminist movement move beyond its fascination with essentialism through the recognition that wholeness of the self and commonality with others are asserted (if never completely achieved) through creative action, not realized in shared victimization. Feminist theory at present, especially feminist legal theory, tends to focus on women as passive victims. For example, for MacKinnon, women have been so objectified by men that the miracle is how they are able to exist at all. Women are the victims, the acted-upon, the helpless, until by radical enlightenment they are somehow empowered to act for themselves.[152] Similarly, for West, the "fundamental fact" of women's lives is pain—"the violence, the danger, the boredom, the ennui, the nonproductivity, the poverty, the fear, the numbness, the frigidity, the isolation, the low self-esteem, and the pathetic attempts to assimilate."[153]

This story of woman as victim is meant to encourage solidarity by emphasizing women's shared oppression, thus denying or minimizing difference, and to further the notion of an essential woman—she who is victimized. But as bell hooks has succinctly noted, the notion that women's commonality lies in their shared victimization by men "directly reflects male supremacist thinking. Sexist ideology teaches women that to be female is to be a victim."[154] Moreover, the story of woman as passive victim denies the ability of women to shape their own lives, whether for better or worse. It also may thwart their abilities. Like Minnie Bruce Pratt, reluctant to look farther than commonality for fear of jeopardizing the comfort of shared experience, women who rely on their victimization to define themselves may be reluctant to let it go and create their own self-definitions.

At the individual level, black women have had to learn to construct themselves in a society that denied them full selves. Again, Zora Neale Hurston's writings are suggestive. Though Hurston plays with being her "colored self" and again with being "the eternal feminine with its string of beads,"[155] she ends *How It Feels to Be Colored Me* with an image of herself as neither essentially black nor essentially female, but simply

> a brown bag of miscellany propped against a wall. Against a wall in company with other bags, white, red and yellow. Pour out the contents, and there is discovered a jumble of small things priceless and worthless. A first-water diamond, an empty spool, bits of broken glass, lengths of string, a key to a door long since crumbled away, a rusty knife-blade, old shoes saved for a road that never was and never will be, a nail bent under the weight of things too heavy for any nail, a dried flower or two still fragrant. In your hand is the brown bag. On the ground before you is the jumble it held—so much like the jumble in the bags, could they be emptied, that all might be dumped in a single heap and the bags refilled without altering the content of any greatly. A bit of colored glass more or less would not matter. Perhaps that is how the Great Stuffer of Bags filled them in the first place—who knows?[156]

Hurston thus insists on a conception of identity as a construction, not an essence—something made of fragments of experience, not discovered in one's body or unveiled after male domination is eliminated.

This insistence on the importance of will and creativity seems to threaten feminism at one level, because it gives strength back to the concept of autonomy, making possible the recognition of the element of consent in relations of domination, and attributes to women the power that makes culpable the many ways in which white women have actively used their race privilege against their sisters of color. Although feminists are correct to recognize the powerful force of sheer physical coercion in ensuring compliance with patriarchal hegemony, we must also "come to terms with the ways in which women's culture has served to enlist women's support in perpetuating existing power relations."[160]

However, at another level, the recognition of the role of creativity and will in shaping our lives is liberating, for it allows us to acknowledge and celebrate the creativity and joy with which many women have survived and turned existing relations of domination to their own ends. Works of black literature like *Beloved, The Color Purple,* and *Song of Solomon,* among others, do not linger on black women's victimization and misery; though they recognize our pain, they ultimately celebrate our transcendence.

Finally, on a collective level this emphasis on will and creativity reminds us that bridges between women are built, not found. The discovery of shared suffering is a connection more illusory than real; what will truly bring and keep us together is the use of effort and imagination to root out and examine our differences, for only the recognition of women's differences can ultimately bring feminist movement to strength. This is hard work, and painful work; but it is also radical work, real work. As Barbara Smith has said, "What I really feel is radical is trying to make coalitions with people who are different from you. I feel it is radical to be dealing with race and sex and class and sexual identity all at one time. I think *that* is really radical because it has never been done before."[163]

D. Epilogue: Multiple Consciousness

I have argued in this article that gender essentialism is dangerous to feminist legal theory because in the attempt to extract an essential female self and voice from the diversity of women's experience, the experiences of women perceived as "different" are ignored or treated as variations on the (white) norm. Now I want to return to an earlier point: that legal theory, including feminist legal theory, has been entranced for too long and to too great an extent by the voice of "We the People." In order to energize legal theory, we need to subvert it with narratives and stories, accounts of the particular, the different, and the hitherto silenced.

Whether by chance or not, many of the legal theorists telling stories these days are women of color. Mari Matsuda calls for "multiple consciousness as jurisprudential method";[164] Patricia Williams shows the way with her multilayered stories and meditations.[165] These writings are healthy for feminist legal theory as well as legal theory more generally. In acknowledging "the complexity of messages implied in our being,"[166] they begin the task of energizing legal theory with the creative struggle between Funes and We the People: the creative struggle that reflects a multiple consciousness.

Notes

1. Ntozake Shange, *no more love poems #4,* in For Colored Girls Who Have Considered Suicide / When the Rainbow Is Enuf 45 (1977). . . .

2. Jorge Luis Borges, Labyrinths: Selected Stories and Other Writings 59 (D. Yates & J. Irby eds. 1964).

3. *Id.* at 63–64.

4. *Id.* at 64.

5. *Id.* at 65.

6. *Id.* at 66.

7. James Boyd White, When Words Lose Their Meaning 232 (1984).

8. *Id.* at 240.

9. CYNTHIA OZICK, *Innovation and Redemption: What Literature Means*, in ART AND ARDOR 238, 244 (1983).

10. Robert M. Cover, *Violence and the Word*, 95 YALE L.J. 1601, 1601 (1986): *see also* Robert Weisberg, *The Law-Literature Enterprise*, 1 YALE J.L. & HUMANITIES 1, 45 (1988) (describing how students of legal interpretation are initially drawn to literary interpretation because of its greater freedom, and then almost immediately search for a way to reintroduce constraints).

11. *See* Peter Goodrich, *Historical Aspects of Legal Interpretation*, 61 IND. L.J. 331, 333 (1986) (arguing that legal interpretation is theological in derivation and "unjustifiably authoritarian in its practice").

12. Henry Louis Gates, Jr., *Editor's Introduction: Writing "Race" and the Difference It Makes*, in "RACE," WRITING AND DIFFERENCE 1, 16 (H.L. Gates, Jr. ed. 1986).

13. Mari J. Matsuda, *When the First Quail Calls: Multiple Consciousness as Jurisprudential Method*. 11 WOMEN'S RTS. L. REP. 7, 9 (1989).

14. Teresa de Lauretis, *Feminist Studies/Critical Studies: Issues, Terms, and Contexts*, in FEMINIST STUDIES/CRITICAL STUDIES 1, 8 (T. de Lauretis ed. 1986).

15. C. OZICK, *supra* note 9, at 247.

16. Matsuda, *supra* note 13, at 9.

17. *Id.* at 8.

18. AUDRE LORDE, *Age, Race, Class, and Sex: Women Redefining Difference*, in SISTER OUTSIDER 114, 120 (1984).

19. For example, in 1851, Sojourner Truth told the audience at the woman's rights convention in Akron, Ohio: "That man over there says women need to be helped into carriages, and lifted over ditches, and to have the best place everywhere. Nobody ever helps me into carriages, or over mud-puddles, or gives me any best place! And ain't I a woman? Look at me! Look at my arm! I have ploughed, and planted, and gathered into barns, and no man could head me! And ain't I a woman? I could work as much and eat as much as a man—when I could get it—and bear the lash as well! And ain't I a woman? I have borne thirteen children, and seen them most all sold off to slavery, and when I cried out with my mother's grief, none but Jesus heard me! And ain't I a woman?" Address by Sojourner Truth (1851) *reprinted in* BLACK WOMEN IN NINETEENTH-CENTURY AMERICAN LIFE: THEIR WORDS, THEIR THOUGHTS, THEIR FEELINGS 234, 235 (B.J. Loewenberg & R. Bogin eds. 1976).

20. I use "black" rather than "African-American" because some people of color who do not have African heritage and/or are not Americans nevertheless identify themselves as black, and in this essay I am more interested in stressing issues of culture than of nationality or genetics. I use "black" rather than "Black" because it is my contention in this essay that race and gender issues are inextricably intertwined, and to capitalize "Black" and not "Woman" would imply a privileging of race with which I do not agree.

21. For a discussion of white racism in the suffrage movement, see ANGELA Y. DAVIS, WOMEN, RACE AND CLASS 110-26 (1981); PAULA GIDDINGS, WHEN AND WHERE I ENTER: THE IMPACT OF BLACK WOMEN ON RACE AND SEX IN AMERICA 159-70 (1984). *See also* P. GIDDINGS, *supra*, at 46-55 (white racism in the abolitionist movement).

22. *See, e.g.*, A. DAVIS, *supra* note 21; BELL HOOKS, AIN'T I A WOMAN? BLACK WOMEN AND FEMINISM (1981); BELL HOOKS, FEMINIST THEORY: FROM MARGIN TO CENTER (1984) [hereinafter B. HOOKS, FEMINIST THEORY]; BELL HOOKS, TALKING BACK: THINKING FEMINIST, THINKING BLACK (1989) [hereinafter B. HOOKS, TALKING BACK]; GLORIA I. JOSEPH & JILL LEWIS, COMMON DIFFERENCES: CONFLICTS IN BLACK AND WHITE FEMINIST PERSPECTIVES (1981); THIS BRIDGE CALLED MY BACK: WRITINGS BY

RADICAL WOMEN OF COLOR (C. Moraga & G. Anzaldúa 2d ed. 1983) [hereinafter THIS BRIDGE CALLED MY BACK]; Hazel V. Carby, *White Woman Listen! Black Feminism and the Boundaries of Sisterhood,* in THE EMPIRE STRIKES BACK: RACE AND RACISM IN 70S BRITAIN 212 (Centre for Contemporary Cultural Studies ed. 1982); Martía C. Lugones & Elizabeth V. Spelman, *Have We Got a Theory for You! Feminist Theory, Cultural Imperialism and the Demand for "The Woman's Voice,"* 6 WOMEN'S STUD. INT'L F. 573 (1983).

23. *See, e.g.,* de Lauretis, *supra* note 14, at 9 (characterizing the feminist identity as "multiple, shifting, and often self-contradictory").

24. Christine A. Littleton, *Feminist Jurisprudence: The Difference Method Makes* (Book Review), 41 STAN. L. REV. 751, 764 (1989). MacKinnon's definition of feminist method is the practice of "believing women's accounts of sexual use and abuse by men." CATHARINE A. MACKINNON, *Introduction: The Art of the Impossible,* in FEMINISM UNMODIFIED 1, 5 (1987). Littleton argues that MacKinnon's major contribution to feminist jurisprudence has been "more methodological than programmatic." Littleton, *supra,* at 753–54. In Littleton's view, "the essence of MacKinnon's view on 'feminisms' comes down to a single choice: feminist method or not." *Id.* at 752–53.

25. *See* Jane Flax, *Postmodernism and Gender Relations in Feminist Theory,* 12 SIGNS 621, 633 (1987). . . .

27. Rich defines white solipsism as the tendency to "think, imagine, and speak as if whiteness described the world." ADRIENNE RICH, *Disloyal to Civilization: Feminism, Racism, Gynephobia,* in ON LIES, SECRETS, AND SILENCE 275, 299 (1979).

28. [ELIZABETH V.] SPELMAN, [INESSENTIAL WOMAN: PROBLEMS OF EXCLUSION IN FEMINIST THOUGHT 4 (1988)].

29. Elizabeth Spelman lists five propositions which I consider to be associated with gender essentialism: "1. Women can be talked about 'as women.' 2. Women are oppressed "as women." 3. Gender can be isolated from other elements of identity that bear on one's social, economic, and political position such as race, class, ethnicity: hence sexism can be isolated from racism, classism, etc. 4. Women's situation can be contrasted to men's. 5. Relations between men and women can be compared to relations between other oppressor/oppressed groups (whites and Blacks, Christians and Jews, rich and poor, etc.), and hence it is possible to compare the situation of women to the situation of Blacks, Jews, the poor, etc." *Id.* at 165.

30. *See* Deborah K. King, *Multiple Jeopardy, Multiple Consciousness: The Context of a Black Feminist Ideology,* 14 SIGNS 42, 51 (1988). . . .

31. E. SPELMAN, *supra* note [28], at 159.

35. C. MACKINNON, *Desire and Power,* in FEMINISM UNMODIFIED, *supra* note 24, at 46, 49.

36. *Id.* at 48.

37. [Catharine A.] MacKinnon, [*Feminism, Marxism, Method, and the State: An Agenda for Theory,* 7 SIGNS 515, 516 (1982) (hereinafter MacKinnon, *Signs I*)] (footnote omitted).

38. *Id.*

39. C. MACKINNON, *supra* note 24, at 3.

40. *Id.* Thus, MacKinnon disagrees both with feminists who argue that women and men are really the same and should therefore be treated the same under the law, and with feminists who argue that the law should take into account women's differences. Feminists who argue that men and women are "the same" fail to take into account the unequal power relations that underlie the very construction of the two genders. Feminists who want the law to recognize the "differences" between the genders buy into the account of women's "natural difference," and therefore (inadvertently) perpetuate dominance under the name of inherent difference. *See id.* at 32–40, 71–77.

41. [Catharine A.] MacKinnon, [*Feminism, Marxism, Method and the State: Toward Feminist Jurisprudence*, 8 SIGNS 635, 638 (1983) (hereinafter MacKinnon, *Signs II*)].

42. *Id.* at 639.

43. *Id.*

44. *See* C. MACKINNON, *Difference and Dominance: On Sex Discrimination*, in FEMINISM UNMODIFIED, *supra* note 24, at 32, 45.

45. MacKinnon, *Signs I, supra* note [37], at 523.

46. *See* C. MACKINNON, *supra* note 24, at 16.

47. Although MacKinnon's explicit position is that until women are free from male domination, we simply don't know what we might be like, as Katharine Bartlett notes, in *Feminism Unmodified* MacKinnon "speaks of 'women's point of view,' 'woman's voice,' woman's 'distinctive contribution,' of standards that are 'not ours,' of empowering women 'on our own terms,' and of what we 'really want.' These references all suggest a reality beyond social construct that women will discover once freed from the bonds of oppression." Katharine T. Bartlett, *MacKinnon's Feminism: Power on Whose Terms?* (Book Review), 75 CALIF. L. REV. 1559, 1566 (1987) (citations omitted).

48. *See, e.g.*, MacKinnon, *Signs II, supra* note [41], at 639 n.8 ("This feminism seeks to define and pursue women's interest as the fate of all women bound together. It seeks to extract the truth of women's commonalities out of the lie that all women are the same.").

49. MacKinnon, *Signs I, supra* note [37], at 516 n.*.

50. C. MACKINNON. *On Exceptionality: Women as Women in Law*, in FEMINISM UNMODIFIED, *supra* note 24, at 70, 76.

51. MacKinnon, *Signs I, supra* note [37], at 518 & n.3.

52. *Id.* at 537 n.54.

53. C. MACKINNON, *supra* note 24, at 3.

54. *Id.* at 2.

55. C. MACKINNON, *Whose Culture? A Case Note on Martinez v. Santa Clara Pueblo*, in FEMINISM UNMODIFIED, *supra* note 24, at 63.

56. Santa Clara Pueblo v. Martinez, 436 U.S. 49, 71-72 (1978).

57. C. MACKINNON, *supra* note 55, at 66.

58. *Id.* at 68.

59. *Id.* at 67.

60. *Id.* at 68.

61. As she did. *See* Martinez v. Santa Clara Pueblo, 402 F. Supp. 5, 11 (D.N.M. 1975), *rev'd.* 540 F.2d 1039 (10th Cir. 1976), *rev'd.* 436 U.S. 49 (1978).

62. The district court hints that such questions were decided on a case-by-case basis. *Id.* at 16. Why was an ordinance thought necessary?

64. C. MACKINNON, *supra* note 55, at 69.

66. MacKinnon, *Signs I, supra* note [37], at 520 n.7.

67. The reference is to an article in *Newsweek* called *Feminism: "The Black Nuance,"* NEWSWEEK, Dec. 17, 1973, at 89-90; *cf.* E. SPELMAN, *supra* note [28], at 114-15 (describing article in the *New York Times* in which the women are white and the blacks are men).

68. MacKinnon recognizes a similar process in Marxism, whereby gender oppression becomes merely a variant form of class oppression. *See* MacKinnon, *Signs I, supra* note [37], at 524-27. What MacKinnon misses is that her own theory reduces racial oppression to a mere intensifier of gender oppression.

69. *See, e.g.*, C. MACKINNON, *supra* note [24], at 169. ("Defining feminism in a way that connects epistemology with power as the politics of women's point of view, [the discovery of feminism] can be summed up by saying that women live in another world: specifically, a world of *not* equality, a world of inequality.").

70. MacKinnon, *Signs I, supra* note [37], at 530. Yet, having acknowledged that black women have never been "women," MacKinnon continues in the article to discuss "women," making it plain that the "women" she is discussing are white.

71. Applied to men, however, the word "black" ameliorates: MacKinnon concedes that black men are not quite as bad as white men, although they are still bad, being men. For instance, in a footnote she qualifies her statement that *"[P]ower to create the world from one's point of view is power in its male form,"* *id.* at 537, with the recognition that black men have "less" power: "But to the extent that they cannot create the world from their point of view, they find themselves unmanned, castrated, literally or figuratively." *Id.* at 537 n.54. The last clause of this statement appears, puzzlingly, to be a reference to lynching; but it was not for *failing* to create the world but for the more radical sin of *making the attempt* that black men were "literally castrated."

72. *Id.* at 540 n.59. Similarly, in *Feminism Unmodified*, MacKinnon reminds us that the risk of death and mutilation in the course of a botched abortion is disproportionately borne by women of color, C. MACKINNON, *Not by Law Alone: From a Debate with Phyllis Schlafly*, in FEMINISM UNMODIFIED, *supra* note 24, at 21, 25, but only in the context of asserting that "[n]one of us can afford this risk," *id.*

73. TONI MORRISON, THE BLUEST EYE (1970).

74. *Id.* at 14.

75. *Id.* at 57.

76. *Id.* at 64.

77. "It had occurred to Pecola some time ago that if her eyes, those eyes that held the pictures, and knew the sights—if those eyes of hers were different, that is to say, beautiful, she herself would be different. Her teeth were good, and at least her nose was not big and flat like some of those who were thought so cute. If she looked different, beautiful, maybe [her father] would be different, and Mrs. Breedlove too. Maybe they'd say, 'Why, look at pretty-eyed Pecola. We mustn't do bad things in front of those pretty eyes.' " *Id.* at 34.

78. MacKinnon, *Signs II, supra* note [41], at 646.

79. *Id.* at 646 n.22; *see also* C. MACKINNON, *A Rally Against Rape*, in FEMINISM UNMODIFIED, *supra* note 24, at 81, 82 (black women are raped four times as often as white women): DIANA RUSSELL, SEXUAL EXPLOITATION 185 (1984) (black women, who comprise 10% of all women, accounted for 60% of rapes reported in 1967).

Describing SUSAN BROWNMILLER, AGAINST OUR WILL: MEN, WOMEN AND RAPE (1976), MacKinnon writes, "Brownmiller examines rape in riots, wars, pogroms, and revolutions; rape by police, parents, prison guards; and rape motivated by racism—seldom rape in normal circumstances, in everyday life, in ordinary relationships, by men as men." MacKinnon, *Signs II, supra* note [41], at 646.

80. MacKinnon, *Signs II, supra* note [41], at 653: *cf.* SUSAN ESTRICH, REAL RAPE 3 (1987) (remarking, while telling the story of her own rape, "His being black, I fear, probably makes my account more believable to some people, as it certainly did with the police."). Indeed, Estrich hastens to assure us, though, that "the most important thing is that he was a stranger." *Id.*

81. *See* ALICE WALKER, *Advancing Luna—and Ida B. Wells*, in YOU CAN'T KEEP A GOOD WOMAN DOWN 93 (1981) ("Who knows what the black woman thinks of rape? Who has asked her? Who *cares?*").

82. As Barbara Omolade notes: "To [the white slave holder the black woman slave] was a fragmented commodity whose feelings and choices were rarely considered: her head and her heart were separated from her back and her hands and divided from her womb and vagina. Her back and muscle were pressed into field labor where she was forced to work with men and work like men. Her hands were demanded to nurse and

nurture the white man and his family as domestic servant whether she was technically enslaved or legally free. Her vagina, used for his sexual pleasure, was the gateway to the womb, which was his place of capital investment—the capital investment being the sex act and the resulting child the accumulated surplus, worth money on the slave market." Barbara Omolade, *Hearts of Darkness,* in POWERS OF DESIRE: THE POLITICS OF SEXUALITY 354 (A. Snitow, C. Stansell & S. Thompson eds. 1983).

83. *See* JACQUELINE JONES, LABOR OF LOVE, LABOR OF SORROW 150 (1985). . . .

84. *See* Jennifer Wriggins, *Rape, Racism, and the Law,* 6 HARV. WOMEN'S L.J. 103, 118 (1983).

85. Susan Estrich gives an example: When a black man raped a white woman, the death penalty was held to be justified by the Virginia Supreme Court; but when a black man raped a black woman, his conviction was reversed, on the grounds that the defendant's behavior, "though extremely reprehensible, and deserving of punishment, does not involve him in the crime which this statute was designed to punish." Christian v. Commonwealth, 64 Va. (23 Gratt.) 954, 959 (1873), *quoted in* S. ESTRICH, *supra* note 80, at 35–36. On the intertwining of gender and race oppression in the law of rape and its connection to lynching, see Jacquelyn Dowd Hall, *"The Mind that Burns in Each Body": Women, Rape, and Racial Violence,* in POWERS OF DESIRE: THE POLITICS OF SEXUALITY, *supra* note 82, at 328; Wriggins, *supra* note 84, at 103. On the intertwining of gender and race oppression in the miscegenation laws, see Karen A. Getman, *Sexual Control in the Slaveholding South: The Implementation and Maintenance of a Racial Caste System,* 7 HARV. WOMEN'S L.J. 115 (1984). *See generally* Paul A. Lombardo, *Miscegenation, Eugenics, and Racism: Historical Footnotes to* Loving v. Virginia, 21 U.C. DAVIS L. REV. 421 (1988).

86. Hazel V. Carby, *"On the Threshold of Woman's Era": Lynching, Empire, and Sexuality in Black Feminist Theory,* in "RACE," WRITING, AND DIFFERENCE, *supra* note 12, at 301, 309.

87. Carby notes, "Those that remained silent while disapproving of lynching were condemned by Wells for being as guilty as the actual perpetrators of lynching." *Id.* at 308. . . .

88. Carby, *supra* note 86, at 306 (discussing Anna Julia Cooper, *A Voice from the South* (1892). . . .

89. S. ESTRICH, *supra* note 80, at 107 n.2.

90. Wriggins, *supra* note 84, at 121 n.113. According to the study, "the average sentence received by Black men, exclusive of cases involving life imprisonment or death, was 4.2 years if the victim was Black, 16.4 years if the victim was white." *Id.* I do not know whether a white man has ever been sentenced to death for the rape of a black woman, although I could make an educated guess as to the answer.

91. A. DAVIS, *supra* note 21, at 174.

92. For example, Susan Brownmiller describes the black defendants in publicized Southern rape trials as "pathetic, semiliterate fellows." S. BROWNMILLER, *supra* note 79, at 237, and the white female accusers as innocent pawns of white men, *see, e.g., id.* at 233 ("confused and fearful, they fell into line"). . . .

93. *See* Carby, *supra* note 86, at 307 (citing Ida B. Wells, *Southern Horrors,* (1892), *reprinted in* IDA B. WELLS, ON LYNCHINGS 5–6 (1969)) (miscegenation laws, directed at preventing sexual relations between white women and black men, "pretended to offer 'protection' to white women but left black women the victims of rape by white men and simultaneously granted to these same men the power to terrorize black men as a potential threat to the virtue of white womanhood").

94. Barbara Omolade, *Black Women and Feminism,* in THE FUTURE OF DIFFERENCE 247, 248 (H. Eisenstein & A. Jardine eds. 1980).

95. 3 WIS. WOMEN'S L.J. 81 (1987).
96. *Id.* at 140.
97. *Id.*
98. *Id.* at 141.
99. 55 U. CHI. L. REV. 1 (1988).
100. *Id.* at 3. West further posits a "fundamental contradiction" in women's experience equivalent to the "fundamental contradiction" posited by some critical legal scholars between autonomy and connection; whereas men experience a fundamental contradiction between autonomy and connection, women experience a fundamental contradiction between invasion and intimacy. *See id.* at 53–58.
101. *Id.* at 2.
102. *Id.*
104. I have taken this analysis from Nancy Fraser and Linda Nicholson's analysis of Nancy Chodorow's work. Nancy Fraser & Linda Nicholson, *Social Criticism Without Philosophy: An Encounter Between Feminism and Postmodernism,* in UNIVERSAL ABANDON? THE POLITICS OF POSTMODERNISM 83, 96 (A. Ross ed. 1988). *See generally* NANCY CHODOROW, THE REPRODUCTION OF MOTHERING: PSYCHOANALYSIS AND THE SO-CIOLOGY OF GENDER (1978).
106. THIS BRIDGE CALLED MY BACK, *supra* note 22.
107. *Id.* at 232.
108. *Id.* at 234.
111. Feminist essentialism also strengthens the wall between the genders. The binary character of essentialism tends to make men into enemies, rather than beings who are also crippled by the dominant discourse, though in different ways. Compare this to Joan C. Williams's view in *Deconstructing Gender,* 87 MICH L. REV. 797, 841 (1989) ("'To break free of traditional gender ideology, we need at the simplest level to see how men nurture people and relationships and how women are competitive and powerful.'").
124. A. LORDE, *supra* note 18, at 122.
125. b. HOOKS, TALKING BACK, *supra* note 22, at 11–12.
126. 14 SIGNS 5 (1988).
127. *Id.* at 5.
128. *Id.* at 6–7.
129. *Id.* at 6.
130. *Id.*
131. *Id.* at 11.
132. *Id.* at 10.
133. *Id.* at 24.
134. *Id.* at 22.
135. Donna Haraway, in her essay *A Manifesto for Cyborgs: Science, Technology, and Socialist Feminism in the 1980s,* 15 SOCIALIST REV. 65 (1985), argues that postmodernist theorists (who reject the idea of a "self" altogether, preferring to speak instead of multiple "subject positions") offer feminists the chance to abandon the dream of a common language and the power games of guilt and innocence in favor of "a powerful infidel heteroglossia." *Id.* at 101. Haraway's symbol for this alternate path is the cyborg, a being that transgresses the familiar boundaries of nature vs. culture, animate vs inanimate, and born vs. made. She suggests that "'women of color' might be understood as a cyborg identity, a potent subjectivity synthesized from fusions of outsider identities," *id.* at 93, and that the writings of women of color are a tool for subverting Western culture without falling under its spell, *id.* at 94.
136. [Martha] Minow, [*The Supreme Court 1986 Term—Foreword: Justice Engendered,* 101 HARV. L. REV. 10, 34–38 (1987)].

137. ZORA NEALE HURSTON, *How It Feels to Be Colored Me*, in I LOVE MYSELF WHEN I AM LAUGHING . . . AND THEN AGAIN WHEN I AM LOOKING MEAN AND IMPRESSIVE 152 (A. Walker ed. 1979).

138. *Id.* at 153.

139. *Id.* at 154.

140. *Id.*

141. *Id.*

142. Z. HURSTON, *What White Publishers Won't Print*, in I LOVE MYSELF WHEN I AM LAUGHING . . . AND THEN AGAIN WHEN I AM LOOKING MEAN AND IMPRESSIVE, *supra* note 137, at 169.

143. *Id.* at 179.

146. [Barbara] Johnson, [*Thresholds of Difference: Structures of Address in Zora Neale Hurston*, in "RACE," WRITING, AND DIFFERENCE, *supra* note 12], at 323–24.

151. TONI MORRISON, SULA 52 (1974).

152. As Andrew Ross has noted, even the female "collaborators" MacKinnon attacks with fury are seen as stupid, not as wrong or evil. Andrew Ross, *Politics Without Pleasure* (Book Review), 1 YALE J.L. & HUMANITIES 193, 200 (1989).

153. West, *supra* note 95, at 143.

154. B. HOOKS, FEMINIST THEORY, *supra* note 22, at 45.

155. Z. HURSTON, *supra* note 137, at 155.

156. *Id.*

160. Williams, *supra* note 111, at 829. [Joan] Williams, for instance, analyzes how women use women's culture against themselves, "as they do every time a woman 'chooses' to subordinate her career 'for the good of the family' and congratulates herself on that choice as a mature assessment of her own 'priorities.' " *Id.* at 830.

Black women have often actively embraced patriarchal stereotypes in the name of racial solidarity. *See* P. GIDDINGS, *supra* note 21, at 322–23 (discussing women's concessions to male chauvinism in the civil rights movement of the 1960s): A. LORDE, *supra* note 18, at 119–21 (discussing refusal to confront sexism and homophobia within the black community).

163. [Barbara] Smith & [Beverly] Smith, [*Across the Kitchen Table: A Sister-to-Sister Dialogue*, in THIS BRIDGE CALLED MY BACK, *supra* note 22], at 126.

164. Matsuda, *supra* note 13, at 9.

165. *See, e.g.*, Patricia J. Williams, *Alchemical Notes: Reconstructing Ideals from Deconstructed Rights*, 22 HARV. C.R.-C.L. L. REV. 401 (1987); Williams, *supra* note 126.

166. Williams, *supra* note 126, at 24.

12

Feminist Jurisprudence:
Grounding the Theories [1990]

Patricia A. Cain

. . .

Feminist Method and Feminist Legal Scholarship

. . .

Feminist Method

Recent feminist legal scholarship emphasizes the importance of feminist method. While it is not clear whether feminist method is, in fact, limited to consciousness-raising, nor whether it should be, there does appear to be general agreement that feminist method begins with the primacy of women's experience. Listening to women and believing their stories is central to feminist method. If we are careful to listen to women when they describe the harms they experience as women, we are likely to get the legal theory right (i.e., perceive the problem correctly and propose the right solutions).

Consider Carol Gilligan's pathbreaking work in psychology.[21] Feminist method led Gilligan to suggest new theories regarding women's moral development. Gilligan's method was to listen to female experience as female experience—and not merely as other-than-male experience. Gilligan listened to women tell their own stories. She did not force the stories into pre-formed male categories. Because she *really* listened, she uncovered a "different voice" than that heard by her male colleagues. . . .

Catharine MacKinnon may be the feminist legal scholar who has most consistently focused on the importance of feminist method. Feminist method, for MacKinnon, means women listening to other women.[27] Women, as they listen to each other, tend to discover a commonality of experience. Uncovering the fact of women's common experiences creates new knowledge.

MacKinnon listened to women's common experience of sexual harassment and built a legal theory that reflected that experience.[29] In May, 1975, Working Women United held a "Speak-Out" on sexual harassment.[30] Women told their

263

stories of being treated as sex objects at work. They spoke of the unarticulated job requirements for women, requirements regarding physical attractiveness and sexual availability. The organization reported that 70% of the women who responded to their survey had experienced some sexual harassment on the job.[31] During this part of the 1970s, individual women also began to bring their claims regarding sexual harassment to the courts.[32]

MacKinnon, beginning with the data of real women's experience,[33] and building on the arguments put forth by feminist litigators, developed a legal theory that characterized sexual harassment as a form of sex discrimination that ought to be covered by Title VII. A theory was necessary because existing jurisprudence did not recognize sexual harassment as a harm which the law should remedy.[34] The theory revealed the male bias of the law (ignoring harms that only occur to women) and proposed a revision: a remedy for sexual harassment harms under Title VII.

Feminist Legal Scholarship

. . . My particular concern is whether the "women's experience" that informs feminist legal theory excludes lesbian experience. I will briefly discuss what I consider to be the three stages of feminist legal scholarship[35] and will review what impact, if any, lesbian experience has had on the development of each of these stages.

1. Stage One: Formal Equality and Reproductive Rights

The period from 1963 to 1966 is generally cited as the beginning of the modern day women's movement, sometimes described as the second wave of feminism.[36] A number of important events occurred during this period.[37] Betty Friedan's book, *The Feminine Mystique*, was published in 1963. The same year, the Equal Pay Act was enacted.[38] In 1964, Title VII[39] was enacted, prohibiting sex discrimination in employment. Both statutes exhibit a commitment to the principle of equal opportunity. However, early evidence indicated that the Equal Employment Opportunity Commission was less than fully committed to the principle as applied to women.[40] For example, in 1965, the Commission ruled that employers could employ sex-segregated advertising, despite the clear statutory language to the contrary.[41] In response, a new national women's activist group was formed in 1966, the National Organization for Women (NOW).[42]

In the beginning, NOW's agenda focused on formal equality in the public arena. The organization avoided issues concerning sexual and reproductive freedom.[44] Some members became concerned when NOW began to consider supporting abortion rights. They split off and formed the Women's Equity Action League (WEAL).[45] NOW adopted a pro-abortion stance shortly thereafter.[46] However, its leaders found the issue of lesbianism to be more problematic.[47] Lesbian feminists who "came out" in the early days of the movement were "disinherited" by their sisters.[48] In the mainstream of the movement, the word "lesbian" was shunned.[49]

In the late 1960s, as the modern women's movement rallied together and began to litigate for women's equality, fewer than 5% of all lawyers were women and fewer than 2% of all law professors were women.[50] Feminist legal scholarship during this period, to the extent it existed at all, reflected the goals of the concurrent women's movement. Such scholarship tended to focus on equality in the public sphere and to argue that women should be treated the same as men.

Feminists who were concerned with reproductive freedom necessarily had to deal with the ways in which women were different from men. However, much early feminist legal scholarship was written from a viewpoint that implicitly approved the male norm. Specific concern for lesbian issues is missing from this scholarship. To the extent lesbians are no different from heterosexual women, they were, of course, silently included in the fight for equality.[54] But the differences between the experience of lesbians and heterosexual women were irrelevant in the fashioning of feminist legal theory during Stage One.

2. Stage Two: Women Are Different from Men

Once women began to be treated like men, people began to notice that women really are not like men. Women are most noticeably not like men when they are pregnant. Stage Two theorists began to develop theories of equality that could account for certain differences between women and men.[55] At a minimum, they argued, equality theory should account for the fact that women get pregnant.[56] Lesbians are as biologically different from men as heterosexual women are.[57] Thus, while the focus on difference remained limited to biological differences between women and men, lesbian experience had no special insights to offer.

Some theorists in Stage Two have suggested that women are different from men in ways that go beyond biology. Some cultural feminists,[58] for example, have claimed that the experience of mothering results in social and psychological gender differences.[59] Women, because they give birth and nurture, tend to be more connected and caring than men.

Following the lead of Carol Gilligan, some feminist legal theorists began to focus on ways that woman's "different voice" has been ignored by the law. They pointed out that, because the law is masculine, it reflects values of autonomy rather than connection and caring.[60] Then they argued that the law should recognize and protect specifically female values.[61]

Catharine MacKinnon, another Stage Two legal theorist,[62] also has argued that men and women are different, but the difference is that men dominate and women are subordinate.[63] Which came first, dominance or difference, is an unimportant question, in her view. The important thing is to end the dominance.[64] Legal arguments that pose the issue as one of difference between the sexes are not likely to end the dominance. MacKinnon calls for a paradigm shift, away from differences in biology, differences in experience, differences in essence, to the only difference that really matters: the difference in power. Her "inequality" approach to sex discrimination recognizes the imbalance in power between men and women. "Practices which express and reinforce the social inequality of women to men are clear cases of sex-based discrimination . . . ."[65] Sexual harassment is one such practice.[66]

One might expect cultural feminists and dominance theorists who engage in legal scholarship (such as Gilligan and MacKinnon, respectively) to acknowledge the relevance of lesbian experience in their writings. It is particularly surprising to discover the invisible lesbian problem in the work of cultural feminists. In disciplines other than law, feminist theorists working to reclaim women's culture and its values have often focused on lesbian community.[67] But in legal scholarship, discussions of female value focus on "woman as mother."[68]

Robin West's article, *Jurisprudence and Gender,*[69] is a prime example of the problem. West posits that current (masculine) jurisprudence is based on the concept of human beings as separate from each other and that this "separation thesis" forms the core of both liberal and critical male legal theories. Feminist theory, in contrast, views human beings as primarily connected to one another. Both cultural and radical feminists use this "connection thesis." West begins her article with four examples of women's primary and material experience with connection: (1) pregnancy; (2) heterosexual penetration; (3) menstruation; and (4) breastfeeding.[70] Despite West's awareness of the pressure on all women to be heterosexual,[71] her list of "connection" experiences ignores specifically lesbian experiences of "connection."

Furthermore, West's two categories of feminist thought, cultural and radical, are constructed in such a way as to exclude lesbian feminists. West defines cultural feminists as those who focus on the mother-child connection as the source of women's greater capacity for caring and nurturance. Professor West does not necessarily align herself with these cultural feminists.[72] But I worry that in creating her two categories of feminists (cultural feminists and radical/ dominance feminists), she ignores those lesbian feminists who are attempting to develop women's community (connections to other women)[73] and to reclaim feminist value as encompassing both separation and connection.[74]

Dominance theorists also tend to ignore lesbian experience. Catharine MacKinnon, for example, has argued that women are constantly and always subordinated to men.[75] In MacKinnon's view, any special abilities for caring and connection come, not from the positive aspects of motherhood, but from the negative aspects of subordination.[76] Women build webs of connection to survive the subordination. "Women value care because men have valued us according to the care we give them . . . ."[77]

To the claim that lesbian experience is different, that lesbians are not subordinate to men, that their care is not male-directed, MacKinnon appears to have two different responses. Her first response is that exceptions do not matter. MacKinnon's intent is to offer a critique of the structural condition of women as sexual subordinates and not to make existential claims about all women.[78] It does not affect her theory that *all* women are not always subordinated to men.[79] Thus, for MacKinnon, lesbian experience of non-subordination is simply irrelevant.

Her second response is more troubling. It goes beyond the assertion that lesbian experience is irrelevant; it denies the claim that lesbian experience is free from male domination.

Some have argued that lesbian sexuality—meaning here simply women having sex with women, not with men—solves the problem of gender by eliminating men from women's voluntary sexual encounters. Yet women's sexuality remains constructed under conditions of male supremacy; women remain socially defined as women in relation to men; the definition of women as men's inferiors remains sexual even if not heterosexual, whether men are present at the time or not.[80]

I find this passage objectional for several reasons. My primary objection is that MacKinnon has defined lesbian sexuality to suit her purposes (*"simply* women having sex with women"—i.e., with nothing else changed except that a woman replaces a man). Although I do not dispute that lesbian couples can sometimes ape their heterosexual counterparts, I am infuriated by MacKinnon's silencing of the rest of lesbian experience. Where is MacKinnon's feminist method? To whom does she choose to listen? Would it not enrich her theory to recognize the reality of non-subordination that some lesbians claim as their experiential reality and ask about its relevance to her underlying theory?[81] And yet, because her theory is premised on a single commonality among women, sexual subordination, MacKinnon fails to see the relevance of the lesbian claim to non-domination, even when it stands—literally—in front of her.[82]

The exclusion of lesbian experience from feminist legal theory is also documented in Clare Dalton's recent summary of feminist legal thought.[83] Dalton describes present aspirations to feminist jurisprudence as falling within two camps: "woman as mother" theories and "woman as sexual subordinate" theories.[84] Neither camp embraces lesbian experience as central to the formation of theory. I suspect Professor Dalton's description is accurate. I can find no major "theory piece" by a legal scholar that focuses on the experience of adult women loving each other as the core experience for building a legal theory premised on caring and connection.[85] And although "woman as sexual subordinate" theorists[86] are more likely to acknowledge the fact of lesbian existence,[87] they focus on a critique of male dominance rather than on lesbian bonding as a possible alternative to male dominance.[88]

3. Stage Three: Postmodernism

Borrowing from Clare Dalton, I call the third stage of feminist legal theory "postmodernism."[89] Postmodern thought challenges notions such as objectivity and universality. The postmodern "knowing self" is subjective, concrete and particular, constructed through the lived experiences of the subject.

Postmodern feminism is generally associated with French feminists, such as Helene Cixous, Luce Irigaray, and Julia Kristeva.[90] The influence of Simone de Beauvoir's work[91] on these theorists is evident.[92] Beauvoir's existential analysis of woman as "other" is conceived by postmodern feminists as enabling women to critique the dominant culture. Being "other" allows women to understand "plurality, diversity, and difference."[93]

From a postmodern perspective, feminist theory is inadequate when limited by the perception that there is one essential commonality among all women. Cultural feminists who focus on "woman" solely as "mother" (actual or cultural) do not speak to the full complexity of female experience. Radical feminists, such as MacKinnon, who focus on "woman" solely as "sexual subordinate" also speak limited truths.[94] Good feminist theory ought to reflect the real differences in women's realities, in our lived experiences. These include differences of race,[95] class, age, physical ability, and sexual preference.

Postmodern legal theorists will want to reject the limitations caused by any categorization. Although they will want to listen to the reality of lesbian experience, these theorists will not be inclined to build a grand theory based on the concept of "woman" as "lesbian." In the final part of this essay, I offer some thoughts about the potential relevance of lesbian experience to the postmodern development of feminist legal theory.

The Retelling

I believe that current feminist legal theory is deficient and impoverished because it has not paid sufficient attention to the real life experiences of women who do not speak the "dominant discourse."[96] Elsewhere I have urged that feminist law teaching ought to include "listening to difference" and "making connections."[97] Here I urge the same for feminist legal scholarship.

Most feminist legal theorists, by focusing on sameness and difference, have fallen into either the assimilationist trap (all women are the same as men/all women are the same) or the essentialist trap (all women are different from men in one essential way/all women are different, but what counts is their essential commonality). The only difference between assimilationists and essentialists is that the former ignore the reality of differences whereas the latter say that differences generally do not matter. The two concepts, assimilationism and essentialism, collapse into each other to the extent they treat women as a single class that is essentially the same.

Elizabeth Spelman describes the essentialist's solution to the "differences" problem in feminist theory: "The way to give proper significance to differences among women is to say that such differences simply are less significant than what women have in common. This solution is very neat, for it acknowledges differences among women only enough to bury them."[98] The difficulty arises when an individual essentialist theorist must determine the content of this commonality which is so significant that it trumps differences. When white, straight, economically-privileged feminists name the commonality, and ignore differences, the result may be that all women are assimilated into a single class of white, straight, middle-class women.

It is not enough to name the differences of race, class, and sexuality. The differences need to be understood. Much recent feminist legal scholarship includes the perfunctory footnote, dropped the first time the essential category "woman" is mentioned, which acknowledges the differences of race and class, and sometimes of sexual preference. Such politically correct footnotes name the differences, but I see no evidence in the accompanying texts that the differences matter. Scholarship that nominally recognizes differences, but still categorizes "woman" from a single perspective is stuck in the assimilationist/ essentialist trap.

I do not mean to ignore the importance of our commonalities. It is valuable to identify the similarities among all women. When we identify what we have in common, we begin to build bridges and connections. Yet if we ignore the differences, we risk distorting those connections, because any connection that fails to recognize differences is not a connection to the *whole* of the other self. A normative principle that honors only what I have in common with each of you fails to respect each of you for the individual woman that you are. To respect you, despite your difference, is an insult. Such respect is not respect for your difference, but only for our sameness. Such respect belittles your difference and says it does not matter. Such "respect" falls into the assimilationist/essentialist trap.

Let me give you an example. A white law professor says to her Black female colleague: "Sometimes I forget that you are Black. Sometimes I think of you as white."[99] The comment is meant as a compliment, but it denies the real life experience of the Black woman to whom it is addressed. It says, ultimately, "what I respect in you is only what you have in common with me."

Now let me give you an example out of lesbian experience. A lesbian college teacher proposes a course entitled "The Outsider in Twentieth-Century American Literature." The course is to include writings of lesbians and gay men, as well as other outsiders, such as persons who have been in mental institutions or prisons. In discussing the potential course, the teacher's (presumably) heterosexual colleagues dismiss the notion that an author's sexuality might be an important aspect of her or his writing, claiming that sexuality is no different from "a thousand other things" that might influence the writer.[100] None of the teacher's colleagues considers "having to live as a 'different' person in a heterosexist culture"[101] as a factor important to one's writing.

Adrienne Rich, a lesbian poet, echoes the same theme in the following story:

> Two friends of mine, both artists, wrote me about reading the "Twenty-One Love Poems" with their male lovers, assuring me how "universal" the poems were. I found myself angered, and when I asked myself why, I realized that it was anger at having my work essentially assimilated and stripped of its meaning, "integrated" into heterosexual romance. That kind of "acceptance" of the book seems to me a refusal of its deepest implications. The longing to simplify . . . to assimilate lesbian experience by saying that "relationship" is really all the same, love is always difficult—I see that as a denial, a kind of resistance, a refusal to read and hear what I've actually written, to acknowledge what I am.[102]

There is a commonality between Adrienne Rich and her heterosexual artist friends. They all experience love and relationship. Yet even if some portion of the love experience is universal, the heterosexual world will never understand the gay and lesbian world if we all focus on the commonality, the universal. To claim that lesbians are the same as heterosexual women or that Black women are the same as white women is to fall into the assimilationist/essentialist trap. Such claims deny the reality of our differences by ignoring or discounting them. Yet it is not enough to recognize and name the differences among us as women. We must also understand those differences.

I ask those of you . . . who are heterosexual to focus on an important love relationship in your life. This could be a present relationship or a past one, or even the relationship you hope to have. I ask you: how would you feel about this relationship if it had to be kept utterly secret? Would you feel "at one with the world" if a slight mistake in language ("we" instead of "I") could lead to alienation from your friends and family, loss of your job? Would you feel at one with your lover if the only time you could touch or look into each other's eyes was in your own home—with the curtains drawn? What would such self-consciousness do to your relationship?

I use the following exercise to demonstrate to my students our different points of view. First I ask each student to write down three self-descriptive nouns or adjectives, to name three aspects of her (or his) personal self.[103] When they have finished writing, we go around the room and each student reads the three choices aloud. For my women students, the list almost always includes either the word woman or female. Thus, we share a perception of self as female. The meaning of female may vary, but it is significant that we all view the fact that we are women as one of the three most important facts about ourselves.

As to the rest of the list, there are important differences. For example, no white woman ever mentions race, whereas every woman of color does. Similarly, straight women do not include "heterosexual" as one of the adjectives on their lists, whereas lesbians, who are open, always include "lesbian" as one of the words on their lists. The point is, not only are we different from each other in such obvious ways as race and sexuality, but we perceive our differences differently.

The results of my exercise are not surprising. Because of the pervasive influences of sexism, racism, and heterosexism, white, heterosexual women think of gender as something that sets them apart, as something that defines them, whereas neither race nor sexuality seems to matter much. Yet if neither race nor sexuality matters much to a white, heterosexual woman, how can she begin to understand the ways in which it matters to others who are different from her in these dimensions?

I wonder sometimes whether heterosexual women really understand the role that heterosexuality plays in the maintenance of patriarchy. Indeed, I sometimes wonder whether lesbians really understand. And yet, if feminist legal theory is to provide meaningful guidance for the abolition of patriarchy, feminist theorists must understand heterosexuality as an institution and not merely as the dominant form of sexuality.

Adrienne Rich illuminated the problem years ago in her brilliant critique of heterosexuality:[104]

> [I]t is not enough for feminist thought that specifically lesbian texts exist. Any theory or cultural/political creation that treats lesbian existence as a marginal or less 'natural' phenomenon, as mere 'sexual preference,' or as the mirror image of either heterosexual or male homosexual relations, is profoundly weakened thereby . . . .

. . . .

. . . Feminist research and theory that contributes to lesbian invisibility or marginality is actually working against the liberation and empowerment of woman as a group.[105]

Adrienne Rich encourages us to look at heterosexuality from a new perspective, from the perspective of the "lesbian possibility." The invisibility of lesbian existence, however, removes the lesbian possibility from view. If there are no lesbians, the only possibility is heterosexuality. Men will assume all women are equally available as sex partners. Women will choose men and never question that choice.

If the choice is never questioned, can it be an authentic choice? Do heterosexual women really choose men or are they victims of false consciousness? And if they are victims of false consciousness, then how do we know that most women are heterosexual? Might they not choose otherwise if they were truly free to choose?[106]

Marilyn Frye offers a challenge to feminist academics and I want to echo her in repeating it here for feminist legal theorists:

I want to ask heterosexual academic feminists to do some hard analytical and reflective work. To begin with, I want to say to them:

I wish you would notice that you are heterosexual.

I wish you would grow to the understanding that you choose heterosexuality.

I would like you to rise each morning and know that you are heterosexual and that you choose to be heterosexual—that you are and choose to be a member of a privileged and dominant class, one of your privileges being not to notice.

I wish you would stop and seriously consider, as a broad and longterm feminist political strategy, the conversion of women to a woman-identified and woman-directed sexuality . . . .[107]

Frye reports that a typical response by heterosexual women to such inquiries is that, although they may understand what she is saying, they cannot just up and decide to be lesbian.[108] I, too, have women colleagues and friends who similarly respond, with a shake of the head, that they are hopelessly heterosexual, that they just are not sexually attracted to women.

Frye says that she wants to ask such women (and so do I), "Why not? Why don't women turn you on? Why aren't you attracted to women?"[109] These are serious questions. Frye encourages heterosexual women to consider the origins of their sexual orientation:

The suppression of lesbian feeling, sensibility, and response has been so thorough and so brutal for such a long time, that if there were not a strong and widespread inclination to lesbianism, it would have been erased from human life. There is so much pressure on women to be heterosexual, and this pressure is both so pervasive and so completely denied, that I think heterosexuality cannot come naturally to many women; I think that widespread heterosexuality among women is a highly artificial product of the patriarchy. . . . I want heterosexual women to do intense and serious consciousness-raising and exploration of their own personal histories and to find out how and when in their own development the separation of women from the erotic came about for them. I would like heterosexual women to be as actively curious about how and why and when they became heterosexual as I have been about how and why and when I became lesbian.[110]

Silence

Engage in self-reflection.

[Did she really mean that? Am I supposed to sit here and consider lesbianism as a possibility? . . . Why not? . . . And if I do consider it, but choose men anyway, is my choice more authentic? What about tomorrow? Do I choose again?]

[She doesn't understand. I did choose. Twenty years ago I chose for the children. Does that make my choice inauthentic? What does my choice mean for me today?]

[What about those of us who choose to live alone, who reject intimacy altogether? Am I choosing to be lesbian if I reject men or only if I choose women? As a woman alone, how am I perceived?]

[To take lesbianism seriously, do I have to reject men? Can I choose both women and men?]

[What is all this about choice? I've been a lesbian all my life. I never chose it. I've just lived my life as it was.]

Connections

The most consistent feminist claim, at least since the publication of Simone de Beauvoir's *The Second Sex*, is that knowledge of reality has been constructed from a male-centered standpoint. From their position as outsider, women have questioned that reality, because women's life experiences differ—often dramatically—from those of men. The most cohesive and challenging critiques of male-centered reality have been made by women from standpoints that are exactly opposite, experientially, from those of men.[111] One such critique is made by cultural feminists from the "woman as mother" standpoint. Another is made by other radical feminists from the "woman as sexual subordinate" standpoint.

The fact that so many women can identify common life experiences that are ignored by the male version of reality makes any critique based on such common experiences compelling and powerful. But theorists ought to resist transforming a critical standpoint into a new all-encompassing version of reality. Indeed, my fear is that what started as a useful critique of one privileged (male) view of reality may become a substitute claim for a different privileged (female) view of reality.

Catharine MacKinnon, for example, critiques the patriarchy from a "woman as sexual subordinate" standpoint. As compelling as her critique is, it should not be viewed as the one and only existential reality for women. And yet MacKinnon herself is so committed to this standpoint that she sometimes seems to claim it as the only reality for women.[112]

MacKinnon's theory is that woman's subordination is universal and constant, but not necessarily inevitable.[113] She cautions against building theory on the basis of Carol Gilligan's discovery of woman's "different voice" because the women Gilligan listened to were all victims of the patriarchy. Thus, MacKinnon is wary of assigning value to their moral voice. As she explains,

> [b]y establishing that women reason differently from men on moral questions, [Gilligan] revalues that which has accurately distinguished women from men by making it seem as though women's moral reasoning is somehow women's, rather than what male supremacy has attributed to women for its own use. When difference means dominance as it does with gender, for women to affirm differences is to affirm the qualities and characteristics of powerlessness. . . . To the extent materialism means anything at all, it means that what women have been and thought is what they have been permitted to be and think. Whatever this is, it is not women's, possessive.[114]

When MacKinnon espoused these beliefs regarding women's subordination and inauthenticity in a dialogue with Gilligan at the now somewhat infamous "Mitchell Lecture" at Buffalo, Mary Dunlap (a lesbian), who was also a speaker at the event, interrupted. Dunlap said:

> I am speaking out of turn. I am also standing, which I am told by some is a male thing to do. But I am still a woman—standing.
> I am not subordinate to any man! I find myself very often contesting efforts at my subordination—both standing and lying down and sitting and in various other positions—but I am not subordinate to any man! And I have been told by Kitty MacKinnon that women have never *not* been subordinate to men. So I stand here an exception and invite all other women here to be an exception and stand.[115]

MacKinnon has subsequently described this event as "a stunning example of the denial of gender,"[116] claiming that Dunlap was saying, "all women who are exempt from the condition of women, all women who are not women, stand with me."[117] I believe MacKinnon misinterpreted Dunlap's reaction. Dunlap's claim that her experiential reality is often free of male domination was not a denial of the existence of male power, nor a statement that she had risen above other women. It was merely a statement of fact about her reality, a statement she felt compelled to make because MacKinnon's description of "what is" had continued to exclude Dunlap's reality.

Dunlap's reality is not irrelevant to feminist theory. Mary Dunlap, and I, and other lesbians who live our private lives removed from the intimate presence of men do indeed experience time free from male domination. When we leave the male-dominated public sphere, we come home to a woman-identified private sphere. That does not mean that the patriarchy as an institution does not exist for us or that the patriarchy does not exist during the time that we experience freedom from male domination. It means simply that we experience significant periods of nonsubordination, during which we, as women, are free to develop a sense of self that is our own and not a mere construct of the patriarchy.[118]

Nor do we work at this experience of nonsubordination and creation of authentic self to set ourselves apart from other women. We are not asserting a "proud disidentification from the rest of [our] sex and proud denial of the rest of [our] life."[119] The struggle is to make nonsubordination a reality for all women, and the reality of nonsubordination in some women's lives is relevant to this struggle. The reality of nonsubordination in lesbian lives offers the "lesbian possibility" as a solution.

At the same time, I believe MacKinnon's claim that all women are subordinate to men all the time is a fair claim upon which to critique the male version of reality, because subordination is such a pervasive experience for women. Her claim gives her a valid standpoint for her critique even though it is not experientially true for all women. Similarly, I believe Robin West's claim that all women are "connected" to life is a fair claim upon which to critique the male version of the "separation thesis." But I do not believe that the "connection thesis" is true of all women.[120] Feminist legal theorists must be careful not to confuse "standpoint critiques" with existential reality. And the theorist who has not confused the two must also be careful to prevent her readers from making the confusion.

The problem with current feminist theory is that the more abstract and universal it is, the more it fails to relate to the lived reality of many women.[121] One problem with much feminist legal theory is that it has abstracted and universalized from the experience of heterosexual women. Consider again Marilyn Frye's challenge to heterosexual academic feminists: "I wish you would notice that you are heterosexual. I wish you would grow to the understanding that you choose heterosexuality . . . that you are and choose to be a member of a privileged and dominant class, one of your privileges being not to notice."[122]

Marilyn Frye's challenge was specifically addressed to heterosexual women. When I elected to adopt her challenge at the Women and the Law Conference (and in this essay), I was choosing a "lesbian standpoint" to critique the dominant reality in the same way that some cultural feminists have chosen a "mother standpoint" to critique patriarchy. My intent was not to convert a roomful of women to lesbianism. It was to raise everyone's self-consciousness about our different "standpoints." Feminist legal theory must recognize differences in order to avoid reinforcing lesbian invisibility or marginality, i.e., impeding "the liberation and empowerment of woman as a group."[123]

My "lesbian standpoint" enables me to see two versions of reality.[124] The dominant reality, which I experience as "theirs," includes the following: lesbians are not mothers, all women are dominated by men, male relationships are valuable and female relationships are not, lesbian is a dirty word, lesbians are sick, women who live alone desire men, women who live together desire men, no one knows a lesbian, lesbians don't have families, all feminist legal theorists are heterosexual, all women in this room are heterosexual, lesbians are sex, most women are heterosexual and not lesbian.

By contrast, the reality that I live, the reality I call "mine," includes the following: some mothers are lesbian, many women are lesbian, many lesbian women are not dominated by men, many women do not desire men, lesbian is a beautiful word, lesbians are love, love is intimacy, the heterosexual/lesbian dichotomy is false, all lesbians are born into families, lesbians are family, some feminist legal theorists are lesbian, lesbians are brave.

Why is the lesbian so invisible in feminist legal theory? Why is "my reality" so different from "their reality?" And which reality is true? For the postmodernist, the last question is meaningless. But the first two are not.

Notes

21. C. Gilligan, In a Different Voice: Psychological Theory and Women's Development (1982).

27. For a full discussion of consciousness-raising as method and the relationship between method and politics, see chapters five and six of MacKinnon's most recent book. C. MacKinnon, [Toward a Feminist Theory of the State 83–125 (1989) (hereinafter C. MacKinnon, Feminist Theory of State)].

29. This theory is advanced in C. MacKinnon [Sexual Harassment of Working Women: A Case of Sex Discrimination (1979) (hereinafter C. MacKinnon, Sexual Harassment)].

30. Silverman, *Sexual Harassment: Working Women's Dilemma*, in Building Feminist Theory 84 (Longman ed. 1981).

31. Silverman, *supra* note 30, at 86. A subsequent survey conducted by *Redbook* magazine elicited 9,000 voluntary responses. Ninety percent of the respondents reported experiences of sexual harassment on the job. C. MacKinnon, Sexual Harassment, *supra* note [29], at 26.

32. *See, e.g.,* Tomkins v. Public Serv. Elec. & Gas Co., 568 F.2d 1044 (3d Cir. 1977); *see also* Taub, Book Review, 80 Colum. L. Rev. 1686, 1687 (1980) (reviewing C. MacKinnon, Sexual Harassment, *supra* note [29]).

33. She credits her sources as including the files of Working Women United as well as individual cases of sexual harassment brought to court. C. MacKinnon, Sexual Harassment, *supra* note [29], at xiv.

34. Sexual harassment claimants lost in the original round in the lower courts, but these cases were reversed on appeal. Taub, *supra* note 32, at 1687. The Supreme Court finally validated the theory that sexual harassment is a harm covered under Title VII in Meritor Sav. Bank v. Vinson, 477 U.S. 57 (1986).

35. These three stages track Clare Dalton's discussion of the development of feminist legal thought in Dalton, *Where We Stand: Observations on the Situation of Feminist Legal Thought*, 3 Berkeley Women's L.J. 1 (1988).

36. The first wave of feminism occurred at the end of the 19th century and marks the beginning of the women's movement. Some writers speak of the women's movement as though it began in the 1960s, thereby distorting history and ignoring a much longer feminist tradition. The goals accomplished in the first wave included the passage of married women's property acts and the enactment of the 19th amendment granting women suffrage. For a good, yet brief, discussion of feminist history (herstory), *see* Bender, [*A Lawyer's Primer on Feminist Theory and Tort*, 38 J. Legal Educ. 3, 12–15 (1988)].

37. Although the modern women's movement owes much to the first wave of feminism, it also owes much to the civil rights and the peace movements of the late 1950s and the 1960s. *See generally* S. Evans, Born for Liberty 263–85 (1989).

38. Equal Pay Act of 1963, 29 U.S.C. § 206 (1982).

39. Civil Rights Act of 1964, 42 U.S.C. § [2000e] (1982).

40. "EEOC commissioners and staff . . . expressed a general belief that the addition of *sex* to the law had been illegitimate—merely a ploy to kill the bill—and that it did not therefore constitute a mandate to equalize women's employment opportunities." C. HARRISON, ON ACCOUNT OF SEX: THE POLITICS OF WOMEN'S ISSUES 1945-1968, at 187 (1988).

41. *Id.* at 188.

42. *Id.* at 192-93. *See also* S. EVANS, *supra* note 37, at 277.

44. C. HARRISON, *supra* note 40, at 198-99.

45. S. EVANS, *supra* note 37, at 278.

46. B. FRIEDAN, [IT CHANGED MY LIFE: WRITINGS ON THE WOMEN'S MOVEMENT 120-22 (1976)].

47. *See id.* at 159. (At a 1970 national feminist demonstration at which participants were asked to wear lavender lesbian armbands as a symbol of solidarity, Friedan refused. "For me . . . the women's movement . . . had nothing whatsoever to do with lesbianism.")

48. S. EVANS, *supra* note 37, at 294. *See generally* LESBIANISM AND THE WOMEN'S MOVEMENT (N. Myron & C. Bunch eds. 1975).

49. NOW was the organization at the center of the women's movement and although its membership included many active lesbians, the organization itself consciously avoided lesbian issues in the early days. Such homophobic attitudes appear to have been worse on the East Coast than on the West Coast. *See* D. MARTIN & P. LYON, LESBIAN WOMAN 256-76 (1972).

50. Fossum, *Women Law Professors*, 1980 AM. B. FOUND. RES. J. 903, 906.

54. Lesbians differed from heterosexual women in one very noticeable respect, however. Lesbians were denied custody of their children because they were deemed unfit mothers. Thus, there is some early separate lesbian-feminist scholarship on custody. *See e.g.*, Hunter & Polikoff, *Custody Rights of Lesbians*, 25 BUFFALO L. REV. 691 (1976); Hitchens & Price, *Trial Strategy in Lesbian Mother Custody Cases: The Use of Expert Testimony*, 9 GOLDEN GATE U.L. REV. 451 (1978-79).

55. *See generally* Kay, *Equality and Difference: The Case of Pregnancy*, 1 BERKELEY WOMEN'S L.J. 1 (1985); Law, *Rethinking Sex and the Constitution*, 132 U. PA L. REV. 955 (1984); Wildman, *The Legitimation of Sex Discrimination: A Critical Response to Supreme Court Jurisprudence*, 63 OR. L. REV. 265 (1984); Williams, *The Equality Crisis: Some Reflections on Culture, Courts, and Feminism*, 8 WOMEN'S RTS. L. REP. 175 (1982).

56. This was the thesis of Ann Scales' first article. Scales, [*Towards a Feminist Jurisprudence*, 56 IND. L.J. 375 (1980-81)].

57. The risk of pregnancy is lower for lesbians, of course. And, statistically, fewer lesbians get pregnant (while they are lesbians) than heterosexual women. Thus, accommodation for pregnancy, although relevant for some lesbians, has never been at the top of the lesbian agenda.

58. By "cultural feminist," I mean (loosely) those feminists who recognize the existence of a separate women's culture, which has values that ought to be reclaimed from the patriarchy. See generally Alison Jaggar's discussion of the politics of radical feminism, which focuses on the reinterpretations and re-conceptions of value by feminists who recognize how women's culture has been devalued by the patriarchy. A. JAGGAR, FEMINIST POLITICS AND HUMAN NATURE 249-55 (1983).

Robin West uses the term "cultural feminist" to include those feminists who believe that "the important difference between men and women is that women raise children and men don't." West, [*Jurisprudence and Gender*, 55 U. CHI. L. REV. 1, 13 (1988)]. Thus, her use of the term is narrower than my understanding of the term. *See infra* notes 69-74 and accompanying text.

59. *See e.g.*, Kuykendall, *Toward an Ethic of Nurturance: Luce Irigaray on Mothering and Power*, in MOTHERING: ESSAYS IN FEMINIST THEORY 263 (J. Trebilcot ed. 1984); Ruddick, *Maternal Thinking*, in MOTHERING: ESSAYS IN FEMINIST THEORY 213 (J. Trebilcot ed. 1984).

60. *See* West, *supra* note [58] at 1. West's claim that the law does not recognize harms that stem from the connected experiences of women is not totally true. Tort claims for loss of consortium are discussed by modern day courts in terms of injury to the relationship. *See, e.g.*, Rodriguez v. Bethlehem Steel Corp., 12 Cal. 3d 382, 525 P.2d 669, 115 Cal. Rptr. 765 (1974). Of course, early recognition of such claims occurred in the days when wives were viewed as the property of their husbands. Thus, the theoretical basis for early claims was property damage rather than relational harm. *See* M. CHAMALLAS & L. KERBER, WOMEN, MOTHERS AND THE LAW OF FRIGHT: A HISTORY 5–6 (Legal History Program Working Papers Series 3, March 1989).

61. Leslie Bender asks, for example, "Why . . . do tort damages recognize financial loss and yet remain reluctant to recognize relational loss . . . ?" Bender, *supra* note [36], at 37.

62. I include in "Stage Two" all theorists who reject the liberal feminist approach of "Stage One," but do not (yet) embrace postmodernism. (*See* discussion of Stage Three *infra* [in the next section].) Because I do embrace postmodernism to the extent it eschews essentialism, universality, and the limits of categorization, I am wary of the categorization I create by placing theorists into what appear to be separate stages of feminist scholarship. I ask the reader to imagine the boundaries as more fluid than my brief identification of the categories/stages suggests.

63. C. MACKINNON, FEMINISM UNMODIFIED 32–45 (1987).

64. "[O]n the first day that matters, dominance was achieved . . . ." *Id.* at 40.

65. C. MACKINNON, SEXUAL HARASSMENT, *supra* note [29], at 174.

66. *Id.*

67. *See generally* A. JAGGAR, *supra* note 58, at 249–302 and sources cited therein. In the field of philosophy, there are works that build ethical theory on women's bonding to other women. *See, e.g.*, J. RAYMOND, A PASSION FOR FRIENDS: TOWARD A PHILOSOPHY OF FEMALE AFFECTION (1986); S. HOAGLAND, LESBIAN ETHICS: TOWARD NEW VALUE (1988).

68. Here, I mean mother in the broad social sense as a person who is nurturing and self-sacrificing.

69. West, *supra* note [58].

70. *Id.* at 3.

71. "Most women are indeed forced into motherhood and heterosexuality." *Id.* at 71.

72. Although she does not include herself in the list of legal scholars who have engaged in "cultural feminist" projects, she explains her "connection thesis," as applied to women, in terms of women's biological connection to pregnancy. Thus, West has been described by Joan Williams as a "biological determinist." Williams, *Deconstructing Gender*, 87 MICH. L. REV. 797, 800 n.11 (1989).

73. *See, e.g.*, M. DALY, PURE LUST (1984); M. DALY, GYN/ECOLOGY (1978).

74. *See, e.g.*, S. HOAGLAND, *supra* note 67.

75. "[I]f you look at . . . whether women have ever not been subordinate to men, . . . as I see it, if bottom is bottom then look on the bottom, and there is where women will be." [DuBois, Dunlap, MacKinnon & Menkel-Meadow, *Feminist Discourse: Moral Values and the Law—a Conversation*, 34 BUFFALO L. REV. 11, 71 (1985) (hereinafter *Feminist Discourse*)].

76. C. MACKINNON, FEMINISM UNMODIFIED, *supra* note 63, at 39; *Feminist Discourse*, *supra* note [75], at 74.

77. C. MacKinnon, Feminism Unmodified, *supra* note 63, at 39.

78. *See, e.g.*, C. MacKinnon, Feminism Unmodified, *supra* note 63, at 55–56, 305–06 n.6.

79. "Structural truths about the meaning of gender may or may not produce big numbers. . . . [T]o say 'not all woman [sic] experience that,' as if that contraindicates sex specificity, . . . is to suggest that to be sex-specific, something must be true of 100 percent of the sex affected." C. MacKinnon, Feminism Unmodified, *supra* note 63, at 55.

80. C. MacKinnon, Feminist Theory of State, *supra* note [27], at 141–42 (footnote omitted).

81. For example, the image of the lesbian in the dominant culture is that of a masculine, often predatory, character, the "butch" of the butch-femme lesbian couple. MacKinnon's references to lesbians often reinforce this stereotype. *See, e.g.*, C. MacKinnon, Feminist Theory of State, *supra* note [27], at 119 (lesbian sex does not necessarily transcend the "erotization of dominance and submission"); C. MacKinnon, Sexual Harassment, *supra* note [29], at 206 (positing a lesbian harasser). I believe MacKinnon does herself (as well as lesbians) a disservice by not acknowledging the reality of co-equal relationships that many lesbians experience. Indeed, the extreme dissonance between traditional male-created concepts of lesbian existence and the reality of much lesbian existence tells us that the patriarchy had constructed lesbianism in a way that supports its norm of enforced heterosexuality. Although MacKinnon recognizes this patriarchal response to lesbianism ("[l]esbians can so violate the sexuality implicit in female gender stereotypes as not to be considered women at all," [C. MacKinnon, Feminist Theory of State, *supra* note 27,] at 110), she never reveals an understanding of lesbian existence different from the patriarchal image of the "butch."

82. I mean this statement literally. Mary Dunlap, a lesbian lawyer, was on a panel at the Buffalo Law School with MacKinnon (and others), entitled "Feminist Discourse, Moral Values and the Law." Responding to MacKinnon's view of "woman," silenced by "man's" foot on her throat, Dunlap rose and said: "I am a woman standing . . . [and] I am not subordinate to any man." MacKinnon failed to acknowledge the potential relevance of Dunlap's life experience as a lesbian to her claim of non-subordination. *See infra* [text accompanying notes 115–117]; *see also* C. MacKinnon, Feminism Unmodified, *supra* note 63, at 221, 305–06 n.6.

83. Dalton, *supra* note 35.

84. These two camps parallel Robin West's prior categorization of feminists as either cultural or radical. West, *supra* note [58].

85. *But see* Reese, *The Forgotten Sex: Lesbians, Liberation, and the Law,* 11 Willamette L.J. 354 (1975) (lesbian-centered critique of areas of the law that ignore the existence of lesbians).

86. *E.g.*, Catharine MacKinnon. *See, e.g.*, C. MacKinnon, Feminism Unmodified, *supra* note 63.

87. *See* C. MacKinnon, Feminist Theory of State, *supra* note [27], at 119; C. MacKinnon, Sexual Harassment, *supra* note [29], at 206. MacKinnon claims that a feminist jurisprudence would recognize that the question of gay and lesbian rights is a question of sex equality rights. C. MacKinnon, Feminist Theory of State, *supra* note [27], at 248. Unfortunately, she does not elaborate on this point other than to articulate the connection between discrimination based on sexuality and discrimination based on gender, a connection that is at the core of her theory.

88. *See, e.g.*, C. MacKinnon, Sexual Harassment, *supra* note [29], at 203–06 (discussing sexual harassment of gay and lesbian employees).

89. Dalton, *supra* note 35.

90. For an excellent overview of postmodern feminism, and of these three French theorists in particular, *see* R. TONG, FEMINIST THOUGHT: A COMPREHENSIVE INTRODUCTION 217–33 (1989).

91. S. DE BEAUVOIR, THE SECOND SEX (1952).

92. They have also been influenced by Jacques Derrida and Jacques Lacan. R. TONG, *supra* note 90, at 219–23.

93. *Id.* at 219.

94. *See* Dalton, *supra* note 35, at 7–8.

95. For an especially good critique of the failure of feminist legal theorists to acknowledge and understand the difference that race makes, *see* Harris, *Race and Essentialism in Feminist Legal Theory*, 42 STANFORD L. REV. 581 (1990).

96. I borrow the phrase "dominant discourse" from Martha Fineman, who argues that current theories of child custody are shaped by the "dominant discourse," a discourse which excludes the mother's experience. Fineman, [*Dominant Discourse, Professional Language, and Legal Change in Child Custody Decisionmaking*, 101 HARV. L. REV. 727, 730 (1988)]. Ironically, I am rebelling against a "dominant discourse" that privileges the experience of motherhood over other experiences of female connections. *See also* West, *supra* note [58], at 28, claiming that cultural feminism, which focuses on the mother-child connection, is "our dominant feminist dogma."

97. Cain, *Teaching Feminist Legal Theory at Texas: Listening to Difference and Exploring Connections*, 38 J. OF LEGAL EDUC. 165 (1988). *See id.* at 171, explaining that if students will listen to each other in a way that encourages identification rather than contrast, then they will "connect" in ways that lead to deeper understanding.

98. Spelman recognizes the limitations of this solution, concluding, "But it doesn't bury them very effectively." E. SPELMAN, INESSENTIAL WOMAN: PROBLEMS OF EXCLUSION IN FEMINIST THOUGHT 3 (1988).

99. This story comes most recently from Pat Williams, although I have heard it from other persons of color. Remarks by Pat Williams, Critical Legal Studies Conference on Feminism, Pine Manor, Massachusetts (June 1985). I also have white friends who have made similar observations to me about persons of color.

Fran Olsen tells me that in 1960 at a Quaker peace camp, they sang the following song: "Oh, there'll be no distinction there; / No, there'll be no distinction there. / We'll all be white / In that heavenly light; / There'll be no distinction there." Letter from Frances Olsen to Patricia Cain (July 19, 1989).

100. Bulkin, *'Kissing/Against the Light': A Look at Lesbian Poetry*, in LESBIAN STUDIES 40–41 (M. Cruikshank ed. 1982).

101. *Id.* (quoting Adrienne Rich).

102. An Interview with Adrienne Rich, quoted in Bulkin, *supra* note 100, at 44–45.

103. I do this in my feminist legal theory class. Most of the students are women.

104. Rich, *Compulsory Heterosexuality and Lesbian Existence*, 5 SIGNS 631 (1980).

105. *Id.* at 632, 647–48 (footnote omitted).

106. Rich asks why, "[i]f women are the earliest sources of emotional caring and physical nurture for both female and male children, . . . the search for love and tenderness in both sexes does not originally lead toward women . . . ." *Id.* at 637.

107. Frye, *A Lesbian Perspective on Women's Studies*, in LESBIAN STUDIES 194, 196 (M. Cruikshank ed. 1982).

108. *Id.*

109. *Id.*

110. *Id.* at 196–97.

111. *See, e.g.,* Hartsock, *The Feminist Standpoint: Developing the Ground for a Specifically Feminist Historical Materialism,* in DISCOVERING REALITY 283-310 (S. Harding & M. Hintikka eds. 1983), arguing that the material differences in men and women's lives determine their relative abilities to see reality.

112. "Although feminism emerges from women's particular experience, it is not subjective or partial, for no interior ground and few if any aspects of life are free of male power." C. MACKINNON, FEMINIST THEORY OF STATE, *supra* note [27], at 116.

113. Indeed, her theory of oppression is so complete that it has been described as "metaphysically perfect." *Feminist Discourse, supra* note [75], at 70 (comment of Ellen DuBois); *see also* Bartlett, *MacKinnon's Feminism: Power on Whose Terms?* (Book Review), 75 CALIF. L. REV. 1559, 1562-63 (1987). MacKinnon herself describes the system of male dominance as "metaphysically *nearly* perfect." C. MACKINNON, FEMINIST THEORY OF STATE, *supra* note [27], at 116 (emphasis added). For a refutation of the inevitability of women's subordination, *see* C. MACKINNON, FEMINISM UNMODIFIED, *supra* note 63, at 305-06 n.6 ("If subordination had to be, it would surely be a waste of time to fight for women's rights.").

114. C. MACKINNON, FEMINIST THEORY OF STATE, *supra* note [27], at 51.

115. *Feminist Discourse, supra* note [75], at 75 (emphasis in original).

116. C. MACKINNON, FEMINISM UNMODIFIED, *supra* note 63, at 305-06 n.6.

117. *Id.*

118. Because I believe the self is developed in relation to others, it matters who the "others" to my self are. If the most intimate "other" is a woman, then the self that I develop in relation to that other is more likely to be woman-identified.

119. C. MACKINNON, FEMINISM UNMODIFIED, *supra* note 63, at 305-06 n.6.

120. Nor does West believe it is true of all women; she specifically disclaims such a position. West, *supra* note [58], at 71.

121. *See generally* E. SPELMAN, *supra* note 98.

122. Frye, *supra* note 107.

123. Rich, *supra* note 104, at 648.

124. And both versions of reality inform my knowledge of the world. As Nancy Hartsock explains: "The concept of a standpoint structures epistemology in a particular way. Rather than a simple dualism, it posits a duality of levels of reality, of which the deeper level or essence both includes and explains the "surface" or appearance, and indicates the logic by means of which the appearance inverts and distorts the deeper reality." Hartsock, *supra* note 111, at 285.

Further Reading for Part Two

Gender and Subjectivity

The most sophisticated analyses of the dilemmas posed by the category of "women" in feminist theory are Denise Riley's *Am I That Name? Feminism and the Category of "Women" in History* (Minneapolis: Univ. of Minnesota Press, 1988) and Elizabeth Spelman's *Inessential Woman: Problems of Exclusion in Feminist Thought* (Boston: Beacon, 1988). A number of essays reflecting the influence of poststructuralism have begun to redefine such basic concepts as "feminism," "identity," and "subjectivity." Many of these are collected in *Coming to Terms: Feminism, Theory, Politics*, ed. Elizabeth Weed (New York: Routledge, 1989); *Feminism as Critique: On the Politics of Gender*, ed. Seyla Benhabib and Drucilla Cornell (Minneapolis: Univ. of Minnesota Press, 1987); and *Feminist Studies/Critical Studies*, ed. Teresa de Lauretis (Bloomington: Indiana Univ. Press, 1986). In addition, a number of essays on gender and subjectivity from the groundbreaking British feminist journal *m/f* have been collected in *The Woman in Question: m/f*, ed. Parveen Adams and Elizabeth Cowie (Cambridge: MIT Press, 1990). For book-length treatments of similar themes, see Jane Flax's *Postmodernism in the Contemporary West* (Berkeley: Univ. of California Press, 1989) and Judith Butler's *Gender Trouble: Feminism and the Subversion of Identity* (New York: Routledge, 1989).

Recently, some feminist legal theorists have begun to incorporate poststructuralist and psychoanalytic theories into their critiques of law. In "Mind's Opportunity: Birthing a Poststructuralist Feminist Jurisprudence," 38 *Syracuse L. Rev.* 1129 (1987), Marie Ashe draws on the work of French theorists Jacques Lacan and Julia Kristeva in her attempt to introduce a psychoanalytic theory of subjectivity into feminist legal theory. In "The Doubly-Prized World: Myth, Allegory, and the Feminine," 75 *Cornell L. Rev.* 644 (1990), Drucilla Cornell combines this same tradition with recent Continental philosophy to develop a critique of feminist theories that equate the Feminine with the bodily experience of women; she urges feminists not to reject the Feminine as purely masculine fantasy, but to reconstruct it as the basis for a feminist ethics. On the much-debated question of whether psychoanalysis is friend or foe to feminism, see Juliet Mitchell's landmark work, *Psychoanalysis and Feminism* (New York: Vintage, 1975), which reappropriates Freudian psychoanalysis for feminism. For a critical overview of Lacan's work from a feminist perspective, see Elizabeth Grosz, *Jacques Lacan: A Feminist Introduction* (New York: Routledge, 1990). Several of Lacan's essays on femininity, edited, with excellent introductions, by Juliet Mitchell and Jacqueline Rose, are collected in *Feminine Sexuality: Jacques Lacan and the École Freudienne*, trans. Jacqueline Rose (New York: Norton, 1985). Some of the best recent essays on psychoanalysis and feminism are collected in *Between Psychoanalysis and Feminism*, ed. Teresa Brennan (New York: Routledge, 1989). In an interesting discussion of feminist critiques of a psychoanalytic analysis of rape,

John Forrester argues that "psychoanalytic and legal discourse are entirely antipathetic." See "Rape, Seduction, Psychoanalysis," in *The Seductions of Psychoanalysis: Freud, Lacan, Derrida* (Cambridge: Cambridge Univ. Press, 1990).

Several of Julia Kristeva's most important feminist essays are collected and introduced in *The Kristeva Reader*, ed. Toril Moi (Oxford: Basil Blackwell, 1987). For two very different collections of essays by a range of French feminists, who have tended to examine questions of the subject more fully than American feminists, see *French Feminist Thought*, ed. Toril Moi (Oxford: Basil Blackwell, 1987) and *New French Feminisms*, ed. Elaine Marks and Isabelle de Courtivron (New York: Schocken, 1981). Further readings on feminist poststructuralist thought follow Part Three of this book.

Subjectivity and Sexuality

Catharine MacKinnon's theory of sexuality was first detailed in her classic article "Feminism, Marxism, Method, and the State: An Agenda for Theory," 7 *Signs* 515 (1982), and elaborated in her most recent book, *Toward a Feminist Theory of the State* (Cambridge: Harvard Univ. Press, 1989). That book, together with her earlier *Feminism Unmodified: Discourses on Life and Law* (Cambridge: Harvard Univ. Press, 1987), continues her project of developing a feminist theory of the state that focuses on "gender-specific abuses" of women such as rape, pornography, domestic violence, and prostitution. See also Andrea Dworkin's *Pornography: Men Possessing Women* (New York: Perigree, 1981) and *Intercourse* (New York: Free Press, 1987).

Among those critical of MacKinnon's views on pornography, primarily on First Amendment grounds, are Thomas Emerson in "Pornography and the First Amendment: A Reply to Professor MacKinnon," 3 *Yale L. & Pol'y Rev.* 130 (1984); Nan D. Hunter and Sylvia A. Law in "Brief Amici Curiae of Feminist Anti-Censorship Taskforce et al. in *American Booksellers Association v. Hudnut*," 21 *U. Mich. J.L. Ref.* 69 (1987); and Nadine Strossen in "The Convergence of Feminist and Civil Liberties Principles in the Pornography Debate," 62 *N.Y.U. L. Rev.* 201 (1987). For a quite different attack on MacKinnon's views that argues that gays and lesbians need more, not less, sexual speech, see Mary Dunlap's "Sexual Speech and the State: Putting Pornography in Its Place," 17 *Golden Gate U.L. Rev.* 359 (1987).

Some feminists have challenged important aspects of radical feminist positions on sexuality. For example, one of Robin West's articles, "The Difference in Women's Hedonic Lives: A Phenomenological Critique of Feminist Legal Theory," 3 *Wis. Women's L.J.* 81 (1987), argues that some women enjoy submissive sexual relationships and that feminists should not assume that hierarchy in sexual relationships is necessarily antifeminist. Karen Newman in "Directing Traffic: Subjects, Object, and the Politics of Exchange," 2 *differences* 41 (Summer 1990), reaches a similar conclusion working from a critical and psychoanalytic tradition, suggesting that loss of subjectivity may be a preferable model of sexual pleasure to one that disavows the "object position." In quite a different vein, Barbara Sichtermann attacks a number of standard feminist positions on matters of "personal" sexuality; see *Femininity: The Politics of the Personal*, trans. Helga Gyer-Ryan (Minneapolis: Univ. of Minnesota Press, 1986).

The diversity and intensity of feminist analyses of sexuality are portrayed in *Powers of Desire: The Politics of Sexuality*, ed. Ann Barr Snitow, Christine Stansell, and Sharon Thompson (New York: Monthly Review, 1983); *Pleasure & Danger: Exploring Female Sexuality*, ed. Carole Vance (New York: Routledge, 1984); and 12 *Heresies* (1981). Two works are particularly excellent in demonstrating the complexity of issues raised by pornography for feminists. See Linda Williams, *Hard Core: Power, Pleasure, and "The Frenzy of the Visible"* (Berkeley: Univ. of California Press, 1990), and *Adult Users Only:*

The Dilemma of Violent Pornography, ed. Susan Gubar and Joan Hoff (Bloomington: Indiana Univ. Press, 1989). See also Judith Butler, "The Force of Fantasy: Feminism, Mapplethorpe, and Discursive Excess," 2 *differences* 105 (1990), and Mariana Valverde, "Beyond Gender Dangers and Private Pleasures: Theory and Ethics in the Sex Debates," 15 *Fem. Stud.* 237 (1989).

Exclusion in Feminist Legal Thought

Classic works raising issues of racism, classism, and exclusion in feminist theory include Angela Davis, *Women, Race, and Class* (New York: Random House, 1981); bell hooks, *Ain't I a Woman: Black Women and Feminism* (Boston: South End Press, 1981); Audre Lorde, *Sister Outsider* (Trumansburg, N.Y.: Crossing Press, 1984); *This Bridge Called My Back: Writings of Radical Women of Color*, ed. Gloria Anzaldúa and Cherríe Moraga (New York: Kitchen Table Press, 1982); *Home Girls: A Black Feminist Anthology*, ed. Barbara Smith (New York: Kitchen Table Press, 1983); and *All the Women Are White, All the Blacks Are Men, but Some of Us Are Brave: Black Women's Studies*, ed. Barbara Smith et al. (Old Westbury, N.Y.: The Feminist Press, 1982). A more recent treatment of black female identity and subjectivity is Deborah King's "Multiple Jeopardy, Multiple Consciousness: The Context of a Black Feminist Ideology," 14 *Signs* 42 (1988). Among the excellent critiques of exclusion specifically in feminist legal thought is Marlee Kline's "Race, Racism, and Feminist Legal Theory," 12 *Harv. Women's L.J.* 115 (1989), and Mari Matsuda's "When the First Quail Calls: Multiple Consciousness as Jurisprudential Method," 11 *Women's Rts. L. Rep.* (1989).

There is less writing on the subject of lesbian exclusion from feminist legal thought, which is especially surprising if Sylvia Law's analysis in "Homosexuality and the Social Meaning of Gender," 1988 *Wis. L. Rev.* 187, is correct—that existing invasive regulations directed against lesbians and gay men reflect not only intolerance toward those groups but the rigidity of gender roles affecting all women in our society. Rhonda Rivera's two-part series "Queer Law: Sexual Orientation in the Mid-Eighties," found at 10 *U. Day. L. Rev.* 459 (1985) (Part I) and 11 *U. Day. L. Rev.* 275 (1986) (Part II), is the basic research tool in this area. A more recent article by Ruthann Robson and S. E. Valentine, "Lov(h)ers: Lesbians as Intimate Partners and Lesbian Legal Theory," 63 *Temp. L. Rev.* 511 (1990), assesses the relationship between lesbians and the law, and especially the problem of "colonization" that arises when lesbians seek to use heterosexual legal tools, such as contracts and marriage, to procure status for their intimate relationships. See also Ruthann Robson, "Lesbian Jurisprudence?" 8 *J. L. & Inequality* 443 (1990). Some excellent writing has been done on lesbian mothers' rights to child custody. One of the most recent is Nancy Polikoff's article, "This Child Does Have Two Mothers: Redefining Parenthood to Meet the Needs of Children in Lesbian-Mother and Other Nontraditional Families," 78 *Geo. L.J.* 459 (1990).

Outside the legal literature, the most well-known essay on heterosexism is Adrienne Rich's "Compulsory Heterosexuality and Lesbian Existence," 5 *Signs* 631 (1980). For a series of responses to this essay, see "On 'Compulsory Heterosexuality and Lesbian Existence': Defining the Issues," by Ann Ferguson, Jacquelyn N. Zita, and Kathryn Pyne Addelson, in *Feminist Theory: A Critique of Ideology*, ed. Nannerl O. Keohane, Michelle A. Rosaldo, and Barbara C. Gelpi (Chicago: Univ. of Chicago Press, 1981). Monique Wittig has also written extensively on the invisibility of compulsory heterosexuality as an institution, especially as it is enforced through discourse, in "The Straight Mind," 1 *Fem. Issues* 103 (Summer 1980), and "One Is Not Born a Woman," 1 *Fem. Issues* (Winter 1981). See also Wittig, *The Lesbian Body*, trans. David Owen (New York: Avon, 1976). Namascar Shaktini provides an insightful discussion of Wittig's work in "Displacing the Phallic Subject: Wittig's Lesbian Writing," in *The Lesbian Issue: Essays from* Signs (Chicago: Univ. of Chicago Press, 1985). For two classic essays on the "difference" of female subjectivity, see Luce Irigaray's essays, "When Our Lips Speak Together" and "This Sex Is Not One," both in *This Sex Which Is Not One*, trans. Catherine Porter with Carolyn Burke (Ithaca, N.Y.: Cornell Univ. Press, 1985).

The themes of exclusion and difference are, of course, tightly linked. For general works exploring the relationship, see *The Future of Difference*, ed. Hester Eisenstein and Alice Jardine (Boston: G. K. Hall, 1980), which collects the most basic essays on theories of gender difference written before 1980, and a collection of essays, *The Difference Within*, ed. Elizabeth Meese and Alice Parker (New York: Methuen, 1988). In law, a recent book by Martha Minow, *Making All the Difference: Inclusion, Exclusion, and American Law* (Ithaca, N.Y.: Cornell Univ. Press, 1990), addresses the subject of difference and exclusion not only with respect to gender but with respect to race, handicap, and other factors as well.

As a counterpoint to the literature that critiques gender essentialism, some feminists have turned to defend essentialism within feminist thought. Robin West's "Feminism, Critical Social Theory and Law," 1989 *U. Chi. Legal F.* 59, offers the most explicit defense of gender essentialism by a feminist legal theorist. For an attempted rehabilitation of essentialism on strategic grounds, see Diana Fuss's *Essentially Speaking: Feminism, Nature and Difference* (New York: Routledge, 1989). Along similar lines, Frances Olsen defends MacKinnon's "grand theory of gender oppression" in "Feminist Theory in Grand Style," 89 *Colum. L. Rev.* 1147 (1989). Kathryn Abrams offers a critical analysis of the strategic defense of this form of essentialism, which she calls "ideological determination," in "Ideology and Women's Choices," 24 *Ga. L. Rev.* 761 (1990).

PART THREE

Feminism and Critical Theory

13

Deconstructing Contract Doctrine [1985]

Clare Dalton

. . .

Doctrine, the Cohabitation
Contract, and Beyond

Doctrinal arguments cast in terms of public and private, manifestation and intent, and form and substance, continue to exert a stranglehold on our thinking about concrete contractual issues. By ordering the ways in which we perceive disputes, these arguments blind us to some aspects of what the disputes are actually about. By helping us categorize, they encourage us to simplify in a way that denies the complexity, and ambiguity, of human relationships. By offering us the false hope of definitive resolution, they allow us to escape the pain, and promise, of continual reassessment and accommodation.

. . . I will illustrate the poverty of traditional doctrinal arguments by examining the use of contract doctrine in recent cases involving the agreements of non-marital cohabitants. . . . Distinctions between private and public realms, between contracts implied-in-fact and contracts implied-in-law, play an important part in the decisions. Interpretive questions and questions about the basis for enforcement—about consideration—also loom large, reiterating the concern with private and public, but couching that concern in the competing terms of subjective and objective, form and substance.

Significantly, the opinions largely ignore the aspect of the public-private debate that appears in contract doctrine as the set of rules governing duress and unconscionability. The concerns of those doctrines—preventing oppression of each party by the other, while preventing oppression of both by the state—are nonetheless highly relevant. For at the heart of these cases lies the problem of power. It is only because the exercise of power in this context is not seen as fitting the traditional rubrics of duress and unconscionability that courts are able to ignore and avoid it.

Once the convoluted play of doctrine in this area has been exposed, we can see that traditional doctrinal formulations are not the only means for understanding how and why decisionmakers reach their decisions. At this point,

other inquiries become both possible and legitimate. In suggesting what some
of those other inquiries might be, my conclusion points toward possible ways
of expanding our thinking about the issues of contract law.

A. *The Cases*

State courts have increasingly confronted cases involving various aspects of
the cohabitation relationship, and their decisions have attracted a fair amount
of scholarly attention. I focus on two such decisions: that of the California
Supreme Court in *Marvin v. Marvin*,[432] and that of the Illinois Supreme Court
in *Hewitt v. Hewitt*.[433]

In *Marvin*,[434] Justice Tobriner addressed the question of whether plaintiff
Michelle Triola, who had lived with the defendant, Lee Marvin, for seven years,
could recover support payments and half the property acquired in Lee Marvin's
name over the course of the relationship. The court found that the plaintiff,
in alleging an oral contract, had stated a cause of action in express contract,
and further found that additional equitable theories of recovery might be
applicable. On remand,[435] the trial court found that there existed neither an
express contract nor unjust enrichment, but awarded the plaintiff equitable
relief in the nature of rehabilitative alimony.[436] The court of appeals then struck
this award on the theory that relief could be granted only on the basis of
express contract or quasi-contract.[437]

The alleged oral agreement provided that plaintiff and defendant would,
while they lived together, combine their efforts and earnings and share equally
any property accumulated. They agreed to present themselves publicly as husband
and wife. Triola also undertook to serve as the defendant's companion, homemaker, housekeeper, and cook. A later alleged modification to the contract
provided that Triola would give up her own career in order to provide these
services; in return, Marvin promised to support Triola for the rest of her life.
The relationship ended when Marvin threw Triola out.[438]

The plaintiff in *Hewitt* was in many respects a more sympathetic figure than
Michelle Triola. When she and Mr. Hewitt were both college students, she
became pregnant. He then proposed that they live together as man and wife,
presenting themselves as such to their families and friends, and that he thereafter
share his life, future earnings, and property with her. She borrowed money
from her family to put him through professional school, worked with him to
establish his practice, bore him three children and raised them, and otherwise
fulfilled the role of a traditional wife. After over fifteen years he left her. She
sought an equal division of property acquired during the relationship and held
either in joint tenancy or in the defendant's name.[439]

The appeals court ruled that she could have an equitable share of the
property if she were able to prove her allegation of an express oral contract,
although it did not preclude the possibility of alternative equitable theories of
recovery in appropriate circumstances.[440] The Supreme Court of Illinois reversed,
basing its decision principally on considerations of public policy.[441]

B. *Express and Implied Agreement*

The opinions in the cohabitation cases indicate that the distinction between the intention-based express contract and the public institution of quasi-contract may be central to the question of whether to grant relief. . . . [H]owever, techniques for interpreting the express contract are indistinguishable from techniques used to determine the presence of a quasi-contractual relationship. If the interpretive techniques employed highlight factors external to the parties and their actual intentions, even express contracts seem very public. If, in contrast, the techniques used have as their stated goal the determination of the parties' intentions, then quasi-contracts appear no less private or consensual than express contracts. The cohabitation opinions employ both public-sounding and private-sounding arguments to reach a variety of conclusions. In some cases courts determine that the parties are bound by *both* real and quasi-contractual obligations, in others that they are bound by neither, in yet others that they are bound by one but not the other. The arguments do not determine these outcomes—they only legitimate them.

In these cases, . . . there is a common presumption that agreements between intimates are not contractual.[442] While this model of association was developed in husband-wife and parent-child cases, non-marital cohabitants are assumed, for these purposes, to have the same kind of relationship.[443] . . . [E]xpress words are taken to be words of commitment but not of contract;[444] conduct that in other circumstances would give rise to an implied-in-fact contract is instead attributed to the relationship.[445] These cases . . . find no unjust enrichment where one party benefits the other.

One possible explanation for this presumption against finding contracts is that it accords with the parties' intentions. It can be argued that cohabitants generally neither want their agreements to have legal consequences, nor desire to be obligated to one another when they have stopped cohabitating. It can further be presented as a matter of fact that their services are freely given and taken within the context of an intimate relationship. If this is so, then a subsequent claim of unjust enrichment is simply unfounded.

This intention-based explanation, however, coexists in the opinions—indeed sometimes coexists within a single opinion—with two other, more overtly public, explanations that rest on diametrically opposed public policies. The first suggests that the arena of intimate relationships is too private for court intervention through contract enforcement to be appropriate. In *Hewitt*, for example, the Illinois Supreme Court suggests that "the situation alleged here was not the kind of arm's length bargain envisioned by traditional contract principles, but an intimate arrangement of a fundamentally different kind."[448]

While it has some intuitive appeal, the argument that intimate relationships are too private for court enforcement is at odds with the more general argument that all contractual relationships are private and that contract enforcement merely facilitates the private relationships described by contract. To overcome this apparent inconsistency, we must imagine a scale of privateness on which business arrangements, while mostly private, are still not as private as intimate arrangements. But then the rescue attempt runs headlong into the other prevailing policy argument, which separates out intimate arrangements because of their peculiarly public and regulated status. Under this view, it is the business relationship that by and large remains more quintessentially private.

According to this second argument, the area of non-marital agreements is too public for judicial intervention. The legislature is the appropriate body to regulate such arrangements; courts may not help create private alternatives to the public scheme. In *Hewitt*, the supreme court directly follows its appeal to the intimate nature of the relationship with an acknowledgement of the regulated, and hence public, character of marriage-like relations.[450] With respect to intimate relations conceived as public, the judiciary can then present itself as either passive or active. The argument for passivity is that judges should "stay out" of an arena already covered by public law. The argument for activity is that judges should reinforce public policy by deterring the formation of deviant relationships, either because they fall outside the legislative schemes organizing familial entitlement and property distribution,[451] or because they offend public morality.[452]

Neither the private nor the public arguments for the absence of contract in this setting are conclusive. Both private and public counterarguments are readily available. If the absence of contract is presented as flowing from party intention, competing interpretations of intention can be used to argue the presence of contract. If, within a more public framework, the court categorizes the concerns implicated by the relationship as private, then an argument can be made that within the boundaries expressly established by legislation, the parties should be free to vary the terms of their relationship without interference by the state.[454] If the focus is the place of cohabitation agreements within the publicly-regulated sphere of intimate relationships, then an argument can be made that certain kinds of enforcement in fact extend and implement public policy rather than derogate from it.[455]

The availability of this range of intention-based and policy-based arguments makes possible virtually any decision. A court can find or not find a "real" contract. It can decide that enforcement of a real contract is or is not appropriate. It can decide that while real contracts should be enforced, there is no basis for awarding quasi-contractual relief in the absence of an expressed intention to be bound. It can decide that even in the absence of real contract, the restitutionary claim of the plaintiff represents a compelling basis for quasi-contractual relief. Further, the competing public and private strands of argument—each of which connects to both enforceability and non-enforceability arguments—can be used within the same opinion or other legal text, without the inconsistencies being so apparent as to undermine the credibility of the final result.

C. Manifestation and Intent

Some identifiable, particular patterns do emerge from this overall confusion of public and private arguments. As with all agreements, for example, every aspect of a cohabitation agreement raises interpretive questions that will drive a court to search for the elusive correspondence between subjective intent and manifested form. Even this most private exercise of contractual interpretation thereby opens the doors to the imposition of public values, norms, and understandings. Two interpretive issues in particular recur in the cases. The courts repeatedly consider how to evaluate the relationships out of which the agreements arise. They also repeatedly consider how to evaluate the role of sex in these relationships and in these agreements. This section explores the very different ways in which the opinions treat these issues, within the range of options made available by current doctrine.

Courts frequently invoke the context of cohabitation relationships to avoid enforcing agreements arising out of them. The argument here is essentially that even if such agreements use language of promise, or commitment, or reciprocal obligation, that language must be understood, *in the intimate context in which it is employed*, as not involving any understanding that one party might use a court to enforce a duty forsaken, or a promise broken.

In theory, if the parties make perfectly clear their intention to be legally bound by their agreement, then their intention governs.[457] But this leaves open the question of when a court will find objective manifestations of such an intention to be bound. Will a written agreement be more susceptible to legal enforcement than an oral one? Will an agreement in which the reciprocal obligations relate to a particular piece of property or to a transaction that can be separated out, however artificially, from the affective context of the relationship convince a court that it has crossed the boundary between intimate unen- forceability and business-like enforceability? These approaches all find some support in the cases,[458] although their manipulability and their imperfect correspondence to questions of motivation and intention are obvious.

A second common theme employing notions of manifestation and intent is the specific role of sex in the parties' arrangement. The boundaries of this debate are set both by the tradition that precludes enforcement of prostitution contracts for reasons of public policy,[459] and by the acknowledgement that even cohabiting parties may form valid contracts about independent matters.[460] In the case of cohabitation agreements, the question therefore becomes whether the sex contemplated by the parties contaminates the entire agreement to the point where it is seen to fall within the model of the prostitution contract, or whether other features of the agreement can be seen as independent and enforceable.[461]

Judges' differing interpretations of virtually identical agreements seem to depend quite openly on either their views of what policy should prevail or their own moral sense. Rarely does a judge even appear to make a thorough attempt to understand and enforce what the parties had in mind. For Justice Underwood in *Hewitt*, for example, nothing but "naivete" could explain the assertion that "there are involved in these relationships contracts separate and independent from the sexual activity, and the assumption that those contracts would have been entered into or would continue without that activity."[462]

Justice Tobriner in *Marvin*, on the other hand, rejects the idea that the sexual relationship between parties to a cohabitation contract renders the contract as a whole invalid. He explicitly uses the divide between objective and subjective, form and substance, to carve out a much larger space for enforceable agreements than that envisaged by Underwood.[463] Tobriner's test has two components: Contracts between non-marital partners are enforceable unless they *explicitly* rest "upon the immoral and illicit consideration of meretricious sexual services."[464] Furthermore, such contracts are unenforceable only *"to the extent"* that they rest on this meretricious consideration.[465]

Tobriner is not so naive as to suppose that the Triola-Marvin agreement did not contemplate a sexual relationship. But he feels that the "subjective contemplation of the parties" is too "uncertain and unworkable" a standard.[466] He relies instead on formal criteria of intent—on the manifestations of agreement alleged by Triola—to determine if his two-part test of enforceability has been met. For the purposes of this analysis Tobriner describes the agreement as follows: "[T]he parties agreed to pool their earnings, . . . they contracted to share equally in all property acquired, and . . . defendant agreed to support plaintiff."[467] None of this strikes Tobriner as necessitating a conclusion that sex invalidates the agreement.[468]

Of course the formal criteria are themselves empty of significance until given meaning by judicial analysis. The very same language construed by Tobriner had been given very different effect in an earlier decision. In *Updeck v. Samuel,* a California District Court of Appeal considered the statement that the woman would make a permanent home for the man and be his companion as indicating precisely the sexual character of the relationship.[469] Unwilling or unable to disapprove *Updeck,* Tobriner is forced to distinguish this case in a fashion that directly undercuts the legitimacy of his stated reliance on form or manifestation. He argues that the *Updeck* agreement was found invalid because the Court "[v]iew[ed] the contract as calling for adultery."[470] But the very act of "viewing" the contract, or interpreting its terms, involves an explanation of substance. The court in *Updeck* supplied sexual substance, while Tobriner supplies economic substance.[471] *Jones v. Daly,*[472] a case subsequent to *Marvin,* provides another striking illustration of the manipulability of form. In *Jones,* which involved a homosexual partnership, a California Court of Appeal denied relief on the ground that an agreement, in other respects almost identical to the *Marvin* agreement, contained the word "lover."[473]

As the courts wrestle with these interpretive questions, we see them apparently infusing a public element, external to the parties' own view of their situation, into their assessment of cohabitation agreements. We also can see how this is a necessary result of the tension between manifestation and intent, of the way in which intent requires embodiment in manifested forms, even while the forms require an infusion of substance before they can yield meaning. Indeed, to accuse judges of moving from the private to the public sphere is only to accuse them of the inevitable. If there is force behind the accusation, it is not *that* they have made the transition from private to public, but that they have made the transition *un-self-consciously,* and that the particular values, norms, and understandings they incorporate are different from the ones we would have favored, or different from the ones we think would correspond with those of one or both of the parties to the agreement.

D. Consideration: Its Substance

Consideration doctrine offers yet other opportunities for the conflation of public and private, and the introduction of competing values, norms, and understandings into the resolution of these cohabitation cases. Just as in the area of interpretation, the crucial additions are judicial conceptions of sexuality, and of woman's role in her relationship with man. Two aspects of consideration doctrine recur in the cases. Each illustrates the proposition that formal consideration doctrine cannot be implemented without recourse to substance. Substance, here as elsewhere, can be provided by assessments of objective value or by investigations into subjective intent. It is with respect to these substantive inquiries that ideas about sexuality and relationship come to play so potentially important a part.

The first use of consideration doctrine in this context shows up in the disinclination of courts to enforce contracts based on "meretricious" consideration.[474] Courts frequently search beyond the express language of the agreement in order to "find" that sex is at the heart of the deal—specifically that the woman is providing sexual services in return for the economic security promised by the man.[475] Insofar as this investigation depends on divining what the parties had in mind, consideration turns on subjective intent. For these purposes, it matters not at all that "intent" has been derived from the judge's own feelings about such relationships, even when the express language of the parties would appear to point in an opposite direction.

The treatment of meretricious consideration also illustrates how consideration may depend on a finding of objective value. When courts refuse to enforce contracts based on the exchange of sexual services for money, they are, for long-standing policy reasons, declining to recognize sexual services as having the *kind* of value that they will honor. This decision, based on an objective measure of value, is no different from the decision that "nominal" consideration will not support a contract.[476] There, too, courts disregard intention in the name of a policy that depends upon societal recognition of certain sorts of values and delegitimation of others.

The second aspect of consideration doctrine of interest in this context is the traditional conclusion that the woman's domestic services cannot provide consideration for the promises made to her by the man. This is usually linked to the idea that the relationship itself is not one the parties see as having a legal aspect. The standard explanation is that the woman did not act in expectation of gain, but rather out of affection, or that she intended her action as a gift.[477]

Tobriner in the *Marvin* decision rejects this conclusion by recasting the issue as one properly belonging in the selfish world of business.[478] Unless homemaking services are considered lawful and adequate consideration for a promise to pay wages, the entire domestic service industry will founder.[479] Just as plainly, such services can provide the consideration for an agreement concerning property distribution.[480] Tobriner thus appeals to the substance of objective value: There is a market in which domestic services receive a price;

when intimates arrange that one will deliver those same services to the other, that promise is therefore capable of supporting a return promise.

Even as Tobriner uses ideas of objective value, however, his reasoning reveals that the ultimate rationale for this aspect of consideration doctrine depends upon arguments of subjective intent. Like the promise in the *Michigan* case,[481] the services could constitute consideration if they were offered with the intention of bargain or exchange. It is only the altruistic context, revealing the beneficent intention, which invalidates them.[482]

Thus, while one route of access into this issue threatens to expose the public determination of what values the law will and will not recognize, that route is apparently closed off by the reminder that it is private intention, not public power, that assigns value. But then the very public role abjured in the context of objective value is played out instead through the "finding" of intent according to criteria that are essentially and inevitably public rather than private.

E. *The Question of Power*

Under duress and unconscionability doctrines, policing the "fair" exchange is tied irretrievably to asking whether each party entered into the contract freely, whether each was able to bargain in equally unconstrained ways, and whether the deal was a fair one.[483] I suppose that any of us would find these questions even harder to answer in the context of intimate relationships than in other contexts—harder in that we would require a much more detailed account of the particulars before we could hazard an opinion, and harder in that even this wealth of detail would be likely to yield contradictory interpretations. Yet we acknowledge the importance of these questions in the area of intimate relations; we do not imagine either that most couples wind up with a fair exchange, or that most couples have equal bargaining power vis-à-vis one another.[484]

The doctrinal treatment of cohabitation agreements, however, like the treatment of contracts in general, usually pays little attention to questions of power and fairness. Duress and unconscionability are the exceptions that prove the rule. Those doctrines identify the only recognized deviations from the supposedly standard case of equal contracting partners. Intimate partners are conceived of as fitting the standard model. One consequence of this conception is that courts can justify the failure to enforce cohabitation arrangements as mere nonintervention, overlooking the fact that the superior position in which nonaction tends to leave the male partner is at least in part a product of the legal system.[485] Another is that courts can idealize the private world in which their "nonintervention" leaves the parties, disregarding the ways in which that world is characterized by inequality and the exercise of private power.[486] Yet another is that courts can talk blithely about the intentions of "the parties" in a fashion that ignores the possibility that one party's intentions are being respected at the expense of the other's.[487]

Not all of the cohabitation contract opinions ignore the issues of fairness and power. They are more likely to receive explicit attention when a judge frankly invokes "public policy" instead of relying exclusively on contract doctrine.

They appear, for example, when the Illinois appeals court in *Hewitt* explains why enforcement of such agreements promotes rather than undermines the institution of marriage.[488] When a judge casts his opinion in traditional doctrinal terms, using intention, for example, or consideration, then any sensitivity he has to questions of power and fairness must be translated—translated, for example, into a willingness to assume that the parties did intend to enter a relationship of reciprocal obligation or that the woman has provided services that require compensation.[489] Frequently this involves construing the male partner's intentions *as if* he were the concerned and equal partner the law assumes him to be.[490] Again, these devices parallel those used by courts across the range of contract decisions. But only when judges move outside the framework of traditional contract doctrine will they be in a position to grapple with the full range of problems posed by these disputes.

There are several ways to begin a richer examination of the cohabitation cases. First, we can learn from the truths underlying contract doctrine while rejecting the idea that that doctrine alone can lead us to correct answers. The dichotomies of public and private, manifestation and intent, form and substance, do touch on troubling questions that are central to our understanding of intimate relationships and the role of the state in undermining or supporting them. The problem with doctrinal rhetoric is twofold. First, it recasts our concerns in a way that distances us from our lived experience of them. Second, the resolution of the cases that the application of doctrine purports to secure offers us a false assurance that our concerns can be met—that public can be reconciled with private, manifestation with intent, form with substance.

Once we realize that doctrinal "resolutions" are achieved only by sleight of hand, consideration of the identified dichotomies helps us to explore more fully the cohabitation agreement. What is the nature of this relationship, or what range of cohabitation arrangements precludes us from making general statements about the nature of the relationship? To what extent do these relationships need protection from authority, and to what extent do they require nurturing by authority? To what extent do they reflect the shared expectations of their participants, and to what extent the imposition of terms by one party on another? How can we harbor intimacy within institutions that offer the flexibility to accommodate individual need, while at the same time providing a measure of predictability and stability? What stake does the society have in limiting the forms of association it will recognize? Given our dependence on our social and cultural context, what freedom does any of us have to reimagine the terms of human association?

Study of the play between public and private, objective and subjective, shows us that these same dichotomies organize not only the strictly doctrinal territory of contract interpretation or consideration, but also the broader "policy" issues that are folded into the cases. Questions of judicial competence, for example, turn out to involve precisely the question of whether a private sphere can be marked off from the public sphere.[491] Similarly, whether enforcement of cohabitation agreements is a pro-marriage or an anti-marriage position turns out to depend on questions of intention and power.[492] Even as this analysis illuminates the policy dimension of the cases, it refutes the claim that the addition of policy considerations can cure doctrinal indeterminacy.

If neither doctrine nor the addition of policy can determine how decision-makers choose outcomes in particular cases, the next question is whether the opinions contain other material that illuminates the decisionmaking process. The dimension of these cohabitation cases that cries out for investigation is the images they contain of women, and of relationship. And since images of women and of relationship are the central concern of feminist theory, I have used that theory as the basis for my enquiry. This does not, of course, foreclose the possibility that other enquiries, in this or other settings, might prove equally possible and promising once doctrine is opened up to make room for them.

I am not claiming that judges decide cohabitation cases on the basis of deeply held notions about women and relationship in the sense that these notions provide a determinate basis for decision. For this to be true, attitudes toward women and relationship would have to be free from contradiction in a way that doctrine and policy are not. I believe instead that these notions involve the same perceived divide between self and other that characterizes doctrine, and are as internally contradictory as any doctrine studied in this Article. My claim, therefore, is only that notions of women and relationship are another source of influence, and are therefore as deserving of attention as any other dimension of the opinions. These notions influence how judges frame rule-talk and policy-talk; in a world of indeterminacy they provide one more set of variables that may persuade a judge to decide a case one way or another, albeit in ways we cannot predict with any certainty.

One introductory caveat is in order. To say that "the opinions" convey images of woman and relationship is to miss the distinction between images that appear to inhere in the doctrine as it has developed, and images woven into the texture of opinions seemingly at the initiative of a particular judge. I think this distinction is worth noting, even though in practice it cannot always be made. It becomes clearest, perhaps, when a judge struggles *against* images he sees embedded in the doctrine, and offers new images that in turn provide him with new doctrinal choices.[493]

One powerful pair of contradictory images of woman paints the female cohabitant as either an angel or a whore. As angel, she ministers to her male partner out of noble emotions of love and self-sacrifice, with no thought of personal gain.[494] It would demean both her services and the spirit in which they were offered to imagine that she expected a return—it would make her a servant.[495] As whore, she lures the man into extravagant promises with the bait of her sexuality—and is appropriately punished for *her* immorality when the court declines to hold her partner to his agreement.[496]

Although the image of the whore is of a woman who at one level is seeking to satiate her own lust, sex—in these cases—is traditionally presented as something women give to men. This is consistent both with the view of woman as angel, and with the different image of the whore as someone who trades sex for money. In either event, woman is a provider, not a partner in enjoyment.[497] When a judge invokes this image, he supports the view that sex contaminates the entire agreement, and that the desire for sex is the only reason for the male partner's promises of economic support. If sex were viewed as a mutually satisfying element of the arrangement, it could be readily separated out from the rest of the agreement. In most cases, the woman's career sacrifices and childrearing and homemaking responsibilities would then provide the consideration for the economic support proffered by the man.

Marriage is often presented in the cases as the only way in which men and women can express a continuing commitment to one another.[498] This suggests that when men do not marry women, they intend to avoid all responsibility for them.[499] Women therefore bear the burden of protecting themselves by declining the irregular relationship.[500] At the same time, the institution of marriage as an expression of caring is portrayed as so fragile that only the most unwavering support by the state will guarantee its survival.[501] This could mean that other expressions of caring would entirely supplant marriage without vigilant enforcement of the socially endorsed forms of relationship, although that would be inconsistent with the portrayal of marriage as the only expression of commitment. Alternatively, it could mean that men and women would not choose to enter relationships of caring without pressure from the state.

These nightmarish images have much in common with what other disciplines tell us men think about women and relationship. The conception of women as either angels or whores is identified by Freud,[502] and supported by feminist accounts.[503] The evil power of female sexuality is a recurrent subject of myth and history.[504] The contrast of men fearing relationship as entrapping, and women fearing isolation, is the subject of Carol Gilligan's work in the psychology of moral development;[505] others have explored the origins of that difference in the context of psychoanalytic theory.[506] Raising these images to the level of consciousness and inquiry therefore seems to me an important aspect of understanding this particular set of cases. It is also a way of stepping beyond the confines of current doctrine and beginning to think about other ways of handling the reciprocal claims cohabitants may make of one another.[507]

Epilogue

The stories told by contract doctrine are human stories of power and knowledge. The telling of these stories—like the telling of any story—is, in one sense, an impoverishing exercise: The infinitely rich potential that we call reality is stripped of detail, of all but a few of its aspects. But it is only through this restriction of content that any story has a meaning. In uncovering the way doctrine orders, and thereby creates, represents, and misrepresents reality, I have suggested and criticized the particular meaning created by doctrinal stories, the particular limitations entailed in the telling of those stories.

My critique is in turn a story, which itself creates order and meaning. My story, too, is subject to the charge that it has reduced the richness of contract law and the multiplicity of its concerns to a few basic elements, that it misrepresents as much as it reveals. And, in fact, I do not believe that my story is the only one that can be told about contract doctrine. I insist only that it is *an* important story to tell.

My story reveals the world of contract doctrine to be one in which a comparatively few mediating devices are constantly deployed to displace and defer the otherwise inevitable revelation that public cannot be separated from private, or form from substance, or objective manifestation from subjective intent. The pain of that revelation, and its value, lies in its message that we can neither know nor control the boundary between self and other. Thus, although my story has reduced contract law to these few basic elements, they are elements that merit close scrutiny: They represent our most fundamental concerns. And the type of analysis I suggest can help us to understand and address those concerns.

By telling my story, I also hope to open the way for other stories—new accounts of how the problems of power and knowledge concretely hamper our ability to live with one another in society. My story both asks why those problems are not currently addressed by doctrine and traditional doctrinal analysis, and suggests how they might be. By presenting doctrine as a human effort at world-making, my story focuses fresh attention on those to whom we give the power to shape our world. My story requires that we develop new understandings of our world-makers as we create them, and are in turn created by them. This kind of inquiry, exemplified for me by feminist theory, can help us see that the world portrayed by traditional doctrinal analysis is already not the world we live in, and is certainly not the only possible world for us to live in. And in coming to that realization, we increase our chances of building our world anew.

Notes

432. 18 Cal. 3d 660, 557 P.2d 106, 134 Cal. Rptr. 815 (1976). *Marvin* also generated a subsequent appeals court decision interesting in its own right. *See* Marvin v. Marvin, 122 Cal. App. 3d 871, 176 Cal. Rptr. 555 (1981).

433. 77 Ill. 2d 49, 394 N.E.2d 1204 (1979). The lower appeals court opinion in *Hewitt*, 62 Ill. App. 3d 861, 380 N.E.2d 454 (1978) (reversing dismissal on grounds that public policy did not disfavor grant of mutually enforceable property rights to knowingly unmarried cohabitants in nonmeretricious relationship), provides a perfect counterpoint to its supreme court successor.

434. 18 Cal. 3d 660, 557 P.2d 106, 134 Cal. Rptr. 815 (1976).

435. Marvin v. Marvin, 122 Cal. App. 3d 871, 176 Cal. Rptr. 555 (1981).

436. *Id.* at 873-74, 176 Cal. Rptr. at 557-58 (reciting facts found by trial court).

437. *Id.* at 875-77, 176 Cal. Rptr. at 558-59.

438. *Marvin*, 18 Cal. 3d at 666, 557 P.2d at 110, 134 Cal. Rptr. at 819.

439. *Hewitt*, 77 Ill. 2d at 52-54, 394 N.E.2d at 1205.

440. *Hewitt*, 62 Ill. App. 3d at 867, 380 N.E.2d at 459.

441. *Hewitt*, 77 Ill. 2d at 65-66, 394 N.E.2d at 1211 (effect of lower court's opinion would be to reinstate common law marriage after legislature had expressly abolished it).

442. Hertzog v. Hertzog, 29 Pa. 465 (1857) . . . .

443. *See* Keene v. Keene, 57 Cal. 2d 657, 668, 371 P.2d 329, 336, 21 Cal. Rptr. 593, 600 (1962).

444. *See Hertzog*, 29 Pa. at 470. . . .

445. *Id.* at 468-70. . . .

448. *Hewitt*, 77 Ill. 2d at 61, 394 N.E.2d at 1209.

450. [*Id.*]

451. *Id.* at 56–58, 394 N.E.2d at 1207–08.

452. *Id.* at 58–59, 394 N.E.2d at 1208.

454. *See, e.g., Hewitt*, 62 Ill. App. 3d at 863–66, 380 N.E.2d at 456–59 (accepting reasoning of Marvin v. Marvin, 18 Cal. 3d 660, 557 P.2d 106, 134 Cal. Rptr. 815 (1976)), *rev'd* 77 Ill. 2d 49, 394 N.E.2d 1204 (1979).

455. *See, e.g., In re* Marriage of Cary, 34 Cal. App. 3d 345, 353, 109 Cal. Rptr. 862, 866 (1973) (court's holding that property should be divided between unmarried couple would not necessarily discourage marriages).

457. *See Balfour*, [1919] 2 K.B. at 574 (Warrington, L.J.) ("It may be, and I do not for a moment say that it is not, possible for such a contract as is alleged in the present case to be made between husband and wife. The question is whether such a contract was made.").

458. For the suggestion that more weight has often been accorded a writing, see, for example, Beal v. Beal, 282 Or. 115, 122, 577 P.2d 507, 510 (1978). For a discussion of evidence of agreement about property distribution between unmarried cohabitants see, for example, Vallera v. Vallera, 21 Cal. 2d 681, 685, 134 P.2d 761, 763 (1943): "Even in the absence of an express agreement to that effect, the woman would be entitled to share in the property jointly accumulated, in the proportion that her funds contributed toward its acquisition. There is no evidence that the parties in the present case made any agreement concerning their property or property rights." (citation omitted.)

This was the court's conclusion despite at least a three-year period of cohabitation during which the woman provided substantial services to the household. *See id.* at 686–87, 134 P.2d at 763–64 (Curtis, J., dissenting in part) (when woman contributes her services in the home, her interest in property accumulated should be protected).

459. *See, e.g., Marvin*, 18 Cal. 3d at 674, 557 P.2d at 116, 134 Cal. Rptr. at 825 (contract to pay for sexual services would be unlawful).

460. *See, e.g., Hewitt*, 77 Ill. 2d at 59, 394 N.E.2d at 1208.

461. *See, e.g., id.* at 59–60, 394 N.E.2d at 1208–09.

462. *Id.* at 60, 394 N.E.2d at 1209.

463. *Marvin*, 18 Cal. 3d at 672, 557 P.2d at 114–15, 134 Cal. Rptr. at 823–24.

464. *Id.* at 669, 557 P.2d at 112, 134 Cal. Rptr. at 821.

465. *Id.* 557 P.2d at 112, 134 Cal. Rptr. at 821 (emphasis in original). Severability as a device for rescuing the cohabitation agreement has proved popular. *See, e.g.,* Rehak v. Mathis, 239 Ga. 541, 544, 238 S.E.2d 81, 82–83 (1977) (Hill, J., dissenting); Donovan v. Scuderi, 51 Md. App. 217, 219, 443 A.2d 121, 123 (Ct. Spec. App. 1982).

466. *Marvin*, 18 Cal. 3d at 672, 557 P.2d at 114, 134 Cal. Rptr. at 823.

467. *Id.* at 674–75, 557 P.2d at 116, 134 Cal. Rptr. at 825.

Tobriner thus shifts his focus away from that involved in his two-part test. He moves from what the parties intended to what consideration the cohabitants provided to support their agreement. He says at one point: "By looking not to such uncertain tests, but only to the consideration underlying the agreement, we provide the parties and the courts with a practical guide to determine when an agreement between nonmarital partners should be enforced." *Id.* at 672, 557 P.2d at 114–15, 134 Cal. Rptr. at 823–24. And in concluding this analysis, he says again: "So long as the agreement does not rest upon illicit meretricious consideration, the parties may order their economic affairs as they choose . . . ." *Id.* at 674, 557 P.2d at 116, 134 Cal. Rptr. at 825.

468. *Id.*, 557 P.2d at 116, 134 Cal. Rptr. at 825.

469. Updeck v. Samuel, 123 Cal. App. 2d 264, 267, 266 P.2d 822, 824 (Dist. Ct. App. 1954) (finding oral contract based on immoral consideration where both parties legally married to other spouses).

470. *Marvin*, 18 Cal. 3d at 671, 557 P.2d at 114, 134 Cal. Rptr. at 823. In *Marvin*, as in *Updeck*, the defendant was legally married to another spouse during at least a portion of the term of his contract with the plaintiff. *Id.* at 667, 557 P.2d at 111, 134 Cal. Rptr. at 820.

471. The one case Tobriner feels compelled to disapprove rather than distinguish is that of Heaps v. Toy, 54 Cal. App. 2d 178, 128 P.2d 813 (Dist. Ct. App. 1942). *See Marvin*, 18 Cal. 3d at 671 n.6, 557 P.2d at 114 n.6, 134 Cal. Rptr. at 823 n.6. In *Heaps*, the court found "contrary to good morals" an agreement under which the woman was to leave her job, refrain from marriage, be a companion to the man and make a permanent home for him, in return for economic support for herself and her child. Tobriner seems to feel that even interpretation must have its limits, and that the *Heaps* court overstepped its limits by reading immorality into this form of agreement.

472. 122 Cal. App. 3d 500, 176 Cal. Rptr. 130 (Ct. App. 1981).

473. . . . *Id.* at 508, 176 Cal. Rptr. at 133. . . . This determination is plainly dependent upon the provision of sexual substance to the form of the agreement, although the court also relies upon arguments of form in finding that the sex cannot be severed from the rest of the agreement: "Neither the property sharing nor the support provision of the agreement rests upon plaintiff's acting as Daly's traveling companion, housekeeper or cook as distinguished from acting as his lover." *Id.* at 509, 176 Cal. Rptr. at 134. Exactly the same could be said, of course, about the agreement at issue in *Marvin*, although the *Jones* court is using the argument to distinguish the case from *Marvin*. . . .

474. *See, e.g.*, Hill v. Estate of Westbrook, 95 Cal. App. 2d 599, 603, 213 P.2d 727, 730 (Dist. Ct. App. 1950); Rehak v. Mathis, 239 Ga. at 543, 238 S.E.2d at 82; Hewitt v. Hewitt, 77 Ill. 2d at 58–59, 394 N.E.2d at 1208; Donovan v. Scuderi, 51 Md. App. at 219, 443 A.2d at 123.

475. . . . The traditional assumptions about the nature of the exchange are at once highlighted and challenged by this comment from the dissenting judge in *Rehak*: "[W]here a man and woman have contracted with each other to cohabit together illegally, a court will not require the woman to perform her promise nor will it require the man to pay for her services. However, where a man hires a maid to clean house for him, his obligation to pay wages is enforceable in court even though he seduces her. . . . I do not find evidence that the female in this case agreed to make house payments in consideration of the male's promise to seduce her or to cohabit with her illegally." 239 Ga. at 544, 238 S.E.2d at 83 (Hill, J., dissenting).

476. *See* RESTATEMENT (SECOND) [OF CONTRACTS] § 71 comment b [1979]. . . .

477. *See, e.g.*, Roznowski v. Bozyk, 73 Mich. App. 405, 408–09, 251 N.W.2d 606, 608 (1977) (in "family relationship," absent "proof of the expectations of the parties, the presumption of gratuity will overcome the usual contract implied by law to pay for what is accepted"); Cropsey v. Sweeney, 27 Barb. 310, 315 (N.Y. App. Div. 1858): "[T]hese services were performed not as a servant, with a view to pay, but from higher and holier motives . . . ."); Roberts v. Roberts, 64 Wyo. 433, 450, 196 P.2d 361, 367 (1948) ("'[T]he relationship as husband and wife negative[s] that of master and servant . . . .'") (quoting Willis v. Willis, 48 Wyo. 403, 437, 49 P.2d 670, 681 (1935)).

478. Marvin v. Marvin, 18 Cal. 3d. 660, 670 n.5, 557 P.2d 106, 113 n.5, 134 Cal. Rptr. 815, 822 n.5 (1976).

479. *Id.*

480. *Id.* at 679, 557 P.2d at 119, 134 Cal. Rptr. at 828 (citing Vallera v. Vallera, 21 Cal. 2d. 681, 686–87, 134 P.2d 761, 763–64 (1943) (Curtis, J., dissenting)).

481. Wisconsin & Mich. Ry. Co. v. Powers, 191 U.S. 379 (1903). . . .

482. There is a subtheme in some of the cases, however, suggesting that in fact homemaking services are of little objective value. In Kinnison v. Kinnison, 627 P.2d

594, 596 (Wyo. 1981), where the parties entered a settlement agreement based on the woman's provision of services in improving a property and managing and maintaining a household, the court stated: "A contract made in settlement of claims is valid even if the claims settled are of doubtful worth." (citations omitted).

Another suggestion, dependent on measures of objective value rather than subjective intent, is that even if the woman's services are not disqualified from counting as consideration by the beneficent intention with which they are provided, they are "balanced out" by the companionship and services provided by the man. This appears to be the reasoning of the trial court in the second *Marvin* decision, in determining that Lee Marvin was not unjustly enriched by his relationship with Michelle Triola. Marvin v. Marvin, 122 Cal. App. 3d 871, 874, 176 Cal. Rptr. 555, 557 (1981) (court of appeals' statement of facts taken from findings of trial court.)

483. In asking these questions, we examine the substance of the deal (according to inevitably suspect measures of equivalence); the behavior of the parties (according to equally suspect standards of good behavior); or the state of mind of the parties (asking questions that lead us back to other evidence of those states of mind, like the outcome of the deal or the behavior of the parties).

484. Our talk about relationship in nonlegal contexts certainly deals at length and in depth with these issues, as we ponder, for example, why relationships are formed and why they fall apart, or what motivates particular decisions within intimate relationships.

485. *See, e.g.*, Taub & Schneider, *Perspectives on Women's Subordination and the Role of Law*, in THE POLITICS OF LAW 117, & especially 118-24 [D. Kairys ed. 1982]; *cf.* Hale, [*Coercion and Distribution in a Supposedly Non-Coercive State*, 38 POL. SCI. Q. 470, at 471-74 (1923)] (legal system places one of contracting parties in superior position by imposing legal duty on other party). . . .

486. Taub & Schneider, *supra* note 485, at 122; *cf.* Coppage v. Kansas, 236 U.S. 1, 15 (1915) (discussing employer-employee relationship. . . .

487. For a thoughtful account that still posits a single contractual intention, shared by both parties, see the California Supreme Court opinion in Marvin v. Marvin, 18 Cal. 3d 660, 675 n.11, 557 P.2d 106, 117 n.11, 134 Cal Rptr. 815, 826 n.11 (1976). Commenting on the second trial court's award, on remand, of rehabilitative alimony, the second opinion of the appeals court challenges that supposition: "[T]here is nothing in the trial court's findings to suggest that such an award is warranted to protect the expectations of *both* parties." Marvin v. Marvin, 122 Cal. App. 3d 871, 876, 176 Cal. Rptr. 555, 558 (emphasis in original) (1981). *See also* Beal v. Beal, 282 Or. 115, 126 n.2, 577 P.2d 507, 512 n.2 (1978) (emphasis in original): "In fact, whatever else may be true of the intentions and expectations of unmarried couples (if these are shared at all) the one thing that may often be inferred with some certainty is that they have chosen *not* to be married and to place themselves within the legal consequences of that relationship."

488. The court stated: "The value of a stable marriage remains unchallenged and is not denigrated by this opinion. It is not realistic to conclude that this determination will "discourage" marriage for the rule for which defendant contends can only encourage a partner with obvious income-producing ability to avoid marriage and to retain all earnings which he may acquire. One cannot earnestly advocate such a policy." Hewitt v. Hewitt, 62 Ill. App. 3d 861, 868-69, 380 N.E.2d 454, 460 (1978).

489. *See, e.g., Marvin*, 18 Cal. 3d at 684, 557 P.2d at 122-23, 134 Cal. Rptr. at 831-32.

490. *Id.* at 683, 557 P.2d at 121, 134 Cal. Rptr. at 830 (suggesting presumption "'that the parties intended to deal fairly with each other'") (quoting Keene v. Keene, 57 Cal. 2d 657, 674, 371 P.2d 329, 339, 21 Cal. Rptr. 593, 603 (1962) (Peters, J., dissenting)). This is essentially the tactic challenged by the second opinion of the appeals court in

Marvin, 122 Cal. App. 3d at 876–77, 176 Cal. Rptr. at 559; *see also* Kozlowski v. Kozlowski, 80 N.J. 378, 390–91, 403 A.2d 902, 909 (1979) (Pashman, J., concurring) (supporting presumption of fair dealing); Carlson v. Olson, 256 N.W.2d 249, 255 (Minn. 1977): "The trial court found that the parties had lived together for over 21 years, had raised a son to maturity, and had held themselves out to the public as husband and wife. The home and some personal property were in joint tenancy. Thus, the trial court was justified in finding that on all the facts of this particular case the parties intended that their modest accumulations were to be divided on an equal basis . . . ."

491. The Supreme Court of Illinois in the *Hewitt* case used the traditional argument that policy in this area should be left to the legislature—that the judiciary should stay out of "public policy in the domestic relations field." *Hewitt*, 77 Ill. 2d at 61, 394 N.E.2d at 1209 (citations omitted). The appeals court doubted the validity of the distinction between intervention and nonintervention, or "public" enforcement of the agreement, and "private" nonenforcement: "[A]lthough the courts proclaim that they will have nothing to do with such matters, the proclamation in itself establishes, as to the parties involved, an effective and binding rule of law which tends to operate purely by accident or perhaps by reason of the cunning, anticipatory designs of just one of the parties." *Hewitt*, 62 Ill. App. 3d at 867, 380 N.E.2d at 459 (quoting West v. Knowles, 50 Wash. 2d 311, 316, 311 P.2d 689, 693 (1957)).

492. The appeals court in *Hewitt* thought that *not* enforcing agreements of this sort would encourage the income-producing party to avoid marriage, and favor the cunning. *See supra* notes 488, 491. The supreme court said: "We cannot confidently say that judicial recognition of property rights between unmarried cohabitants will not make that alternative to marriage more attractive by allowing the parties to engage in such relationships with greater security." *Hewitt*, 77 Ill. 2d at 61–62, 394 N.E.2d at 1209.

493. Justice Tobriner does this consistently in his opinion in Marvin v. Marvin, 18 Cal. 3d 660, 557 P.2d 106, 134 Cal. Rptr. 815 (1976).

494. *See, e.g.,* Cropsey v. Sweeney, 27 Barb. 310, 314–15 (N.Y. App. Div. 1858) ("[H]er long, devoted, faithful love, and services, as a *wife* and *mother*, will not permit us to say that she is legally entitled to receive pay for those services *as a servant*.") (emphasis in original); Roberts v. Roberts, 64 Wyo. 433, 450, 196 P.2d 361, 367 (1948) ("'[T]he relationship as husband and wife negative[s] that of master and servant . . . .'") (citation to Stewart v. Waterman, 97 Vt. 408, 414, 123 A. 524, 526 (1924), in Willis v. Willis, 48 Wyo. 403, 437, 49 P.2d 670, 681 (1935)).

495. "The law would do injustice to the plaintiff herself, by implying a promise to pay for these services; and respect for the plaintiff herself, as well as for the law, compels us to [deny her relief]." Cropsey v. Sweeney, 27 Barb. at 315.

496. "From plaintiff's own lips and from her own petition, the court was informed that she and the defendant lived together or cohabited together without the benefit of marriage and in this court's judgment she 'committed iniquity' and the court concludes that her action 'arises out of an immoral transaction.'" Roach v. Buttons, 6 FAM. L. REP. (BNA) 2355 (Tenn. Ch. Ct. Feb. 29, 1980) (quoting Q. POMEROY, A TREATISE ON EQUITY JURISDICTION §§ 397–404, at 737–61 (4th ed. 1918)). That her partner has equally participated in immoral conduct but is rewarded by a decision not to enforce the agreement is simply irrelevant. *See, e.g.,* Kinnison v. Kinnison, 627 P.2d 594, 596, 599 (Wyo. 1981) (Rooney, J., dissenting).

497. The point is not that courts ruminate openly about the nature of the sexual relationship between the cohabitants whose agreements they oversee. As clarified in the following text, provision of sex by the man to the woman is never suggested as the consideration for the provision of sex for the woman to the man. The implication is, therefore, that women are not benefited by, or do not enjoy, the sex—but provide it

for ulterior motives such as economic support. For another example of judicial reliance on traditional assumptions, see the dissenting opinion of Justice Hill in *Rehak v. Mathis*, quoted *supra* note 475.

498. *See, e.g.*, Vallera v. Vallera, 21 Cal. 2d 681, 685, 134 P.2d 761, 763 (1948) (where woman denied maintenance and share of property acquired in man's name during relationship, "[e]quitable considerations arising from the reasonable expectation of the continuation of benefits attending the status of marriage entered into in good faith are not present"); Roach v. Buttons, 6 FAM. L. REP. (BNA) 2355 (Tenn. Ch. Ct. Feb. 29, 1980) ("[M]arriage is a legal state or legal relationship between two persons of the opposite sex and, as aforesaid, certain mutual benefits flow one to the other as a result of the marriage contract. . . . If plaintiff had married defendant, these rights and benefits would have been hers, but she entered into a relationship that is not sanctioned by Natural or Divine Law.").

499. *See, e.g.*, Baker v. Baker, 222 Minn. 169, 171–72, 23 N.W.2d 582, 583–84 (1946) ("Where the arrangement under which the parties lived together was a meretricious one, the court will grant no relief, . . . [I]n such a situation, there is no implied obligation on the part of the man to compensate the woman for household services rendered by her.") (citations omitted); *see also supra* note 487 (discussing judicial analysis of contractual intention in cohabitation arrangements).

500. This suggestion arises out of the notion that the relationship is one equally chosen and therefore equally avoidable. The Illinois Supreme Court in Hewitt v. Hewitt, 77 Ill. 2d at 58, 394 N.E.2d at 1207, questions whether "legal rights closely resembling those arising from conventional marriages, can be acquired by those who deliberately choose to enter into what have heretofore been commonly referred to as illicit or meretricious relationships . . . ." *See also* Roach v. Buttons, 6 FAM. L. REP. (BNA) at 2355 ("[S]he voluntarily and with her eyes open entered into an illicit relationship . . . ."); Kinnison v. Kinnison, 627 P.2d 594, 597 (Wyo. 1981) (Rooney, J., dissenting): "[T]he plain fact exists that both parties have assumed a relationship that is recognizable in law, morals and public policy *only* if the legal requirements for such relationship are met. For either of them to ask the courts to disregard this fact but sanction an aspect flowing from such relationship is impertinent."

501. For a court to enforce a cohabitation agreement would be "but another failure by the court to maintain the standards and principles upon which our society and nation were founded and which are essential to their successful continuance." Kinnison v. Kinnison, 627 P.2d at 597 (Rooney, J., dissenting). Justice Underwood, for the Supreme Court of Illinois in *Hewitt*, 77 Ill. 2d at 58, 394 N.E.2d at 1207–08, uses rhetorical questions to suggest a parade of horribles: "Will the fact [of enforcement] . . . encourage formation of such relationships and weaken marriage as the foundation of our family-based society? . . . And still more importantly: what of the children born of such relationships? . . . What of the sociological and psychological effects on them of that type of environment?"

502. XI S. FREUD, *A Special Type of Choice of Object Made by Men*, in THE STANDARD EDITION OF THE COMPLETE PSYCHOLOGICAL WORKS OF SIGMUND FREUD 165 (J. Strachey trans. & ed. 1957); XI S. FREUD, *On the Universal Tendency to Debasement in the Sphere of Love*, in *id.* at 179.

503. *See, e.g.*, A. DWORKIN, WOMAN HATING (1974).

504. *Id.*, *see especially* 31–46, 118–50.

505. C. GILLIGAN [IN A DIFFERENT VOICE 24–63 (1982)] ("Images of Relationship").

506. N. CHODOROW, [THE REPRODUCTION OF MOTHERING: PSYCHOANALYSIS AND THE SOCIOLOGY OF GENDER (1978)]; D. DINNERSTEIN, [THE MERMAID AND THE MINOTAUR: SEXUAL ARRANGEMENTS AND HUMAN MALAISE (1976)].

507. It may not be possible, ultimately, to "transcend" the kinds of categories our current ways of thinking and imagining condemn us to use in order to make sense of our experience. But being self-conscious about the particular *set* of categories inhering in particular doctrine may at least enable us to expand our repertoire, and enlarge the number of concrete alternatives available to us in this context, even while recognizing the limits of our culture.

14

Statutory Rape: A Feminist
Critique of Rights Analysis [1984]

Frances Olsen

Introduction

A man accused of raping his wife may feel that his privacy rights are being violated; a woman may feel that she is sexually exploited by pornography even if it is viewed privately. The right to privacy and the right to protection exist in fundamental conflict—a conflict that illustrates the contradiction between freedom of action and security that recurs throughout our legal system. Privacy assures the freedom to pursue one's own interests; protection assures that others will not harm us. We want both security and freedom, but seem to have to choose between them. Our historical experience with censorship warns us to be wary of state protection; our experience with domestic violence warns us to be wary of privacy. An individual may be just as oppressed by the state's failure to protect him as by the state's restraint of his freedom for the sake of protecting another. Every difficult legal or political decision can be justified as either protecting freedom or protecting security and attacked as either undermining security or undermining freedom.[5]

This conflict between freedom and security implicates two important and related controversies—the debate between liberals and critical legal scholars over rights analysis and the debate among feminists over sexuality. The central problem of the rights debate is that many social reforms appear to be based on rights, yet every theory of rights that has been proposed can be shown to be internally inconsistent or incoherent.[6] The central problem of the sexuality debate is that women are oppressed by moralistic controls society places on women's sexual expression, yet women are also oppressed by violence and sexual aggression that society allows in the name of sexual freedom.

Rights theory does not indicate which of the two values—freedom or security—the decisionmaker should choose in a given case. Because it cannot transcend this fundamental conflict of values, rights theory does not offer an adequate basis for legal decisions.

Moreover, thinking in terms of rights encourages a partial and inadequate analysis of sexuality. Just as rights theory conceptualizes a society composed of self-interested individuals whose conflicting interests are mediated by the state, it conceptualizes the problem of sexuality as a question of where social controls should end and sexual freedom should begin. Libertines and moralists alike tend to think of sexuality as a natural, presocial drive that is permitted or repressed by society; they disagree only over where to draw the line between freedom and social control. At one extreme, social control is limited to requiring consent of the participants; the realm of sexual freedom should extend to all consensual sexual activity. At the other extreme, freedom is limited to pro-creational sex within marriage; social control should restrict sexuality outside this realm.

The important issue, however, is not where to draw such a line, but the substance and meaning that we give to sexuality. Unfortunately, feminists who set out to discuss sexuality find their arguments trivialized into a line-drawing debate. Some feminists focus on the sexist nature of social control and assert that in practice it means social control of women. Other feminists focus on the sexist nature of sexual freedom and point out that freedom means freedom for men to exploit women. But the fundamental issue addressed by both sides— the nature of sexuality and our ability to reconstruct it—is ultimately redefined through rights analysis as a question about the location of the boundary between sexual freedom and social control. In this way, feminists who are or should be engaged in a joint or parallel project of challenging the dominant definition of sexuality come to perceive themselves as opposing one another. Feminists on one side of the debate accuse those on the first of contributing to their own oppression through "false consciousness." Another set of polemical charges is that the feminists on one side are overly preoccupied with violence and sexual domination and those on the other are defending male supremacy at the expense of women. . . .

Statutory Rape Laws and Feminist Thought

Statutory rape laws provide a concrete example of the advantages and disadvantages of rights analysis. These laws pose a classic political dilemma for feminists. On one hand, they protect females; like laws against rape, incest, child molestation, and child marriage, statutory rape laws are a statement of social disapproval of certain forms of exploitation. To some extent they reduce abuse and victimization. On the other hand, statutory rape laws restrict the sexual activity of young women and reinforce the double standard of sexual morality.[70] The laws both protect and undermine women's rights, and rights arguments can be used to support, attack, or urge changes in the laws.

Although feminists initially supported such laws, in recent years they have been among the most trenchant critics of gender-based statutory rape laws. I examine their two major objections to the laws: that they restrict women and that they reinforce sexist stereotypes.[71] To illustrate the indeterminacy of rights analysis, I suggest a variety of rights-oriented arguments that could be made in favor of very different revisions of gender-based statutory rape laws. Although some of the revisions are more appealing than others, rights analysis does not explain why this is so. The problem is not that one is unable to choose among equally persuasive arguments, but that the basis for the choices one makes and urges upon others has little or nothing to do with the abstract categories employed in rights analysis. . . .

A Feminist Critique of Gender-Based Statutory Rape Laws

California's law against "unlawful sexual intercourse" is typical of the gender-based statutory rape laws that remain on the books in a minority of states. The California statute prohibits any "act of sexual intercourse accomplished with a female not the wife of the perpetrator, where the female is under the age of 18 years."[84]

Feminists charge that statutes such as this one are harmful to women on both a practical and an ideological level. First, as an effort to control the sexual activities of young women, statutory rape laws are an unwarranted governmental intrusion into their lives and an oppressive restriction upon their freedom of action. An unmarried woman under eighteen cannot legally have intercourse in California. Whether the prohibition is enforced by prosecuting her partner or by prosecuting her as an aider and abettor, the statute interferes with the sexual freedom of the underage female. In the language of rights analysis, statutory rape laws violate the female's right to privacy and her right to be as free sexually as her male counterpart.

Feminists' second common objection to statutory rape laws is ideological. Gender-based statutory rape laws reinforce the sexual stereotype of men as aggressors and women as passive victims. The laws perpetuate the double standard of sexual morality. For males, sex is an accomplishment; they gain something through intercourse. For women, sex entails giving something up. Further, for the myth of male sexual accomplishment to exist, some females must give in. The double standard divides females into two classes—virgins and "bad girls" who may be exploited with impunity. Even if young women need more protection from sexual coercion and exploitation than the laws against forcible rape and incest provide, many feminists nevertheless oppose gender-based laws. They argue that males and females should be protected equally and that gender-based laws stigmatize women as weaker than men. In terms of rights theory, gender-based statutory rape laws violate the right of all women to be treated equally to men.

Although these two objections to statutory rape laws are analytically distinct, they nonetheless are related. Ideology affects people's lives, and daily life can limit and reshape ideology. The restrictive aspects of statutory rape laws are particularly objectionable because they exalt female chastity and treat women as lacking in sexual autonomy. This view of women both provides a reason (although a false and pernicious one) for state restrictions upon young women's sexual freedom and reinforces damaging stereotypes. At the same time, the laws imply that young men do not need the protection that they afford. This implication reinforces the ideology that sex is okay for young men; it also means that some women will have to be available to have sex with them.

The state restricts the young woman's sexual behavior for reasons related to sexist notions of what makes females valuable. The state does not merely restrict the young woman's freedom; it also treats her sexuality as a thing that has a value of its own and must be guarded. By refusing to grant women autonomy and by protecting them in ways that men are not protected, the state treats women's bodies—and therefore women themselves—as objects. Men are treated differently. Their bodies are regarded as part of them, subject to their free control.

Changing Statutory Rape Laws to Protect Women's Rights

There are several ways statutory rape laws could be altered to overcome these grounds for objection. There are at least two ways the laws could be altered to free young women from state-enforced sexual constraint and four ways the laws could be changed to help overcome debilitating stereotypes.

1. Freeing Women from Sexual Constraints

(a) Disempowering the state.—The simplest way to prevent statutory rape laws from restricting women's sexual freedom and treating women as objects would be to repeal the laws or declare them unconstitutional. This approach would support the rights of young women by freeing them from one form of state domination and giving them the same status as adult women.

Unfortunately, invalidating statutory rape laws altogether and putting young women in the same position as adult women might undermine the right of young women to be free of unwanted sexual contact. Adult women occupy a position of pervasive economic and social subordination to men. Adult women are seduced, pressured, coerced, and even forced into unwanted sexual relations, for which they have no legal recourse. Underage females might discover that although the abolition of statutory rape laws would protect their rights against the state, it would remove some of their already-minimal protection against individual men. Young women and their sexuality would still be treated as objects, but instead of being controlled by state legislation, sex would be "taken" from them by individual men, one at a time.[92] Nice as it is to be freed from state oppression, domination by private individuals can be equally oppressive. Despite their negative aspects, statutory rape laws may provide some protection for females. Recognizing this, even opponents of such laws support some form of age-of-consent statute—at least to protect six-year-olds, if not twelve-year-olds.

Statutory rape laws can also protect females against forms of oppression that other laws do not reach. For example, statutory rape laws may prohibit certain instances of sexual assault that should be considered illegal, but cannot be prosecuted as forcible rape.[94] Similarly, abuses of authority that do not fit the statutory definition of incest may be punishable under statutory rape laws.[95]

(b) Empowering women.—Instead of restricting women's freedom, it might be possible to protect women by empowering them against male coercion.[96] This alternative would free women from state domination without removing all protection against private domination. For example, statutory rape laws could be amended or interpreted to give the underage woman control over the prosecution decision. Such a law could either permit charges to be brought only upon the woman's complaint or require that they be dropped upon her request. Either version would increase the protective aspects of statutory rape laws and reduce the negative, repressive aspects. A young woman would be free to engage in sex or accept the protection of statutory rape laws. Her characterization of a sexual encounter as voluntary intercourse or as rape would be determinative.[101] Although giving the woman control over prosecution would not guarantee that her decision would be her choice and not coerced, it might at least enable her to play the various pressures against one another.

Despite its merits, many feminists would oppose this revision of statutory rape laws because it would treat women differently from men and therefore could stigmatize all women by implying that underage women are vulnerable and in need of protection. But the ideological significance attached to the label "vulnerable" depends in good measure upon the concrete context in which the label is attached and the practical effect of the labeling. Women rightly object when their alleged vulnerability is used as an excuse to deny them certain opportunities or to foreclose choices that should be available to them. Statutory rape laws that gave a young woman power over the prosecution decision, however, would treat her vulnerability as a reason to empower her against coercion rather than to take power away from her.

Nevertheless, it is certainly possible that women would be stigmatized as well as empowered. Indeed, it may be impossible to predict whether the ideological damage to women from being treated as vulnerable would in the long run outweigh the practical and ideological advantages of empowerment.[106]

2. Overcoming Debilitating Stereotypes

The second feminist objection to statutory rape laws is that they stigmatize women and reinforce sexist stereotypes. There are at least four possible solutions to this problem.

(a) *Abolition.*—One could meet the objection that statutory rape laws perpetuate debilitating sexual stereotypes by abolishing the laws. Although this approach might increase the practical basis for the woman-as-powerless-victim stereotype by allowing more young women to be victimized by male aggression, it would at least avoid ideological reinforcement of the stereotype.

(b) *Effective enforcement.*—If it were possible to enforce or revise statutory rape laws so that they actually prevented men from victimizing women, the stereotypes might become so false that they would lose their power. This approach imposes significant risks, however. Legal reform may be insufficient to prevent victimization; laws alone seldom change behavior. Moreover, in our present society, it may be impossible to empower women without stigmatizing them.

In a sense, this second approach is the converse of the first. The first proposal would undermine the stereotype of men as aggressors and women as victims but allow the reality; the second would support the stereotype but undermine the reality.

(c) *Simple extension.*—A third approach—criminalizing sexual intercourse when either party is underage—would seem neither to stigmatize women nor to reinforce sexist stereotypes. This approach benefits underage males by protecting them from being pressured into premature sex and harms them by curtailing their freedom.

Although this change seems to address the issue of stereotyping, it obscures the issue of social power. Extending the age-of-consent laws to males may effect merely a cosmetic change, without altering images or practices under the law. Moreover, it leaves untouched the repressive aspects of statutory rape laws. In our present society, these repressive aspects hurt females more than males. Extension of the legal rule to males might not bring extension of these repressive aspects. This solution therefore is actually less neutral than it initially appears.

(d) *Extension with age gap.*—As a variation of the third approach, one could decriminalize most sex between teenagers but extend protection to minors of both sexes against exploitation by an older person. For example, statutory rape laws might provide criminal penalties for anyone who engaged in sexual intercourse with a minor four or more years younger than the person charged.[111] Such a law would restrict freedom less than the previous proposal because it would allow teenagers to engage in sexual intercourse with partners near their own age. In addition, the law would provide for criminal prosecution in many of the worst kinds of exploitative situations, but would avoid overt sexual stereotyping. Unfortunately, such a law would not address the problem of male sexual aggression that characterizes society at large. Underage males are likely to relate to underage females in illegitimate ways, just as their older counterparts relate to adult women in illegitimate ways.

. . .

A commitment to establish and protect rights for women provides us with little guidance in deciding whether to support any particular statutory rape law or to oppose all statutory rape laws. Even if we artificially simplify our task by focusing only upon the rights of women, we cannot determine how to protect these rights. Rights analysis does not help us as an analytic tool because it is indeterminate. Every effort to protect young women against private oppression by individual men risks subjecting women to state oppression, and every effort to protect them against state oppression undermines their power to resist individual oppression.

Further, any acknowledgment of the actual difference between the present situation of males and females stigmatizes females and perpetuates discrimination. But if we ignore power differences and pretend that women and men are similarly situated, we perpetuate discrimination by disempowering ourselves from instituting effective change. The strategy of protecting rights runs afoul of the conflict between rights as freedom of action and rights as security; the strategy of promoting equality runs afoul of the conflict between formal equality of opportunity and substantive equality of outcome.

Despite the circularity of arguments about rights and equality, however, effective reforms do take place and do change people's lives. Some of the proposed changes in statutory rape laws are better than others. It is even possible that most feminists would agree on the best change. But this agreement would not be reached by discovering the "real" meaning of women's rights or by logically deducing the "true implications" of gender equality. Rather, it would rest upon sociological calculations and political and moral commitments. An abstract commitment to women's rights does not help us decide concrete cases.

In general, rights analysis is merely indeterminate; it contributes nothing to the resolution of concrete cases. In the context of statutory rape laws, however, I would argue that the use of rights analysis has had a more negative effect. The Supreme Court's decision in *Michael M. v. Superior Court*[114] shifted the terrain of debate in such a way that the use of rights analysis to discuss statutory rape laws tends now to be politically debilitating. . . .

A New Feminist Critique of Michael M.

I believe that the most useful question to be asked in evaluating *Michael M.* is whether the case—including the plurality, concurring, and dissenting opinions—tends to mask and legitimate conditions of social existence that are hurtful and damaging to women. I conclude that it does, and thus I condemn it.

The opinions imply that there are two sharply distinct categories of sexual relations that together comprise all of sexuality. There is equal, consensual sexual intercourse on one hand,[194] and bad, coercive sex imposed upon a female by a male aggressor on the other hand. But these two categories constitute a continuum of sexual relations; there is no bright line between them. Although most women do seek sexual contact with men, heterosexual behavior in our society is seldom fully voluntary; sex is usually to some extent imposed on females by males. Perhaps sixteen-year-old girls are not especially helpless, but they—and women as a group—are systematically dominated by men as a group. This inequality is deeply implicated in popular notions of eroticism and sexiness.[195]

The *Michael M.* opinions mystify the power relations involved in sexual intercourse by assuming that it is an equal activity. Most feminists would agree that sexual intercourse should be more equal. One might wish that men and women were doing more the same thing when they had intercourse—that they were experiencing the same risks and sharing the same pleasures. There may even be occasions on which one should treat sexual intercourse as though it were an equal activity, because to do so might bring about good changes. But it is not helpful to pretend that sexual intercourse is normally equal.[197] This pretense is an unexamined assumption buried in the *Michael M.* opinions.

The decision in *Michael M.* did not have to mystify sexual intercourse or legitimate the status quo. The case could have been an occasion to examine conditions of sexuality in a society of gender hierarchy.[198] Male sexual aggression could have been exposed as oppressive and illegitimate. Michael's coercive male initiative could have been generalized and delegitimated. Justice Blackmun was correct in noting that Michael was not engaged in especially deviant behavior—

behavior that is properly criminalized because it is so different from everyday sexual interaction. But this should be a condemnation of everyday behavior, rather than a reason to find Michael blameless. Distinguishing Michael's behavior from acceptable male initiative may serve to legitimate everyday coercive sex. But using it as an example of the destructive and coercive elements in sexual relations might delegitimate present sexual arrangements and encourage change.[199]

Conclusion: Toward a New Feminist Jurisprudence

In an earlier article, I tried to open a conversation about means of breaking out of the dichotomy between family and market and about alternatives to this conceptual scheme.[200] I would like to continue that effort here in the same speculative vein, focusing now on the related dichotomy between freedom and security.

Rights analysis and the dominant image of sexuality both try to create realms of freedom for the individual. Both employ a counter-notion of restraint in order to create this realm of freedom. The state restrains the freedom of some to protect the freedom of others. Social controls of sexuality are said to offer similar protection. Under the dominant view, sexuality is a realm of freedom rendered safe by a cordon of state protection designed to assure that sexual behavior is consensual.

Rights analysis sees the individual in social isolation. The risks inherent in human interaction are pretended away by the formal processes of allocating entitlements and drawing lines to settle social conflict. Feminist rights analysis generally pretends that there are no differences between men and women and attempts to advance women by giving them the rights men have. The related attitude toward sexuality pretends that males are not sexually aggressive and attempts to advance women by allowing them to participate in sex as men do. Rights analysis is *modified*—though not basically changed—by feminist arguments for special treatment. The sexual analogue to special treatment recognizes males as aggressive but acts as though merely expanding social control, without changing the nature of social control, will provide a real answer.

One group of feminists focuses on women's ability to be independent sexual actors and to achieve a degree of autonomy; like other oppressed groups, women can and do make the best of what is available to them. Other feminists point out that women's sexuality exists as it does because it is created out of social conditions of oppression. It is wrong, these feminists argue, to interpret women's sexuality as self-expression or autonomy, as though sexism did not exist. What seems to be a split between feminist activists arises from the fact that in conditions of sexual inequality, women are oppressed by both sexual freedom and societal control of sexuality. Sexual freedom turns out to be freedom for men to exploit women; the burden of social control of sexuality falls primarily upon women. Of course, all culture is formed under conditions of various limitations and scarcity and much of culture is created under conditions of external domination. But this doesn't answer the question how to make the best of it and go on. Instead of arguing about which is worse—men's exploitation of women or the state's repression of women—let us devise strategies to overcome both.

To go beyond liberal-legalism, we should stop trying to fit our goals into abstract rights arguments and instead call for what we really want. Similarly, regarding sexuality we should recognize the problems with both social control and sexual freedom and call for a reconstruction of sexuality altogether. As MacKinnon points out, liberalism treats law as a neutral arbiter between conflicting interests and supports state intervention on behalf of women as abstract persons with abstract rights.[201] Just as we must scrutinize the content of these liberal notions, we must scrutinize the content of sexual freedom and social control.

The answer does not lie, however, in a wholehearted embrace of the critique of rights. Although the critique is useful in pointing out the fundamental indeterminacy of rights claims, it sometimes fails to critique the impoverished forms of "community" forced on women. The conditions cannot be changed as long as women are oppressed. When the critique of rights does not recognize the importance of gender, it oversimplifies bourgeois' individualism. Most criticisms of the critique of rights oversimplify the critique of rights by failing to see it as an attack on the entire system that makes rights seem necessary.

Nor is it helpful merely to fiddle with the location of the boundary between sexual freedom and social control. Instead, we must recognize the problem within each of the "spheres" as presently defined. The critique of social control of women and of freedom for men to exploit women is really a way of getting at the broader complaint about the *quality* of sexual freedom and the *nature* of social control. The sexuality debate is focused most sharply by discussion of pornography. Attempts to ban obscene materials can increase their erotic power—social control can be sexy. In response to this concern, some feminists have constructed a new analysis of pornography, an analysis that focuses on the harm pornography does to women[202] rather than on the lack of "redeeming social value" of obscene materials. In a partial attempt to get at the problem of social control, many antipornography feminists reject criminal enforcement typical of obscenity law and attempt to empower the women who are hurt by pornography by giving them a civil cause of action against the pornographer.[204] Although this shift seems to me clearly a step in the right direction, just as giving underage women power over statutory rape prosecutions would be a step in the right direction, neither goes far enough in critiquing the nature of social control. On the other side, most anti-antipornography feminists fail to recognize the extent to which the attack on pornography is an attack on the notion or definition of sexual freedom. The attack on pornography is thus an attack on the whole system of sexuality, a system defined by and for men and designed in such a way that women are silenced, terrorized, or both.

"Repression theory" may capture some aspects of what is wrong with social control in our society, but it also gives ideological support for freeing male sexual aggression and delegitimates women's refusal to respond. Similarly, theories dependent on the oppressiveness of sex capture what is wrong with one realm—sexual freedom—but give ideological support to the oppressive aspects of the other realm; they justify controlling women and delegitimate women's expression of desire.

Even though sex is, to a great extent, eroticized violence and domination, celibacy is no choice for women. It is not enough to empower women to resist male coercion in all its forms; we must also create new choices for women. Suppose, for example, that most men in a particular society wanted sexual intercourse to be an event without emotional entanglements—isolated sex— and that most women wanted sexual intercourse to lead to a strong emotional commitment—sex in exchange for love. Women as a group could alter the societal conditions of sex if they acted jointly,[206] but women acting alone would not have this power. Individual women would not necessarily be any better off if they simply chose not to engage in sex under these conditions than they would be if they just made the best of the sex that was offered. If women did engage in sex, that sex would not be freely chosen, but would be exploitative.

Sexuality is socially constructed. In our male-dominated society, it has been constructed to serve the complex interests of men. Sexuality serves women's interests, if at all, only incidentally, as women can fit in and make the best of what's available.

Isolated sex, promoted by pornography and advertising, and sex in exchange for love, promoted by romance magazines, have both been eroticized, but this does not mean that either is good, natural, or inevitable. Both constructs of sex are obviously incomplete—stunted in complementary ways. Isolated sex seems more destructive in general than sex for love and is certainly more closely related to violence and exploitation. Sex for love, however, may be just as destructive for those who seek it. We cannot start from scratch or write on a clean slate, but we can start with the best of what we have and go on from there. I believe that the best of what we have is sex as an expression of an equal, sharing relationship.[208] There are things we can do to support and further eroticize this conception of sexuality. Ending the subordination of women is one important step in the right direction. Although violence and domination have been eroticized in our society, sex is more complicated. It is defined, or created, in a male-dominated culture, but there are nooks and crannies in which the beginnings of a new sexuality can be discovered.

Notes

5. For example, allowing a woman to sue a pornographer who allegedly caused her to be raped can be justified as enforcement of her right to security, or it can be attacked as violating the pornographer's first amendment right to free expression (or unspecified right to make money). Denying the woman a cause of action can be justified as granting freedom to the pornographer, or it can be attacked as violating the rape victim's right to security.

6. *See, e.g.,* Tushnet, *An Essay on Rights,* 62 TEXAS L. REV. 1363, 1375–82 (1984). It could be argued that rights analysis has a consistency in that people with power have rights and those without do not. For example, some feminists argue that the conflict between rights as security and rights as freedom is made less sharp by privileging men— giving them both freedom and security while depriving women of both. Men can be

secure from women and free to exploit women as long as women do not have rights. As description, this may be all too true, but it does not affect the critique of rights as an analytic tool nor does it argue in favor of conceptualizing social struggles in terms of rights.

70. The double standard of sexual morality has two important aspects. First, nonmarital sex, or sexual activity separated from emotional commitment, is considered desirable for men but devaluing for women. The second aspect is a corollary of the first: some women have to be "immoral" in order to serve as sexual partners for males outside of marriage. Thus, women are categorized as moral or immoral, good girls or bad girls, virgins or whores, wife material or playmate material.

71. It is important to consider a third ground upon which the statutes might be attacked. It can be argued that the statutes legitimate the pervasive reality of male sexual aggression by attempting to police a border between "good" shared sex and "bad" coercive sex. In fact, there is no clear distinction; the exploitative content of so much of sexuality in our society pervades all of its forms. Outlawing certain forms of male coercion to protect particularly vulnerable females can be seen cynically as necessary to prevent us all from becoming aware of the relationship of domination and submission that is built into our basic definitions of heterosexuality. As Catharine MacKinnon puts it: "[I]s ordinary sexuality, under conditions of gender inequality, to be presumed healthy? What if inequality is built into the social conceptions of male and female sexuality, of masculinity and femininity, of sexiness and heterosexual attractiveness? . . . [M]ale sexual desire itself may be aroused by female vulnerability . . . . [S]exual intercourse normally occurs between economic (as well as physical) unequals." C. MACKINNON, [SEXUAL HARASSMENT OF WORKING WOMEN: A CASE OF SEX DISCRIMINATION 219 (1979)]. Sexual intercourse also normally occurs between older men with some social power and younger, less powerful women. MacKinnon concludes: "In this context, the apparent legal requirement that violations of women's sexuality appear out of the ordinary before they will be punished helps prevent women from defining the ordinary conditions of their own consent." *Id.* By isolating those cases in which it is obvious that a young woman had no meaningful choice and that her sexuality was expropriated, statutory rape laws may pacify women by encouraging them to believe that their own choices are voluntary and that they are not exploited in their sexual encounters.

84. CAL. PENAL CODE § 261.5 (West Supp. 1981).

92. Laws and judicial decisions that establish the home and sexuality as spheres of privacy can be seen as protecting the right of individual men to oppress individual women. *See* MacKinnon, [*Feminism, Marxism, Method, and the State: Toward Feminist Jurisprudence*, 8 SIGNS: J. WOMEN IN CULTURE & SOC'Y 635, 656–57 (1983) (hereinafter *Toward Feminist Jurisprudence*)]. Catharine MacKinnon has noted the similarities between the Marxist assertion that workers' labor is expropriated from them and the feminist assertion that women's sexuality is expropriated from them. *See* MacKinnon, *Feminism, Marxism, Method, and the State: An Agenda for Theory*, 7 SIGNS: J. WOMEN IN CULTURE & SOC'Y 515, 515 (1982). For an excellent development of the notion that a woman does not own or control her sexuality, but merely acts as its trustee, see L. CLARK & D. LEWIS, RAPE: THE PRICE OF COERCIVE SEXUALITY (1977).

94. *See* Comment, [*The Constitutionality of Statutory Rape Laws*, 72 UCLA L. REV. 757, 811 (1980)].The testimony at the preliminary hearing in Michael M. v. Superior Court, 450 U.S. 464 (1981), provides one example. The male hit the female in the face two or three times as she resisted his efforts at sexual intercourse. Presumably this could not be prosecuted as forcible rape because before intercourse took place the female gave what is considered legal consent. According to Sharon, "I just said to myself, 'Forget it' and I let him do what he wanted to do. . . ." *Id.* at 485 n.* (Blackmun, J., concurring).

To the State's argument that prosecutors would "commonly invoke [the statutory rape] statute only in cases that actually involve a forcible rape," *id.* at 501 (Stevens, J., dissenting), Justice Stevens responded that this would result in "convicting a [rape] defendant on evidence that is constitutionally insufficient." *Id.* . . .

95. Some incest laws do not protect adopted children and many do not apply to nonrelatives acting *in loco parentis*—such as a parent's nonmarital roommate. *See, e.g.,* CAL. PENAL CODE § 225 (West Supp. 1984); TEX. PENAL CODE ANN. § 25.02 (Vernon 1983).

96. The question whether the coercive apparatus of the state can be used effectively on behalf of women or whether attempts to do so will always divert, coopt, or patronize women has been treated in literature on rape, wife beating, and sexual harassment. *See* MacKinnon, *Introduction,* 10 CAP. U.L. REV. i, viii (Spring 1981); M. Freeman, Violence Against Women: Does the Legal System Provide Solutions or Itself Constitute the Problem? 12 n.161 (1980) (original version of Freeman, [3 CAN. J. FAM. L. 219 (1980)]; *see also* S. SCHECTER, WOMEN AND MALE VIOLENCE 125, 185-202, 241-55 (1982) (arguing that grass-roots movements may be coopted and subverted by government enforcement efforts).

101. Under present laws of forcible rape, the man's characterization of the encounter as consensual or forced is too often determinative. A man's actual belief that the woman consented to intercourse may be a defense, as long as his belief was not grossly unreasonable. *See* Note, [*Shifting the Communication Burden: A Meaningful Consent Standard in Rape,* 6 HARV. WOMEN'S L.J. 143, 144-45 (1983)].

106. The ideological damage would also include reinforcement of the damaging sexist stereotype of the woman who tempts a man into sexual contact and then cries rape.

111. Such a law would rest on the assumption that the evil to be addressed is the coercion of a younger person by an older person. Thus, the age differential approach may be seen as an effort to criminalize intercourse that is presumed to be exploitative, using the age differential as a proxy for exploitation. . . .

114. 450 U.S. 464 (1981).

194. According to this view, statutory rape laws may criminalize "good, equal" sexual intercourse in order to reduce the incidence of teenage pregnancy.

195. Professor MacKinnon offers the most effective statement of this position. *See* C. MACKINNON, *supra* note [71], at 219; MacKinnon, *Not a Moral Issue,* 2 YALE L. & POL'Y REV. 321, 342-45 (1984).

197. It is a mistake to believe that feminists have only two choices: to reject a generalization about women and call it an "outmoded stereotype," or to accept the generalization and embrace it as true and good. *See* Freedman [*Sex Equality, Sex Difference, and the Supreme Court,* 92 YALE L.J. 913, 931-45 (1983)] (discussing these choices). Instead, feminists can acknowledge the elements of truth in the generalization and attempt to change the conditions that make it true. For a sociological study demonstrating that the behavior of men and women has not changed as much as one might think, see P. BLUMSTEIN & P. SCHWARTZ, [AMERICAN COUPLES (1983)].

198. The transcript of Michael's preliminary hearing, *see Michael M.,* 450 U.S. at 483-88 n.* (Blackmun, J., concurring) . . . constitutes an indictment of the warped human relations that take place in a gender-stratified society. The testimony captures the confused yearnings for closeness and the frustrated anger that can make adolescence such a painful time—for both females and males—in our society.

199. For a discussion of how difficult it may be to resist legitimating the status quo, see Olsen, *Socrates on Legal Obligation: Legitimation Theory and Civil Disobedience,* 18 GA. L. REV. 929, 950-57 (1984).

One of the basic premises underlying most feminist legal writing is that we can move toward a more just and equal society by establishing rights for women and enforcing these rights. This is sometimes thought to require only the equal application of sex-neutral rules; at other times it is asserted that fairness can be achieved only by balancing competing rights or by refining our system of rules to make them neutral in practice as well as in form. In either case, the basic strategy is to establish a system of impartial rules that will apply equally to all and thus ensure that we can pursue our individual goals without harming one another.

But feminist legal criticism is most successful as it moves away from these notions and into the risky territory of real concerns that are political rather than neutral or impartial. Abstract rights and neutral rules are devices used by feminists to deny what we really want while getting what we want indirectly.

200. *See* Olsen, [*The Family and the Market: A Study of Ideology and Legal Reform,* HARV. L. REV. 1497, 1560 & n.241 (1983)].

201. *See* MacKinnon, [*Toward Feminist Jurisprudence, supra* note 92], at 642.

202. *See* MacKinnon, [*Not a Moral Issue*], *supra* note 195.

204. At least two city councils recently enacted ordinances empowering women to take such action. *See* Minneapolis, Minn., Ordinance Amending tit. 7, chs. 139, 141, Minneapolis Code Ordinances Relating to Civil Rights (Dec. 30, 1983) (vetoed 1984); Indianapolis, Ind., General Ordinances 24 (April 23, 1984) (amended June 1984). The Indianapolis ordinance was declared unconstitutional in American Booksellers Ass'n v. Hudnut, [771 F.2d 323, *aff'd mem.* 475 U.S. 1001, *reh. den.* 475 U.S. 1132 (1986)].

206. *Cf.* ARISTOPHANES, LYSISTRATA (depicting a successful sex strike by women, but to war, not to change social conditions of sexuality).

208. I don't know what sexuality might become in a nonsexist society. I offer these speculations simply as an opening statement. They do not result from or depend upon the critique presented in this Article, nor does that critique in any sense depend upon these speculations. I would hope that the reader who finds my reconstruction of sexuality unappealing will not discount my critique, but will instead propose an alternative reconstruction.

15

The Dialectic of Rights and Politics: Perspectives from the Women's Movement [1986]

Elizabeth M. Schneider

. . .

The Debate on Rights

The idea that legal rights have some intrinsic value is widespread in our culture. A rights claim can make a statement of entitlement that is universal and categorical. This entitlement can be seen as negative because it protects against intrusion by the state (a right to privacy), or the same right can be seen as affirmative because it enables an individual to do something (a right to choose whether to bear a child). Thus, a rights claim can define the boundaries of state power and the entitlement to do something, and, by extension, provide an affirmative vision of human society. Rights claims reflect a normative theory of the person, but a normative theory can see the rights-bearing individual as isolated or it can see the individual as part of a larger social network. Recently, legal scholars, in particular CLS and feminist scholars, have debated the meanings of rights claims and have questioned the significance of legal argumentation focused on rights.

CLS scholars question whether rights claims and rights discourse can facilitate social reconstruction. The CLS critique has several interrelated themes which flow from a more general critique of liberalism. CLS scholars argue that liberalism is premised on dichotomies, such as individual and community or self and other, that divide the world into two mutually exclusive spheres. Rights claims only perpetuate these dichotomies, which, to CLS scholars, limit legal thinking and inhibit necessary social change. CLS scholars base their critique of rights on the inherently individualistic nature of rights under legal liberalism, the "reification" of rights generally, and the indeterminate nature of rights claims.

CLS scholars argue that rights are "permeated by the possessive individualism of capitalist society."[22] Because rights "belong" to individuals—rights rhetoric portrays individuals as "separated owners of their respective bundles of rights[23]—they are necessarily individualistic." This notion of ownership delimits the boundaries of state authority from that of individual autonomy, the self from other. Rights discourse tends to overemphasize the separation of the individual from the group, and thereby inhibits an individual's awareness of her connection to and mutual dependence upon others.

CLS scholars also see rights discourse as taking on a "thing-like" quality—a fixed and external meaning—that "freezes and falsifies" rich and complex social experience.[25] This "attribution of a thing-like or fixed character to socially constructed phenomena," called reification, "is an essential aspect of alienated consciousness, leading people to accept existing social orders as the inevitable 'facts of life.' "[26] This process thus gives people a sense of "substitute connection" and an illusory sense of community that disables any real connection. Finally, these scholars see rights claims as indeterminate because argumentation based on rights does not solve the problem of how to resolve conflicts between rights and cannot transform social relations.

CLS scholars criticize the use of rights claims by social movement groups on related grounds. They argue that the use of rights discourse by a social movement group and the consequent reliance on rights can keep people passive and dependent upon the state because it is the state which grants them their rights. Individuals are only allowed to act—to "exercise their rights"—to the degree to which the state permits. Legal strategies based on rights discourse, then, tend to weaken the power of a popular movement by allowing the state to define the movement's goals. Rights discourse obscures real political choice and determination. Further, it fosters social antagonisms by magnifying disagreement within and conflicts between groups over rights. From a strategic perspective, then, reliance on rights by social movements can be politically debilitating. . . .

Some feminist critiques of rights see rights claims as formal and hierarchical—premised on a view of law as patriarchal. From this perspective, law generally, and rights particularly, reflect a male viewpoint characterized by objectivity, distance, and abstraction. As Catharine MacKinnon, a leading exponent of this position writes, "Abstract rights will authorize the male experience of the world."[40] . . .

Some legal writers see similarities between the CLS critique of rights based on "liberal legalism" and the feminist critique based on "patriarchy." Both liberal legalism and patriarchy rely upon the same set of dichotomies. Further, the critiques usefully emphasize the indeterminacy of rights, and the ways in which rights discourse can reinforce alienation and passivity. Both critiques highlight the ways in which rights discourse can become divorced from political struggle. They appropriately warn us of the dangers social movements and lawyers encounter when relying on rights to effect social change.

But both critiques are incomplete. They do not take account of the complex, and I suggest dialectical, relationship between the assertion of rights and political struggle in social movement practice. They see only the limits of rights, and fail to appreciate the dual possibilities of rights discourse. Admittedly, rights discourse can reinforce alienation and individualism, and can constrict political vision and debate. But, at the same time, it can help to affirm human values, enhance political growth, and assist in the development of collective identity.

By failing to see that both possibilities exist simultaneously, these critiques have rigidified, rather than challenged, the classic dichotomies of liberal thought—law and politics, individual and community, and ultimately, rights and politics. Radical social theory, such as CLS and feminist scholarship, must explore the dialectical dimensions of each dichotomy, not reinforce the sense that the dichotomies are frozen and static. Radical social theory must explain how these dichotomies can be transcended.

Dialectics and Praxis as Methodology: The Examples of Feminist Theory and Feminist Legal Practice

My perspective on rights is grounded in a view of the dialectical nature of consciousness and social change and a view that theory and practice must be understood as interrelated. . . . My effort is to transcend the purported oppositions of rights and politics, theory and practice, individual and community, and to understand their dialectical relationship. In this way, I . . . describe how two purportedly contradictory notions can, at the same time, be inextricably linked to one another, such as the liberating and constraining aspects of rights discourse. Rights discourse may sometimes appear to be distinct from politics and an obstacle to political growth, but it is actually part of the larger process of political struggle.

The concept of dialectics has shaped much of contemporary social theory and has developed different meanings and uses. Most significantly here, it stands for the idea of the process, connection, and opposition of dualities, and for subsequent change and transcendence. The dialectical approach that I use . . . explores the process which connects ideas that appear to be in opposition to one another. One "moment" in the process gives rise to its own negation, and "out of this negativity, emerges a 'moment' which at once negates, affirms, and transcends the 'moment' involved in the struggle."[50] Thus, an idea may be both what it appears to be and something else at the same time; the idea may contain the seeds of its own contradiction, and ideas that appear to be in opposition may really be the same or connected. At any given "moment," ideas may appear to be connected or in opposition because this connection or opposition exists in only one stage of a larger process. The dialectical process is not a mechanical confrontation of an opposite from outside, but an organic emergence and development of opposition and change from within the "moment" or idea itself.

The critiques of rights that I have described suffer from an analysis that divorces theory from practice. Rights are analyzed in the abstract, viewed as static—as a form of legal theory separate from social practice—and then criticized for being formal and abstract. My approach to rights views theory and practice as dialectically related, and I look to the philosophical concept of praxis to describe this process. The fundamental aspect of praxis is the active role of consciousness and subjectivity in shaping both theory and practice, and the dynamic interrelationship that results. . . . [M]y focus on praxis impels me to explore how rights claims can flow from and express the political and moral aspirations of a social movement group, how rights claims are experienced or perceived in social movement practice, and how rights discourse impacts on social movement practice generally. . . .

. . . Both feminist theory and feminist legal practice exemplify aspects of this methodological perspective and shape my approach to rights. . . . Feminist theory is characterized by an emphasis on dialectical process and the interrelationship of theory and practice. Feminist theory emphasizes the value of direct and personal experience as the place that theory should begin, as embodied in the phrase "the personal is political." This phrase reflects the view that the realm of personal experience, the "private" which has always been trivialized, particularly for women, is an appropriate and important subject of public inquiry, and that the "private" and "public" worlds are inextricably linked. The notion of consciousness-raising as feminist method flows from this insight. In consciousness-raising groups, learning starts with the individual and personal (the private), moves to the general and social (the public), and then reflects back on itself with heightened consciousness through this shared group process. Consciousness-raising as feminist method is a form of praxis because it transcends the theory and practice dichotomy. Consciousness-raising groups start with personal and concrete experience, integrate this experience into theory, and then, in effect, reshape theory based upon experience and experience based upon theory. Theory expresses and grows out of experience but it also relates back to that experience for further refinement, validation, or modification.

The idea of consciousness-raising as a method of analysis suggests an approach to social change which recognizes dynamic tension, reflection, and sharing as essential aspects of growth. Feminist theory values this process which starts with experience, generalizes through self-reflection and evaluation, and then returns to experience. This dialectical process transcends the oppositions of self and other, public and private, individual and community, and is simultaneously grounded in an understanding that any connections between these apparent dualisms will be only partial and tentative, and that distinctions will again emerge.

Feminist theory thus reveals the social dimension of individual experience and the individual dimension of social experience. . . .

The fact that this process begins with the self, and then connects to the larger world of women, is important. For feminists, theory is not "out there," but rather is based on the concrete, daily, and "trivial" experiences of individuals, and so emerges from the shared experience of women talking. Because feminist theory grows out of direct experience and consciousness actively asserting itself, feminist theory emphasizes context and the importance of identifying experience and claiming it for one's own.

Feminist theory involves a particular methodology, but it also has a substantive viewpoint and political orientation. Recognizing the links between individual change and social change means understanding the importance of political *activity*, not just theory. Theory emerges from practice and practice then informs and reshapes theory. At the same time, because of its dialectical cast, feminist theory encompasses a notion of process that encourages a grounded and reflective appreciation of this interrelationship—its possibilities and limits, visions and defeats. . . .

Towards a Dialectical Understanding of Rights and Politics: Women's Rights and Feminist Struggle

. . . A dialectical perspective . . . sees rights and politics as part of a . . . dynamic [and] complex . . . process characterized by the possibility that rights discourse can simultaneously advance and obscure political growth and vision. A dialectical view of rights develops the expressive, transformative, and prob-lematic aspects of rights. . . .

. . . Rights discourse can be an alienated and artificial language that constricts political debate. But it can also be a means to articulate new values and political vision. The way in which a social movement group uses the rights claim and places it in a broader context affects the ability of rights discourse to aid political struggle. Rights discourse and rights claims, when emerging from and organically linked to political struggle, can help to develop political consciousness which can play a useful role in the development of a social movement.

Rights discourse can express human and communal values; it can be a way for individuals to develop a sense of self and for a group to develop a collective identity. Rights discourse can also have a dimension that emphasizes the interdependence of autonomy and community. It can play an important role in giving individuals a sense of self-definition, in connecting the individual to a larger group and community, and in defining the goals of a political struggle, particularly during the early development of a social movement. . . .

Recent experience with claims of legal rights for women suggests the importance of understanding the relationship between rights and political struggle from a dialectical perspective. This experience demonstrates the richly textured process by which a social movement group articulates political demands through a rights claim and the way in which that claim affects the development of the group. Most significantly, the experience of the women's rights movement simultaneously reveals the communal possibilities of rights and underscores the limits of political strategy focused on rights. . . .

. . . A claim of right can make a political statement and transmit a powerful message concerning "the kind of society we want to live in, the kind of relations among people we wish to foster and the kind of behavior that is to be praised or blamed. [It] is a moral claim about how human beings should act toward one another."[182] . . . [O]n an individual level, a claim of right can be an assertion of one's self-worth and an affirmation of one's moral value and entitlement. Claims of women's rights are "a way for a woman to make a claim about herself and her role in the world."[183]

The women's rights movement has had an important affirming and individuating effect on women's consciousness. The articulation of women's rights provides a sense of self and distinction for individual women, while at the same time giving women an important sense of collective identity. Through this articulation, women's voices and concerns are heard in a public forum and afforded a legal vehicle for expression.

But rights claims do not only define women's individual and collective experience, they also actively shape public discourse. Claims of equal rights and reproductive choice, for example, empowered women. Women as a class had not previously been included within the reach of the fourteenth amendment. Women's concerns now rose to the level of constitutional (serious, grown-up) concerns. By claiming rights, women asserted their intention to be taken seriously in society. . . . Women's interests, previously relegated to the private sphere, and therefore outside the public protection of the law, now received the protection of the Constitution. The claims reinforced on a powerful ideological level that the "personal is political" and changed previously private concerns into public ones that needed to be dealt with by the society at large.

The public nature of rights assertion is especially significant because of the private nature of discrimination against women. The locus of women's subordination is frequently the private and individual sphere—the home and family—and is thus perceived as isolated and experienced in isolation. Women also tend to see individual fault rather than to identify a systemic pattern of social discrimination. . . . The assertion of rights claims and use of rights discourse help women to overcome this sense of privatization and of personal blame which has perpetuated women's subordination. Rights claims and rights discourse have thus had a self-defining aspect as well as a collective dimension because the inner experience of the right ties the individual and her particular experiences to the larger experiences of women as a class. Rights claims assert women's selfhood collectively, thereby giving women a sense of group identity and pride; they make manifest the fact that women can act and claim their place in history. . . .

At the same time, the women's movement's experience with rights suffers from some of the problems discussed by rights critics. First, in some sense the idea of equal rights, although radical in conception, has not captured the scope and depth of the feminist program. Women's rights have been, in a sense, "too little" for the women's movement, although perhaps "too much" for society. Feminists understand that genuine equality for women will not be achieved simply by winning rights in court. Rather, equality requires social reconstruction of gender roles within the workplace and the family. Rights claims, however, do not effectively challenge existing social structures. Reflecting on the reproductive rights experience, Rosalind Petchesky wrote:

> [T]he concept of "rights," [is,] in general, a concept that is inherently static and abstracted from social conditions. Rights are by definition claims staked within a given order of things. They are demands for access for oneself, or for "no

admittance" to others; but they do not challenge the social structure, the social relations of production and reproduction. The claim for "abortion rights" seeks access to a necessary service, but by itself it fails to address the social relations and sexual divisions around which responsibility for pregnancy and children is assigned. In real-life struggles, this limitation exacts a price, for it lets men and society neatly off the hook.[203]

Second, the articulation of a right can, despite a movement's best efforts, put the focus of immediate political struggle on winning the right in court. Thus, even if one is concerned with and understands the need for social reconstruction, it is hard to sustain an understanding of short term goals at the same time. The concreteness and immediacy of legal struggle tends to subsume the more diffuse role of political organizing and education. Thus, while there has been a positive attitude toward the use of legal rights in court as an aspect of law reform work, the problems with rights have caused the women's movement to view the use of rights with some ambivalence.

Third, since women's rights formulations oblige the state to act, serious questions about the appropriate role of the state in the context of women's rights have emerged. Women's rights litigators argue that by fighting for women's rights in the courts they do not exclusively rely on the state. However, feminist skepticism over the ability of the state to help women understandably heightens concern over feminist law reform efforts both in the courts and the legislatures.

Finally, despite some substantive gains in the legal treatment of women, rights claims generally have had only limited success in the courts. . . . For example, even though women's rights to reproductive choice have improved, access to those rights for poor women and especially poor women of color has not been adequately protected. More generally, even with concrete legal gains, it is not clear how the lives of most women, particularly poor women and women of color, have changed. Certainly women's economic realities have not improved.

Yet in some areas of women's rights, there have been important victories for individual women, for women as a class, and for the development of substantive legal doctrine. Public consciousness of sex discrimination in the law, for example, has increased. Looking at the gains and losses together, I believe that the struggles around legal rights have moved the women's movement forward and reinforced a sense of collective experience for the movement. . . .

Rights to Equality and Reproductive Choice

The women's rights movement articulated women's right to equal treatment as a claim of equal protection under the fourteenth amendment, and women's right to procreative freedom as a claim of liberty and privacy under the due process clause of the fourteenth amendment. The way in which equality and reproductive rights issues were formulated by women and distorted and limited by the courts raises serious questions about how rights claims affect social movements.

The issue of equal treatment poses the theoretical problem of sameness and difference. Equal protection of the law is guaranteed only to those who are similarly situated. Thus, the issue for equality theory is comparative—who is the same as whom. In deciding this issue of comparability, difficult questions must be considered concerning whose standards are the norm, whether women and men really are different, what differences are real (biologically based or socially constructed), and whether these differences, if they do exist, really matter.

The comparative equal rights approach has had limited political and doctrinal success in the courts and legislatures. . . . [D]espite efforts by feminist litigators to formulate women's rights claims as if no differences existed between men and women, the Supreme Court has read in differences. [In addition], the Supreme Court has viewed equality claims as distinct from reproductive choice claims. Despite the vigorous efforts of feminist litigators to argue that pregnancy discrimination violates equality principles, the Supreme Court has held that since the capacity to become pregnant is "unique" to women, rules concerning pregnancy do not violate equal protection.[223] Thus, despite widespread acknowledgement by the women's movement of the centrality of pregnancy and reproductive choice to women's subordination, pregnancy and reproductive choice have not been seen by the Court as problems of equality.

The movement for reproductive choice played a critical role in the early development of the women's movement. In the early 1970s large groups of women organized to demonstrate against state laws that criminalized abortion and to challenge abortion laws in the courts. Although feminists articulated this "women's right" as a right to liberty, the Supreme Court in *Roe v. Wade*[226] decided the issue on privacy grounds. Thus, in *Roe*, a woman's right to choose whether to have an abortion was seen as a woman's private decision, which left her free from state and medical interference in the first trimester, but allowed the state's interest in the decision to increase in the second trimester and eventually outweigh her interest in the third trimester.

The development of women's rights to equality and reproductive choice [has] had an important ideological effect on the women's rights movement, but the doctrinal evolution of these rights, as the reproductive rights example suggests, has muddied their ideological meaning. First, feminist commentators widely believe that the Court's distinct theoretical articulation of reproductive control as a right to privacy separate from equality constrains political analysis on both a practical and ideological level and reinforces ideological separation of deeply interrelated oppression.

Second, feminist commentators find the very articulation of the women's right to procreative freedom as a matter of privacy to be problematic, because it reinforces and legitimizes the public and private dichotomy which historically has been damaging to women. For women, the domestic sphere and sexuality—primary areas of subordination—have been viewed as private and unregulated. Although the right has a powerful collective dimension which could be used to emphasize group values as well as to develop the strands of individual autonomy, as interpreted by the Court, it is primarily individualistic in that it simply protects an individual's right to choose. Most significantly, analyzing the right to reproductive choice as a right of privacy emphasizes the process of decision making, which entails a balancing of interests throughout the term of the pregnancy, rather than the importance of abortion itself, which concerns the control that a woman should have over her own body and life decisions.

On the other hand, the impact on social movements of a court's particular decision or doctrinal formulation cannot be easily measured. For example, how do we know what effect the doctrinal limitations which the Supreme Court has placed on the right to reproductive choice has had on the consciousness and politics of the women's movement? How do we know that the Court's rejection of the right to liberty and the narrower characterization of the reproductive right as a right of privacy have not affected the women's movement's understanding, for instance, of issues of doctor-patient relationships or state-funded abortion? Winning the right to procreative choice in the Supreme Court certainly helped many women regardless of the particular doctrinal formulation developed. Winning it as a right of privacy may have given some activists a false sense of security, but it has led others to greater insights into the mutable nature of the legal right to choose.

Ultimately, women's rights formulations by both feminists and the courts are best considered from a dialectical perspective. On an ideological level, the formulation of women's rights in both the equality and reproductive rights contexts has simultaneously expanded and limited our perspective on women's subordination. In both contexts, the articulation of the right was necessary to allow new contradictions to unfold.

The equal rights focus of the early women's movement is a good example. The emphasis on equal rights, which reflected an egalitarian strain in the women's movement and has historically dominated the women's movement, was adopted for several reasons. The contemporary women's movement grew out of the civil rights struggle. Thus, there was a strategic orientation to analogize to the civil rights experience, this time struggling to include sex within the ambit of the fourteenth amendment and to ensure passage of the equal rights amendment. The women's movement also recognized the risks of asserting a distinct women's perspective and asserting differences because difference had historically led to paternalism and exclusion.

This emphasis on equality rights, however, although understandable, arguably narrowed the movement's focus and constricted its vision of possible change. It certainly tended to cause women to analyze their experience from a comparative perspective and to stress political debate over equal treatment with men, rather than over empowerment, self-actualization, or "women-centered" perspectives generally. This limitation on the scope of equality rights was also encouraged by the fact that many of the plaintiffs raising and benefitting from equal rights claims were men. The factual context of much litigation that featured an individual plaintiff's attempt to "get" something from society, such as military dependents' benefits, increased social security, property tax exemptions, or admission to a sex-segregated nursing school, appeared to narrow the focus of equality rights even further.

Moreover, because the women's movement articulated its equality concerns using a rights language that frequently becomes symbolic and reified, the movement's ability to account for the range of potential political strategies and to determine appropriate reforms in any given area became more difficult. The equal rights perspective also made it easier for women to avoid the complex question of biological and social differences. Finally, some argue that the pervasiveness of an equality perspective contributed to an emphasis within the women's movement on the "symbolic" equality of rules that reflected formal, as opposed to substantive, fairness and justice.

Nevertheless, the struggle over equal rights was a necessary development for the women's movement. Through the beginning efforts to articulate equal rights, the women's movement acquired a broader and clearer understanding of what it wanted, what obstacles it faced, how deep the phenomenon of sexism went, and how hard it was to affect meaningful change. The movement also learned about the limitations and inadequacies of rights to perform the prerequisite economic and social reconstruction for meaningful change for women. The development of an equality perspective enabled women to understand the tenacity of "neutral" standards based on male experience and legitimized discussion of equality within public discourse.

Further, both the legal movements for equal rights and reproductive rights emerged organically out of the women's movement. At the grass roots level, the movement helped to shape legal strategies, particularly for reproductive rights. The articulation of these rights expressed a collective project that began with a description of women's experience, translated that experience into legal formulation, and through that formulation asserted a demand for power.

In a certain sense, these claims, articulated in the language of rights, have advanced the political development and organizing potential of the movement, and expanded and concretized the consciousness of feminist activists and litigators. By thus providing a public vehicle for expressing what women want, the rights struggle clarified and heightened the debates within the movement itself and then turned these insights back into theory. . . .

Both the right to equality and the right to reproductive choice are rights derived from the contexts of political struggle and feminist organization. Both rights emerged from a radical feminist vision that equality was not limited to formal legal treatment or assimilation of women into male roles, but rather required the radical restructuring of society. The expression of these visions began with the formulation of rights claims in the courts. Yet even though these visions have neither been nor could be achieved in the courts, their introduction through rights claims started the "conversation" in society at large about women's roles and women's subordination under the law.

The radical impulse behind the notion of women's equality and reproductive control, then, is powerful. By concretizing an abstract idea and situating it within women's experience, these rights claims did not simply "occupy" an existing right, but rather modified and transformed the nature of the right. These claims, then derived from concrete struggle and political vision, articulate a notion of collective experience. They do not simply reflect an individual woman's claim, but rather have a communal dimension that can expand opportunities for women as a class.

Sexual Harassment and Battering

Both the concept of sexual harassment and the notion of legal protection for battered women emerged directly from feminist thinking on issues of sexuality in the 1970s. Both areas suggest the importance of legal thinking tied to political struggle and to the experience of women themselves.

The history of sexual harassment is an important example of the creative development of rights.[253] The experience of what is now called sexual harassment did not even have a name until feminist thinkers provided it with one. Widely practiced, it was viewed as a normal and inevitable activity of men when exposed to female co-workers. The idea of sexual harassment as a harm, and as an experience that was not simply normal, private, or individual to one woman, was developed through the work of feminist theorists and litigators. This work gave formerly private and hidden experience a public dimension and so legitimized it as a subject of public discourse.

Sexual harassment defined an injury to an individual woman and to women as a class from a woman's perspective. It emerged out of feminist perceptions and theories about the role of sexuality and from an effort to name and define women's experience and oppression. It developed as part of an effort to assist women in asserting control over their sexuality. The concept of sexual harassment and the definition of harm that developed reflected the methodology of consciousness-raising applied to law.

At the same time, the articulation of claims of sexual harassment has led to the unfolding of new problems, arising in part because of the very gains realized in the recognition of sexual harassment as a cognizable wrong. These new dilemmas concern the scope of employer liability, visions of women as sexual victims, not actors, and victim-precipitation.[260] These tensions highlight important concerns which can then reshape theory and so push feminist analysis forward.

The assertion of rights for battered women developed as an outgrowth of the women's movement experience and the insights of feminist theory. In the 1970s, projects to help battered women suddenly appeared throughout the United States, and by the 1980s a real national battered women's movement existed. Legal claims emerging from this movement, based on the right of battered women to protection from abuse, revealed important dimensions of patriarchy. The movement sought to change police practices, develop legislation to criminalize battering, enforce the victim's rights, and increase a victim's protection and legal options. Some of these legislative reforms made particularly creative connections between battering and patriarchy as, for example, state legislation which used money from marriage license fees to fund battered women's shelters. The claim that women had a right not to be battered, a right to require husbands to leave the house, and a right to get orders of protection emerged from the efforts of feminist activists and thinkers to define the problem of battering.

Both the articulation of the right to be free from sexual harassment and claims for legal protection of battered women appear more affirmative and less problematic than the previous rights struggle over equality. Legal challenges involving equality have not explicitly argued for the social reconstruction necessary to help women achieve sufficient freedom and equality. The legal formulation of the battered women and sexual harassment rights claims, however, flows more directly from the political statement that these claims of right make than does the formulation of equal rights claims. Is it because the political message and demand of these claims is narrower, simpler, or clearer? Is it because these claims have done better, thus far, in the courts? Or is it because the development of both legal rights is at an earlier stage than that of equality and reproductive rights? Both sexual harassment and battered women's rights emerged directly out of collectively developed political theory and practice concerning patriarchy and sexuality. The theory exposed new harms and expanded understanding by labeling these previously private issues as public harms. The claims of right reflected a shared political understanding that women needed to be free from sexual subordination and violence and made important statements about women's autonomy. Moreover, the scope of both rights as articulated by feminist litigation was broad. For example, sexual harassment claims did not simply rest on the employment treatment of individual women, but rather on a broader understanding of how a workplace environment can be tainted by sexual harassment and innuendo, and therefore harm all women who work there. In addition, the claims as articulated recognized the connection between the individual and collective components of the claim. Similarly, in the battered women context, the idea that women needed ex parte orders of protection and that police owed a duty of care to battered women transcended the individual dimension of the claim and illuminated the problems of patriarchy.

Further, the articulation of these rights claims developed feminist theory in several important ways. For example, in the battered women's movement, claims of right in both civil and criminal contexts raised important questions for feminists about how to view the state. The claims sharpened debate over the role of law in modifying the public and private dichotomy, especially given the historic absence of law in the area of domestic relations generally. Debates over whether feminists should support criminalization and other reform efforts within the criminal justice system to ameliorate the problem of battering clarified the need for a feminist theory of the state that neither expressly relied upon nor rejected the state. These debates underscored the ideological function of criminalization in defining battery as a public and not a private harm, and heightened the movement's analysis of reforms for battered women. For instance, reforms could focus on the individual "bad" man, or the individual woman's "victimization," but they then would not address the shared experience of battered women, the common problems of patriarchy, the conditions that create or perpetuate violence against women, or the economic and social resources—jobs, child care, housing—that battered women need to free themselves from dependence.

Some within the battered women's movement have been sensitive to these tensions and have recognized the need for litigation and legal reforms in the context of political organizing and education. These advocates have sought to consider reform efforts within a theoretical framework that focuses on the political effect and message of these efforts. Such an approach evaluates a reform based on whether it helps to redress the balance of power within the family, emphasize the broader experience of sex discrimination within the family (rather than individual victimization), and challenge the public and private dichotomy. Most significantly, this approach evaluates whether a particular reform helps to strengthen the women's movement and organize more women. This approach underscores the role that rights claims can play in furthering political development.

In both the areas of sexual harassment and legal treatment of battered women, rights claims have strengthened public consciousness on the issues and illuminated broader political perceptions of patriarchy and sexual subordination. The women's movement has begun to reshape the law in women's terms and has thus exposed new dilemmas and challenges. This effort to reshape law through the articulation of legal rights has been an important aspect of the political struggle around these issues.

A Dialectical Perspective Reconsidered

What does an examination of the practice and experience of the women's rights movement reveal about rights? Does it suggest that a dialectical approach to the relationship between rights and politics is appropriate? I want to draw some implications for theory from the women's movement's experience with rights and relate this experience to the earlier discussion of a dialectical perspective.

The women's movement's experience with rights shows how rights emerge from political struggle. The legal formulation of the rights grew out of and reflected feminist experience and vision and culminated in a political demand for power. The articulation of feminist theory in practice in turn heightened feminist consciousness of theoretical dilemmas and at the same time advanced feminist theoretical development. This experience, reflecting the dynamic interrelationship of theory and practice, mirrored the experience of the women's movement in general.

This analysis of the women's rights movement, shaped by an understanding of praxis, reveals a conception of both the process through which rights are formulated as well as the content of the rights themselves. The process had been "regenerative" as rights were developed in the "middle," not at the "end," of political dialogue. Rights were the product of consciousness-raising and were often articulated by both political activists and lawyers translating and explaining their own experience. Further, rights asserted in the context of the women's movement enabled women to develop an individual and collective identity as women and to understand the connection between individual and community. The articulation of rights, then, has been a means of projecting, reflecting, and building upon a burgeoning sense of community developing within the women's movement.

The content of these rights contained both individual and communal dimensions. A particular right did not simply benefit a particular woman, but rather benefitted women as a class. Rights claims illuminated and expressed experiences of women as a class because newly developed perceptions of women's experience defined and gave meaning to the individual claims of rights. . . .

In fairness, it could be said that the content of women's rights in all these areas was "traditional" or individualistic. But this characterization minimizes the importance of context. Since rights in the women's movement experience emerged in the middle of "conversation," and began a process of articulating political vision connected to political program, their meaning and content have been closely tied to the political practice of the women's movement. If the rights claim is part of a larger process and the movement believes that the rights claim expresses its vision, the claim is likely to have a greater impact on the movement itself. If the movement sees rights claims as an integral part of the struggle, but not the exclusive focus, the process of rights assertion will more likely activate, than pacify, the social movement. . . .

The articulation of rights claims energized the women's movement and started the conversation. But once a right is articulated, or even won, the issues change. How will the right be applied? How will it be enforced? Women's rights have been necessary for the political development of women, particularly because they combat the privatization of women's oppression. However, rights, although they must vigorously be fought for, cannot perform the task of social reconstruction. The present economic crisis for women in this country underscores the need for a radical redefinition of social and economic responsibility and a restructuring of work and family which would transform the lives of women, particularly the many women who live in poverty. Rights, even rights which are interdependent, can only begin to help people organize themselves and identify with larger groups. . . .

The experience of rights in the women's movement supports the need for a perspective on rights and politics grounded in a dialectical sensibility, a view that allows us to acknowledge both the universal, affirming, expressive, and creative aspects of rights claims and at the same time, maintain a critical impulse towards rights. We must hold on to and not seek to deny the contradictions between the possibilities and the limits of rights claims and discourse. In the women's movement, a wide range of feminist activists and commentators have participated in a broad critique of rights analysis, both on theoretical and practical levels. A common theme of these critiques has been the need to strengthen legal challenges for equal rights while at the same time not limiting our vision to a narrow conception of rights. We need to continue to strive for a political strategy that expresses a politics and vision of social reconstruction sensitive to women's real concerns. Legal strategy must be developed in the context of political strategy. It should attack formal doctrinal barriers which inhibit the recognition of the interconnectedness of women's oppression and look at the particular factual context of discrimination in shaping legal responses.

A struggle for rights can be both a vehicle of politics and an affirmation of who we are and what we seek. Rights can be what we make of them and how we use them. The experience of rights assertion in the women's movement can move us forward to a self-reflective recognition of the importance and the limitations of political and legal strategy that utilizes rights.

Notes

22. Lynd, Communal Rights, 62 Tex. L. Rev. 1417, 1418 (1984). . . .

23. Olsen, [Statutory Rape: A Feminist Critique of Rights Analysis, 63 Tex. L. Rev. 387, 393 (1984)].

25. Gabel & Kennedy, Roll Over Beethoven, 36 Stan. L. Rev. 1, 3–6 (1984). . . .

26. Gabel & Harris [Building Power and Breaking Images: Critical Legal Theory and the Practice of Law, 11 N.Y.U. Rev. Law & Soc. Change 369, 373 n.10 (1982–83)].

40. MacKinnon, [Feminism, Marxism, Method and the State: Toward Feminist Jurisprudence, 8 Signs: J. Women Culture & Soc'y 635, 658 (1983)].

50. [R. Bernstein, Praxis and Action 20–21 (1971)].

182. [Olsen, supra note 23, at 391.]

183. Id.

203. R. Petchesky, Abortion and Woman's Choice 7 (1984) (footnote omitted). . . .

223. Geduldig v. Aiello, 417 U.S. 484, 492–97 (1974). . . .

226. 410 U.S. 113 (1973).

253. For the history of the development of sexual harassment as a legal claim, see generally C. MacKinnon, [Sexual Harassment of Working Women (1979)]; MacKinnon, Introduction, Symposium: Sexual Harassment, 10 Cap. U.L. Rev. i (1981).

260. See Meritor Sav. Bank v. Vinson, 106 S. Ct. 2399, 2406–09 (1986).

16

Feminist Critical Theories [1990]

Deborah L. Rhode

. . .

I. Theoretical Premises

Critical feminism, like other critical approaches, builds on recent currents in social theory that have made theorizing increasingly problematic. Post-modern and post-structural traditions that have influenced left legal critics presuppose the social construction of knowledge.[8] To varying degrees, critics within these traditions deny the possibility of any universal foundations for critique. Taken as a whole, their work underscores the cultural, historical, and linguistic construction of human identity and social experience.[9]

Yet such a theoretical stance also limits its own aspirations to authority. For feminists, this post-modern paradox creates political as well as theoretical difficulties. Adherents are left in the awkward position of maintaining that gender oppression exists while challenging our capacity to document it.[10] Such awkwardness is, for example, especially pronounced in works that assert as unproblematic certain "facts" about the pervasiveness of sexual abuse while questioning the possibility of any objective measure.[11]

To take an obvious illustration, feminists have a stake both in quantifying the frequency of rape, and in questioning the conventional definitions on which rape statistics are based. Victims of sexual assault by acquaintances often respond to questions such as, "Have you ever been raped?" with something like, "Well . . . not exactly." What occurs in the pause between "well" and "not exactly" suggests the gap between the legal understanding and social experience of rape, and the ways in which data on abuse are constructed, not simply collected.[12]

Although responses to this dilemma vary widely, the most common feminist strategies bear mention. The simplest approach is to decline to address the problem—at least at the level of abstraction at which it is customarily formulated. The revolution will not be made with slogans from Lyotard's *Postmodern Condition,* and the audiences that are most in need of persuasion are seldom interested in epistemological anxieties. Critiques of existing ideology and in-stitutions can proceed under their own standards without detailed discussions of the philosophy of knowledge. Yet, even from a purely pragmatic view, it is helpful to have some self-consciousness about the grounding for our claims about the world and the tensions between our political and methodological commitments.

Critical feminism's most common response to questions about its own authority has been reliance on experiential analysis. This approach draws primarily on techniques of consciousness-raising in contemporary feminist organizations, but also on pragmatic philosophical traditions. A standard practice is to begin with concrete experiences, integrate these experiences into theory, and rely on theory for a deeper understanding of the experiences.[13] One distinctive feature of feminist critical analysis is, as Katharine Bartlett emphasizes, a grounding in practical problems and a reliance on "practical reasoning."[14] Rather than working deductively from abstract principles and overarching conceptual schemes, such analysis builds from the ground up. Many feminist legal critics are also drawn to narrative styles that express the personal consequences of institutionalized injustice.[15] Even those commentators most wedded to broad categorical claims usually situate their works in the lived experience of pornography or sexual harassment rather than, for example, in the deep structure of Blackstone's *Commentaries* or the fundamental contradictions in Western political thought.[16]

In part, this pragmatic focus reflects the historical origins and contemporary agenda of feminist legal theory. Unlike critical legal studies, which began as a movement within the legal academy and took much of its inspiration from the Grand Theory of contemporary Marxism and the Frankfurt School, feminist legal theories emerged against the backdrop of a mass political movement. In America, that struggle has drawn much of its intellectual inspiration not from overarching conceptual schemes, but from efforts to provide guidance on particular substantive issues. As Carrie Menkel-Meadow has argued, the strength of feminism "originates" in the experience of "*being* dominated, not just in thinking about domination," and in developing concrete responses to that experience.[17] Focusing on women's actual circumstances helps reinforce the connection between feminist political and analytic agendas, but it raises its own set of difficulties. How can critics build a unified political and analytical stance from women's varying perceptions of their varying experiences? And what entitles that stance to special authority?

The first question arises from a longstanding tension in feminist methodology. What gives feminism its unique force is the claim to speak from women's experience. But that experience counsels sensitivity to its own diversity across such factors as time, culture, class, race, ethnicity, sexual orientation, and age. As Martha Minow has noted, "[c]ognitively we need simplifying categories, and the unifying category of 'woman' helps to organize experience, even at the cost of denying some of it."[18] Yet to some constituencies, particularly those who are not white, heterosexual, and economically privileged, that cost appears prohibitive since it is their experience that is most often denied.

A variation of this problem arises in discussions of "false consciousness." How can feminists wedded to experiential analysis respond to women who reject feminism's basic premises as contrary to *their* experience? In an extended footnote to an early article, Catharine MacKinnon noted:

> Feminism aspires to represent the experience of all women as women see it, yet criticizes antifeminism and misogyny, including when it appears in female form. . . . [Conventional responses treat] some women's views as unconscious conditioned reflections of their oppression, complicitous in it. . . . [T]his approach criticizes the substance of a view because it can be accounted for by its determinants. But if both feminism and antifeminism are responses to the condition of women, how is feminism exempt from devalidation by the same account? That feminism is critical, and antifeminism is not, is not enough, because the question is the basis on which we know something is one or the other when women, all of whom share the condition of women, disagree.[19]

Yet having raised the problem, MacKinnon declined to pursue it. As a number of feminist reviewers have noted, MacKinnon has never reconciled her unqualified condemnation of opponents with her reliance on experiential methodology.[20]

The issue deserves closer attention particularly since contemporary survey research suggests that the vast majority of women do not experience the world in the terms that most critical feminists describe.[21] Nor do these feminists agree among themselves about which experiential accounts of women's interests should be controlling in disputes involving, for example, pornography, prostitution, surrogate motherhood, or maternity leaves.[22]

A related issue is how any experiential account can claim special authority. Most responses to this issue take one of three forms. The first approach is to invoke the experience of exclusion and subordination as a source of special insight. According to Menkel-Meadow, the "feminist critique starts from the experiential point of view of the oppressed, dominated, and devalued, while the critical legal studies critique begins—and, some would argue, remains—in a male-constructed, privileged place in which domination and oppression can be described and imagined but not fully experienced."[23] Yet such "standpoint" theories, if left unqualified, present their own problems of privilege. There remains the issue of whose standpoint to credit, since not all women perceive their circumstances in terms of domination and not all who share that perception agree on its implications. Nor is gender the only source of oppression. Other forms of subordination, most obviously class, race, ethnicity, and sexual orientation, can yield comparable, and in some instances competing, claims to subjugated knowledge. To privilege any single trait risks impeding coalitions and understating other forces that constitute our identities.[24]

A second feminist strategy is to claim that women's distinctive attributes promote a distinctive form of understanding. Robin West has argued, for example, that

> [t]here is surely no way to know with any certainty whether women have a privileged access to a way of life that is more nurturant, more caring, more natural, more loving, and thereby more moral than the lives which both men and women presently pursue in the public sphere, including the legal sphere of legal practice, theory, and pedagogy. But it does seem that whether by reason of sociological role, psychological upbringing or biology, women are *closer* to such a life . . . .[25]

Such claims occur in more muted form in much of the legal scholarship that draws on relational strands of feminist theory. This line of analysis, popularized by Carol Gilligan, argues that women tend to reason in "a different voice"; they are less likely than men to privilege abstract rights over concrete relationships and are more attentive to values of care, connection, and context.[26] The strength of this framework lies in its demand that values traditionally associated with women *be valued* and that legal strategies focus on altering societal structures, not just assimilating women within them. Such an approach can yield theoretical and political cohesiveness on initiatives that serve women's distinctive needs.

Yet such efforts to claim an authentic female voice illustrate the difficulty of theorizing from experience without essentializing or homogenizing it. There is no "generic woman,"[27] or any uniform "condition of women."[28] To divide the world solely along gender lines is to ignore ways in which biological constraints are experienced differently by different groups under different circumstances. If, as critical feminists generally maintain, women's experience has been shaped through culturally contingent patterns of subordination, no particular experience can claim universal authentic status. Moreover, to emphasize only the positive attributes traditionally associated with women is to risk overclaiming and oversimplifying their distinctive contributions. Most empirical work on moral reasoning and public values discloses less substantial gender differences than relational frameworks generally suggest. These frameworks also reinforce dichotomous stereotypes—such as males' association with abstract rationality and females' with empathetic nurturance—that have restricted opportunities for both sexes.

Such concerns underpin those strands of critical feminism that focus on challenging rather than celebrating sex-based difference. The virtue of their approach lies in revealing how legal ideology has misdescribed cultural constructions as biological imperatives. Yet the strengths of this framework also suggest its limitations. Affirmations of similarity between the sexes may inadvertently institutionalize dominant social practices and erode efforts to build group solidarity. Denying difference can, in some contexts, reinforce values that critics seek to change.

A more promising response to the "difference dilemma," and to more general questions about feminist epistemology, is to challenge the framework in which these issues are typically debated. The crucial issue becomes not difference, but the difference difference makes. In legal contexts, the legitimacy of sex-based treatment should not depend on whether the sexes are differently situated. Rather, analysis should turn on whether legal recognition of gender distinctions is likely to reduce or reinforce gender disparities in power, status, and economic security. Since such issues cannot be resolved in the abstract, this strategy requires contextual judgments, not categorical choices. It asks which perspective on difference can best serve particular theoretical or practical objectives, and recognizes that there may be tradeoffs between them. Such an approach demands that feminists shift self-consciously among needs to acknowledge both distinctiveness and commonality between the sexes and unity and diversity among their members.

On the more general question of what validates any particular feminist claim, the first step is to deconstruct the dualistic framework of truth and falsehood in which these issues are often discussed. As postmodernist theorists remind us, all perspectives are partial, but some are more incomplete than others.[33] To disclaim objective standards of truth is not to disclaim all value judgments. We need not become positivists to believe that some accounts of experience are more consistent, coherent, inclusive, self-critical, and so forth. Critical feminism can illuminate the process by which claims about the world are constituted as well as the effects of marginalizing women and other subordinate groups in that process. Such a framework can subject traditional forms of argument and criteria of relevance to sustained scrutiny. It can challenge exclusionary institutions in which knowledge is constructed. And it can press for social changes that would encourage deeper understanding of our experience and the forces that affect it.

Although critical feminists by no means speak with one voice on any of these issues, part of our strength lies in building on our differences as well as our commonalities. Precisely because we do not share a single view on this, or other more substantive concerns, we need theories but not Theory. Our objective should be multiple accounts that avoid privileging any single universalist or essentialist standpoint. We need understandings that can resonate with women's shared experience without losing touch with our diversity. The factors that divide us can also be a basis for enriching our theoretical perspectives and expanding our political alliances. Any framework adequate to challenge sex-based oppression must simultaneously condemn the other forms of injustice with which it intersects.

What allies this method with other critical accounts is its skepticism toward everything, including skepticism. Critical feminist theories retain a commitment to locate judgment within the patterns of social practice, to subject that judgment to continuing critique, and to promote gender equality as a normative ideal. Those commitments may take us in multiple directions but, as Martha Minow maintains, they are unifying commitments nonetheless.[34]

II. Liberal Legalism

For CLS theorists, the most frequent unifying theme is opposition to a common target: the dominance of liberal legalism and the role law has played in maintaining it. On this issue, critical feminism offers more varied and more ambivalent responses. This diversity in part reflects the diversity of perspectives within the liberal tradition. The target appearing in many critical legal studies accounts, and in some critical feminist analyses, is only one version of liberal legalism, generally the version favored by law and economics commentators. Under a more robust framework, many inequalities of greatest concern to feminists reflect limitations less in liberal premises than in efforts to realize liberalism's full potential.[36]

From both a philosophical and pragmatic standpoint, feminist legal critics have less stake in the assault on liberalism than CLS. Their primary target is gender inequality, whatever its pedigree, and their allies in many concrete political struggles have come as often from liberal as from radical camps. Thus, when critical feminist theorists join the challenge to liberal legalism, they often do so on somewhat modified grounds. Their opposition tends to focus on the particular form of liberalism embodied in existing legal and political structures and on the gender biases it reflects.

Although they differ widely in other respects, liberal theorists generally begin from the premise that the state's central objective lies in maximizing individuals' freedom to pursue their own objectives to an extent consistent with the same freedom for others. Implicit in this vision are several assumptions about the nature of individuals and the subjectivity of values. As conventionally presented, the liberal state is composed of autonomous, rational individuals. Their expressed choices reflect a stable and coherent understanding of their independent interests. Yet, while capable of full knowledge of their own preferences, these liberal selves lack similar knowledge about others. Accordingly, the good society remains as neutral as possible about the meaning of the good life: It seeks simply to provide the conditions necessary for individuals to maximize their own preferences through voluntary transactions. Although liberal theorists differ widely about what those background conditions entail, they share a commitment to preserving private zones for autonomous choices, free from public intervention.[37]

Critical feminist theorists have challenged this account along several dimensions. According to theorists such as West, these liberal legalist selves are peculiarly masculine constructs—peculiarly capable of infallible judgments about their own wants and peculiarly incapable of empathetic knowledge about the wants of others.[38] Classic liberal frameworks take contractual exchanges rather than affiliative relationships as the norm. Such frameworks undervalue the ways social networks construct human identities and the ways individual preferences are formed in reference to the needs and concerns of others. For many women, a nurturing, giving self has greater normative and descriptive resonance than an autonomous, egoistic self.[39]

Critical feminists by no means agree about the extent, origins, or implications of such gender differences. Some concept of autonomy has been central to the American women's movement since its inception, autonomy from the constraints of male authority and traditional roles. How much emphasis to place on values of self-determination and how much to place on values of affiliation have generated continuing controversies that cannot be resolved at the abstract level on which debate has often foundered.[40] Even critical feminists who agree about the significance of difference disagree about its causes and likely persistence. Disputes center on how much importance is attributable to women's intimate connection to others through childbirth and identification with primary caretakers, how much to cultural norms that encourage women's deference, empathy, and disproportionate assumption of nurturing responsibilities, and how much to inequalities in women's status and power.[41]

Yet despite these disagreements, most critical feminists share an emphasis on the importance of social relationships in shaping individual preferences.

From such a perspective, no adequate conception of the good society can be derived through standard liberal techniques, which hypothesize social contracts among atomistic actors removed from the affiliations that give meaning to their lives and content to their choices.

This feminist perspective points up a related difficulty in liberal frameworks, which critical theorists from a variety of traditions have noted. The liberal assumption that individuals' expressed preferences can be taken as reflective of genuine preferences is flatly at odds with much of what we know about human behavior. To a substantial extent, our choices are socially constructed and constrained; the desires we develop are partly a function of the desires our culture reinforces. As long as gender plays an important role in shaping individual expectations and aspirations, expressed objectives cannot be equated with full human potential. Women, for example, may "choose" to remain in an abusive relationship, but such choices are not ones most liberals would want to maximize. Yet a liberal legalist society has difficulty distinguishing between "authentic" and "inauthentic" preferences without violating its own commitments concerning neutrality and the subjectivity of value.

Similar problems arise with the legal ideology that underpins contemporary liberal frameworks. In its conventional form, liberal legalism assumes that appropriate conduct can be defined primarily in terms of adherence to procedurally legitimate and determinate rules, that law can be separated from politics, and that spheres of private life can be insulated from public intrusion. Critical feminism challenges all of these assumptions on both empirical and normative levels.

The feminist critique joins other CLS work in denying that the rule of law in fact offers a principled, impartial, and determinate means of dispute resolution. Attention has centered both on the subjectivity of legal standards and the gender biases in their application. By exploring particular substantive areas, feminists have underscored the law's fluctuation between standards that are too abstract to resolve particular cases and rules that are too specific to result in principled, generalizable norms.[45] Such explorations have also revealed sex-based assumptions that undermine the liberal legal order's own aspirations.

These limitations in conventional doctrine are particularly apparent in the law's consistent analysis of gender difference. Decisionmakers have often reached identical legal results from competing factual premises. In other cases, the same notions about sexual distinctiveness have yielded opposite conclusions. Identical assumptions about woman's special virtues or vulnerabilities have served as arguments for both favored and disfavored legal treatment in criminal and family law, and for both including and excluding her from public roles such as professional occupations and jury service. For example, although courts and legislatures traditionally assumed that it was "too plain" for discussion that sex-based distinctions in criminal sentencing statutes and child custody decisions were appropriate, it was less plain which way those distinctions cut. Under different statutory schemes, women received lesser or greater punishments for the same criminal acts and in different historical periods were favored or disfavored as the guardians of their children.[47]

The law's traditional approach to gender-related issues has not only yielded indeterminate interpretations, it has allowed broad mandates of formal equality to mask substantive inequality. Part of the problem with "difference" as an organizing principle is that legal decisionmakers do not always seem to know it when they see it. Once of the most frequently noted illustrations is the Supreme Court's 1974 conclusion that pregnancy discrimination did not involve gender discrimination or even "gender as such"; employers were simply distinguishing between "pregnant women and non-pregnant persons."[48] So too, although most contemporary divorce legislation promises "equal" or "equitable" property distributions between spouses, wives have in practice received neither equality nor equity. In the vast majority of cases, women end up with far greater caretaking responsibilities and far fewer resources to discharge them.[49]

Such indeterminacies and biases also undermine the liberal legalist distinction between public and private spheres. From a critical feminist view, the boundary between state and family is problematic on both descriptive and prescriptive grounds. As an empirical matter, the state inevitably participates in determining what counts as private and what forms of intimacy deserve public protection. Governmental policies concerning childcare, tax, inheritance, property, welfare, and birth control have all heavily influenced family arrangements. As Fran Olsen and Clare Dalton have noted, the same legal decisions regarding intimate arrangements often can be described either as intervention or nonintervention depending on the decisionmakers' point of view. For example, a refusal to enforce unwritten cohabitation agreements can be seen as a means of either preserving or intruding on intimate relationships.[50]

Conventional public/private distinctions present normative difficulties as well. Contrary to liberal legalist assumptions, the state's refusal to intervene in private matters has not necessarily expanded individual autonomy; it has often simply substituted private for public power. Courts' failure to recognize unwritten agreements between cohabitants or to enforce support obligations and rape prohibitions in ongoing marriages has generally enlarged the liberties of men at the expense of women.[51]

Critical feminism does not, however, categorically renounce the constraints on state power that liberal legalism has secured. Rather, it denies that conventional public/private dichotomies provide a useful conceptual scheme for assessing such constraints. As the following discussion of rights suggests, judgments about the appropriate scope of state intervention require a contextual analysis, which takes account of gender disparities in existing distributions of power. In this, as in other theoretical contexts previously noted, we need less reliance on abstract principles and more on concrete experience.

A similar point emerges from one final challenge to liberal legalism. Building on the work of moral theorists such as Carol Gilligan, Annette Baier, and Sarah Ruddick, some commentators have questioned the primacy that this culture attaches to formal, adversarial, and hierarchical modes of dispute resolution.[52] A legal system founded on feminist priorities—those emphasizing trust, care, and empathy—should aspire to less combative, more conciliatory, procedures.

Yet as other feminist critics have noted, an appeal to empathetic values leaves most of the difficult questions unanswered. With whom should legal decisionmaking empathize when individual needs conflict?[53] And what procedural protections should be available to monitor those judgments? One risk is that conciliation between parties with unequal negotiating skills, information, and power can perpetuate those inequalities.[54] Judicial systems that have aspired to more nurturing processes, such as juvenile and family courts, have often reinforced patriarchal assumptions and sexual double standards.[55] Norms appropriate to our vision of justice in an ideal state may not be the best way to get us there.

Here again, a critical feminist approach to procedural values demands contextual judgment. To further the substantive objectives that critical feminism seeks, its greatest challenge lies at the pragmatic level; its task is to design frameworks more responsive to the experiences of subordinate groups. A crucial first step is to deconstruct the apparent dichotomy between formalism and informalism that has traditionally structured debate over alternative dispute resolution processes. Since neither approach has adequately responded to women's experiences and concerns, we cannot rest with debunking both possibilities or choosing the least objectionable alternative. Rather, as is true with debates over substantive rights, we need to reimagine the range of procedural options and to challenge the broader system of sex-based subordination that constrains their exercise.

III. Rights

One central difference between critical feminism and other critical legal theory involves the role of rights. Although both bodies of work have challenged liberal legalism's reliance on formal entitlements, feminist accounts, like those of minority scholars, have tended more toward contextual analysis than categorical critique.

Most CLS scholarship has viewed rights-based strategies as an ineffective and illusory means of progressive social change. While sometimes acknowledging the importance of basic political liberties in preserving opportunities for dissent, critical legal theorists have generally presented the liberal rights agenda as a constraint on individual consciousness and collective mobilization. Part of the problem arises from the indeterminacy noted earlier. Feminist commentators such as Fran Olsen have joined other critical theorists in noting that rights discourse cannot resolve social conflict but can only restate it in somewhat abstract, conclusory form. A rights-oriented framework may distance us from necessary value choices and obscure the basis on which competing interests are accommodated.[57]

According to this critique, too much political energy has been diverted into battles that cannot promise significant gains. For example, a decade's experience with state equal rights amendments reveals no necessary correlation between the standard of constitutional protection provided by legal tribunals and the results achieved.[58] It is unlikely that a federal equal rights amendment would have insured the vast array of substantive objectives that its proponents frequently claimed. Supporters' tendencies to cast the amendment as an all-purpose prescription for social ills—the plight of displaced homemakers, the feminization of poverty, and the gender gap in earnings—have misdescribed the problem and misled as to the solution.[59]

A related limitation of the liberal rights agenda involves its individualist premises and restricted scope. A preoccupation with personal entitlements can divert concern from collective responsibilities. Rights rhetoric too often channels individuals' aspirations into demands for their own share of protected opportunities and fails to address more fundamental issues about what ought to be protected. Such an individualistic framework ill serves the values of cooperation and empathy that feminists find lacking in our current legal culture.

Nor are mandates guaranteeing equality in formal rights adequate to secure equality in actual experience as long as rights remain restricted to those that a predominately white upper middle class male judiciary has been prepared to regard as fundamental. No legal structure truly committed to equality for women would end up with a scheme that affords extensive protection to the right to bear arms or to sell violent pornography, but not to control our reproductive lives.[61]

In a culture where rights have been defined primarily in terms of "freedoms from" rather than "freedoms to," many individuals lack the resources necessary for exercising rights to which they are formally entitled. Such problems are compounded by the costs and complexities of legal proceedings and the maldistribution of legal services available to enforce formal entitlements or prevent their curtailment. By channeling political struggles into legal disputes, rights-based strategies risk limiting aspirations and reinforcing dependence on legal decisionmakers.

Yet while acknowledging these limitations, critical feminism has also emphasized certain empowering dimensions of rights strategies that other CLS work discounts. As theorists including Kimberlé Crenshaw, Christine Littleton, Elizabeth Schneider, and Patricia Williams have argued, legal rights have a special resonance in our culture.[63] The source of their limitations is also the source of their strength. Because claims about rights proceed within established discourse, they are less readily dismissed than other progressive demands. By insisting that the rule of law make good on its own aspirations, rights-oriented strategies offer a possibility of internal challenge that critical theorists have recognized as empowering in other contexts.

So too, critiques that focus only on the individualist premises of rights rhetoric obscure its collective dimensions. The dichotomies often drawn between rights and relationships or rights and responsibilities are highly exaggerated. Rights not only secure personal autonomy, they also express relationships between the individual and the community. Just as rights can impose responsibilities, responsibilities can imply rights. Often the concepts serve identical ends: a right to freedom from discrimination imposes a responsibility not to engage in it. Discarding one form of discourse in favor of another is unlikely to alter the foundations of our legal culture. Moreover, for subordinate groups, rights-based frameworks have supported demands not only for individual entitlements but also for collective selfhood. For example, women's right to reproductive autonomy is a prerequisite to their social equality; without control of their individual destinies, women cannot challenge the group stereotypes and role constraints that underpin their subordinate status. Claims of right can further advance collective values by drawing claimants within a community capable of response and demanding that its members take notice of the grievances expressed.

For critical feminism, the most promising approach is both to acknowledge the indeterminate nature of rights rhetoric and to recognize that, in particular circumstances, such rhetoric can promote concrete objectives and social empowerment. Too often, rights have been abstracted from their social context and then criticized as abstract. Yet however manipulable, the rubric of autonomy and equality have made enormous practical differences in the lives of subordinate groups. Undermining the conceptual foundations of rights like privacy, on which women's reproductive choice has depended, involves considerable risks. Even largely symbolic campaigns, such as the recent ERA struggle, can be highly important, less because of the specific objective they seek than because of the political mobilization they inspire. Like the suffrage movements a half century earlier, the contemporary constitutional battle offered women invaluable instruction in both the limits of their own influence and the strategies necessary to expand it.

Whatever its inadequacies, rights rhetoric has been the vocabulary most effective in catalyzing mass progressive movements in this culture. It is a discourse that critical feminists are reluctant to discard in favor of ill-defined or idealized alternatives. The central problem with rights-based frameworks is not that they are inherently limiting but that they have operated within a limited institutional and imaginative universe. Thus, critical feminism's central objective should be not to delegitimate such frameworks but rather to recast their content and recognize their constraints. Since rights-oriented campaigns can both enlarge and restrict political struggle, evaluation of their strategic possibilities requires historically situated contextual analysis.

On this point, feminists join other critical theorists in seeking to build on the communal, relational, and destabilizing dimensions of rights-based arguments.[66] Claims to self-determination can express desires not only for autonomy but also for participation in the communities that shape our existence. If selectively invoked, the rhetoric of rights can empower subordinate groups to challenge the forces that perpetuate their subordination.

IV. Alternative Visions

One final issue on which critical feminism often parts company with other critical theory involves the construction of alternative visions of the good society. Although both traditions reflect considerable ambivalence about the value of such projects, the focus of concern varies. Most critical theory that has attempted to construct alternative visions assumes away the problems with which feminists have been most concerned or opens itself to the same challenges of indeterminacy that it has directed at other work. Partly for these reasons, feminist legal critics have devoted relatively little attention to idealized programs. Rather, their efforts have centered on identifying the values that must be central to any affirmative vision and the kinds of concrete legal and institutional transformations that such values imply.

A recurrent problem with most progressive utopian frameworks involves their level of generality. Objectives are often framed in terms of vague, seemingly universal aspirations—such as Roberto Unger's appeal to a world free "from deprivation and drudgery, from the choice between isolation from other people and submission to them."[67] Such formulations leave most of the interesting questions unanswered. How are such ideals to be interpreted and implemented under specific circumstances, how are interpretive disputes to be resolved, and how are gender relations to be reconstructed?

In response to such questions, a standard critical strategy is to specify conditions under which answers would be generated. Habermas' ideal speech situation has been perhaps the most influential example. Under his theory, beliefs would be accepted as legitimate only if they could have been acquired through full uncoerced discussion in which all members of society participate. Some critical feminists, including Drucilla Cornell and Seyla Benhabib, draw on similar conversational constructs.[68]

Such strategies are, however, problematic on several levels. One difficulty involves the level of abstraction at which the ideals are formulated. It is not self-evident how individuals with diverse experiences, interests, and resources will reach consensus or how their agreements can be predicted with enough specificity to provide adequate heuristic frameworks. Strategies emphasizing uncoerced dialogue have often assumed away the problems of disparate resources and capacities that parties bring to the conversation. Given the historical silencing of women's voices, many critical feminists have been unsatisfied by approaches that are themselves silent about how to prevent that pattern from recurring.

A related difficulty stems from idealists' faith in dialogue as the primary response to social subordination. Alternative visions that proceed as if the central problem were our inability to imagine such alternatives often understate the material conditions that contribute to that inability. Many feminists have no difficulty imagining a world without pervasive sexual violence or the feminization of poverty; the difficulty lies in commanding support for concrete strategies that would make that vision possible. It is, of course, true that we cannot be free from coercive institutional structures as long as we retain an ideology that legitimates them. But neither can we rid ourselves of that ideology as long as such structures limit our ability to challenge it.

In response to this dilemma, critical feminism has tended to focus on particular issues that implicate both material and ideological concerns. Rather than hypothesizing some universal utopian program, feminist legal critics have generally engaged in more concrete analysis that challenges both structural inequalities and the normative assumptions that underlie them. In evaluating particular strategies, critical feminism focuses on their capacity to improve women's social and economic status; to reach those women most in need; and to enhance women's self-respect, power, and ability to alter existing institutional arrangements.

For example, the struggle for comparable pay for jobs of comparable worth presents direct opportunities to increase women's financial security. The campaign has helped reveal the cultural undervaluation of "women's work," has exposed gender and racial bias in employers' own criteria for compensation, and has aided workplace organizing efforts. Pay equity initiatives have also raised broader questions about market principles and social priorities. How should we reward various occupational and worker characteristics and how should those decisions be made? Are we comfortable in a society that pays more to parking attendants than child care attendants, whatever the gender composition of those positions? The struggle for comparable worth could spark a rethinking of the scope in inequality and the ideologies that sustain it.

The feminist focus on concrete issues has avoided an idealized vision that must inevitably change in the course of change. Feminist legal critics have been less interested in predicting the precise role that gender would play in the good society than in undermining its role in this one. Whether sex would ultimately become as unimportant as eye color or whether some sex-linked traits and affiliations would endure is not an issue on which more speculation seems fruitful. Since what is now problematic about gender relations is the disparity in power, we cannot fully anticipate the shape of those relations in an ideal world where, by definition, such disparities do not exist. At utopian as well as practical levels, critical feminism is unwilling to remain trapped in debates about women's commonality with or difference from men. Its commitment is neither to embrace nor to suppress difference but to challenge the dualism and make the world safe for differences.

Although we cannot know *a priori* what the good society will be, we know more than enough about what it will not be to provide a current agenda. It will not be a society with sex-based disparities in status, power, and security. Nor will it be a society that denies many of its members substantial control over the terms of their daily existence. To realize its full potential, feminism must sustain a vision concerned not only with relations between men and women, but also with relations among them. The commitment to sexual equality that gave birth to the women's movement is necessary but not sufficient to realize the values underlying it. Those values place critical feminism in both tension and alliance with aspirations that other critical legal theory expresses.

Notes

8. Critics such as Francois Lyotard invoke the term post-modernism to describe the present age's collapse of faith in traditional Grand Narratives. Since the Enlightenment, these metanarratives have sought to develop principles of objective science, universal morality, and autonomous art. For discussion of post-modernism's denial that categorical, noncontingent, abstract theories derived through reason or human nature can serve as the foundation for knowledge, see JEAN FRANCOIS LYOTARD. THE POSTMODERN CON-

DITION (1984); POST-ANALYTIC PHILOSOPHY (J. Rajchmand & C. West eds. 1985); Nancy Fraser & Linda Nicholsen, *Social Criticism Without Philosphy: An Encounter Between Feminism and Postmodernism,* in UNIVERSAL ABANDON?: THE POLITICS OF POSTMODERNISM 83 (A. Ross ed. 1988); Sandra Harding, *The Instability of the Analytical Categories of Feminist Theory,* 11 SIGNS 645 (1986); David Luban, *Legal Modernism,* 84 MICH. L. REV. 1656 (1986); Robin West, *Feminism, Critical Social Theory and Law,* 1989 U. CHIC. LEGAL F. 59.

Post-structuralism, which arises from and contributes to this post-modern tradition, refers to theories of interpretation that view meaning as a cultural construction mediated by arrangements of language or symbolic form. What distinguishes post-structuralism from other interpretive schools is the premise that these arrangements are unstable and contradictory, and that readers create rather than simply discover meaning. For a useful overview, see CHRISTOPHER NORRIS, DECONSTRUCTION: THEORY AND PRACTICE (1982); Peter Fitzpatrick & Alan Hunt, *Critical Legal Studies: Introduction,* 14 J.L. & SOC'Y 1 (1987); David Kennedy, *Critical Theory, Structuralism and Contemporary Legal Scholarship,* 21 NEW ENG. L. REV. 209 (1986).

9. J.F. LYOTARD, *supra* note 8; Jane Flax, *PostModernism and Gender Relations in Feminist Theory,* 12 SIGNS 621 (1987). Critical legal studies scholars have responded in varying ways, ranging from Roberto Unger's and Jürgen Habermas's continued embrace of universalist claims, to Duncan Kennedy's reliance on deconstructive technique. *Compare* ROBERTO MANGABEIRA UNGER, KNOWLEDGE AND POLITICS (1975) *and* JÜRGEN HABERMAS, LEGITIMATION CRISIS (1975) *with* Peter Gabel & Duncan Kennedy, *Roll Over Beethoven,* 36 STAN. L. REV. 1 (1984).

10. As Nancy Cott notes, "in deconstructing categories of meaning, we deconstruct not only patriarchal definitions of 'womanhood' and 'truth' but also the very categories of our own analysis—'woman' and 'feminism' and 'oppression' " (*quoted in* Frances E. Macia-Lees, Patricia Sharpe & Colleen Ballerino Cohen, *The Postmodernist Turn in Anthropology: Cautions From a Feminist Perspective,* 15 SIGNS 7, 27 (1989)).

11. *Compare* C. MACKINNON, [FEMINISM UNMODIFIED 81–92 (1987)] (discussing the social construction of rape and sexual violence) *with id.* at 23 (asserting "facts" about its prevalence). *See also* CATHARINE A. MACKINNON, TOWARD A FEMINIST THEORY OF THE STATE 100 (1989) (acknowledging without exploring the difficulty).

12. For discussion of the "not really" phenomena, see *id.* and DIANA E. H. RUSSELL, RAPE IN MARRIAGE 44–48, 207 (1982).

13. According to Catharine MacKinnon, "Consciousness raising is the major technique of analysis, structure of organization, method of practice, and theory of social change of the women's movement." Catharine A. MacKinnon, *Feminism, Marxism, Method and the State: An Agenda for Theory,* 7 SIGNS 515, 519 (1982); *see also* Nancy Hartsock, *Fundamental Feminism: Process and Perspective,* 2 QUEST 67, 71–79 (1975); Elizabeth M. Schneider, *The Dialectic of Rights and Politics: Perspectives from the Women's Movement,* 61 N.Y.U. L. REV. 589, 602–03 (1986).

14. See, for example, the work of Amelie Rorty, discussed in Katharine T. Bartlett, *Feminist Legal Methods,* 103 HARV. L. REV. 829 (1990); Margaret Jane Radin, *The Pragmatist and the Feminist,* 63 S. CAL. L. REV. [1699] (1990).

15. *See, e.g.,* Patricia Williams, *Spirit Murdering the Messenger: The Discourse of Fingerpointing as the Law's Response to Racism,* 42 U. MIAMI L. REV. 127 (1987); Mari J. Matsuda, *Public Response to Racist Speech: Considering the Victim's Story,* 87 MICH. L. REV. 2320 (1989); Robin L. West, *The Difference in Women's Hedonic Lives: A Phenomenological Critique of Feminist Legal Theory,* 3 WIS. WOMEN'S L.J. 81 (1987).

16. *See* Duncan Kennedy, *The Structure of Blackstone's Commentaries,* 28 BUFFALO L. REV. 205 (1979); R. M. UNGER, *supra* note 9.

17. [Carrie] Menkel-Meadow, [*Feminist Legal Theory, Critical Legal Studies, and Legal Education or "The Fem-Crits Go to Law School,"* 38 J. LEGAL EDUC. 61 (1988)]; *see also* MacKinnon, *supra* note 13; West *supra* note 15.

18. Martha Minow, *Feminist Reason: Getting It and Losing It,* 38 J. LEGAL EDUC. 47, 51 (1988).

19. [Catharine A. MacKinnon, *Feminism, Marxism, Method, and the State: Toward Feminist Jurisprudence,* 8 SIGNS 635, 637 n.5 (1983).] For a similar point, see C. MACKINNON, [TOWARD A FEMINIST THEORY OF THE STATE], *supra* note 11, at 115–16.

20. *See* West, *supra* note 15, at 117–18. For critiques of MacKinnon's position in works such as *On Collaboration,* in FEMINISM UNMODIFIED, *supra* note [11], at 198–205, see Katharine T. Bartlett, *MacKinnon's Feminism: Power on Whose Terms?* (Book Review), 75 CALIF. L. REV. 1559, 1564 (1987); Christina B. Whitman, *Law and Sex* (Book Review), 86 MICH. L. REV. 1369, 1399–1400 (1988). . . .

21. *See, e.g.,* D. RHODE, JUSTICE AND GENDER 66 (1989); Lisa Belkin, *Bars to Equality of Sexes Seen as Eroding Slowly.* N. Y. Times, Aug. 20, 1989, at 1, 16 (61% of wives felt husbands did less than fair share of house work; 70% of women with full time jobs felt women had equal or better chance of promotion than men where they worked; and only 39% of Black women and 22% of white women believed organized women's groups had made their lives better); *Rosy Outlook Among Women Ages 18 to 44,* San Francisco Examiner, Aug. 23, 1988, at A7, col. 3 (finding that nearly 90% of women of childbearing ages are satisfied with their lives). For more qualitative research, see SPOUSE, PARENT, WORKER: ON GENDER AND MULTIPLE ROLES (F. Crosby ed. 1987).

22. For differences on pornography, compare West, *supra* note 15, at 134–39 with MACKINNON, [FEMINISM UNMODIFIED], *supra* note [11], at 127–213. For differences on maternity policies, compare [Lucinda M. Finley, *Transcending Equality Theory: A Way out of the Maternity and the Workplace Debate,* 86 COLUM. L. REV. 1118 (1986)], Herma Hill Kay, *Equality and Difference: The Case of Pregnancy,* 1 BERKELEY WOMEN'S L.J. 1 (1985), and Reva B. Siegel, *Employment Equality Under the Pregnancy Discrimination Act of 1978,* 94 YALE L.J. 929 (1984–1985) (student author) with Nadine Taub, *From Parental Leaves to Nurturing Leaves,* 13 N.Y.U. REV. L. & SOC. CHANGE 381 (1985) and Wendy W. Williams, *Equality's Riddle: Pregnancy and the Equal Treatment/Special Treatment Debate,* 13 N.Y.U. REV. L. & SOC. CHANGE 325 (1984–85). For differences on prostitution, see sources cited in D. RHODE, JUSTICE AND GENDER, *supra* note [21], at 257–62. For differences on surrogate motherhood, see *id.* at 223–29, and MARTHA A. FIELD, SURROGATE MOTHERHOOD (1988).

23. Menkel-Meadow, *supra* note [17], at 61.

24. For standpoint theory, see e.g., NANCY C. HARTSOCK, MONEY, SEX & POWER: TOWARD A FEMINIST HISTORICAL MATERIALISM 117–18, 135, 231–47 (1983). For a critique of such theories, see SANDRA HARDING, THE SCIENCE QUESTION IN FEMINISM 163–96 (1986); Bartlett, *supra* note 14.

25. West, *supra* note 8, at [83].

26. *See* CAROL GILLIGAN, IN A DIFFERENT VOICE (1982); MARY FIELD BELENKY, BLYTHE MCVICKAR CLINCHY, NANCY RULE GOLDBERGER & JILL MATTUCK TARULE, WOMEN'S WAYS OF KNOWING (1986); Colker, [*Feminism, Sexuality, and Self: A Preliminary Inquiry into the Politics of Authenticity,* 68 B.U.L. REV. 217 (1988)]; Carrie Menkel-Meadow, *Portia in A Different Voice: Speculations on a Women's Lawyering Process,* 1 BERKELEY WOMENS L.J. 39 (1985).

27. The phrase is Elizabeth V. Spelman's in INESSENTIAL WOMAN: PROBLEMS OF EXCLUSION IN FEMINIST THOUGHT 187 (1988). *See also* ADRIENNE RICH, *Disloyal to Civilization: Feminism, Racism, Gynephobia,* in ON LIES, SECRETS AND SILENCE 275 (1979).

28. MacKinnon, *supra* note [19], at 637 n.5. *quoted in* text accompanying note 19 *supra*.

33. *See* BARBARA HERRNSTEIN SMITH, CONTINGENCIES OF VALUE 94, 166–79 (1988); Flax, *supra* note 9; Fraser & Nicholsen, *supra* note 8, at 91; Mary E. Hawkesworth, *Knower, Knowing, Known: Feminist Theory and Claims of Truth*, 14 SIGNS 533, 557 (1989) (arguing that "[i]n the absence of claims of universal validity, feminist accounts derive their justificatory force from their capacity to illuminate existing social relations [and] to demonstrate the deficiencies of alternative interpretations").

34. Martha Minow, *Beyond Universality*, 1989 U. CHI. LEGAL. F. 115. . . .

36. For example, although Susan Okin criticizes John Rawls's work for its assumptions about egoism and his insensitivity to gender inequalities, she believes that his framework can be consistent with feminist principles. *See* Susan Moller Okin, *Reason and Feeling in Thinking About Justice*, 99 ETHICS 229, 230, 248 (1989). For a contrary view, see Mari Matsuda, *Liberal Jurisprudence and Abstracted Visions of Human Nature: A Feminist Critique of Rawls' Theory of Justice*, 16 N.M.L. REV. 613 (1986). *See generally* CHARLES LARMORE, PATTERNS OF MORAL COMPLEXITY 107–29 (1987) (arguing that liberalism understood as a political rather than metaphysical doctrine need not appeal to individualism as a general value); Robin L. West, *Liberalism Rediscovered: A Pragmatic Definition of the Liberal Vision*, 46 U. PITT. L. REV. 673 (1985).

37. *See* JOHN RAWLS, A THEORY OF JUSTICE (1971); Ronald Dworkin, *Liberalism*, in PUBLIC AND PRIVATE MORALITY 113 (S. Hampshire ed. 1978); BRUCE ACKERMAN, SOCIAL JUSTICE IN THE LIBERAL STATE (1980). *See generally* Steven Shiffrin, *Liberalism, Radicalism, and Legal Scholarship*, 30 UCLA L. REV. 1103 (1983); West, *supra* note 36.

38. Robin West, *Economic Man and Literary Woman: One Contrast*, 39 MERCER L. REV. 867 (1988).

39. A. JAGGAR, [FEMINIST POLITICS AND HUMAN NATURE 21–22 (1983)]; Virginia Held, *Feminism and Moral Theory*, in WOMEN AND MORAL THEORY 111 (E. Kittay & D. Meyers eds. 1987); Susan Moller Okin, *Humanist Liberalism*, in LIBERALISM AND THE MORAL LIFE 39 (N. Rosenblum ed. 1989); Robin West, *Jurisprudence and Gender*, 55 U. CHI. L. REV. 1 (1988).

40. *See, e.g.,* West, *supra* note 39, at 36; Jennifer Nedelsky, *Reconceiving Autonomy: Sources, Thoughts and Possibilities*, 1 YALE J.L. & FEMINISM 7 (1989); *see also* Kathryn Jackson, *And Justice for All? Human Nature and the Feminist Critique of Liberalism*, in WOMEN AND A NEW ACADEMY 122 (J. O'Barr ed. 1989) (arguing that dualistic approaches fail adequately to recognize the interdependence of values such as autonomy and care).

41. Compare the focus on childbirth in West, *supra* note 39, at 2–3, with the emphasis on identification with primary caretakers in NANCY CHODOROW, THE REPRODUCTION OF MOTHERING: PSYCHOANALYSIS AND THE SOCIOLOGY OF GENDER 7 (1978); DOROTHY DINNERSTEIN, THE MERMAID AND THE MINOTAUR 5 (1976); the attention to stereotypes in CYNTHIA FUCHS EPSTEIN, DECEPTIVE DISTINCTIONS (1988); and the focus on power in *Feminist Discourse, Moral Values and the Law—A Conversation*, 34 BUFFALO L. REV. 11, 71–72 (1985) (comments of MacKinnon).

45. *See* Clare Dalton, *An Essay in the Deconstruction of Contract Doctrine*, 94 YALE L.J. 997, 1106–08 (1985).

47. Territory v. Armstrong, 28 Haw, 88 (1924) (upholding greater statutory penalties for males than females convicted of adultery); Wark v. Maine, 266 A.2d 62, 64–65 (Me. 1970) (upholding greater statutory penalties for males than females convicted of escape from penal institutions), *cert. denied*, 400 U.S. 952 (1970); Ex parte Gosselin, 141 Me. 412, 421, 44 A.2d 882, 885–86 (1945) (upholding greater statutory penalties for females than males convicted of misdemeanors such as intoxication); Commonwealth v. Daniel, 210 Pa. Super. 156, 232 A.2d 247 (1967), *rev'd*, 430 Pa. 642, 243 A.2d 400 (1968)

(invalidating statute that gave judges greater discretion to consider exonerating circumstances for males than females convicted of robbery). For changes in custody provisions, see Fran Olsen, *The Politics of Family Law*, 2 LAW & INEQUALITY 1, 12–19 (1984).

48. Geduldig v. Aiello, 417 U.S. 484, 497 n.20 (1974); *see also* General Elec. Co. v. Gilbert, 429 U.S. 125 (1976).

49. LENORE J. WEITZMAN, THE DIVORCE REVOLUTION (1985); Herma Hill Kay, *Equality and Difference: A Perspective on No-Fault Divorce and Its Aftermath*, 56 U. CIN. L. REV. 1, 60–65 (1987); Deborah L. Rhode & Martha Minow, *Reforming the Questions, Questioning the Reforms: Feminist Perspectives on Divorce Reform*, in DIVORCE REFORM AT THE CROSS-ROADS [191] (S. Sugarman & H. Kay eds. 1990).

50. Dalton, *supra* note 45, at 1107; Frances E. Olsen, *The Myth of State Intervention in the Family*, 18 U. MICH. J.L. REF. 835 (1985).

51. *See* MICHAEL D.A. FREEMAN & CHRISTINA M. LYON, COHABITATION WITHOUT MARRIAGE: AN ESSAY IN LAW AND SOCIAL POLICY (1983); DIANA E.H. RUSSELL, RAPE IN MARRIAGE 17–24 (1982); Olsen, *supra* note 50, at 843–58; Marjorie Maguire Shultz, *Contractual Ordering of Marriage: A New Model for State Policy*, 70 CALIF. L. REV. 204 (1982).

52. C. GILLIGAN, *supra* note 26; Annette Baier, *Trust and Antitrust*, 96 ETHICS 231, 247–53 (1986); Sara Ruddick, *Maternal Thinking*, 6 FEMINIST STUD. 342 (1980); *see* Lynne N. Henderson, *Legality and Empathy*, 85 MICH. L. REV. 1574 (1987); Menkel-Meadow, *supra* note 26.

53. Toni [Massaro], *Empathy, Legal Storytelling, and the Rule of Law*, 87 MICH. L. REV. 2104 (1989).

54. *See* Janet Rifkin, *Mediation from a Feminist Perspective: Promise and Problems*, 2 LAW & INEQUALITY 21 (1984). For example, the National Center on Women and Family Law maintains that because wives in divorce cases do not have equal financial and social power they cannot assert equal bargaining power in informal settings without representation by counsel. *See* Carol Lefcourt, *Women, Mediation, and Family Law*, 18 CLEARINGHOUSE REV. 266 (1984). Similarly, researchers in domestic violence cases have found that mediation often perpetuates attitudes that perpetuate abuse because it implies that assaultive behavior does not justify criminal sanctions and that parties bear equal responsibility for preventing it. Lisa G. Lerman, *Mediation of Wife Abuse Cases: The Adverse Impact of Informal Dispute Resolution on Women*, 7 HARV. WOMEN'S L.J. 57 (1984).

55. Judith Resnik, *On the Bias: Feminist Reconsiderations of the Aspirations for Judges*, 61 S. CAL. L. REV. 1877, 1926–33 (1988); Rifkin, *supra* note 54.

57. *See generally* [Olsen, *Statutory Rape: A Feminist Critique of Rights Analysis*, 63 TEX. L. REV. 387 (1984); Peter Gabel, *The Phenomenology of Rights-Consciousness and the Pact of the Withdrawn Selves*, 62 TEX. L. REV. 1563 (1984); Mark Tushnet, *An Essay on Rights*, 62 TEX. L. REV. 1363, 1382–84 (1984)]; sources cited in note 66 *infra*; THE POLITICS OF LAW: A PROGRESSIVE CRITIQUE [D. Kairys ed. 1982]; Adelaide Villamore, *The Left's Problems With Rights*, 9 LEGAL STUD. F. 39 (1985).

58. *See generally* Dawn-Marie Driscoll & Barbara J. Rouse, *Through a Glass Darkly: A Look at State Equal Rights Amendments*, 12 SUFFOLK U.L. REV. 1282, 1308 (1978); D. RHODE, JUSTICE AND GENDER, *supra* note [21], at 92.

59. *See* D. RHODE, JUSTICE AND GENDER, *supra* note [21]; Catharine A. MacKinnon, *Unthinking ERA Thinking* (Book Review), 54 U. CHI. L. REV. 759 (1987).

61. *Compare* U.S. CONST. amend. II *and* American Booksellers Ass'n v. Hudnut, 771 F.2d 323 (7th Cir. 1985), *aff'd*, 475 U.S. 1001 (1986), *with* Webster v. Reproductive Health Servs., 109 S. Ct. 3040 (1989), *and* Harris v. McRae, 448 U.S. 297 (1980).

63. Kimberlé Williams Crenshaw, *Race, Reform, and Retrenchment: Transformation and Legitimation in Antidiscrimination Law*, 101 HARV. L. REV. 1331, 1366–69 (1988); Schneider, *supra* note 13; Patricia J. Williams, *Alchemical Notes: Reconstructing Ideals From Deconstructed Rights*, 22 HARV. C.R.-C.L. L. REV. 401 (1987).

66. *See* Staughton Lynd, *Communal Rights*, 62 TEX. L. REV. 1417 (1984); Roberto Mangabeira Unger, *The Critical Legal Studies Movement*, 96 HARV. L. REV. 561, 612–16 (1983).

67. *See* Unger, *supra* note 66, at 651; *see also* R. UNGER, *supra* note 9, at 18, 24. For a critical review of such generalized aspirations, see B. HERRNSTEIN SMITH, *supra* note 33, at 81–114.

68. *See* Seyla Benhabib. *The Generalized and the Concrete Other*, in FEMINISM AS CRITIQUE 92–94 [S. Benhabib & D. Cornell eds. 1987]; *see also* J. HABERMAS, *supra* note 9; Richard J. Bernstein, *Philosophy in the Conversation of Mankind*, in HERMENEUTICS AND PRAXIS 54, 82 (R. Hollinger ed. 1985).

Further Reading for Part Three

Some feminists were deeply involved in the early stages of the critical legal studies movement and contributed what have become classic works in how the "neutral" concepts of law help to structure patriarchy. See, e.g., Nadine Taub and Elizabeth Schneider, "Perspectives on Women's Subordination and the Role of Law," and Diane Polan, "Toward a Theory of Law and Patriarchy," both in *The Politics of Law: A Progressive Critique*, ed. David Kairys (New York: Pantheon, 1982 and 1990); Janet Rifkin, "Toward a Theory of Law and Patriarchy," 3 *Harv. Women's L.J.* 83 (1980); and Frances Olsen, "The Family and the Market: A Study of Ideology and Legal Reform," 96 *Harv. L. Rev.* 1497 (1983).

The most concise introduction to critical legal studies (CLS) remains Robert Gordon, "New Developments in Legal Theory," in *The Politics of Law: A Progressive Critique*, ed. David Kairys (New York: Pantheon, 1982 and 1990). The two leading CLS symposiums are found at 36 *Stan. L. Rev.* 1 (1984) and 6 *Cardozo L. Rev.* 693 (1985); also see *Critical Legal Studies*, ed. Allan Hutchinson (Totowa, N.J.: Rowman & Littlefield, 1987). Mark Kelman's *A Guide to Critical Legal Studies* (Cambridge: Harvard Univ. Press, 1987) provides in monograph form an overview of the dominant themes in critical legal scholarship. Roberto Unger's *Knowledge and Politics* (New York: Free Press, 1974), a critique of classic liberal philosophy and psychology, laid the groundwork for a critical approach to law, while Unger's *The Critical Legal Studies Movement* (Cambridge: Harvard Univ. Press, 1986) is a rigorously argued but idiosyncratic view of the movement. For a feminist account of the relationship between critical legal studies and feminism, see Carrie Menkel-Meadow, "Feminist Legal Theory, Critical Legal Studies, and Legal Education or 'The Fem-Crits Go to Law School,'" 38 *J. Legal Educ.* 61 (1988).

A deconstructive methodology, which in the United States is associated primarily with the work of French philosopher Jacques Derrida, is one of the hallmarks of critical legal studies. Newcomers to Derrida might find it easiest to begin with his *Of Grammatology*, trans. G. Spivak (Baltimore: Johns Hopkins Univ. Press, 1976), which has a long but excellent introduction by Gayatri Spivak. Other important essays include "Structure, Sign, and Play in the Discourse of the Human Sciences," in *Writing and Difference*, trans. Alan Bass (Chicago: Univ. of Chicago Press, 1987), which marks the transition from structuralism to poststructuralism, and "Differance," in *Margins of Philosophy*, trans. Alan Bass (Chicago: Univ. of Chicago Press, 1982). For a discussion of deconstruction in a legal context, see Christopher Norris, "Law, Deconstruction, and the Resistance to Theory," 15 *J.L. & Soc'y* 166 (1988), and Daniel Williams, "Law, Deconstruction, and Resistance: The Critical Stance of Derrida and Foucault," 6 *Cardozo Arts & Entertainment L.J.* 359 (1988). Derrida's writings on law include "Before the Law," his reading of Franz Kafka's parable of that name, in *Kafka and the Contemporary Critical Performance: Centenary Readings*, ed. Alan Udoff (Bloomington: Indiana Univ. Press, 1987), and his

"Force of Law: The Mystical Foundations of Authority," published together with the other papers presented at the Cardozo Law School conference on "Deconstruction and the Possibility of Justice," in 11 *Cardozo L. Rev.* 919 (1990). For a feminist discussion of the powers and limitations of deconstruction, see Leslie Rabine, "A Feminist Politics of Non-Identity," and the other articles in 13 *Fem. Stud.* (Spring 1988), a special issue on deconstruction.

Another hallmark of critical theory is its emphasis on the relationship between power and knowledge and the importance of local as opposed to grand narrative, both themes associated with the work of Michel Foucault. See his *Discipline and Punish* (New York: Pantheon, 1979); *The History of Sexuality, Vol. 1: An Introduction* (New York: Pantheon, 1980); and *Power/Knowledge: Selected Interviews and Other Writings, 1972–1977* (New York: Pantheon, 1981). For a variety of feminist responses to Foucault, see *Feminism and Foucault: Reflections on Resistance*, ed. Irene Diamond and Lee Quinby (Boston: Northeastern Univ. Press, 1988), and in law, Robin West, "Feminism, Critical Social Theory and Law," 1989 *Univ. Chi. Legal F.* 59.

One focus for application of feminist deconstruction has been the concept of motherhood and the politics of reproduction. *Reproductive Technologies: Gender, Motherhood, and Medicine*, ed. Michelle Stanworth (Minneapolis: Univ. of Minnesota Press, 1987), exemplifies some of the scholarship in this area. See also two books by Mary O'Brien: *The Politics of Reproduction* (Boston: Routledge & Kegan Paul, 1981) and *Reproducing the World: Essays in Feminist Theory* (Boulder, Colo.: Westview, 1989). In *The Ties That Bind: Law, Marriage, and the Reproduction of Patriarchal Relations* (London: Routledge & Kegan Paul, 1984), Carol Smart addresses more specifically the role of law in reinforcing the dependence of women. Among the most interesting examples of feminist legal scholarship addressing issues of motherhood and reproduction using a deconstructive analysis to establish relationships between law and power are Marie Ashe's "Law-Language of Maternity: Discourse Holding Nature in Contempt," 22 *New Eng. L. Rev.* 521 (1988), and "Zig-Zag Stitching and the Seamless Web: Thoughts on 'Reproduction' and the Law," 13 *Nova L. Rev.* 355 (1989).

The attack by critical legal scholars on rights has been contested from a number of perspectives. For more affirmative appraisals of rights discourse, see Pat Williams, "Alchemical Notes: Reconstructing Ideals from Deconstructed Rights," and Mari Matsuda, "Looking to the Bottom: Critical Legal Studies and Reparation," both in 22 *Harv. C.R.-C.L. L. Rev.* (1987); Christine Littleton, "Equality Across Difference: A Place for Rights Discourse," 3 *Wis. Women's L.J.* 189 (1987); Martha Minow, "Rights for the Next Generation: A Feminist Approach to Children's Rights," 9 *Harv. Women's L.J.* 1 (1986); and Judy Scales-Trent, "Black Women and the Constitution: Finding Our Place, Asserting Our Rights," 24 *Harv. C.R.-C.L. L. Rev.* 9 (1989).

For a wide-ranging, lucid introduction to the concept of postmodernism, see David Harvey's *The Condition of Postmodernity* (Oxford: Basil Blackwell, 1989). Classic articulations of postmodernism include Jurgen Habermas, "Modernity: An Incomplete Project," in *The Anti-Aesthetic*, ed. Hal Foster (Port Townsend, Wash.: Bay Press, 1983); Fredric Jameson, "Postmodernism, or the Cultural Logic of Late Capitalism," 146 *New Left Review* 53 (July–August 1984); and Jean Lyotard, *The Postmodern Condition* (Minneapolis: Univ. of Minnesota Press, 1984). Some of the best feminist essays that find postmodernism both useful and problematic include Nancy Fraser and Linda Nicholson's "Social Criticism Without Philosophy: An Encounter Between Feminism and Postmodernism," Jane Flax's "Postmodernism and Gender Relations in Feminist Theory," and Susan Bordo's "Feminism, Postmodernism, and Gender-Scepticism," all found in *Feminism/Postmodernism*, ed. Linda Nicholson (New York: Routledge, 1990). Also see Toril Moi, "Feminism and Postmodernism:

Recent Feminist Criticism in the United States," in *British Feminist Thought: A Reader*, ed. Terry Lovell (Oxford: Basil Blackwell, 1990). For a thought-provoking consideration of how the concept of postmodernism might be useful to an analysis of race and racism, see bell hooks, *Yearning: Race, Gender, and Cultural Politics* (Boston: South End Press, 1990).

PART FOUR

Turning Feminist Method Inward

17

Feminist Reason: Getting It and Losing It [1988]

Martha Minow

As white women ignore their built-in privilege of whiteness and define [woman] in terms of their own experience alone, then women of Color become "other," the outsider whose experience and tradition is too "alien" to comprehend.

—Audre Lorde[1]

Judges and lawyers in the contemporary legal system in the United States, like managers in other systems of knowledge and control, treat their own points of reference as natural and necessary. Judges' preoccupation with neutrality, for example, especially notable in constitutional and statutory equality jurisprudence, upholds existing institutional arrangements while shielding them from open competition with alternatives. Thus, the Supreme Court recently sustained as "neutral" a state law denying unemployment benefits to a woman out of work due to pregnancy despite a federal statute forbidding discrimination on the basis of pregnancy in state grants of unemployment benefits. The Court reasoned that the state denied the woman benefits under a rule that also denies benefits to others who leave their jobs for reasons unrelated to the employer. The state's rule thus "incidentally disqualifies pregnant or formerly pregnant claimants as part of a larger group."[2]

Feminists have shown how such assertions of neutrality hide from view the use of a male norm for measuring claims of discrimination. Adopting such feminist critiques can deepen the meaning of equality under law. I advocate developing similar feminist critiques in contexts beyond gender, such as religion, ethnicity, race, handicap, sexual preference, socioeconomic class, and age.[3] Yet attempts to advance feminist analyses in new contexts come up against unstated assumptions about other traits—assumptions embedded in prevailing feminist arguments. In critiques of the "male" point of view and in celebrations of the "female," feminists run the risk of treating particular experiences as universal and ignoring differences of racial, class, religious, ethnic, national, and other situated experiences.

357

Thus, feminist analyses have often presumed that a white, middle-class, heterosexual, Christian, and able-bodied person is the norm behind "women's" experience. Anything else must be specified, pointed out. This set of assumptions recreates the problem feminists seek to address—the adoption of unstated reference points that hide from view a preferred position and shield it from challenge by other plausible alternatives. These assumptions also reveal the common tendency to treat differences as essential, rather than socially constructed, and to treat one's own perspective as truth, rather than as one of many possible points of view.

Feminism has contributed to the campaign that challenges the convergence between knowledge and power. Feminists question assertions of knowledge that owe their effectiveness to the power wielded by those making the assertions. Some feminists, however, assert as reality claims that hide the power of those doing the claiming. This essay thus pursues the perpetual critique initiated by feminist work while also searching, as feminists do, for practical justice, not just more theory.

I. Insights

Feminists have contributed incisive critiques of the unstated assumptions behind political theory, law, bureaucracy, science, and social science that presuppose the universality of a particular reference point or standpoint.[4] In field after field of human thought, feminist work exposes the dominance of conceptions of human nature that take men as the reference point and treat women as "other," "different," "deviant," or "exceptional." Male psychology, feminist theorists argue, is the source in a male-dominated society of conceptions of rational thought that favor abstraction over particularity and mind over body. Similarly, the assumption of autonomous individualism behind American law, economic and political theory, and bureaucratic practices rests on a picture of public and independent man rather than private—and often dependent, or interconnected—woman.[6] The norms and the dynamics of the natural world— the way its biological, evolutionary, and even chemical and physical properties are explained—embody unstated male reference points.

Feminist work confronts the power of naming and challenges both the use of male measures and the assumption that women fail by them. If, at times, feminists appear contradictory, arguing both for the right of women to be included and treated like men and for the right to have special treatment (which valorizes women's differences), feminists have an explanation. The inconsistency lies in a world and set of symbolic constructs that have simultaneously used men as the norm and denigrated any departure from the norm. Thus, feminism demands the dual strategy of challenging the assumptions that women are too different from the unstated male norm to enjoy male privileges and that women's differences actually justify denial of privileges or benefits. For over a century now, feminists have claimed that distinctive aspects of women's experiences and perspectives offer resources for constructing more representative, more empathic, more creative, and, in general, better theories, laws, and social practices.

II. New Claims, Old Risks

As many feminist theorists are beginning to recognize, our critique runs the great risk of creating a new standpoint that is equally in danger of projecting the experience of some as though it were universal.[10] By urging the corrective of women's perspective, or even a feminist standpoint, feminists may jeopardize our challenge to simplifications, essentialism, and stereotypes.

Many feminists acknowledge that women fall into every category of race, religion, class, and ethnicity, and vary in sexual preference, handicapping conditions, and other sources of assigned difference.[11] Any claim to speak from women's point of view, or to use women as a reference point, threatens to obscure this multiplicity by representing a particular view as the view of all.[12] Some have expressly argued that sexism is more fundamental than racism.[13] This claim is disturbing because it suggests not just that feminists may fail to take account of other forms of oppression or domination beyond sexism but that they may fail to take account of women's own experiences in all their variety. Elizabeth V. Spelman persuasively argues that we ought to be "skeptical about any account of gender relations which fails to mention race and class or consider the possible effects of race and class differences on gender: for in a world in which there is racism and [classism], obscuring the workings of race and class are likely to involve—whether intentionally or not—obscuring the workings of racism and classism."[16] Focusing on the same danger, Nancy Fraser and Linda Nicholsen conclude that there is neither one "feminist method" nor one feminist epistemology, "since women's oppression is not homogenous in content, and since it is not determined by one root, underlying cause."[17] Audre Lorde puts it powerfully: "Some problems we share as women, some we do not. You fear your children will grow up to join the patriarchy and testify against you, we fear our children will be dragged from a car and shot down the street, and you will turn your backs upon the reasons they are dying."[18]

III. Why Do We Make the Mistake We Identify in Others?

Such critiques of feminism are internal, voiced by feminists, admonishing feminists. In a sense, the method of consciousness-raising—personal reporting of experience in communal settings to explore what has not been said—enables a practice of self-criticism among feminists even about feminism itself. Yet why, when it comes to our own arguments and activities, do feminists forget the very insights that animate feminist initiatives, insights about the power of unstated reference points and points of view, the privileged position of the status quo, and the pretense that a particular is the universal?

Perhaps our own insights elude us because of our attraction to simplifying categories, our own psychodynamic development, our unconscious attachment to stereotypes, and our participation in a culture in which contests over power include contests over what version of reality prevails.[20] We are afraid of being overwhelmed, which is what full acknowledgement of all people's differences may portend. Cognitively, we need simplifying categories, and the unifying category of "woman" helps to organize experience, even at the cost of denying some of it.[21] Ideas that defy neat categories are difficult to hold on to, even though the idea itself is about the tyranny of categories.[22] We especially attach ourselves to such categories as male/female because of our own psychological development in a culture that has made gender matter, and our own early constructions of personal identity forged in relationship to parents who made gender matter.[23]

Feminist activities themselves also reveal relationships between knowledge and power. Feminists are no more free than others from the stereotypes in cultural thought.[24] White feminists may well carry unconscious stereotypes about people of color, and similar stereotypes may divide women of different religions, political persuasions, abilities and disabilities, and sexual preferences.[25] Some stereotypes may be an unconscious cultural inheritance, but they also may be clues to who has power to define agendas and priorities within feminist communities.[26] Ignoring differences among women may permit the relatively more privileged women to claim identification with all discrimination against women while also claiming special authority to speak for women unlike themselves.[27]

Finally, we share the version of reality that has for the most part prevailed in the entire culture. Not only does this instill conceptions of difference and stereotypic thinking, it also gives us internal scripts about how to argue, and indeed, how to know. The dominant culture has established certain criteria for theories, for legal arguments, for scientific proofs—for authoritative discourse. These established criteria are the governing rules. If we want to be heard— indeed, if we want to make a difference in existing arenas of power—we must acknowledge and adapt to them, even though they confine what we have to say or implicate us in the patterns we claim to resist.

IV. The Example of Pregnancy

The Supreme Court's treatment of issues concerning pregnancy and the workplace highlights the power of the unstated male norm in analyses of problems of difference. In 1975, the Court accepted an argument based on a male norm in striking down a Utah statute that disqualified a woman from receiving unemployment compensation for twelve weeks before the expected date of childbirth and for six weeks after childbirth, even if her reasons for leaving work were unrelated to the pregnancy.[29] Although the capacity to become pregnant is a difference between women and men, this fact does not justify treating women and men differently on matters unrelated to the pregnancy. That is, if men are used as the norm, any woman who can perform like a man should be treated like a man. A woman cannot be denied unemployment compensation for different reasons than a man would be.

What happens, though, to the woman's difference—the occasion of pregnancy? May the fact of this difference justify different treatment? What is equal treatment for the woman who is correctly identified, not stereotyped, and who differs from nonpregnant persons in ways that are relevant to the workplace? It was on this issue that the reliance on the male norm reached such a notorious result in the Supreme Court, twisting the meaning of sex discrimination to use male experience to measure discrimination against women. The Court considered, both as a statutory and a constitutional question, whether discrimination in health insurance plans on the basis of pregnancy amounted to discrimination on the basis of sex. In both instances, the Court answered negatively because pregnancy marks a division between the groups of pregnant and nonpregnant persons, and women fall in both categories.[30] Only from a point of view that treats pregnancy as a strange occasion, rather than a present, bodily potential, would its relationship to female experience be made so tenuous; and only from a vantage point that treats men as the norm would the exclusion of pregnancy from health insurance coverage seem unproblematic and free from forbidden gender discrimination.

With judicial decisions such as these, litigators working for women's rights have discovered that unless we fit our claims into existing doctrines, we are unlikely to be understood, much less to succeed.[32] Yet trying to fit women's experiences into categories forged with men in mind reinstates gender differences by treating the male standard as unproblematic. Feminist attacks on the problem face a double risk. Either we reinvest unstated male norms with legitimacy by trying to extend them to women, or we criticize those norms and posit a new, female norm that may be insensitive to the variety of women's experiences. A critique of the Supreme Court's decisions in *Geduldig* and *Gilbert*, for instance, runs the risk of positing a new essential female experience to counter the Court's conclusion that pregnancy is not sufficiently related to the female experience to count as a basis for sex discrimination. The Court was correct in noting that not all women at all times are pregnant. Indeed, some women will never become pregnant, and some who already have will never again. The medical, social, and psychological meanings of pregnancy vary by individual, and so do needs for medical and other treatment. Further, some women may argue that excluding health benefits for pregnancy is far less burdensome to them than denying them work leaves to care for a dependent parent, or restricting health benefits to the primary worker and spouse and excluding other intimate household members. Reformers approaching the issues of pregnancy and the workplace and seeking both litigation and legislation to establish women's right to pregnancy benefits and leaves may merely carve a new norm that produces new exclusions.

Political and legal reactions to past victories pose the real danger that legal decisions may grow worse for women and minority men. We are more likely than ever to attempt to frame conventional arguments that can succeed in the courts and legislatures, both of which enshrine convention. Arguments that women are just like men—and deserve to be treated like men—reappear when legal and political authorities reject arguments that mainstream institutions should be revamped to include women's experiences.

When formerly excluded groups such as women want to be recognized or represented in mainstream, established institutions, our own efforts at reform become most vulnerable to the version of reality that has in the past excluded us. We risk becoming tokens, and taking our meanings and identities from those who have let us in.

A similar problem arises in the production of knowledge. In established academic institutions, what has counted as theory meets criteria of coherence, value neutrality, and abstraction that themselves may embody the false universalism that feminists criticize. Yet to be counted by establishment institutions as theory, feminist approaches must resemble the objects of their attack. This may be why Jane Flax notes that "We cannot re-vision the world with the tools we have been given."[36] We risk becoming embroiled in what we critique, entranced by what we would demystify.

The problem is a familiar one—criticism's preoccupation with the subject of the criticism. When the subject of criticism is authoritativeness, the critic faces the special dilemma of how to claim authority while rejecting its usual forms of subduing and vanquishing others. Feminists, no less than anyone else, and perhaps more than people who have felt at home in the prevailing conceptions of reality, want something to hang on to, some sense of the validity of our own perceptions and experience, some certainty—not more experiences of doubt. Yet, each form of certainty hazards a new arrogance, projecting oneself, one's own experience, or one's own kind as the model for all.

Thus, feminists make the mistake we identify in others—the tendency to treat our own perspective as the single truth—because we share the cultural assumptions about what counts as knowledge, what prevails as a claim, and what kinds of intellectual order we need to make sense of the world. Like the systems of politics, law, and empiricism feminists criticize for enthroning an unstated male norm, feminist critiques tend to establish a new norm that also seeks to fix experience and deny its multiplicity.[41]

V. A Pointed Effort to See Points of View

No new principle or rule can solve the problem: challenging the hidden privileging of one perspective privileges another in its place. Instead we need a stance, one that helps us accept complexity but not passivity. As people who judge others and who face the judgments of others, we should challenge any ready assignment of "difference" that seems to allocate benefits or burdens as though the results were natural rather than chosen. This means doubting words and concepts that we take for granted, and looking to the consequences when we do use them. A useful strategy is to pay attention to competing perspectives on a given problem, and to challenge unstated points of view that hide their assumptions from open competition with others. In sum, we need to pay attention to what we give up as well as what we embrace.

Rather than creating a new female norm for use in claiming equality, I suggest that we contest the ready association of sameness with equality and difference with inferiority. Similarly, we could take challenges to differential treatment as occasions to assess not difference but treatment, not individual and group traits but social arrangements that make those traits seem to matter.

Again, let us take pregnancy and the workplace as an example. Although tortured in its framework and controverted in its results, the Supreme Court's 1987 decision in *California Federal Savings and Loan Association v. Guerra*,[43] represents an effort to remake an apparent issue of neutrality toward gender differences in the workplace into an issue of neutrality toward gender differences in the conjunction between work and family. In so doing, the Court—and the legislatures whose enactments the Court construed—converted the difference question into a challenge to prevailing social arrangements that had made a gender difference significant. I will explain and defend the Court's decision but also suggest alternative locutions to avoid the Court's contortions in the future.

Before the initiation of the *Cal. Fed.* lawsuit, Lillian Garland asserted protection under a state statute requiring employers to provide employees with an unpaid pregnancy disability leave of up to four months. The state commission had construed the state law to establish a qualified right to reinstatement in the job after the leave. While her case was pending with the state commission, Garland's employer, California Federal Savings and Loan Association, joined with others to seek a declaration from federal court that the state statute was inconsistent with and therefore preempted by Title VII's prohibition against discrimination on the basis of sex. The case thus put directly at issue the meaning of the Pregnancy Discrimination Act of 1978, the Congressional rejoinder to the Supreme Court's refusal to treat pregnancy discrimination as a violation of Title VII.[44] Triggering debates that fractured the Court and the women's rights community, the suit questioned whether the federal ban against discrimination on the basis of pregnancy allows treating pregnant workers like other workers, or instead allows special treatment. Thus framed, the problem treats men as the norm and presumes a workplace designed for men or for people who never become pregnant. Any effort to remake the workplace to accommodate pregnancy would be "special treatment" and would not be neutral with regard to the workplace. Yet a ban against such accommodation, focused on pregnancy, leaves in place the male norm that makes women and pregnancy seem "different."

The majority for the Court understood this and construed the statute to permit employers to remove barriers in the workplace that had disadvantaged pregnant people compared with others.[45] Most important, Justice Marshall's opinion for the Court shifted from the comparison between men and women in the workplace to a comparison of men and women in the conjunction of their workplace and family lives. "By 'taking pregnancy into account,' California's pregnancy disability leave statute allows women, as well as men, to have families without losing jobs."[46]

The majority's second rationale—that the state and federal laws are compatible because employers may comply with both by providing comparable reinstatement benefits to men and women following leaves for reasons such as pregnancy— uses women's experience as the benchmark.[47] The Court called for equal treatment of men and women and permitted the state's elected representatives to determine the minimum threshold level for such treatment. By allowing this legislative alteration of the employers' obligation to workers, the Court unmasked the employers' effort to rely on the federal law for what it was—an attempt to implant the male norm as the reference for workplace equality. Although the task of asserting the permissible significance of gender-linked characteristics remains, the Court successfully resisted the role of reinstating social arrangements that had made gender difference at the workplace significant.

How can the *Cal. Fed.* decision be reconciled with the Court's decision in *Wimberly* one week later to permit a state to refuse benefits to a woman unemployed because of her pregnancy, despite a federal law banning discrimination because of pregnancy in unemployment benefits? On one level, the cases are perfectly compatible. In both instances, the Court read federal antidiscrimination requirements to permit states legislative latitude to set minimum benefit levels at any chosen point, so long as pregnancy was not singled out as the basis for granting or withholding benefits.[50] On another level, however, the cases diverge significantly. Unlike *Cal. Fed.*, in which the Court used a guarantee against pregnancy discrimination to establish the pregnant person as the point of comparison, in *Wimberly* the Court superimposed a neutral nondiscrimination demand on a workplace world and a state statute that were modeled without pregnancy in mind.[51] The Court in *Wimberly* treated the federal equality statute as a neutrality requirement, although the baseline social arrangements are not neutral about the consequences of gender and/or class differences. But in *Cal. Fed.* the Court treated a federal equality statute as a requirement to eliminate obvious discrimination against women and to guard against new discriminations against men not by keeping women's lot small but by improving men's lot as well.

As if to demonstrate that the Court knows how to move beyond pretended neutrality to guard against discrimination even in the context of unemployment benefits involved in *Wimberly*, at just about the same time the Court required accommodation of an individual's religious beliefs in making unemployment benefits available. In *Hobbie v. Unemployment Appeals Commission v. Florida*,[52] the Court concluded that the Free Exercise Clause forbids denial of unemployment-compensation benefits to a woman discharged when she refused because of her sincerely-held religious beliefs to work certain scheduled hours.[53] The Court reached this conclusion despite the even more explicit—and Constitutional—demand for neutrality in the context of religion. For the Court also concluded that the award of benefits under these circumstances—accommodating an individual's religious beliefs—does not violate the Establishment Clause.[54]

What the Court did in *Cal. Fed.* and in *Hobbie* was to pay attention to what is lost when power reinforces a version of reality that coincides with dominant social arrangements. The standard analysis would compare alternate perspectives to the unstated norm encased in the dominant social relations and then ask whether exclusion of the "different" perspectives contravenes a legal commitment to equality.[55] In these cases, in contrast, the Court took seriously versions of reality at odds with the structure of social arrangements: the perspectives of pregnant women and of religious individuals whose needs are not embedded in the rules of employers and the laws governing unemployment benefits. At the same time, the Court construed the federal obligations to permit state experimentation and judicial obligations to allow legislative initiative with an important limitation. Existing social arrangements are no more privileged or immune from challenge than any competing arrangement when confronting allegations of burdens based on a personal or group difference.

Discussing legal disputes in terms of how existing social arrangements appear in light of competing minority and majority perspectives would have the advantage of exposing initial answers to the same scrutiny. An explicit inquiry into these matters would help guard against the risk that new answers might reestablish a preference for one point of view disguised as the necessary and natural arrangement. The California employers may well face new claims that benefits comparable to the qualified reinstatement guarantee following pregnancy leave include a variety of reinstatement conditions not just for men but also for women facing short-term leave demands for reasons other than pregnancy.

Feminist insights into the power of unstated norms demand just this perpetual reconsideration of the point of view buried within social arrangements and in critiques of them, the point of view that makes some differences matter and others irrelevant. Otherwise, outsiders who become insiders simply define new groups as "other." Taking the point of view of people labeled "different" is one way to move beyond current difficulties in treating differences as real and consequential. Generating vivid details about points of view excluded from or marginalized by particular institutions is another. Seeking out and promoting participation by voices typically unheard are also crucial if equality jurisprudence is to mean more than enshrining the point of view of those sitting on the bench. The concerted and persistent search for excluded points of view and the acceptance of their challenges are equally critical to feminist theory and practice. Otherwise, feminists will joint the ranks of reformers who have failed to do more than impose their own point of view.

The more powerful we are, the less able we are to see how our own perspective and the current structure of our world coincide. That is just one of our privileges. Another is that we can put and hear questions without questioning ourselves. The more marginal we feel, the more likely we are to glimpse a contrast between other people's perceptions of reality and our own. Yet we still may slip into the world view of the more powerful because their view is more apt to be validated and because we often would like to be like them. It is hard to hang on to these insights because we prefer to have our perceptions validated: we need to feel acknowledged and confirmed. But when we fail to take the perspective of another, we deny just that acknowledgment and confirmation in return.

Notes

1. Audre Lorde, Age, Race, Class, and Sex: Women Redefining Difference, in Sister Outsider 114, 117 (Trumansburg, N.Y., 1984).

2. Wimberly v. Labor and Indus. Relations Comm'n of Missouri, 107 S. Ct. 821, 825 (1987). This decision received far less attention than the Court's decision a week earlier unholding California's statutory requirement of unpaid pregnancy disability leaves with

a qualified right to reinstatement. California Fed. Savings and Loan Ass'n v. Guerra, 107 S. Ct. 683 (1987), which I discuss *infra* text accompanying notes 43–4[7].

3. See Martha Minow, The Supreme Court 1986 Term—Foreword: Justice Engendered, 101 Harv. L. Rev. 10, 11–12 (1987).

4. See, e.g., Simone de Beauvoir. The Second Sex (New York, 1952); Carol Gilligan, In a Different Voice: Psychological Theory and Women's Development (Cambridge, Mass., 1982); Kathy E. Ferguson, The Feminist Case Against Bureaucracy (Philadelphia, 1984); Nancy C. M. Hartsock, Money, Sex, and Power: Toward a Feminist Historical Materialism (New York, 1983, 1985); Alison M. Jaggar, Feminist Politics and Human Nature (Totowa, N.J., 1983); Evelyn F. Keller, Reflections on Gender and Science (New Haven, 1985); Catharine MacKinnon, Feminism, Marxism, Method, and the State: An Agenda for Theory, 7 Signs 515 (1982), and Feminism, Marxism, Method, and the State: Toward Feminist Jurisprudence, 8 Signs 635 (1983); Jean Baker Miller, Toward a New Psychology of Women (Boston, 1976); Susan Moller Okin, Women in Western Political Thought (Princeton, N.J., 1979). I draw on these works in the following summary.

6. In addition to the sources cited *supra* note 4, see Frances Olsen, The Family and the Market, 96 Harv. L. Rev. 1497 (1983); Mary Joe Frug, Re-Reading Contracts: A Feminist Analysis of a Contracts Casebook, 34 Am. U. L. Rev. 1065 (1985).

10. Audre Lorde puts it this way: "By and large within the women's movement today, white women focus upon their oppression as women and ignore differences of race, sexual preference, class and age. There is a pretense to a homogeneity of experience covered by the word [sisterhood] that does not in fact exist." Lorde, *supra* note 1, at 116. See also bell hooks, Ain't I a Woman: Black Women and Feminism 194–195 (Boston, 1981) (white females bring racism to feminism); Barbara Omolade, Black Women and Feminism, *in* The Future of Difference, ed. Hester Eisenstein & Alice Jardine, 247, 255 (New York, 1980) (black experience needed in feminism for black women to pursue dialogue with white feminists); Iris Marion Young, Social Movements, Difference and Social Policy, presented at Feminist Moral, Political and Legal Theory, 56 U. Cin. L. Rev. 535 (1987) (discussions of difference within women's movement mirror puzzles generated by assertion of difference in all oppressed social movements). Sandra Harding states her view of the problem: "[T]he feminist standpoint epistemologies appear committed to trying to tell the 'one true story' about ourselves and the world around us that the postmodernist epistemologies regard as a dangerous fiction." Sandra G. Harding, The Science Question in Feminism 195 (Ithaca, N.Y., 1986). See Gloria I. Joseph & Jill Lewis, Common Differences: Conflicts in Black and White Feminist Perspectives (New York, 1982); Home Girls: A Black Feminist Anthology, ed. Barbara Smith (New York, 1983); With Wings: Anthology of Literature By and About Women with Disabilities, ed. Marsha Saxton & Florence Howe (New York, 1987).

11. Other obvious differences among women include language, nationality, age, height, appearance. Consider also politics. See, e.g., Kristin Luker, Abortion and the Politics of Motherhood 127–46 (Berkeley, Calif., 1983) (comparing backgrounds and outlooks of profile and prochoice activists).

12. This poses a special dilemma for feminism, which has celebrated "women's experience" as the touchstone for a new source of authority. If this authority speaks only for the individual, not for the group of women, how can it counter the predominant structures of societal authority? Barbara Johnson describes the dilemma that ensues in discussion of feminist pedagogy: "[I]t would be impossible to deny that female experience has been undervalidated. On the other hand, the moment one assumes one knows what female experience is, one runs the risk of creating another reductive appropriate—an appropriate that consists in the reduction of experiences as self-resistance." Barbara Johnson, A World of Difference 46 (Baltimore, 1987).

13. See Richard Wasserstrom, Racism, Sexism and Preferential Treatment: An Approach to the Topics, 24 UCLA L. Rev. 581, 581–615 (1977); Lawrence Thomas, Sexism and Racism, Some Conceptual Differences 90 Ethics 239 (1980).

16. Elizabeth V. Spelman, Inessential Woman: Problems of Exclusion in Feminist Thought [80–113] (Boston, Beacon Press, [1988]).

17. Nancy Fraser & Linda Nicholson, Social Criticism Without Philosophy: An Encounter Between Feminism and Postmodernism, *in* The Institution of Philosophy: A Discipline in Crisis? ed. Avner Cohen & Marcelo Descal (Totowa, N.J., 198[9]). Fraser and Nicholson nonetheless conclude that feminism can continue to mean something: a commitment to actual diversity, and a complex, multilayered feminist solidarity. See also Harding, *supra* note 10, at 194 ("By giving up the goal of telling 'one true story,' we embrace instead the permanent partiality of feminist inquiry").

18. Lorde, *supra* note 1, at 119. And, "As a black lesbian feminist comfortable with the many different ingredients of my identity, and a woman committed to racial and sexual freedom from oppression, I find I am constantly being encouraged to pluck out some one aspect of myself and present this as the meaningful whole, eclipsing or denying the other parts of self. But this is a destructive and fragmenting way to live." *Id.*

20. See Minow, *supra* note 3, in which I draw especially on work by William James, Felix Cohen, George Lakoff, Ludwig Wittgenstein, Nancy Chodorow, D. W. Winnicott, Ernest Becker, Charles Lawrence, Sanford Gilman, Erving Goffman, Stephen Jay Gould, Karl Mannheim, E. P. Thompson, Steven Lukes, and Barbara Christian.

21. George Lakoff suggests that this simplifying process works even in our development of unstated prototypes that give form to seemingly general linguistic categories. We discover the prototype when we use adjectives to modify the general category, adjectives that reveal the unstated norm. For example, the term "working mother" modifies the general category "mother," revealing that the general term carries an unstated assumption of the norm (a woman who cares for her children full time without pay); if the normal meaning is not intended, it must be explicitly modified. George Lakoff, Women, Fire, and Dangerous Things 80–81 (Chicago, 1987). The politicization of this very example, through arguments such as "every mother is a working mother," challenges the unstated prototype and also challenges its replacement by another unstated prototype. This essay, in a sense, seeks to challenge the unstated prototype behind feminism.

22. See Caren Kaplan, Deterritorializations: The [Rewriting] of Home and Exile in Western Feminist Discourse, Cultural Critique 187 (Spring 1987) (goal is to make a world of possibilities out of the experience of displacement). This point currently occupies debates among literary theorists who fear the routinization of deconstruction. See, e.g., Johnson, *supra* note 12.

23. This is the insight advanced by Nancy Chodorow's work. See Nancy Chodorow. The Reproduction of Mothering (Berkeley, Calif., 1978), and Mothering, Male Dominance, and Capitalism, *in* Capitalist Patriarchy and the Case for Socialist Feminism, ed. Zillah R. Eisenstein, 83 (New York, 1979). Chodorow underplays, however, the significance of early formation of racial, religious, and national identities, which are layered into the psychodynamic process of individuation with perhaps as much power as gender identities.

24. See Adrienne Rich, Blood, Bread, and Poetry 230 (New York, 1986); Elizabeth Spelman, Theories of Race & Gender: The Erasure of Black Women, 5 Quest 36, no. 4 (1982); Michael Omni & Howard Winant, By the Rivers of Babylon: Race in the United States: Part One, 13 The Socialist Rev. 31 (September-October 1983).

25. Majority and minority women may each have stereotypes of one another, but the majority's stereotypes of the minorities carry more power to implement the exclusion and control that stereotypes imply.

26. It may be a characteristic of white privilege to deny difference among women because admitting difference would mean overcoming stereotypes and giving up power,

not through the mere tokenism of letting some women of color in but by actually giving up control over the definition of priorities. Audre Lorde attributes this phenomenon to white women's opportunities and temptations to share some of white men's power. Lorde, *supra* note 1, at 118. Emphasizing gender rather than other sources of difference and oppression may actually be a tool of social control.

27. "It is because white middle-class women have something at stake in not having their racial and class identity be made and kept visible that we [must question accepted feminist positions on gender identity]." Spelman, *supra* note 16[, at 112]; see also *id.* at [57–79].

29. Turner v. Dep't of Employment Sec. of Utah, 423 U.S. 44 (1975) (decided on due process grounds).

30. Geduldig v. Aiello, 417 U.S. 484, 496–97 n.20 (1974) (equal protection); General Electric Co. v. Gilbert, 429 U.S. 125, 136–40 (1976) (Title VII).

32. Inventive lawyering remakes old categories to capture women's experience, as in the use of discrimination doctrine to recognize the harm of sexual harassment. See Catharine A. MacKinnon, Sexual Harassment of Working Women (New Haven, 1979).

36. Jane Flax, Mother-Daughter Relationships, *in* Eisenstein & Jardine, *supra* note 10, at 20, 38.

41. In short, feminist work risks the danger of a new certainty, and the danger of certainty "is that it turns against the generous impulse to open oneself up to the other, and truly listen, to risk, the chance that we might be wrong." Drucilla Cornell, The Poststructuralist Challenge to the Ideal of Community, 8 Cardozo L. Rev. 989, 1018 (1987). Is there a different approach?

43. 107 S. Ct. 683 (1987).

44. 42 U.S.C. § 2000e(k) (1982). See discussion of Gilbert, *supra* text accompanying note 30.

45. See 107 S. Ct. at 694.

46. *Id.*

47. That this solution will impose costs on employers—costs that will undoubtedly be shifted to nonpregnant workers—should not be denied. But neither should this consequence be misunderstood: the costs of *failing* to accommodate pregnant workers— along with perhaps less calculable costs from underemploying women—are also borne by employers and shifted to individuals, partially adjusted by the social welfare system. To the extent that pregnant women have shouldered the costs of a workplace that has not accommodated them, the legislation requiring accommodation marks a decision not to create new costs but to spread existing costs more widely.

50. This reading follows the second rationale in the *Cal. Fed.* majority opinion, which rejects the challenge to the state statute on the ground that employers could comply with the federal antidiscrimination requirement by providing comparable benefits to nonpregnant persons as well.

51. *Wimberly*, 107 S. Ct. 821, 825 (1987). "[I]f a State adopts a neutral rule that incidentally disqualifies pregnant or formerly pregnant claimants as part of a larger group, the neutral application of that rule cannot readily be characterized as a decision made 'solely on the basis of pregnancy.' "

52. 107 S. Ct. 1046 (1987).

53. The employer had argued that Hobbie's refusal to work during her religious Sabbath amounted to misconduct and rendered her ineligible for benefits under a statute limiting compensation to persons who become "unemployed through no fault of their own." *Id.* at 1048. The Court rejected this attribution of fault to Hobbie and reasoned instead that the employer caused the conflict between work and belief by refusing to accommodate her religious practices.

54. *Id.* at 1049, 1051.

55. *Hobbie* involved the First Amendment's religious clauses and yet also presented a critical equality claim: Did this individual suffer unlawful discrimination, differential treatment, because of her religious beliefs? I believe that greater efforts to borrow across fields and reason by analogy would advance especially the jurisprudence of equality. Because different people are situated differently in relation to questions of difference and equality, they may perceive instances of discrimination in one context they would miss in another. "[N]either the whole of truth nor the whole of good is revealed to any single observer, although each observer gains a partial superiority of insight from the peculiar position in which he stands." William James, On a Certain Blindness in Human Beings, *in* James, [On Some of Life's Ideals 3, 46 (New York, 1900)]. We could all learn, then, about the varieties of discrimination from the partial superiority of our own different sympathies.

18

Feminist Legal Methods [1990]

Katharine T. Bartlett

.   .   .

I. Introduction

In what sense can legal methods be "feminist"? Are there specific methods that feminist lawyers share? If so, what are these methods, why are they used, and what significance do they have to feminist practice? Put another way, what do feminists mean when they say they are doing law, and what do they mean when, having done law, they claim to be "right"?

Feminists have developed extensive critiques of law and proposals for legal reform. Feminists have had much less to say, however, about what the "doing" of law should entail and what truth status to give to the legal claims that follow. These methodological issues matter because methods shape one's view of the possibilities for legal practice and reform. Method "organizes the apprehension of truth; it determines what counts as evidence and defines what is taken as verification."[4] Feminists cannot ignore method, because if they seek to challenge existing structures of power with the same methods that have defined what counts within those structures, they may instead "recreate the illegitimate power structures [that they are] trying to identify and undermine."[5]

Method matters also because without an understanding of feminist methods, feminist claims in the law will not be perceived as legitimate or "correct." I suspect that many who dismiss feminism as trivial or inconsequential misunderstand it. Feminists have tended to focus on defending their various substantive positions or political agendas, even among themselves. Greater attention to issues of method may help to anchor these defenses, to explain why feminist agendas often appear so radical (or not radical enough), and even to establish some common ground among feminists.

As feminists articulate their methods, they can become more aware of the nature of what they do, and thus do it better. Thinking about method is empowering. When I require myself to explain what I do, I am likely to discover how to improve what I earlier may have taken for granted. In the process, I am likely to become more committed to what it is that I have improved. . . .

II. Feminist Doing in Law

When feminists "do law," they do what other lawyers do: they examine the facts of a legal issue or dispute, they identify the essential features of those facts, they determine what legal principles should guide the resolution of the dispute, and they apply those principles to the facts. This process unfolds not in a linear, sequential, or strictly logical manner, but rather in a pragmatic, interactive manner. Facts determine which rules are appropriate, and rules determine which facts are relevant. In doing law, feminists like other lawyers use a full range of methods of legal reasoning—deduction, induction, analogy, and use of hypotheticals, policy, and other general principles.

In addition to these conventional methods of doing law, however, feminists use other methods. These methods, though not all unique to feminists, attempt to reveal features of a legal issue which more traditional methods tend to overlook or suppress. One method, asking the woman question, is designed to expose how the substance of law may silently and without justification submerge the perspectives of women and other excluded groups. Another method, feminist practical reasoning, expands traditional notions of legal relevance to make legal decisionmaking more sensitive to the features of a case not already reflected in legal doctrine. A third method, consciousness-raising, offers a means of testing the validity of accepted legal principles through the lens of the personal experience of those directly affected by those principles. . . .

A. Asking the Woman Question

A question becomes a method when it is regularly asked. Feminists across many disciplines regularly ask a question—a set of questions, really—known as "the woman question,"[23] which is designed to identify the gender implications of rules and practices which might otherwise appear to be neutral or objective.
. . .

1. The Method. The woman question asks about the gender implications of a social practice or rule: have women been left out of consideration? If so, in what way; how might that omission be corrected? What difference would it make to do so? In law, asking the woman question means examining how the law fails to take into account the experiences and values that seem more typical of women than of men, for whatever reason, or how existing legal standards and concepts might disadvantage women. The question assumes that some features of the law may be not only nonneutral in a general sense, but also "male" in a specific sense. The purpose of the woman question is to expose those features and how they operate, and to suggest how they might be corrected.

Women have long been asking the woman question in law. . . . Within the judicial system, Myra Bradwell was one of the first to ask the woman question when she asked why the privileges and immunities of citizenship did not include, for married women in Illinois, eligibility for a state license to practice law.[27] The opinion of the United States Supreme Court in Bradwell's case evaded the gender issue,[28] but Justice Bradley in his concurring opinion set forth the "separate spheres" legal ideology underlying the Illinois law:

> [T]he civil law, as well as nature herself, has always recognized a wide difference in the respective spheres and destinies of man and woman. Man is, or should be, woman's protector and defender. The natural and proper timidity and delicacy which belongs to the female sex evidently unfits it for many of the occupations of civil life. The constitution of the family organization . . . indicates the domestic sphere as that which properly belongs to the domain and functions of womanhood.[29]

Women, and sometimes employers, continued to press the woman question in challenges to sex-based maximum work-hour legislation,[30] other occupation restrictions,[31] voting limitations,[32] and jury-exemption rules.[33] The ideology, however, proved extremely resilient.

Not until the 1970's did the woman question begin to yield different answers about the appropriateness of the role of women assumed by law. The shift began in 1971 with the Supreme Court's ruling on a challenge by Sally Reed to an Idaho statute that gave males preference over females in appointments as estate administrators.[34] Although the Court in *Reed* did not address the separate spheres ideology directly, it rejected arguments of the state that "men [are] as a rule more conversant with business affairs than . . . women,"[35] to find the statutory preference arbitrary and thus in violation of the equal protection clause.[36] This decision was followed by a series of other successful challenges by women arguing that beneath the protective umbrella of the separate spheres ideology lay assumptions that disadvantage women in material, significant ways.[37]

Although the United States Supreme Court has come to condemn explicitly the separate spheres ideology when revealed by gross, stereotypical distinctions, the Court majority has been less sensitive to the effects of more subtle sex-based classifications that affect opportunities for and social views about women. The Court ignored, for example, the implications for women of a male-only draft registration system in reserving combat as a male-only activity.[38] Similarly, in upholding a statutory rape law that made underage sex a crime of males and not of females, the Court overlooked the way in which assumptions about male sexual aggression and female sexual passivity construct sexuality in limiting and dangerous ways.[39]

Pregnancy has been a special problem for the Court. In 1974, Carolyn Aiello and other women asked the woman question by challenging California's singling-out of pregnancy as virtually the only medical condition excluded from its state employee disability plan.[40] Revealing a telling blindness, the Supreme Court's answer to the question defined the relevant groups to compare in a way that severed the connection between gender and pregnancy. "The program divides potential recipients into two groups—pregnant women and nonpregnant persons."[41] Although only women are in the first group, "the second includes members of both sexes."[42] Because women as well as men are in the group who could receive benefits under the plan, the Court concluded that the exclusion of "pregnant persons" could not be discrimination based on sex.[43]

Dissatisfied, feminists continued to refine the woman question about pregnancy, and increasingly supplied their own clear answers to the questions they posed: Do exclusions based on pregnancy disadvantage women? (Of course, because only women can become pregnant.) What are the reasons for singling out pregnancy for exclusion? (Because the inclusion of pregnancy is costly; usually it is also a voluntary condition.) Are other disabilities costly? (Yes.) Are other covered disabilities voluntary? (Yes, some are, like cosmetic surgery and sterilization.)[44] Are there other reasons for treating pregnancy differently? (Well, now that you mention it, pregnant women should be home, nesting.)[45]

Feminists' persistent questioning led to an Act of Congress in 1978, The Pregnancy Discrimination Act,[46] which established the legal connection between gender and pregnancy. The nature of that connection remains contested. Do rules granting pregnant women job security not available to other workers violate the equality principle that has been broadened to encompass pregnancy? The Supreme Court has said "no."[47] Although feminists have split over whether women have more to lose than to gain from singling out pregnancy for different, some would say "favored," treatment,[48] they agree on the critical question: what are the consequences for women of specific rules or practices?

Feminists today ask the woman question in many areas of law. They ask the woman question in rape cases when they ask why the defense of consent focuses on the perspective of the defendant and what he "reasonably" thought the woman wanted, rather than the perspective of the woman and the intentions she "reasonably" thought she conveyed to the defendant.[49] Women ask the woman question when they ask why they are not entitled to be prison guards on the same terms as men[50] [or] why the conflict between work and family responsibilities in women's lives is seen as a private matter for women to resolve within the family rather than a public matter involving restructuring of the workplace.[51]. . . Asking the woman question reveals the ways in which political choice and institutional arrangement contribute to women's subordination. Without the woman question, differences associated with women are taken for granted and, unexamined, may serve as a justification for laws that disadvantage women. The woman question reveals how the position of women reflects the organization of society rather than the inherent characteristics of women. As many feminists have pointed out, difference is located in relationships and social institutions—the workplace, the family, clubs, sports, childrearing patterns, and so on—not in women themselves.[53] In exposing the hidden effects of laws that do not explicitly discriminate on the basis of sex, the woman question helps to demonstrate how social structures embody norms that implicitly render women different and thereby subordinate.

Once adopted as a method, asking the woman question is a method of critique as integral to legal analysis as determining the precedential value of a case, stating the facts, or applying law to facts. "Doing law" as a feminist means looking beneath the surface of law to identify the gender implications of rules and the assumptions underlying them and insisting upon applications of rules that do not perpetuate women's subordination. It means recognizing that the woman question always has potential relevance and that "tight" legal analysis never assumes gender neutrality.

2. The Woman Question: Method or Politics. Is asking the woman question really a method at all, or is it a mask for something else, such as legal substance, or politics? The American legal system has assumed that method and substance have different functions, and that method cannot serve its purpose unless it remains separate from, and independent of, substantive "bias." Rules of legal method, like rules of legal procedure, are supposed to insulate substantive rules from arbitrary application. Substantive rules define the rights and obligations of individuals and legal entities (what the law is); rules of method and procedure define the steps taken in order to ascertain and apply that substance (how to invoke the law and to make it work). Separating rules of method and procedure from substantive rules, under this view, helps to ensure the regular, predictable application of those substantive rules. Thus, conventional and reliable ways of working with substantive rules permit one to specify in advance the consequences of particular activities. Method and process should not themselves have substantive content, the conventional wisdom insists, because method and process are supposed to protect us from substance which comes, "arbitrarily," from outside the rule. Within this conventional view, it might be charged that the method of asking the woman question fails to respect the necessary separation between method and substance. Indeed, asking the woman question seems to be a "loaded," overtly political activity, which reaches far beyond the "neutral" tasks of ascertaining law and facts and applying one to the other.

Of course, not only feminist legal methods but *all* legal methods shape substance;[55] the difference is that feminists have been called on it. Methods shape substance, first, in the leeway they allow for reaching different substantive results. Deciding which facts are relevant, or which legal precedents apply, or how the applicable precedents should be applied, for example, leaves a decisionmaker with a wide range of acceptable substantive results from which to choose. The greater the indeterminacy, the more the decisionmaker's substantive preferences, without meaningful methodological constraints, may determine a particular outcome.[56] Not surprisingly, these preferences may follow certain patterns[57] reflecting the dominant cultural norms.

Methods shape substance also through the hidden biases they contain. A strong view of precedent in legal method, for example, protects the status quo over the interests of those seeking recognition of new rights. The method of distinguishing law from considerations of policy, likewise, reinforces existing power structures and masks exclusions or perspectives ignored by that law.[59] The endless academic debates over originalism, interpretivism, and other theories of constitutional interpretation demonstrate further that methodological principles convey substantive views of law and make a difference to legal results.

Does recognition of the substantive consequences of method make the distinction between method and substance incoherent and pointless? If methods mask substance, why not dispose with method altogether and analyze every legal problem as one of substance alone? There is both a practical and a normative reason to treat legal methods as at least *somewhat* distinct from the substance of law. The practical reason is the virtual impossibility of thinking directly from substance to result in law, except in the most superficial of senses, without methods. Consider, for example, whether a rule against discrimination in the workplace against women with children applies only to hiring policies, or whether it requires particular employee benefits, such as on-the-job childcare or liberal parenting-leave policies. In resolving this question, how relevant are such factors as the previous application of other antidiscrimination rules, the childrearing responsibilities actually born by a claimant, or by mothers in general, the cost of particular benefits to employers, or the possible ramifications of the rule as applied for the free market system? Further substantive rules will help to resolve these issues, but even their application assumes some set of background principles about which facts matter and which sources of interpretation are available to decisionmakers.

Such background principles, or methods, are not only inevitable, but desirable, because they can help to preserve the integrity of the substantive rules which the legal system produces. Feminists, as well as nonfeminists, have a stake in this integrity. As Toni Massaro points out, not all substantive rules are bad rules,[61] and feminists will want to ensure faithful application of the good ones. Whether all decisionmakers can be entirely faithful to the methodological constraints imposed upon them, the existence of these constraints can make a difference.

The real question is neither whether there is such a thing as method—method is inevitable—nor whether methods have substantive consequences—also inevitable—but whether the relationship between method and substance is "proper."[63] Some relationships are improper. A purely result-oriented method in which decisionmakers may decide every case in order to reach the result they think most desirable, for example, improperly exerts no meaningful constraints on the decisionmaker. Also improper is a method that imposes arbitrary or unjustified constraints, such as one that requires a decisionmaker to decide in favor of all female claimants or against all employers.

In contrast, the method of asking the woman question establishes a justifiable relationship to legal substance. This method helps to expose a certain kind of bias in substantive rules. Asking the woman question does not require decision in favor of a woman. Rather, the method requires the decisionmaker to search for gender bias and to reach a decision in the case that is defensible in light of that bias. It demands, in other words, special attention to a set of interests and concerns that otherwise may be, and historically have been, overlooked. The substance of asking the woman question lies in *what* it seeks to uncover: disadvantage based upon gender. The political nature of this method arises only because it seeks information that is not supposed to exist. The claim that this information may exist—and that the woman question is therefore necessary—is political, but only to the extent that the stated or implied claim that it does not exist is *also* political.

Asking the woman question confronts the assumption of legal neutrality, and has substantive consequences only if the law is not gender-neutral. The bias of the method is the bias toward uncovering a certain kind of bias. The bias disadvantages those who are otherwise benefited by law and legal methods whose gender implications are *not* revealed. If this is "bias," feminists must insist that it is "good" (or "proper") bias, not "bad."[64]

3. Converting the Woman Question into the Question of the Excluded. The woman question asks about exclusion. Standing alone, and as usually posed in feminist legal method, it asks about the exclusion of women. Feminists have begun to observe, however, that any analysis using the general category of woman is itself exclusionary, because it treats as universal to women the interests and experiences of a particular group of women—namely white, and otherwise privileged women.[65]. . .

It is not surprising that white women, identifying the oppression they experience primarily as gender-based, have come to describe their feminism as a politics of "women." It is also not surprising that in a movement which grounds its claims to truth in experience, white women would develop a feminism that closely corresponds to their own experiences as white women. Like the male world that feminists seek to expose as partial, the world of feminism betrays the partiality of its makers.

The problem is how to correct this failing while maintaining feminism's ability to analyze the social significance of gender. . . .

To correct feminism's exclusionary failing, [Elizabeth] Spelman suggests that in speaking of "women," the speaker should name explicitly which women she means.[69] This suggestion deserves intensive efforts, though the job is anything but easy. The category of women includes innumerable other categories, and the mention of any of these categories will leave unmentioned many others. One cannot talk about "black women" (as Spelman often does), for example, without implying that one is talking about *heterosexual* black women. One cannot talk about heterosexual black women without implying that one is talking about heterosexual able-bodied women. Any category, no matter how narrowly defined, makes assumptions about the remaining characteristics of the group that fail to take account of members of the group who do not have those characteristics. Spelman's suggestion, therefore, requires distinctions between those categories that should be separately recognized, and those that need not be. The speaker can make such distinctions based upon her understanding about which characteristics are most important to recognize given current social realities. But this is tricky business that requires great sensitivity to multiple, invisible forms of exclusion that many people face. The privileged who attempt this business must recognize the ever-present risks of solipsism without succumbing to a paralyzing paranoia about those risks.[71]

Using the "woman" question as a model for deeper inquiry into the consequences of overlapping forms of oppression could also help to correct the problem Spelman identifies. This inquiry would require a general and far-reaching set of questions that go beyond issues of gender bias to seek out other bases of exclusion: what assumptions are made by law (or practice or analysis) about those whom it affects? Whose point of view do these assumptions reflect? Whose interests are invisible or peripheral? How might excluded viewpoints be identified and taken into account?

Extended beyond efforts to identify oppression based only upon gender, the woman question can reach forms of oppression made invisible not only by the dominant structures of power but also by the efforts to discover bias on behalf of women alone. These forms of oppression differ from gender subordination in kind as well as in degree, and those who have not experienced them are likely to find them difficult to recognize. The difficulty in recognizing oppression one has not experienced, however, makes the necessity of a "method" all the more apparent. As I indicated earlier, a method neither guarantees a particular result nor even the right result. It does, however, provide some discipline when one seeks something that does not correspond to one's own interests.

Will this expanded inquiry dilute the coherence of gender critique? Far from it. As Spelman writes, fine-tuning feminism to encompass the breadth and specificity of oppressions actually experienced by different women—and even some men—can only make feminism clearer and stronger.[72] Coherence, or unity, is possible only when feminism's underlying assumptions speak the truth for many, not a privileged few.

B. Feminist Practical Reasoning

Some feminists have claimed that women approach the reasoning process differently than men do.[74] In particular, they say that women are more sensitive to situation and context, that they resist universal principles and generalizations, especially those that do not fit their own experiences, and that they believe that "the practicalities of everyday life" should not be neglected for the sake of abstract justice.[75] Whether these claims can be empirically sustained, this reasoning process has taken on normative significance for feminists, many of whom have argued that individualized factfinding is often superior to the application of bright-line rules, and that reasoning from context allows a greater respect for difference and for the perspectives of the powerless. In this section, I explore these themes through a discussion of a feminist version of practical reasoning.

1. The Method. As a form of legal reasoning, practical reasoning has many meanings invoked in many contexts for many different purposes. . . . [A] version of practical reasoning . . . that I call "feminist practical reasoning" . . . combines some aspects of a classic Aristotelian model of practical deliberation with a feminist focus on identifying and taking into account the perspectives of the excluded. . . .

(a) Practical reasoning.—According to Amélie Rorty, the Aristotelian model of practical reasoning holistically considers ends, means, and actions in order to "recognize and actualize whatever is best in the most complex, various, and ambiguous situations."[80] Practical reasoning recognizes few, if any, givens. What must be done, and why and how it should be done, are all open questions, considered on the basis of the intricacies of each specific factual context. Not only the resolution of the problem, but even what counts as a problem emerges from the specifics of the situation itself, rather than from some foreordained definition or prescription.

   Practical reasoning approaches problems not as dichotomized conflicts, but
as dilemmas with multiple perspectives, contradictions, and inconsistencies.
These dilemmas, ideally, do not call for the choice of one principle over another,
but rather "imaginative integrations and reconciliations,"[82] which require attention to particular context. Practical reasoning sees particular details not as
annoying inconsistencies or irrelevant nuisances which impede the smooth
logical application of fixed rules. Nor does it see particular facts as the *objects*
of legal analysis, the inert material to which to apply the living law. Instead,
new facts present opportunities for improved understandings and "integrations."
Situations are unique, not anticipated in their detail, not generalizable in advance.
Themselves generative, new situations give rise to "practical" perceptions and
inform decisionmakers about the desired ends of law.[83]

   The issue of minors' access to abortion exemplifies the generative, educative
potential of specific facts. The abstract principle of family autonomy seems
logically to justify a state law requiring minors to obtain their parents' consent
before obtaining an abortion. Minors are immature and parents are the individuals
generally best situated to help them make a decision as difficult as whether to
have an abortion. The actual accounts of the wrenching circumstances under
which a minor might seek to avoid notifying her parent of her decision to
seek an abortion, however, demonstrate the practical difficulties of the matter.
These actual accounts reveal that many minors face severe physical and emotional
abuse as a result of their parents' knowledge of their pregnancy. Parents force
many minors to carry to term a child that the minor cannot possibly raise
responsibly; and only the most determined minor will be able to relinquish
her child for adoption, in the face of parental rejection and manipulation.[84]
Actual circumstances, in other words, yield insights into the difficult problems
of state and family decisionmaking that the abstract concept of parental autonomy
alone does not reveal.

   Practical reasoning in the law does not, and could not, reject rules. Along
the specificity-generality continuum of rules, it tends to favor less specific rules
or "standards," because of the greater leeway for individualized analysis that
standards allow. But practical reasoning in the context of law necessarily works
from rules. Rules represent accumulated past wisdom, which must be reconciled
with the contingencies and practicalities presented by fresh facts. Rules provide
signposts for the appropriate purposes and ends to achieve through law.[86] Rules
check the inclination to be arbitrary and "give constancy and stability in
situations in which bias and passion might distort judgment. . . . Rules are
necessities because we are not always good judges."[87]

   Ideally, however, rules leave room for the new insights and perspectives
generated by new contexts. As noted above, the practical reasoner believes that
the specific circumstances of a new case may dictate novel readings and applications
of rules, readings and applications that not only *were not*, but *could not* or
should not have been determined in advance.[88] In this respect, practical reasoning
differs from the view of law characteristic of the legal realists, who saw rules
as open-ended by necessity, not by choice. The legal realist highly valued
predictability and determinacy, but assumed that facts were too various and

unpredictable for lawmakers to frame determinate rules. The practical reasoner, on the other hand, finds undesirable as well as impractical the reduction of contingencies to rules by which all disputes can be decided in advance.

Another important feature of practical reasoning is what counts as justification. . . . Practical reasoning . . . demands more than *some reasonable* basis for a particular legal decision. Decisionmakers must offer their *actual* reasons—the same reasons "that form its effective intentional description."[93] This requirement reflects the inseparability of the determinations of means and ends; reasoning is itself part of the "end," and the end cannot be reasonable apart from the reasoning that underlies it. It reflects, further, the commitment of practical reasoning to the decisionmaker's acceptance of responsibility for decisions made. Rules do not absolve the decisionmaker from responsibility for decisions. There are choices to be made and the agent who makes them must admit to those choices and defend them.[94]

(b) Feminist practical reasoning.—Feminist practical reasoning builds upon the traditional mode of practical reasoning by bringing to it the critical concerns and values reflected in other feminist methods, including the woman question. The classical exposition of practical reasoning takes for granted the legitimacy of the community whose norms it expresses, and for that reason tends to be fundamentally conservative.[95] Feminist practical reasoning challenges the legitimacy of the norms of those who claim to speak, through rules, for the community. No form of legal reasoning can be free, of course, from the past or from community norms, because law is always situated in a context of practices and values. Feminist practical reasoning differs from other forms of legal reasoning, however, in the strength of its commitment to the notion that there is not one, but many overlapping communities to which one might look for "reason." Feminists consider the concept of community problematic, because they have demonstrated that law has tended to reflect existing structures of power. Carrying over their concern for inclusionism from the method of asking the woman question, feminists insist that no one community is legitimately privileged to speak for all others. Thus, feminist methods reject the monolithic community often assumed in male accounts of practical reasoning, and seek to identify perspectives not represented in the dominant culture from which reason should proceed.

Feminist practical reasoning, however, is not the polar opposite of a "male" deductive model of legal reasoning. The deductive model assumes that for any set of facts, fixed, pre-existing legal rules compel a single, correct result. Many commentators have noted that virtually no one, male or female, now defends the strictly deductive approach to legal reasoning.[100] Contextualized reasoning is also not, as some commentators suggest,[101] the polar opposite of a "male" model of abstract thinking. All major forms of legal reasoning encompass processes of both contextualization and abstraction. Even the most conventional legal methods require that one look carefully at the factual context of a case in order to identify similarities and differences between that case and others. The identification of a legal problem, selection of precedent, and application of that precedent, all require an understanding of the details of a case and how they relate to one another. When the details change, the rule and its application are likely to change as well.

By the same token, feminist methods require the process of abstraction, that is, the separation of the significant from the insignificant. Concrete facts have significance only if they represent some generalizable aspect of the case. Generalizations identify what matters and draw connections to other cases. I abstract whenever I fail to identify every fact about a situation, which, of course, I do always.[104] For feminists, practical reasoning and asking the woman question may make more facts relevant or "essential" to the resolution of a legal case than would more nonfeminist legal analysis. For example, feminist practical reasoning deems relevant facts related to the woman question—facts about whose interests particular rules or legal resolutions reflect and whose interests require more deliberate attention. Feminists do not and cannot reject, however, the process of abstraction. Thus, though I might determine in a marital rape case that it is relevant that the wife did not want sexual intercourse on the day in question, it will probably not be relevant that the defendant gave a box of candy to his mother on St. Valentine's Day or that he plays bridge well. No matter how detailed the level of particularity, practical reasoning like all other forms of legal analysis requires selecting and giving meaning to *certain* particularities. Feminist practical reasoning assumes that no a priori reasons prevent one from being persuaded that a fact that seems insignificant *is* significant, but it does not require that every fact be relevant. Likewise, although generalizations that render detail irrelevant require examination, they are not a priori unacceptable.

Similarly, the feminist method of practical reasoning is not the polar opposite of "male" rationality. The process of finding commonalities, differences, and connections in practical reasoning is a rational process. To be sure, feminist practical reasoning gives rationality new meanings. Feminist rationality acknowledges greater diversity in human experiences[106] and the value of taking into account competing or inconsistent claims.[107] It openly reveals its positional partiality by stating explicitly which moral and political choices underlie that partiality,[108] and recognizes its own implications for the distribution and exercise of power.[109] Feminist rationality also strives to integrate emotive and intellectual elements[110] and to open up the possibilities of new situations rather than limit them with prescribed categories of analysis. Within these revised meanings, however, feminist method is and must be understandable. It strives to make more sense of human experience, not less, and is to be judged upon its capacity to do so.

* * *

[2]. Feminist Practical Reasoning: Method or Substance? . . . Do feminists reason contextually in order to avoid the application of rules. . . to which they substantively object? Or can the substantive consequences of feminist practical reasoning be justified as a proper means of moving from rules to results in specific cases?

Whether the relationship between feminist practical reasoning and legal substance is a "proper" one depends upon some crucial assumptions about legal decisionmaking. If one assumes that methods can and should screen out political and moral factors from legal decisionmaking, practical reasoning is not an appropriate mode of legal analysis. To the contrary, its open-endedness would seem to provide the kind of opportunity for deciding cases on the basis of political or moral interests that method, operating independently from substance, is supposed to eliminate.

On the other hand, if one assumes that one neither can nor should eliminate political and moral factors from legal decisionmaking, then one would hope to make these factors more visible. If political and moral factors are necessarily tied into any form of legal reasoning, then bringing those factors out into the open would require decisionmakers to think self-consciously about them and to justify their decisions in the light of the factors at play in the particular case.

Feminists, not surprisingly, favor the second set of assumptions over the first. Feminists' substantive analyses of legal decisionmaking have revealed to them that so-called neutral means of deciding cases tend to mask, not eliminate, political and social considerations from legal decisionmaking.[134] Feminists have found that neutral rules and procedures tend to drive underground the ideologies of the decisionmaker, and that these ideologies do not serve women's interests well. Disadvantaged by hidden bias, feminists see the value of modes of legal reasoning that expose and open up debate concerning the underlying political and moral considerations. By forcing articulation and understanding of those considerations, practical reasoning forces justification of results based upon what interests are actually at stake.

The "substance" of feminist practical reasoning consists of an alertness to certain forms of injustice that otherwise go unnoticed and unaddressed. Feminists turn to contextualized methods of reasoning to allow greater understanding and exposure of that injustice. Reasoning from context can change perceptions about the world, which may then further expand the contexts within which such reasoning seems appropriate, which in turn may lead to still further changes in perceptions. The expansion of existing boundaries of relevance based upon changed perceptions of the world is familiar to the process of legal reform. The shift from *Plessy v. Ferguson*[135] to *Brown v. Board of Education*,[136] for example, rested upon the expansion of the "legally relevant" in race discrimination cases to include the actual experiences of black Americans and the inferiority implicit in segregation. Much of the judicial reform that has been beneficial to women, as well, has come about through expanding the lens of legal relevance to encompass the missing perspectives of women and to accommodate perceptions about the nature and role of women. Feminist practical reasoning compels continued expansion of such perceptions.

C. *Consciousness-Raising*

Another feminist method for expanding perceptions is consciousness-raising.[139] Consciousness-raising is an interactive and collaborative process of articulating one's experiences and making meaning of them with others who also articulate their experiences. As Leslie Bender writes, "Feminist consciousness-raising creates knowledge by exploring common experiences and patterns that emerge from shared tellings of life events. What were experienced as personal hurts individually suffered reveal themselves as a collective experience of oppression."[140]

Consciousness-raising is a method of trial and error. When revealing an experience to others, a participant in consciousness-raising does not know whether others will recognize it. The process values risk-taking and vulnerability over caution and detachment. Honesty is valued above consistency, teamwork over self-sufficiency, and personal narrative over abstract analysis. The goal is individual and collective empowerment, not personal attack or conquest.

Elizabeth Schneider emphasizes the centrality of consciousness-raising to the dialectical relationship of theory and practice. "Consciousness-raising groups start with personal and concrete experience, integrate this experience into theory, and then, in effect, reshape theory based upon experience and experience based upon theory. Theory expresses and grows out of experience but it also relates back to that experience for further refinement, validation, or modification."[141] The interplay between experience and theory "reveals the social dimension of individual experience and the individual dimension of social experience"[142] and hence the political nature of personal experience.[143]

Consciousness-raising operates as feminist method not only in small personal growth groups, but also on a more public, institutional level, through "bearing witness to evidences of patriarchy as they occur, through unremitting dialogues with and challenges to the patriarchs, and through the popular media, the arts, politics, lobbying, and even litigation."[144] Women use consciousness-raising when they publicly share their experiences as victims of marital rape, pornography, sexual harassment on the job, street hassling, and other forms of oppression and exclusion, in order to help change public perceptions about the meaning to women of events widely thought to be harmless or flattering.

Consciousness-raising has consequences, further, for laws and institutional decisionmaking more generally. Several feminists have translated the insights of feminist consciousness-raising into their normative accounts of legal process and legal decisionmaking. Carrie Menkel-Meadow, for example, has speculated that as the number of women lawyers increases, women's more interactive approaches to decisionmaking will improve legal process.[149] Similarly, Judith Resnik has argued that feminist judging will involve more collaborative decisionmaking among judges.[150] Such changes would have important implications for the possibilities for lawyering and judging as matters of collective engagement rather than the individual exercise of judgment and power.

The primary significance of consciousness-raising, however, is as meta-method. Consciousness-raising provides a substructure for other feminist methods— including the woman question and feminist practical reasoning—by enabling feminists to draw insights and perceptions from their own experiences and those of other women and to use these insights to challenge dominant versions of social reality.

. . . As consciousness-raising has matured as method, disagreements among feminists about the meaning of certain experiences have proliferated. Feminists disagree, for example, about whether women can voluntarily choose heterosexuality, or motherhood; or about whether feminists have more to gain or lose from restrictions against pornography, surrogate motherhood, or about whether women should be subject to a military draft. They disagree about each other's roles in an oppressive society: some feminists accuse others of complicity in the oppression of women. Feminists disagree even about the method of consciousness-raising; some women worry that it sometimes operates to pressure women into translating their experiences into positions that are politically, rather than experientially, correct.

These disagreements raise questions beyond those of which specific methods are appropriate to feminist practice. Like the woman question and practical reasoning, consciousness-raising challenges the concept of knowledge. It presupposes that what I thought I knew may not, in fact, be "right." How, then, will we know when we *have* got it "right"? Or, backing up one step, what does it mean to *be* right? And what attitude should I have about that which I claim to know? . . .

III. Feminist Knowing in Law

A point—perhaps *the* point—of legal methods is to reach answers that are legally defensible or in some sense "right." Methods themselves imply a stance toward rightness. If being right means having discovered some final, objective truth based in a fixed physical or moral reality, for example, verification is possible and leaves no room for further perspectives or for doubt. On the other hand, if being right means that one has expressed one's personal tastes or interests which have no greater claim to validity than those of anyone else, being right is a rhetorical device used to assert one's own point of view, and verification is both impossible and pointless.

In this section, I explore several feminist explanations for what it means to be "right" in law.[158] I look first at a range of positions that have emerged from within feminist theory. These include the three positions customarily included in feminist epistemological discussions: the rational/empirical position, standpoint epistemology, and postmodernism.[159] In addition I examine a fourth stance called positionality,[160] which synthesizes some aspects of the first three into a new, and I think more satisfactory, whole. I evaluate each position from the same pragmatic viewpoint reflected in the feminist methods I have described: how can that position help feminists, using feminist methods, to generate the kind of insights, values, and self-knowledge that feminism needs to maintain its critical challenge to existing structures of power and to reconstruct new, and better, structures in their place? These criteria are admittedly circular: I evaluate theories of knowledge by how well they make sense in light of that which feminists claim as knowledge and in light of the methods used to obtain knowledge. This circularity, however, is consistent with one of the central features of the version of feminism I advocate. Any set of values and truths, including those of feminists, must make sense within the terms of the social realities that have generated them. Any explanation of that verification must also operate in the context in which verifications take place—in practice.

A. The Rational/Empirical Position

Feminists across many disciplines have engaged in considerable efforts to show how, by the standards of their own disciplines, to improve accepted methodologies. These efforts have led to the unraveling of descriptions of women as morally inferior, psychologically unstable, and historically insignificant—descriptions these disciplines long accepted as authoritative and unquestionable.

Similarly, feminists in law attempt to use the tools of law, on its own terms, to improve law. . . . [F]eminists often challenge assumptions about women that underlie numerous laws and demonstrate how laws based upon these assumptions are not rational and neutral, but rather irrational and discriminatory. When engaged in these challenges, feminists operate from a rational/empirical position that assumes that [existing] law is not objective, but that identifying and correcting its mistaken assumptions can make it more objective.

When feminists challenged employment rules that denied disability benefits to pregnant women, for example, they used empirical and rational arguments about the similarity between pregnancy and other disabilities. Faced with state laws designed to address the disadvantages experienced by pregnant women in the workplace, some feminists argued that such "special treatment" for pregnant women reinforces stereotypes about women and should be rejected under the equality principle. Other feminists argued that pregnancy affects only women and that lack of accommodation for it will prevent women from achieving equality in the workplace. Each side of the debate defended a different concept of equality, but the underlying argument focused upon which is the most rational, empirically sound and legally supportable interpretation of equality. . . .

Feminists also argue that particular reforms in child custody law would more rationally meet the law's express purpose of protecting the best interests of the child. Some feminists favor the tender-years doctrine or the maternal-preference rule, on the ground that women are likely to be the actual caretakers of children, and that the bias against women of the white, male judges who decide custody cases makes such a rule necessary to give women a fair shot at custody. Other feminists argue that applying the best-interests-of-the-child test on a case-by-case basis will produce the fairest and most neutral child-custody decisions. Still other feminists advocate a primary caretaker presumption on the empirical ground that a child's primary caretaker is most likely to be the parent in whose custody the child's best interests lies, and that this standard minimizes the potential intimidation that can be exercised against a risk-averse parent who has invested the most in the child's care. Finally, some feminists favor rules that promote joint custody, based upon empirical claims about which rules best serve the interests of children and women.

All of these arguments from the rational/empirical stance share the premise that knowledge is accessible and, when obtained, can make law more rational. The relevant empirical questions are often very difficult ones: if parents, usually men, who fall behind in their child support obligations face almost certain jail sentences, will they be more likely to make their child support payments on time? If state law singles out pregnancy as the only condition for which job security is mandated, how much additional resistance to hiring women, if any, is likely to be created, and what impact on the stereotyping of women, if any, is likely to result? The rational/empirical position presumes, however, that answers to such questions can be improved—that there is a "right" answer to get—and that once gotten, that answer can improve the law.

Some feminists charge that improving the empirical basis of law or its rationality is mere "reformism" that cannot reach the deeper gendered nature of law. This charge unfortunately undervalues the enormous transformation in thinking about women that the empirical challenge to law, in which all feminists have participated, has brought about. Feminist rational/empiricism has begun to expose the deeply flawed factual assumptions about women that have pervaded many disciplines, and has changed, in profound ways, the perception of women in this society. Few, if any, feminists, however, operate entirely within the rational/empirical stance, because it tends to limit attention to matters of factual rather than normative accuracy, and thus fails to take account of the social construction of reality through which factual or rational propositions mask normative constructions. Empirical and rational arguments challenge existing assumptions about reality and, in particular, the inaccurate reality conveyed by stereotypes about women. But if reality is not representational or objective and not above politics, the method of correcting inaccuracies ultimately cannot provide a basis for understanding and reconstructing that reality. The rational/empirical assumption that principles such as objectivity and neutrality can question empirical assumptions within law fails to recognize that knowability is itself a debatable issue. I explore positions that challenge, rather than presuppose, knowability in the following sections.

B. *Standpoint Epistemology*

The problem of knowability in feminist thought arises from the observation that what women know has been determined—perhaps overdetermined—by male culture. Some of the feminists most concerned about the problem of overdetermination have adopted a "standpoint epistemology"[177] to provide the grounding upon which feminists can claim that their own legal methods, legal reasoning, and proposals for substantive legal reform are "right."

Feminist standpoint epistemology identifies woman's status as that of victim, and then privileges that status by claiming that it gives access to understanding about oppression that others cannot have. It grounds this privilege in the contention that pain and subordination provide the oppressed "with a motivation for finding out what is wrong, for criticizing accepted interpretations of reality and for developing new and less distorted ways of understanding the world."[178] The experience of being a victim therefore reveals truths about reality that non-victims do not see.

> Women know the world is out there. Women know the world is out there because it hits us in the face. Literally. We are raped, battered, pornographed, defined by force, by a world that begins, at least, entirely outside us. No matter what we

think about it, how we try to think it out of existence or into a different shape for us to inhabit, the world remains real. Try some time. It exists independent of our will. We can tell that it is there, because no matter what we do, we can't get out of it.[179]

Feminists have located the foundation of women's subordination in different aspects of women's experiences. Feminist post-Marxists find this foundation in women's activities in production, both domestic and in the marketplace; others emphasize women's positions in the sexual hierarchy, in women's bodies, or in women's responses to the pain and fear of male violence. Whatever the source, however, these feminists claim that the material deprivation of the oppressed gives them a perspective—an access of knowledge—that the oppressors cannot possibly have.

Standpoint epistemology has contributed a great deal to feminist understandings of the importance of our respective positioning within society to the "knowledge" we have. Feminist standpoint epistemologies question "the assumption that the social identity of the observer is irrelevant to the 'goodness' of the results of research," and reverse the priority of a distanced, "objective" standpoint in favor of one of experience and engagement.[185]

Despite the valuable insights offered by feminist standpoint epistemology, however, it does not offer an adequate account of feminist knowing. First, in isolating gender as a source of oppression, feminist legal thinkers tend to concentrate on the identification of woman's true identity beneath the oppression and thereby essentialize her characteristics. Catharine MacKinnon, for example, in exposing what she finds to be the total system of male hegemony, repeatedly speaks of "women's point of view,"[186] of "woman's voice,"[187] of empowering women "on our own terms,"[188] of what women "really want,"[189] and of standards that are "not ours."[190] Ruth Colker sees the discovery of women's "authentic self"[191] as a difficult job given the social constructions imposed upon women, but nonetheless, like MacKinnon, insists upon it as a central goal of feminism. Robin West, too, assumes that woman has a "true nature" upon which to base a feminist jurisprudence.[192]

Although the essentialist positions taken by these feminists often have strategic or rhetorical value,[193] these positions obscure the importance of differences among women and the fact that factors other than gender victimize women. . . .

. . . [S]tandpoint epistemologists also tend to presuppose too narrow a view of privilege. I doubt that being a victim is the only experience that gives special access to truth. Although victims know something about victimization that non-victims do not, victims do not have exclusive access to truth about oppression. The positions of others—co-victims, passive bystanders, even the victimizers— yield perspectives of special knowledge that those who seek to end oppression must understand.

Standpoint epistemology's claim that women have special access to knowledge also does not account for why all women, including those who are similarly situated, do not share the same interpretations of those situations—"a special explanation of non-perception."[196] One account argues that the hold of patriarchal ideology, which "intervenes successfully to limit feminist consciousness,"[197] causes "false consciousness." Although feminist legal theorists rarely offer this explanation explicitly, it is implicit in theories that associate with women certain essential characteristics, variance from which connotes a distortion of who women really are or what they really want.[198]

False consciousness surely does not satisfactorily explain women's different perceptions of their experiences. Such an explanation negates the standpoint claim that experience itself, not some external or objective standard, is the source of knowledge. In addition, to suggest that one's consciousness is "false," and thus another's "true," is at odds with the assumption of MacKinnon and others that male patriarchy has totally constructed women's perceptions for its own purposes.[199] If male patriarchy is as successful as MacKinnon claims, on what basis can some women pretend to escape it?

MacKinnon herself recognizes the infeasibility of false consciousness as an explanation for women's different perceptions;[200] yet throughout her writings, her branding of women with whom she does not agree as collaborators[201] and rejection of the suggestion that feminism is either subjective or partial implies this explanation.[202] Colker is sensitive to the problem of selecting one version of women's experience as politically correct, but she also remains trapped in the contradiction between the claim that women have "authentic selves" and the claim that they are victims of someone else's fantasy.[203]

A final difficulty with standpoint epistemology is the adversarial we/they politics it engenders. Identification from the standpoint of victims seems to require enemies, wrongdoers, victimizers.[204] Those identified as victims ("we") stand in stark contrast to others ("they"), whose claim to superior knowledge becomes not only false but suspect in some deeper sense: conspiratorial, evil-minded, criminal. You (everyone) must be either with us or against us. Men are actors—not innocent actors, but evil, corrupt, irredeemable. They conspire to protect male advantage and to perpetuate the subordination of women.[205] Even women must choose sides, and those who chose badly are condemned.[206]

This adversarial position hinders feminist practice. It impedes understanding by would-be friends of feminism and paralyzes potential sympathizers. Even more seriously, it misstates the problem that women face, which is not that men act "freely" and women do not, but that both men and women, in different but interrelated ways, are confined by gender. The mystifying ideologies of gender construction control men, too, however much they may also benefit from them. As Jane Flax writes, "Unless we see gender as a social relation, rather than as an opposition of inherently different beings, we will not be able to identify the varieties and limitations of different women's (or men's) powers and oppressions within particular societies."[209] In short, gender reform must entail not so much the conquest of the now-all-powerful enemy male, as the transformation of those ideologies that maintain the current relationships of subordination and oppression.

C. Postmodernism

The postmodern or poststructural critique of foundationalism resolves the problem of knowability in a quite different way. While standpoint epistemology relocates the source of knowledge from the oppressor to the oppressed, the postmodern critique of foundationalism questions the possibility of knowledge, including knowledge about categories of people such as women. This critique rejects essentialist thinking as it insists that the subject, including the female subject, has no core identity but rather is constituted through multiple structures and discourses that in various ways overlap, intersect, and contradict each other. Although these structures and discourses "overdetermine" woman and thereby produce "the subject's experience of differentiated identity and . . . autonomy,"[212] the postmodern view posits that the realities experienced by the subject are not in any way transcendent or representational, but rather particular and fluctuating, constituted within a complex set of social contexts. Within this position, being human, or female, is strictly a matter of social, historical, and cultural construction.

Postmodern critiques have challenged the binary oppositions in language, law, and other socially-constituting systems, oppositions which privilege one presence—male, rationality, objectivity—and marginalize its opposite—female, irrationality, subjectivity. Postmodernism removes the grounding from these oppositions and from all other systems of power or truth that claim legitimacy on the basis of external foundations or authorities. In so doing, it removes external grounding from any particular agenda for social reform. In the words of Nancy Fraser and Linda Nicholson, postmodern social criticism "floats free of any universalist theoretical ground. No longer anchored philosophically, the very shape or character of social criticism changes; it becomes more pragmatic, ad hoc, contextual, and local."[215] There are no external, overarching systems of legitimation; "[t]here are no special tribunals set apart from the sites where inquiry is practiced." Instead, practices develop their own constitutive norms, which are "plural, local, and immanent."[216]

The postmodern critique of foundationalism has made its way into legal discourse through the critical legal studies movement. The feminists associated with this movement have stressed both the indeterminacy of law and the extent to which law, despite its claim to neutrality and objectivity, masks particular hierarchies and distributions of power. These feminists have engaged in deconstructive projects that have revealed the hidden gender bias of a wide range of laws and legal assumptions. Basic to these projects has been the critical insight that not only law itself, but also the criteria for legal validity and legitimacy, are social constructs rather than universal givens.

Although the postmodern critique of foundationalism has had considerable influence on feminist legal theory, some feminists have cautioned that this critique poses a threat not only to existing power structures, but to feminist politics as well. To the extent that feminist politics turns on a particular story of woman's oppression, a theory of knowledge that denies that an independent, determinate reality exists would seem to deny the basis of that politics. Without a notion of objectivity, feminists have difficulty claiming that their emergence from male hegemony is less artificial and constructed than that which they have cast off, or that their truths are more firmly grounded than those whose accounts of being women vary widely from their own. Thus, as Deborah Rhode observes, feminists influenced by postmodernism are "left in the awkward position of maintaining that gender oppression exists while challenging [their] capacity to document it."[221]

Feminists need a stance toward knowledge that takes into account the contingency of knowledge claims while allowing for a concept of truth or objectivity that can sustain an agenda for meaningful reform. The postmodern critique of foundationalism is persuasive to many feminists, whose experiences affirm that rules and principles asserted as universal truths reflect particular, contingent realities that reinforce their subordination. At the same time, however, feminists must be able to insist that they have identified unacceptable forms of oppression and that they have a better account of the world free from such oppression. Feminists, according to Linda Alcoff, "need to have their accusations of misogyny validated rather than rendered 'undecidable.'"[222] In addition, they must build from the postmodern critique about "how meanings and bodies get made," Donna Haraway writes, "not in order to deny meanings and bodies, but in order to build meanings and bodies that have a chance for life."[223]

To focus attention on this project of rebuilding, feminists need a theory of knowledge that affirms and directs the construction of new meanings. Feminists must be able to both deconstruct *and construct* knowledge. . . .

D. Positionality

Positionality is a stance from which a number of apparently inconsistent feminist "truths" make sense. The positional stance acknowledges the existence of empirical truths, values and knowledge, and also their contingency. It thereby provides a basis for feminist commitment and political action, but views these commitments as provisional and subject to further critical evaluation and revision.

Like standpoint epistemology, positionality retains a concept of knowledge based upon experience. Experience interacts with an individual's current perceptions to reveal new understandings and to help that individual, with others, make sense of those perceptions. Thus, from women's position of exclusion, women have come to "know" certain things about exclusion: its subtlety; its masking by "objective" rules and constructs; its pervasiveness; its pain; and the need to change it. These understandings make difficult issues decidable and answers non-arbitrary.

Like the postmodern [stance], however, positionality rejects the perfectibility, externality, or objectivity of truth. Instead, the positional knower conceives of truth as situated and partial. Truth is situated in that it emerges from particular involvements and relationships. These relationships, not some essential or innate characteristics of the individual, define the individual's perspective and provide the location for meaning, identity, and political commitment. Thus, for example, the meaning of pregnancy derives not just from its biological characteristics, but from the social place it occupies—how workplace structures, domestic arrangements, tort systems, high schools, prisons, and other societal institutions construct its meaning.

Truth is partial in that the individual perspectives that yield and judge truth are necessarily incomplete. No individual can understand except from some limited perspective. Thus, for example, a man experiences pornography as a man with a particular upbringing, set of relationships, race, social class, sexual preference, and so on, which affect what "truths" he perceives about pornography. A woman experiences pregnancy as a woman with a particular upbringing, race, social class, set of relationships, sexual preference, and so on, which affect what "truths" she perceives about pregnancy. As a result, there will always be "knowers" who have access to knowledge that other individuals do not have, and no one's truth can be deemed total or final.

Because knowledge arises within social contexts and in multiple forms, the key to increasing knowledge lies in the effort to extend one's limited perspective. Self-discipline is crucial.[229] My perspective gives me a source of special knowledge, but a limited knowledge that I can improve by the effort to step beyond it, to understand other perspectives, and to expand my sources of identity.[230] To be sure, I cannot transcend my perspective; by definition, whatever perspective I currently have limits my view. But I can improve my perspective by stretching my imagination to identify and understand the perspectives of others.[231]

Positionality's requirement that other perspectives be sought out and examined checks the characteristic tendency of all individuals—including feminists—to want to stamp their own point of view upon the world. This requirement does not allow certain feminist positions to be set aside as immune from critical examination.[233] When feminists oppose restrictive abortion laws, for example, positionality compels the effort to understand those whose views about the sanctity of potential human life are offended by assertion of women's unlimited right to choose abortion. When feminists debate the legal alternative of joint custody at divorce, positionality compels appreciation of the desire by some fathers to be responsible, co-equal parents. And (can it get worse?) when feminists urge drastic reform of rape laws, positionality compels consideration of the position of men whose social conditioning leads them to interpret the actions of some women as "inviting" rather than discouraging sexual encounter.

Although I must consider other points of view from the positional stance, I need not accept their truths as my own. Positionality is not a strategy of process and compromise that seeks to reconcile all competing interests. Rather, it imposes a twin obligation to make commitments based on the current truths and values that have emerged from methods of feminism, and to be open to previously unseen perspectives that might come to alter these commitments. As a practical matter, of course, I cannot do both simultaneously, evenly, and perpetually.[234] Positionality, however, sets an ideal of self-critical commitment whereby I act, but consider the truths upon which I act subject to further refinement, amendment, and correction.

Some "truths" will emerge from the ongoing process of critical reexamination in a form that seems increasingly fixed or final. Propositions such as that I should love my children, that I should not murder others for sport, or that democracy is as a general matter better than authoritarianism seem so "essential" to my identity and my social world that I experience them as values that can never be overridden, even as standards by which I may judge others.[235] These truths, indeed, seem to confirm the view that truth does exist (it must; these things are true) if only I could find it. For feminists, the commitment to ending gender-based oppression has become one of these "permanent truths." The problem is the human inclination to make this list of "truths" too long, to be too uncritical of its contents, and to defend it too harshly and dogmatically.

Positionality reconciles the existence of reliable, experience-based grounds for assertions of truth upon which politics should be based, with the need to question and improve these grounds. The understanding of truth as "real," in the sense of produced by the actual experiences of individuals in their concrete social relationships, permits the appreciation of plural truths. By the same token, if truth is understood as partial and contingent, each individual or group can approach its own truths with a more honest, self-critical attitude about the value and potential relevance of other truths.

The ideal presented by the positionality stance makes clear that current disagreements within society at large and among feminists—disagreements about abortion, child custody, pornography, the military, pregnancy, motherhood, and the like—reflect value conflicts basic to the terms of social existence. If resolvable at all, these conflicts will not be settled by reference to external or pre-social standards of truth. From the positional stance, any resolutions that emerge are the products of human struggles about what social realities are better than others. Realities are deemed better not by comparison to some external, "discovered" moral truths or "essential" human characteristics, but by internal truths that make the most sense of experienced, social existence. Thus, social truths will emerge from social relationships and what, after critical examination, they tell social beings about what they want themselves, and their social world, to be.[236] As Charles Taylor writes, "What better measure of reality do we have in human affairs than those terms which on critical reflection and after correction of the errors we can detect make the best sense of our lives?"[237]

In this way, feminist positionality resists attempts at classification either as essentialist . . . or relativistic. . . . . Donna Haraway sees relativism and essentialism, or what she calls totalization, as mirror images, each of which makes seeing well difficult: "Relativism and totalization are both 'god tricks' promising vision from everywhere and nowhere equally and fully . . . ."[239] Positionality is both nonrelative and nonarbitrary. It assumes some means of distinguishing between better and worse understanding; truth claims are significant or "valid" for those who experience that validity. But positionality puts no stock in fixed, discoverable foundations. If there is any such thing as ultimate or objective truth, I can never, in my own lifetime, be absolutely sure that I have discovered it. I can know important and non-arbitrary truths, but these are necessarily mediated through human experiences and relationships. There can be no universal, final, or objective truth; there can be only "partial, locatable, critical knowledges";[241] no aperspectivity—only improved perspectives.

Because provisional truth is partial and provisional, the nature of positional truth-seeking differs from that assumed under either a relativist or an essentialist stance. Positional meanings are what Moira Gatens calls meanings in "*becoming* rather than being, [in] *possibilities* rather than certainty and [in] meaning or *significance* rather than truth."[242] The attitude of positional understanding assumes that arrival is not possible; indeed, there is no place at which we *could* finally arrive. Truth-seeking demands "ceaseless critical engagement"; as Gatens writes, "there cannot be an unadulterated feminist theory which would announce our arrival at a place where we could say we are 'beyond' patriarchal theory and patriarchal experience."[243] Not only is truth unfixed, but the human capacity to attain it is limited. Iris Murdoch's Socrates captures the point dynamically: "We put the truth into a conceptual picture because we feel it can't be expressed in any other way; and then truth itself forces us to criticize the picture."[244]

A stance of positionality can reconcile the apparent contradiction within feminist thought between the need to recognize the diversity of people's lives and the value in trying to transcend that diversity. Feminists, like those associated with the critical legal studies movement, understand that when those with power pretend that their interests are natural, objective and inevitable, they suppress and ignore other diverse perspectives. This understanding compels feminists to make constant efforts to test the extent to which they, also, unwittingly project their experiences upon others. To understand human diversity, however, is also to understand human commonality. From the positional stance, I can attain self-knowledge through the effort to identify not only what is different, but also what I have in common with those who have other perspectives. This effort, indeed, becomes a "foundation" for further knowledge.[245] I achieve meaning in my own life when I come to know myself in knowing others.[246] In fact, it is when I cease to recognize my mutual relatedness with others that I inevitably project my own experiences upon them to make "identification with them impossible."[247]

Because of its linkage between knowledge and seeking out other perspectives, positionality provides the best foothold from which feminists may insist upon both the diversity of others' experiences, and their mutual relatedness and common humanity with others. This dual focus seeks knowledge of individual and community, apart and as necessarily interdependent. . . . Positionality locates the source of community in its diversity and affirms Frank Michelman's conclusions about human commonality: "The human universal becomes difference itself. Difference is what we most fundamentally have in common."[249]

All three of the methods [I have discussed] affirm, and are enhanced by, the stance of positionality. In asking the woman question, feminists situate themselves in the perspectives of women affected in various ways and to various extents by legal rules and ideologies that purport to be neutral and objective. The process of challenging these rules and ideologies, deliberately, from particular, self-conscious perspectives, assumes that the process of revealing and correcting various forms of oppression is never-ending. Feminist practical reasoning, likewise, exposes and helps to limit the damage that universalizing rules and assumptions can do; universalizations will always be present, but contextualized reasoning will help to identify those currently useful and eliminate the others. Consciousness-raising links that process of reasoning to the concrete experiences associated with growth from one set of moral and political insights to another. Positional understanding enhances alertness to the special problems of oppressive orthodoxies in consciousness-raising, and the insights developed through collaborative interaction should remain open to challenge, and not be held hostage to the unfortunate tendency in all social structures to assume that some insights are too politically "correct" to question.

Positional understanding requires efforts both to establish good law and to keep in place, and renew, the means for deconstructing and improving that law. In addition to focusing on existing conditions, feminist methods must be elastic enough to open up and make visible new forms of oppression and bias. Reasoning from context and consciousness-raising are self-renewing methods that may enable continual new discoveries. Through critical practice, new methods should also evolve that will lead to new questions, improved partial insights, better law, and still further critical methods.

IV. Conclusion: Feminist Methods as Ends

I have argued that feminist methods are means to feminist ends: that asking the woman question, feminist practical reasoning, and consciousness-raising are methods that arise from and sustain feminist practice. Having established the feminist stance of positionality, I now want to expand my claim to argue that feminist methods are also ends in themselves. Central to the concept of positionality is the assumption that although partial objectivity is possible, it is transitional, and therefore must be continually subject to the effort to reappraise, deconstruct, and transform. That effort, and the hope that must underlie it, constitute the optimistic version of feminism to which I adhere. Under this version, human flourishing means being engaged in the world through the kinds of critical yet constructive feminist methods I have described. These methods can give feminists a way of doing law that expresses who they are and who they wish to become.

This is, I contend, a goal central to feminism: to be engaged, with others, in a critical, transforming process of seeking further partial knowledges from one's admittedly limited habitat. This goal is the grounding of feminism, a grounding that combines the search for further understandings and sustained criticism toward those understandings. Feminist doing is, in the sense, feminist knowing. And vice versa.

Notes

4. MacKinnon, [*Feminism, Marxism, Method, and the State: An Agenda for Theory*, 7 SIGNS 515, 527 (1982) (hereinafter MacKinnon, *Agenda for Theory*)].

5. Singer, *Should Lawyers Care About Philosophy?* (Book Review), 1989 DUKE L.J. [1752, 1753].

23. *See, e.g.*, Gould, *The Woman Question: Philosophy of Liberation and the Liberation of Philosophy*, in WOMEN AND PHILOSOPHY: TOWARD A THEORY OF LIBERATION 5 (C. Gould & M. Wartofsky eds. 1976) (discussing the woman question in philosophy); Hawkesworth, *Feminist Rhetoric: Discourses on the Male Monopoly of Thought*, 16 POL. THEORY 444, 452–56 (1988) (examining the treatment of the woman question in political theory). The first use of the term "woman question" of which I am aware is in S. DE BEAUVOIR, THE SECOND SEX at xxvi (1957).

27. *See* Bradwell v. Illinois, 83 U.S. (16 Wall.) 130 (1873). For a detailed historical analysis of the *Bradwell* case, see Olsen, *From False Paternalism to False Equality: Judicial Assaults Feminist Community, Illinois 1869–1985*, 84 MICH. L. REV. 1518 (1986).

28. The Court declared, simply, that the privileges and immunities clause did not apply to her claim, and that the fourteenth amendment did not transfer protection of the right to practice law to the federal government. *See Bradwell*, 83 U.S. (16 Wall.) at 138–39.

29. *Id.* at 141 (Bradley, J., concurring in the judgment).

30. *See* Muller v. Oregon, 208 U.S. 412 (1908) (upholding against an employer challenge an Oregon statute prohibiting employment of women in certain establishments for more than ten hours per day). "That woman's physical structure and the performance of maternal functions place her at a disadvantage in the struggle for subsistence is obvious," the *Muller* court declared. *Id.* at 421. "[H]istory discloses the fact that woman has always been dependent upon man. . . . [S]he is so constituted that she will rest upon and look to him for protection; that her physical structure and a proper discharge of her maternal functions . . . justify legislation to protect her from the greed as well as the passion of man." *Id.* at 421–22.

31. *See* Goesaert v. Cleary, 335 U.S. 464 (1948) (upholding a Michigan statute distinguishing between wives and daughters of owners of liquor establishments and all other women, and prohibiting the latter from serving as bartenders).

32. *See, e.g.*, Minor v. Happersett, 88 U.S. (21 Wall.) 162, 178 (1874) (holding that the right to vote was not among the privileges and immunities of United States citizenship and thus states could limit "that important trust to men alone"); *In re* Lockwood, 154 U.S. 116 (1894) (upholding Virginia's reading of its statute providing that any "person" admitted to practice in any state could also practice in Virginia, to mean any "male" person).

33. Gwendolyn Hoyt challenged Florida's automatic exemption of women from juries. *See* Hoyt v. Florida, 368 U.S. 57 (1961). Although women in Florida had a right to serve on juries, the automatic exemption meant that they did not have the same duty to serve as men; consequently, the jury of "peers" made available to women defendants systematically underrepresented women. In denying Hoyt's challenge to a jury that had no women, the Supreme Court reiterated Justice Bradley's reasoning in *Bradwell* focusing on the special role and responsibilities of woman: "Woman is still regarded as the center of home and family life." *Id.* at 62.

34. *See* Reed v. Reed, 404 U.S. 71 (1971).

35. Brief for Appellee at 12, *Reed* (no. 70-4). The Idaho court's opinion, which the Supreme Court reversed, had suggested that the Idaho legislature might reasonably have concluded that "in general men are better qualified to act as an administrator than are women." Reed v. Reed, 93 Idaho 511, 514, 465 P.2d 635, 638 (1970).

36. *See Reed*, 404 U.S. 71.

37. *See, e.g.*, Stanton v. Stanton, 421 U.S. 7 (1975) (holding that a sex-based difference in age of majority for purposes of child support obligations by parents is not justified by the assumption that girls tend to mature and marry earlier than boys and have less need to continue their education); Frontiero v. Richardson, 411 U.S. 677 (1973) (plurality opinion) (rejecting a rule requiring a female member of the armed services to prove her spouse's dependency while automatically assuming the dependency of the spouse of a male member as not justified by a conclusion that a husband in our society is generally the breadwinner). . . .

38. *See* W. Williams, [*The Equality Crisis: Some Reflections on Culture, Courts, and Feminism*, 7 WOMEN'S RTS. L. REP. 175, 181–90 (1982)] (criticizing Rostker v. Goldberg, 453 U.S. 57 (1981), which upheld a male-only draft registration requirement on the ground that only men were eligible for combat).

39. *See id.* (criticizing Michael M. v. Superior Ct., 450 U.S. 464 (1981), which upheld a statute criminalizing male, but not female, involvement in underage sex on the grounds that the state had a legitimate interest in preventing illegitimate teenage pregnancies, which only males can cause); Olsen, [*Statutory Rape: A Feminist Critique of Rights*, 63 TEX. L. REV. 387 (1987)] (same).

40. *See* Geduldig v. Aiello, 417 U.S. 484 (1974).

41. *Id.* at 497 n.20.

42. *Id.*

43. *See id.* at 496–97 ("There is no risk from which men are protected and women are not."). The Court adopted this same conclusion in reviewing a challenge to the exclusion of pregnancy from a private employer's disability plan under title VII. *See* General Elec. Co. v. Gilbert, 429 U.S. 125 (1976).

44. *See Geduldig,* 417 U.S. at 499–500 (Brennan, J., dissenting).

45. *See* Bartlett, *Pregnancy and the Constitution: The Uniqueness Trap,* 62 CALIF. L. REV. 1532 (1974); Comment, Geduldig v. Aiello: *Pregnancy Classifications and the Definition of Sex Discrimination,* 75 COLUM. L. REV. 441 (1975); *see also* W. Williams, *supra* note [38], at 190–200 (reviewing the Supreme Court's stereotyped notions of women).

46. The Pregnancy Discrimination Act became § 701(k) of title VII. "The terms 'because of sex' or 'on the basis of sex' include, but are not limited to, because of or on the basis of pregnancy, childbirth, or related medical conditions; and women affected by pregnancy, childbirth, or related medical conditions shall be treated the same for all employment-related purposes, including receipt of benefits under fringe benefit programs, as other persons not so affected but similar in their ability or inability to work . . . ." 42 U.S.C. § 2000e (1982).

47. *See* California Fed. Sav. & Loan Ass'n v. Guerra, 479 U.S. 272 (1987).

48. *Compare* W. Williams, *Equality's Riddle: Pregnancy and the Equal Treatment/ Special Treatment Debate,* 13 N.Y.U. REV. L. & SOC. CHANGE 325, 370–74 (1984–1985) [hereinafter W. Williams, *Equality's Riddle*] (noting, with qualifications, the advantages of an equal-treatment approach) *with* Krieger & Cooney, *The Miller-Wohl Controversy: Equal Treatment, Positive Action and the Meaning of Women's Equality,* 13 GOLDEN GATE U.L. REV. 513 (1983) (arguing that women have more to gain from the special-treatment approach). Chris Littleton has recast this debate in terms of "symmetrical" vs. "asymmetrical" models of equality. *See* Littleton, [*Reconstructing Sexual Equality,* 75 CALIF. L. REV. 1279, 1291–301 (1987)]. The line-up of feminist groups on each side of California Federal Savings & Loan Association v. Guerra, 479 U.S. 272 (1987), demonstrates the breadth of the division on the equal-treatment/special-treatment issue. *See* Strimling, *The Constitutionality of State Laws Providing Employment Leave for Pregnancy: Rethinking Geduldig After Cal Fed,* 77 CALIF. L. REV. 171, 194 n.108 (1989). . . .

49. *See* S. ESTRICH, REAL RAPE 92–104 (1987).

50. *See* W. Williams, *supra* note [38], at 188 n.75 (criticizing Dothard v. Rawlinson, 433 U.S. 321 (1977)).

51. *See* Dowd, *Work and Family: The Gender Paradox and the Limitations of Discrimination Analysis in Restructuring the Workplace,* 24 HARV. C.R.-C.L. L. REV. 79 (1989); Olsen, *The Family and the Market: A Study of Ideology and Legal Reform,* 96 HARV. L. REV. 1497 (1983); Taub, *From Parental Leaves to Nurturing Leaves,* 13 N.Y.U. REV. L. & SOC. CHANGE 381 (1985); J. Williams, *Deconstructing Gender,* [87 MICH. L. REV. 797 (1989)]; W. Williams, *Equality's Riddle, supra* note [48], at 374–80.

53. *See, e.g.,* S. DE BEAUVOIR, *supra* note 23; Harris, [*Race and Essentialism in Feminist Legal Theory,* 42 STAN. L. REV. 581, 612 (1990)]; Littleton, *supra* note [48], at 1306–07; Minow, [*The Supreme Court, 1986 Term—Foreword: Justice Engendered,* 101 HARV. L. REV. 10, 34–37 (1987)].

55. *See* Mossman, *Feminism and Legal Method: The Difference It Makes*, 3 WIS. WOMEN'S L.J. 147, 163–65 (1987). . . .

56. [*Id.*] at 158.

57. Judith Resnik, for example, has shown how distinguishing a question of law from a question of fact may have systematic effects on which kinds of litigants win or lose lawsuits at the appellate level. *See* Resnik, *Tiers*, 57 S. CAL. L. REV. 837, 998–1005, 1013–14 (1984).

59. *See* Mossmann, *supra* note 55, at 157–58; Singer, *The Player and the Cards: Nihilism and Legal Theory*, 94 YALE L.J. 1, 30–33 (1984).

61. *See* Massaro, *Empathy, Legal Storytelling, and the Rule of Law: New Words, Old Wounds?*, 87 MICH. L. REV. 2099, 2120 (1989) ("Discretion may license a decisionmaker to ignore the rules we think are worthy of support, in favor of her private agenda or personal experiential understanding.").

63. . . . . *See* Cover, [*For James Wm. Moore: Some Reflections on a Reading of the Rules*, 84 YALE L.J. 718, 721 (1975)].

64. *See* Cain, *Good and Bad Bias: A Comment on Feminist Theory and Judging*, 61 S. CAL. L. REV. 1945 (1988).

65. *See* E. SELMAN, [INESSENTIAL WOMAN: PROBLEMS OF EXCLUSION IN FEMINIST THOUGHT (1988)]; Harris, [*Race and Essentialism in Feminist Legal Theory*, 42 STAN. L. REV. 581 (1990)]; Minow, *supra* note [53, at 10]. . . .

69. *See* [E. SPELMAN, *supra* note 65] at 186.

71. *See* D. FUSS, ESSENTIALLY SPEAKING: FEMINISM NATURE & DIFFERENCE 1 (1989) (arguing that the "perceived threat of essentialism" fosters paranoia that "foreclose[s] more ambitious investigations of specificity and difference").

72. *See* E. SPELMAN, *supra* note [65], at 175–77.

74. *See* C. GILLIGAN, IN A DIFFERENT VOICE: PSYCHOLOGICAL THEORY AND WOMEN'S DDEVELOPMENT (1982); M. BELENKY, B. CLINCHY, N. GOLDBERGER & J. TARULE, WOMEN'S WAYS OF KNOWING: THE DEVELOPMENT OF SELF, VOICE, AND MIND (1986); Menkel-Meadow, *Portia in a Different Voice: Speculations on a Women's Lawyering Process*, 1 BERKELEY WOMEN'S L.J. 39 (1985); Sherry, *Civic Virtue and the Feminine Voice in Constitutional Adjudication*, 72 VA. L. REV. 543 (1986).

75. M. BELENKY, B. CLINCHY, N. GOLDBERGER & J. TARULE, *supra* note 74, at 149.

80. A. RORTY, MIND IN ACTION 272 (1988). . . .

82. A. RORTY, *supra* note 80, at 274. . . .

83. *See* M. NUSSBAUM, THE FRAGILITY OF GOODNESS: LUCK AND ETHICS IN GREEK TRAGEDY AND PHILOSOPHY 301–05 (1986). Nussbaum writes that ethical choice must be "seized in a confrontation with the situation itself, by a faculty that is suited to confront it as a complex whole." *Id.* at 300–01.

84. *See* Brief for Petitioners at 6–25, Hodgson v. Minnesota, 110 S. Ct. 400 (1989) (Nos. 88-1125 & 88-1309).

86. *See* M. NUSSBAUM, *supra* note 83, at 305.

87. *Id.* at 304.

88. *See* [*id.*] at 298–306. . . .

93. A. RORTY, *supra* note 80, at 283; *see also* Michelman, [*The Supreme Court, 1985 Term—Foreword: Traces of Self-Government*, 100 HARV. L. REV. 4, 31 (1986)] (linking having one's own reasons for action with the positive or ethical notion of freedom); Singer *supra* note 59, at 32 (arguing that judges should "feel free honestly to express what they really were thinking about when they decided the case" in order to "clarify the moral and political views at stake in legal controversies"). For a general discussion of the problem of judicial candor, which also collects the standard scholarly positions

on this subject, see Shapiro, *In Defense of Judicial Candor*, 100 HARV. L. REV. 731 (1987).

94. On the desirability of accepting this kind of responsibility, see Singer, [*Legal Realism Now*, 76 CALIF. L. REV. 465, 533 (1988)]. *See also* Michelman, *supra* note [93], at 15, 35 (criticizing objective legal standards for absolving decisionmakers of responsibility for the fates of individual parties); Mossman, *supra* note 55, at 157–58 (criticizing neutral principles of interpretation for carrying with them the "absense of responsibility on the part of the male judges for any negative outcome"); Sunstein, [*Interest Groups in American Public Law*, 38 STAN. L. REV. 29, 69–72 (1985)] (proposing that rationality review should consider only the real, not the hypothetical, reasons for legislation). On the unavoidability of taking responsibility, see B. SMITH, CONTINGENCIES OF VALUE: ALTERNATIVE PER- SPECTIVES FOR CRITICAL THEORY 159–60 (1988), which argues that "since the contingency of all value cannot be evaded, whoever does the *urging* cannot ultimately suppress, or ultimately evade taking responsibility for, the *particularity* of the perspective from which he does so." *Id.* (emphasis in original).

95. *See* Singer, *supra* note [94], at 540. . . .

100. *See, e.g.*, Bennett, *Objectivity in Constitutional Law*, 132 U. PA. L. REV. 445, 495 (1984) . . . ; Stick, *Can Nihilism Be Pragmatic?*, 100 HARV. L. REV. 332, 363–65 (1986) . . . .

101. *See, e.g.*, Matsuda, *Liberal Jurisprudence and Abstracted Visions of Human Nature: A Feminist Critique of Rawls' Theory of Justice*, 16 N.M.L. REV. 613, 618–24 (1986); Menkel-Meadow, *supra* note 74, at 45–46; Scales, [*The Emergence of Feminist Jurisprudence: An Essay*, 95 YALE L.J. 1373, 1376–78 (1986)].

104. Martha Nussbaum addresses the need for generalizations based upon past experience as well as new detail; she states that practical wisdom would be "arbitrary and empty" if every situation were truly "new and nonrepeatable." M. NUSSBAUM, *supra* note 83, at 306. Nussbaum views the relationship between the universal and the particular as one of "two-way illumination": "Although . . . the particular takes priority, they are partners in commitment and share between them the honors given to the flexibility and responsiveness of the good judge." *Id.*; *see also* Gould, *supra* note 23, at 25–31 (developing a concept of "concrete universality" requiring appreciation of and general- izations about both similarities and differences among concrete situations).

106. *See* Minow, *supra* note [53], at 60–61; *see also* J. Williams, *Deconstructing Gender*, *supra* note [51], at 805 ([describing the "new epistemologists" who favor] "a new kind of rationality, one not so closely tied to abstract, transcendental truths, one that does not exclude so much of human experience as Western rationality traditionally has done").

107. *See* Minow, *supra* note [53], at 61–62; *see also* Wiggins, *Deliberations and Practical Reason*, in PRACTICAL REASONING 144, 145 (J. Raz ed. 1978) (arguing that practical reasoning must account for competing claims).

108. *See* Haraway, *Situated Knowledges: The Science Question in Feminism and the Privilege of Partial Perspective*, 14 FEMINIST STUD. 575, 590 (1988). . . .

109. *See* [*id.*] at 590; Minow, *supra* note [53], at 65–66; *see also* Flax, [*Postmodernism and Gender Relations in Feminist Theory*,] 12 SIGNS 621, 633 (1987)] (describing the need to be sensitive to interconnections between knowledge and power); Minow & Spelman, [*Passion for Justice*, 10 CARDOZO L. REV. 37, 57–60 (1988)] (calling for "a direct human gaze between those exercising power and those governed by it"); Gabel & Harris, *Building Power and Breaking Images: Critical Theory and the Practice of Law*, 11 N.Y.U. REV. L. & SOC. CHANGE 369, 375 (1982–1983) (suggesting a focus on "counter- hegemonic" law practice that draws attention to issues of power distribution).

110. *See* M. BELENKY, B. CLINCHY, N. GOLDBERGER & J. TARULE, *supra* note 74, at 134, 176–82; *see also* Brennan, *Reason, Passion, and "The Progress of the Law,"* 10

CARDOZO L. REV. 3 (1988) (noting that rational judicial decisionmaking requires passion); M. NUSSBAUM, *supra* note 83, at 307–09.

134. *See, e.g.,* Minow, *supra* note [53], at 34–45 (describing how unstated norms and assumptions about differences affect substantive legal decisionmaking); Mossman, *supra* note 55, at 156–63 (arguing that traditional methods of characterizing the legal issue, choosing legal precedent and interpreting statutes mask political choices); *see also* Kairys, *Legal Reasoning,* in THE POLITICS OF LAW: A PROGRESSIVE CRITIQUE 11–17 [D. Kairys ed. 1982] (arguing that the stare decisis principle serves primarily an ideological rather than a functional role); Gabel & Harris, *supra* note 109, at 373 (arguing that legal reasoning is an "ideological form of thought" that *"presupposes* both the existence of and the legitimacy of existing hierarchical institutions" (emphasis in original)); Singer, *supra* note 59, at 6, 30–39, 43–47 (arguing that legal reasoning obscures political and moral commitment and fails to transcend contradictory value choices).

135. 163 U.S. 537 (1896).

136. 347 U.S. 483 (1954).

139. Catharine MacKinnon sees consciousness-raising as *the* method of feminism. "Consciousness-raising is the major technique of analysis, structure of organization, method of practice, the theory of social change of the women's movement." MacKinnon, *Agenda for Theory, supra* note [4], at 519. Many feminist legal thinkers have emphasized the importance of consciousness-raising to feminist practice and method. *See, e.g.,* Law, *Equality: The Power and Limits of the Law* (Book Review), 95 YALE L.J. 1769, 1784 (1986); Matsuda, *supra* note 101, at 618–22; Scales, *supra* note [101], at 1401–02; Schneider, [*The Dialectic of Rights and Politics: Perspectives from the Women's Movement,* 61, N.Y.U. L. REV. 589, 602–04 (1986)]. For historical perspectives on consciousness-raising in the American women's movement, see C. HYMOWITZ & M. WEISSMAN, A HISTORY OF WOMEN IN AMERICA 351–55 (1978); and G. LERNER, [THE MAJORITY FINDS ITS PAST: PLACING WOMEN IN HISTORY 42–44 (1979)].

140. Bender, *A Lawyer's Primer on Feminist Theory and Tort,* 38 J. LEGAL EDUC. 3, 9 (1988) (citations omitted); . . .

141. Schnieder, *supra* note [139], at 602 (footnote omitted).

142. *Id.* at 603.

143. *See id.* at 602–04. Hence the feminist phrase: "The personal is the political." MacKinnon's explanation of this phrase is perhaps the best: "It means that women's distinctive experience as women occurs within that sphere that has been socially lived as the personal—private, emotional, interiorized, particular, individual, intimate—so that what it is to *know* the *politics* of woman's situation is to know women's personal lives." MacKinnon, *Agenda for Theory, supra* note [4], at 535.

144. Bender, *supra* note 140, at 9–10. In a recent example of litigation as consciousness-raising, three women filed a lawsuit against *Hustler Magazine* for "libel, invasion of privacy, intentional infliction of emotional injury, 'outrage,' " and various civil rights claims, following publication of a pornographic cartoon and photographs. Some of this material referred specifically to anti-pornography activist Andrea Dworkin, who was one of the plaintiffs. *See* Dworkin v. Hustler Magazine, Inc., 867 F.2d 1188 (9th Cir. 1989). The lawsuit, which was dismissed on motion for summary judgment, sought $150 million in damages for both direct harm caused to the women who are the subjects of such pornographic material, and the indirect harm of the material to other women "who are afraid to exercise [political freedoms on behalf of women] for fear of an ugly, pornographic representation of them appearing in such a magazine." *Id.* at 1191. The plaintiffs in this case probably did not expect to prevail on their claims, or to be awarded damages on the scale they sought. Such a lawsuit, however, can contribute to public education and dialogue on the issues it raises. Parties, of course, are subject to sanctions for pursuing

"frivolous" litigation. In *Dworkin*, the Ninth Circuit denied a request for double costs and attorneys' fees pursuant to rule 38 of the *Federal Rules of Appellate Procedure* and 28 U.S.C. § 1912, but suggested that if the plaintiffs raise similar contentions in subsequent cases, sanctions may be appropriate. *See* 876 F.2d at 1200–01.

149. *See* Menkel-Meadow, *supra* note 74, at 55–58.

150. *See* Resnik, *On the Bias: Feminist Reconsiderations of the Aspirations for Our Judges*, 61 S. CAL. L. REV. 1877, 1942–43 (1988); *see also* Sherwin, *Philosophical Methodology and Feminist Methodology: Are They Compatible?*, in FEMINIST PERSPECTIVES: PHILO-SOHPICAL ESSAYS ON METHOD AND MORALS 13, 19 (L. Code, S. Mullett & C. Overall eds. 1988) (linking consciousness-raising with interactive processes of thought).

158. Separating attitude about knowledge from the knowledge itself might appear a hopeless task. My attitude toward knowing is, in a sense, a claim about what I know. Moreover, my attitude about knowing, like other claims, may itself be strategic. *Cf.* C. WEEDON, FEMINIST PRACTICE AND POSTSTRUCTURALIST THEORY 131–35 (1987) (offering a strategic rationale for a radical feminist critique); W. Williams, *Equality's Riddle, supra* note 48, at 351–52 (justifying equal-treatment over special-treatment theory for tactical reasons). Despite the analytical overlap, the separation of issues of attitude from other knowledge claims enables greater focus on these issues.

159. Sandra Harding, Mary Hawkesworth, and others use these categories. *See* S. HARDING, THE SCIENCE QUESTION IN FEMINISM 24–28 (1986); Hawkesworth, *Knowers, Knowing, Known: Feminist Theory and Claims of Truth*, 14 SIGNS 533, 535–37 (1989). I define these categories somewhat differently than either Harding or Hawkesworth to reflect the categories into which feminists doing law have seemed to fall.

In using these categories, I am mindful of Leslie Bender's observation that labels and categorizations are divisive and cause ideas to "become fixed instead of remaining fluid and growing." Bender, *supra* note 140, at 5 n.5. Regretfully, I find the labels necessary to order, describe and clarify differences in ways of thinking. . . .

160. This term I have adapted from Linda Alcoff's description of the appropriate feminist view toward the concept of "woman." *See* Alcoff, [*Cultural Feminism Versus Post-Structuralism: The Identity Crisis in Feminist Theory*, 13 SIGNS 405, 428–36 (1988)].

177. Sandra Harding finds the roots of the standpoint approach in Hegel's analysis of the relationship between master and slave, which was elaborated by Engels, Marx, and Lukacs, and extended to feminist theory by Jane Flax, Hilary Rose, Nancy Hartsock, and Dorothy Smith. *See* S. HARDING, *supra* note 159, at 26.

178. A. JAGGAR, FEMINIST POLITICS AND HUMAN NATURE 370 (1983).

179. C. MACKINNON, [FEMINISM UNMODIFIED 57 (1987)].

185. S. HARDING, *supra* note 159, at 162.

186. *See* C. MACKINNON, *supra* note [179], at 88, 91, 160.

187. *See id.* at 195.

188. *See id.* at 22.

189. *See id.* at 83.

190. *See id.* at 76.

191. *See* Colker, [*Feminism, Sexuality and Self: A Preliminary Inquiry into the Politics of Authenticity* (Book Review), 68 B.U.L. REV. 217, 218 (1988)].

192. *See* West, [*Jurisprudence and Gender*, 55 U. CHI. L. REV. 1, 4 (1988)]. West devoted an earlier article to the need for a "phenomenological critique" of women's subjective experiences, which West suggested could be accomplished by women "speaking the truth about the quality of our internal lives." West, [*The Difference in Women's Hedonic Lives: A Phenomenological Critique of Feminist Legal Theory*, 3 WIS. WOMEN'S L.J. 81, 144 (1987)]. In *Jurisprudence and Gender*, West seems to have partially resolved the ambiguities she earlier saw in women's nature to find women's experience to be one

of connection in contrast to the experience of separation presupposed in all modern legal theory. *See* West, [*Jurisprudence and Gender*], at 1–3; *see also* West, *Feminism, Critical Social Theory and Law*, 1989 U. CHI. LEGAL F. 59, 96 (rejecting the anti-essentialism of critical social theory).

Other feminists also assume that women have an essential, discoverable identity, but do not seem to claim a privileged knowledge based on this identity. *See, e.g.*, Finley, *Transcending Equality Theory: A Way out of the Maternity and the Workplace Debate*, 86 COLUM. L. REV. 1118, 1139–40 (1986) (attributing certain unique, "mystical" qualities to pregnancy); Sherry, *supra* note 74, at 584–85 [(defining basic feminine sense of self)] . . . .

193. *See* D. FUSS. *supra* note 71, at 20 (distinguishing between "deploying" essentialism for strategic purposes and "lapsing into" essentialism by mistake).

196. Charles Taylor uses this phrase in describing the general phenomenon of false consciousness, *See* C. TAYLOR, PHILOSOPHY AND THE HUMAN SCIENCES 95 (1985).

197. Z. EISENSTEIN, [FEMINISM AND SEXUAL EQUALITY: CRISIS IN LIBERAL AMERICA 153 (1984)].

198. *See* Colker, *supra* note [191], at 217–22, 217 n.2 (declaring that feminists aspire to discover their authentic selves). West labels mistakes in describing women's realities as "false," *see* West, [*Hedonic Lives, supra* note 192], at 114, or as "lies," *see id.* at 126, 127, 144.

199. *See, e.g.*, MacKinnon, [*Feminism, Marxism, Method, and the State: Toward Feminist Jurisprudence*, 8 SIGNS 635, 638 (1983)] (describing male domination as "metaphysically nearly perfect").

200. *See id.* at 637–38 n.5. MacKinnon also rejects the explanation that women's different perceptions are based upon different subjective experiences; as constructions of men, she argues, women cannot be subjects. *See id.* Having rejected both of these explanations, MacKinnon concludes that women's different perceptions are proof of women's contradictory situation: "Feminism affirms women's point of view by revealing, criticizing, and explaining its impossibility," *Id.* at 637. I accept this conclusion, but do not think it is consistent with MacKinnon's other work which reflects the false-consciousness view.

201. *See* C. MACKINNON, *supra* note [179], at 198–205, 216–28.

202. *See* C. MACKINNON, TOWARD A FEMINIST THEORY OF THE STATE 116 (1989).

203. *See* Colker, *supra* note [191], at 255–60.

204. Mary Hawkesworth associates this linkage with the "rhetoric of oppression." *See* Hawkesworth, *supra* note 23, at 445–48. In another article, Hawkesworth describes a related phenomenon whereby feminist treatments of knowledge shift "from a recognition of misinformation about women to a suspicion concerning the dissemination of disinformation about women." Hawkesworth, *supra* note 159, at 538–39.

205. Thus, MacKinnon writes, "men author scripts to their own advantage" and "set conditions" which maintain their own power and the subordination of women. *See* MacKinnon, *Sexuality, Pornography and Method: "Pleasure Under Patriarchy*," 99 ETHICS 314, 316 (1989). Although sometimes careful to distinguish male power as a system from the power individual men have, or do not have, *see* Littleton, *supra* note [48], at 1318, Chris Littleton also frequently slips into the conspiratorial mode. *See id.* at 1302 ("[T]he terms of social discourse have been set by men who, actively or passively, have ignored women's voices . . . ."); *id.* at 1333 (suggesting that men have "[taken] the best for themselves and assign[ed] the rest to women"); *see also* C. MACKINNON, *supra* note [179], at 198–205, 216–28.

206. For an example of how bitter exchanges between feminists carried on in this framework can become, see *The 1984 James McCormich Mitchell Lecture: Feminist Discourse, Moral Values, and the Law—A Conversation*, 34 BUFFALO L. REV. 11, 68–

76 (1985). MacKinnon extends her side of the argument in C. MACKINNON, *supra* note [179], at 305 n.6. For an insightful feminist commentary on this exchange, see Colker, cited above in note [191], at 249–50.

209. [Flax, *supra* note 109], at 641. As Flax also writes, women cannot be "free of determination from their own participation in relations of domination such as those rooted in the social relations of race, class, or homophobia," while men are not. *Id.* at 642.

211. See Alcoff, *supra* note [160], at 415–16; Schultz, *Room to Maneuver (f)or a Room of One's Own? Practice Theory and Feminist Practice*, 14 LAW & SOC. INQUIRY 123, 132 (1989).

212. Coombe, *Room For Manoeuver: Toward a Theory of Practice in Critical Legal Studies*, 14 LAW & SOC. INQUIRY 69, 85 (1989).

215. Fraser & Nicholson, [*Social Criticism Without Philosophy: An Encounter Between Feminism and Postmodernism*, in UNIVERSAL ABANDON? THE POLITICS OF POSTMODERNISM 85 (A. Rossi ed. 1988)].

216. *Id.* at 87.

221. D. RHODE, [*Feminist Critical Theories*, 42 STAN. L. REV. 617, 620 (1990)].

222. Alcoff, *supra* note [160], at 419.

223. Haraway, *supra* note 108, at 580.

229. A number of legal writers in other theoretical contexts have sought to incorporate the notion of effort as a component of truth-seeking. *See, e.g.*, B. JACKSON, LAW, FACT AND NARRATIVE COHERENCE 5 (1988) (emphasizing "integrity in relation to one's own subjectivity"); Cornell, [*Post-Structuralism, the Ethical Relation, and the Law*, 9 CARDOZO L. REV. 1587, 1625 (1988)] (describing "a self that constantly seeks to divest itself of sovereign subjectivity"); Minow, *supra* note [53], at 95 (advocating "deliberate attention to our own partiality"); Schultz, *supra* note 211, at 137 (describing "the practice of 'self-consciousness' "); Sherwin, *supra* note 150 (urging "suspicion" of examinations limited to one's own perspective); *see also* Donovan, *Beyond the Net: Feminist Criticism As a Moral Criticism*, DENVER Q., Winter 1983, at 56 (describing Iris Murdoch's orientation toward increasing one's sense of realities beyond the self); Lewis, *From This Day Forward: A Feminine Moral Discourse of Homosexual Marriage*, 97 YALE L.J. 1783, 1792 (1988) ("Stretching the moral imagination is a question of willpower . . . .").

230. Neither postmodernism nor standpoint epistemology fosters or even makes possible this attitude. The privilege that standpoint epistemology grants to a particular perspective leaves little reason to look beyond that perspective for further truth. Postmodernism, by denying any meaningful basis for making qualitative judgments between perspectives, leaves no reason to stretch beyond one's current perspective in order to improve it.

231. One might question, as does Barbara Hernstein Smith, whether, given one's dependence on one's perspective, it is possible to will one's choices about perspective. *See* B. SMITH, *supra* note 94, at 176. I argue here, however, that the will to transcend one's perspective helps to enlarge or transform that perspective, even though at any point in the never-ending transformation one is configured by a single, limiting perspective.

233. The absence of a self-critical account is the principal difficulty I have with Christine Littleton's presentation of feminist method (interpreting Catharine MacKinnon) as that of believing women's accounts of sexual use and abuse by men. *See* Littleton, [*Feminist Jurisprudence: The Difference Method Makes* (Book Review), 41 STAN. L. REV. 751, 764–65 (1989)]. Neither Littleton nor MacKinnon bring into their discussions of feminist method the necessity for feminists to be critical of themselves or of other women. *See id.* at 764–65; MacKinnon, *Agenda for Theory, supra* note [4], at 510. Self-criticism does not even enter into their respective discussions of consciousness-raising,

where it could play an enormously valuable role. *See* Schneider, *supra* note [139], at 602. Although feminists want to give full voice to women whose accounts of their experiences have for so long been ignored or devalued, feminists cannot assume that women's accounts will always be truthful or valid, or for that matter that men's accounts will always be untruthful or invalid.

234. This ideal seems beyond human capacity, because people must act upon judgments as if those judgments are correct, and the need for stability seems to require that they deem some judgments true, at least for a time. As Chris Schroeder told me, "Continual reappraisal is impossible, except for God, who has no need for it."

235. One of the most well-known, and most powerful, of lists of such propositions was invented by Arthur Leff, who concluded both that truth is humanly constructed, and that some standards could be known: "All I can say is this: it looks as if we are all we have. Given what we know about ourselves, and each other, this is an extraordinarily unappetizing prospect; looking around the world, it appears that if all men are brothers, the ruling model is Cain and Abel. Neither reason, nor love, nor even terror, seems to have worked to make us 'good,' and worse than that, there is no reason why anything should. Only if ethics were something unspeakable by us, could law be unnatural and therefore unchallengeable. As things now stand, everything is up for grabs.

Nevertheless: / Napalming babies is bad. / Starving the poor is wicked. / Buying and selling each other is depraved. / Those who stood up to and died resisting Hitler, Stalin, Amin, and Pol Pot—and General Custer too—have earned salvation. / Those who acquiesced deserve to be damned. / There is in the world such a thing as evil. / [All together now:] Sez who? / God help us." Leff, *Unspeakable Ethics, Unnatural Law*, 1979 DUKE L.J. 1129, 1249. Charles Taylor refers to values that are incomparably more important than others—those that define my identity and give "me a sense of wholeness, of fulness of being as a person or self"—as "hypergoods." C. TAYLOR, SOURCES OF THE SELF: THE MAKING OF THE MODERN IDENTITY 63 (1989).

236. Charles Taylor describes this concept as the "best account" we have of ourselves. *See* C. TAYLOR, *supra* note 235, at 58. Nel Noddings calls it "the best picture I have of myself." *See* N. NODDINGS, CARING: A FEMININE APPROACH TO ETHICS AND MORAL EDUCATION 5 (1984); *see also* Johann, [*An Ethics of Emergent Order*, in JAMES M. GUSTAFSON'S THEOCENTRIC ETHICS 109 (H. Beckley & C. Swezey eds. 1988)] (arguing that reasoned ethical values are those which "fulfill our quest for good order"); Kay, *Preconstitutional Rules*, 42 OHIO ST. L.J. 187, 207 (1981) (arguing that principles of constitutional interpretation should "attempt to shape the unruly facts of the world and of our natures into such forms as will best serve our own purposes"); Leff, *supra* note 235, at 1249 (arguing that by speaking ethics, we can challenge law, and make ourselves better).

237. C. TAYLOR, *supra* note 235, at 57.

239. Haraway, *supra* note 108, at 584.

241. *Id.*

242. Gatens, *Feminism, Philosophy and Riddles Without Answers*, in FEMINIST CHALLENGES 13, 26 (C. Pateman & E. Gross eds. 1986) (emphasis in original).

243. *Id.* at 29.

244. I. MURDOCH, *Above the Gods: A Dialogue About Religion*, in ACASTOS: TWO PLATONIC DIALOGUES 85 [1986]; *see also* B. SMITH, *supra* note 94 at 179 (" '[T]he best' is always both heterogeneous and variable: . . . it can never be better than a state of affairs that remained more or less than good *for some people*, or got considerably better for many of them *in some respects*, or became, *for a while*, rather better on the whole." (emphasis in original)).

245. *See, e.g.*, Cornell, *Toward a Modern/Postmodern Reconstruction of Ethics*, 133 U. PA. L. REV. 291, 360–68 (1986); Holler, *Is There a Thou "Within" Nature? A Dialogue*

with H. Richard Niebuhr, 17 J. RELIGIOUS ETHICS 81, 83 (1989); Minow, [*Learning to Live with the Dilemma of Difference: Bilingual and Special Education,* LAW & CONTEMP. PROBS. 157, 206 (Spring 1985)]; *see also* Gabel, *Creationism and the Spirit of Nature,* TIKKUN, Sept.-Oct. 1987, at 62 (arguing that we can know "with certainty" from "our own fundamental need for the confirmation and love of others," that "this need fundamentally motivates all living things").

246. *See* Gabel, *supra* note 245, at 59-60 (stating that we can only understand, and correct, ourselves, by approaching others as "differentiated presences like ourselves and putting ourselves in their place in order to comprehend them").

247. Holler, *supra* note 245, at 82. Holler writes: "insofar as we are severed from the community of diverse beings, we are unaware of our own being, and, like Narcissus, we will see that community only in our own image." *Id.* at 83.

249. Michelman, *supra* note [93], at 32. . . .

19

Subordination, Rhetorical Survival Skills, and Sunday Shoes: Notes on the Hearing of Mrs. G. [1990]

Lucie E. White

. . .

The profound political intervention of feminism has been . . . to redefine the
very nature of what is deemed political. . . . The literary ramifications of this
shift involve the discovery of the rhetorical survival skills of the formerly unvoiced.
Lies, secrets, silences, and deflections of all sorts are routes taken by voices or
messages not granted full legitimacy in order not to be altogether lost.[1]

In 1970 the Supreme Court decided *Goldberg v. Kelly*.[2] The case, which
held that welfare recipients are entitled to an oral hearing prior to having their
benefits reduced or terminated, opened up a far-reaching conversation among
legal scholars over the meaning of procedural justice. All voices in this
conversation endorse a normative floor that would guarantee all persons the
same formal opportunities to be heard in adjudicatory proceedings, regardless
of such factors as race, gender, or class identity. Beyond this minimal normative
consensus, however, two groups of scholars have very different visions of what
procedural justice would entail. One group, seeing procedure as an *instrument*
of just government, seeks devices that will most efficiently generate legitimate
outcomes in a complex society.[3] Other scholars, however, by taking the perspective
of society's marginalized groups, give voice to a very different—I will call it a
"humanist"—vision. According to this vision, "procedural justice" is a normative
horizon rather than a technical problem. This horizon challenges us to realize
the promise of formal procedural equality in the real world. But this horizon
may beckon us even farther than equality of access to current adjudicatory
rituals. It may invite us to create new legal and political institutions that will
frame "stronger," more meaningful opportunities for participation[4] than we can
imagine within a bureaucratic state.[5] *Goldberg* can be read to pre-figure this
humanist vision of procedural justice. The Court's decision to mandate prior
oral hearings for welfare recipients suggests "the Nation's basic commitment"

to both substantive equality and institutional innovation in participation opportunities, in order to "foster the dignity and well-being of *all* persons within
its borders."[6]

I . . . assum[e] that the meaningful participation by all citizens in the
governmental decisions that affect their lives—that is, the humanist vision—
reflects a normatively compelling and widely shared intuition about procedural
justice in our political culture. [There is] a disjuncture between this vision and
the conditions in our society in which procedural rituals are actually played
out. Familiar cultural images and long-established legal norms construct the
subjectivity and speech of socially subordinated persons as inherently inferior
to the speech and personhood of dominant groups. Social subordination itself
can lead disfavored groups to deploy verbal strategies that mark their speech
as deviant when measured against dominant stylistic norms. These conditions—
the web of subterranean speech norms and coerced speech practices that
accompany race, gender, and class domination—undermine the capacity of many
persons in our society to use the procedural rituals that are formally available
to them. Furthermore, bureaucratic institutions disable *all* citizens—especially
those from subordinated social groups—from meaningful participation in their
own political lives.

This disjuncture between the norm of at least *equal*—if not also *meaningful*—
participation opportunities for all citizens and a deeply stratified social reality
reveals itself when subordinated speakers attempt to use the procedures that
the system affords them. . . .

I. The Shaping of Subordinate Speech

Linguists have repeatedly noted significant differences between the speech
of dominant and subordinated groups within the same broad language communities. Particularly in the context of gender, such differences, both in language
practice and in *beliefs* about how men and women speak, have been documented
across many cultures.[48] In an influential essay published in 1975, linguist Robin
Lakoff asked *why* men and women are often presumed—and observed—to speak
differently.[49] In seeking an answer to this question, she suggested that the
speech of men and women might be motivated by two contrasting goals, the
"transmission of factual knowledge" and "politeness," which correspond to two
contrasting verbal styles.

Lakoff links the first of these styles to the typical speech habits of men. In
this style, the speaker's primary goal is to inform the listener of new information
"by the least circuitous route."[50] The speaker will use succinct, unambiguous,
declarative sentences—unqualified factual propositions ordered according to a
linear logic.[51] These features convey the speaker's authority. They announce
his autonomous power to make truthful statements about the world.

Lakoff claims that a contrasting "polite" style, crafted to sustain *connection*
with the listener, typifies the speech of women. Polite speech does not announce
the speaker's own authority; rather, it enacts her deference to her listener and

garners "some intuition about his feelings toward [her]."[52] The "polite" speaker gives her listener great linguistic latitude to determine what she, the *speaker*, means to say. She does so by adding features to declarative sentences that render them ambiguous. These "hedges," as Lakoff calls them,[53] include a rising, questioning intonation, "tag questions,"[54] excessive modals or hyper-polite circumlocutions,[55] and semantically ambiguous adjectives or intensifiers.[56] All of these hedges undercut the claim to authority that is implicit in declarative syntax. They cede to the listener the power to determine what the speaker has to say.

Lakoff's essay has stimulated a vast literature of responses.[57] Some of her critics dispute Lakoff's negative evaluation of women's language.[58] These critics seek in women's speech habits a powerful utopian alternative to male language and male logic.[59] Other critics have begun to document the speech strategies of the economically and racially subordinated women who were excluded from Lakoff's sample.[60] Their work suggests that "women's language" is best understood as the array of speech *strategies* that women—as well as other subordinated speakers—have devised to manage verbal encounters with more powerful Others. The common variable in these encounters is not the speaker's gender identity. Rather, it is the imbalance *between* two speakers in social power.

The work of legal anthropologist William O'Barr lends support to this broad thesis.[61] In observing courtroom testimony, he found that women are more likely than men to use the verbal features that Lakoff labels "women's language."[62] Yet these features correlate more strongly with the speaker's social status than with gender *per se*.[63] Based on this data, O'Barr surmised that women—as well as minority and working class men—tend to use "women's language" not because of any biological or cultural predisposition to speak differently, but rather because these speakers tend to occupy "relatively powerless social positions."[64]

O'Barr has also examined the narrative logic of *pro se* litigants' speech.[65] He has identified two typical storytelling strategies, which he calls "relational" and "rule-oriented."[66] Litigants who use a relational framework do poorly in court because the logic of their stories clashes with the rule-breach-injury logic in which judges have learned to conceptualize legal claims. O'Barr found that socially powerless speakers, already disadvantaged by their verbal style, tend to use this relational logic to structure their testimony.[67] Thus, on the level of story as well as sentence, powerless speakers tend to use speech strategies that increase their disempowerment.

Another O'Barr study casts some empirical light on the feminist debate over the *value* of "women's language." Using simulated jury trials, O'Barr found that jurors are likely to assess speakers who use "powerless" language as less credible, competent, intelligent, or trustworthy than speakers who use typically "male" speech patterns.[68] W. Lance Bennett and Martha Feldman have drawn similar conclusions from qualitative observations of actual trials. Their work also suggests that jurors from dominant groups will sometimes find subordinate speakers to lack credibility *not* because of the substance of their testimony, but rather because of the non-dominant linguistic and narrative conventions that they use.[69] . . .

UConn Co-op
Save your receipts for Refunds/Rebates

632	632	0.70
	Goodies, Candy	
632	632	0.10
	Goodies, Candy	
101	9780813312484 0-8133-124	37.00
	FEMINIST LEGAL THEORY	

SUB TOTAL	37.80
SALES TAX	0.05
TOTAL	37.85
Discover	37.85

Acct# 6011001280640121 APPROVAL 18

SA   556   191 09:08:36 04/23/01 9848
Your Cashier Was: JEAN   ST# 9
Member # 030649279

Thank You for shopping UConn Co-op!

In reflecting on his research, O'Barr has concluded that language practice and social power have a complex, recursive relationship.[71] Socially powerless speakers do not have the luxury of confrontation—or even clarity—when they speak. Avoiding verbal commitment, training one's voice to anticipate the other's pleasure—such moves can defuse the risk of retaliation from a more powerful Other. Yet these strategies offer protection at the cost of confessing, and compounding, the speaker's lack of power.[72] . . .

II. The Story of Mrs. G.

With one lingering exception,[74] our laws of evidence and procedure now treat the speech of all persons according to the same formal rules, regardless of the speaker's gender, ethnicity, or social class. Indeed, the notion that the law *should* value speech according to the speaker's gender or caste reads more like a footnote from history than a serious claim; it lies far outside the bounds of current debate over procedural and evidentiary norms. Yet a range of evidence suggests that women and other subordinated groups do not in fact participate in legal proceedings as frequently or as fluently as socially dominant groups.

. . .[F]or many speakers who are stigmatized by gender, race, or caste—those unwilling or unable to assume the role of a social male—the lived experience of inequality undermines the formal guarantee of an equal opportunity to participate in the rituals of the law. Mrs. G. is one of this majority. Through her story we can trace how the complex realities of social inequality undermine the law's formal promise of procedural justice.

A. The Story[78]

Mrs. G. is thirty-five years old, Black, and on her own. She has five girls, ranging in age from four to fourteen. She has never told me anything about their fathers; all I know is that she isn't getting formal child support payments from anyone. She lives on an AFDC[79] grant of just over three hundred dollars a month and a small monthly allotment of Food Stamps. She probably gets a little extra money from occasional jobs as a field hand or a maid, but she doesn't share this information with me and I don't ask. She has a very coveted unit of public housing, so she doesn't have to pay rent. She is taking an adult basic education class at the local community action center, which is in the same building as my own office. I often notice her in the classroom as I pass by.

The first thing that struck me about Mrs. G., when she finally came to my office for help one day, was the way she talked. She brought her two oldest daughters with her. She would get very excited when she spoke, breathing hard and waving her hands and straining, like she was searching for the right words to say what was on her mind. Her daughters would circle her, like two young mothers themselves, keeping the air calm as her hands swept through it. I haven't talked with them much, but they strike me as quite self-possessed for their years.

At the time I met Mrs. G., I was a legal aid lawyer working in a small community in south central North Carolina. I had grown up in the state, but had been away for ten years, and felt like an outsider when I started working there. I worked out of two small rooms in the back of the local community action center. The building was run-down, but it was a store front directly across from the Civil War Memorial on the courthouse lawn, so it was easy for poor people to find.

There were two of us in the office, myself and a local woman who had spent a few years in Los Angeles, working as a secretary and feeling free, before coming back to the town to care for her aging parents. Her family had lived in the town for generations. Not too long ago they, and most of the other Black families I worked with, had been the property of our adversaries—the local landowners, businessmen, bureaucrats, and lawyers. Everyone seemed to have a strong sense of family, and of history, in the town.

In the late 1960s, the town had erupted into violence when a local youth who had read some Karl Marx and Malcolm X led some five thousand people down the local highway in an effort to integrate the county swimming pool. He had been charged with kidnapping as a result of the incident and had fled to Cuba, China, and ultimately Detroit. My colleague would talk to me about him in secretive tones. Her father was one of those who sheltered him from justice on the evening of his escape. I think she expected that one day he would come back to take up the project that was abandoned when he fled.

Since World War II, the town had been a real backwater for Black people. People told me that it was a place that was there to be gotten out of, if you could figure out how. Only gradually, in the 1980s, were a few African American families moving back into the area, to take up skilled jobs in chemicals and electronics. But the lives of most Blacks in the county in the early 1980's could be summed up by its two claims to fame. It was the county where the state's arch-conservative senior Senator had grown up. Locals claimed that the Senator's father, the chief of police at one time, was known for the boots he wore and the success he had at keeping Black people in their place. It was also the county where Steven Spielberg filmed *The Color Purple*. By the time Spielberg discovered the county, the dust from the 1960s had long since settled, and the town where I worked had the look of a sleepy Jim Crow village that time had quite entirely passed by.

Mrs. G. and two daughters first appeared at our office one Friday morning at about ten, without an appointment. I was booked for the whole day; the chairs in the tiny waiting room were already filled. But I called her in between two scheduled clients. Mrs. G. looked frightened. She showed me a letter from the welfare office that said she had received an "overpayment" of AFDC benefits. Though she couldn't read very well, she knew that the word "overpayment" meant fraud. Reagan's newly appointed United States attorney, with the enthusiastic backing of Senator Jesse Helms, had just announced plans to prosecute "welfare cheats" on the full extent of the law. Following this lead, a grand jury had indicted several local women on federal charges of welfare fraud. Therefore, Mrs. G. had some reason to believe that "fraud" carried the threat of jail.

The "letter" was actually a standardized notice that I had seen many times before. Whenever the welfare department's computer showed that a client had received an overpayment, it would kick out this form, which stated the amount at issue and advised the client to pay it back. The notice did not say why the agency had concluded that a payment error had been made. Nor did it inform the client that she might contest the county's determination. Rather, the notice assigned the client a time to meet with the county's fraud investigator to sign a repayment contract and warned that if the client chose not to show up at this meeting further action would be taken. Mrs. G.'s meeting with the fraud investigator was set for the following Monday.

At the time, I was negotiating with the county over the routine at these meetings and the wording on the overpayment form. Therefore, I knew what Mrs. G. could expect at the meeting. The fraud worker would scold her and then ask her to sign a statement conceding the overpayment, consenting to a 10 percent reduction of her AFDC benefits until the full amount was paid back, and advising that the government could still press criminal charges against her.

I explained to Mrs. G. that she did not have to go to the meeting on Monday, or to sign any forms. She seemed relieved and asked if I could help her get the overpayment straightened out. I signed her on as a client and, aware of the other people waiting to see me, sped through my canned explanation of how I could help her. Then I called the fraud investigator, canceled Monday's meeting, and told him I was representing her. Thinking that the emergency had been dealt with, I scheduled an appointment for Mrs. G. for the following Tuesday and told her not to sign anything or talk to anyone at the welfare office until I saw her again.

The following Tuesday Mrs. G. arrived at my office looking upset. She said she had gone to her fraud appointment because she had been "afraid not to." She had signed a paper admitting she owed the county about six hundred dollars, and agreeing to have her benefits reduced by thirty dollars a month for the year and a half it would take to repay the amount. She remembered I had told her not to sign anything; she looked like she was waiting for me to yell at her or tell her to leave. I suddenly saw a woman caught between two bullies, both of us ordering her what to do.

I hadn't spent enough time with Mrs. G. the previous Friday. For me, it had been one more emergency—a quick fix, an appointment, out the door. It suddenly seemed pointless to process so many clients, in such haste, without any time to listen, to challenge, to think together. But what to do, with so many people waiting at the door? I mused on these thoughts for a moment, but what I finally said was simpler. I was furious. Why had she gone to the fraud appointment and signed the repayment contract? Why hadn't she done as *we* had agreed? Now it would be so much harder to contest the county's claim: we would have to attack *both* the repayment contract *and* the underlying overpayment claim. Why hadn't she listened to me?

Mrs. G. just looked at me in silence. She finally stammered that she knew she had been "wrong" to go to the meeting when I had told her not to and she was "sorry."

After we both calmed down I mumbled my own apology and turned to the business at hand. She told me that a few months before she had received a cash settlement for injuries she and her oldest daughter had suffered in a minor car accident. After medical bills had been paid and her lawyer had taken his fees, her award came to $592. Before Mrs. G. cashed the insurance check, she took it to her AFDC worker to report it and ask if it was all right for her to spend it. The system had trained her to tell her worker about every change in her life. With a few exceptions, any "income" she reported would be subtracted, dollar for dollar, from her AFDC stipend.

The worker was not sure how to classify the insurance award. After talking to a supervisor, however, she told Mrs. G. that the check would not affect her AFDC budget and she could spent it however she wanted.

Mrs. G. cashed her check that same afternoon and took her five girls on what she described to me as a "shopping trip." They bought Kotex, which they were always running short on at the end of the month. They also bought shoes, dresses for school, and some frozen food. Then she made two payments on her furniture bill. After a couple of wonderful days, the money was gone.

Two months passed. Mrs. G. received and spent two AFDC checks. Then she got the overpayment notice, asking her to repay to the county an amount equal to her insurance award.

When she got to this point, I could see Mrs. G. getting upset again. She had told her worker everything, but nobody had explained to her what she was supposed to do. She hadn't meant to do anything wrong. I said I thought the welfare office had done something wrong in this case, not Mrs. G. I thought we could get this mess straightened out, but we'd need more information. I asked if she could put together a list of all the things she had bought with the insurance money. If she still had any of the receipts, she should bring them to me. I would look at her case file at the welfare office and see her again in a couple of days.

The file had a note from the caseworker confirming that Mrs. G. had reported the insurance payment when she received it. The note also showed that the worker did not include the amount in calculating her stipend. The "overpayment" got flagged two months later when a supervisor, doing a random "quality control" check on her file, discovered the worker's note. Under AFDC law, the insurance award was considered a "lump sum payment." Aware that the law regarding such payments had recently changed, the supervisor decided to check out the case with the state quality control office.

He learned that the insurance award did count as income for AFDC purposes under the state's regulations; indeed, the county should have cut Mrs. G. off of welfare entirely for almost two months on the theory that her family could live for that time off of the insurance award. The lump sum rule was a Reagan Administration innovation designed to teach poor people the virtues of saving money and planning for the future. Nothing in the new provision required that clients be warned in advance about the rule change, however. Only in limited circumstances was a state free to waive the rule. Without a waiver, Mrs. G. would have to pay back $592 to the welfare office. If the county didn't try to collect the sum from Mrs. G., it would be sanctioned for an administrative error.

I met again with Mrs. G. the following Friday. When I told her what I had pieced together from her file, she insisted that she had asked her worker's permission before spending the insurance money. Then she seemed to get flustered and repeated what had become a familiar refrain. She didn't want to make any trouble. She hadn't meant to do anything wrong. I told her that it looked to me like it was the welfare office—and not her—who had done something wrong. I said I would try to get the county to drop the matter, but I thought we might have to go to a hearing, finally, to win.

Mrs. G. had been in court a few times to get child support and to defend against evictions, but she had never been to a welfare hearing. She knew that it was not a good idea to get involved in hearings, however, and she understood why. Fair hearings were a hassle and an embarrassment to the county. A hearing meant pulling an eligibility worker and several managers out of work for a few hours, which—given the chronic under-staffing of the welfare office—was more than a minor inconvenience. It also meant exposing the county's administrative problems to state-level scrutiny.

Front-line eligibility workers were especially averse to hearings because the county's easiest way to defend against its own blunders was to point to the worker as the source of the problem. As a result, the workers did all they could to persuade clients that they would lose, in the end, if they insisted on hearings.

The prophesy was self-fulfilling, given the subtle and diffuse retaliation that would often follow for the occasional client who disregarded this advice.

I could tell that Mrs. G. felt pressure from me to ask for a hearing, but she also seemed angry at the welfare office for asking her to pay for their mistake. I said that it was her decision, and not mine, whether to ask for the hearing, and reassured her that I would do my best to settle the matter, no matter what she decided. I also told her she could drop the hearing request at any time, for any reason, before or even after the event. When she nervously agreed to file the hearing request, I didn't second-guess her decision.

My negotiations failed. The county took the position that the worker should have suspended Mrs. G.'s AFDC as soon as the client had reported the insurance payment. This mistake was "regrettable," but it didn't shift the blame for the overpayment. Mrs. G.—and not the county—had received more welfare money than she was entitled to. End of discussion. I then appealed to state officials. They asked if the county would concede that the worker told Mrs. G. she was free to spend her insurance award as she pleased. When county officials refused, and the details of this conversation did not show up in the client's case file, the state declined to intervene. Mrs. G. then had to drop the matter or gear up for a hearing. After a lot of hesitation, she decided to go forward.

Mrs. G. brought all five of her girls to my office to prepare for the hearing. Our first task was to decide on a strategy for the argument. I told her that I saw two stories we could tell. The first was the story she had told me. It was the "estoppel" story, the story of the wrong advice she got from her worker about spending the insurance check. The second story was one that I had come up with from reading the law. The state had laid the groundwork for this story when it opted for the "life necessities" waiver permitted by federal regulations. If a client could show that she had spent the sum to avert a crisis situation, then it would be considered "unavailable" as income, and her AFDC benefits would not be suspended. I didn't like this second story very much, and I wasn't sure that Mrs. G. would want to go along with it. How could I ask her to distinguish "life necessities" from mere luxuries, when she was keeping five children alive on three hundred dollars a month, and when she had been given no voice in the calculus that had determined her "needs."

Yet I felt that the necessities story might work at the hearing, while "estoppel" would unite the county and state against us. According to legal aid's welfare specialist in the state capital, state officials didn't like the lump sum rule. It made more paper work for the counties. And, by knocking families off the federally financed AFDC program, the rule increased the pressure on state and county-funded relief programs. But the only way the state could get around the rule without being subject to federal sanctions was through the necessities exception. Behind the scenes, state officials were saying to our welfare specialist that they intended to interpret the exception broadly. In addition to this inside information that state officials would prefer the necessities tale, I knew from experience that they would feel comfortable with the role that story gave to Mrs. G. It would place her on her knees, asking for pity as she described how hard she was struggling to make ends meet.

The estoppel story would be entirely different. In it, Mrs. G. would be pointing a finger, turning the county itself into the object of scrutiny. She would accuse welfare officials of wrong, and claim that they had caused her injury. She would demand that the county bend its own rules, absorb the overpayment out of its own funds, and run the risk of sanction from the state for its error.

As I thought about the choices, I felt myself in a bind. The estoppel story would feel good in telling, but at the likely cost of losing the hearing, and provoking the county's ire. The hearing officer—though charged to be neutral— would surely identify with the county in this challenge to the government's power to evade the costs of its own mistakes. The necessities story would force Mrs. G. to grovel, but it would give both county and state what they wanted to hear— another "yes sir" welfare recipient.

This bind was familiar to me as a poverty lawyer. I felt it most strongly in disability hearings, when I would counsel clients to describe themselves as totally helpless in order to convince the court that they met the statutory definition of disability. But I had faced it in AFDC work as well, when I taught women to present themselves as abandoned, depleted of resources, and encumbered by children to qualify for relief. I taught them to say yes to the degrading terms of "income security," as it was called—invasions of sexual privacy, disruptions of kin-ties, the forced choice of one sibling's welfare over another's. Lawyers had tried to challenge these conditions, but for the most part the courts had confirmed that the system could take such license with its women. After all, poor women were free to say no to welfare if they weren't pleased with its terms.

As I contemplated my role as an advocate, I felt again the familiar sense that I had been taken. Here I was, asking Mrs. G. to trust me, talking with her about our conspiring together to beat the system and strategizing together to change it. Here I was, thinking that what I was doing was educative and empowering or at least supportive of those agendas, when all my efforts worked, in the end, only to teach her to submit to the system in all of the complex ways that it demanded.

In the moment it took for these old thoughts to flit through my mind, Mrs. G. and her children sat patiently in front of me, fidgeting, waiting for me to speak. My focus returned to them and the immediate crisis they faced if their AFDC benefits were cut. What story should we tell at the hearing, I wondered out loud. How should we decide? Mechanically at first, I began to describe to her our "options."

When I explained the necessities story, Mrs. G. said she might get confused trying to remember what all she had bought with the money. Why did they need to know those things anyway? I could tell she was getting angry. I wondered if two months of benefits—six hundred dollars—was worth it. Maybe paying it back made more sense. I reminded her that we didn't have to tell this story at the hearing, and in fact, we didn't have to go to the hearing at all. Although I was trying to choose my words carefully, I felt myself saying too much. Why had I even raised the question of which story to tell? It was a tactical decision—not the kind of issue that clients were supposed to decide. Why hadn't I just told her to answer the questions that I chose to ask?

Mrs. G. asked me what to do. I said I wanted to see the welfare office admit their mistake, but I was concerned that if we tried to make them, we would lose. Mrs. G. said she still felt like she'd been treated unfairly but—in the next breath— "I didn't mean to do anything wrong." Why couldn't we tell both stories? With this simple question, I lost all pretense of strategic subtley or control. I said sure.

I asked for the list she had promised to make of all the things she bought with the insurance money. Kotex, I thought, would speak for itself, but why, I asked, had she needed to get the girls new shoes? She explained that the girls' old shoes were pretty much torn up, so bad that the other kids would make fun of them at school. Could she bring in the old shoes? She said she could.

We rehearsed her testimony, first about her conversation with her worker regarding the insurance award and then about the Kotex and the shoes. Maybe the hearing wouldn't be too bad for Mrs. G., especially if I could help her see it all as strategy, rather than the kind of talking she could do with people she could trust. She had to distance herself at the hearing. She shouldn't expect them to go away from it understanding why she was angry, or what she needed, or what her life was like. The hearing was their territory. The most she could hope for was to take it over for a moment, leading them to act out her agenda. Conspiracy was the theme she must keep repeating as she dutifully played her role.

We spent the next half hour rehearsing the hearing. By the end, she seemed reasonably comfortable with her part. Then we practiced the cross-examination, the ugly questions that—even though everyone conceded to be irrelevant—still always seemed to get asked . . . questions about her children, their fathers, how long she had been on welfare, why she wasn't working instead. This was the part of these sessions that I disliked the most. We practiced me objecting and her staying quiet and trying to stay composed. By the end of our meeting, the whole thing was holding together, more or less.

The hearing itself was in a small conference room at the welfare office. Mrs. G. arrived with her two oldest daughters and five boxes of shoes. When we got there the state hearing officer and the county AFDC director were already seated at the hearing table in lively conversation. The AFDC director was a youngish man with sandy hair and a beard. He didn't seem like a bureaucrat until he started talking. I knew most of the hearing officers who came to the county, but this one, a pale, greying man who slouched in his chair, was new to me. I started feeling uneasy as I rehearsed how I would plead this troubling case to a stranger.

We took our seats across the table from the AFDC director. The hearing officer set up a portable tape recorder and got out his bible. Mrs. G.'s AFDC worker, an African American woman about her age, entered through a side door and took a seat next to her boss. The hearing officer turned on the recorder, read his obligatory opening remarks, and asked all the witnesses to rise and repeat before god that they intended to tell the truth. Mrs. G. and her worker complied.

The officer then turned the matter over to me. I gave a brief account of the background events and then began to question Mrs. G. First I asked her about the insurance proceeds. She explained how she had received an insurance check of about six hundred dollars following a car accident in which she and her oldest daughter had been slightly injured. She said that the insurance company had already paid the medical bills and the lawyer; the last six hundred dollars was for her and her daughter to spend however they wanted. I asked her if she had shown the check to her AFDC worker before she cashed it. She stammered. I repeated the question. She said she may have taken the check to the welfare office before she cashed it, but she couldn't remember for sure. She didn't know if she had gotten a chance to talk to anyone about it. Her worker was always real busy.

Armed with the worker's own sketchy notation of the conversation in the case file, I began to cross-examine my client, coaxing her memory about the event we had discussed so many times before. I asked if she remembered her worker telling her anything about how she could spend the money. Mrs. G. seemed to be getting more uncomfortable. It was quite a predicament for her, after all. If she "remembered" what her worker had told her, would her story expose mismanagement in the welfare office, or merely scapegoat another Black woman, who was not too much better off than herself?

When she repeated that she couldn't remember, I decided to leave the estoppel story for the moment. Maybe I could think of a way to return to it later. I moved on to the life necessitates issue. I asked Mrs. G. to recount, as best she could, exactly how she had spent the insurance money. She showed me the receipts she had kept for the furniture payments and I put them into evidence. She explained that she was buying a couple of big mattresses for the kids and a new kitchen table. She said she had also bought some food—some frozen meat and several boxes of Kotex for all the girls. The others in the room shifted uneasily in their chairs. Then she said she had also bought her daughters some clothes and some shoes. She had the cash register receipt for the purchase.

Choosing my words carefully, I asked why she had needed to buy the new shoes. She looked at me for a moment with an expression that I couldn't read. Then she stated, quite emphatically, that they were Sunday shoes that she had bought with the money. The girls already had everyday shoes to wear to school, but she had wanted them to have nice shoes for church too. She said no more than two or three sentences, but her voice sounded different—stronger, more composed—than I had known from her before. When she finished speaking the room was silent, except for the incessant hum of the tape machine on the table and the fluorescent lights overhead. In that moment, I felt the boundaries of our "conspiracy" shift. Suddenly I was on the outside, with the folks on the other side of the table, the welfare director and the hearing officer. The only person I could not locate in this new alignment was Mrs. G.'s welfare worker.

I didn't ask Mrs. G. to pull out the children's old shoes, as we'd rehearsed. Nor did I make my "life necessities" argument. My lawyer's language couldn't add anything to what she had said. They would have to figure out for themselves why buying Sunday shoes for her children—and saying it—was indeed a "life necessity" for this woman. After the hearing, Mrs. G. seemed elated. She asked me how she had done at the hearing and I told her that I thought she was great. I warned her, though, that we could never be sure, in this game, who was winning, or even what side anyone was on.

We lost the hearing and immediately petitioned for review by the chief hearing officer. I wasn't sure of the theory we'd argue, but I wanted to keep the case open until I figured out what we could do.

Three days after the appeal was filed, the county welfare director called me unexpectedly, to tell me that the county had decided to withdraw its overpayment claim against Mrs. G. He explained that on a careful review of its own records, the county had decided that it wouldn't be "fair" to make Mrs. G. pay the money back. I said I was relieved to hear that they had decided, finally, to come to a sensible result in the case. I was sorry they hadn't done so earlier. I then said something about how confusing the lump sum rule was and how Mrs. G.'s worker had checked with her supervisor before telling Mrs. G. it was all right to spend the insurance money. I said I was sure that the screw up was not anyone's fault. He mumbled a bureaucratic pleasantry and we hung up.

When I told Mrs. G. that she had won, she said she had just wanted to "do the right thing," and that she hoped they understood that she'd never meant to do anything wrong. I repeated that they were the ones who had made the mistake. Though I wasn't sure exactly what was going on inside the welfare office, at least this crisis was over.

B. The Terrain

Mrs. G. had a hearing in which all of the rituals of due process were scrupulously observed. Yet she did not find her voice welcomed at that hearing. A complex pattern of social, economic, and cultural forces underwrote the procedural formalities, repressing and devaluing her voice. Out of that web of forces, [I see] three dominant themes, all of them linked, sometimes subtly, to Mrs. G.'s social identity as poor, Black and female. The first theme is *intimidation*. Mrs. G. did not feel that she could risk speaking her mind freely to welfare officials. She lived in a community in which the social hierarchy had a caste-like rigidity. As a poor Black woman, her position at the bottom accorded her virtually no social or political power. She depended on welfare to survive and did not expect this situation to change in the future. She was simply not situated to take action that might displease her superiors. The second theme is *humiliation*. Even if Mrs. G. could find the courage to speak out at the hearing, her words were not likely to be heard as legitimate, because of the language she had learned to speak as a poor woman of color, and because of the kind of person that racist and gendered imagery portrayed her to be. The final theme is *objectification*. Because Mrs. G. had little voice in the political process that set the substantive terms of her welfare eligibility, the issues that she was constrained to talk about at the hearing bore little relation to her own feelings about the meaning and fairness of the state's action. . . .

.   .   .

C. The Route Taken: Evasive
Maneuvers or a Woman's Voice?

. . . Each of these forces attaches a specific social cost to her gender and race identity. The caste system implements race and gender ideology in social arrangements. The "fraud issue" revives misogynist and racist stereotypes that had been forced, at least partly, underground by the social movements of the 1960s and 1970s. And the welfare system responds to gender and race-based injustice in the economy by constructing the poor as Woman—as an object of social control. Given the power amassed behind these forces, we might predict that they should win the contest with Mrs. G. for her voice.

Yet . . . [i]f we re-center our reading on Mrs. G., as a woman shaping events, unpredictably, to realize her own meanings, we can no longer say with certainty what the outcome will be. We cannot tell who prevailed at the hearing, or where the power momentarily came to rest. Rather, what we see is a sequence of surprising moves, a series of questions. Why did Mrs. G. return to the lawyer after meeting with the fraud investigator to sign a settlement agreement? Why did she depart from the script she had rehearsed for the hearing, to remain silent before her own worker, and to speak about Sunday shoes? And why did the county finally abandon its claim to cut her stipend?[96]

1. Why Did Mrs. G. Return to the Lawyer? The lawyer[143] thought she understood the answer to this question. In her view, Mrs. G.'s life had taught her that to be safe, she must submit to her superiors. Mrs. G. was faced with conflicting commands from the welfare agency and the legal aid office. So, like the archetypical woman, shaped to mold herself to male desire, Mrs. G. said "yes" to everything the Man asked. She said yes when the lawyer asked her to go through with a hearing, yes again when the fraud investigator asked her to drop it, and yes once more when the lawyer demanded her apology. In the lawyer's view, this excess of acquiescence had a sad, but straightforward meaning. It marked Mrs. G.'s lack of social power: this woman could not risk having a point of view of her own.

Yet the lawyer was not situated to see the whole story. Though she aspired to stand beside Mrs. G. as an equal, she also sought to guard her own status—and the modicum of social power that it gave her. She *saw* Mrs. G. as a victim because that was the role she needed her client to occupy to support her own social status. For if Mrs. G. was indeed silenced by the violence around her, she could then be dependent on the lawyer's expertise and protection, and therefore compliant to the lawyer's will. With such clients, the lawyer could feel quite secure of her power, and complacent about the value of her work.

But Mrs. G.'s survival skills were more complex, more subtle, than the lawyer dared to recognize. There might be another meaning to Mrs. G.'s ambivalence about what she wanted to do. Perhaps she was *playing* with the compliance that all of her superiors demanded. By acquiescing to both of the system's opposed orders, she was surely protecting herself from the risks of defiance. But she was also undermining the value—to them—of her own submission. By refusing to claim any ground as her own, she made it impossible for others to subdue her will.

Self-negation may not have been the *only* meaning that Mrs. G. felt positioned to claim. She finally *came back* to the lawyer, repudiated the settlement, determined to pursue her case. Was this merely one more deft move between two bureaucrats, searching them both for strategic advantage while secretly mocking the rhetoric of both spheres? Or did Mrs. G. finally get fed up at the unfairness of the welfare, and at her own endless submission? When she returned to the lawyer, she was offered a bargain. She might get money, and some limited protection from the welfare, if she went along with the hearing plan. But she might have also heard the lawyer to promise something different from this *quid pro quo*. In her talk of rights and justice, the lawyer offered Mrs. G. not just money, but also vindication. In going forward with the hearing, was Mrs. G. simply making a street-wise calculation to play the game the lawyer offered? Or was she also giving voice to a faint hope—a hope that one day she might really have the legal protections she needed to take part in the shaping of justice?

2. Why Did Mrs. G. Depart from Her Script? The lawyer had scripted Mrs. G. as a victim. That was the only strategy for the hearing that the lawyer, within the constraints of her own social position, could imagine for Mrs. G. She had warned her client to play the victim if she wanted to win. Mrs. G. learned her lines. She came to the hearing well-rehearsed in the lawyer's strategy. But in the hearing, she did not play. When she was cued to perform, without any signal to her lawyer she abandoned their script.

The lawyer shared with Mrs. G. the oppression of gender, but was placed above Mrs. G. in the social hierarchies of race and class. The lawyer was paid by the same people who paid for welfare, the federal government. Both programs were part of a social agenda of assisting, but also controlling, the poor. Though the lawyer had worked hard to identify with Mrs. G., she was also sworn, and paid, to defend the basic constitution of the *status quo*. When Mrs. G. "misbehaved" at the hearing, when she failed to talk on cue and then refused to keep quiet, Mrs. G. pointed to the ambiguity of the legal aid lawyer's social role. Through her defiant actions, Mrs. G. told the lawyer that a conspiracy with a double agent is inevitably going to prove an unstable alliance.

The lawyer had tried to "collaborate" with Mrs. G. in devising an advocacy plan. Yet the terms of that "dialogue" excluded Mrs. G.'s voice. Mrs. G. was a better strategist than the lawyer—more daring, more subtle, more fluent— in her own home terrain. She knew the psychology, the culture, and the politics of the white people who controlled her community. She knew how to read, and sometimes control, her masters' motivations; she had to command this knowledge—this intuition—to survive. The lawyer had learned intuition as a woman, but in a much more private sphere.[150] She was an outsider to the county, and to Mrs. G.'s social world. Mrs. G.'s superior sense of the landscape posed a subtle threat to the lawyer's expertise. Sensing this threat, the lawyer steered their strategic "discussion" into the sphere of her own expert knowledge. By limiting the very definition of "strategy" to the manipulation of legal doctrine, she invited Mrs. G. to respond to her questions with silence. And, indeed, Mrs. G. did not talk freely when the lawyer was devising their game-plan. Rather, Mrs. G. waited until the hearing to act out her own intuitions. Although she surely had not plotted those actions in advance, she came up with moves at the hearing which threw everyone else off their guard, and may have proved her the better *legal* strategist of the lawyer-client pair.[151]

The disarming "strategy" that Mrs. G. improvised at the hearing was to appear to *abandon* strategy entirely. For a moment she stepped out of the role of the supplicant. She ignored the doctrinal pigeonholes that would fragment her voice. She put aside all that the lawyer told her the audience wanted to hear. Instead, when asked to point a finger at her caseworker, she was silent. When asked about "life necessities," she explained that she had used her money to meet *her own* needs. She had bought her children Sunday shoes.

a. Her silence before her caseworker. When the lawyer asked Mrs. G. about the conversation with her caseworker regarding the insurance payments, Mrs. G. had nothing to say. The lawyer, smarting from her own rejection, felt that Mrs. G. was protecting a vulnerable Black sister with her silence—at her own, and her lawyer's expense. But perhaps something else was going on. Unlike Mrs. G., the caseworker had earned self-respect in the system. Mrs. G. and her like—desperately poor, with no formal schooling, burdened by too many children, "abandoned" by their men—cast a stigma on this woman because of the common color of their skin. Did this woman command a different kind of power over Mrs. G. than the white masters—a power that felt like shame, rather than fear? Perhaps Mrs. G. was not willing to flaunt her own degradation before this woman, as the lawyer demanded.[152] Perhaps she was not willing to grovel—pointing fingers, showing off tattered shoes, listing each of her petty expenses—before this distant, disapproving sister. Perhaps Mrs. G.'s silence before this other Black woman, and her talk about Sunday shoes, expressed a demand—and an affirmation—of her own dignity.

b. *Her talk about Sunday shoes.* When Mrs. G. talked about Sunday shoes, she was talking about a life necessity. For subordinated communities, physical necessities do not meet the minimum requirements for a human life. Rather, subordinated groups must create cultural practices through which they can elaborate an autonomous, oppositional consciousness. Without shared rituals for sustaining their survival and motivating their resistance, subordinated groups run the risk of total domination—of losing the *will* to use their human powers to subvert their oppressor's control over them. Religion, spirituality, the social institution of the Black Church, has been one such self-affirming cultural practice for the communities of African American slaves, and remains central to the expression of Black identity and group consciousness today. By naming Sunday shoes as a life necessity, Mrs. G. was speaking to the importance of this cultural practice in her life, a truth that the system's categories did not comprehend.

At the same time that Mrs. G.'s statement affirmed the church, it condemned the welfare system. By rejecting the welfare's definition of life necessities, she asserted her need to have a say about *the criteria* for identifying her needs. Her statement was a demand for meaningful participation in the political conversations in which her needs are contested and defined. In the present welfare system, poor women—the objects of welfare—are structurally excluded from those conversations. When Mrs. G. insisted on her need to say for herself what her "life necessities" might be, she expanded, for a moment, the accepted boundaries of those conversations.

Mrs. G.'s statement also spoke to a third dimension of her "life necessity." When Mrs. G. talked about buying Sunday shoes, she defied the rules of legal rhetoric—the rule of relevancy, the rule against "rambling," the unwritten rule that told her to speak like a victim if she wanted to win. Had Mrs. G. spoken the language that was proper for her in the setting, her relevant, logical, submissive, hyper-correct responses to their questions might have been comprehended. But, by dutifully speaking the language of an institution from which subordinated groups have historically been excluded and in which Mrs. G. felt herself to have no stake, her voice would have repeated, and legitimated, the very social and cultural patterns and priorities that had kept her down. Had she been a *respectful* participant in the legal ritual, Mrs. G. would have articulated someone else's need, or pleasure, rather than her own.

Mrs. G. did not boycott the hearing altogether. Rather, in her moment of misbehavior, she may have been standing her ground within it. Although she appeared, at first, to be deferring to the system's categories and rules, when she finally spoke, she animated those categories with her own experience. She stretched the category of "life necessity" to express her own values, and turned it around to critique the welfare's systemic disregard of her own point of view.

By talking about Sunday shoes, Mrs. G. claimed, for one fragile moment, what was perhaps her most basic "life necessity." She claimed a position of equality in the speech community—an equal power to take part in the *making* of language, the making of shared categories, norms, and institutions—as she spoke through that language about her needs.

When Mrs. G. claimed this power, she affirmed the feminist insight that the dominant languages do *not* construct a closed system, from which there can be no escape. Although dominant groups may control the *social institutions* that regulate these languages, those groups cannot control the *capacity* of subordinated peoples to speak. Thus, women have evaded complete domination through their *practice* of speaking, like Mrs. G. spoke at her hearing, from their own intuitions and their own experience. Feminist writers have drawn three figures—play, archaeology, and poetry—to describe this emancipatory language practice.[160]

When Mrs. G. construed "life necessities" to include Sunday shoes, she turned the hearing into a place where she could talk, on a par with the experts, about her "needs." For a moment she defied the rigid official meaning of necessity, and refused to leave nameless the values and passions that gave sense to her life. Adrienne Rich describes the process:

> For many women, the commonest words are having to be sifted through, rejected, laid aside for a long time, or turned to the light for new colors and flashes of meaning: power, love, control, violence, political, personal, private, friendship, community, sexual, work, pain, pleasure, self, integrity. . . . When we become acutely, disturbingly aware of the language we are using and that is using us, we begin to grasp a material resource that women have never before collectively attempted to repossess. . . .[161]

Mrs. G. might want to add "participation" and "need" to the poet's list.

3. How Was Mrs. G.'s Voice Heard? The third question that the story raises is the ending. The story tells us that the hearing officer ruled against Mrs. G., and then the county welfare department decided to drop the case, restoring her full stipend. But the text does not say how the men across the table experienced the hearing, or why the county eventually gave in. Did Mrs. G.'s paradoxical "strategy" disarm her audience? Did she draw a response from her audience that was different—more compelling—than the pity that her lawyer had wanted to play upon? Did her presentation of herself as an independent, church-going woman, who would exercise her own judgment, and was willing to say what she needed—did these qualities make the men fear her, respect her, regard her for a moment as a person, rather than a case? Did they feel a moment of anger—about the ultimately powerless roles that they were assigned to play in the bureaucracy that regulated all of their lives? Were these men moved, by the hearing, to snatch her case from the computer and subject it to their own human judgment? If this is indeed what happened—and we do not know—would Mrs. G., in retrospect, have wished the story to end that way? Or was this moment of benign discretion a double-edged precedent— more dangerous to her people than the computer's reliable indifference?

We do not know why the county decided to drop Mrs. G.'s case. What we do know, however, is that after the hearing Mrs. G. remained a Black, single mother on welfare—poor, dependent, despised.[162] Mrs. G.'s unruly participation at her hearing was itself political action. Yet it was an act that did little to change the harsh landscape which constricts Mrs. G. from more sustained and more effective political participation. Substantial change in that landscape will come only as such fragile moments of dignity are supported and validated by the law. . . .

III. What Kind of Process for Mrs. G.?

Like all stories, the story of Mrs. G. is ambiguous. The only clear lesson that it teaches is negative: removing formal barriers to participation is not enough in our stratified society to achieve procedural justice, even in the modest sense of enabling all persons to participate in the rituals of their self-government on an *equal* basis. Although Mrs. G. finally "won" her hearing, it was a fragile victory, more attributable to the mysteries of human character than to the rule of law. Even after that victory, she was still obstructed from meaningful participation[165] in her own self-governance—not by overt legal barriers, but by deeply rooted conditions of social inequality. Is it asking too much of our Constitution to enlist its normative authority to challenge those conditions? *Goldberg v. Kelly* speaks, in its margins, to this unsettling possibility. The majority opinion quotes an article which observes that "the prosecution of a [welfare] appeal demands a degree of security, awareness, tenacity, and ability which few dependent people have."[167] The opinion also states that "[t]he opportunity to be heard must be tailored to the capacities and circumstances of those who are to be heard."[168] What would it mean to tailor procedures to take account of the "insecurity" that gets in the way when Mrs. G., and other "dependent" people seek to be heard? It is far beyond the scope of this essay—indeed, it may be beyond the scope of the possible—to provide a definitive answer to that question. Instead, in closing, I will return to the three local forces that obstructed Mrs. G.'s participation. I will point toward a few themes that Mrs. G. might herself suggest for countering those forces.

A. Challenging the Grounds of Intimidation

Perhaps the greatest barrier to Mrs. G.'s participation is her well-founded fear of retaliation. A substantial first step toward countering this barrier was taken when legal representation was made available to her. Without skilled advocates, poor people cannot invoke the laws that already forbid intentional retaliation. But even with access to lawyers, subordinated groups would need stronger and more sensitive laws to give them any real protection against the threat of retaliation. The penalties against retaliation must be increased, and the enforcement mechanisms simplified. The definition of retaliation and the methods of proof must be designed from the claimant's, rather than the perpetrator's point of view. And the claimant must be shielded from the risk of further retaliation for seeking relief.

In order to feel safe to speak out at a hearing, however, Mrs. G. needs more than *post hoc* remedies against overt acts of retaliation. She also needs to feel economically secure, economically independent. She needs to feel confident enough of her future that threats of economic punishment will have no bite. The social policies that might create such conditions are vigorously contested, and the political will that might enact them is not apparent. Without such economic security, however, *post hoc* measures to deter retaliation will never fully dismantle the barrier that intimidation imposes to her speech. For as long as Mrs. G. remains dependent on the pleasure of her masters for her next meal, she will continue to plot her words—and her silences—to speak *their* will, rather than hers.

B. Challenging the Imagery that Sustains Subordination

The second force that impedes Mrs. G.'s participation is negative cultural imagery of gender, race, and class. This imagery dwells in the minds of her superiors. But it is also through these images that Mrs. G. understands herself, and learns to undermine her own voice. Mrs. G. was under the sway of these negative images when she repeatedly apologized to her lawyer for doing something wrong. These internalized images also led Mrs. G. to use "powerless" language at her hearing, language that might deflect overt violence, but at the expense of confirming her subordination. It is not easy to imagine mechanisms to protect Mrs. G. from the negative stereotypes that pervade the culture and distort her speech.

As a first step, lawyers and judges can be educated about the risk that race- and gender-linked speech habits will impact on credibility assessment. William O'Barr suggests that lawyers might coach witnesses to use socially dominant modes of speech. Judges might intervene during hearings to restate the testimony of "powerless" speakers. In cases where the social gap between witness and factfinder is extreme, the law might guarantee interpreters, or require corrective jury instructions, or even amend evidence rules to address the subtle distortions that dialect differences are likely to cause.[172] Bennett and Feldman suggest the use of expert witnesses to educate juries about the risk that they might discredit testimony because of social barriers encoded into a witness's speech.[173] We could go beyond such educational measures, to require that the fact-finder *share* the perspective[174]—the social location[175]—of the claimant, particularly in a context like welfare hearings where the claimant is likely to come from a marginalized social group. All such proposals would run an obvious risk, however, of deepening the already profound chasms in perspective between dominant and subordinated social groups in this society.

A more ambitious reform agenda would expand the logic of proof so that the conversational and narrative styles of subordinated groups are no longer deemed "irrelevant" to the decision process. Uncertain, Other-oriented speech might be revalued in legal rituals that seek to build community rather than punish the transgression of legal rules. Informal processes carry serious risks in the welfare context, however, where the power difference between the individual claimant and the government is so great.

Even if any of these reforms could be implemented, however, none would address the hardest question that racist and gendered cultural imagery poses. Are the images themselves so central to Mrs. G.'s subordination that the law should challenge those images directly, even at the risk of silencing or chilling speech? This question has erupted into bitter political controversy within subordinated communities and impassioned debates among constitutional scholars. We may wish to avoid getting caught up in this debate. But if we take Mrs. G.'s experience seriously, the law's appropriate response to racist imagery marks an empirical, strategic, and normative conundrum that we cannot avoid.

C. *Confining Bureaucracy*

Beyond the obvious injustice imposed by racism and gender looms the much more complex obstacle posed to the participation of all citizens by a structural momentum I have called bureaucracy. To dismantle the bureaucratic barrier— to imagine an alternative template for the organization of complex, "post-industrial" institutions—entails a much more daring reconstructive project than simply to realize the promise of formal equality. Can we reimagine the economy as a network of face to face deliberations, among citizens, about the production and allocation of social wealth? Can we reimagine our mature, liberated selves as interdependent beings, rather than lonely souls embattled by the selfish demands of others? And as women, weary from incessant connectedness, do we even want to?

Neither the answers to those questions, nor the project of creating post-bureaucratic institution, are easy. Such institutions will be neither feasible nor desirable in every domain of social life. Their creation cannot be driven by ideological presuppositions about what the future should be; indeed, misguided leaps forward have proved disastrous. Rather, the relocation of bureaucratized governance in participatory institutions must proceed cautiously, experimentally, guided by local knowledge rather than grand design. In diverse locales, gradual steps toward new institutional forms—democratic experiments in the workplace, in housing, in education, and in the community—are under way.

Perhaps a second "constitutional revolution" will eventually map these changes onto the charter of our government, superseding the bureaucratized normative vision of the New Deal regulatory state by a less holistic vision of power. Such a transformation must receive substantial support from the state, through reforms that protect against race and gender bias and reduce the risk of retaliation when poor people dare to speak out. Reforms that will dismantle the barriers to Mrs. G.'s political participation. But beyond that crucial economic and cultural support, the shape of post-bureaucratic institutions will not come from the traditional architects of the law. It will come instead from the diverse, localized institution-building activities that poor Black single women with children—citizens—undertake for themselves, on their own ground.

Notes

1. B. Johnson, *Is Writerliness Conservative?*, in A WORLD OF DIFFERENCE 25, 31 (1987).

2. 397 U.S. 254 (1970). . . .

3. This position was endorsed by the Supreme Court in Matthews v. Eldridge, 424 U.S. 319 (1976) (directing courts to balance accuracy, administrative costs, and other factors to determine the minimal procedures constitutionally required before the state can infringe a liberty or property interest). . . .

4. *See* B. BARBER, STRONG DEMOCRACY: PARTICIPATORY POLITICS FOR A NEW AGE (1984).

5. Prominent among the legal scholars engaged in articulating this vision of process are Martha Minow and Frank Michelman. *See, e.g.,* Minow, *Interpreting Rights: an Essay for Robert Cover,* 96 YALE L.J. 1860 (1987); Minow, *The Supreme Court 1987 Term— Foreword: Justice Engendered,* 101 HARV. L. REV. 10 (1987); Michelman, *The Supreme Court 1986 Term—Foreword: Traces of Self-Government,* 100 HARV. L. REV. 4 (1986); Michelman, *Formal and Associational Aims in Procedural Due Process,* in NOMOS, DUE PROCESS 126 (J. Pennock & J. Chapman eds. 1977); Michelman, *The Supreme Court and Litigation Access Fees: The Right to Protect One's Rights,* 1973 DUKE L.J. 1153.

6. Goldberg v. Kelly, *supra* note 2, at 264–65 (emphasis added). . . .

48. Major works of feminist linguistic scholarship from the last two decades include D. CAMERON, FEMINISM AND LINGUISTIC THEORY (1985); LANGUAGE, GENDER, AND SOCIETY (B. Thorne, C. Kramarae & N. Henley eds. 1983); C. KRAMARAE, WOMEN AND MEN SPEAKING (1981); WOMEN AND LANGUAGE IN LITERATURE AND SOCIETY (S. McConnell-Ginet, R. Borker & N. Furman eds. 1980); M. KEY, MALE/FEMALE LANGUAGE (1975); and LANGUAGE AND SEX: DIFFERENCE AND DOMINANCE (B. Thorne & N. Henley eds. 1975). For an overview and critique of feminist linguistic investigation, see Elshtain, *Feminist Discourse and its Discontents,* in FEMINIST THEORY: A CRITIQUE OF IDEOLOGY 127–145 (N. Keohane, M. Rosaldo, & B. Gelpi eds. 1981), and McConnell-Ginet, *Difference and Language: A Linguist's Perspective,* in THE FUTURE OF DIFFERENCE 156–166 (H. Eisenstein & A. Jardine eds., 1987). For a survey of linguistic data about gendered features in non-Western languages, see Bodine, *Sex Differentiation in Language,* in LANGUAGE AND SEX: DIFFERENCE AND DOMINANCE 130 (B. Thorne & N. Henley eds. 1975).

49. R. LAKOFF, LANGUAGE AND WOMAN'S PLACE (1975). Lakoff based her conclusions on introspection and intuition about the speech of white, middle class professional women like herself, rather than on rigorous field studies. *Id.* at 4 ("I have examined my own speech and that of my acquaintances, and have used my own intuitions in analyzing it.").

50. *Id.* at 71.

51. *See id.* In characterizing this style, Lakoff draws heavily from H.P GRICE, THE LOGIC OF CONVERSATION (1968).

52. LAKOFF, *supra* note 49, at 70.

53. *Id.* at 53.

54. For example, "It's time for dinner, isn't it?"

55. For example, "Wouldn't it be a good idea if you could leave me alone."

56. For example, "That seemed kinda all right."

57. Virtually every linguistic and political claim of Lakoff's has stimulated further research. The technical studies include Brend, *Male-Female Intonation Patterns in American English,* in LANGUAGE AND SEX: DIFFERENCE AND DOMINANCE, *supra* note 48, at 84–87, and B. PREISLER, LINGUISTIC SEX ROLES IN CONVERSATION: SOCIAL VARIATION IN THE EXPRESSION OF TENTATIVENESS IN ENGLISH (1986). For a broad critique of Lakoff's method and conclusions, *see* Kramarae, *Women's Speech: Separate but Unequal?* in LANGUAGE AND SEX: DIFFERENCE AND DOMINANCE, *supra* note 48, at 43–56. For a

comprehensive bibliography of the linguistics literature scrutinizing Lakoff's claims, see LANGUAGE, GENDER, AND SOCIETY, *supra* note 48, at 233-252. . . .

58. *See, e.g.,* B. Thorne & N. Henley, *Difference and Dominance: An Overview of Language, Gender, and Society,* in LANGUAGE AND SEX: DIFFERENCE AND DOMINANCE, *supra* note 48, at 25-26 ("[A]lthough stressing the primacy of social rather than linguistic change, Lakoff seems to argue that equality *should* entail women using the 'stronger' forms now associated with men.") (emphasis in original).

59. These critics argue that women's speech can show us how to use language to negotiate truly *human* meanings, which are inescapably ambivalent, by attending to the Other, rather than by imposing an imperial truth on a captive audience. Furthermore, they claim that it is only by revaluing women's language, culture, and life experience that we can talk concretely about *what* norms and visions should motivate the feminist political project in the long term. *See, e.g.,* Kramarae, *Women's Speech: Separate but Unequal?, supra* note 48, at 43-56; Fishman, *Interaction: The Work Women Do,* in LANGUAGE, GENDER, AND SOCIETY, *supra* note 48, at 89.

Lakoff's critics are correct to remind us that feminists must debate ultimate visions. However, at the same time we must make hard decisions about the concrete steps that might lead forward. It is to this "transitional" question that Lakoff speaks when she suggests that women should learn to speak like males if they want to command power in the present-day public world. In her view, because dominant-group males control the public sphere, setting the standards for public discourse, women's verbal hedges are *heard* as confessions of their lack of power. This debate between Lakoff and her critics is but one example of a broader discussion among feminists about whether the historical practices of women should be regarded as symptoms of gender oppression or lauded as the signifiers of alternative feminist values. . . .

60. *See* the essays in LANGUAGE AND POWER (C. Kramarae, M. Schulz & W. O'Barr eds. 1984). *See also* Nichols, *Women in their Speech Communities,* in WOMEN AND LANGUAGE IN LITERATURE AND SOCIETY, *supra* note 48, at 140 (documenting contrasts between women speakers in different speech communities and conversational settings, which the author relates to such variables as social role and activities); Nichols, *Linguistic Options and Choices for Black Women in the Rural South,* in LANGUAGE, GENDER, AND SOCIETY, *supra* note 48, at 54; Scott, *The English Language and Black Womanhood: a Low Blow at Self-esteem,* 2 J. AFRO-AMERICAN ISSUES 218 (1974); Stanback, *Language and Black Woman's Place: Toward a Description of Black Women's Communication* (paper presented at meeting of Speech Communication Association, Lousiville, Ky., 1982).

61. *See* Lind & O'Barr, *The Social Significance of Speech in the Courtroom,* in LANGUAGE AND SOCIAL PSYCHOLOGY (H. Giles & R. St.Clair eds. 1979); Conley, O'Barr & Lind, *The Power of Language: Presentational Style in the Courtroom,* 1978 DUKE L.J. 1375; Erickson, Lind, Johnson & O'Barr, *Speech Style and Impression Formation in a Court Setting: The Effects of "Powerful" and "Powerless" Speech,* 14 J. EXPERIMENTAL SOC. PSYCH. 266 (1978).

62. O'Barr refers to the linguistic features that Lakoff associates with women— including hedges, hesitation forms, polite forms, question intonation and intensifiers— as "powerless" speech forms. *See* Conley, O'Barr & Lind, *supra* note 61, at 1379-80.

63. O'Barr & Atkins, *Women's Language" or "Powerless Language?",* in WOMEN AND LANGUAGE IN LITERATURE AND SOCIETY, *supra* note 48, at 93, 102-03 ("[W]e are able to find *more* women toward the high end of the continuum [measuring the frequency of Lakoff's "powerless forms" that occurred in their speech]. Next, we noted that all the women who were aberrant . . . had something in common—an unusually high social status. . . . [T]hey were typically well-educated, professional women of middle-class background. A corresponding pattern was noted among the aberrant men. . . .[T]hey

tended to be men who held either subordinate, lower-status jobs or were unemployed."). The data also suggested that those speakers who were more familiar with a courtroom setting were likely to use a lower proportion of powerless features.

64. *Id.* at 104.

65. *See* O'Barr & Conley, *Litigant Satisfaction versus Legal Adequacy in Small Claims Court Narratives,* 19 LAW & SOC'Y REV. 661 (1985); Conley & O'Barr, *Rules versus Relationships in Small Claims Disputes,* in CONFLICT TALK (A. Grimshaw ed. 19[90]). . . .

66. *Rules versus Relationships, supra* note 65, at [178–79] ("A *relational* account emphasizes status and relationships, and is organized around the litigant's efforts to introduce these issues into the trial. A *rule-oriented* account emphasizes rules and laws, and is tightly structured around these issues. . . . Rule-oriented accounts mesh better with the logic of the law and the courts. They . . . concentrate on the issues that the court is likely to deem relevant to the case. . . . By contrast, relational accounts are filled with background details that are presumably relevant to the litigant, but not necessarily to the court, and emphasize the complex web of relationships between the litigants rather than legal rules or formal contracts") (emphasis in original).

67. *Id.* at [194] ("[U]se of the rule-oriented approach correlates with exposure to the sources of social power. . . . Such exposure is in turn differentially distributed between men and women and among the members of various classes and ethnic groups. . . . Indeed, the rule-oriented relational continuum may be the discourse-level manifestation of the power-powerless stylistic continuum").

68. The study was conducted with both male and female witnesses reading prepared scripts of "powerful" and "powerless" testimony. Among both gender groups, credibility was significantly enhanced when "powerful" speech was used. The baseline assessment of the male witnesses, as a group, was consistently, though only slightly, more favorable than that of the females. *See* O'Barr & Atkins, *supra* note 63.

69. *See* W. BENNETT & M. FELDMAN, RECONSTRUCTING REALITY IN THE COURT-ROOM: JUSTICE AND JUDGMENT IN AMERICAN CULTURE 171 (1981). . . .

71. O'Barr, *Asking the Right Questions about Language and Power,* in LANGUAGE AND POWER, supra note 60, at 262, 266.

72. "Robin Lakoff states the dilemma as some women might experience it: "[T]he acquisition of this special type of speech [women's speech, or powerless speech] will later be an excuse others use to keep her in a demeaning position, to refuse to take her seriously as a human being. . . . So a girl is damned if she does, damned if she doesn't. If she refuses to talk like a lady, she is ridiculed and subjected to criticism as unfeminine; if she does learn, she is ridiculed as unable to think clearly, unable to take part in a serious discussion: in some sense, as less than fully human. These two choices which a woman has—to be less than a woman or less than a person—are highly painful." *See* Lakoff, *supra* note 49, at 5–6.

74. This exception is in the area of rape law. . . .

78. This story is based upon my work as a legal aid lawyer in North Carolina from 1982 to 1986. Certain details have been changed to avoid compromising client confidentiality.

79. Aid to Families with Dependent Children, 42 U.S.C. §§ 601, 615 (1982).

[96]. Although I base this section on two years of intensive work with women in the social location of Mrs. G., this section should properly be a conversation with her, rather than an imaginative projection based on my own experience with her. Such a project, however, is beyond the scope of the Article, as it is beyond the bounds of much feminist scholarship. This limitation in my method deserves close attention, because it raises the broad question of how feminist scholars might write about subordination—

about gender—without making other women into objects of study, and keeping for themselves the power to name problems and imagine solutions. In this essay, I mark this question by rejecting the universalizing rhetoric of "normal" scholarship and writing stories instead. But my story—about Mrs. G.'s claim to name her own needs—does not attend to her as a subject any more than the grandiose prescriptions of the policy engineers. My storytelling still guards the power to interpret firmly in my own hands.

A feminist alternative to this monologic approach to scholarship would entail conversation and translation, rather than observation and pronouncement. It would entail dialogue with the other subject and then the *mutual* creation of forms for expanding that discussion to a wider audience. The participants would themselves devise the appropriate method for that communication in each situation. In some cases, it might be a quantitative study, using mainstream social science methodology, or an essay in the discourse of academic philosophy. In other cases, however, the communication might take a quite different form. For two accounts in which groups, working with outsiders, chose drama as their "method" for communicating their analysis of their own political situation, see White, *To Learn and Teach: Lessons from Driefontein on Lawyering and Power*, 1989 WISC. L. REV. 699 and White, *Mobilizing on the Margins of Litigation*, 16 N.Y.U. REV. L. & SOC. CHANGE 535 (1987–88).

143. As I begin this critique of the lawyer's perspective, I must note the ambiguity of my own position in this project. As Mrs. G.'s lawyer, I appeared in her story. Yet I also wrote that story, and I now prepare to read it. The reader should ask what feelings and events I might have left out of the narrative of Mrs. G. because I was not situated to perceive them. Although this reading purports to comment on how the lawyer's viewpoint was limited in the story, my interpretation of the lawyer's limitations is itself shaped by my own present social location and concerns. What questions does this reading pose to the story, and what issues does my reading conceal from view?

150. The behaviors labelled "intuition" are among the strategies that subordinates use to manage an unequal power relationship. *See, e.g.,* Snodgrass, *Women's Intuition: The Effect of Subordinate Role on Interpersonal Sensitivity.* 49 J. PERSONALITY & SOC. PSYCHOLOGY 146 (1985). . . .

151. Some readers have suggested that Mrs. G.'s testimony at the hearing simply shows how well the adversarial instrument works. They suggest that the ancient trappings of due process, the formality, the oath, confrontation, urged her, finally, to tell the truth. Her case file noted that the crucial conversation between herself and her caseworker *had* taken place, even if the file did not document this conversation in detail. In the hearing Mrs. G. equivocated about this uncontested fact. And her children's "everyday" shoes were there at the hearing for everyone to examine. The question of whether she *needed* to replace them was not a simple question of reconstructing the historical record.

152. This discussion does not imply that the social worker's imagined judgment of Mrs. G. is fair. Rather, it suggests that Mrs. G. made her statement at the hearing in the context of the complex relationship between these two women, a relationship that none of the other actors had access to.

160. The figure of play connotes an exuberant, unruly approach toward conventions of discourse which can disarm an oppressive language-system, reanimating it with women's experiences. Patricia Yaeger elaborates in HONEY-MAD WOMAN: EMANCIPATORY STRATEGIES IN WOMEN'S WRITING 18 (1988)]: "[P]layfulness and word play are very much at issue in the woman writer's reinvention of her culture. . . . [P]lay itself is a form of aesthetic activity in which . . . what has been burdensome becomes—at least momentarily— weightless, transformable, transformative. As women play with old texts, the burden of the tradition is lightened and shifted; it has the potential for being remade."

The figure of archaeology refers to the collective searching of private memories and the shared past to uncover the suppressed meanings that are latent in familiar words. Mary Daly invokes archaeology in GYN/ECOLOGY (1978) at 24 when she describes how, in her writing, she searches for the hidden powers of words: "Often I unmask deceptive words by dividing them and employing alternate meanings for prefixes. . . . I also unmask their hidden reversals, often by using less known or "obsolete" meanings. . . . Sometimes I simply invite the reader to listen to words in a different way. . . . When I play with words I do this attentively, deeply, paying attention to etymology, to varied dimensions of meaning, to deep Background meanings and subliminal associations."

The third figure that guides this emancipatory language practice is poetry—coaxing the language just beyond its systemic boundaries, toward images and understandings that both expand, and challenge, its rule. Used in this sense, poetry is closely connected to consciousness raising—the feminist method in which women, through their *practice* of talking together about their own experience, create the common language which makes that talking possible. *See* T. DE LAURETIS, ALICE DOESN'T: FEMINISM, SEMIOTICS, CINEMA (1984) (defining consciousness raising as "the collective articulation of one's experience of sexuality and gender . . . [which] has produced, and continues to elaborate, a radically new mode of understanding the subject's relation to social-historical reality. Consciousness raising is the original critical instrument that women developed toward such understanding, the analysis of social reality and its critical revision"). Consciousness raising places new demands on the language because, through it, women grope to share feelings that have previously gone unnamed. When those feelings find words, poetry is produced. As Audre Lorde expresses the matter in her essay, *Poetry is Not a Luxury*: "We can train ourselves to respect our feelings and to transpose them into a language so they can be shared. And where that language does not yet exist, it is our poetry which helps to fashion it." *See* A. LORDE, SISTER OUTSIDER 37-38 (1984).

161. A. RICH, *Power and Danger: Works of a Common Woman*, in ON LIES, SECRETS, SILENCE 247 (1977).

162. Perhaps by collaborating more fully with Mrs. G. as we theorize about her, we could better comprehend the "doubleness" of her subordination—her power *and* her pain—without being caught between the inadequate paradigms of structural determinism on the one hand and unfettered human agency on the other. . . .

165. My use of this term throughout the essay presumes a moral and political theory through which we can distinguish between "meaningful" or "authentic" and "distorted" or "inauthentic" participation. *See* Sunstein, *Legal Interference with Private Preferences*, 53 U. CHI. L. REV. 1129 (1986) (discussing possible normative grounds for the law's interference with the expressed preferences of individual citizens). Habermas' theory of communicative action provides a powerful possibility, particularly if the insights of his feminist critics are also taken into account. *See* J. HABERMAS, [THE THEORY OF COMMUNICATIVE ACTION (T. McCarthy trans. 1984); Habermas, *Law as Medium and Law as Institution*, in DILEMMAS OF LAW IN THE WELFARE STATE (G. Teubner ed. 1985)]. *But see* Cornell, *Toward a Modern/Postmodern Theory of Ethics*, 133 U. PA. L. REV. 291 (1985); Fraser, *What's Critical about Critical Theory? The Case of Habermas and Gender*, in FEMINISM AS CRITIQUE: ON THE POLITICS OF GENDER 31-55 [(S. Benhabib & D. Cornell eds. 1987)] (showing how Habermas presumes the basic social structures of patriarchy in his theory of "life worlds"); Young, *Impartiality and the Civic Public: Some Implications of Feminist Critiques of Moral and Political Theory*, in FEMINISM AS CRITIQUE, [*supra*, at 67-73] (critiquing Habermas' vision of communicative rationality for its failure to take account of the opacity of language and the irreducible heterogeneity of any speech community).

167. Goldberg v. Kelly, *supra* note 2, at 269 & n. 16, citing to Wedermeyer & Moore, *The American Welfare System*, 54 CALIF. L. REV. 326, 342 (1966).

168. Goldberg v. Kelly, *supra* note 2, at 253-54.

172. *See* Conley, O'Barr & Lind, *supra* note 61, at 1395-99, for speculation about how this proposal might work in the courtroom. There is a problem, of course, that such a remedy might itself exacerbate the perceived status difference between the witness and her audience.

173. *See* W. Bennet & M. Feldman, *supra* note 69, at 179. Experts might also work behind the scenes, helping lawyers take account of language and cultural barriers in preparing their cases, or providing the court with guidance on the venue issue or the jury selection process.

174. *See* Resnik, *On the Bias: Feminist Reconsiderations of the Aspirations for our Judges*, 61 S. CAL. L. REV. 1877 (1988) (critiquing the norm of judicial neutrality in light of feminist theories).

175. This might mean sharing demographic characteristics such as class, race, ethnicity, gender, age, disability, or sexual orientation. It might mean sharing membership in a localized geographic community, such as a housing project or a neighborhood. Alternatively, it might mean sharing an identity as "clients" in a particular social program, such as AFDC or a public school.

Further Reading for Part Four

A great deal of attention has been paid by feminist scholars to questions of methodology. *Feminism and Methodology*, ed. Sandra Harding (Bloomington: Indiana Univ. Press, 1987), emphasizes methodology in the social sciences; *Women, Knowledge, and Reality: Explorations in Feminist Philosophy*, ed. Ann Garry and Marilyn Pearsall (Winchester, Mass.: Unwin Hyman, 1989), deals specifically with philosophical method; and Sandra Harding's *The Science Question in Feminism* (Ithaca, N.Y.: Cornell Univ. Press, 1986) is the leading feminist work on feminist methodology in the natural sciences.

The first sustained examination of feminist method among contemporary feminist legal scholars was Catharine MacKinnon's analysis of consciousness-raising, in "Feminism, Marxism, Method, and the State: An Agenda for Theory," 7 *Signs* 515 (1982). This discussion was extended in her most recent book *Toward a Feminist View of the State* (Cambridge: Harvard Univ. Press, 1989). MacKinnon's approach to feminist method raises questions of authenticity, which are examined in two very different ways in Ruth Colker's "Feminism, Sexuality, and Self: A Preliminary Inquiry into the Politics of Authenticity," 68 *Boston U. L. Rev.* 217 (1988), and in Christine Littleton's "Feminist Jurisprudence: The Difference Method Makes," 41 *Stan. L. Rev.* 751 (1989).

Efforts to develop a feminist legal methodology that could be more easily related to existing legal methods include Catharine Wells, "Situated Decisionmaking," 63 *So. Cal. L. Rev.* 1727 (1990), and Mary Jane Mossman, "Feminism and Legal Method: The Difference It Makes," 3 *Wis. Women's L.J.* 147 (1987). See also Heather Wishik's "To Question Everything: The Inquiries of Feminist Jurisprudence," 1 *Berkeley Women's L.J.* 64 (1986), which pursues "asking the woman question" as a legal method.

An increasing amount of feminist legal scholarship is autobiographical, particularly that of black feminist lawyers. Patricia Williams in much of her work integrates autobiography, metaphor, and legal analysis. Some of her best-known articles are integrated in her book-length autobiographical work, *Alchemy of Race and Rights* (Cambridge: Harvard Univ. Press, 1991). Regina Austin in "Sapphire Bound!" 1989 *Wis. L. Rev.* 539, and Mari Matsuda in "Public Response to 'Racist Speech': Considering the Victim's Story," 87 *Mich. L. Rev.* 2320 (1989), also use personal narrative effectively to break conventional cognitive barriers to understanding the marginalization and the resistance of minority women. For an excellent analysis of how personal narrative might be used to litigate cases on behalf of lesbians, gays, and feminists generally, see Elizabeth Schneider, Mary Dunlap, Michael Lavery, and John Gregory, "Lesbians, Gays, and Feminists at the Bar: Translating Personal Experience into Effective Legal Argument," 10 *Women's Rts. L. Rep.* 107 (1988).

Personal narratives have also been particularly successful in highlighting issues of violence and the law. Susan Estrich in *Real Rape* (Cambridge: Harvard Univ. Press,

1986), for example, begins a comprehensive analysis of rape law with an account of her own rape. Robin West uses stories of other women's lives, both in "The Difference in Women's Hedonic Lives: A Phenomenological Critique of Feminist Legal Theory," 2 *Wis. Women's L.J.* 81 (1987), and in "Feminism, Critical Social Theory, and Law," 1989 *U. Chi. Legal F.* 59, to explore questions of authenticity in women's sexual lives and to demonstrate the pervasiveness of violence against women. See also Christine Littleton's "Women's Experience and the Problem of Transition: Perspectives on Male Battering of Women," 1989 *U. Chi. Legal F.* 23. Other works dealing with the method of narrative in law and in feminist theory include Lynne Henderson, "Legality and Empathy," 85 *Mich. L. Rev.* 1574 (1987), and Jane Cohen, "The Arrival of the Bee Box: Feminism, Law, and Literature," 13 *Harv. Women's L.J.* 345 (1990).

Recent interest in legal pragmatism has overlapped with feminist efforts for greater contextual judgments (or "practical reasoning") in the law. For recent writings on this subject, see *Symposium on the Renaissance of Pragmatism in American Legal Thought,* 62 *So. Cal. L. Rev.* 1569 (1990), and for an explicitly feminist approach, see Margaret Jane Radin's "The Pragmatist and the Feminist," 62 *So. Cal. L. Rev.* 1699 (1990).

For a direct application of feminist legal method to the problem of racism, sexism, and homophobia in law school classrooms, see Ann E. Freedman's "Feminist Legal Method in Action: Challenging Racism, Sexism, and Homophobia in Law School," 24 *Ga. L. Rev.* 849 (1990).

Several excellent collections address the relationship between feminism, epistemology, and method. See *Discovering Reality: Feminist Perspectives on Epistemology, Metaphysics, Methodology, and Philosophy of Science,* ed. Sandra Harding and Merrill B. Hintikka (Dordrecht, Holland: D. Reidel Publishing Co., 1983); *Feminist Perspectives: Philosophical Essays on Method and Morals,* ed. Lorraine Code, Sheila Mullett, and Christine Overall (Toronto: Univ. of Toronto Press, 1988); and *Gender/Body/Knowledge: Feminist Reconstructions of Being and Knowing,* ed. Alison Jaggar and Susan Bordo (New Brunswick, N.J.: Rutgers Univ. Press, 1989).

How feminist theory relates to feminist politics is a theme that runs through much of the feminist works presented in this book and cited for further reading. Nancy Fraser's *Unruly Practices: Power, Discourse, and Gender in Contemporary Social Theory* (Minneapolis: Univ. of Minnesota Press, 1989) is a particularly successful attempt to join critical social theory with feminist practice, an attempt that culminates in the articulation of a "politics of need" for translating justified needs claims into social rights. Other feminists have focused on the limits of law and legal method to achieve deep gender reform in our society. Two examples are Martha L. Fineman's "Challenging Law, Establishing Differences: The Future of Feminist Legal Scholarship," 42 *Fla. L. Rev.* 25 (1990), and Carol Smart's *Feminism and the Power of Law* (London: Routledge, 1989).

About the Book
and Editors

Our understanding of the law and its potential for reforming social and political norms was dramatically reshaped in the 1980s by the intellectual movement known as feminist legal theory. What makes this new theory so important is the far-reaching challenge it poses to the assumptions embedded in traditional legal doctrine and method as well as the light it sheds on how these assumptions so consistently undercut efforts toward fundamental gender change. Feminist legal theory also suggests how feminist practice might move toward strategies capable of fostering more effective, fundamental reform.

In a carefully balanced and thoughtfully edited collection of classic and new, cutting-edge papers, Katharine T. Bartlett and Rosanne Kennedy present some of the most provocative and diverse work in this exciting field. The selections reveal the influences of feminist work in philosophy, psychoanalysis, political theory, and literary criticism, among other fields. These disciplines have enriched legal theory and provided feminist scholars with more and sharper tools, and the results, as evidenced in this book, are impressive and encouraging. They are also sobering, in that they force the realization that there is much theoretical and practical work yet to be done, under constraints we are only beginning to fully comprehend.

For students of the law, for anyone interested in women's issues, for experienced scholars, and for newcomers, *Feminist Legal Theory* is not just essential reading but an enduring reference work.

Katharine T. Bartlett is professor of law at Duke University School of Law and the author of many articles on family law and feminist legal theory. **Rosanne Kennedy** is a lecturer in women's studies and English at Australian National University and is currently writing in the area of feminist theory and cultural studies.

About the Contributors

Katharine T. Bartlett is professor of law at Duke University. A former legal services attorney, Bartlett writes on family law subjects, especially child custody, as well as feminist legal theory.

Patricia A. Cain is professor of law at the University of Iowa. Cain brings a lesbian perspective to feminist legal theory. A long-time activist in the lesbian feminist community, she is currently working on a legal history of the lesbian and gay rights movement.

Kimberle Crenshaw is acting professor of law at the University of California at Los Angeles. A pioneer in the area of critical race theory, Crenshaw writes and lectures frequently on legal issues of race and gender.

Clare Dalton is professor of law at Northeastern University. Dalton was a leader in joining feminist jurisprudence to critical legal theory, transforming them both in the process. Her most recent work is on bioethics and law and on domestic violence.

Angela P. Harris is acting professor of law at the University of California at Berkeley. She teaches courses in criminal law, civil rights, and contemporary American legal theory and is interested in the relationship among race, gender, and class in legal theory and in social life.

Christine A. Littleton is professor of law at the University of California at Los Angeles. A feminist activist and litigator as well as scholar, Littleton was cofounder in 1984 of West Coast Fem-Crits, a study group of feminist critical legal scholars, and in 1989 helped to found the Southern California Women's Law Center. Littleton writes on a wide range of topics relating to women, including domestic violence and equality theory.

Catharine A. MacKinnon is professor of law at the University of Michigan. MacKinnon, a feminist lawyer, scholar, and activist, has conceptualized sexual harassment as sex discrimination and, with Andrea Dworkin, conceived ordinances recognizing pornography as a violation of women's civil rights. Her books include *Sexual Harassment of Working Women* (1979), *Feminism Unmodified* (1987), and *Toward a Feminist Theory of the State* (1989).

Martha Minow is professor of law at Harvard University. In addition to her leading articles in feminist theory, she writes and lectures extensively on topics relating to the disabled and children. She is the author of *Making All the Difference*, which examines issues of exclusion and inclusion across a broad spectrum of American law.

Frances Olsen is professor of law at the University of California at Los Angeles. She is an internationally known scholar and a long-time activist who represented Native Americans throughout their seventy-one-day uprising at Wounded Knee in 1973, established the first feminist pro-bono law office in Denver, and helped to organize feminist legal scholars ("fem-crits") in the Boston area and in California. She has been a visiting professor of law at both Harvard and the University of Michigan, a fellow at Oxford, and a Senior Fulbright Professor at the University of Frankfurt. Her articles have been published throughout the United States and Europe.

Deborah L. Rhode is professor of law and former director of the Institute for Research on Women and Gender at Stanford University. Her scholarship spans a number of topics relating to women and the law, some of it consolidated in her book *Justice and Gender* (1989). She has also edited a collection of essays under the title *Theoretical Perspectives on Sexual Difference* (1990).

Elizabeth M. Schneider is professor of law at Brooklyn Law School. For many years a litigator for the Center for Constitutional Rights in New York City, Schneider focuses in her scholarship on the relationship between feminist theory and practice. She is an expert on legal issues relating to battered women.

Vicki Schultz is assistant professor of law at the University of Wisconsin. Formerly an attorney in the U.S. Department of Justice Civil Rights Division, Schultz writes at the boundary of feminist theory and legal practice. Her current work focuses on job segregation and sexual harassment, examining the relationship between law, gender, work, and identity.

Robin West is professor of law at the University of Maryland. In addition to her groundbreaking work in feminist jurisprudence, she also writes and speaks frequently on matters of constitutional law, political and literary theory, and legal interpretation.

Lucie E. White is acting professor of law at the University of California at Los Angeles. Following her experience in a poverty law practice, White specializes in the areas of clinical legal education, welfare law, and feminist legal theory.

Joan C. Williams is professor of law at American University. Williams writes extensively in such diverse areas as legal history, nonfoundationalist theory, feminist jurisprudence, and local government law.

Patricia J. Williams is associate professor at the University of Wisconsin. Professor Williams lectures widely and writes extensively on questions of identity and subjectivity as they relate to race and gender. *The Alchemy of Race and Rights* is her recent book on these subjects.

Wendy W. Williams is associate dean and professor of law at Georgetown University. Cofounder in 1973 of San Francisco–based Equal Rights Advocates, Williams has litigated major women's rights cases before the United States Supreme Court and has been involved in important legislative advocacy efforts as well. Her best-known writing concerns issues of pregnancy discrimination and worker protection policies.

Index